WRITER'S ENCYCLOPEDIA

Third Edition

WRITER'S ENCYCLOPEDIA

From the Editors of Writer's Digest

WRITER'S DIGEST BOOKS
CINCINNATI, OHIO

Writer's Encyclopedia, Third Edition. Copyright © 1996 Writer's Digest Books. Printed and bound in the United States of America. All rights reserved. No part of this book may be reproduced in any form or by any electronic or mechanical means including information storage and retrieval systems without permission in writing from the publisher, except by a reviewer, who may quote brief passages in a review. Published by Writer's Digest Books, an imprint of F&W Publications, Inc., 1507 Dana Ave., Cincinnati, Ohio 45207. (800) 289-0963.

This hardcover edition of *Writer's Encyclopedia, Third Edition* features a "self-jacket" that eliminates the need for a separate dust jacket. It provides sturdy protection for your book while it saves paper, trees and energy.

Other fine Writer's Digest Books are available from your local bookstore or direct from the publisher.

00 99 98 97 96   5 4 3 2 1

Library of Congress Cataloging-in-Publication Data

Writer's encyclopedia / edited by Amanda Boyd . . . [et al.]—3rd ed.
   p. cm.
  Rev. ed. of: Writing, A to Z. 1990.
  Includes bibliographical references.
  ISBN 0-89879-749-7 (alk. paper)
  1. Authorship—Dictionaries. 2. Mass media—Dictionaries.
I. Boyd, Amanda II. Title: Writing, A to Z.
PN141.W72   1996
808'.02'03—dc20   95-53299
                                                        CIP

Edited by Amanda Boyd, Thomas Clark, Peter Blocksom, Jo Gilbert, Bruce Woods, Megan Lane
Interior and cover designed by Sandy Conopeotis Kent

TABLE OF CONTENTS

ACKNOWLEDGMENTS

3rd Edition Editors: Amanda Boyd, Thomas Clark, Peter Blocksom, Jo Gilbert, Bruce Woods, Megan Lane

Contributing Editors:
Connie Achabal, Rose Adkins, Richard Balkin, Phyllis Ball, Joan Bloss, John Brady, Bill Brohaugh, Anita Buck, Colleen Cannon, Carol Cartaino, Debbie Cinnamon, Bernadine Clark, Sally Davis, Henry Dorfman, Kathryn Falk, Bill Francois, Beth Franks, Jean Fredette, Don Herman, Jo Hoff, Nancy Kersell, Barb Kuroff, Dave Luppert, Bob Lutz, Tom McCormack, Mary Mangold, Victor Martin, Leonard Meranus, Paul Nathan, Robert Orben, Miriam Phelps, Kirk Polking, Mert Ransdell, Yuri Rasovsky, Hugh Rawson, Richard Rosenthal, P. J. Schemenaur, Victor Schmalzer, John Tebbel, W.B. Wallis, Howard I. Wells III, the editorial associates of Writer's Digest School and Writer's Digest Criticism Service, and the authors and friends of Writer's Digest Books.

PREFACE

Writing is an art, a craft, a business. It is the persuasive power of advertising, the lyrics of a song, the pages of a novel we can't stop reading. And each writing specialty has its idioms to be mastered. This reference work brings together in one volume all the terms, techniques, procedures and trade expressions you'll need to know, whether your interest is publishing, broadcasting, films, lecturing, the theater, advertising or public relations.

Arranged in simple alphabetical format, *Writer's Encyclopedia* is meant to be your experienced fellow writer, editorial colleague, marketing manager, reference librarian, knowledgeable teacher—available for instant consultation, no matter what your question. Whether you read the book straight through, flip along at random or search for specific answers, we hope its definitions will lead you to a better understanding of the craft of writing.

More than 100 entries have been added to this third edition. Many of these deal with resources newly available to writers—online services, the Internet and CD-ROMs to name a few. Entries from previous editions have been extensively revised, with new information added and helpful examples included.

While revising these existing entries we drew on the material published in *Writer's Digest* and *Writer's Yearbook*, the advice of published authors and other experts, along with hundreds of references on specialized types of writing. The editors have tried to give readers a general understanding of each topic; readers who want more detailed information on individual subjects will find additional sources listed at the end of some entries. These references are incorporated into the bibliography at the end of the book.

In this third edition, the editors continue to use the traditional "he" for readability. Women writers and editors are as prominent as men in each of the disciplines covered by this book, but we found the use of "he or she" and other various contractions awkward and distracting.

Kirk Polking, a former *Writer's Digest* editor, created this book to answer the question "Where do I find out what *that* means?" We hope that your search leads not only to answers, but to action—to writing.

Amanda Boyd
Thomas Clark
Peter Blocksom
Jo Gilbert
Bruce Woods
Megan Lane

AA. Acronym for *author's alteration*, refers to text corrections or emendations made by the writer on galleys or page proofs. Typographical errors, known as printer's errors (PEs), are not counted as part of author's alterations. The author's contract indicates the percentage of the text that may be changed by the author at a given stage in the production process; the author must pay for any alterations made after that percentage has been reached. Also called *author's alts. (See: Author's alteration clause.)*

A&R (artists' and repertoire) representative. Working either independently or on a record company staff, an A&R representative traditionally finds potential acts and matches artists with songs to be recorded. However, the duties in this position vary widely, and the A&R representative may also seek out artists, choose the engineer for each recording project or find an appropriate studio, among other tasks.

In recent years, the number of musical groups that continuously record and compose together has increased. Since they know their own style and music, such groups need little guidance from an A&R representative. In working with this kind of group, the representative typically serves to budget the album.

ABC. *(See: Broadcast networks.)*

Abridged Readers' Guide to Periodical Literature. A shortened form of the *Readers' Guide to Periodical Literature*, this index lists magazines usually found in elementary school libraries, which are its primary subscribers. The *Abridged Readers' Guide* currently indexes eighty-two magazines. *(See:* Readers' Guide to Periodical Literature.)

Abridgment. A shortened form of literary work, in which the major themes of the original are kept. Books are abridged for faster and easier reading. The Reader's Digest Condensed Books are the most notable examples of abridgment; *The Reader's Digest Bible,* for instance, is 40 percent shorter than the 850,000-word Revised Standard Version. Although well-known passages have been left intact, the editors excised what they described as the "repetition, rhetoric and redundancy" of the complete work. *(See: Abstract; Pony.)*

Abstract. An abstract is a synopsis of a piece of nonfiction writing, such as an article, document, speech or statement. It summarizes the main points of the publication in the same order that the writer has presented them. Abstracts are published with their respective articles (especially in scientific and professional journals) and in some indexes to periodicals. Indexes that contain abstracts sometimes use the word *abstracts* in their titles instead of the word *index; Psychological Abstracts* is an example. (*See: Periodicals, indexes to.*)

A/C (adult contemporary). A term used in the music business to refer to a particular category of popular music. Also known as *middle-of-the-road* and *easy listening* music, A/C songs are melodic and easy to listen to, as the alternate name implies. They are composed for and performed at lower volumes and slower tempos than rock music. Most A/C songs have lyrics, but some are purely instrumental, such as *Chariots of Fire*, the theme from the movie of the same name.

Billboard, a trade magazine of the music industry, publishes weekly charts listing the titles of the one hundred current best-selling singles in this category. Songs by artists as diverse as Simon and Garfunkel, Elton John, Stevie Wonder and Dolly Parton have appeared on *Billboard*'s chart.

Academy of American Poets. This organization exists to "encourage, stimulate and foster the production of American poetry." The Academy awards $20,000 fellowships to poets of proven merit, the Lamont Poetry Selection for a poet's second book, the Walt Whitman Award for a poet's first book and more than 120 College and University Prizes around the country. Its New York City activities include poetry readings and literary walking tours. The Academy is located at 177 E. Eighty-seventh St., New York, NY 10128. (212) 427-5665.

Account executive. The advertising agency contact person who acts as a liaison between the client and the agency's creative and media buyer departments.

In radio advertising, an account executive is a radio station representative who calls on the station's advertisers to service their accounts.

Accrediting Council on Education in Journalism and Mass Communication (ACEJMC). This organization accredits college and university journalism programs and elicits cooperation between schools and industry for the advancement of journalism education. The Council publishes lists of ACEJMC-accredited programs and accrediting standards. ACEJMC annual meetings are held each May and September. Contact their headquarters for location.

This organization was formerly called the American Council on Education for Journalism. ACEJMC is headquartered at University of Kansas Stauffer-Flint Hall, Lawrence, KS 66045.

Acknowledgment page. The page of a book on which the author credits sources of assistance. Acknowledgments are customarily given to people or institutions who have helped with research, writing, editing, or typing, and to sources of copyrighted material that have been quoted in the book. Some publishers now shy away from the overly personal, gushy acknowledgments popular in the past.

Acronym. A word formed from the initial letters of a proper name or a series of words referring to one thing. Examples of acronyms are *MASH*, for Mobile Army Surgical Hospital; *SASE*, for self-addressed, stamped envelope; and *ZIP* (as in ZIP code), for Zone Improvement Program. Writers generally use acronyms in this way: Spell out the entire phrase initially, follow it with the acronym in parentheses and use only the acronym thereafter. Two sources of standard acronyms are *New Acronyms, Initialisms and Abbreviations* and *Brands and Their Companies*, both of which are available in libraries.

Across the board. Refers to a radio program or commercial used five, six or seven days a week that is scheduled to be broadcast at the same time every day.

Adaptation. This term refers to the process of rewriting a composition (e.g., novel, story, film, article, play) into a form suitable for some other medium, such as TV or the stage. Since the copyright owner has the exclusive right to adapt his own work, anyone else wishing to adapt the material must get permission from the original owner or whomever he may have assigned the adaptation rights to. This is the basis for the sale (usually by his agent or publisher) of various subsidiary rights. (*See: Rights for sale.*)

Addresses, sources of. To gather authoritative and current information, the writer must sometimes contact a person who is prominent in a given field. When a noted person's address is not directly available, librarians can often furnish directories that contain the necessary information, or an organization with which the

person is affiliated will be able to supply an address.

A book author, for example, can be reached in care of his publisher; a magazine writer, through the magazine(s) he writes for. *Writer's Directory* and *Contemporary Authors* are two sources of writers' addresses. Addresses of scientists are listed in *American Men and Women of Science* and *World Who's Who in Science*. Similarly, addresses of artists and others who work in the field of art can be found in *Who's Who in American Art*. A university professor can usually be located at the university he is affiliated with. If his current affiliation is unknown, he may be listed in the *National Faculty Directory*.

To find the address of an attorney outside his own city, the writer should consult the *Martindale-Hubbell Law Directory*, which contains information on individual attorneys and law firms. The address of a physician can be obtained from the *American Medical Directory* (published by the American Medical Association).

Clergymen can be located through the home offices of their respective denominations. Sports figures can be reached through the teams or professional sports organizations they play on or are associated with. A librarian can assist the researcher in finding directories of such organizations.

Freelancers who want to contact government offices, corporations, colleges, banks, national unions, transportation companies, media and other business services will find fifty thousand selected entries in the *National Directory of Addresses and Telephone Numbers*, published in paperback by General Information, Inc.,

New York. Of course, if the writer knows the city in which the expert is located, he can consult an out-of-town phone book, available in most large public libraries.

Celebrity Service, Inc., aids researchers in locating celebrities not listed in directories. (*See: Celebrity addresses; Lawyers, where to find.*)

Adjective. An adjective is a word that describes, qualifies, restricts or changes the meaning of the noun or pronoun it modifies. Adjectives offer a means of adding specific description and color to writing. The simplest way to use an adjective is to place it directly in front of the noun it modifies—the dented, red Volkswagen—but that's not always the most interesting way. Vern Sneider described in *Writer's Digest* five variations of "the adjectival idea": (1) an adjective combined with a prepositional phrase, e.g., "Maria, *heavy with child*"; (2) the relative clause with relative pronoun and verbs understood, e.g., "it was an island, (that was) *unimportant except to its inhabitants*"; (3) the participial phrase, e.g., "Harry, *having completed four years of college*"; (4) the absolute phrase, e.g., "John, (with) *a gun in his hand*"; and (5) the ablative absolute, e.g., "the whistle *having blown.*"

Many writers feel that it is more effective to use precise nouns, rather than rely on adjectives; overuse of adjectives is a common writing flaw.

Additional information: any handbook on English grammar and composition, such as *Harbrace College Handbook* or *Essentials of English.*

Ad-lib. Music or spoken parts used extemporaneously in a radio or TV program; elements that are used but are not indicated on the script.

Adult fiction. A novel or story in which the subject matter is often sexually explicit. (*See: Erotica; Pornography.*)

Advance. A sum of money that a publisher pays a writer(s) prior to the publication of a book. The advance represents compensation for the time and effort to be expended writing the book, and it usually reflects the publisher's expectation of the work's prospective sales. It is usually paid in installments, such as one-half on signing the contract; one-half on delivery of a complete and satisfactory manuscript. When royalties begin to accrue, the publisher withholds the amount of the advance paid to the author before making royalty payments.

The writer and/or his agent negotiates the advance against royalties, and its provisions are incorporated into the book contract. In the instance that an advance is actually larger than the royalties ultimately collected, the contract usually specifies that the advance is nonreturnable. The contract may also provide for protection against a publisher's trying to recoup all or part of the advance if for some reason he decides not to issue a book.

Advances vary with the type of book, the author's writing ability, his reputation and the book idea itself. They may be nonexistent in some cases, as low as $2,000-$4,000 for a fledgling writer, or from $15,000 to more than a million dollars for a veteran in the field. The publisher sometimes figures the advance as a function of the price of the book times the royalty percentage times the estimated advance sale. Thus, an estimated four-thousand-copy advance sale of a $13.95 book with a 10 percent of list price starting royalty might produce an advance offer to the author of a maximum of $5,600. A writer's advances generally rise from book to book, as his audience increases. (*See: Book contract; Book publishing economics.*)

Advance sale. This publishing term refers to the commitments to buy made by bookstores or wholesalers before the formal publication date of a particular book. To make advance sales, a publisher's representative supplies information on forthcoming books to buyers. Publishers also circulate direct-mail catalogs listing and describing forthcoming publications so that individual consumers can place orders in advance. Data from the very earliest advance sales, especially the orders placed by the major bookstore chains, help the publisher estimate the print order for a book.

Adventure story. A genre of fiction in which action is the key element, overshadowing characters, theme and setting. (Even though *adventure story* is the name of the genre, the term refers to articles, novels and nonfiction books as well.)

The conflict in an adventure story is often man against nature. A secondary plot that reinforces this kind of conflict is sometimes included. In Alistair MacLean's *Night Without End*, for example, the hero, while investigating a mysterious Arctic air crash, also finds himself dealing with espionage, sabotage and murder.

In recent years, adventure novels have been in demand, and novels and stories alike have begun to borrow elements from spy stories and war stories.

Papillon, by Henri Charrier, and *Annapurna*, by Maurice Herzog, are two examples of nonfiction adventure stories, while *Hunt for Red October* and *Flight of the Intruder* are adventure novels. Some publishers have produced series of books under imprints such as "Men of Action," "Hawk," "Destroyer" and other lines.

Men's, young adults', children's, religious and women's magazines all publish adventure stories. *Novel & Short Story Writer's Market* lists editors' needs and payment rates for writers.

Advertiser control of media. Because advertisers provide a substantial portion of media revenue, they sometimes try to exert influence on the editorial aspects of media presentations. They might try to suppress a news story unfavorable to them or influence editors to give their products favorable treatment in magazines.

Most editors working in print media will vigorously defend their ideological independence from advertisers, although the industry has experienced occasional lapses.

Television producers, on the other hand, are placed under more pressure by their sponsors. Advertisers hire celebrities to advertise products on their own shows; ensure that their product, as opposed to a similar one, is used in the program; and may censor controversial characters and philosophies featured in teleplays. (*See: Advertorial.*)

Advertising, agencies and profits. (*See: Figure 1.*)

Advertising, copyrighted. Copyright protection for print media advertisements is granted when the work is created. Published and unpublished advertisements may be registered at the U.S. Copyright Office by depositing a copy of the work along with the appropriate application and filing fee. Prior to March 1989, a copyright notice was required on all published works, to maintain protection. While the copyright notice is no longer mandatory, it is still important to show ownership and to rebut claims of innocent infringement.

Parts of an advertisement, such as original jingles, illustrations, photos and copy, are eligible for copyright protection, as are many objects used in advertisements, such as original works of art, dolls, games and maps. Anyone—a radio or TV station or an advertiser who has the right to control a program's content—can be held responsible for copyright infringement when using the copyrighted material of others in an unauthorized fashion. (*See: Copyright; Copyright notice; Copyright, Register of.*)

Advertising copywriters. Writers whose purpose is selling products or services for clients through written or spoken copy. These writers prepare newspaper and magazine ads, brochures, billboards, radio and TV commercials, annual reports and anything else that is used to sell a product or service.

Copywriters work for advertising agencies or for the advertising departments of companies. Copy chiefs tend to prefer applicants with liberal arts/English backgrounds and retail or marketing research experience. Desirable personality traits include: an ability to get along with others, a spirit of inventiveness and the discipline to work long hours under pressure.

Freelance copywriters develop their own clients by contacting people and organizations that advertise. Department stores, catalog houses, shopping centers, art studios, printing companies and political campaigns afford opportunities for copywriters. Sample copy presented to these advertisers to solicit their business should deal with the merchandise or service they offer and should be slanted to reflect their particular advertising "image" (e.g., institutional copy for banks and hotels would be different from the action words and catchy headlines for sportswear).

Salary scales for ad copywriters vary with company size and the availability of competent writers. Successful freelance copywriters work to gain the confidence of steady clients. Some employers hire by the day or the hour. Those writers with experience may choose to quote a price for a job before accepting it.

One advantage of copywriting for advertising may well be the growth and flexibility it offers the writer. Freelancers often work at home, sometimes during their spare time from other employment. They can move from one ad job to another with relative ease once they establish a portfolio. Though advertising copywriters get no bylines of their own, they are known and have visibility within the advertising community they serve.

FIGURE 1

ADVERTISING AGENCIES' COSTS AND PROFITS

The following figures represent percentages of gross income unless otherwise stated, based on a survey of 343 advertising agencies in 1988:

Rent, light and depreciation 10.64%

Other operating expenses 16.23%

Total payroll 60.47%

Payments into retirement plans 1.23%

Insurance for employee benefit 2.81%

Total expenses 95.69%

Operating profit 4.31%

Gross income comprises commissions, agencies' service charges and fees. Figures are averages for agencies of all sizes. Source: Annual studies of advertising agencies' costs and profits conducted by American Association of Advertising Agencies.

Additional information: *Jobs and Opportunities for Writers; Standard Directory of Advertisers; Standard Directory of Advertising Agencies.*

Advertising freelance services. Freelance writers and editors can take advantage of several methods of advertising without purchasing ads in publications. Direct-mail brochures can be sent to any printers, businesses or agencies that the freelancer perceives as prospective clients. A résumé and a portfolio are effective means of introducing work to a client in person. Similarly, copies of articles can be sent to acquaintances or associates, such as librarians, editors and professors, to keep them current on a writer's career.

The writer can obtain a listing in a directory such as *Literary Market Place* or *Working Press of the Nation.* Another method of direct advertising is to post business cards or other notices at suitable locations.

Finally, public speaking offers a way for many writers to make themselves known. (*See: Business cards; Speechwriting; Stationery.*)

Advertorial. Advertising presented in such a way as to resemble editorial material. Even though it may contain the same kind of information that might have been written as an editorial feature in a magazine, it is paid for by an advertiser, and the word "advertising" usually appears in small type at the top of each page.

The Association of Business Publishers has guidelines for the use of these special advertising supplements.

Advice columns. Besides the well-known personal advice columns of twin sisters Ann Landers and Abigail Van Buren, there are numerous other specialized advice columns in U.S. newspapers. A list of those columns, their authors and the syndicates that handle them appears in the *Editor & Publisher Syndicate Directory*, described in this book. Freelancers who have an idea for a specialized advice column usually try for sales to their local and regional papers before approaching a national syndicate. (*See:* Editor & Publisher Syndicate Directory; *Self-syndication; Syndicated column.*)

Affiliate. A local radio or TV station that has a contract with a network to carry certain programs.

Agents, comedians'. A writer interested in submitting gag material to a well-known comedian should first try contacting him through a club at which or a TV show on which he's appearing. If that doesn't work, the writer must approach the comic through a personal manager. The National Conference of Personal Managers, at 10231 Riverside Dr., Toluca Lake, CA 91602, or 1650 Broadway, New York, NY 10019, may be able to provide information on which personal manager represents which comedian. (*See:* Variety.)

Agents, literary. (*See: Figure 2.*) Writers' business representatives. As marketing experts in the publishing field, they sell book outlines or manuscripts, negotiate royalty advances, and contract terms for writers. They know what publishers are buying and which books are selling; therefore, they can often speed up the purchase of material. They know editors' tastes and serve as liaisons between them and authors with appropriate ideas.

Most legitimate agents earn their money by deducting commissions from the manuscripts they sell. Commission rates on U.S. material range from 10-15 percent. When a U.S. agent deals with a foreign agent on the writer's behalf, the commission is at least 20 percent. Agents represent writers in any kind of literary output but generally do not handle poetry, verse, articles, short stories, cartoons or fillers because of the low commissions they generate. Most agents do not charge reading and evaluation fees if they consider a work salable. Some agents specializing in handling the beginning writer's work, however, charge fees for reviewing manuscripts, since their opportunities for commissions on sales are more limited.

There are many ways to find an agent. The most direct approach is to query by mail. Query letters should contain an outline of the project and the qualifications of the writer. (Complete manuscripts should not be sent to an agent at this point.) Since it is not unusual for an agent's client list to include as many as sixty authors to whom he is responsible, an agent may not be interested in taking on another client unless the project is compelling. A self-addressed, stamped envelope should accompany the request

FIGURE 2

AGENTS, LITERARY

WHAT I LOOK FOR IN A NEW WRITER CLIENT
by Oscar Collier, Collier Associates

*I*n my imagination I have found an ideal new client. He has talent, imagination, the drive to make money—and is willing to listen to advice.

The new client has read my listing in either *Writer's Market* or *Novel & Short Story Writer's Market,* so he knows the kind of books I represent and doesn't send me juveniles, textbooks or trivia books. Although I'm not against erotic scenes in novels, I don't handle pornography. The client realizes that I, like an editor, look for a strong new angle on a good subject. The initial approach to an agent by a prospective new client is always by letter—not a phone call—with appropriate details on past publishing history and type of current work seeking representation.

Though canny and self-reliant, this new client is willing to establish a relationship based on trust. The client trusts me and knows I wouldn't have started working with him unless I like his writing. While I can't offer detailed editorial criticism, I do make suggestions when I see that a manuscript needs some changes or additions and this ideal client won't be wounded, but *will* argue back if there is justified disagreement.

The new client is considerate of my time—an agent's main resource—but still is not too shy to call when it's important. Under normal circumstances I'd hope not to get called more than once a month by each of my clients. Letters are always preferred.

The client will bounce back from rejections, knowing I will make submissions to every likely prospect for any work that has broad appeal. The client reads rejection letters but doesn't take them too seriously unless several editors make the same criticism. A writer needs a combination of resilience and patience. Just as it takes time to write a book, so it can take time to sell it. But if I'm lucky enough to make a quick sale, I hope the client won't think I'm a wizard, able to sell anything I handle. Each new sale is just as hard as the one before—or maybe, harder.

This ideal client respects me enough to use his full writing power when writing me a letter. What is the point of being in the literary business if I don't get any interesting letters? A writer should regard anything he writes as an example of his style, whether a business letter or a multivolume saga.

Finally, I truly appreciate it when a client remembers throughout our association that ours is a business relationship. Friendship can happen, but it is not the basic connection between writer and agent. I expect performance from a client, just as the client expects performance from me. So I guess what I look for most of all in a new client is a continuing flow of commercial ideas and strong work—the real key to writing success.

for the agent's consideration of the proposed work.

Lists of agents are published in the annual directories *Guide to Literary Agents* and *Literary Market Place.* Some agents advertise their services in writers' magazines. In addition, editors, friends and teachers can often recommend suitable agents. (*See: Association of Authors' Representatives.*)

Agents, TV. The TV business is unlike publishing in that a writer interested in breaking into TV writing usually approaches producers through an agent; most TV producers will not consider unsolicited manuscripts from a writer. TV agents, like literary agents, work on a commission (10-15 percent on domestic sales).

Names of agents who have regular contact with TV producers are maintained in the files of the Writers Guild of America, West, 7000 W. Third St., Los Angeles, CA 90048. Agents willing to work with previously unproduced writers are listed in *Writer's Market.* (*See: Agents, literary.*)

AKA. Acronym for *also known as.* It is used in connection with writers' pen names, and sometimes appears in bibliographies of a writer's works, e.g., Erle Stanley Gardner (aka A.A. Fair). (*See: Pen name.*)

All rights. Some magazines buy all rights to the articles, stories and poems they acquire from freelancers. They indicate this policy either in their listings in *Writer's Market* or on the checks they issue for manuscripts. Magazines with this policy will, in some cases, return all but first

North American serial rights to the author on request.

Under the old copyright law, a publisher was presumed to have bought all rights to a manuscript unless the author and the publisher agreed otherwise. Under the current law, which went into effect in 1978, the publisher is presumed to have bought only one-time rights unless the author and the publisher have agreed otherwise.

A work-for-hire agreement, which concerns assigned rather than unsolicited work, includes the purchase of all rights. The writer has no power to negotiate future rights when such an agreement has been made. The purchase of all rights without such an agreement, on the other hand, usually concerns unsolicited work, the rights to which may sometimes be regained by the author, as mentioned above. Listings in *Writer's Market* indicate editors' policies on rights. (*See: Copyright; Rights to manuscripts; Work made for hire.*)

Alternate (or alternate selection). In book club offerings, a book that, though not a main selection, is called to the special attention of the club's membership. A book club's catalog sometimes promotes more than one alternate.

The first time an alternate selection is offered, it is featured—given special treatment in the book club's bulletin. In later months, it becomes part of the backlist of alternate selections, and so is given a short descriptive entry in the bulletin. Like a main selection, an alternate means additional sales for the author. (*See: Book club selection; Book clubs; Selection [or main selection].*)

Alternative weekly. A weekly paper, usually a tabloid, that is distinguished from a suburban or small-town weekly by its urban readership, concern with urban issues and political liberalism. Alternative weeklies are the offspring of the underground papers of the 1960s. Most of their readership is aged from the late teens to the early forties; live in an urban central core of downtown and inlying suburbs; and are college-educated.

Alternative weeklies are published in major cities, particularly cities on either coast and cities with a revitalized inner city. They are characterized by in-depth coverage and analysis of news and controversial topics not covered or barely covered by the daily newspapers. A great advantage to alternative weeklies is that, since they are not the local newspaper of record, they can pick and choose the stories to cover. Alternative weeklies also report on the particular arts their readers follow, in greater depth than most dailies can.

The quality of writing in an alternative weekly is generally high; the pay, generally low. Alternative weeklies can be either easy or difficult markets to break into, depending on the individual paper's reputation, but they are an excellent training ground for young writers.

Some of the most successful and respected alternative weeklies are the Chicago *Reader* and the San Francisco *Bay Guardian.*

America Online. Usually referred to as "AOL," America Online is one of the largest online services, with more than two million members as of early 1995. Known for the ease of use of its excellent graphic interface, AOL serves subscribers using DOS, Windows and Macintosh operating systems. It offers a wide range of activities and information, from research (including some access to the Internet's World Wide Web, WWW), to games, to late-breaking news. AOL is a commercial service, and thus charges a set monthly fee plus an hourly charge for time used over and above the free monthly allotment of online time. For additional information, or to request a set of disks to install America Online on your computer, call (800) 822-6364 (*See: Electronic mail; Internet; Online service.*)

American Academy & Institute of Arts & Letters. The National Institute of Arts & Letters was established in 1898 to further literature and the fine arts in the U.S. The American Academy of Arts & Letters, founded by the Institute in 1904, is a self-perpetuating group of fifty members chosen for special recognition in literature, art and music. Eminent foreign artists, writers and composers are elected as honorary members.

The Institute encourages excellence in the arts by conferring a number of awards and honors for works meriting praise. Many of the awards have been established in memory of a distinguished practitioner of a particular craft: e.g., the Sue Kaufman Prize for First Fiction; the Marjorie Peabody Waite Award, given to an older writer for continuing achievement; and the Witter Bynner Poetry Prize. Other awards have been established to recognize achievement in other fields, such as the Award of Merit Medal given to an outstanding novelist, poet or dramatist. The Academy also sponsors fellowships—e.g., the Rome Fellowship in literature at the American Academy in Rome.

Some of the awards are accompanied by cash prizes and/or medals. Most of them may not be applied for but are awarded by decision of the Academy members. Further details of the awards are given in the annual *Literary Market Place*. Recipients of the various awards are listed in recent editions of *Literary and Library Prizes*.

American Book Awards. Established in 1978 to recognize outstanding literary achievement by contemporary American authors without restriction for race, sex, ethnic background or genre. The purpose is to acknowledge the excellence and multicultural diversity of American writing. The awards are nonprofit. There are no categories, and winners are accorded equal status.

Literary Market Place details submission dates and contact persons for more information about the American Book Awards. (*See: National Book Critics Circle.*)

American Book Trade Directory. This directory, available in most public libraries, lists bookstores in the U.S. and Canada by state or province and city. It lists—in addition to the address, phone number and name of owner (or manager)—the types of books and other products carried by bookstores. The directory also includes the names and addresses of book and magazine wholesalers, national distributors of paperbacks and other book trade information. Writers who self-publish their books use the annual to find stores that are likely prospects for their work.

American Booksellers Association (ABA). An organization of fifty-five hundred retail bookstores whose goals are to facilitate bookstore operations; educate members in their trade through seminars and workshops; foster greater numbers of book sales; and sustain harmonious relations between booksellers and publishers.

The ABA publishes the weekly *Newswire,* the monthly *American Bookseller,* the biennial *Sidelines Directory,* the biennial *Basic Book List* and *A Manual on Bookselling: How to Open and Operate Your Own Bookstore* (third edition), which is distributed by Crown Publishers. It convenes annually and is the largest publishing-related meeting of the year, attended by foreign as well as domestic publishers, packagers and agents.

ABA headquarters are located at 137 W. Twenty-fifth St., New York, NY 10001. (*See:* Basic Book List.)

American Dialect Society (ADS). This group, founded in 1889, is made up of scholars who study not only the English language in North America, but languages that influence or are influenced by English in this region. The Society has research committees that report on new words, proverbial sayings, regionalisms and linguistic geography, non-English dialects, and usage.

Membership currently comprises eight hundred individuals and institutions. People interested in the goals and activities of the organization are qualified to join; members must pay dues, however.

The ADS holds an annual meeting and other, regional meetings. Its publications include *American Speech*, published quarterly; *Publication of the American Dialect Society* (PADS), published occasionally; and *Newsletter of the American Dialect Society* (NADS), published in January, May and October.

This organization sponsors the five-volume *Dictionary of American Regional English* (DARE). The Society's publications are sources for half the dictionary's content.

While fiction writers are always cautioned to use dialect sparingly, the use of an apt word or phrase to pinpoint a certain section of the country can add flavor and credibility to a work. Writers with questions about regionalisms, for example, may find the Society's research helpful. The Society's headquarters are % the English Department, Mac-Murray College, Jacksonville, IL 62650. (*See:* Dictionary of American Regional English *[DARE].*)

American Library Association (ALA).
A forty-eight-thousand-member organization of libraries, library trustees, individual librarians and other individuals interested in libraries.

According to the American Library Association, the Association is "an organization with the overarching objective of promoting and improving library services and librarianship. The priorities are access to information, legislation/funding, intellectual freedom, public awareness and personnel resources."

ALA's committees include Instruction in the Use of Libraries, Intellectual Freedom, Professional Ethics, Publishing and Research. It publishes *Booklist*, semimonthly;

American Libraries, eleven times per year; *Choice*, eleven times per year; books; and pamphlets.

The Association holds an annual convention and an annual midwinter meeting. The address of ALA is 50 E. Huron St., Chicago, IL 60611.

American Medical Writers' Association (AMWA).
Members of this organization are medical writers, editors, publishers, administrators, audiovisualists and pharmaceutical and public relations professionals concerned with effective communication about medicine and allied sciences. The Association publishes a newsletter, a journal, a membership directory and a freelance directory. Awards for medical books and medical films are given; a conference is held annually. The address of the AMWA is 9650 Rockville Pike, Bethesda, MD 20814.

American Society of Indexers (ASI).
The 750 members of ASI strive to encourage communication concerning developments in the field and to stimulate members to improve their professional capacities. Besides indexers, members include librarians, editors, publishers and organizations that employ indexers.

Committees of the group include Education, Getting Started as an Indexer, Indexer Economics and Indexer-Publisher Relations.

Publications include *The Indexer*, a journal published in affiliation with the Society of Indexers (England); the ASI newsletter; and the *Register of Indexers*, a list of indexers available for freelance assignments.

The address of the ASI is 1700

Eighteenth St., N.W., Washington, DC 20009.

American Society of Journalists and Authors (ASJA).

The ASJA is a nation-wide organization of more than six hundred independent nonfiction writers. It encourages high standards of nonfiction writing, takes a strong stand against practices denigrating the freelance writer's professional status, holds educational conferences and meetings, offers awards for outstanding accomplishments and examines issues that concern the freelance writer and the reading public. ASJA publishes a monthly newsletter for its members, a "Code of Ethics and Fair Practices," an annual membership directory and books on writing. By sending $12.95 to the address below, writers can receive *The ASJA Handbook: A Writer's Guide to Ethical and Economic Issues.*

The American Society of Journalists and Authors was formerly called the Society of Magazine Writers. ASJA is located at 1501 Broadway, Suite 302, New York, NY 10036. (*See: Dial-a-Writer.*)

American Society of Journalists and Authors Code of Ethics. (*See: Figure 3.*)

American Society of Magazine Editors (ASME).

The seven hundred members of ASME are senior editors on magazines. The organization presents national magazine awards, sponsors a magazine internship program, holds seminars and luncheons and publishes an occasional newsletter for members. ASME convenes annually. Its address is 575 Lexington Ave., New York, NY 10022.

American Society of Media Photographers (ASMP).

(Formerly the Society of Photographers in Communications.) Established in 1944, this organization comprises more than five thousand members worldwide. General members have had at least three years' experience following their first published work; they are involved in advertising, documentary photography and photojournalism.

Freelancers may wish to inquire if there is an ASMP photographer in their area to recommend to an editor on an article idea for which they're not equipped to provide illustrations themselves. The address of the American Society of Media Photographers (ASMP) is 419 Park Ave., S., #1407, New York, NY 10016.

American Society of Newspaper Editors (ASNE).

The membership of this group is made up of one thousand daily newspaper editors in the U.S. and Canada, who hold positions such as managing editor executive editor, associate editor and editorial page editor. Committees include Freedom of Information and Press-Bar. The organization meets annually.

ASNE publishes the *Bulletin of ASNE* nine times per year, and *Problems of Journalism—ASNE Proceedings* annually. The mailing address of the ASNE is P.O. Box 17004, Washington, DC 20041.

American Society of Picture Professionals (ASPP).

Since 1966, this organization of more than six hundred members has brought together people involved in all areas of the photographic profession including photo researchers, photo editors,

FIGURE 3

AMERICAN SOCIETY OF JOURNALISTS AND AUTHORS
CODE OF ETHICS AND FAIR PRACTICES

PREAMBLE

Over the years, an unwritten code governing editor-writer relationships has arisen. The American Society of Journalists and Authors has compiled the major principles and practices of that code that are generally recognized as fair and equitable.

The ASJA has also established a Committee on Editor-Writer Relations to investigate and mediate disagreements brought before it, either by members or by editors. In its activity this committee shall rely on the following guidelines.

1. TRUTHFULNESS, ACCURACY, EDITING

The writer shall at all times perform professionally and to the best of his or her ability, assuming primary responsibility for truth and accuracy. No writer shall deliberately write into an article a dishonest, distorted or inaccurate statement.

Editors may correct or delete copy for purposes of style, grammar, conciseness or arrangement, but may not change the intent or sense without the writer's permission.

2. SOURCES

A writer shall be prepared to support all statements made in his or her manuscripts, if requested. It is understood, however, that the publisher shall respect any and all promises of confidentiality made by the writer in obtaining information.

3. IDEAS AND PROPOSALS

An idea shall be defined not as a subject alone, but as a subject combined with an approach.

A proposal of an idea ("query") by a professional writer shall receive a personal response within three weeks. If such a communication is in writing, it is properly viewed and treated as business correspondence, with no return postage or other materials required for reply.

A writer shall be considered to have a proprietary right to an idea suggested to an editor.

4. ACCEPTANCE OF AN ASSIGNMENT

A request from an editor that the writer proceed with an idea, however worded and whether oral or written, shall be considered an assignment. (The word "assignment" here is understood to mean a definite order for an article.) It shall be the obligation of the writer to proceed as rapidly as possible toward the completion of an assignment, to meet a deadline mutually agreed upon, and not to agree to unreasonable deadlines.

5. CONFLICT OF INTEREST

The writer shall reveal to the editor, before acceptance of an assignment, any actual or potential conflict of interest, including but not limited to any financial interest in any product, firm or commercial venture relating to the subject of the article.

6. REPORT ON ASSIGNMENT

If in the course of research or during the writing of the article, the writer

continued on next page

FIGURE 3 (CONTINUED)

AMERICAN SOCIETY OF JOURNALISTS AND AUTHORS
CODE OF ETHICS AND FAIR PRACTICES

concludes that the assignment will not result in a satisfactory article, he or she shall be obliged to so inform the editor.

7. *WITHDRAWAL*
Should a disagreement arise between the editor and writer as to the merit or handling of an assignment, the editor may remove the writer on payment of mutually satisfactory compensation for the effort already expended, or the writer may withdraw without compensation and, if the idea for the assignment originated with the writer, may take the idea elsewhere without penalty.

8. *AGREEMENTS*
The practice of written confirmation of all agreements between editors and writers is strongly recommended, and such confirmation may originate with the editor, the writer, or an agent. Such a memorandum of confirmation should list all aspects of the assignment including subject, approach, length, special instructions, payments, deadline and guarantee (if any). Failing prompt contradictory response to such a memorandum, both parties are entitled to assume that the terms set forth therein are binding.

All terms and conditions should be agreed upon at the time of assignment, with no changes permitted except by written agreement signed by both parties.

9. *REWRITING*
No writer's work shall be rewritten without his or her advance consent. If an editor requests a writer to rewrite a manuscript, the writer shall be obliged to do so but shall alternatively be entitled to withdraw the manuscript and offer it elsewhere.

10. *BYLINES*
Lacking any stipulation to the contrary, a byline is the author's unquestioned right. All advertisements of the article should also carry the author's name. If an author's byline is omitted from a published article, no matter what the cause or reason, the publisher shall be liable to compensate the author financially for the omission.

11. *UPDATING*
If delay in publication necessitates extensive updating of an article, such updating shall be done by the author, to whom additional compensation shall be paid.

12. *REVERSION OF RIGHTS*
A writer is not paid by money alone. Part of the writer's compensation is the intangible value of timely publication. Consequently, reasonable and good-faith efforts should be made to schedule an article within six months and publish it within twelve months. In the event that circumstances prevent such timely publication, the writer should be informed within twelve months as to the publication's continued interest in the article and plans to publish it. If publication is unlikely, the manuscript and all rights therein should revert to

continued on next page

FIGURE 3 (CONTINUED)

AMERICAN SOCIETY OF JOURNALISTS AND AUTHORS
CODE OF ETHICS AND FAIR PRACTICES

the author without penalty or cost to the author.

13. PAYMENT FOR ASSIGNMENTS
An assignment presumes an obligation upon the publisher to pay for the writer's work upon satisfactory completion of the assignment, according to the agreed terms. Should a manuscript that has been accepted, orally or in writing, by a publisher or any representative or employee of the publisher, later be deemed unacceptable, the publisher shall nevertheless be obliged to pay the writer in full according to the agreed terms.

If an editor withdraws or terminates an assignment, due to no fault of the writer, after work has begun but prior to completion of the manuscript, the writer is entitled to compensation for work already put in; such compensation shall be negotiated between editor and author and shall be commensurate with the amount of work already completed. If a completed assignment is not acceptable, due to no fault of the writer, the writer is nevertheless entitled to payment; such payment, in common practice, has varied from half the agreed-upon price to the full amount of that price.

14. TIME OF PAYMENTS
The writer is entitled to full payment for an accepted article within thirty days of delivery. No article payment, or any portion thereof, should ever be subject to publication or to scheduling for publication.

15. EXPENSES
Unless otherwise stipulated by the editor at the time of an assignment, a writer shall assume that normal, out-of-pocket expenses will be reimbursed by the publisher. Any extraordinary expenses anticipated by the writer shall be discussed with the editor prior to incurring them.

16. INSURANCE
A magazine that gives a writer an assignment involving any extraordinary hazard shall insure the writer against death or disability during the course of travel or the hazard, or, failing that, shall honor the cost of such temporary insurance as an expense-account item.

17. LOSS OF PERSONAL BELONGINGS
If, as a result of circumstances or events directly connected with a perilous assignment and due to no fault of the writer, a writer suffers loss of personal belongings or professional equipment or incurs bodily injury, the publisher shall compensate the writer in full.

18. COPYRIGHT, ADDITIONAL RIGHTS
It shall be understood, unless otherwise stipulated in writing, that sale of an article manuscript entitles the purchaser to first North American publication rights only, and that all other rights are retained by the author. Under no circumstances shall an independent writer be required to sign a so-called ''all rights transferred'' or

continued on next page

FIGURE 3 (CONTINUED)

AMERICAN SOCIETY OF JOURNALISTS AND AUTHORS
CODE OF ETHICS AND FAIR PRACTICES

"work made for hire" agreement as a condition of assignment, of payment, or of publication.

19. *REPRINTS*
All revenues from reprints shall revert to the author exclusively, and it is incumbent upon a publication to refer all requests for reprint to the author. The author has a right to charge for such reprints and must request that the original publication be credited.

20. *AGENTS*
An agent may not represent editors or publishers. In the absence of any agreement to the contrary, a writer shall not be obliged to pay an agent a fee on work negotiated, accomplished, and paid for without the assistance of the agent. An agent should not charge a client a separate fee covering "legal" review of a contract for a book or other project.

21. *TV AND RADIO PROMOTION*
The writer is entitled to be paid for personal participation in TV or radio programs promoting periodicals in which the writer's work appears.

22. *INDEMNITY*
No writer should be obliged to indemnify any magazine or book publisher against any claim, actions, or proceedings arising from an article or book, except where there are valid claims of plagiarism or copyright violation.

23. *PROOFS*
The editor shall submit edited proofs of the author's work to the author for approval, sufficiently in advance of publication that any errors may be brought to the editor's attention. If for any reason a publication is unable to so deliver or transmit proofs to the author, the author is entitled to review the proofs in the publication's office.

© 1991, American Society of Journalists and Authors, Inc.

---

stock agents, museum curators, librarians, historians, designers and photographers. "The ASPP provides a forum about the use, purchase and sale of still images, promotes high professional standards, maintains a Code of Fair Practice in the business of picture research and handling, and cooperates with organizations that have similar interests." Five chapters based in New York, Boston, Washington DC, Chicago and San Francisco offer programs, panel discussions, speakers, tours and chapter meetings to the members. All members receive a quarterly magazine, a News Digest, a membership directory, and a newsletter from their local chapter. ASPP's main office is located at 2025 Pennsylvania Ave., N.W., #226, Washington, DC 20006.

American Translators Association (ATA). This international organization of thirty-five hundred members advocates improvement of professional standards and encourages professional training. Its members are categorized as follows: *active* (citizens or permanent residents of the U.S. who are professional translators or interpreters or who work in related fields), *associate* ("individuals who are interested in the objectives of ATA but who are not eligible for active membership"), *student* (full-time students at accredited institutions; must be thirty years of age or under), *institutional, corporate* and *sustaining*. According to the pamphlet "Guide to ATA," the "ATA actively discourages anyone from joining it primarily to obtain employment or freelance assignments."

The *ATA Chronicle* is a monthly publication for organization members.

Awards presented by the ATA are the Alexander Gode Medal, for "outstanding achievement in the profession"; the Lewis Galantiere Prize, for literary translation; the Distinguished Service Plaque, for "outstanding and dedicated service to the American Translators Association"; and the Academic Programs Fund, given to a student or group of students.

The American Translators Association convenes annually to exchange ideas and to discuss common problems. Its headquarters are at 1735 Jefferson Davis Highway, Suite 903, Arlington, VA 22202-3413.

Anecdote. A short narrative revealing a curious, amusing or insightful incident that illustrates a point or reinforces an idea. Anecdotes frequently contain dialogue, provide explicit detail and sometimes incorporate plays on words or humorous endings. It is a glimpse of life that is often used to "humanize" a topic.

An anecdote may be biographical, or it may result from the writer's observation. It is used in virtually all article writing, in addition to being salable in itself as a filler.

Here, for example, is an anecdote as it appeared in a column by Robert Sylvester in the New York *Sunday News*:

The other day a truck, a cab and a private car managed to ram each other at Fifth Avenue and 48th Street. The three drivers were using some pretty strong language. A newcomer to the onlookers' circle asked: "Anybody hurt?"

"Not yet," said another bystander.

Examples of anecdotes are available in any issue of *Reader's Digest* in departments titled, "Life in These United States," "Humor in Uniform," "Campus Comedy" and "All in a Day's Work."

Angle. In TV and motion picture scripts, a designation of camera position used to highlight a dramatic scene. It could be either straight forward or an oblique camera angle. The expression *angle on* is used to indicate the major subject of the scene the camera should emphasize. Both terms are typed in all caps.

Annotation. Notes that explicate or augment a text. Ancient or reconstructed or symbolically dense literature is frequently published in annotated editions, e.g., Chaucer, Shakespeare, collections of folktales, translations of classics or of national literature, Joyce and the poetry of Pound and Eliot.

An annotated bibliography briefly describes and/or evaluates the listed works to better aid the reader in researching a topic.

Announcement. In radio advertising, another word for *commercial* or *spot.*

Annual report. The financial statement published at the end of each fiscal year by a corporation or institution. It often contains corporate histories, executive profiles and other information for which freelance writers are sometimes employed. (*See: Seasonal jobs for writers.*)

Anonymity of sources. Confidentiality between journalists and certain sources is important to the media's function of gathering and disseminating news: If a reporter reveals a source, he risks losing the confidence of the person who was his source, as well as his reputation among potential sources.

The court trial represents a common situation in which reporters are asked to reveal their sources of information. Although no federal law protects writers from such requests, some states have *shield laws,* or laws that give reporters the right to keep their sources confidential. However, shield law privileges apply to freelance writers only in some states. (*See: Attribution; Free press vs. fair trial; Shield laws.*)

Antagonist. The primary character in a story or novel with whom the hero or heroine is in conflict. (*See: Protagonist.*)

Anthology. A collection of selected writings by various authors, or a gathering of works by one author.

A freelancer who sells a publisher on an anthology becomes the editor of the collection. As such, he usually includes an introduction highlighting the purpose of the work. Upon a publisher's acceptance of the writer's proposal for a new anthology, a contract is written outlining the term of cash advances, royalty schedules and permission fees. Royalty schedules depend on whether the book retails as hardbound or paperback and on the permission fees, which are negotiated between the publisher and the editor.

Permission must be secured to use previously copyrighted material in an anthology. Before the current copyright law took effect in 1978, most copyrights were held by the magazine in which the work originally appeared. Now, they may be owned by either the original author or the publisher, depending on what rights the author sold. Books, of course, are usually copyrighted in the name of the author, so reprint requests on work in books would be sent to the author in care of the publisher. Reprint fees depend on the original author's reputation and the source of the original publication. Materials in uncopyrighted U.S. government journals are available for reprint without cost. (Since the government itself sometimes may pick up copyrighted material for reprint, the author/editor should be on the lookout for copyright notices. If there are none, the material is in the public domain.)

Upon receipt of permission to use copyrighted materials, the anthologist selects a consistent method of indicating which materials in the collection have been previously copyrighted, usually on an "Acknowledgments" page preceding the table of contents. The anthology may be copyrighted in the name of the publisher or the author/editor, depending on the type of book and the terms of the contract.

The contents of the anthology may be arranged in a number of ways, depending on the subject matter and the editor's view of how the reader would use the book. It may be chronological (for textbooks), alphabetical (by author), categorical or any other organization.

Anticlimax. The part of a novel, story or play that follows the resolution of the climax. Its purpose is usually merely to satisfy the reader's curiosity regarding subsequent events in the characters' lives. The reader's interest level drops sharply from the climax to the anticlimax, which is usually a letdown for most readers. (*See: Climax.*)

Antihero. An antihero, or nonhero, is a protagonist that lacks traditional heroic qualities such as strength, valor and nobility of mind and spirit. Found primarily in modern fiction, drama and cinema, an antihero is not ordinarily an admirable or heroic figure: He might even be a coward, a clod or a crook. Nevertheless, an antihero is generally likeable because, while he might not live by society's values, he is true to the personal moral code that he has established. The comic strip character Charlie Brown is something of an antihero, as is the hardboiled, coarse but streetwise Sam Spade character in Dashiell Hammett's *The Maltese Falcon*. The protagonists in many of Kurt Vonnegut's novels are antiheroes; Woody Allen is adept at creating engaging antiheroes in his films. (*See: Protagonist.*)

Article. A nonfiction prose composition that appears in a magazine or newspaper. (Articles printed in newspapers are often called *feature stories* to distinguish them from straight news.)

A successful article begins with an idea that may come from almost anywhere—a friend, an item in a newspaper, an observation. The writer mulls over the idea, does some market research to determine what, if anything, has recently been written about the subject, then hones the idea into a *theme*—the precise subject of an article. While a theme may be a complex one, it is very important that the writer think it through and find a sufficiently narrow aspect of it to discuss in proper depth; this is the *peg* of the article. (The peg determines not only how extensively the writer will treat the topic, but also where he will market the article—and vice versa. An article on liverworts, for example, marketed to a local Sunday magazine rather than to *Smithsonian,* not only would require a regional peg, but also would have to be written in much simpler language and briefly explain even basic natural processes to a less sophisticated readership.)

After finding a solid peg, the writer researches the piece, both at the library for background and by conducting interviews. (Research may also uncover a more promising peg; the writer should be alert for this.) He then begins to organize his material into an article.

Most articles have a four-part structure. The *lead,* or opening paragraph, is crucial to capturing reader interest; a good lead clearly sets forth the problem or situation the article deals with and demonstrates (directly or indirectly) why the reader should read the piece. If the lead has not directly stated the theme or explained the reader's stake in the piece (for instance, if the lead were an anecdote), then the next *theme* paragraph must do so. Succeeding paragraphs, the *body* of the article, develop the theme using quotes and anecdotes (and sometimes statistics) where appropriate. The *conclusion* should relate back to the lead in some way, by concluding the opening anecdote, by answering questions raised at the beginning or by summarizing the main points of the article.

If the article demands extensive research, some magazine editors may request the author's bibliography so that the research department can verify the facts presented in the article. (*See: Essay; Feature.*)

Article rejection terms. When rejecting an article, the editor may indicate the piece lacks "authority." By that, he may mean: (1) the writer used only material from previously published sources instead of interviewing original sources himself; (2) statements that are apparently opinion are not documented; (3) the article lacks, or contains too few, quotes from experts; or (4) conclusions presented in the article do not arise logically from the previous statements. Other editors might say that an ar-

ticle is "flat." By this, they usually mean the article lacks dialogue, local color, anecdotes, moving passages of forceful argument or proper pacing and flow of ideas.

Another article rejection term might be the article is too "slight." This usually means that the treatment of the subject is too general, or without any meaty new angles to make it different from other articles on the subject.

Arts review. A critical reaction to a popular or classical cultural event. Some forms of art that are typically reviewed are concerts, plays, films, records and exhibits. A review should be constructed from the critic's personal, analytical reaction, although audience response may also be mentioned in the piece.

A reviewer must be informed about the art form he writes about, because a good review gives insight into, as well as an account of, a performance or exhibit. By the same token, preparation for the specific event to be reviewed is necessary. The critic can read a play script or book before attending a play or movie; similarly, a critic should be knowledgeable about other records or concert performances by an artist.

In a newspaper review, certain facts, such as time, place, dates and credits, are often placed in the first paragraph; the decision as to which facts are necessary and where they are placed, of course, varies with the editor.

An arts review of a play, film, etc., mentions the plot but should refrain from revealing the outcome if that is essential to enjoying the work. The reviewer also evaluates the plot, the interpretation of the theme and the technical skill displayed. In the case of a live performance, the critic can sometimes meet the performers and directors to ask questions and to take photos to accompany his piece.

Arts reviews are used by newspapers and magazines. For a newspaper assignment, a writer should query an arts or entertainment editor. (A weekly, because it is less likely to have a staff person handling reviews and imposes less deadline pressure, is a better place to start than a daily.) Payment for a review in a weekly ranges from $15 to $35; in a daily, from $45 and up. In addition, the reviewer usually receives tickets to the event.

National trade magazines specializing in the arts use reviews from different parts of the U.S.; a writer querying such a magazine should include sample summary reviews of a month's events in his area. Payment for this type of work is about $35 for a beginner, and up to $100 for an experienced correspondent.

Records and related printed material are supplied free of charge by record companies, but a reviewer who requests them must prove that he has published work in this field. The contact for review copies of new records is the promotion and publicity department of a record company. (*See: Book review; Criticism; Drama criticism; Restaurant review.*)

ASCAP. (*See: Performing rights organizations.*)

Aside. A speech, or perhaps just a line, in a play in which a character reveals his thoughts aloud. When an aside is delivered, other characters are on stage besides the speaker; the audience understands that for the purposes of the drama, the other characters do not hear the speaker's aside. The technique is not used very often in contemporary drama. (*See: Soliloquy.*)

Assignment, writing on. Writing on assignment is almost always done by writers who have already established a reputation with particular editors. The magazine requests that a freelance writer do a story on a subject it has conceived. It also may set a word length, a focus, a fee and a kill fee.

Beginning writers rarely get assignments; however, a beginner in a unique situation, such as that of having access to a celebrity, may sometimes obtain an assignment from a magazine. Unlike the established writer, the beginner must usually submit his work unassigned and on speculation, with no guarantee of a purchase.

Professional freelance writers may write on assignment, not only for magazines, but for businesses, book publishers and others as well. (*See: Kill fee; On spec.*)

Associated Business Writers of America (ABWA). A subsidiary of The National Writers Club. This group serves as a link between writers specializing in business and editors of business magazines. NWC/ABWA holds periodic workshops. Its publications include newsletters and market reports, published monthly; and the annual *Professional Freelance Writer's Directory.* The ABWA's address is 1450 S. Havana, Suite 620, Aurora, CO 80012.

Associated Press (AP). Established in 1848, the Associated Press is the oldest international news service, with a staff of three thousand reporters, photographers, editors, technicians and administrative personnel. There are more than two hundred AP bureaus worldwide, engaged in the gathering and distribution of world, national, regional and state news. The AP is a nonprofit cooperative owned by its American newspaper members. AP supplies information and photographs via satellite, wire, ocean cable, landline and radio to some ten to fifteen thousand newspapers and broadcasters around the world. AP Radio Network in Washington is the audio arm of this news company.

As a cooperative news service, the AP has the right to reprint any local news stories or photographs that originate with member papers. In the case of a freelance story rewritten and published by the AP, the writer of the original receives no additional payment from the news organization. When a story is copyrighted, however, AP makes reprint arrangements before running the story. The AP does not routinely make use of freelance material, however.

The AP convenes annually. Its headquarters are at 50 Rockefeller Plaza, New York, NY 10020. (*See: United Press International.*)

Associated Writing Programs. An association of colleges and universities that offer undergraduate and graduate programs in creative writing. The Association publishes a newsletter, an annual anthology of student work, and a catalog describing 250 writing programs in the U.S. and Canada.

The Association's purposes include enhancing the quality of literary education and helping writers and teachers get jobs. Students who want to major in creative writing can find appropriate colleges in the geographical areas of their choice by writing the Association.

Its current headquarters are at Tallwood House, Mail Stop 1E3, George Mason Univ., Fairfax, VA 22030.

Association for Education in Journalism and Mass Communications (AEJMC). An organization of twenty-five hundred college and university professors, professionals and students, whose goals are to improve techniques in teaching journalism and the overall quality of journalism itself. The AEJMC conducts research on and stays abreast of enrollment in journalism programs. In addition, it maintains a list of people seeking teaching positions, as well as a list of positions open in the field.

Publications of the Association include *Journalism Abstracts,* published annually; *Journalism Educator, Journalism Monographs* and *Journalism Quarterly,* all published quarterly; and *Journalism* newsletter, published six times a year. Committees include AEJMC-American Newspaper Publishers Association Cooperative on Journalism Education, Journalism Language Skills, Professional Freedom and Responsibility, Publications, Research, Status of Women in Journalism Education and Teaching Standards.

The AEJMC meets annually. Its headquarters are at the University of

South Carolina, College of Journalism, 1621 College St., Columbia, SC 29208.

Association of American Publishers (AAP).

The more than three hundred members of this organization publish trade books, textbooks, reference books and books for a general audience, as well as teaching materials.

AAP operates a library of materials on book publishing and presents the Curtis G. Benjamin Award for creative publishing. In addition, it publishes the *AAP Newsletter.*

Committees within the Association include Copyright, Education for Publishing, Freedom to Read, International Freedom to Publish, New Technology and Postal.

The group's seven divisions, based on members' interests and areas of greatest sales volume, are general publishing, college, school, professional and scholarly, mass paperback, direct marketing/book club and international.

AAP holds a spring annual meeting and a fall divisional meeting. Its offices are at 220 E. Twenty-third St., New York, NY 10010.

Association of American University Presses (AAUP).

A group of scholarly publishers operating at colleges and universities, AAUP exists to assist and counsel its members, conduct research, inform the public through public information programs, act as a medium through which members can exchange information, and manage workshops and seminars. It is active in soliciting funds in the form of grants from foundations to keep university presses in existence.

The Association currently has one hundred members.

AAUP publishes *Exchange,* a quarterly newsletter; an annual directory; books; and handbooks. Its committees include Books, Catalogs and Ads; Copyright; Education and Training; Marketing; and Systems and Information Technology.

The Association convenes annually in June. Its headquarters are at 584 Broadway, Suite 410, New York, NY 10012. (*See: University press.*)

Association of Authors' Representatives (AAR).

A voluntary professional organization for agents that resulted from the merger of Independent Literary Agents Association (ILAA) and Society of Authors' Representatives (SAR). This organization has a strong code of ethics—which the AAR enforces—for its members. As of January 1, 1996, AAR member agents will not be allowed to charge reading fees for manuscripts. For a list of members and the code of ethics, send $5 and an SAE with two first-class stamps to Association of Authors' Representatives, 10 Astor Place, Third Floor, New York, NY 10003.

Association of Editorial Businesses (AEB).

Companies that specialize in editorial services, such as writing, editing, proofreading, indexing and research, belong to this organization. The AEB, which was established in 1980, exists to uphold professionalism, to improve standards in editorial quality and in business dealings, to conduct research and to educate its members and the public. It publishes a newsletter and a membership directory and meets monthly.

The AEB's headquarters are at 116 Fourth St., S.E., Washington, DC 20003.

Association of Independent Video and Filmmakers, Inc. (*See: Videotape.*)

As-told-to article or book.

This term refers to a ghostwritten, first-person narrative, for which the writer is given an "as-told-to" or "with" joint byline; or credit on the acknowledgment page. This technique lends itself to at least three types of accounts: the dramatic personal experience, the opinion on some matter of public interest by an authority and the commentary or personal revelation by a celebrity.

One of the best idea sources for possible co-authors of as-told-to articles and books is the newspaper or newsmagazine. A writer "sells" the idea to the subject and together they settle the financial arrangements. If the two write and sell an article, the subject may get the public recognition while the author gets the check from the publication. Or they may split fifty-fifty. In the case of a book, the split of advance and royalties varies. The writer (sometimes with the help of an agent or literary lawyer) often negotiates in writing the sharing of proceeds to suit his particular situation, depending on which person—the subject or the writer—contributes more to the salability of the project. Some professional writers prefer to get 75 percent of the advance and take less than 75 percent of the royalties, in case the book does not sell as well as expected and to cover their work on the book "up front."

After completing the manuscript, the writer obtains a signed release from the subject giving permission for publication. (*See: Ghostwriting.*)

Atmosphere.

A term describing the overall effect or mood of a piece of writing. It is a combination of setting, descriptive details and dialogue (if any). It includes both physical and psychological details and is achieved not only by the choice of words but also by the pacing of sentences. A successfully evoked atmosphere heightens the reader's emotional response.

For example, the bleak setting of Arthur Miller's *Death of a Salesman* and the emphasis on familial allegiance in Mario Puzo's *The Godfather* create atmosphere for those works.

Attribution.

A term that refers to the writer's or reporter's stating the source of a direct quote.

Attribution is important because it lends credibility to a story. However, whether to use a speaker's actual name in attribution can cause a dilemma for the writer when his material pertains to personal or controversial subjects, or when the interviewee has designated particular bits of information as "not for attribution."

A method of solving the writer's problem is to print the direct quote while using a descriptive phrase or a professional title to name the source. For example, certain information about news in Washington might be attributed to "a prominent White House aide." (*See: Off the record.*)

Auction (of a manuscript). Publishers sometimes bid for the acquisition of a book manuscript that has excellent sales prospects. Before such an auction, which is private, takes place, the author's agent submits the manuscript simultaneously to various publishers. Publishers' bids are for the amount of the author's advance, plus other considerations such as guaranteed dollar amounts to be used for advertising and promotion, royalty percentages, agreement for the publisher to take smaller shares of paperback revenue, and the like.

In recent years, runaway bidding on some blockbuster books has resulted in considerable financial success for some authors. However, when a publisher pays an extremely high advance for one author's book, he has few funds for promotional and other expenses for others' books, which can cause those works to suffer.

This practice was begun by literary agent Scott Meredith in about 1950 when, armed with a book his agency considered particularly strong, he phoned and saw many publishers about it rather than just one publisher, giving them a two-week bidding deadline. All publishers at that time had the strict policy of considering submissions only on an exclusive basis, but Meredith felt that this policy was protective for publishers but very unfair for writers, who sometimes had to wait through years of slow readings and rejections, getting through only a handful of publishers and perhaps never reaching the firm ready to buy the manuscript.

A number of publishers flatly refused to consider the manuscript if other publishers were also considering it. Other publishers, however, agreed to read the manuscript if that was the only way they were going to get to see it, and in time the literary auction became established practice in the field. Today, virtually all "hot" books—books by major authors and unusual or unusually good books by new or newer authors—are auctioned.

The title of that first auctioned book? Unfortunately, neither Scott Meredith nor his staff could remember, since, said Meredith, "the first time we tried an auction, I had no idea I was doing anything historic."

Today, of course, book publishers themselves auction books to paperback houses and book clubs.

Audio Video Market Place (AVMP). This directory refers the writer to organizations and services connected to the audiovisual industry, which comprises films, slide-tape programs, audio cassettes, etc. The largest of the directory's sections, "Producers, Distributors, and Services," has both geographic and classified listings for writers seeking contacts in the audiovisual field. Other sections of the directory of particular interest to writers are "Periodicals" and "Reference Books."

A cross-index section contains the names of people and organizations listed in the book.

Listings in *Audio Video Market Place* include names, addresses, telephone numbers, names of personnel and descriptive data about the companies and services.

Audiovisual communication. Audiovisual communication is writing for the voice and ear as well as the eye. Its format may be motion pictures, video and slide tapes, filmstrips, audio cassettes or whatever new forms technology brings us. Its purpose, like writing for print, is to entertain and/or inform.

The audiovisual communicator faces challenges different from those of conventional writers. He strives to achieve a balance between copy and visuals. His script persuades the viewer to his point of view not just with dialogue or narration, but also with lighting, camera angles, music, sound effects (or silence)—all of the nonverbal techniques that are largely emotional in appeal.

A typical script is divided into two columns. One is labeled "picture" or "video," in which the writer indicates everything the viewer will see. This includes a description of the scene, camera directions, etc. The other column, labeled "sound" or "audio," contains the words spoken in narration or dialogue plus indications of sound effects, music, etc.

Audiovisual markets include business, industry, government, education, medicine, religion—virtually any group with a motive and the money to reach an audience. Before querying a potential audiovisual producer, the writer should find out the company's current needs and previous productions as described in the "Scriptwriting" chapter of *Writer's Market* and the producer's current catalog.

Before beginning a script, the writer consults with the client, who outlines the purpose, the budget and the target audience.

Payment rates for audiovisual writers vary. While the Writers Guild of America has established rates for theatrical and TV material, payment for nontheatrical audiovisual filmscripts usually depends on the producers and clients. The going rates are listed in the "Scriptwriting" section of *Writer's Market* and vary from a flat fee to a percentage of the production cost. (*See: Figure 4; Film writing, nontheatrical; Screenwriting.*)

Authorized biography. An authorized biography is an account of a person's life, written with the subject's complete cooperation. Such cooperation involves in-depth interviews, anecdotes from family and friends (and sometimes enemies) and access to personal records/correspondence. If the subject is dead, authorization comes from his family or the executor of his estate.

When writing an authorized account, the biographer secures the subject's approval before the work is published. In addition, the writer sometimes shares with him the byline, advance and royalties. Some authorized biographies are simply puffery and are panned by critics for lack of objectivity. (*See: Biography; Unauthorized biography.*)

Author's alteration clause. This book contract clause spells out the amount of changes (in terms of a percentage of the typesetting cost) an author is allowed to make on galleys or page proofs. Usually, if the author makes changes totaling more than 10 percent of the cost of typesetting, charges for the overage are deducted from future royalties. (*See: AA.*)

FIGURE 4

AUDIOVISUAL
SCRIPT SAMPLE

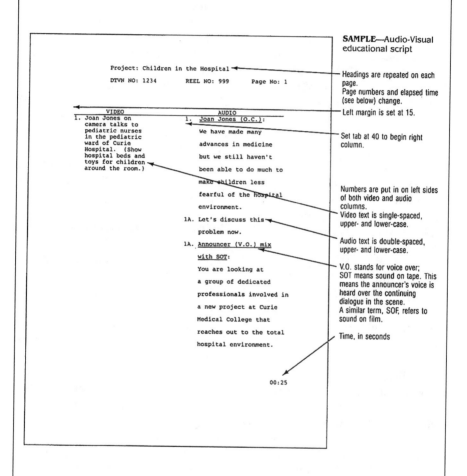

SAMPLE—Audio-Visual
educational script

Project: Children in the Hospital

DTVN NO: 1234   REEL NO: 999   Page No: 1

Headings are repeated on each page.
Page numbers and elapsed time (see below) change.
Left margin is set at 15.

VIDEO	AUDIO

1. Joan Jones on camera talks to pediatric nurses in the pediatric ward of Curie Hospital. (Show hospital beds and toys for children around the room.)

1. Joan Jones (O.C.):

We have made many

advances in medicine

but we still haven't

been able to do much to

make children less

fearful of the hospital

environment.

1A. Let's discuss this

problem now.

1A. Announcer (V.O.) mix

with SOT:

You are looking at

a group of dedicated

professionals involved in

a new project at Curie

Medical College that

reaches out to the total

hospital environment.

00:25

Set tab at 40 to begin right column.

Numbers are put in on left sides of both video and audio columns.
Video text is single-spaced, upper- and lower-case.

Audio text is double-spaced, upper- and lower-case.

V.O. stands for voice over; SOT means sound on tape. This means the announcer's voice is heard over the continuing dialogue in the scene.
A similar term, SOF, refers to sound on film.

Time, in seconds

The script sample on this page is reprinted from the book: *The Writer's Digest Guide to Manuscript Formats,* published by Writer's Digest Books. Copyright © 1987 by Dian Dincin Buchman and Seli Groves.

Author's copies. An author usually receives about ten free copies of his own hardcover book from the publisher; more from a paperback firm. He can obtain additional copies at a price that has been reduced by an author's discount. (*See: Author's discount.*)

Author's discount. A reduction in cost of a book—usually by 40 percent of the retail price—given to the author of that book. An author may wish to buy books from the publisher and sell them, at a profit, to individuals and groups to which the publisher may not have easy access but the author does—as, for example, when he is a frequent lecturer at various conventions or workshops related to the book's topic. This provision, however, must be covered by the contract, and when large quantities of books are involved, better discounts are possible. Author's discounts on textbooks may average 20-25 percent rather than 40 percent. (*See: Author's copies.*)

Authors Guild. A national professional organization made up of more than sixty-five hundred book authors and magazine writers. It is involved in issues such as free speech, copyright and taxes, and has represented the writer in such matters before Congress and in the courts. The Guild also provides writers with information about publishers' contract provisions for advances, royalties, subsidiary rights, etc.

Applicants for membership to the Guild are generally required to have published either one book at an established American house within seven years of their applica-tion, or three fiction or nonfiction pieces in a general circulation magazine within the previous eighteen months of their application for membership.

The Guild meets every February in New York City. Its committees include the Book Contract Committee and the Children's Book Committee, and it publishes a bulletin five times per year.

All Authors Guild members also belong to the Authors League of America, which comprises the Authors Guild and the Dramatists Guild. The Guild headquarters are located at 330 W. Forty-second St., New York, NY 10036. (*See: Authors League of America.*)

Author's information forms. After signing with a book publisher, an author may be asked to complete two or more forms: One provides the publisher with his social security number for tax purposes, while another questionnaire seeks promotion information on the author (such as education and career accomplishments), and on the book's subject matter. The publisher uses this information to write book jacket copy and send publicity releases to the author's hometown newspapers and college alumni publications, and to any professional organization newsletters or other publications related to the author's background. Authors should take great care to provide as much good descriptive copy about the book and as many sales and publicity leads as possible.

Authors League of America. This 14,700-member professional organization comprises the Authors Guild's sixty-five hundred book authors and magazine writers and the Dramatists Guild's eight thousand playwrights. The Guilds publish and distribute (to members only) the *Dramatists Guild Quarterly* and *Newsletter* and the *Authors Guild Bulletin* which, along with other printed materials, provide information on contract terms, copyright, libel and other legal and professional matters affecting writers. The ALA's headquarters are at 330 W. Forty-second St., New York, NY 10036. (*See: Authors Guild; Dramatists Guild.*)

Author's tour. (*See: Book-promotion tour; Promotion by author.*)

Autobiography. A book-length account of a person's life written by the subject himself. An autobiography is usually set down in the form of narrative recollections of those people and events in his life that the writer considers interesting. Some celebrities' autobiographies really *are* written by the subject—*Sweet Life: Adventures on the Way to Paradise,* by Barry Manilow—while others are opportunities for professional writer-collaborators, such as *Breaking the Surface,* by Greg Louganis with Eric Marcus.

People who are not well known and who want to publish an autobiography must have either an exceptionally unusual or fascinating life or fine writing style, or both, to interest a commercial publisher. (*See: Biography.*)

Autographing party. An autographing party is a promotional device that is provided by publishers, usually to authors of books with bestseller po-

tential. The author appears at bookstores or book departments and autographs each copy of his book, as it is sold, for individual customers.

It is unlikely that an autograph party would be held for a book by a new author, since the publisher's profit would not justify the cost. However, an author may decide to promote his book independently of the publisher; in such a case, he could take it upon himself to arrange a local autographing party through a bookstore or department store chain. (*See: Promotion by author; Publishing party.*)

Availability list. In radio advertising, a list maintained by the traffic manager; it indicates the amount of time that can be sold.

Avant-garde. A kind of writing in which the subject matter or style shows a break from tradition. *Avant-garde,* which literally means *foreguard* in French, is often used to refer to experimental writing.

As a noun, this term applies to the group of people in a field (such as writers or artists) whose work is unconventional. (*See: Magazine, alternative.*)

Aviation/Space Writers Association (AWA). This nine hundred-member organization is made up of writers and editors involved in books, newspapers, magazines, radio, TV and public relations for and about the aviation/space industry. The AWA presents annual awards for writing, public relations, public affairs, company communications, visual communications and helicopter heroism. Its publications include a newsletter published four times per year and a manual containing a membership list. An annual meeting/news conference is held.

The headquarters of the AWA are at 17 S. High St., Suite 1200, Columbus, OH 43215. (*See: Council of Writers Organizations.*)

Awk. Copyeditor's mark, suggesting to the author that a particular word, phrase or sentence is awkward, and proposing a clarification.

Back matter. (*See: Book manuscript preparation and submission.*)

Background information, books of. Nonfiction writers who need statistical or factual data to support their arguments can find such information in the *Information Please Almanac* and similar one-volume almanacs, *The Statistical Abstract of the United States,* and in references such as *Facts on File,* which deals with news events indexed by subject, person and country. While reference books provide a good starting search for factual information, encyclopedias, travel books, magazines, newspapers—almost anything—can provide the writer with background information.

When writing a book set in Rome, for example, the writer who wants to add authenticity to the fiction may find detailed background in a travel guide. A writer doing a nonfiction piece on breast cancer would want to get background information from publications about breast cancer, medical journal reports and recent magazine articles on the subject.

Reference books of facts are just a starting place to look for background information on a subject. (*See: Periodicals, indexes to.*)

Backlist. The publishing term for a group of previously published books that are still in print a year after publication. Backlist books are available from the publisher, but not usually from bookstores except on special order; some independent bookstores, however, do carry backlist titles.

The ABA *Basic Book List* includes those backlist books that continue to sell well enough to be carried by bookstores.

Backstory. Biographical information about a fictional character. A realistic past gives the writer a strong foundation of motivations and goals to use when building the story and establishing the character. Actors use backstory to give their portrayals more realism.

Basic Book List. An annual publication of the American Booksellers Association listing books with sales records. The *Basic Book List* recommends titles in various categories that might complete a bookseller's stock, balance his inventory or fill a void in a subject area. Though the list is designed to assist booksellers, it may also be used by writers as an adjunct to bestseller lists, to get a feel for the books that sell consistently in certain subject areas.

The *Basic Book List* is compiled by a panel of booksellers who update, revise and expand the previous year's list, and consider title and category suggestions submitted by other booksellers. It is available in some public libraries, some bookstores and from the American Booksellers Association.

Bay Area Writing Project (BAWP). This program for teachers of writing was founded at the University of California, Berkeley, in 1974 and has influenced other universities throughout the U.S. to establish similar programs. In conjunction with BAWP, the programs are known as the National Writing Project Network.

BAWP exists to instruct teachers how to teach writing. Participants, who teach in colleges, secondary schools and elementary schools, gather during the summer for a five-week session. The program consists of presentations by the students (teachers), small group discussions, exposure to new ideas and to research findings, and writing. To be eligible, teachers must submit recommendations and prove that they have had successful teaching experience. Those who attend receive a stipend and college credit. After the summer session, teachers take part in a follow-up program during the school year; they are paid for acting as consultants to school districts.

Some assumptions underlying the philosophy of the program are that most teachers are unaware of the knowledge that exists in the field of teaching writing, that teachers have not been adequately prepared to teach writing and that anyone who teaches writing must write himself.

BAWP publishes monographs written by teacher-consultants. A list of publications, as well as information on how to obtain them, is available from the Publications Department, Bay Area Writing Project, 5627 Tolman Hall, University of California, Berkeley, CA 94720. (*See: National Writing Project.*)

Beat. In a motion picture, TV or radio script, a one-count pause in the action or in a character's speech.

Belles lettres. Literally "beautiful letters," usually referring to literature of the fine arts, as distinguished from scientific or technical writings.

Berne Union or Berne Convention. An international union for the protection of literary artistic works, to which many countries throughout the world belong. On March 1, 1989, the U.S. became a member, thus making available to its nationals copyright protection in the foreign countries that are members of the convention. Similarly, works by nationals of those countries become eligible for copyright protection of their works in the U.S. In amending the U.S. copyright law to come into compliance with the Berne Convention, the primary change was that a copyright notice on the work after March 1, 1989, was not *mandatory*. For practical purposes in preventing infringement, however, writers are urged to continue to use the copyright notice (©, name, year). (*See: International Copyright Convention.*)

Best Books for Children: Preschool Through Grade 6. A guide to children's fiction and nonfiction books, which is aimed at librarians and used to begin collections, to add to or judge existing collections, to help children to choose books, and to compile bibliographies and reading lists. The majority of books described in this volume are those written for children in preschool through the sixth grade, but some can be used by junior high school students as well. There are books intended for pleasure reading as well as those designed to fit into a school curriculum.

This guide is useful to writers of children's books in showing them the existing competition in selected subject matter. The Fifth Edition, published in 1994, contains approximately fifteen thousand entries, divided into thirty-four sections, many of which contain subsections. Examples of section headings are "Books for Beginning Readers," "Mythology," "The Arts and Language," "Folklore," "Personal Development" and "The Sciences."

Entries contain data such as title, author and illustrator of the book; grade levels for which the book is appropriate; publication date; publisher; cost; information on the book's format, i.e., *LB* for library binding or *paper* for paperback; and an annotation.

Best Books for Children was begun in 1959 as a series of annual books. In 1978, it took on its present subtitle, changed format and became a hardbound volume.

The best markets. Beginning writers frequently ask the editors of Writer's Digest Books what is the "best" market to write for. For beginners, nonfiction represents by far the largest *number* of markets, since magazines contain predominantly articles these days, not stories. Obviously, the larger circulation magazines *pay* more, but these also demand a higher level of professionalism and experience. Smaller circulation

magazines pay less, but fewer writers are competing for the editors' checks.

Nonfiction books, too, are usually easier for a new writer to sell than novels.

Writing for films and TV is lucrative but usually demands residence near a film production center, and specialized skills.

There is no one answer to the question of "best" markets. Many novelists never earn more royalties than their advances, while others are millionaires. Some film and TV writers hunger to have their names on a book, even though their annual freelance income far surpasses that of the average book author.

Each writer must serve an apprenticeship of both finding his own voice and learning about the marketplace through trial and error submissions. A new architect doesn't get his first job as designer of a skyscraper office/hotel/retail shops complex; there are no shortcuts for the writer either. There are Cinderella stories of previously unknown writers who became overnight successes, but investigation usually uncovers a long period of development that preceded that sudden fame.

Best-seller lists. Lists that appear in *Publishers Weekly, USA Today,* the *New York Times Book Review* section and the book pages of local newspapers are compiled from sales figures reported by bookstores, bookstore chains, wholesalers and distributors. They don't usually report sales of Bibles, cookbooks and other specialized books. A good summary of the year's best-selling hardcover, trade paperback and mass market paperback sales appears in the annual statistics issue of *Publishers Weekly,* which is published in March each year.

Bibliography. Most publishers of general interest trade books prefer a bibliography and appendix to footnotes for citing sources used in book research. Textbook formats, on the other hand, are more likely to include footnotes.

In one style for writing bibliographic entries suggested by the University of Chicago Press's *The Chicago Manual of Style,* the components are listed in the following order: name of author (with last name first), title of book (set in italics), city of publication, publishing company, date of publication (year only). The following example demonstrates the proper form, including punctuation, according to *The Chicago Manual of Style:* Provost, Gary. *Make Your Words Work.* Cincinnati: Writer's Digest Books, 1994.

The book *Words Into Type* suggests the following order for bibliographic references to articles: author's name (surname first), the title of the article (in quotation marks), publication title (in italics), the volume number, date of issue and page number. Example: Childe, V. Gordon. "War in Prehistoric Societies." *Sociological Review,* Vol. XXXIII (1941), pp. 126-38.

People who write or edit scientific books or journals should note that these publications usually have a different system from publications related to the humanities. They should query the particular editors they work with about methods of citing sources.

Bilingual edition. A book that is printed—either wholly or partially—in two languages. When a single publisher produces such editions, the author and the translator usually share the royalties. (*See: Translation rights.*)

Bimonthly. Referring to something that takes place once every two months, such as a magazine published bimonthly.

This word is sometimes confused with *semimonthly,* which refers to a publication issued twice a month. (*See: Biweekly; Semimonthly.*)

Biographical novel. A life story documented in history and transformed into fiction through the insight and imagination of the writer. This type of novel melds the elements of biographical research and historical truth into the framework of a novel complete with dialogue, drama and mood. A biographical novel resembles historical fiction, save for one aspect: Characters in a historical novel may be fabricated and then placed into an authentic setting; characters in a biographical novel have actually lived.

Several identifying characteristics distinguish the biographical novel. First is the writer's choice of a subject he values and whose life is naturally traversed with the substance of a novel—e.g., recurring themes, human conflicts, triumphs and defeats. Another distinction is the writer's painstaking study of the human condition and everyday life of the subject and his time. Finally, the biographical novel unfolds as if it were happening at this moment. A classic example of a biographical novel would be Irving Stone's *Lust for Life,* the story of Vincent Van Gogh.

Biographical references. The standard references for biographical research that are available in most public libraries include: *Biography Index,* which refers the reader to books and periodicals containing biographical material; *Marquis Who's Who Publications/Index to All Books,* which covers the people listed in most of the Marquis directories such as *Who's Who in America, Who Was Who in America,* and specialized directories such as *Who's Who in Finance and Industry;* and *Current Biography,* with articles on prominent people in national and international affairs. Other sources include the *International Who's Who, Webster's Biographical Dictionary* and *American Men and Women of Science. Biography News* is a monthly publication that contains material from American newspapers about people prominent in the news.

Writers interested in looking up their favorite authors can refer to volumes such as: *Author Biographies, Twentieth Century Authors, Contemporary Authors* and *Journalist Biographies Master Index. (See: Writers, biographical directories of.)*

Biography. An account of a person's life (or the lives of a family or close-knit group) written by someone other than the subject(s). The work is set within the historical framework (i.e., the unique economic, social and political conditions) existing during the subject's life.

A biography can detail the lives of people living or dead. Its subjects are people who inspire, repel, attract or intrigue.

A biography may take several forms. The traditional or narrative biography begins with a subject's birth and proceeds chronologically through his life. Or it may open with some dramatic or character-revealing episode and later bring in his early life. A life story may also take a topical format, in which various aspects of the subject's life are detailed in designated chapters. Finally, a biography may be written in essay form, wherein the author writes in the first person and includes his own comments about the subject.

Characteristics of the modern biography include an opening scene or statement establishing the subject's prominence or suggesting a reason for the biography, suppositions about the subject's subconscious life, and probes into the subject's personality.

The average length of an adult biography runs from three to four hundred manuscript pages. (*See: Authorized biography; Autobiography; Collective biography; Juvenile biography; Memoir; Unauthorized biography.*)

Biweekly. Referring to something that takes place once every two weeks, such as a magazine published biweekly. This word is sometimes confused with *semiweekly,* which refers to a publication issued twice a week. (*See: Bimonthly; Semiweekly.*)

Black humor. A kind of humor that concentrates on social issues and social outcasts. It is somber and destructive in tone. Black humor comments on societal problems through grotesque and nightmarish means.

Bruce Jay Friedman, editor of the anthology *Black Humor,* describes this form as one that goes beyond satire. He holds that since the modern world contains elements of the absurd, satire is no longer the province of the novelist, but rather of the journalist; out of the fiction writer's groping for new territory black humor evolved.

Black humor is found in all media. The Evelyn Waugh novel *The Loved One* is a classic example of black humor, as is the Emmeline Grangerford segment in *The Adventures of Huckleberry Finn.* Some playwrights and filmmakers deal exclusively in black humor—Brendan Behan and Sam Shepard, in *The Hostage* and *Buried Child,* respectively, are just two of many dramatists who rely on the form, and filmmaker John Waters has acquired a large cult following with movies such as *Pink Flamingos* and *Female Trouble.* Even artists and cartoonists—such as Edward Gorey and Gahan Wilson—have developed distinctive black-humor styles.

Black writers. Although over the centuries the nature of race relations in the U.S. has kept unknown numbers of black writers from being published, blacks have nevertheless made invaluable contributions to American literature. The struggle against racial prejudice and the resultant economic, political and social disadvantage has given rise to a rich and powerful black literature; while most black writers have never been commercially successful, many have received critical acclaim, and proponents of black literature have rediscovered—and in some cases republished—the work of fine black writers of the past.

One of the most important black forms is the autobiography. Frederick Douglass's 1845 narrative of his life as a slave and escape to the North helped popularize the Abolitionist movement. Other black writers and political figures who have published influential autobiographical works include Booker T. Washington, James Baldwin, Richard Wright, Malcolm X, Eldridge Cleaver and Gwendolyn Brooks.

Around the turn of the last century, Paul Lawrence Dunbar was one of the most widely read poets in America; Charles W. Chestnutt achieved critical success among the literary realists but failed to find a popular audience and gave up literature. The Harlem Renaissance of the 1920s and 1930s sparked admiration for black art forms among blacks and educated whites alike; the best-known Harlem writers included Countee Cullen, Claude McKay (who wrote *Home to Harlem,* the first best-seller by a black writer), Zora Neale Hurston and Langston Hughes. In the 1940s, Richard Wright published *Native Son* and *Black Boy.*

The struggle for black civil rights in the 1950s was in part fueled by, and helped produce, important black literature. Gwendolyn Brooks received the first Pulitzer Prize awarded to a black for her second book of poems, *Annie Allen.* In 1952, Ralph Ellison published *Invisible Man,* widely regarded as the finest novel of the postwar era. James Baldwin produced his first novel, *Go Tell It on the Mountain,* and his first collection of essays, *Notes of a Native*

Son, and went on to become the most successful black writers of the 1950s and 1960s.

It was in the late 1950s and early 1960s that a number of important black plays were first produced: Lorraine Hansberry's *A Raisin in the Sun* (1958); Ossie Davis's *Purlie Victorious* (1961); in 1964, Baldwin's *Blues for Mister Charlie* and LeRoi Jones's *Dutchman,* two spectacularly angry plays, were produced within months of each other.

Among the most important contemporary black writers are poet/novelist Ishmael Reed, poet/playwright Ntozake Shange and fiction writers Alice Walker, Toni Cade Bambara and Toni Morrison.

Bleed. Printed copy or an illustration that, to attract the reader's attention, reaches to one or more edges of the page.

Bleeds are found more often in books and magazines than in newspapers. According to the number of edges on the page where material bleeds, an illustration or print copy is called a one-, two-, three-, or four-side bleed. *Bleed* can be used as a verb or noun: Printing or an illustration *bleeds,* the designer *bleeds* an ad, and printing or an illustration that bleeds is called a *bleed.*

Blind writers' resources. The National Library Service for the Blind and Physically Handicapped, a division of the Library of Congress, lends talking books (on discs and cassette), Braille reading materials and Braille and large-print music to print-handicapped persons. Novels, nonfiction books and general interest magazines are available, as is information on handicap conditions. Reading materials are distributed and returned by postage-free mail.

Talking Book Topics and *Braille Book Review,* two bimonthly magazines published by the Library of Congress, announce the latest reading materials produced for visually and physically handicapped readers. People interested in borrowing the service's material must complete an application and have it signed by a physician or other professional working in a school, hospital, nursing home, rehabilitation center or other institution. Applications are available from the National Library Service for the Blind and Physically Handicapped, Library of Congress, Washington, DC 20542, and may be submitted either to the Library of Congress or to a regional or subregional library. (A list of regional and subregional libraries can be obtained from the Library of Congress.)

Blockbuster. A book that is a commercial success. *Blockbuster* is defined differently by different publishers, depending on the size of the latter. To a large publishing house, a blockbuster is a book with hardcover sales in the hundred thousands and paperback reprints in the millions, that is placed on national bestseller lists, and for which other subsidiary rights are sold. Another publishing term for *blockbuster* is *big book.* Blockbuster books by authors such as Tom Clancy and Mary Higgins Clark have made them millionaires.

Blurb. The copy on paperback book covers or hardcover book dust jackets. Blurbs can either give information about the book and the author or promote the book by featuring testimonials from book reviewers or well-known people in the book's field.

In fields other than publishing, *blurb* sometimes refers to any overstated advertisement or publicity release.

The word *blurb* was first used in 1907 by humorist Gelett Burgess. The jacket of his book *Are You a Bromide?* carried a picture of a young woman (which was customary for novels of that period) and textual matter mentioning ''Miss Belinda Blurb.''

BMI. (*See: Performing rights organizations.*)

Book club selection. For a book sold through a book club, the royalty is usually 10 percent of the book club member's price for hardcover books and 8 percent for paperbacks. If the book is a premium (a book offered at a low price to recruit new members), the royalty is 5 percent or 4 percent of the member's price. Royalties are usually split fifty-fifty by author and publisher on net sums received. Similarly, the advance varies according to the size of the club and whether the book is offered to members as a main or an alternate selection.

One large book club reports that its selections are chosen on the basis of entertainment/interest (as perceived by in-house editors) and members' response to previous books offered in the same category. (*See: Book clubs.*)

Book clubs. A book club offers books on selected subjects to its members

at a discounted price; it purchases such books from the publisher at a special price—in some cases at cost plus a royalty. Large clubs may print their own editions from duplicates of the publisher's films.

Acceptance by a major book club is a very positive factor for an author, since it brings the book to a large number of people throughout the country at the same time; but even selection by a small book club can enhance his royalties. The usual contract between author and publisher stipulates a fifty-fifty split of proceeds from book club sales.

The sale of book club rights is almost invariably made by the publisher. Book club selection usually comes about in one of two ways: The publisher may send advance galleys of a book to the club; or the club director, having read about forthcoming publication of a title he feels would interest his members, may request them from the publisher.

Larger book clubs usually print special editions for their members. Some clubs print cheaper editions; others print editions equal in quality to the publisher's. Smaller clubs may simply request the publisher to add a number of copies to his printing.

An advance for a large book club's main selection averages $50,000; a medium-sized club, from $5,000 to $10,000; a large book club's alternate selection yields an advance of from $2,500 to $25,000. But an author's royalties can vary from as little as $100 from a small, specialized book club to five or six figures if the book is a major book club selection.

Book contract. A legal agreement between author and publisher defining their commitments and establishing the financial terms of their partnership, including the advance, rights and royalties from the manuscript accepted for publication.

The typical publisher's contract is a standard form that allows for some of the terms, as well as the author's name and the book's title, to be filled into blanks. Many contracts mention the approximate length of the book (number of words) if it has not yet been fully written or if expansion has been requested by the editor.

The specific terms of a contract vary from publisher to publisher, depending on whether the author is a first-time writer or an established professional; whether the author has an agent; the topic; the publisher's estimate of the book's sales potential; and other factors. The usual royalty payment for hardcover books is 10 percent of the retail price on the first five thousand copies; 12½ percent on the next five thousand copies; and 15 percent thereafter. Advances vary by type of book, author's reputation, and sales prospects for the book. The book is copyrighted in the name of the author by the publisher.

Most contracts grant the publisher exclusive distribution of the book in a designated territory (e.g., the U.S., the world), and for a defined period of time (usually as long as the book remains in print). The sale of subsidiary rights is also provided for. In any case, the author's share of the subsidiary rights is usually no less than 75 percent on foreign editions, 50 percent on paperback and book club sales, and 90 percent on TV and movie sales.

Changes in book contracts may be negotiated by the author himself or with the help of an agent or lawyer. The Authors Guild, a professional organization offering guidance on the financial matters of writers, makes available to its members a sample contract designed to educate writers to the legalese of the book contract. This sample also provides recommendations on contract terms to seek that would be ideal for the author. (*See: Figure 5.*)

Book distribution. Major book publishers have their own salespeople calling on bookstores and wholesalers—e.g., Baker & Taylor and Ingram—and ship books directly to stores. Smaller companies hire independent book salespeople to represent them and contract with book distributing companies and wholesalers to ship to bookstores. A list of such publishers' representatives, wholesalers and distributors appears in *Literary Market Place*. A list of hardcover book and paperback wholesalers, set up geographically, appears in *The American Book Trade Directory*, which also lists geographically all bookstores in the U.S. and Canada and describes the types of books they carry.

When ordering books from a distributor, a buyer, such as a bookstore, must allow several weeks between the time the order is placed and the time delivery can be made. This fact is significant for teachers ordering books for classes and for authors who receive inquiries about the availability of their books.

Book distribution by author. An author who self-publishes a book and wishes to distribute it to trade bookstores,

FIGURE 5

BOOK CONTRACT TERMS

A beginner negotiating his first book contract may not be able to get his publisher to agree to all of the following terms, but *Writer's Digest* recommends them as parts of a standard to shoot for.

THE GRANT CLAUSE

Author's basic grant to the publisher should cover only English language book publication rights in the United States, Canada, and the Philippines. Should not grant "all rights" nor "the work."

ROYALTIES

Should be based on the retail list price, not the publisher's net price. For hardcover trade books, should not be lower than 10% on the first 5,000 copies; 12½% on the next 5,000; and 15% thereafter. (The writer may have to split his 10% with the illustrator in juvenile picture books; textbooks and juveniles may pay a lower rate.) Trade paperback royalties should be no less than 6% of list price on the first 20,000 copies and 7½% thereafter. Original mass market paperback royalties should be no less than 6% on net copies sold (distribution less returns).

THE ADVANCE

Should be nonreturnable, with the final payment due on submission of manuscript rather than publication of book.

SUBSIDIARY RIGHTS

Author's share should be no less than 80% on British edition, 75% on foreign editions, 50% on paperback reprint and book club sales; 90% on movie and TV sales; 90% on first serial (prepublication) rights and no less than 50% on second serial sales.

PAYMENTS

Statements of accounting and payments (if any) should be made semiannually.

WARRANTY CLAUSES

Author should only be liable if judgment is recovered in a suit against the publisher. (Author will be called upon to provide documentation for defense purposes, however.)

COPYRIGHT

Should be in the author's name.

OPTION CLAUSE

If one is given, should only grant the publisher an option to publish the next book on terms to be negotiated by the parties (not on the same terms provided in the current contract). The option clause should be keyed to submission of a *proposal* for the next work, not on submission of the next work itself. The publisher should be required to say yea or nay to the new proposal within 30-60 days.

TERMINATION

Author should be entitled to recover his rights if the book is no longer available for sale through regular trade channels or listed in the publisher's catalogue, and is not reprinted within six months after the author requests termination of rights.

PUBLICATION DATE

Should be within one year from delivery of manuscript.

EDITOR'S NOTE: Sample U.S. and foreign contracts are available for $.75 and $.50 respectively, plus a No. 10 self-addressed, stamped envelope from the Association of Authors' Representatives, 10 Astor Place, Third Floor, New York, NY 10003. New York residents must include sales tax. A helpful guide for the use of authors negotiating contracts with book publishers is available to members of the Author's Guild. See Author's Guild entry in this book.

schools or libraries will find lists of wholesalers and sales representatives for hardcover and paperback books in *Literary Market Place* and *The American Book Trade Directory*, available in most libraries. There are also some helpful sections on book distribution in the various books about self-publishing. For the titles of such books, check the *Subject Guide to Books In Print* under the category "Publishers and Publishing."

Book doctor. A freelance editor hired by a writer, agent or book editor who is skilled in analyzing any problems that exist in a book manuscript or proposal, and offering solutions to those problems. Book doctors often give advice on structure, characterization, dialogue, plotting and organization, or perform simple cutting, restructuring or line editing.

Before hiring a freelance editor, writers should ask to see a previous critique, the book doctor's professional résumé, names of books acquired and edited and references. A letter of agreement should itemize what services the book doctor will provide, when the services will be completed and how the fee should be paid (usually half up front and half on delivery).

Fees vary, but generally, a book doctor will charge $600-$2,00 for a 20- to 35-page detailed critique of a 400-page manuscript; and $35-$150 per hour for line editing, cutting or revising a manuscript or proposal.

Writers can locate potential book doctors by writing The National Writer's Union (873 Broadway, Suite 203, New York, NY 10003) for suggestions or Editorial Freelancers Association (71 N. Twenty-third St.,

New York, NY 10010) for directories that list members' specialties; and consulting *Literary Market Place* under Editorial Services.

Book editor. (*See: Book publishing jobs.*)

Book indexing. A nonfiction book author is often expected to provide his own index or have the cost of its preparation deducted from his royalties. When the author does not provide his own index, publishers often delegate this task to freelancers. The freelancer who seeks an indexing job usually must be located in the same general area as the publisher.

Freelancers looking for indexing jobs should consult *Literary Market Place*, an annual directory available at most libraries, which lists book publishers in the U.S. and Canada cross-indexed by geographic region. Another section in this directory, "Editorial Services," presents an opportunity for freelancers to announce their services to publishers and printers. (*See: Index; Indexing.*)

Book Industry Study Group, Inc. (BISG). This is a not-for-profit association of firms and individuals representing various sectors of the book trade. Incorporated in 1976, the group includes publishers, manufacturers, suppliers, wholesalers, retailers, librarians and others engaged in the development, production and dissemination of books. The Group promotes and supports research in and about the book industry. Its members share data and work to develop information useful to all segments of the industry. BISG publishes annual research reports on book industry trends in its aim to increase readership, improve book distribution and expand members' markets.

Information specifying membership criteria, dues and current activities of BISG is available by contacting its Managing Agent at 160 Fifth Ave., New York, NY 10010.

Book jacket and paperback cover copy. A freelance writer can make $75-$100 and up writing cover copy for books.

A book jacket copy assignment usually consists of two parts: back cover copy and flap copy, both front and back. Flap copy generally summarizes the content of the book and mimics the author's style. Back cover copy for novels may offer a brief description of the main characters and their motivations. Nonfiction back cover—or flap—copy often highlights the book's features.

A freelancer interested in writing cover copy begins by querying various publishing houses to find out which ones use freelancers. (Most New York publishing houses require that the freelancer live in New York City.) An editor may offer a writer with no related experience a book on speculation, in which case the writer will be paid for the assignment only if the copy is used. In other cases, an editor may ask the writer to rework copy that's already been written: The writer may not be paid for this work, but if it is acceptable, it may lead to future cover copy assignments.

Before starting, the cover copy writer should ask the editor for copies of readers' reports of the book and sample jackets of other books in the same line, both of which will provide the writer with key words and ideas for cover copy. Generally, a freelancer can work faster on creating copy for nonfiction books, since, although he must read the whole book, much of the key material he'll need is in the table of contents. (*See: Blurb; Sell copy.*)

Book manuscript preparation and submission. A book manuscript comprises three parts: front matter, back matter and text. Two items of front matter are absolutely required for nonfiction books: a manuscript title page and a table of contents. If the book includes tables or illustrations, the front matter should include a list of illustrations. Other front matter includes the dedications, acknowledgments, preface or foreword and the introduction. Pages of front matter are not formally numbered.

A nonfiction book's back matter consists of all or some of the following sections: appendices, endnotes, bibliography, glossary and index(es). Not all are required for every book; publisher's guidlines will vary.

The text is the manuscript. Each page is numbered in the upper right corner. Margins on all sides of the text should measure at least one inch. The manuscript should be typed double-spaced, on standard weight paper (except erasable bond), using either a typewriter with a new ribbon or a word processor or computer printer using serif type. Editors will accept computer printouts as long as they are laser-quality or letter-quality; near letter-quality dot-matrix printouts are generally acceptable, but aren't necessarily appreciated.

Each manuscript chapter begins

on a new page, leaving blank the top third of the page above the centered chapter number. The chapter title is placed two lines below. The author's last name, a shortened form of the book's title and a chapter number should be typed in the upper left margin of every text page. The pages of the manuscript are numbered consecutively from beginning to end. The phrase "The End" is typed three lines below the last line of text. This format is also used for fiction book manuscripts.

A query letter is the preferred communication for first contact with an editor concerning a nonfiction book. Clips should be included when appropriate. A query letter usually receives a faster response than the submission of a complete manuscript. If an editor asks for more information, he may request the complete manuscript or a detailed proposal and three consecutive sample chapters of the manuscript.

Fiction editors may prefer your first communication to be anything from a query letter to a synopsis or plot summary to a complete manuscript. See individual publisher's listings in *Writer's Market* for more specific submission information.

When submitting a proposal or manuscript, always include a self-addressed envelope with sufficient postage for the return of the manuscript. (*See: Manuscript preparation and submission; Nonfiction books, marketing.*)

Additional information: *The Writer's Digest Guide to Manuscript Formats.*

Book producer (book packager). An entrepreneur whose function is to engage writers, designers and editors to create a book and deliver it either as a manuscript or "ready for printing" to a publisher who markets it.

Book producers are likely to package certain kinds of books: how-to and reference books that call on the talents of many experts, books whose impact depends greatly on graphic layout and novels that originate in paperback.

Book producers may think of an idea for a book or book series, or they may work up a detailed outline of a subject presented to them. They usually contract with a veteran writer and sell the publication rights for an advance. Many, if not most, packaged books are done for a flat fee. Royalties are sometimes paid, but scales vary widely. They are almost always less than the standard 10-12½-15 percent. Usually, the royalty from the publisher is included in the unit price per copy agreed upon by packager and publisher. The writer then has a separate contract with the packager.

The producer is usually acknowledged on the title or copyright page of the book.

There are currently more than two hundred book producers in the U.S., most of them small enterprises in the Northeast. Fifty-five of them have banded together as the American Book Producers Association. A directory of the ABPA's membership is available by contacting them at 160 Fifth Ave., Suite 604, New York, NY 10010.

Among the best-known packagers in the trade is Lyle Kenyon Engel, who contracted with John Jakes for the first books in the Kent Family

Chronicles, published by Jove Publications.

Book promotion. The job of devising strategies for selling books. Book promotion is a joint project between publisher and author. A publisher's duties usually include advertising a book by sending review copies and press releases to book reviewers and—where budgeted—planning the author's tours.

The best advertising is word-of-mouth by satisfied buyers/readers, but giving a book exposure via TV, radio and newspaper feature interviews with the author builds an audience not only for a specific book, but often generates a following for the author himself. Other face-to-face promotional tools include authors' visits to bookstores and speeches to special-interest groups. Author input—contacts, suggested avenues of promotion, etc.—is most helpful to the publisher, as the author is usually an expert in his field. (In fact, marketing suggestions from the author in his original book proposal may help sway the publisher toward acceptance.)

Books are also effectively promoted through book club sales (more than one hundred clubs in the U.S.); some newspaper advertising is used, too, usually with the publisher and the bookseller splitting the cost. Posters, bookmarks, circulars and other promotion and advertising theoretically are allocated a percentage (usually 10 percent) of the book's projected net sales income. (In practice, some authors' books get more; other authors', less.) Reviews of specialized books in publications for readers who are prospective buyers of the book are useful, and if a book has a news angle, a promotional press conference may be arranged.

If a book is self-published, the writer may hire a publicist or handle a promotion campaign himself. He may also solicit the help of friends and/or place ads (with order form coupons) in targeted publications. He also identifies local and regional organizations that might welcome a personal introduction to his book through a speaking engagement. (*See: Autographing party; Book clubs; Mid-list books; Promotion by author; Talk shows.*)

Book proposal. (*See: Nonfiction books, marketing; Novels, marketing.*)

Book publisher organizational chart. (*See: Figure 6.*)

Book publisher reader's report. (*See: Figure 7.*)

Book publisher's royalty statement. (*See: Figure 8.*)

Book publishing economics. (*See: Figure 9.*)

Book publishing, history of. Although civilized man attempted to record information as early as 3500 B.C., when the Sumerians wedged cuneiform inscriptions onto clay tablets, it was the Romans, teaching slaves to work as copyists, who increased production of rolls so that as many as one thousand copies of a popular work could be produced and distributed throughout their world.

The formatting of modern books

FIGURE 6

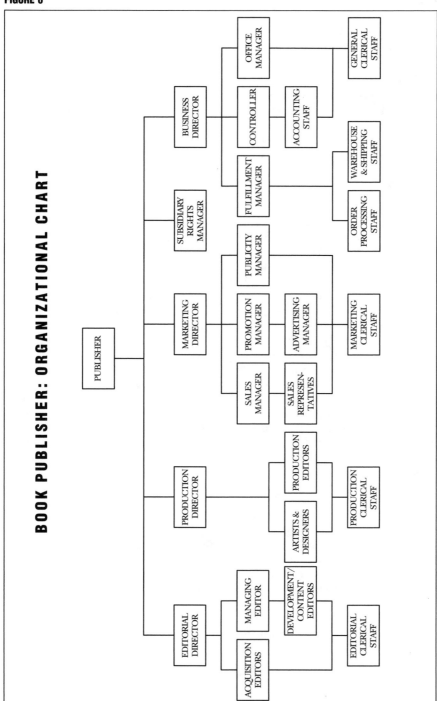

BOOK PUBLISHER: ORGANIZATIONAL CHART

FIGURE 7

BOOK PUBLISHER READER'S REPORT

*H*ere is an example of the kind of report that would be prepared on a submission by an editor at a book publishing house. Some such reports would suggest rejecting a manuscript. Others, like this, are recommendations for publication. This book report was prepared by editor Anne Savarese, and the book was edited by George Witte. It was published with the same title by St. Martin's Press in 1989 and was well reviewed.

THE BODY'S MEMORY
BY JEAN STEWART
This is a moving, gracefully written novel. While the story is told with a blend of journal entries, third-person narratives, and poems, the loosely chronological order of events gives it coherence. Kate is an appealing character: she describes her surgery and resulting disability with honesty, intelligence, and imagination. As she records her thoughts and examines the facts of her illness, she also takes a critical look at both her present situation and her past: by discussing her solitary years in Maine, her love affairs, or her suicide attempt, for example, she helps me see her not as "a cancer patient," but as a woman learning to deal with cancer and its effects. The author's way of mixing Kate's journal entries with occasional narratives from other characters' points of view enriches the story and makes it more than a fictionalized autobiography.

The author uses rich detail and candid emotion throughout the book, and I found it easy to identify with her struggle as she moves through diagnosis, surgery, recovery, and independent life as a disabled person. Her increasing awareness of public discrimination against the disabled is enlightening, especially because she comes from the perspective of a formerly able-bodied person.

The last thirty pages of the book, however, seem to cover too much material too quickly. Most events in the book take place at intervals of several months, but suddenly three years have gone by, and Kate is using the wheelchair she resisted for so long (p.152). I felt as though I'd missed out on something: after accompanying her through the long recovery, I was surprised that she would skip over three years in a few paragraphs. Because these last pages discuss her political awakening, they are one of the most interesting parts of the book, but she seems to hurry through them. She summarizes without the sense of immediacy that she maintains through the rest of the novel. Sometimes her discussion seems too general (pp.166-68), or too brisk (e.g. her decision to use the wheelchair, pp. 173-74).

In general, however, I think this book would be a source of strength for disabled people, their families, and friends, and might also appeal to feminists and general readers.

FIGURE 8

BOOK PUBLISHER'S
ROYALTY STATEMENT

Joe Bloome
100 Sunshine Street
Anywhere, CA 92601

Title: *How To Write Novels That Sell*   Retail Price: $15.95
Royalty earnings for period of July 1 to December 31, 1989.

TYPE OF SALE	UNITS SOLD	ROYALTY RATE	AMOUNT EARNED
Regular edition	1,650	10% of retail price	$2,631.75
Book Club rights		50% of advance of $3,187.50	1,593.75
Second serial		50% of $1,000.00	500.00
Japanese translation		50% of advance of $2,000	1,000.00
L.A. Times Syndicate		50%	300.00
		Total earnings	$6,025.50
Adjustments			
Advances			(4,000.00)
Permission fees paid			(152.73)
Books purchased			(85.93)
Net Amount Due—Check Enclosed			$1,786.84

EDITOR'S NOTE: This is an example of what a royalty statement on a mythical nonfiction book might look like. Many books, of course, do not have subsidiary sales such as those shown here; others might have more.

can be traced to the *codex*, a flat manuscript made up of several folded sheets of parchment or vellum (dried animal skin) and bound on one side. Dating from the first century A.D., the codex remained the typical book of the Middle Ages, during which monks wrote, lettered and circulated codex books, primarily with other monks for scholarly use.

John Dessauer notes in the "The Past is Prologue" chapter of *Book Publishing: What It Is, What It Does,* that two vital developments in the fifteenth century—the introduction of linen paper and the invention of movable type—resulted in widespread printing and distribution of books. "By 1500 books were paginated and title pages listed publishers' imprints and dates of publication much as they do today. In 1501 Aldus Manutius designed the first small book which thereafter re-

FIGURE 9

BOOK PUBLISHING ECONOMICS

*F*reelance authors should be aware of the expenses that publishers face in producing their books and that influence the royalties publishers pay. After the writing of a book is completed, there are editorial costs and expenses for production, promotion, and distribution that must be financed.

Following is a chart detailing the hypothetical expenditures of a publisher. It outlines figures for a hardcover nonfiction book written by a previously unpublished author.

NONFICTION BOOK BY NEW AUTHOR

Print order: 15,000 copies (Hardcover, 6"×9", 272 pages)

Retail list price: $15.00

Cost to bookstore (47% average bookstore discount): $7.95

	PUBLISHER'S EXPENSES	*PUBLISHER'S INCOME*	*AUTHOR'S INCOME*
12,000 books sold over lifespan of book at publisher's income of $7.95 each, less 5% bad debt: $7.55		$90,600	
2,000 returned bookstore copies sold at remainder prices		3,200	
1,000 unsold (review, author, and office copies; damaged; otherwise unsalable)		0	
Author's advance against royalties	$ 3,000		$ 3,000
Royalties (10%, 12½%, 15% of retail price* on first, second, and third 5,000 copies; less advance)			
• for first 5,000 copies: 5,000 × 10% of $15.00 = $7,500			
• for second 5,000 copies: 5,000×12½% of $15.00 = $9,375			
• for additional 2,000 copies: 2,000×15% of $15.00 = $4,500			
• total royalties $21,375			
• less $3,000 advance $3,000			
royalties paid to author $18,375	18,375		18,375
Publishing expenses:			
a. editorial costs (editor's work with author on this book plus a pro-rata share of cost of reading all the other manuscripts that were not publishable)	15,000		
b. production costs (personnel, design, typesetting, paper, paste-up, printing, and binding)	26,800		

FIGURE 9 (CONTINUED)

	PUBLISHER'S EXPENSES	PUBLISHER'S INCOME	AUTHOR'S INCOME
c. cost of carrying inventory	2,800		
d. advertising, publicity, and promotion plus overhead pro-rata share of these departments—marketing, order processing, shipping, labor.	15,000		
Salespeople's commissions (based on varying commissions to wholesalers, sales reps calling on bookstores, the publisher's own "house" accounts and direct consumer sales) averaging 7% of publisher's net income	6,342		
Pro-rata share of other administrative costs (bookkeeping, clerical, comptroller, employee benefits, rent, taxes, general overhead, pro-rated among all the titles published that year)	5,000		
Publisher's net profit $1,483 (1.6% profit before taxes)	$92,317	$93,800	$21,375

*Some publishers pay royalties based on net receipts, not retail prices.

The preceding chart represents the finances of the publishing of a trade hardcover nonfiction book. (Print order on a novel could be as low as 3,000–5,000 copies.) As you can see, the publisher could have invested his $92,317 in something other than a book and gotten a greater percentage of return on his money. Why does he do it? In hopes of finding books on which he can earn subsidiary rights income from paperback reprinters, book clubs, foreign translations. Those subsidiary sales and reprint editions of his own on some books help the publisher make up for the loss and minimal profit on other books. Trade book publishers average about 8% profit before taxes.

Textbooks, trade paperbacks, and books sold only by direct mail would have different economics. In mass paperback book publishing, a typical print order would call for 150,000–1,000,000 copies, and up to 50% of books could be returned unsold. The author's royalties for an original paperback are generally from 6%–10% of the retail price; a paperback reprint of a hardcover book could split royalties 50/50 between author and original publisher.

placed the large and awkward codex." An estimated one thousand printers had published about thirty thousand editions of different books before the end of the fifteenth century in western Europe. Some nine million volumes were in existence.

According to Dessauer, modern publishing began in the eighteenth century when the general population of the western world began to recognize and appreciate the knowledge to be gained from books. Several of the great encyclopedias, including the English *Britannica*, were founded during this century, and many countries established circulating libraries around this period, which made books more accessible to the public. The British Copyright Act of 1710 weakened the power of the monopolistic printers of the time and enabled authors to negotiate for more favorable financial terms.

Many of today's active American publishing houses were founded during the nineteenth century, including John Wiley and Sons (1807), HarperCollins (1817), Houghton, Mifflin (1832), G.P. Putnam's Sons (1838), Rand McNally (1856), and Doubleday, now part of Bantam Doubleday Dell (1897). J.B. Lippincott was founded even earlier (1792).

It was the post-World War II period—characterized by an educational boom and general prosperity of the country—that determined the shape and character of the contemporary publishing industry. The post-World War II period brought a boom in the modern paperback book industry, which had been originated by Pocket Books in 1939, and the emergence in the 1950s of the "quality" trade paperback industry (serious nonfiction and literary classics), which served the needs of the ever-increasing student enrollments at the elementary, high school and college levels.

The 1960s saw continued growth in the industry: Many publishing houses were acquired by corporations seeking to diversify or expand the market for other related products; many more new bookstores opened, new book clubs were established to cater to specialized consumer interests, and mass paperback sales increased. More people than ever bought books.

The general economic recession in the 1970s hit the book publishing industry particularly hard.

Lewis A. Coser, Charles Kadushin, and Walter W. Powell comment on this in *Books: The Culture and Commerce of Publishing*, noting the mergers of softcover and hardcover houses, the formation of film company/book publishing combines, and other media mergers.

Coser, Kadushin and Powell point out that "multimedia mergers in trade publishing have created an environment in which books, films and even TV programs, are viewed as constituent parts of a media package" and writers would do well to keep that in mind.

There are currently more than thirty thousand book publishing companies in the U.S. New York, Boston, Philadelphia and Chicago have long been the hubs of publishing; in recent years, the West Coast has increased its role as a publishing locale.

Book publishing companies and their vital statistics (i.e., addresses, what they publish, number of titles, etc.) are listed in the annual *Writer's Market* and *Literary Market Place*. In addition, the *Publishers' Trade List Annual* is a reference of current backlisted books of publishing companies, policies of book publishers and their related products. (*See: Paperbacks, history of.*)

Additional information: *Book Publishing: What It Is, What It Does*; *Books: The Culture and Commerce of Publish-*

ing, History of Book Publishing in the United States.

Book publishing industry sales. (*See: Figure 10.*)

Book publishing jobs, editorial. Editorial titles and functions vary significantly from one publishing house to another, depending on the size and type (i.e., trade publisher, paperback house, university press, textbook publisher) of the organization. In general, the larger the publishing house, the more differentiated and specialized the editorial functions. In smaller publishing organizations, editorial positions are often less clearly defined, and editors may have a variety of duties and responsibilities.

In a medium-sized publishing house there is a fairly standard set of editorial positions that may be adapted by larger and smaller houses, depending on their specific needs. The Editor in Chief or Chief Editor (sometimes called the Executive Editor or Editorial Director) is primarily an executive rather than an editor in the traditional sense. He is responsible for coordinating and supervising all of the organization's editorial activities and functions. Duties are largely managerial: delegating work to the editorial staff, conducting staff meetings and taking responsibility for editorial budget, policymaking and personnel management. The Editor in Chief also works closely with the publisher and marketing department of the organization to create new book ideas and other publishing projects.

Senior Editors are experienced staff members who work closely with authors and their agents in contracting books and other publishing projects. Senior Editors are also very involved in creating and proposing ideas for new books and other publishing projects. A Senior Editor may have the title of Acquiring or Sponsoring Editor.

The Managing Editor or Production Editor is a liaison between the editorial and production departments of a publishing organization. He is responsible for coordinating a manuscript through all phases of production—copyediting, design and manufacture—to bound book.

The people who do substantive editing of manuscripts are known by various titles: Associate Editors, Assistant Editors, Developmental Editors. Depending on their specific position in the publishing house, these editors may be involved in reading and reporting on incoming manuscripts, doing in-depth editing and rewriting of manuscripts and preparing the final revision of a manuscript to send to the copyeditor.

Editorial Assistants, often novices in the business, perform clerical and routine editorial duties such as typing, filing and opening and routing mail. In addition to basic clerical duties, however, many editorial assistants are assigned to work directly with copy, taking on editing and rewriting responsibilities. The distinction between editors and editorial assistants is thus sometimes blurred.

Other positions in publishing are held either by full-time staff members or freelancers, depending on the size of the publishing house. Copyeditors polish the style, grammar and spelling of manuscripts, and are responsible for composition

FIGURE 10

BOOK PUBLISHING INDUSTRY SALES, ESTIMATED 1994
(IN MILLIONS)

CATEGORY	1993	1994	% INCREASE 1993-94	CAGR 1987-94
Trade (total)	$5,023.3	$5,470.8	9.0%	10.5%
Adult Hardbound	2,553.6	2,801.3	9.7	11.0
Adult Paperbound	1,333.6	1,499.0	12.4	10.9
Juvenile Hardbound	767.4	751.3	-2.1	6.7
Juvenile Paperbound	368.7	419.2	13.7	15.1
Religious (total)	931.5	978.0	5.0	6.3
Bibles, Testaments, Hymnals and Prayerbooks	259.3	275.6	6.3	6.5
Other Religious	672.2	702.4	4.5	6.2
*Professional (total)	3,106.7	3,320.5	6.9	**
Business	490.3	510.9	4.2	**
Law	1,128.1	1,177.7	4.4	**
Medical	622.7	707.4	13.6	**
Technical, Scientific, Other	865.6	924.5	6.8	**
Mass Market Paperbacks	1,359.8	1,392.4	2.4	6.2
Book Clubs	804.7	873.9	8.6	3.7
University Press	292.9	325.7	11.2	9.6
El-Hi Texts	2,318.1	2,155.8	-7.0	3.5
College Texts	2,140.4	2,176.8	1.7	5.0
Standardized Tests	146.8	156.5	6.6	6.0
Mail-Order Publications	601.2	557.3	-7.3	-2.3
Subscription Reference	602.0	641.3	6.5	5.6
Other Sales (Including AV)	452.5	457.2	1.0	.9
TOTALS	**$17,993.7**	**$18,791.8**	**4.4%**	**6.4%**

Source: Association of American Publishers
CAGR: Compound Annual Growth Rate

* Professional figures based on 1992-1993
**CAGR not available

matters such as typeface style and consistency of design. Proofreaders check printed copy against original, noting every letter, word and symbol. Although proofreading usually means checking for typographical and spelling errors, proofreaders are often asked to query editors on questionable points that may have slipped by previous readers.

Unlike the preceding two jobs, indexing is almost always performed by a freelancer working outside the company.

To qualify for the jobs described above, one generally needs a college degree. While most editors have an English, journalism or liberal arts degree, a background in these areas is not required. Many textbook publishers, for example, seek editors with educational or teaching backgrounds in the type of books they publish: science, math, political or social science, etc. One survey revealed that, in hiring editors, publishers are not as interested in educational background as they are in evidence of curiosity and intelligence in a candidate, since editorial positions involve primarily on-the-job training. As John Dessauer notes in *Book Publishing: What It Is, What It Does*: "Although a number of academic programs throughout the country offer courses on book publishing, most of the education and training given to employees in the industry is imparted on the job."

Customarily, jobs in publishing provide lower pay than do those in other business fields; what they offer instead is prestige and psychic rewards. According to *Publishers Weekly*, the average salary for a secretary/assistant editor with three years' experience is $18,300. Copyeditors average $22,700, and executive/managing editors, $39,200. Freelance copyeditors, proofreaders and indexers usually receive an hourly rate for assignments.

Newcomers to the publishing industry are often required to begin at clerical jobs, regardless of educational background. (*See: Book indexing; Continuing education; Copyeditor; Editing, freelance; Editor, acquisitions; Editor, content; Editor, production; Editors; Indexing.*)

Book publishing jobs, publicity. The publicity department of a publishing organization offers job opportunities for individuals with writing skills. Since the goal of the publicity department is to secure media coverage for the publishing house's books and other products, publicists are primarily responsible for creating press releases describing books and their authors, as well as developing special feature stories about books and authors, intended for distribution to newspapers, magazines and broadcast media. In some publishing houses, the publicity department is responsible for writing the copy that appears on a book's dust jacket.

In addition to these duties, members of the publicity department also send out review copies of new publications, arrange radio and TV appearances for authors, coordinate authors' promotional tours and autographing parties, and perform related promotional duties such as creating book catalogs, book ads, etc. The publicity department serves a public relations function as well, sending out press releases about the company's activities, sometimes preparing annual reports, and keeping up to date a complete biographical file of authors and book reviews for use by critics, students and writers.

Publicists in the book publishing industry are generally paid between $15,000 and $50,000, depending on the size and locale of the publishing house and the specific duties involved in the job. (*See: Autographing party; Book promotion; Book publishing jobs, editorial; Promotion by author.*)

Book review. An analytical, evaluative account of a work, usually by a person qualified to comment on its literary merit and/or subject matter. The review conveys an opinion and supports that critical judgment with evidence from the book's content. In the case of nonfiction, the review considers aspects such as the accuracy of the facts, the organization of the information and the complete-

ness of the bibliography and index. For fiction, the review comments on plot development, the unity of theme, the credibility of the characters and the effect of the whole work on the reader. Book reviews may also contain the following: some background information about the author, a comparison of the book with others in the field and an appraisal of the book in terms of the author's intended purpose.

Book reviews appear in general interest newspapers and magazines as well as professional journals. Payments vary: Compensation may range from only a copy of the book reviewed to fees of $35–$300 and more in the case of larger circulation magazines and newspapers. (*See: Arts review; Criticism.*)

Book reviews, indexes to. For reviews of books on general topics, the researcher should consult the *Book Review Digest* or *Book Review Index. Readers' Guide to Periodical Literature*, in volumes from 1976 on, lists book reviews in a separate section at the end of the book. *The New York Times Index* and *Popular Periodicals Index* both list book reviews within the text, under the category "book reviews."

There are also indexes that list reviews of books in specialized fields.

If a book review was written too recently to have been cataloged in an index, it is best to consult a recent issue of a magazine with a book review department, or consumer review publications such as the *New York Times Book Review, New York Review of Books,* and *Times Literary Supplement.* (*See: Book review; Periodicals, indexes to.*)

Book revision for second edition (terms). The contract between author and book publisher generally has a revision clause, a built-in provision regarding subsequent editions. Therefore, the author is usually obligated to do a revision or have its cost—if done by another writer for a flat fee—deducted from his royalties on the new edition. Whether a new advance is offered depends on whether the revision involves an excessive amount of work and whether the book needs revising very frequently.

In the case of a second author's revising of the published work of another—for example, an author who is asked by a publisher to revise a book of a deceased author—the author who does the revision faces two alternative methods of payment: either a flat fee or a percentage of the royalties due the original author. The payment method would depend on the amount of work involved and what kind of agreement can be negotiated between the freelancer and the original author or his heirs.

Bookkeeping. (*See: Recordkeeping.*)

Booklist. *Booklist* is a semimonthly trade magazine for librarians published by the American Library Association (ALA). In addition to reviews of books for both adults and young people, the magazine also reviews films, recordings, reference books and U.S. government publications.

One of its regular features is a column reviewing first novels, through which the fiction writer can discover which publishers publish what kinds of novels. *Booklist* is available in most libraries; its publisher's address is

American Library Association, 50 E. Huron St., Chicago, IL 60611.

Book-promotion tour. Publishers sometimes send authors on promotional tours that include personal and/or media appearances. Only authors who have reached celebrity status or whose books are projected blockbusters are sent on such tours. Some self-promotion tips for authors are given in books on self-publishing, which are listed in *Subject Guide to Books In Print* under the category "Publishers and Publishing."

Books published by subject/format. (*See: Figure 11.*)

Books, tapes of. Cassette tapes of books can be listened to when one is driving, working or otherwise occupied so that reading is impossible. Regular trade publishers that are now offering books on cassettes include Bantam, Random House, Simon & Schuster and Warner Publishing; also, Books on Tape, Inc., P.O. Box 7900, Newport Beach, CA 92660.

Bookstore directories. (*See:* American Book Trade Directory.)

Bound galleys. A prepublication— often paperbound—edition of a book, usually prepared from photocopies of the final galley proofs; also known as "bound proofs." Designed for promotional purposes, bound galleys serve as the first set of review copies to be mailed out. Many consumer review publications such as *The New York Times Book Review* section, *Publishers Weekly* and others have a long lead time and require copies well in advance of publication

to synchronize the review with the book's arrival in stores.

Occasionally, bound galleys are distributed to sales representatives and wholesale or chain store book buyers; these are sometimes called *special reader editions.* A few bound galleys may also be sent to experts in the book's subject field, or to well-known individuals whose endorsements may help sell a book, to solicit testimonials or dust jacket blurbs for second and third editions of the book. (*See: Page proof; Prepublication review; Review copy; Testimonial.*)

Brand name author. A well-known author who has acquired a large following. The term is often associated with authors of certain types of fiction—mysteries, gothics, science fiction, etc. Any brand name author's book is likely to be a good seller, since readers search out new books by a writer whose style they admire.

British spelling and usage. George Bernard Shaw once remarked that America and England are two nations divided by a common language, and American writers need to keep those differences in mind when writing for publications in Great Britain. As examples, some British spellings are *colour, practise, civilisation, cheque* (the document) and *theatre.* In England, a mechanical device used to transport people or objects from one level to another is called a *lift,* while in America, it is known, of course, as an *elevator.* To the British, *holiday* means what *vacation* means to Americans.

The *Oxford English Dictionary,* available in most libraries, is a source of British spellings of English

FIGURE 11

BOOKS PUBLISHED BY SUBJECT/FORMAT
A COMPARISON, 1989 VS. 1993

CATEGORY	1989 ALL HARDBOUND AND TRADE PAPER			1993 ALL HARDBOUND AND TRADE PAPER		
	NEW BOOKS	NEW EDITIONS	TOTALS	NEW BOOKS	NEW EDITIONS	TOTALS
Agriculture	464	94	558	434	101	535
Art	1,358	202	1,560	1,345	181	1,526
Biography	1,855	261	2,116	1,778	204	1,982
Business	1,163	386	1,549	1,088	332	1,420
Education	871	164	1,035	1,040	162	1,202
Fiction	3,131	182	3,313	3,014	107	3,121
General Works	1,937	331	2,268	1,565	244	1,809
History	2,093	438	2,531	1,962	338	2,300
Home Economics	740	161	901	684	114	798
Juveniles	4,867	170	5,037	4,796	223	5,019
Language	454	118	572	529	161	690
Law	802	292	1,094	807	336	1,143
Literature	1,988	281	2,269	1,919	224	2,143
Medicine	2,765	653	3,418	2,367	702	3,069
Music	306	67	373	312	63	375
Philosophy, Psychology	1,652	298	1,950	1,466	209	1,675
Poetry, Drama	1,053	64	1,117	948	50	998
Religion	2,306	269	2,575	2,247	372	2,619
Science	2,698	574	3,272	2,187	481	2,668
Sociology, Economics	6,907	1,005	7,912	6,443	1,004	7,447
Sports, Recreation	801	142	943	872	130	1,002
Technology	2,196	477	2,673	1,714	460	2,714
Travel	515	173	688	329	149	478
Total	**42,922**	**6,802**	**49,724**	**39,846**	**6,347**	**46,193**

MASS MARKET PAPERBACKS						
Fiction			2,628			2,298
Nonfiction			1,094			1,266
Total			**3,722**			**3,564**

Reprinted from the March 8, 1991, and March 20, 1995, issues of Publishers Weekly, *published by Cahners Publishing, a division of Reed Publishing USA © 1991, 1995 Reed Publishing USA.*

words, as is *Brewer's Dictionary of Phrase and Fable*, which defines words, idioms and phrases used in the English language. One of the most recent books Americans might find very useful is *Britishisms: A Dictionary of Words, Idioms and Phrases Characteristic of British English*, by Lawrence Holofcener.

Broadcast networks. TV and radio networks are groups of stations over which programs are broadcast simultaneously. They can assist the writer doing research by providing transcripts of and other information about their programs. Writers may contact these networks at the following addresses.

The American Broadcasting Company (ABC), 47 W. Sixty-sixth St., New York, NY 10023.

CBS, Inc. (the Columbia Broadcasting System), 524 W. Fifty-seventh St., New York NY 10019.

Fox Broadcasting Company, 1211 Avenue of the Americas, New York, NY 10036.

The Mutual Broadcasting System, 1755 S. Jefferson Davis Highway, Arlington, VA 22202.

The National Broadcasting Co., Inc. (NBC), 30 Rockefeller Plaza, New York, NY 10112.

National Public Radio (NPR), 2025 M St., N.W., Washington, DC 20036.

Public Broadcasting Service (PBS), 1320 Braddock Place, Alexandria, VA 22314.

Turner Broadcasting System, Inc. (a cable system), 1 CNN Center, Box 105366, Atlanta, GA 30348. (*See: Transcripts of broadcasts.*)

Broadcasting directories. *Broadcasting/Cablecasting Yearbook* gives details on the ownership and operation of radio, TV and cable TV stations throughout the U.S. and Canada. It is arranged geographically by state or province and by city, and includes additional information on program producers, market areas, etc. It is published by *Broadcasting* magazine, 1705 De Sales St., N.W., Washington, DC 20036.

Names of staff personnel at radio and TV stations throughout the country are included in Volume 3 of *Working Press of the Nation*, and a directory of *Cable* (TV) *Contacts*. Both directories are described in detail under their titles in this book.

Directories of programs featuring authors as guests are published by companies such as *Directory of Experts, Authorities and Spokespersons*, 2500 Wisconsin Ave., Suite 930, N.W., Washington, DC 20007, and a nationwide directory, *TV and Cable Publicity Outlets*, 2200 Sansom St., Philadelphia, PA 19103.

Radio and TV programs that feature book reviews and/or author interviews are also listed in *Literary Market Place*, described under its title in this book. (*See:* Cable Contacts*; Directories;* Literary Market Place; Working Press of the Nation.)

Bulletin board. On an online service or the Internet, bulletin boards (BBS) are places where one can post his or her opinions, usually on a prescribed subject. These will often develop into slow-motion ''conversations,'' in which one writer may answer another's post two days later, and be answered in turn days after that. Some bulletin boards take the form of ongoing collaborative stories and can test a writer's creativity and spontaneity. (*See: Online service.*)

Business and industry as it employs writers. People seeking full-time writing jobs may wish to look to business and industry, which employ them in advertising, public relations, sales, training, company publications, handbook/manual and speechwriting work.

In this kind of work, the writer serves as a link between the company and its dealers or customers and the public. He can be either a generalist or a specialist, and his education, experience and interests should guide him in selecting where he will work.

To approach a corporation, one

should write to its personnel manager, enclosing a résumé and writing samples with the letter. Speculative copy may also be added (an article or advertisement) on subjects of interest to that company or industry, or a portfolio of published work. A trainee with a bachelor's degree can expect to start at $18,000–$20,000. More experienced writers average $37,000, depending on the size of the company. (*See: Advertising copywriters; Company publication; Financial writing; Ghostwriting speeches; Public relations [PR] manager; Technical writing; Jobs for writers.*)

Business cards. A writer's business card can help him obtain new clients when he makes personal calls on local prospects, or remind present clients of his availability. Business cards should display the writer's name, address, telephone number and an indication of his services, e.g., "freelance writer" or "editorial services." A freelance writer may create a company name for his business and include it as well.

In some cases, e.g., if a writer works as a stringer for a publication, the publisher may provide the writer with business cards. Independent writers may have cards designed professionally and/or printed by a quick-print service. (*See: Stationery.*)

Business side of writing. Writers tend to concentrate on creating and too often ignore administrative details. But freelance writers are essentially small businesspeople, and that role demands the management of many sides of an enterprise. (Of course, an independently wealthy writer or a writer who has attained considerable

financial success can hire an accountant, a secretary or other assistants, but the majority of writers, especially early in their careers, are one-person operations.)

Financial matters usually left to an employer are the freelancer's own responsibility. For example, he must deduct federal, state—and sometimes city—taxes from his income, save for his retirement and pay social security tax. Similarly, insurance fees are paid out of a freelancer's own income, not by an employer. In some areas, the writer must obtain a license to operate a small business.

Devising personal and business budgets can be complicated by the fact that the freelancer's income is irregular, but these administrative tasks, though time consuming, are necessary to the freelancer's success.

Keeping records of expenses is essential for figuring tax deductions, as well as for collecting reimbursements from publishers on assignments involving travel, for example. (*See: Recordkeeping; Taxes.*)

Business writer/client agreement. (*See: Figure 12.*)

Business writing. A term that includes the copy found in business magazines, in-house publications, speeches, annual reports, newsletters, position papers, press releases, catalogs and brochures and pamphlets used in public relations, advertising and fundraising. Business writing is clear, accurate and usually positive. Its purpose is to get a message across quickly and economically.

The craft of business writing is applicable not only to business and

FIGURE 12

BUSINESS WRITER AGREEMENT

This is an agreement between _____ (name) doing business as

_____ (business name and address) _____ (hereinafter "business

name") and _____ (client name) _____

located at _____ (address) _____

(hereinafter "Client").

    1. *PROFESSIONAL SERVICES:* _____agrees to perform the following ser-

vices for Client and Client agrees to retain and hire _____ to perform

the following services: _____

_____

_____

    2. *CONSIDERATION:* Client shall pay to _____ for the services

referenced as follows: _____ (for example $ _____ per hour for all services)

_____

Client shall pay to _____ a deposit in the amount of

$ (⅓ estimate) upon signing of this Agreement. For any sums due above

the deposit, Client will pay promptly upon receipt of the statement

of _____ . Client agrees to pay interest at the rate of 15 percent per annum

for any statement that is not paid within thirty days of its date.

    3. *MISCELLANEOUS:* Unless Client notifies within ten days that services are unac-

ceptable, Client is indicating services are acceptable. In the event that Client fails

to pay pursuant to the terms of this Agreement and _____

hires counsel or a collection agency to collect the consideration due, Client

agrees to pay a reasonable sum for attorney's fees or collection costs as well as

expenses incurred in the collection process.

    Nothing contained herein shall create an employment relationship between

the parties. _____ is an independent contractor.

DATED this _____ day of _____, 19___ .

_____

_____

_____

Client

_____

Reprinted courtesy Mary Westheimer, PWS Writing/Editing, Phoenix AZ

---

industry but also to nonprofit institutions such as churches and hospitals, as well as community associations and professional societies. Though businesses often have their own writing staffs, freelancers who can meet pressing needs may be welcomed. Freelance business writers know the background of the company or organization they write for; they know the group's objectives and its intended audience. Because business writing is often closely tied with a graphic presentation of the message, knowledge of layout, photography, typography and printing are extra pluses for a freelance business writer.

Payment depends on the availability of good business writers, specific market needs, size of the company and scope of the assignment. Rates generally range from $100 to $200 per day or more; for smaller projects the beginning business writer can expect $25-$60 per hour. Current average rates for specific business writing assignments (speeches, catalogs, etc.) are listed in *Writer's Market* in the section ''How Much Should I Charge?''

Organizations representing business writers include Associated Business Writers of America (ABWA) and International Association of Business Communicators (IABC). These business writers' groups are described, under their names, in this book.

Additional information: *Directory of Corporate Affiliations; Dun & Bradstreet Reference Book of Corporate Managements; Standard & Poor's Register of Corporations, Directors and Executives.*

Byline. Most magazines publish an author's name with his article or story or poem, and in some small publications, this may be his only ''payment.'' But any such pieces— along with paid-for, bylined publications—are useful additions to the writer's portfolio in gaining recognition among editors and readers.

A well-established, prolific writer may occasionally have more than one article in the same issue of a publication, and in that case, he usually uses a pseudonym with one of the pieces.

Bylines are generally not given for research work, although the writer may receive contributor credit. When a ghostwriter works on a first-person confession-type piece, his byline may be replaced by an as-told-to credit. (*See: As-told-to article or book; Pseudonym.*)

Cable Contacts. A directory listing major market cable systems, satellite networks, independent producers, news services and multiple system operators. It includes guest/information/product usage on the various cable systems, plus technical requirements (such as kinds of tape for submissions), subscriber figures and program placement opportunities. The directory contains approximately 800 pages and is published annually in October by Larimi Communications Associates, Ltd., 165 W. Ninety-first St., New York, NY 10024. (*See: Broadcasting directories.*)

Caldecott Medal. This award is offered annually by the American Library Association to honor the artist who has illustrated what it considers to be the most significant American picture book for children published in the preceding year. Established in 1938, the Caldecott Medal was the first award created with the purpose of giving recognition to a book's illustrator. The award is named for the famous nineteenth-century English illustrator Randolph Caldecott who, together with his wife and a colleague, began a new era of picture books for young people.

Publishers send a copy of each of their picture books published for children to the ALA's Association for Library Service to Children, whose committee makes the choice.

The award itself is a bronze medal presented at the annual ALA conference, usually in June. The face of the medal carries a reproduction of an original Caldecott illustration; the reverse side is an illustration of "four and twenty blackbirds baked in a pie" and an inscription, "For the most distinguished American picture book for children."

A list of the prize-winning books appears in *Literary and Library Prizes.*

Camera. A valuable accessory for writers, the camera has many potential uses. A camera is an effective instrument for increasing not only the likelihood of an actual sale but also for increasing the fee an editor will pay; it can be used to take fast, accurate fiction research notes, e.g., showing how a person looks or details of a setting; and it may also be used to tell a story mostly with pictures, accompanied by minimal text.

Though the choice of camera equipment is a personal one, the basic outfit for a freelance writer usually begins with a 35mm single-lens-reflex camera equipped with a "normal" 50mm lens. A flash unit, collapsible tripod and an equipment bag to carry them in complete the basic requirements. Depending on the writer's taste and expertise and on whether the equipment is bought new or used, the total cost of a basic system may range from $119 to $485. From this starter outfit, the writer's collection of equipment grows with his experience. (A wide-angle lens and a telephoto lens are valuable additions to any system.)

To supplement the instruction book that comes with a camera, salespeople in camera or department stores can usually provide basic hands-on instruction at the time of (and after the) purchase. Often, such stores also sell beginners' books in photo-taking, which can be helpful.

Camera and equipment descriptions and price ranges are available in magazines such as *Petersen's Photography* and *Popular Photography*. Places to sell individual photos or photo series are detailed in *Photographer's Market*.

Canadian Authors Association (CAA). The CAA exists "to work for protection of Canadian writers and other artists producing copyrightable material; to act as a spokesman before Royal Commissions and official enquiries; and to sponsor a system of awards, and otherwise encourage work of literary and artistic merit."

Active members are writers of books, plays, short stories, articles, poetry, TV, radio scripts and other forms, who have produced "a sufficient body of work." Associate members are beginning writers and others who have an interest in Canadian literature. All members belong to the national Association and have the option of joining one of sixteen branches, which sponsor speeches by authors and panel discussions. The CAA holds an annual meeting. Members receive a subscription to the *Canadian Author and Bookman,* a quarterly magazine.

This organization strives for re-form of copyright laws, tax laws and book contracts. It publishes a guide to Canadian markets for writers.

Although membership is open to everyone, only Canadian writers are eligible for awards. The Vicky Metcalf Award is presented annually by the CAA to honor excellence in children's literature. The author judged to have the best body of work receives $10,000, best short story receives $3,000 and the editor of the short story receives $1,000. In addition, the CAA Literary Awards, sponsored by Harlequin Enterprises Limited, are presented in the categories of fiction, nonfiction, poetry and drama. A CAA Literary Award is a silver medal and $5,000.

The Canadian Authors Association is at 275 Slater St., #500, Ottawa, Ontario K1P 5H9, Canada.

Canadian Society of Children's Authors, Illustrators and Performers (CANSCAIP). This organization of 1,270 members promotes development of Canadian children's culture and support for writers, illustrators and performers working in this field. CANSCAIP also sponsors a conference the last week in October and publishes *CANSCAIP News,* which includes member profiles, market news and information about professional concerns. An associate, or nonpublished, membership is $25 and professional, or published, membership is $60. CANSCAIP can be contacted at 35 Spadina Rd., Toronto, Ontario M5R 2S9, Canada.

Cap. An abbreviation for *capital,* used by proofreaders to indicate that a letter or letters printed in lower case should be capital letters. *Cap.* is written in the margin on galleys or page proofs and accompanies the symbol of three parallel lines underscoring the erroneous letter. (*See: Proofreader's marks/symbols.*)

Caption (cutline). Explanatory text that accompanies a photograph or illustration. Composing captions for pictures is an important part of the writer/photojournalist's responsibility when submitting material for publication. A good caption complements the photograph, forming a visual unit that is understandable even without the body text. In submissions, photo quality is paramount, but captions may also influence an editor (and the subsequent magazine reader) to read the accompanying article.

Captions for pictures in news articles consist of identifying the who/what/where/why/how of the photograph. Captions for photographs in magazines and books must not only identify the photo subject, but also induce the reader to want to read the magazine article or the book text they accompany.

When prints are submitted for publication, captions (including picture credits) are often typed on separate pieces of paper and taped to the back of each photo. Other photojournalists number the photographs and provide a separate caption sheet, keyed to the numbers. Caption length may range from one to hundreds of words, depending on the publication's style.

It is important not to write on the backs of photos with pencils or ball point pens (the marks go right through and can be seen on the other side) and not to paperclip anything to photos, another common way of damaging them. Stiff cardboard, of course, should be used to protect the photos in the mailing package.

Careers in writing. The various opportunities for careers in writing fields such as advertising, magazines, newspapers, public relations, publishing, radio, teaching and TV are discussed throughout this book.

It is important to note that although people in all fields of writing have some skills in common, most writers have particular personality traits that make them more suitable for one field than another.

For example, the kind of personality needed by an advertising copywriter who is a great idea generator and a facile writer is different from that required by a nonfiction book writer who can organize a mass of research material and over a protracted period of time write a well-thought-out but highly readable book.

The publications *Toward Matching Personal and Job Characteristics* and the *Occupational Outlook Handbook*, which can be used in career decisions, are available in the government and business departments of most public libraries. They detail job requirements, working conditions and special personal qualifications needed beyond education in the field. (*See: Jobs for writers.*)

Carpal tunnel syndrome. (*See: Repetitive stress injury.*)

Cart. A shortened form of *cartridge*; a tape loop similar to an 8-track tape, used by radio stations to store commercials, PSAs, etc.; one advertiser's commercials per cartridge. On a broadcast cartridge, when a commercial has been played, the tape automatically recycles itself to the beginning of that spot or stops at the beginning of the next spot on the cartridge.

Cartoon. A drawing or sketch, usually intended to be humorous, that satirizes or comments on a person, situation or subject of popular interest. In form, a cartoon usually consists of a line drawing and a caption (gag line) that work together to express an idea. (Some cartoons make a point without a caption, however.) Cartoons rely on the spontaneous reactions of their readers; readership studies show that cartoons rank near the top of the list of what people read in magazines and newspapers. The successful cartoonist is tuned in to current events. He knows the editorial slant of a particular publication and he understands its readers.

There are many cartoon types, each requiring a different perspective. The *political cartoon* presents an issue—often through caricature—in such a way that the reader quickly grasps the artist's opinion on the issue. The *gag cartoon*—the kind most often found in magazines—often jokes about social trends or plays on trendy phrases or catchwords; some gag cartoonists specialize in situation-pictures without words. *Comic strip* cartoonists use panel drawings and balloon dialogue to set up and deliver their jokes and commentary.

Freelance cartoonists have many potential markets for their work. The annuals *Artist's Market* and *Writer's Market* list specific magazines, newspapers, greeting card companies, book publishers, ad agencies, etc., that solicit cartoons. (*Writer's Market* also lists cartoonists who solicit gag ideas on which they can base cartoon drawings—and for which they pay a commission to the writer when the cartoon sells.) In the magazine market, the cartoonist earns from $5 to more than $100 per cartoon. A few magazines pay only in contributor's copies. (*See: Comics writing; Gag writing.*)

Category fiction. A term used to include all the various labels attached to types of fiction. Category tags name popular fiction writing as mystery, spy, suspense, western, Gothic, religious, historical, science fiction, etc. Category publishing houses include: Harlequin (romance), Greenleaf Classics (erotica) and large paperback publishers such as Avon, Bantam, and Pocket Books (which publish books in several categories) among the many others listed in *Novel & Short Story Writer's Market.* (*See: Fiction.*)

CATV writing. Writing for programs distributed on a community antenna TV system. Cable TV began in 1949–1950 as a way—via a cable of electrically conducting wires—to bring TV service to communities outside the reach of broadcast signals. Because the cable construction minimizes electrical interference from outside sources, it soon spread to other communities that wanted to receive more stations and obtain better reception from the regular stations. There are currently more than nine thousand cable systems in the U.S.

CATV systems represent *potential*

markets for generalist writers, playwrights, poets, juvenile specialists, cartoonists, feature writers and ad writers. CATV managers (directors of original programming) may be receptive to writers' local interest ideas, news and features geared to a well-defined audience. In addition, the Federal Communications Commission has established provisions for government, private and public access channels for which writers may be needed.

The *Broadcasting/Cablecasting Yearbook*, available in most libraries, lists location, ownership and management of every system in the U.S. Yellow Pages directories also pinpoint local cable networks. (*See: Broadcasting directories;* Cable Contacts.)

CBS. (*See: Broadcast networks.*)

CD-ROM. Compact Disc, Read-Only Memory. In this format, information and/or games are stored on a compact disc. However, these discs can only be read by a special disc player. (*See: Electronic publishing.*)

Celebrity addresses. Some well-known people's home or business addresses are available through *Who's Who* or other biographical directories. Writers may also reach celebrities through Celebrity Service, Inc., 1780 Broadway, Suite 300, New York, NY 10019. This firm provides the name and telephone number of a celebrity's personal manager, agent or press agent; at present, the writer pays $50 for one name and $10 for each additional name or $250 per month (subscription rate). Celebrity Service, Inc., also publishes the biennial *Celebrity Service International Contact Book.* (*See: Research sources, directories of.*)

Censorship, literary. Most censorship in the U.S. concerns publications for use in schools and alleged pornography in books for the mass market. According to a report by the American Library Association, reports of books having been removed or threatened to be removed from libraries averaged one hundred per year in the early 1970s, three hundred per year in the late 1970s and approximately one thousand per year in the early 1980s.

Although censorship has always existed to some degree, the criteria for proposing that books be banned seem to shift with societal trends. In the late 1960s and early 1970s racism, sexism and other forms of discrimination were considered objectionable; in the 1980s and 1990s, it is often material alleged to be anti-American, antifamily or obscene that is challenged. While educators traditionally have chosen books for use by schoolchildren for their literary value and for their handling of controversial topics in what they consider to be a tasteful manner, some conservative lobbying groups emerged in the early 1980s as opponents of certain works of literature.

P.E.N. and the Author's Guild are two of several writers organizations that speak out against censorship by sponsoring lectures and readings and involving themselves in court cases by filing friend-of-the-court briefs. (*See: Freedom of the press.*)

Census Bureau, Department of Commerce. The Bureau of the Census in the U.S. Department of Commerce is the primary agency of the federal government engaged in the collection and production of general-purpose statistics. It takes the national censuses of population, housing, agriculture, retail and wholesale trade, service industries, manufacturers, mineral industries, transportation, construction industries and governments. The Bureau also conducts monthly, quarterly and annual surveys on some of the same subjects. An inquirer may learn from the Bureau, for instance, which cities in the U.S. have the highest crime rates, or what the country's annual growth rate of coal consumption is. The Bureau can provide information about the number of single-parent households in the U.S. or the employment statistics for U.S. psychologists. These are just a few examples of the wealth of statistical information the Census Bureau makes available.

The Bureau publishes an average of two thousand titles a year. Among the more popular is the *Statistical Abstract of the United States,* an annual summary of American social, economic and political data. This reference volume is available at any library; it may also be purchased from the Government Printing Office (GPO).

The Bureau also publishes "Telephone Contacts for Data Users," a list of names and phone numbers of individual analysts in each subject area. The list can be obtained free from the Customer Services Branch (DUSD), Bureau of the Census, Washington, DC 20233.

cf. Abbreviation for the Latin word *confer,* which translates to *compare.*

Used in footnotes and text material, *cf.* points out a related subject to the reader, e.g., "Most researchers agree that alcohol can adversely affect the unborn child (cf. alcoholism)."

Chain magazine publishers. (*See: Magazine publishers, multiple.*)

Character. The unique set of traits and features that form the nature of a fictional person. For example, the *character* of Falstaff is the blend of physical attributes, feelings, thoughts and actions that readers recognize as distinctly his.

Characters that the reader will remember start with a basis of reality. The writer takes a trait, the mannerisms or perhaps the appearance of someone he has known and adds to and embellishes it, drawing from his imagination. Sometimes a character is a composite. Often a character reflects the writer's own background or fantasies.

The character's motivation, the "why" of his behavior, is revealed through his dialogue and actions. He is the sum of everything that has happened to him in his fictional life: a character with flesh and blood and genuine emotions who brings the validity of truth to a work of fiction.

Writer Damon Knight, in *Creating Short Fiction,* advises the following background exercises for creating characters: writing biographical sketches of them; writing a scene that would give the reader insight into a character; and writing a scene that involves two of the story's characters who are similar to each other, pointing out their differences. In the story itself, Knight suggests describing a character from the viewpoint of another character or of two different characters, and showing a character in a scene that includes part of his daily routine.

Knight offers the following advice on inventing original characters: "Each time you write a scene from the viewpoint of one of your characters, imagine yourself inside that person's head. Exactly what is that person seeing right now—what is she hearing? What other sensations is she aware of? What is she thinking? Remembering? What impulses does she suppress? What does she notice while another person is speaking? What is her mood? Is she elated, depressed, or what?"

Character change. Every short story or novel necessarily involves a change in the central character. Just as real-life people do, fictional characters undergo change as a result of their experiences. At the end of a story, the writer may show that a character is in a different situation or has a different attitude, but the alteration within the fictional person is always brought about as the logical result of his experience. (*See: Consequence, a sense of; Incident.*)

Characterization. The process of creating an image of a person in drama, fiction or narrative poetry in such a way that the reader believes in his authenticity. Characterization—the consistent evolution of a character—both generates plot (conflict) and results from it.

The writer uses various methods of character development. He may give the reader a picture of a person by describing his appearance, man-

ners and mood. Or he may let a character "speak for himself" in the form of dialogue. The writer may cultivate a character's nature by showing what he does and how he acts; in the same vein, he may indicate to the reader how the character reacts to people and situations around him. Finally, the writer may portray a character's effect on others in the story.

The writer achieves a successful characterization when the fictional person becomes so credible that he exists as a real person for the reader. (*See: Character.*)

Chases' Calendar of Annual Events. A reference booklet that lists and describes events and observances of each day of the year; each day's events are listed alphabetically under the date heading. Entries cover events worldwide; national and religious holidays are included, as well as famous birthdays, traditional holidays, festivals, fairs, promotional events, week-long and month-long observances, and other happenings. Some listings give the name and address of a contact who can supply further information on the event or observance. The booklet also contains a general cross-index by subject.

A sample of listings in the 1993 *Calendar* includes "Amelia Earhart Atlantic Crossing Anniversary" (May 20); "Punxsutawney Groundhog Festival" (June 20-26); "National Bed Check Month" (Sept. 1-30); and "Humbug Day" (Dec. 21).

Writers may find this directory helpful in inspiring ideas for seasonal articles.

Chase's Calendar of Annual Events is

published by Best Publications, 180 N. Michigan Ave., Chicago, IL 60601. (*See: Seasonal material.*)

Chat. When two or more people converse, in "real time," using computers and modems. Most commercial online services, as well as the Internet itself, feature a variety of "chat rooms." Once you've logged into such a location, you'll be able to see a list of the screen names of the others participating. Anything you type and enter will then be seen, in the flow of typed conversation in the "room," by the other participants, and thus a conversation can develop. Online chat room topics can vary widely, from current affairs to cooking; some chat rooms are specifically designed as "MUDDs" (Multi-User Dungeons and Dragons), and participants in these develop characters to suit the rooms, often writing detailed backgrounds for the characters and participating in ongoing, convoluted storylines. Chat would seem to be a better *subject* for writers, or simply a practice ground, rather than a useful research tool. (*See: Online service.*)

Chat room. An electronic "location," either on a commercial online service or on the Internet, where computer users can converse by way of instantaneously exchanged, typed messages. Such conversations are perhaps most significant in that they remove prejudices from the interactions (it's impossible to truly know the race, sex or age of the person you chat with), and also lack such auxiliary communication tools as gesture, inflection and intonation. (*See: Emoticon.*)

Check contract. A statement endorsed on the back of a publisher's check in payment to an author, indicating what rights are being purchased to an article, story or poem in a magazine. (While a copyright is the property of the author, he sells a publisher the contractual rights to use his manuscript in certain ways.) An author who endorses a check contract may be simultaneously signing a legal contract.

In the case in which a previous agreement concerning rights has been made in correspondence between publisher and author, and the endorsement runs counter to that agreement, the author may endorse the check but cross out the publisher's notation. In this way, he is not bound by unagreed-to obligations imposed by the check contract.

If the endorsement carries a message to the effect that any alteration of it voids the check, then the author has no choice but to return the check, remind the publisher (with a photocopy of their previous agreement), and request that a new check be issued showing the correct rights bought. (*See: Rights to manuscripts.*)

Children as writers. A number of magazines solicit articles, poems, stories and drawings from young people. Some child writers begin their careers by being published in special children's sections of newspapers and magazines, then branch out into magazines that suit their interests.

Editors agree that articles written by children need original ideas, slants and attention to grammar. They also suggest that the young writer develop persistence and a thick skin and find a family member or friend to serve as a critic—attributes that are essential to writers of all ages.

Publications that contain sections created by children include the *Christian Science Monitor, Highlights for Children, Scholastic Scope* and *Wee Wisdom Magazine. Turtle* and *Stone Soup* are magazines consisting entirely of work by children. Also, *Seventeen, Straight* and *Tiger Beat* sometimes accept material written by teenagers. Each of these magazines has individual editorial needs and submission requirements. With material written by children, it is often necessary to include a statement from a parent or teacher attesting to its originality.

The *Market Guide for Young Writers* lists publications that accept submissions from young writers, as well as contests, profiles of editors, and answers to the questions asked most often by young writers.

Writer's Market, in the section "Juvenile," lists additional magazines written for children. (*See: Children's Writer's & Illustrator's Market.*)

Children's Book Council (CBC). This association of publishers of children's books works with groups in other fields through joint committees to create children's book programs. The CBC sponsors an annual Children's Book Week in November and supports an examination library that contains reference works and children's trade books published during the past three years. Beginning in 1983, the CBC sponsors *Everychild: The American Conference*, a national meeting about books and other media that also includes exhibits of materials.

This organization publishes annotated bibliographies of children's books, available free for a 6½″ × 9½″ self-addressed, stamped envelope. These lists include "Children's Choices," compiled annually and based on schoolchildren's voting on books selected by publishers; "Outstanding Science Trade Books for Children"; and "Notable Children's Trade Books in the Field of Social Studies." When requesting these publications, envelopes should be coded as follows: "Att'n.: NSTA" for the list of science books and "Att'n: NCSS" for the list of social studies books. (A request for both lists must include first-class postage for three ounces.) For *Children's Choices* list, send a 9″ × 12″ self-addressed envelope with postage for four ounces to "Att'n: *Children's Choices,* International Reading Association, 800 Barksdale Road, Box 8139, Newark, DE 19714. "Writing Books for Children and Young Adults" and two annually revised lists—the "Members List" of editors' names and "Members' Publishing Programs" featuring brief descriptions of each publisher's list—are other publications of the CBC that may be obtained for a self-addressed, stamped envelope. The address of the Children's Book Council is 568 Broadway, New York, NY, 10012.

Children's Media Market Place (CMMP). A biennial directory that lists organizations and individuals in various categories of communications for children. Listings include names, addresses and telephone numbers of personnel, as well as a description of the audience, services and products of the company, agency or group.

CMMP contains sections on book publishers, periodical publishers (which include "Periodicals for Children," "Periodicals for Professionals & Parents," and "Review Journals & Services"), book clubs, bookstores, audiovisual producers, agents, TV and radio stations and distributors of TV programs. The sections "Public Library Coordinators of Children's & Young Adult Services," "State School Media Officers," and "Examination Centers" deal with individuals and organizations that select books for public libraries and school libraries. Also included in the book are a section on federal grants, a calendar of events and a bibliography of works about children's media.

The section "Names & Numbers Index to Children's Media Sources" lists individuals, companies and other organizations.

Children's theater. The term used to refer to plays written to entertain young people. Full-length dramas written for children's theater usually have performance times of an hour or longer (but not too much longer). Dramatized fairy tales (*The Wizard of Oz, The Snow Queen*) and original scripts (modern comedies, historical sagas) written for children are not usually intended to be acted by young people.

The children's theater playwright knows his young audience well. He uses vivid language, lively stage behavior, attention-getting devices and dialogue that neither preaches nor moralizes. He attempts to grip his audience's attention at the outset of the play. He concentrates on ideas/themes that are understandable by children, but never underestimates the depth of perception in his audience may have.

The children's playwright submits his script, along with specific costume or prop needs and unique staging requirements, to producers. Multiple submissions of plays to amateur and touring companies, college experimental groups, contests and church organizations are common. Some beginning playwrights allow amateur productions of their work for limited fees to gain exposure for their work.

When a play has been successfully produced, the playwright may submit it (along with its reviews) to a play publisher who, on accepting the work, markets it—usually through a catalog. *Writer's Market* offers information on producers and publishers that solicit plays for young audiences as well as producers of films and audiovisual materials for children. *Songwriter's Market* identifies markets for musicals. (*See: Play royalties; Plays for young actors.*)

Children's Writer's & Illustrator's Market. This annual directory for children's writers and illustrators contains listings for categories such as audiovisual aids, songs, coloring books, comic books and puzzles, in addition to magazine and book publishers. It also includes markets for writing *by* children; lists of Caldecott and Newbery award-winning books; artwork samples; a detailed "Business of Writing & Illustrating" article; subject and age-level indexes; and many other features to help writers and illustrators market their work in this field.

City magazine. A regional publication reflecting the people, services, institutions and unique environment of a metropolitan area. City magazines are generally upbeat publications willing to look analytically at a city's many themes. Though some "city-mags" began as chamber-of-commerce-type publications, whose "boosterism" articles discussed only the best and brightest aspects of the city, the most successful magazines are now independent operations free of the restraints of public relations.

City magazines share similar philosophies because of their common denominator—people and cities. They are not strictly news, business or local interest journals; rather, they are periodicals offering in-depth pieces on the background, significance and effect of area happenings. They also present lifestyles, distinct personalities and local-color situations that might otherwise go unnoticed. Because they are not usually in competition with each other, city magazines frequently copy and imitate each other's ideas and formats.

They are published mainly for the middle- and upper-class, well-educated, sophisticated reader interested in various aspects of life in the city. Writers must know the particular demographics of their readership and tackle subjects appealing to that audience. Current popular offerings include service articles, exposés, how-to's, community calendars, columns—even pieces that take on a popular urban cause, such as neighborhood safety.

The city magazine represents a potentially fruitful market for freelancers. (There are currently more than two hundred city magazines nationwide, most of them supported by populations of one million or more. Smaller cities, if they are both diverse and booming, may also provide suitable ground for a magazine.) Because local newspapers are usually in competition with city magazines for advertising, stories and readers, newspaper staff writers are not generally permitted to write for area city magazines; moreover, city magazines usually carry few staff writers of their own.

Payment for articles depends on the magazine's profitability, its size, management, budget and talent pool. For major features, writers may earn $100–$500. For shorter articles and columns, the price is usually about half the major feature rate. Most city magazines do not pay by the word. *Writer's Market* highlights potential markets and their requirements.

Classical music. Established, formal, elegant and precise musical art forms. Throughout history, different styles of classical music have predominated, such as the work of J.S. Bach of the baroque period (1600–1750), Wolfgang Amadeus Mozart of the classical period (1750–1820); Felix Mendelssohn of the romantic period (1820–1920); and Arnold Schoenberg and Igor Stravinsky of the twentieth century.

Cliché. A trite word or phrase that lacks originality or impact because of frequent and prolonged use. Clichés clutter a manuscript and should be avoided, except when used deliberately as sarcasm or as a revealing commentary through the dialogue of a particular character.

"Cool as a cucumber" and "green with envy" are examples of clichés.

Climax. The climax, as the result of all the events that have preceded it, is the most intense point in the story line of a fictional work. (A novel or play may contain more than one climax; however, a short story should include only one.)

A climax represents the peak of emotional response from the reader as well as the turning point in the story's action. It always follows a crisis, but when time elapses between the two occurrences, the event is called an *anticlimax* instead of a climax. (*See: Crisis.*)

CLIO awards. These awards of the advertising industry were named for Clio, one of the muses of Greek mythology, who is described as "the proclaimer and glorifier of great accomplishments and deeds." They are given annually for best U.S. TV, radio, cable TV, print, packaging design, and specialty advertising, and for best international TV/cinema, radio, print and packaging design. The best entries receive CLIO statuettes; the finalists, certificates.

Criteria for judging are effectiveness of communication of sales message, appeal and/or taste, and use of production techniques. In 1995, 260 statuettes were awarded out of more than thirteen thousand entries. The competition is open to all ads in all media. Deadline is December 1 for material produced from January 1 to November 30. For material produced in December, deadline is January 2. CLIO Awards are presented in New York City in June.

Inquiries may be addressed to CLIO Awards, 336 E. Fifty-ninth St., New York, NY 10022; the office can be reached by phone at (212) 683-4300.

Clip. In journalistic terms, a sample of a writer's published work, usually from a newspaper or magazine. Editors often indicate that *clips* or *clippings* should be mailed or presented in person when applying for a job.

A clip can also be a piece cut out of a newspaper or magazine for any other reason. For example, freelance writers may keep files of clips for article ideas and research. (*See: Tearsheet.*)

Clip art. Camera-ready drawings on various subjects. Clip art firms sell booklets of clip art to editors of small publications, publicists at nonprofit organizations and others who need inexpensive illustrations. Clip art firms include companies such as Dynamic Graphics, Inc., 6000 N. Forest Park Dr., Peoria, IL 61614.

Some current subscription prices are $376.38 per year and $29.50 per month. (*See: Copyright-free art.*)

Clipping services. These firms employ people to read thousands of U.S. newspapers and magazines and clip items for writers or publishers on selected subjects.

While some publishing companies provide copies of reviews to authors whose books they publish (and may hire a clipping service for this purpose), some authors prefer to engage a service on their own for a certain book, or to collect newspaper or magazine clippings on a subject they're researching that's in the news.

Costs for the service are usually a set fee plus an additional amount for each clip provided. Current charges at one major national firm, for example, are $140 per month for three months' service plus $.85 per clipping.

Many such firms are listed in the Manhattan Yellow Pages telephone directory under "Clipping Bureaus."

Close shot. In a motion picture or TV script, this direction indicates that the camera should emphasize an actor or object by singling him or it out to fill the screen. When an extremely close shot is needed, the term *tight shot* is used. Both terms are typed in all caps. (*See: Close-up.*)

Close-up. A camera direction indicating that the subject is seen at close range. In a close-up of a person, only the head or the head and shoulders are in view. *Close-up* can be abbreviated *CU*. A related camera direction is *extreme close-up* or *XCU*. Both terms are typed in all caps. (*See: Close shot.*)

Co-author. When more than one writer is an author of a book, the multiple bylines appear on the text and the jacket, and the royalties usually are shared proportionate to the individual authors' contributions to the salability of the book. When a writer works with a subject or expert who is not a writer, the division of

royalty income again depends on how much each party contributed to the book. (*See: As-told-to article or book; Collaboration.*)

Coins, illustrations of. Coins of the U.S. and foreign countries that are represented in photographs, illustrations, motion pictures or slides, "may be used for any purpose including advertising," according to the U.S. Department of the Treasury. (*See: Money, illustration of.*)

Collaboration. In the writing field, this term refers to the act of working with one or more persons in a joint enterprise involving research and writing. The writer may collaborate with various people: another writer, an editor, illustrator, technical person, photographer, celebrity or musician.

Both fiction and nonfiction can be written as collaborative efforts. Writing in this way succeeds when careful planning accompanies the choice of a partner. Collaborators share similar motivations for the work, feel comfortable with brainstorming sessions, and are willing to give and take in writing, revising, editing and marketing. In the case of the co-written manuscript, writers generally share the workload and agree to an equitable split of the income and title page credits according to what percentage of the work's salability depends on each person's contributions.

Three categories of collaboration are especially appropriate for nonfiction. (1) The as-told-to manuscript is ghostwritten in the first person, with the writer getting an as-told-to byline. Income is often split fifty-fifty, but this is negotiable depending on the creative contributions of each party to the salability of the work. (2) The ghostwritten work exists where the writer does the job of telling someone's story, usually for a set fee, and with no accompanying credits. Books by politicians and stage personalities are often ghostwritten. (3) The anthology is collated by a writer acting as an editor, who gets contributors to write chapters for the work or himself secures reprint permissions for published material. Fees for the contributors are deducted from the publisher's advance to the author or paid from a publisher's fund set up for that purpose; the writer/editor gets the royalties.

Whatever the collaborative agreement or genre of writing, the collaborators draw up a contract providing for division of the rights and income from the work. More complex contracts give attention to the effect that disability or death of one of the collaborators would have on the work and whether/how to progress with the project. Several forms of collaboration contracts are described in *Entertainment, Publishing, and the Arts: Agreement and the Law.* (*See: Anthology; As-told-to article or book; Ghostwriting; Musical.*)

Collective biography. A volume of biographical sketches of individuals in similar professions, related persuasions or parallel life circumstances. Example: *Winners on the Tennis Court*, by William S. Glickman. The successful collective biography knits the individual accounts together in a meaningful way by suggesting common threads among the lives of the profiled persons.

Writers who would like to see which publishers are currently producing biographies can refer to the book publishers section of *Writer's Market* and the "Biography" category of the *Subject Guide to Books in Print.* (*See: Biography.*)

College textbook publishers, largest. (*See: Figure 13.*)

Colloquial language. (*See: Dialogue; Informal writing style.*)

Colophon. The term *colophon* is sometimes used interchangeably with *logo* as the publisher's identifying mark or symbol on the book's title page, jacket and binding. It can also be a brief description or discussion of some or all of the elements of a high-quality book's design and production: the designer, typeface, printer, printing process and paper stock.

For example, the colophon to *The Lone Pilgrim*, a collection of stories by Laurie Colwin, credits the typesetter, the printer and the designer, and gives the following note on the type: "The text of this book was set in Intertype Garamond, a modern rendering of the type first cut by Claude Garamond (1510–1561). Garamond was a pupil of Geofroy Tory and is believed to have based his letters on the Venetian models, although he introduced a number of important differences, and it is to him we owe the letter that we know as 'old style.' He gave to his letters a certain elegance and a feeling of movement that won for their creator an immediate reputation and the patronage of Francis I of France."

FIGURE 13

LARGEST US COLLEGE TEXTBOOK PUBLISHERS
1993 ESTIMATED REVENUES AND RANK
(DOLLARS IN MILLIONS)

RANK 1993/1992		PUBLISHER	COLLEGE REVENUES 1993	1992	CHANGE
1	2	The Thompson Corp.	$ 289.5	$ 267.2	8.3%
2	1	Simon & Schuster*	289.2	298.8	-3.2%
3	3	McGraw-Hill	232.0	228.0	1.8%
4	4	Times Mirror	186.0	176.2	5.6%
5	5	Addison-Wesley	164.0	160.0	2.4%
6	6	Harcourt General	151.1	148.0	2.1%
7	7	HarperCollins	130.0	130.0	0.0%
8	8	John Wiley & Sons	91.0	86.8	4.8%
9	9	Houghton Mifflin	90.1	81.2	11.0%
10		Macmillian**	90.0	128.0	NM
TOTAL			$1712.9	$1704.4	0.5%

*Sales include two months of Macmillan revenues.
**Sales estimate reflects a 10-month period.

©1994 SIMBA Information, Inc. Wilton, Connecticut. Reprinted with permission. Unauthorized copying prohibited.

This type of colophon is usually located at the back of a book. (*See: Logo.*)

Color in writing. (*See: Local color.*)

Columbia Journalism Review. (*See: Media reviewers.*)

Column. A short newspaper or magazine piece that deals specifically with a particular field of interest, or broadly with an issue or circumstance of far-reaching scope. A good column is written clearly and succinctly. Columns appear with bylines on a regular basis (daily, weekly, etc.) and usually run 350–500 words in newspapers. They may be written exclusively for one newspaper or magazine; they may be marketed by a syndicate; or they may be self-syndicated by the writer.

Columns generally fall into two types. The first is the column written by an expert in a particular subject area. From education and/or experience the writer knows a topic and is able to come up with new slants and fresh approaches to inform interested readers about his specialty. Columns dealing with subjects such as gardening, business, child care, and fitness are currently popular.

The second kind of column is written by a person expert in the observation of humans and their activities. This writer views the routine and the ordinary with a keen perspective. His columns may be humorous or serious and usually appeal to mass audiences.

Beginning writers are more likely to find success in writing and selling a special-interest column than in attempting to write columns in the style of Art Buchwald or Erma Bombeck. Publishers and editors of weekly and daily newspapers, county tabloids and independent newsletters are receptive to "focused" columns likely to generate and sustain interest among their unique readerships.

Local newspaper column rates currently range from $.80 per column-inch to $5 for a weekly publication and from $7.50 to $25 or more for dailies, depending on their circulation. *Writer's Market* details rates for local, syndicated and self-syndicated columns. (*See: Self-syndication; Syndicated column.*)

Column-inch. In a printed publication, the area whose boundaries are the width of the column and one inch of depth. This measurement is used in selling advertisements and is also used by some small newspapers as a guideline for paying correspondents.

Comedy writing. This category includes special material composed of gags and routines written to be performed by a comedian. Comedy writing begins with a premise or theme, such as the financial dilemmas of an oil sheik. This subject is developed into a routine, a four- to five-minute bit with appropriate gags. Its purpose is to amuse an audience. Subjects for comedy material range from the absurd to the unexpected, from the ungarnished to the pompous; there is very little that cannot be slanted to make people laugh. Suc-cessful comedy writing is visual in that it conjures amusing images in the minds of an audience.

Comedy material is geared to the style and practice of a comedian. The comedy writer submits his work to a market, i.e., a specific comedian who he feels is best suited to delivering it successfully. The freelance comedy writer usually contacts "big-name" comics and entertainers through clubs where they appear or through the TV networks on which they perform. However, would-be comedy writers use whatever means they can to bring their work to the attention of comedians. One writer, who worked as a tailor in a shop in the Manhattan theater district, started out leaving gags in the pockets of suits left at the shop by well-known comedians. Trade papers such as *Variety* and *Show Business* may also reveal who a well-known comic's personal or theatrical manager is. Writers looking for comics in smaller cities may be able to contact them by phone when they appear in town at a nightclub or hotel. If no comedians routinely perform in an area, comedy material may be sold to local disc jockeys, TV personalities and newspapers.

Producers of TV situation comedies and variety shows also need comedy material. Sitcom producers look for comedy plots and situations in which to put their characters; variety show producers want sketches and monologues for their stars. Both sitcoms and variety shows, however, are usually written by staff writers, not freelancers.

Rates for freelance comedy writers vary according to the popularity and income of the comedian. Nightclub performers currently pay $2–$25 for each gag; $150 and up per minute for routines. New comics offer only slim rates to writers for five-minute routines, but some comedians pay $2,500 and more for a five-minute stint from an established comedy writer. (*See: Gag writing; Humor.*)

Additional information: *Comedy Writing Secrets.*

Come-to-realize story. A short story in which the main character's learning or changing occurs entirely within his mind. This kind of story cannot be dramatically effective because the character never takes action as a result of his new insight. Because of this weakness, editors often reject come-to-realize stories.

For example, such a story may end when a newly successful young pianist (the main character) realizes that without the untiring encouragement of the self-sacrificing mother he has all but forgotten, he would be nothing. He feels deep remorse and resolves to write his mother at once. This ending lacks drama because it's all mental, but the story could be effective if the pianist were to *do something*. He may telephone his mother, for example, even though it's 2:00 A.M. where she lives, confess his neglect, and tell her he's sending air fare (which the reader knows he can ill afford) for her to join him for his Vienna debut. (*See: Character change; Short story.*)

Comic relief. A literary device in which a humorous scene or comment is injected into a work that is generally serious. Although it is used in fiction, comic relief is especially associated with drama: It serves to release the audience's tension brought about by previous scenes and to amplify the tragic elements of the story.

Comic relief is used in *Hamlet* to relieve the feeling of doom created by Ophelia's and Polonius's deaths, and Hamlet's despondent state. Just after the audience learns of Ophelia's drowning, a comic scene is inserted in which two clowns exchange witticisms as they dig the young woman's grave.

In the contemporary drama *The Night of the Iguana*, Tennessee Williams uses comic relief in the persons of the German family who are residents at the same hotel as the hero. By what they wear, how they act and what they say, the characters always bring a laugh and momentarily slow the play's pace.

Comics writing. This job involves creating and writing copy for stories told in a comics/graphic art technique—an extremely versatile technique used for advertising, for instructional material, for educational material and other nonfiction, and for fiction of all sorts—action-adventure stories, fantasy, science fiction, humor, Westerns, horror, drama, romance, etc.

Comics reach all ages and levels effectively and are properly considered a communications medium in their own right. Like TV and motion pictures, comics are a visual medium; however, comics can be absorbed at the reader's own pace, and material can be reread and reviewed easily and conveniently.

Comics writers have a number of unique devices at their disposal. Smooth-bordered "balloons" indicate that the words enclosed are spoken; scalloped balloons indicate thoughts. (A "pointer" on the side or bottom of the balloon identifies which character is speaking or thinking.) Captions enclosed in ruled boxes provide whatever narration is needed to augment the illustrations. Whether a comics writer's work is a short vignette, a series of multipanel strips or a book-length project, he must succeed in covering a lot of ground in a small space and in only two or three sentences at a time.

A writer interested in creating comic book scripts submits a plot idea to the editor. If it is approved, he is assigned to submit a synopsis of three to twenty pages for the editor's appraisal. At this stage, the editor sometimes requests that the writer make corrections. (If, for certain reasons, the project is abandoned, a kill fee may be involved.)

Then the *penciler* takes over, interpreting the story in drawings. He spends from one to four weeks at this task, after which his work (called the *pencils*) is submitted to the editor. The writer then receives the drawings so that he can *script* the pages by typing the dialogue and captions for them (on a separate sheet) and indicating where on each page the copy is to be placed.

The editor then rechecks the work; the writer may be asked to make revisions. If he lives a considerable distance from the publisher, he may not see the copy after this stage because of the time involved in sending it back and forth.

The next step, lettering the copy and drawing borders around the panels, is the job of a *letterer*. Then the drawings are *inked*—traced over with India ink—either by the penciler (who drew them originally) or by yet another person, an *inker*. Coloring, proofreading and designing the cover are the final steps to producing a comic book.

An alternate method involves the writer, upon approval of his plot, creating a "full script," which includes all dialogue, captions and descriptions of the required pictures on a panel-by-panel basis. The full script, once approved by the editor, is sent on to the artist, letterer, etc., for completion of the comic.

Payment for comics averages $35–$50 a page—although some well-established, steady contributors to some comic companies receive more per page and earn $20,000–$100,000 or more a year. Most of the major comic book publishers—such as DC Comics, Inc. and Marvel Comics—are in the New York area; their addresses are in the Manhattan telephone book.

Comment song. A kind of song in a musical that provides commentary on (or opinion of) the action of the story. A well-known comment song is "Sunrise, Sunset," from *Fiddler on the Roof.* (*See: Musical.*)

Commission person. An independent salesperson of books, sometimes also called a publisher's representative. This type of salesperson is used by some small publishing houses, from which he receives a commission rather than a salary. A commission person may be engaged by several publishers at once. Some work with assistants and others work alone.

The work of a commission person involves usually regional travel to bookstores. A list of Publishers Representatives appears in the directory *Literary Market Place.*

Commissioned writing. (*See: Assignment, writing on.*)

Committee of Small Magazine Editors & Publishers (COSMEP). COSMEP is an association of publishers of small magazines and books. Its fourteen hundred members strive to increase the promotion and distribution of their publications. COSMEP sponsors an exhibit service, publishes a monthly newsletter and convenes annually. Its headquarters can be reached at P.O. Box 703, San Francisco, CA 94101.

Comp. Abbreviation for *complimentary copy.* An author receives a certain number of comps of his own book from his publisher.

Publishers sometimes supply other authorities on the book's subject with comps so that they can review the book or provide testimonial quotes for advertising copy. Authors do not receive royalties on these comp copies or the copies sent to book reviewers.

Magazine publishers usually maintain a complimentary subscription list for their regular advertisers, prospective advertisers, regular correspondents and contributing editors. (*See: Author's copies; Pre-publication review.*)

Company publication. This is an institutional publication taking one of two forms. One, the *internal,* is designed primarily to promote good employee relations within a company. The second, an *external,* is pub-

lished for dealers, distributors and/or stockholders to keep them informed about a company's progress. A company publication may be produced as a general notice, letter, newsletter, newspaper, magazine or annual report.

Company publications are also known as *house organs,* but that term is not preferred by editors.

Freelance writers can serve as contributors to or editors of company publications. However, many businesses depend on their own staff members to produce these publications. (*See: Business writing.*)

Complaints against publishers. The writer's grievance most often heard at Writer's Digest Books is publishers' failure to return manuscripts (even when a self-addressed, stamped enveloped has been enclosed). Another common complaint is that the publisher has neglected to respond to a query letter. In addition, nonpayment on the part of publishers seems to be increasingly common, according to the editor of *Writer's Market.*

For writers who have been unsuccessful in getting responses to their own follow-up letters to the editor and/or the publisher, *Writer's Market* operates a complaint service dealing with grievances against the organizations listed in the directory. The editors are prepared to intercede for the writer in two areas only: (1) cases in which a promised payment for accepted material has not been delivered or has been delivered only in part, and (2) cases in which the writer has received no report on solicited material. Writers must enclose both a self-addressed, stamped

FIGURE 14

COMPLAINTS AGAINST
PUBLISHERS/AGENTS

*T*he types of complaints received most often by the editors of *Writer's Market* about publisher or agent listings in that publication or the market columns of *Writer's Digest* are these:

No report on manuscript or query...45%
Nonreturn of material with self-addressed, stamped envelope.....................10%
Nonpayment or late payment for magazine article/story............................15%
Complaint about level of service provided for fee by agent.........................10%
Nonpayment royalty (including no royalty report)..3%
Dissatisfaction with subsidy publishing: lack of communication,
    product, promotion, sales, etc. 1%
Accepted manuscript not yet published after lengthy wait...........................6%
Mail returned from post office (mss, follow-up letters), addressee
    unknown/no forwarding address..5%
Miscellaneous (Market needs not those reflected in *WM/WD* listings,
    change in policy, incorrect addresses, other)..5%
                                                           100%

---

envelope and photocopies of correspondence that verify their claims. The service can solve approximately 50 percent of the writer-publisher conflicts brought to its attention, according to an estimate by the *Writer's Market* editor.

If the publisher in question is not listed in *Writer's Market*, there are other possible options. The writer (1) may be able to file a claim in small claims court; (2) can consult an attorney about the existence of a long-arm law in his state by which to sue the publisher in the writer's state; or (3) can notify the U.S. Postmaster in the city where the publisher is located about possible mail fraud. Sending a copy of such a letter to the publisher sometimes encourages the publisher to come forth with the payment.

Similarly, when other kinds of legal problems are involved, the writer is referred to a legal service such as Volunteer Lawyers for the Arts or the attorney general of the state in which the publisher does business. (*See: Editorial ethics; Figure 14; "Long-arm" law; Volunteer Lawyers for the Arts.*)

Composite character. With this device, a nonfiction writer combines the experiences and attitudes of several real people into one character. He creates a composite either to protect individual identities or to avoid having numerous people make similar comments. In such cases, of course, he mentions this fact in his covering letter to the editor, who should, of course, alert the reader to the use of the device.

Among the earliest examples of

this new journalism technique was an article about prostitution written by *New York* magazine writer Gail Sheehy, in which the hustler she called Redpants was actually a composite of the many hustlers she interviewed over several weeks.

CompuServe. One of the original, and still among the most successful, commercial online services, Compu-Serve is available to computer users on DOS, Windows and Macintosh operating systems. It is highly regarded as a research tool, though its interface might not be as easy to maneuver around in as those of America Online and eWorld. For information, or to order CompuServe installation software, call (800) 848-8990. (*See: Electronic Mail; Internet; Online service.*)

Conceit. A particularly striking or imaginative extended image or metaphor found most often in poetry, especially in Elizabethan verse and the work of the seventeenth-century metaphysical poets. Robert Frost's poem "Departmental," in which a community of ants is treated as a bureaucracy, is a modern conceit. (*See: Metaphor.*)

Concept. A general statement regarding a screenplay or teleplay. It is usually created before the outline or treatment is written. A concept, which is a general idea about a situation or a character in a story, is more vague and less developed than a premise, which indicates the story's beginning, middle and resolution. (*See: Premise; Screenwriting; Television script; Television writing.*)

Condensation and copyright law. (*See: Adaptation.*)

Confession. The confession is a first-person story in which the narrator is involved in an emotional situation that encourages sympathetic reader identification, concluding with the affirmation of a morally acceptable theme. The basic story themes of love, anger or fear, based on everyday problems, are intended primarily for female readers ranging in age from pre-teen to senior citizen, although there is a small male readership as well. Published for the most part without bylines, confession stories give the writer the advantage of anonymity, especially with regard to writing freely about personal problems. While following basic story structure, confessions are generally introspective episodes written with sincerity, rather than tongue-in-cheek sophistication. Confessions run from 1,500 to 12,000 words long, the greatest demand being for 5,000 to 6,000-word stories.

Confessions are written in one of two structural formats. The formula confession begins with the narrator facing, or about to face, an identifiable problem that has arisen through some character flaw or "wrong" attitude—sufficiently motivated to ensure reader sympathy. The viewpoint character muddles through obstacles en route to an emotionally satisfying solution. This "sin-suffer-repent" format is still used in the standard confession, but it is less melodramatic than in the original stories of sixty years ago; today the narrator profits from his experience and reaches new maturity.

The nonformula story deals with

a narrator struggling to solve a problem that has occurred through no fault of his own. In either confession format, the "lesson learned" and consequent growth in human understanding are meant to stimulate growth in the reader.

Confessions can also be classified by subject matter. One common type of confession is in the *family problem* category. There is also the *inspirational* story, in which the narrator overcomes some handicap, and the *documentary*, which explores a problem (often medical) or dispels a myth with up-to-date, authoritative information. The *tabloid* confession is usually a frank sexual account that does not depend on reader identification. The *romance* story emphasizes dating and courtship, rather than sex. There is also room for humor, the supernatural and suspense writing in the confession writer's craft.

Currently about twenty confession magazines are on the stands, averaging eight or nine stories an issue. Rates usually run from $.03 to $.05 per word, paid on publication. Both *Writer's Market* and *Novel & Short Story Writer's Market* give details on submission requirements. (*See: First-person short story.*)

Conflict. Conflict is one of the prime ingredients of fiction. It usually represents some obstacle to the main character's goals; for the reader to be concerned about the resolution of the conflict, that resolution must have consequence for the main character.

Any conflict in fiction can be defined by one of five themes. Although we're using the traditional expression "man," all these themes

apply to either men or women. *Man against himself* can be manifest in a character's conflicting emotions, which sometimes involves a battle with the conscience. Many of Henry James's protagonists—for instance, John Marcher in "The Beast in the Jungle"—live in such inner turmoil. The conflict of *man against man* can take either a psychological or physical form; it places a goal or the well-being of the main character in jeopardy because of another character. In *Wuthering Heights*, for example, Heathcliff is in conflict with practically every other character.

When a writer places *man against environment*, something in the character's societal surroundings—a city, a government, a social class—causes the conflict; the American naturalistic writers of the late nineteenth and early twentieth centuries—Theodore Dreiser and Stephen Crane, for example—were preoccupied with this problem. Similarly, natural surroundings can threaten a character; in this type of conflict—*man against nature*—the opposition to the protagonist can be either a natural setting or a natural disaster. Jack London's "To Build a Fire" is a classic story of conflict with nature.

A fictional situation may also place *man against the machine*. Since machines do not possess volition, there are few pure examples of such conflict; but the Frank Norris muckraking novel *The Octopus*, which deals with the sprawling prewar American railway system, can be read as man versus technology. (*See: Climax; Crisis; Plot.*)

Conflict of interest. This is an issue of ethics that confronts newspaper editors and reporters, as well as free-lance writers. Its basic cause is the simultaneous need to serve readers and to maintain associations with other businesses.

Conflict of interest can occur when a reporter or newspaper uses information obtained in the gathering of news for his/their own benefit, or suppresses or distorts news for his/their own or someone else's benefit. When a newspaper reporter moonlights at a public relations job, for example, or writes speeches for political candidates, what he is doing in his second job—promoting products or people—may interfere with his fair and accurate reporting of the news in his first job. Other conflicts involve a newsperson's appearance in commercials; a reporter's writing about a news event he was somehow involved in; journalists' working for the CIA; and a newspaper or magazine including or omitting copy to satisfy advertisers.

For freelancers, conflict of interest is presented by some freebies and junkets (typically offered to writers on travel, food and cosmetics, who must attempt objective reporting despite the financial support of the supplier). On the other hand, a magazine, for example, may be backing a political candidate and so refuse to publish a negative story about him. That may not be "objective," but the magazine is under no obligation to be so. Its editors can pick and choose what they want to publish, what slant they want to take, etc., whereas a newspaper is expected to print the news—unslanted and in its entirety, with no angles concealed. (*See: Press trip.*)

Conglomerates—book publishers. In recent years, some book publishers have been purchased by companies unrelated to publishing, thereby joining conglomerates. Although some corporate owners grant a certain amount of autonomy to publishers, others subject them to restrictions that may prove harmful to beginning authors. For example, a publishing house that is part of a conglomerate may be less likely to gamble on a first novel.

On the other hand, as Dean Koontz points out in *How to Write Best-Selling Fiction*, conglomerate takeovers in the past fifteen years have strongly influenced publishers' advertising and marketing techniques, so that some books are exposed to a much larger audience than they were in the past. This situation can, of course, increase the writer's income.

Literary Market Place listings for book publishers indicate if they are a subdivision of a parent company, which may be either another publishing firm or a corporation unrelated to publishing. (*See: Book promotion; Magazine publishers, multiple.*)

Congressional Directory. This volume, available in most libraries, furnishes the names and addresses of all current members of Congress, along with details on committee assignments, federal agencies, members of the judiciary, foreign representatives and consular offices in the U.S., and other data. Of particular interest to writers are the names of all reporters or photographers (and the publications and broadcast media they represent) who are accredited to the press galleries in Congress. Representatives of consumer and specialized magazines are included, as well as newspapers, wire services, radio and TV networks, and station representatives. (*See: Press galleries.*)

Consent. (*See: Libel.*)

Consequence, a sense of. *Esquire*'s fiction editor, Rust Hills, reminds fiction writers that "Whatever happens must happen to someone and must have consequence to him. A lot can happen in a story or novel—a man can be shot by another man or go crazy in the jungle—but if there is no sense of the consequence of these events to someone, then they might as well go unrecounted; they are artistically pointless." Fiction writers need always examine their stories to see that the conflicts faced and resolved by their characters leave readers with this sense of consequence. (*See: Conflict; Plot.*)

Consulting. Writers who have developed specialties can serve as consultants to businesses, educational institutions and other organizations that produce their own films, books and other materials. A consultant's big advantage to a company is objectivity: He is freer to criticize and suggest changes than an employee is, and he can concentrate solely on his task without taking the time to become part of an operation. A consultant does not have to go to staff meetings, which enables him to produce relatively more than staffers in the same amount of time. A consultant also need not be concerned with office politics or with internal advancement.

The usual qualifications for a con-

sultant, according to consultant Richard A. Stemm, include a combination of formal education, practical experience and seasoning; and the ability to maintain a mental storehouse of information and experiential knowledge.

Stemm advises the would-be full-time consultant to prepare for a consulting career one or two years before he actually begins a practice. Preparation consists of becoming acquainted with the necessary jargon and with jobs at all levels in the field, reading trade journals and attending meetings of professional organizations.

Experts disagree on the best approach. Some say marketing consulting services through indirect means is preferable to directly approaching a prospective client. A consultant can make his name known through articles in trade journals and by giving seminars and speeches. He can also contact professional acquaintances for leads. As his experience increases, the consultant is likely to receive referrals.

On the other hand, the direct approach of advertising in trade journals is also recommended.

A consultant's fees are based on the comparable amount he is capable of earning as an employee. Since he must earn enough to cover insurance and other benefits that would be paid an employee by a corporation, he increases the hourly rate he is capable of receiving by two and a half to three times. Expenses required by the consultant for out-of-town travel and lodging are paid for by the client, but the cost of commuting to and from the client's office (when the distance is fifty miles or less) is paid for by the consultant. Billing procedures vary, and many consultants request that part of the total fee be paid in advance.

The *Consultants and Consulting Organizations Directory* lists individuals and organizations in 135 fields. Names, addresses, telephone numbers and descriptions of services are included in the listings, which are cross-referenced by geographic location, subject, names of people and names of companies. Specialist writer-consultants who want to be listed should contact the publisher (Gale Research Company, Book Tower, Detroit, MI 48226) regarding eligibility requirements.

Consumer magazines. Those publications aimed at the reader of general interest, sport, hobby or other specialized consumer interest material; as opposed to magazines aimed toward business, professional and trade interests.

Contest writing. This term is usually applied to the short, original entries that are submitted in competition for prize and profit. Contest writing usually involves composing prose or rhyme, often in response to a request for a product-praising statement, jingle, slogan, name or caption. It uses parodies, analogies and take-offs on current speech as well as triad constructions (Our apples are *selected* for their flavor, *inspected* for their quality and *protected* for your pleasure) to make a point or sell a product.

Contest writers understand the particular requirements of various games and respond with the necessary research to produce concise, fluent, catchy entries. They vie for prizes of money, vacations or product samples. Participants equip themselves with the tools of the literary trade—standard dictionary, thesaurus, rhyming dictionary. They recognize that judges often look for timely, topical writing.

Contest announcements appear in newspapers, magazines, company publications, even in grocery stores. Several publications of interest to contest writers are listed in *The Newsletter Yearbook Directory*, and books on how to be successful in contest writing are listed under "Rewards (Prizes, Etc.)" in the *Subject Guide to Books In Print.*

The National Contesters Association (NCA) represents people interested in contest writing. It sponsors an annual meeting and publishes a bulletin for members. Information can be obtained by writing the Association at 346 City View Dr., Fort Lauderdale, FL 33311, for a self-addressed, stamped envelope. (*See: Contests, writing.*)

Contests, writing. While "contest writing" usually refers to the short statements or jingles composed for prizes or money, other contests are open to writers working in a variety of literary forms. The directory *Gadney's Guide to 1500 International Contests, Festivals and Grants in Film and Video, Photography, TV-Radio Broadcasting, Writing, Playwriting and Journalism* is one such detailed compilation. Four individual directories of *How to Enter and Win Fiction Writing Contests, Film Contests, Nonfiction/Journalism Contests* and *Video and Audio Contests* by Alan Gadney have been published by Facts on File Publications. Other sources are the "Contests and Awards" section of *Novel & Short Story Writer's Market* and "Prize Contests Open" in *Literary Market Place.*

Literary contests offer writers an incentive (prestige, money) and a self-imposed deadline by which to produce a specific manuscript that may also have other marketing potential after the contest is over.

Some literary prizes are awarded by sponsoring organizations and cannot be competed for directly by the writer. Many of these are listed in the directory *Literary and Library Prizes.* Information on major literary awards such as the Nobel or Pulitzer Prize is provided in the individual entries in this book.

Continuing education. Writers and professionals in writing-related fields have several options available for keeping abreast of their fields once they have completed their formal college education. (A good liberal arts background is a given for any writer.)

In addition to local universities that may offer classes in professionally related topics, professional organizations offer periodic educational workshops, seminars and conferences. American Women in Radio and Television; Public Relations Society of America; Society of Professional Journalists, Sigma Delta Chi; and Women in Communications, Inc., are a few such organizations.

Folio: The Magazine for Magazine Management sponsors an annual conference for practitioners in magazine and book publishing. In addition, courses such as Harvard's Radcliffe Publishing Procedures

Course and others throughout the country are described in Petersen's *Guide to Book Publishing Courses.* Some programs, such as the Nieman Fellowships in Journalism at Harvard, are specifically designed for working professionals who want to take a year's leave of absence and return to the university for a period of intensive study in their specialty.

Of course, in addition to courses specifically related to careers in writing, freelance writers also seek information and education in new areas of interest about which to write, whether it's a trip to Spain related to a historical novel, or a course in computers for a nonfiction book. (*See: Correspondence courses for writers; National University Continuing Education Association; Publishing, courses in.*)

Continuity. Commercials and other spoken parts of a radio program. Also refers to the spoken part of a commercial. In a motion picture, effective continuity depends on the proper matching of details, movement and dialogue from shot to shot, and the logical and explicit development of plot from scene to scene.

Contract writing. (*See: Ghostwriting.*)

Contributing editor. A person who writes for a magazine on a continuous basis is sometimes called a contributing editor of the magazine and is so listed on the masthead. A contributing editor is typically an expert on a subject of special interest to readers of the magazine he writes for. Usually a contributing editor is an author who has written a number of articles on a freelance basis for a magazine, and whom the editor has chosen because he perceives a need in his audience for this writer's knowledge. A contributing editor may write a regular column for an agreed-on fee or submit ideas for and be given a specific number of article assignments annually.

Contributor's copies. An author's copies of his own work (such as a book) or of the issue of a publication in which his work appears, sent by some publishers either as partial payment or full payment. Literary/little magazines and small presses often pay only in contributor's copies.

Co-op copy. Radio advertising for a store in which a manufacturer's name is mentioned; the spot is paid for partly by the store and partly by the manufacturer. (*See: Cooperative [co-op] advertising.*)

Cooperative (co-op) advertising. Although it could be for any product or service, as it applies most frequently to writers it is a form of print advertising in which a publisher's book is featured in an ad for a particular bookstore. The publisher pays a lower rate for cooperative advertising than he would pay for his own ad, since co-op ads are charged the retail rate (applied to bookstores) rather than the higher national rate (applied to publishers). The publisher and bookstore owner arrange between themselves the way to divide the total cost of the ad; the publisher pays his share of the cost to the bookstore rather than to the newspaper or magazine. In addition, the publisher often supplies a camera-ready ad free to the bookstore. Unfortu-nately for the average writer, a lot of this co-op advertising goes to the bestselling titles for which the bookstores have large inventories, rather than to a first novel or a mid-list book. (*See: Mid-list books.*)

Cooperative publishing. (*See: Co-publishing; Poetry book publishing.*)

Co-publishing. Publication of a book by two publishers (often a hardcover and a paperback publisher; but could also include a U.S. and foreign publisher, a publisher and a foundation, etc.). The term also refers to an agreement, usually underscored by a contract, in which both a book publisher and an author pay for publishing costs and receive profits. Small publishing houses are likely to work under this system.

One advantage of co-publishing is that the author has some influence in the production and promotion of his book. The disadvantage is that he must contribute not only the creative product but a financial investment as well. (*See: Self-publishing.*)

Copyeditor. Copyediting positions are found in book, magazine, journal and newspaper publishing. A copyeditor corrects faulty grammar, spelling and punctuation in a manuscript, and improves readability when necessary. He checks to see that the work conforms to the publisher's style, and that specifications for typefaces and type sizes are correct. (*See: Editing, freelance; Editor, content.*)

Copyfitting. A magazine editor's job that involves calculating how many magazine column-inches a typed manuscript will take up once it is typeset; or, conversely, how much typed copy is needed to fill a fixed amount of magazine space.

Various systems for copyfitting exist, including the em system, the square-inch method and the character-count method. The character-count method is considered the most accurate for magazine and advertising copy, and will be explained here.

To use this system, the editor must know how many characters occupy a typeset line; to find that figure, he consults a *type book*—a system of charts devised by typesetting machine manufacturers for use by printers, editors and art directors. Type books give the correct character count per *pica* (the standard unit of measure for magazine layout; there are six picas in an inch) for every type size a particular typeface is available in.

To find what amount of magazine space a manuscript will fill, the editor first determines the total number of typed characters in the manuscript (each space between words counts as one character). He does this by measuring the line width—pica typewriters type ten characters per inch; elite typewriters, twelve—and either totaling the individual line counts, or finding the average line count and multiplying it by the number of lines in the manuscript. The editor then divides the resultant figure by the number of characters per typeset line (as determined from the chart in the type book) to get the number of typeset lines the copy will occupy.

In facing the other problem—i.e., finding how much copy must be writ-ten to fill a given area—the editor simply reverses the process. He divides the depth of the space to be filled (measured in *points*: twelve points per pica) by the depth of each line (also in points; usually one or two points greater than the type size) to get the number of lines of typeset copy that will fill the space. He multiplies the number of lines by the character count (which he finds in the type book) to get the total character count for the area, then divides by the average number of characters in a typewritten line to get the number of typed lines the copy must be.

While copyfitting is a complicated process to describe, in practice it is relatively simple. An experienced editor can quickly gauge manuscript length and estimate how many column-inches it will be, typeset. Absolute precision in word count is seldom necessary, since magazine layout can usually be adjusted to allow for a little more or less copy.

Copyright. A proprietary right designed to give the creator of a work the power to control that work's reproduction, distribution and public display or performance, as well as its adaptation to other forms.

Teachers, students and others may excerpt parts of copyrighted material for nonprofit use, in some cases, without infringing on copyrights.

The U.S. copyright law extends to literary, musical and dramatic works, works of art, motion pictures and other audiovisual works and sound recordings. Derivative works, or modifications of existing works, are also copyrightable; this includes translations, dramatizations, fictionalizations, screenplays, abridgments and condensations. Compilations, such as magazines or anthologies, are also copyrightable material. U.S. government publications are not copyrightable; however, a freelancer may be able to obtain copyrights on work produced for the government under a grant or contract, i.e., when the writer is not a regular employee of the government. Titles, ideas, jokes and other items are *not* copyrightable.

One change brought about by the Copyright Revision Act of 1976 (which became effective January 1, 1978) is that statutory copyright exists in a work as soon as it is created in tangible form, even if it has not been published, and whether or not it has been registered with the U.S. Copyright Office. (However, even though an unregistered work is copyrighted, registration is required before a writer can bring an infringement suit.) Under the original law, a literary work had to be published to be protected under statutory law; it was protected under common law between the time it was created and the time it was published.

Registration is accomplished through the U.S. Copyright Office, which supplies the registrant with the appropriate application form. The registration fee is currently $20; sometimes a group of works by the same author can be registered for a single fee. A work need not be published to secure copyright registration.

A copyright notice, consisting of the symbol © and/or the word *copyright* (or an abbreviation of it), the copyright owner's name, and the year of publication, may be placed on all copies of a work that are intended to be distributed to the public. Since March 1989, a copyright notice is no longer required to secure protection, but it is still useful to show ownership and to rebut claims of innocent infringement. The prudent author should request that his work appear with an individual copyright notice, especially when no copyright is claimed in the larger work. But when a piece copyrighted by an author appears in a copyrighted publication—a magazine, for example—without the individual's copyright notice, and the publication does not own the copyright to the individual piece, the writer is still usually protected.

The owner of a copyright may transfer his copyright or any part of it to another party. For example, the copyright owner may transfer only the right to translate his work to one individual, and only the right to abridge his work to another. For works copyrighted after January 1, 1978, the copyright owner may, thirty-five years after the transfer took place, regain the rights he has transferred. Publication rights may be regained at the earlier of these two dates: thirty-five years after the date of publication, or forty years after the date of execution of the grant. Termination of a grant must occur within the five-year period that begins at the end of the specified terms.

Copyright protection lasts for the duration of the owner's life plus the fifty years following his death. On collaborative works, the life of the last surviving owner determines the term of copyright, i.e., protection lasts fifty years following the death of the last surviving collaborator. On anonymous works, pseudonymous works, and works made for hire, the copyright expires either seventy-five years after the work's first publication or one hundred years after its creation, whichever is reached first. The term of copyright was revised with the latest law, so those works protected under statutory law as of December 31, 1977 (i.e., covered under the previous law *and published*), retain their original term of protection, twenty-eight years. These works must be renewed before December 31 of the twenty-eighth year for future copyright protection; the new law increases the second term to forty-seven years. (It was previously twenty-eight years.) Works that were not copyrighted prior to January 1, 1978 (and therefore covered under common law), now are protected for a term of the author's life plus the following fifty years; however, the law stipulates that coverage will be in effect until at least December 31, 2002, and if the work is published on or before that date, copyright protection lasts until at least December 31, 2027. In 1994 the oldest book that might still be in copyright would be dated 1919. In 1995, the oldest book possibly still in copyright would be dated 1920.

When a freelance writer creates a work made for hire, the buyer of the work is also usually obtaining the copyright. When a writer works for an organization as an employee and produces creative works as part of his job, the copyright to those works belongs to the employer.

(*See: Berne Union; Copyright notice; Copyright, Register of; Fair use; Figure 15; Figure 16; Infringement of copyright; International copyright; International copyright convention; Public domain; Work made for hire.*)

Copyright Clearance Center. With limited exception, the copyright act of 1978 requires that individuals and institutions wishing to photocopy copyrighted materials must obtain permission to do so from copyright owners. In response to this act, the Association of American Publishers (AAP) established the Copyright Clearance Center to serve as a centralized agency responsible for recording eligible photocopying, granting permission to use registered materials, collecting fees and processing royalty payments. The eighteen hundred members of the CCC include photocopy users (e.g., libraries, research institutes, universities and others who regularly use or distribute photocopy material—as opposed to the single individual who makes one copy for his own use); and copyright owners such as publishers and authors.

The widespread use of photocopying equipment and the increasing development in photocopying technology make it difficult for the CCC to monitor the photocopying of copyrighted materials. The Center estimates that it receives reports of only 6 percent of the photocopying activity for which permission from copyright owners is required. This type of copyright infringement affects not only publishers' earnings, but consequently authors' incomes. The CCC cannot accomplish its established goal—to distribute the full earnings amount to which each publisher-member is entitled—until the reporting volume level rises.

FIGURE 15

COPYRIGHT APPLICATION FORM

FORM TX

UNITED STATES COPYRIGHT OFFICE

REGISTRATION NUMBER

TX   TXU

EFFECTIVE DATE OF REGISTRATION

Month   Day   Year

DO NOT WRITE ABOVE THIS LINE. IF YOU NEED MORE SPACE, USE A SEPARATE CONTINUATION SHEET.

1

TITLE OF THIS WORK ▼

PREVIOUS OR ALTERNATIVE TITLES ▼

PUBLICATION AS A CONTRIBUTION If this work was published as a contribution to a periodical, serial, or collection, give information about the collective work in which the contribution appeared. **Title of Collective Work ▼**

If published in a periodical or serial give: Volume ▼   Number ▼   Issue Date ▼   On Pages ▼

2

a

NAME OF AUTHOR ▼

DATES OF BIRTH AND DEATH
Year Born ▼   Year Died ▼

Was this contribution to the work a "work made for hire"?
☐ Yes
☐ No

AUTHOR'S NATIONALITY OR DOMICILE
Name of Country
OR { Citizen of ▶ _____
Domiciled in ▶ _____

WAS THIS AUTHOR'S CONTRIBUTION TO THE WORK
Anonymous? ☐ Yes ☐ No
Pseudonymous? ☐ Yes ☐ No
If the answer to either of these questions is "Yes," see detailed instructions

NOTE

Under the law, the "author" of a "work made for hire" is generally the employer, not the employee (see instructions) For any part of this work that was "made for hire" check "Yes" in the space provided, give the employer (or other person for whom the work was prepared) as "Author" of that part, and leave the space for dates of birth and death blank.

NATURE OF AUTHORSHIP Briefly describe nature of the material created by this author in which copyright is claimed. ▼

b

NAME OF AUTHOR ▼

DATES OF BIRTH AND DEATH
Year Born ▼   Year Died ▼

Was this contribution to the work a "work made for hire"?
☐ Yes
☐ No

AUTHOR'S NATIONALITY OR DOMICILE
Name of country
OR { Citizen of ▶ _____
Domiciled in ▶ _____

WAS THIS AUTHOR'S CONTRIBUTION TO THE WORK
Anonymous? ☐ Yes ☐ No
Pseudonymous? ☐ Yes ☐ No
If the answer to either of these questions is "Yes," see detailed instructions

NATURE OF AUTHORSHIP Briefly describe nature of the material created by this author in which copyright is claimed. ▼

c

NAME OF AUTHOR ▼

DATES OF BIRTH AND DEATH
Year Born ▼   Year Died ▼

Was this contribution to the work a "work made for hire"?
☐ Yes
☐ No

AUTHOR'S NATIONALITY OR DOMICILE
Name of country
OR { Citizen of ▶ _____
Domiciled in ▶ _____

WAS THIS AUTHOR'S CONTRIBUTION TO THE WORK
Anonymous? ☐ Yes ☐ No
Pseudonymous? ☐ Yes ☐ No
If the answer to either of these questions is "Yes," see detailed instructions

NATURE OF AUTHORSHIP Briefly describe nature of the material created by this author in which copyright is claimed. ▼

3

YEAR IN WHICH CREATION OF THIS WORK WAS COMPLETED This information must be given ◀ Year in all cases.

DATE AND NATION OF FIRST PUBLICATION OF THIS PARTICULAR WORK
Complete this information Month ▶ _____ Day ▶ _____ Year ▶ _____
ONLY if this work has been published.   ◀ Nation

4

COPYRIGHT CLAIMANT(S) Name and address must be given even if the claimant is the same as the author given in space 2.▼

APPLICATION RECEIVED

ONE DEPOSIT RECEIVED

TWO DEPOSITS RECEIVED

REMITTANCE NUMBER AND DATE

DO NOT WRITE HERE
OFFICE USE ONLY

See instructions before completing this space

TRANSFER If the claimant(s) named here in space 4 are different from the author(s) named in space 2, give a brief statement of how the claimant(s) obtained ownership of the copyright.▼

MORE ON BACK ▶ • Complete all applicable spaces (numbers 5-11) on the reverse side of this page.
• See detailed instructions.   • Sign the form at line 10.

DO NOT WRITE HERE

Page 1 of_____ pages

FIGURE 15 (CONTINUED)

COPYRIGHT APPLICATION FORM

EXAMINED BY

FORM TX

CHECKED BY

☐ CORRESPONDENCE
☐ Yes

FOR
COPYRIGHT
OFFICE
USE
ONLY

DO NOT WRITE ABOVE THIS LINE. IF YOU NEED MORE SPACE, USE A SEPARATE CONTINUATION SHEET.

PREVIOUS REGISTRATION Has registration for this work, or for an earlier version of this work, already been made in the Copyright Office?
☐ Yes ☐ No If your answer is "Yes," why is another registration being sought? (Check appropriate box) ▼
☐ This is the first published edition of a work previously registered in unpublished form.
☐ This is the first application submitted by this author as copyright claimant.
☐ This is a changed version of the work, as shown by space 6 on this application.
If your answer is "Yes," give: **Previous Registration Number** ▼   **Year of Registration** ▼

5

DERIVATIVE WORK OR COMPILATION Complete both space 6a & 6b for a derivative work; complete only 6b for a compilation.
a. Preexisting Material Identify any preexisting work or works that this work is based on or incorporates. ▼

b. Material Added to This Work Give a brief, general statement of the material that has been added to this work and in which copyright is claimed. ▼

6

See instructions
before completing
this space

—space deleted—

7

REPRODUCTION FOR USE OF BLIND OR PHYSICALLY HANDICAPPED INDIVIDUALS A signature on this form at space 10, and a check in one of the boxes here in space 8, constitutes a non-exclusive grant of permission to the Library of Congress to reproduce and distribute solely for the blind and physically handicapped and under the conditions and limitations prescribed by the regulations of the Copyright Office: (1) copies of the work identified in space 1 of this application in Braille (or similar tactile symbols); or (2) phonorecords embodying a fixation of a reading of that work; or (3) both.
a ☐ Copies and Phonorecords   b ☐ Copies Only   c ☐ Phonorecords Only

8

See instructions

DEPOSIT ACCOUNT If the registration fee is to be charged to a Deposit Account established in the Copyright Office, give name and number of Account.
Name ▼   **Account Number** ▼

9

CORRESPONDENCE Give name and address to which correspondence about this application should be sent. Name/Address/Apt/City/State/Zip ▼

Area Code & Telephone Number ▶

Be sure to
give your
daytime phone
◀ number

CERTIFICATION* I, the undersigned, hereby certify that I am the
Check one ▶
☐ author
☐ other copyright claimant
☐ owner of exclusive right(s)
☐ authorized agent of
of the work identified in this application and that the statements made
by me in this application are correct to the best of my knowledge.
Name of author or other copyright claimant, or owner of exclusive right(s) ▲

Typed or printed name and date ▼ If this application gives a date of publication in space 3, do not sign and submit it before that date.

date ▶

☞ Handwritten signature (X) ▼

10

MAIL CERTIFI-CATE TO

Name ▼

Number Street Apartment Number ▼

City State ZIP ▼

Certificate will be mailed in window envelope

YOU MUST:
• Complete all necessary spaces
• Sign your application in space 10
SEND ALL 3 ELEMENTS IN THE SAME PACKAGE:
1. Application form
2. Non-refundable $10 filing fee in check or money order payable to Register of Copyrights
3. Deposit material
MAIL TO:
Register of Copyrights
Library of Congress
Washington, DC 20559

11

* 17 U.S.C. § 506(e): Any person who knowingly makes a false representation of a material fact in the application for copyright registration provided for by section 409, or in any written statement filed in connection with the application, shall be fined not more than $2,500.

August 1989—500,000

U.S. GOVERNMENT PRINTING OFFICE: 1989-241-428/00,004

FIGURE 16

COPYRIGHT OFFICE APPLICATION
FORMS AND CIRCULARS
(REVISED NOVEMBER 1994)

APPLICATION FORMS

FORM TX: For published and unpublished nondramatic literary works

FORM SE: For serials, works issued or intended to be issued in successive parts bearing numerical or chronological designations and intended to be continued indefinitely (periodicals, newspapers, magazines, newsletters, annuals, journals, etc.)

FORM PA: For published and unpublished works of the performing arts (musical and dramatic works, pantomimes and choreographic works, motion pictures and other audiovisual works)

FORM VA: For published and unpublished works of the visual arts (pictorial, graphic, architectural and sculptural works)

FORM SR: For published and unpublished sound recordings

FORM RE: For claims to renewal of copyright in works copyrighted under the law in effect through December 31, 1977 (1909 Copyright Act)

FORM GR/CP: An adjunct application to be used for registration of a group of contributions to periodicals in addition to an application Form TX, PA or VA

CIRCULARS

1—Copyright Basics
1B—Limitations on the Information Furnished by the Copyright Office
2—Publications on Copyright
2B—Selected Bibliographies on Copyright
13—Trademarks
15—Renewal of Copyright
22—How to Investigate the Copyright Status of a Work
32—Blank Forms and Other Works Not Protected by Copyright
38C—International Copyright Conventions
40—Copyright Registration for Works of the Visual Arts
44—Cartoons and Comic Strips
55—Copyright Registration for Multimedia Works
62—Copyright Registration for Serials
92—Copyright Law of the United States of America
96—201.20: Methods of Affictation and Positions of the Copyright Notice
96—202.1: Material Not Subject to Copyright
96—202.2: Copyright Notice
96—202.17: Renewals

To strengthen its effectiveness, the CCC is attempting to broaden publisher participation in the organization and to educate and inform the public about copyright law requirements regarding photocopy use. A CCC publication for further reference is *You Can Photocopy and Still Comply with the Copyright Law.*

The address of the Copyright Clearance Center is 27 Congress St., Salem, MA 01970. (*See: Copyright; Fair use.*)

Copyright notice. Consists of the internationally used copyright symbol, © (or the word *copyright* or the abbreviation *Copr.*), the year the work was first published, and the copyright owner's name. It usually is published on the reverse of the title page of a book and on the contents page of a magazine. Prior to March, 1989, a copyright notice was required on all published works to ensure complete protection. The copyright notice is no longer required as a condition of protection, but it is still useful to show ownership and to rebut claims of innocent infringement.

While a copyright exists for works created on or after January 1, 1978, from the moment of creation, the year stated in the copyright notice is generally the year of publication of the work.

Copyright page. (*See: Copyright notice.*)

Copyright, Register of. The U.S. Copyright Office can inform the writer of current fees for copyright registration and for copyright search, a procedure that determines whether a work has been registered with the Office. It can also provide the writer with applications for copyright registration. The Copyright Office can be reached at Register of Copyright, Copyright Office, Library of Congress, Washington, DC 20559, telephone (202) 707-3000.

Forms on which application for registration is made are coded by category of creation. A new form, Form SE, is used by those who wish to register a serial, such as a magazine or newspaper; Form TX is used to register literary work other than drama, as well as nondramatic works to be included in serials and to which the author, rather than the publisher, owns the copyright; Form PA registers a work of the performing arts; with Form GR/CP, a writer applies for registration of a group of pieces intended for periodicals whose copyright is registered separately. Form RE is used to renew registration; Form CA, for a supplementary registration. (*See: Copyright; Copyright notice; Figure 15; Figure 16.*)

Copyright-free art. Examples of art in the styles of different historical periods are compiled into books and sold to editors and publishers. Such illustrations can be used in advertisements, brochures, books and magazines.

Editors of small magazines, company publications, and other publications with limited budgets may find such sources a money-saver.

One source of copyright-free art is Dover Publications, Inc., 31 E. Second St., Mineola, NY 11501. Dover publishes books of old illustrations, borders, ornaments, etc. Another company that produces books of specialized art subjects on gummed repro paper (which can be cut out and pasted down as camera-ready art) is Graphic Products Corp., 1480 S. Wolf Rd., Wheeling, IL 60090. (*See: Clip art.*)

Correspondence courses for writers. Writers may participate in organized study by means of courses conducted through the mail that are designed to provide them with incentives to write and deadlines to keep. Home study courses allow motivated students to further their training in a convenient alternative to the class-room.

There are two main sources for learning through the mail. Some universities offer correspondence courses for writers on both credit and noncredit bases. In addition to writing courses, studies in English, literature, cartooning and photography are available. Other correspondence courses are offered by privately operated schools, which frequently advertise in magazines such as *Writer's Digest.* They teach students how to write for specific commercial markets, e.g., newspapers and magazines. The instructors, who ideally are themselves published writers, critique student work.

Good candidates for correspondence courses are disciplined individuals who work independently and with minimal guidance. They accept the fact that no home study course guarantees future success as a published writer. They choose a specific writing course for its purpose and subject matter; they consider its costs, length of time to complete, quality of instructional material, and the credentials of the instructor.

Education expenses—whether for a college class or a home study course—incurred for improving an individual's performance in a trade or profession are usually tax deductible. (*See: National University Continuing Education Association.*)

Correspondent. (*See: Stringer.*)

Council of Communications Management (formerly Industrial Communications Council). Members work in business and government communication offices or are educators who teach effective communication within organizations. The association aims to promote effective communication techniques and to evaluate trends in the field. A speakers' bureau and placement services are some of its features. It publishes books and a monthly newsletter. A conference is held annually; regional workshops and local meetings are held periodically.

The address is P.O. Box 3970, Grand Central Post Office, New York, NY 10163.

Council of Writers Organizations. This is a group comprising the following writers' organizations: American Society of Indexers, Association of Great Lakes Outdoor Writers, Aviation/Space Writers Association, Computer Press Association, Garden Writers Association of America, Independent Writers of Southern California, Midwest Travel Writers Association, Midwest Writers Association, National Association of Science Writers, North American Ski Journalists Associations, Outdoor Writers Association of America, Philadelphia Writers Organization, Society of American Travel Writers, Travel Journalists Guild, Washington Independent Writers and Writers Union.

The CWO acts as a communications network for member groups, with circulation of a monthly news alert. Member groups are also entitled to receive regular newsletters of other participating members.

Services available through CWO that may not be available through individual memberships include discount legal services and advice for writers on problems of copyright, libel, First Amendment issues and contract negotiation. Free or low-cost income tax advice is also available.

For information on CWO membership, general services and meetings, contact Dixie Franklin, CWO Executive Director, 972 Valley Rd., Marquette, MI 49855.

Council of Writing Program Administrators. This professional organization was established to address the needs of, and disseminate knowledge among, U.S. and Canadian college and university writing program administrators.

The Council publishes a journal two times per academic year; its focus is the professional interests of Council members, which are specialized in that they relate to a combination teaching-administrative objective. Information on the journal can be obtained care of English Department, Miami University, Oxford, OH, 45056. (*See: Associated Writing Programs.*)

Counterplot. (*See: Subplot.*)

Country music. At one time known as "Hillbilly Music," this type of music developed from old English and Scottish ballads brought to the Appalachian Mountain areas during the late eighteenth century. Generally played on stringed instruments such as a guitar, banjo, mandolin, fiddle or autoharp; lyrical subject matter typically includes the rambling man, prison, hard work, love, religion or crime. Artists include Johnny Cash, Garth Brooks, Reba McEntire, Dolly Parton and Kenny Rogers.

Cover letter. A letter accompanying a completed manuscript. A cover letter is especially useful as a reminder when submitting finished material that has been requested by an editor. It is not necessary when there has been no previous correspondence and the manuscript must be judged on the writing style itself, as in the case of fiction or humor.

The cover letter may request an editor's response within a reasonable length of time if the topic is timely. No rates or fees should be mentioned in the letter, since most publications' rates are listed in *Writer's Market*. No biographical information about the writer is included unless the manuscript requires credentials by the author in a specific area of expertise.

Editors generally discourage writers from submitting letters with completed, unsolicited manuscripts.

Creativity. Creativity can be described as the potential of human beings to be inventive and original.

Scientists and lay people alike have long grappled with an explanation of the creative process. What is generally accepted is the belief that every person is creative to some degree, and in some capacity. Whereas intelligence is an individual's capacity to learn and reason, creativity goes beyond the acquisition of knowledge or skill to the development and expression of a unique point of view. Though there is no clear-cut, established relationship between creativity and intelligence, it is fairly certain that creativity does not require a high I.Q.—nor does a high I.Q. guarantee creativity. Rather, the potential for original and imaginative response—creativity—is present in every person having some measure of intellectual ability.

Creativity may be nurtured and cultivated. It is like a muscle that atrophies without exercise. It may be fostered at any stage of life so long as the individual is able to transcend his previous exposure to the trite and the stereotyped. Creativity germinates in a creative atmosphere—that is, a setting, circumstance or situation in which a person is free to apply his energy and enthusiasm to perceiving relationships around him and being conscious of his life experience. For some people, a creative atmosphere might be invoked by reading a book; for others, it might be best stimulated by a quiet walk or the noise of a big city. Establishing a creative environment is as essential to writers and other artists as is possessing the techniques and disciplines of their craft.

The process of creativity may often result in some end product—a written work, a piece of sculpture, a song. The work is in fact "creative" if the process produces a unique result that communicates with its audience on an emotional as well as an intellectual level.

Credit line. The name of the photographer, illustrator, company or institution that supplied a photograph, diagram, chart or artwork to a magazine or book. The name is usually typeset alongside the published illustration or printed with the page number on an acknowledgments page. When a writer obtains illustration material from a business or institution, credit lines may be required

and are usually indicated on the back of the photograph, drawing, etc. Writers should call such requirements to the attention of the editor.

Crisis. In fiction, the word *crisis* refers to part of the plot that represents a turning point. A crisis arises from a conflict, the forces of which take action to effect a turning point. The result of a crisis is a climax, which refers to the degree of emotion elicited from the reader.

A novel can contain a series of crises, but a short story typically contains only one. In a short story, the major character experiences a crisis in two steps: the dark moment/black moment, and the moment of revelation, the latter of which results in a change in the character. (*See: Character change; Climax; Dark moment/black moment.*)

Criticism. This term applies to a piece written to analyze a work of art. Criticism is distinguished from arts reviews in several ways. It is written in a more scholarly tone by a writer who is well versed in the particular art form he writes about. Criticism is usually published in magazines and journals; it would be inappropriate in a newspaper, since most of the general public is not interested in such in-depth analysis. Newspaper reviews necessarily display a different style; lofty language serves only to alienate the newspaper reviewer's readers.

While a review is an account of a performance or work, often providing subjectivity through an audience reaction, criticism depends on the writer's educated perspective for reaction and judgment. Criticism, in contrast with the arts review, discusses the particular work in relation to the art form it reflects.

Karl Shapiro wrote that "a good work of criticism is a work of art about another work of art." A critique can, indeed, stand on its own literary merits. The criticism of George Bernard Shaw, for example, is still read today. His criticism of music has been compiled in *Shaw's Music: The Complete Musical Criticism.* (*See: Arts review; Book review; Drama criticism; Restaurant review.*)

Criticism of manuscript. An evaluation of a written work by a person who, through experience and knowledge of the marketplace, has acquired expertise to judge it objectively. Valuable criticism comes from editors and writers skilled in pointing out strengths and weaknesses in fiction and nonfiction technique. The art of receiving criticism is tied up with being able to distinguish between helpful comments from professionals, and well-meaning but useless or possibly harmful comments from other people who may read the manuscript—and then using the significant remarks accordingly.

Some firms that offer criticism services for writers advertise in *Writer's Digest.* (*See: Self-criticism.*)

Cumulative Book Index: A World List of Books in the English Language (CBI). This publication lists books published in English; its scope is worldwide. Published monthly except August, it has been in existence since 1928. Issues are accumulated annually.

Listings in this index are categorized by author, title and subject. (*See:* National Union Catalog.)

Customs reminders for writers. People returning to the U.S. from abroad are charged a duty on items purchased in foreign countries. The total value of items purchased is assessed in the U.S. and an exemption is granted, the amount of which depends on the country the person has traveled to. Limitations are placed on imports of cars, pets and products bearing certain trademarks.

Foreign-made equipment such as cameras, typewriters and tape recorders taken abroad could be taxed upon the traveler's return to the U.S. To avoid this situation, the writer should be able to provide proof—such as a sales slip—that he purchased the equipment before leaving the U.S. You can obtain a form from U.S. Customs before leaving the country to cover this problem.

More information on customs can be obtained from the Department of the Treasury, U.S. Customs Service, 1301 Constitution Ave., Washington, DC 20229.

Writer-photographers are also cautioned about the possibility of airport x-ray machines fogging their film. They can usually have airport security personnel hand-check their equipment, thus avoiding the risk of such damages.

Cut to. An editing direction. In motion pictures or TV, the shift from one scene to another without using a fade or a dissolve. Also, *cut.* (*See: Dissolve; Fade in; Fade out.*)

Cutline. (*See: Caption [cutline].*)

Cyberpunk. This sub-genre of speculative fiction is usually set in a fictional near-future in which great advances in computer technology are matched by increased violence and human misery. The protagonists are often antiheroes, such as computer hackers or mercenaries, and typically square off against evil in the form of faceless multinational corporations. Willam Gibson (*Neuromancer*) is widely credited with founding the cyberpunk "world."

Cyberspace. The universe of information accessible through a computer and modem. As science fiction author William Gibson described it, cyberspace is a mutually agreed-upon hallucination, a space that isn't a space, yet which we call a space in order to better visualize it. (*See: Internet; Online service; World Wide Web.*)

Dance Critics Association (DCA).

Members of DCA are full-time and freelance dance critics and others interested in dance writing, such as teachers, historians and publicists. Voting members, associate members and student members make up its ranks.

The DCA's committees include Critics' Training and Publications. It publishes the quarterly *DCA Newsletter* and pamphlets such as "Copyright for Newspaper and Magazine Writers," "Training Opportunities for Dance Critics" and "Research Sources for Dance Writers."

DCA's annual conference, usually held in New York City in June, features talks by prominent persons in the field, films, and workshops. According to DCA, the conference provides "a chance for critics and other interested people from across the country to meet together and explore ways to be more effective in their profession."

The address of the Dance Critics Association is 127 W. Eighty-third St., New York, NY 10024. (*See: Council of Writers Organizations.*)

Dark moment/black moment.

This forms a part of the short story structure. At the beginning of the crisis, the protagonist experiences a *dark moment* (also called *black moment*) when his problem has increased to such proportion that he can conceive of no solution for it; moreover, the conflict action in the crisis forces the central character to make a decision that resolves the problem. This decision at the end of the crisis leads to the character change. (*See: Character change; Crisis.*)

Database.

A collection of specialized information stored in a computer. Used by science and industry as research tools since the mid-1950s, and by academic and public libraries since the 1970s, databases permit almost instant access to information that would take hours to locate manually. Databases can be found in libraries, corporations and government agencies.

Depending on the type of information it contains, a database is labeled either numeric or bibliographic. Numeric databases lead the researcher to numbers and statistics, while bibliographic databases lead to citations or summaries of text. *Compustat II*, for example, is a numeric database that houses financial information on industrial companies, banks and utilities. Included are balance sheets, trading data, statements of income, sources of funds and uses of funds. An example of a bibliographic database is *Educational Resources Information Center* (ERIC), which contains citations of documents in the field of education.

When conducting a search, the researcher must state his topic as clearly as possible, using specific keywords to narrow a broad subject. For example, the writer may be researching learning disabilities, but only as they relate to elementary students in public schools. Qualifying the search helps the writer find the most useful information and eliminate the irrelevant.

To find databases that contain relevant information, a writer may consult an index that lists databases. *Computer Readable Data Bases: A Directory & Sourcebook* contains subject and name indexes. *The Directory of Online Databases* contains a name index. Some available databases include *Economic Abstracts International, Federal Index, New York Times Information Bank, National Institute of Mental Health* and *Psychological Abstracts.* Your local librarian can help you find other databases and directories.

Additional Information: *Knowing Where to Look: The Ultimate Guide to Research.*

Daybook. A book in which each page corresponds to a day of the month; used by radio advertising copywriters.

DBA. Acronym for *doing business as.* Sometimes used in connection with a writer's pen name. A writer, for example, may notify his local postmaster and bank manager that he is doing business as _____ (his pen name) so that he will safely receive any mail and be able to cash checks in that business name.

Deadline. A specified date and/or time that an article or news story must be turned in to the editor. The writer's deadline is important in the editor's production schedule, which involves a copyeditor, a typesetter, a printer and other personnel.

In magazine work, a writer has more time between deadlines than he has in newspaper or broadcast newswriting. Short deadlines, of course, require working under pressure, and not all writers can endure the stress of working both quickly and accurately.

Freelance writers learn, with experience, to schedule several projects at once and have them conform to different deadlines. When the freelance writer must miss a deadline, he should inform the editor as soon as he is aware that he needs more time for the project.

Dedication. A brief inscription in a nonfiction book or novel expressing the author's affection or respect for a person or persons, who may or may not be directly related to the subject matter of the book. Dedications usually appear on the right-hand page directly opposite the reverse side of the title page. The dedication page is one of several preliminary pages the writer prepares after a book has been accepted for publication.

Defamation. (*See: Libel.*)

Delphi. Launched in 1983, this is one of the oldest online services. Its primary user base focuses on the personal home user and member-to-member communications. Delphi is also one of the first online services to offer full access to the Internet. (*See: Electronic mail; Internet; Online service.*)

Dénouement. French for "an untying." The *dénouement* of a novel or story follows the climax; it represents the unraveling of the complexities of a plot, and the clarifying of the story's details and misunderstandings.

Derivative works (and copyright). A derivative work is one that has been translated, adapted, abridged, condensed, annotated or otherwise produced by altering a previously created work. Derivative works can take many forms, including plays, motion pictures and revised versions of books.

Before producing a derivative work for publication, it is necessary to secure written permission from the author or the copyright owner of the work on which the new piece will be based. If the original work is in the public domain, however, as in the case of some works first published more than seventy-five years ago or published in an uncopyrighted periodical, permission from the author is not necessary. (*See: Adaptation; Copyright; Novelization; Tie-in.*)

Description. The art of showing the reader how a person, place or thing looks, tastes, feels, sounds, smells or acts. It is more than the amassing of details; it is bringing something to life by carefully choosing and arranging words and phrases to produce the desired effect. Here is an example, from John Steinbeck's *Of Mice and Men*:

On the sand banks the rabbits sat as quietly as little, gray, sculptured stones. And then from the direction of the state highway came the sound of footsteps on crisp sycamore leaves. The rabbits hurried noiselessly for cover. A stilted heron labored up into the air and pounded down river.

Description cannot be objective; it always delivers a specific and intentional graphic message to the reader within the context of the work in which it appears.

Desktop publishing. A method of graphic arts production developed in the early 1980s that allows users to set type, place images and paginate documents using a personal computer. The term came into use in 1984 with the introduction of Aldus PageMaker, the first software for the Apple computer to accomplish production tasks. Many other programs have followed, including the widely used QuarkXPress.

Proposals, newsletters, brochures, booklets, magazines and other publications can be created easily using desktop publishing software. Because of this ease of use, one person can execute tasks that traditionally took several production people. This has allowed smaller magazines to prosper and has made self-publishing a more viable option for writers. (*See: Self-publishing.*)

Detective story. The phrase *detective story* is used by the editors of fact-crime magazines to mean a nonfictional account of a true crime. The term *detective fiction* is used by some mystery magazines to refer to stories in which detectives play a central role. Among book publishers, *novel of suspense* and *thriller* are synonymous, and this type of story may contain elements of mystery, romance and adventure. (*See: Adventure story; Mystery story; Romance novel.*)

Deus ex machina. This term, meaning "a god from the machine," originated in Greek drama, in which playwrights sometimes introduced a god to resolve a problem so that the play could end. These intervening gods descended onto the stage by means of a mechanical device.

Today, *deus ex machina* is used to refer to any unlikely, contrived or trick resolution of a plot in any type of fiction. Critics—and readers—generally object to this technique, which is most commonly used by beginning writers.

Dial-a-Writer. The American Society of Journalists and Authors (ASJA) maintains a writer referral service that can provide experts on a wide variety of subjects: the arts, business and finance, education, health and medicine and many more. Dial-a-Writer will locate professionals to write articles, books, scripts, speeches, annual reports, promotional materials, etc., almost anywhere in the U.S. and overseas.

Writers interested in being referred by Dial-a-Writer must be members of ASJA. Information on membership can be obtained from ASJA, 1501 Broadway, Suite 302, New York, NY 10036, (212) 997-0947. (*See: American Society of Journalists and Authors.*)

Dialect. The language of a particular geographic region, social class or ethnic group is referred to as dialect. Dialect is often used in fiction as a means of characterization. The way a person speaks (i.e., the words he uses, the accent he has, the sentence structure and speech patterns he employs) tells the reader something about his status in life. Dialect helps portray a character's individuality and makes him real and believable. Dialect can clarify the regional setting for a fictional work. For example, "My cah is pahked at the hahbuh" puts the speaker's home within fifty miles of Boston. Dialect may also establish a date or time period for a piece of writing. "Dig it! We've got us one groovy scene . . ." can only suggest the psychedelic 1960s.

To succeed, dialect should be neither so contrived and complicated as to be distracting, nor so sporadic and subtle that it fails to create a consistent, distinct flavor for a character or an entire work. Usually the writer sets the stage by having his characters use certain words or phrases that, in combination with details presented in his other narration, give the reader a picture of the dialect involved. There may be limited phonetic spellings in these introductory passages. Once the characterization is established, dialogue can be typed normally, and it is the speech patterns that convey the image to the reader.

The use of dialect is difficult to accomplish successfully. Most writers, particularly beginners, would do well to avoid this fictive device. (*See: Dialogue;* Dictionary of American Regional English [DARE]*; Idiom.*)

Dialogue. An essential element of fiction, dialogue consists of conversations between two or more people. Every bit of it has a purpose that contributes to the effect of the total work. A great many stories are told essentially through dialogue. The writer may use dialogue to move the plot along. It may serve to distinguish one character from another, or one locale from another. Dialogue may effectively provide the reader with information pertinent to the understanding of the plot. It does not interrupt the story to tell the reader something; it is, in fact, an integral part of the story itself. In addition, it adds color and life to a work. And, from a purely cosmetic point of view, dialogue on a page is more attractive to the reader's eye than solid paragraphs of narration.

Dialogue captures the quirks and peculiarities of characters' speech patterns. It should be appropriate to the speakers and the setting of the action.

The writer uses dialogue to provoke humor, prompt understanding, establish tension or stir emotion more convincingly through the characters' words than through his own. Dialogue conveys a lot of information in a brief amount of time and space. Written dialogue is a compression of "real" conversation because it eliminates most of the nonsense syllables, repetition, pauses, audible sighs and chitchat that occur in actual talk, using only enough to simulate concisely the flavor of the speaker. Like all fictional elements, dialogue creates an illusion of reality.

Beginning writers sometimes try too hard to find substitutes for the verb "said," when that is usually the best choice, except where the verb can be eliminated entirely in short passages where the reader clearly understands who is speaking. (*See: Dialect.*)

Dictionary. A book containing the words of a language, profession, discipline or special interest, arranged alphabetically. Depending on their purpose and scope, dictionaries may supply spellings, pronunciations, meanings, origins and examples of word usage.

Dictionaries differ in approach. "Descriptive" volumes reflect current language practice; they do not attempt to establish standards of usage. *Webster's Third New International Dictionary* is a descriptive work. "Prescriptive" dictionaries, *Webster's Second New International Dictionary* is an example, attempt to dictate word usage by labeling certain words or phrases as "slang" or "vulgar." *The American Heritage Dictionary* and *Random House Dictionary* also use a prescriptive approach.

Depending on the writer's needs and his pocketbook, he has several other choices to make regarding a dictionary. "Unabridged" dictionaries of the English language are comprehensive works, usually with more than 250,000 entries. *The Oxford English Dictionary* is an outstanding example of an unabridged dictionary. "Abridged" dictionaries are taken from the larger edition by the same publisher and contain between 130,000 and 150,000 entries. The "pocket" dictionary comprises concise entries of only commonly used words. "Pronouncing" dictionaries indicate only spelling, pronunciation and syllabification of frequently used words.

Two specialty dictionaries a writer might like to refer to are: *The Dictionary of American Slang* and *The Dictionary Catalogue*, which is a comprehensive list of thousands of dictionaries in the sciences, humanities and social sciences.

Dictionary revisions are usually made every ten years. Editors add newly coined words and new meanings of old words, and delete those words and meanings considered obsolete. Writers may wish to check the copyright date in a dictionary before purchase.

A Dictionary of American Idioms. This reference book, arranged in dictionary form, furnishes the meanings of more than four thousand idioms used in American English.

Entries are arranged in alphabetical order. Within each entry, every meaning of the same idiom is preceded by a different number. The entry information includes variations on the idiom, its part of speech, definition(s), notes on usage, cross-references to synonymous and antonymous idioms, its etymology, and other idioms derived from the entry-heading idiom. Each entry contains a sentence using the idiom, followed by a sentence that conveys the same meaning without using the idiom.

The words *slang, informal, formal, literary, vulgar, substandard, nonstandard, archaic* and *Southern* (or other terms denoting geographic regions) indicate situations/places in which each idiom is used. (*See: Idiom.*)

Dictionary of American Regional English (DARE). This reference work is published in five volumes by the Belknap Press; the first volume appeared in 1983.

DARE entries concentrate on the spoken language of specific regions and social groups of the U.S. They provide information such as the region in which a word is used; its origin; characteristics of people who use the word, such as age, sex, race and education level; and actual quotes from a resident of a particular region using the word. Besides the entries, the DARE includes maps that indicate regions in which a word is used. DARE was compiled using 1,002 questionnaires and informal conversations with 2,752 individuals in local communities in all fifty states. In process since 1965, this work was produced at the University of Wisconsin; Chief Editor is Frederic G. Cassidy.

A fiction writer whose work is set in a particular locale may find research into speech patterns helpful.

Dinner theater. This term describes a production staged in a restaurant where patrons sit at a table and pay one price for dinner and a show. The U.S. has approximately 125 dinner theaters, which seek light, humorous plays designed to appeal to audiences who are interested primarily in entertainment rather than thought-provoking drama.

Plays produced in these theaters are realistic but not too profound; they neither offend the audience nor offer it great insights. Dinner-theater productions are characterized by comic plots that are exaggerated but believable, and sex that is implied but never shown on stage. Profanity, if used at all, is mild.

The physical structure of dinner theaters presents singular limitations to the playwright. The full- or three-quarter-arena stages of most dinner theaters can pose logistical problems, and because most stages are fewer than twenty feet square, crowd scenes cannot be accommodated. Also, the entire theater is likely to be small, so loud noises (such as gunfire) that startle an audience should be avoided.

The following organizations maintain lists of dinner theaters: the American Dinner Theatre Institute, P.O. Box 7057, Akron, OH 44306; and the Foundation for Extension and Development of the American Professional Theatre (FEDAPT), 270 Lafayette St., Suite 810, New York, NY 10012.

Direct marketing/direct response. These two terms are used to include not only direct-mail advertising but also any interactive system that uses an advertising medium to effect a measurable response and/or transaction at any location. This could include coupon ads in magazines, TV ads using a toll-free number or a regular call-in telephone number, and any two-way electronic advertising/ordering system, such as the Warner-Amex QUBE cable TV system.

Direct-mail advertising. Advertising sent to potential customers through the U.S. mail. Direct-mail advertising touts products and services and is also used to generate leads for salespeople, raise funds, etc. Successful direct-mail copy appeals to basic human wants, describes a credible benefit of the product or service, and impels the reader to some direct, immediate action—such as filling out an order card or enclosing a check.

Industrial firms, businesses such as retailers, and fundraising organizations all rely heavily on this technique, as do mail-order companies that sell exclusively by catalog. While large companies and mail-order firms have their own direct-mail advertising copywriting staffs, smaller businesses use freelance copywriters to create their sales letters, brochures, order cards, etc. Even large companies use freelancers for major pieces.

Earnings for freelance direct-mail ad writers vary with the size of a company and the market for a product or service. Copywriters, for example, may earn from $10-$50 per page for catalog copy, depending on the market. Veteran freelancers who create a basic mailing package of letter, brochure, response card and outer envelope design earn from $1,500 to $15,000 (or more) from magazine publishers and other clients. Freelancers whose clients are smaller publishers may earn $300 and up for direct-mail packages.

The yellow pages lists countless goods and services that may be potential clients for freelance direct-mail copywriters. Companies that do much of that writing for clients and may also use freelancers are listed under "Advertising—Direct Mail." Trade journals such as *Advertising Age* frequently carry classified ads seeking direct-mail copywriters. Many of the companies that use direct mail to promote their products and services are members of the Direct Marketing Association, 11 W. Forty-second St., New York, NY 10036-8096. (*See: Direct marketing/direct response.*)

Directories. Two general sources to consult are *The Directory of Directories* and *The Guide to American Directories*, but there are many specialized directories nonfiction writers will find useful; some of these are mentioned in other entries in this book under "Biographical references"; "Business writing"; "Science writing"; and "U.S. government publications." (*See: Directories, writer-related.*)

Directories, writer-related. Directories related to the writing field include the *Media Personnel Directory,* which lists major editorial and business personnel in magazine publishing; and the *Directory of American Poets and Fiction Writers,* which is useful to writers who want to obtain lecture or workshop engagements at colleges and with arts councils. *Working Press of the Nation* is a five-volume set of print- and broadcast-media-related directories; it is described in this book under its title. Newspaper personnel are listed in the *Editor and Publisher International Year Book,* and broadcast employees are detailed in the *Broadcasting/Cablecasting Yearbook.* (*See:* Literary Market Place; Working Press of the Nation; Writers, biographical directories of.)

Dissertations as research sources. Dissertations, often unpublished, can be sources of article or book reference material. A writer has access to these works through *Dissertation Abstracts International,* an international directory of abstracts of dissertations, which are arranged in two sections: humanities and social sciences, and sciences and engineering.

This publication is indexed by keyword and author and is published monthly. The researcher can find *Dissertation Abstracts International* in most libraries, but may have to contact a university to obtain a dissertation itself, or buy a copy (from University Films International) of any dissertation abstracted in DAI.

Dissolve. A motion picture or TV editing direction indicating that one scene should fade away at the same time a new scene fades in. In a dissolve, both scenes overlap each other for a moment. It can be written as *dissolve to.* Both terms are typed in all caps.

Distribution rights. (*See: Book contract.*)

Distributor. A business that buys books from a publisher and resells them to wholesalers, jobbers, retail outlets or individual consumers. (*See: Book distribution.*)

Division (publisher's). Major publishing corporations may produce not only trade books but also lines of books for schools and colleges, as well as reference books and specialized books for professionals. Since each division of a corporation may be responsible for a separate line of books, the writer should be sure he will be dealing with the appropriate division before approaching a publisher. The major divisions of publishing corporations are detailed in *Literary Market Place.* (*See: Conglomerates—book publishers; Magazine publishers, multiple; Trade books.*)

Docudrama. A play, film or TV story in which real contemporary or historical events are blended with the playwright's or screenwriter's imagination to create an entertaining version. Critics say they oversimplify or distort events or the people involved in them; defenders say creative artists have the right to use history and reality as the basis of their fictional representations.

Documentary. A documentary is a nonfiction film in which real people "play" themselves. Its subject matter may be anything from the drilling for oil to the children of migrant workers. Motion picture and TV documentaries either film actual events or recreate situations based on research, factual evidence and information about a subject. Private organizations, large companies and foundations often sponsor the production of documentary films to inform the public or influence their attitude about a certain person, event or social condition.

Though a documentary may or may not have an actual script or narration, much writing is done before it is ready for production. A writer composes a proposal (in effect a two- to three-page query letter) for a producer to present to a sponsor, convincing the sponsor that a particular idea for a documentary is good, that the producer knows just what kind of film is needed, and that he can do the job best. If the proposal is accepted, the writer does a treatment (an outline of the film based on research) and ultimately a script—a blueprint for the film—describing a series of "master scenes" as they would be seen by the audience. The writer may also be involved in detailing a shooting script describing actual shots and camera angles, and finally a narration script after the film has been shot.

As with all audiovisual writing, drawing up documentary scripts is a cooperative venture in which the writer depends on other profession- als to bring his work to life. He creates a series of visual images that tell a story, and the director and producer develop the means to take an audience through the revelation process during which a subject unfolds before them. (*See: Audiovisual communication.*)

Donut. A radio commercial consisting of a jingle sung at the beginning; a "hole" in the middle, where instrumental music is played and copy is read; and more singing at the end.

Double spotting. In broadcasting, using two commercials in the same break, sometimes back to back with nothing intervening.

Down and under. In a radio commercial script, a direction to reduce the volume and music to a background level so that the announcer's voice can be heard.

Drama criticism. An evaluation of a drama written by a reviewer, who gives the reader an idea of the topic of a play and offers an opinion on the success of its execution. The reviewer attempts to discover the intended effect of the work and comments on the form and style of the performance. As an expert in the techniques and conventions of drama, he analyzes actors, sets, lighting, makeup, costume and direction. The reviewer loves theater and, therefore, applauds the superior and chastises the second rate.

Drama criticism both teaches and entertains. Ideally, criticism is informative to both those who have and those who have not seen a performance. It offers one informed reviewer's insights and reactions to what happened on stage. As a kind of feature writing, drama criticism strives to be well written and readable. It does not "talk down" to its readers, nor does it give evaluative comments without supportive evidence from the production. Good drama criticism does not depend heavily on plot summary, and it never gives away an ending if the surprise is essential to enjoying the play.

Drama criticism appears both in daily and weekly newspapers and national magazines. Though some large publications have their own reviewing staffs, there are opportunities for freelance drama critics. Performances worthy of review take place in cities across the country, and local newspapers may welcome a drama "correspondent" to provide reviews of regional performances. In this case, writers should contact the editor of the publication. Magazines may pay little to beginning reviewers, but writers who have proved their worth may earn $50 and more per review. Information on potential magazine markets for drama criticism and related drama features, and the rates they pay, are available in the "Entertainment" section of the annual *Writer's Market.* (*See: Arts review, Playwriting.*)

Dramatic agent. Some agencies specialize in material for theatrical, motion picture and TV presentation. An author who wishes to be represented by such an agent uses the same technique as he does to secure a literary agent—being introduced by recommendation of a writer already represented by the agent, or by his own letter outlining the pub-

lishing and production credits he's already obtained on his work and offering to submit scripts for examination. The dramatic agent's commission is usually 10-15 percent—the same as that of a literary agent—and he negotiates for possible production with theatrical and film producers. (*See: Agents, literary; Agents, TV.*)

Dramatic convention. A contrivance of playwriting and staging that the audience understands is to be taken for reality. Some common dramatic conventions are the *monologue* (in real life, people do not speak so coherently at such length), the *aside* (in which a character gives vital information to the audience, while the other characters onstage are understood not to hear)—even the stage itself (which obviously is not really a battlefield, or a garret). (*See: Aside.*)

Dramatic irony. Dramatic irony refers to the theatrical device in which the audience is made aware of information unknown to some or all of the characters in the play. This information may be about the real identity of a character, his actual intentions or the probable outcome of the play's action. Dramatic irony may be described as putting into a speaker's (character's) mouth words that have for the audience a meaning not intended by the speaker. It depends for effect on the contrast between what the character says or believes and the play's or film's true state of affairs.

Irony based on misunderstanding or partial knowledge is common to both tragedy and comedy. A classic example is Sophocles' tragedy *Oedipus Rex*, in which Oedipus seeks throughout the play to discover and punish the murderer of his father, only to find that he himself is guilty of the crime. Dramatic irony in a tragedy is also called *tragic irony* or *Sophoclean irony.* Dramatic irony in comedy is particularly common in plots involving mistaken identities, such as Shakespeare's *A Comedy of Errors.*

A second type of dramatic irony results when a character's remarks early in a play prove to have quite another meaning later on. After the murder of Duncan in Shakespeare's *Macbeth,* for example, Lady Macbeth says to her husband, "A little water clears us of this deed," yet during the sleepwalking scene, she says that all the waters of the ocean won't cleanse the stain of blood from her hand. (*See: Irony.*)

Dramatic rights. A type of subsidiary rights to a copyrighted created work. They belong to the author unless transferred to someone else. Such rights are usually optioned from a script or book by a director or producer and usually handled by the author's agent, or by his publisher on his behalf.

Dramatic rights, TV rights and motion picture rights are often offered at a percentage of the total price as an option to buy for a specific period of time. The idea is then brought to the attention of individuals or organizations in the industry— actors, directors, studios or TV networks—for possible production. (*See: Rights for sale.*)

Dramatis personae. Literally, "characters of the play." An archaic term for the cast of characters; a modern playwright would not use it unless he meant to be tongue-in-cheek.

Dramatists Guild. A division of the Authors League of America, Inc., this organization includes playwrights, lyricists and composers as members. Active-member status is reached by those who have had a play produced on Broadway, Off-Broadway or on a regional theater's main stage. Associate members have written at least one play; and subscriber members are nonwriters who have an interest in theater.

The Guild sponsors seminars on the business and creative aspects of playwriting, as well as symposia on various aspects of the theater. The latter are led by noted professionals such as Edward Albee and Stephen Sondheim.

Members of the Guild have access to its reference library of materials on plays, playwriting and the theater. They may also participate in a health insurance plan. In addition, the organization advises members on business topics, such as copyright, agents, contracts, options and dealings with producers.

The Dramatists Guild contracts are considered the world's most comprehensive contracts for playwrights. They cover the areas of first-class dramatic plays, first-class dramatico-musical works, Off-Broadway dramatic plays, Off-Broadway dramatico-musical works, regional theater productions, stock tryout productions, review productions and collaborations for both dramas and musicals.

The Approved Production Contract (APC) for playwrights was negotiated between the Dramatists

Guild and the League of American Theaters and Producers. According to its stipulations, the playwright receives 5 percent of the gross weekly box office receipts in royalties rising to 10 percent upon recoupment of the production expenses. (These royalty figures apply to first-class productions, i.e., those staged on Broadway or in other large houses.)

This association publishes the *Dramatists Guild Newsletter,* issued ten times per year, and the *Dramatists Guild Quarterly.*

The Dramatists Guild Headquarters are located at 234 W. Forty-fourth St., Eleventh floor, New York, NY 10036. (*See: Authors League of America.*)

Dramatists Sourcebook. This directory lists not-for-profit professional theaters in America to which playwrights, composers, lyricists and librettists may submit their work. The *Sourcebook* also lists contests and awards, fellowships and grants, conferences and festivals, workshops and residencies and other services for those who create new material for the stage; it is published by the Theatre Communications Group, Inc., 355 Lexington Ave., New York, NY 10017.

Dub. In the radio business, a tape copied from a master tape, sometimes for another station; means *duplicate.*

Dummy. The physical plan for a publication, such as a magazine, book or newspaper. Dummies are constructed at various levels of sophistication, the simplest being a group of blank pages the size and format of the publication, and the most elaborate a printed blueprint of the publication, called a *positive blue dummy.* The purpose of the more elaborate dummy is to show the position of and the area occupied by each piece of copy, illustration, photograph and heading.

An entrepreneur also will use as a dummy a printed sample or section of a proposed new magazine containing articles, stories and advertisements (just as they would appear if the effort got off the ground) to solicit investors and potential advertisers.

Dust jacket copy. Copy describing the book, typically prepared by the editor. Writing it is an important job because later promotion pieces as well as some reviews are likely to be written out of it. (*See: Blurb; Book jacket and paperback cover copy.*)

Easy Listening Formula (ELF). A gauge of listening comprehension, the ELF was developed by Dr. Irving Fang, an expert in determining the "learnability" levels of TV news reports. It is designed to make broadcasters and writers aware of the various degrees of language complexity in their presentations. The formula consists of counting each syllable above one, per word, in any one sentence. For example, Dr. Fang found that Walter Cronkite's scripts had an easy-listening score of less than twelve. That meant no sentence had more than twelve two-or-more-syllable words and was easily understood by the average listener. The most readable newspaper he tested, the *Christian Science Monitor*, also averaged less than twelve. Writers who are writing speeches and/or broadcast copy could use the Easy Listening Formula to keep their sentences from becoming too complex and difficult to listen to and understand. (*See: Readability formulas.*)

Edgar Awards. This group of awards was established in 1945 by the Mystery Writers of America, Inc. to recognize outstanding contributions to various categories of mystery, crime and suspense writing. The Edgar Allan Poe Awards consist of ceramic statuettes of Poe, known as "Edgars." They are awarded annually for the best first mystery novel by an American and the best mystery novel published in America. Edgars are also awarded in categories such as best juvenile mystery novel, best mystery short story, and best mystery motion picture, among others. More information on the Edgar prizes is available from the Mystery Writers of America, Inc., 17 E. Forty-seventh St., Sixth Floor, New York, NY 10017.

Editing. Editing is the art of generating and selecting, compiling and revising literary, photographic or audiovisual material and making it suitable for publication/production. Editors are the "gatekeepers" of publishing. They solicit and read manuscripts and decide what is publishable. Newspaper and magazine editors may write captions, choose which letters to the editors to print, send potentially libelous manuscripts to the company lawyer, and confer with writers and art directors to meet deadlines and stay within budget. Book editors often have many of the same responsibilities, in addition to their duties surrounding new acquisitions and new authors on publishers' lists.

Editing is the skill of knowing what works for an audience, and an editor's primary responsibility is to see that a piece or an entire publication does just that. Whatever his specific duties, he maintains a commitment to his readership. He accepts appropriate material and rejects the rest. On accepting a manuscript, an editor discusses with the writer any significant changes to be made and shows him alterations via the copyedited manuscript or the galley proofs. Ideally, the writer-editor relationship is based on mutual respect for accuracy and good writing. (*See: Copyeditor; Editor, acquisitions; Editor, content; Editor, production.*)

Editing, freelance. Basically three types of freelance editing opportunities are available: proofreading, copyediting and content editing.

A proofreader is responsible for comparing printer's proofs against the original material for the purpose of identifying and correcting errors in the typeset copy. This job requires familiarity with the standard proofreading symbols, as well as with the basic rules of grammar and spelling. Proofreading is painstaking and often tedious; nevertheless, it is an important job that demands both speed and accuracy. Upon accepting a proofreading assignment, the freelancer should ask for an estimate of how long the job should take or how much work he is expected to complete within a specified time. Of the three types of freelance editing opportunities, proofreading pays the least, usually $7-$10 per hour. The fee for a straight proofreading assignment is generally fixed by the publishing house or other client, and is not ordinarily negotiable. Although proofreading may not pay exceptionally well, the job does provide the freelancer with training and experience that can lead to more responsible editorial positions.

Copyediting, a job that pays more than proofreading does, also involves more responsibilities. The copyeditor prepares a manuscript to be typeset, reviewing the material to make sure the text reads well and makes sense. He corrects spelling and grammatical errors; verifies proper names, certain facts and cited references; makes sure that all the manuscript pages and auxiliary material (tables, charts, graphs, etc.) are there; and generally makes the book consistent with the publishing house's own style. The job often requires that the copyeditor recognize and correct factual errors as well as grammatical and style problems; many publishing houses seek copyeditors who have knowledge or experience in a certain field to work on a specific project. The average rate of pay for copyediting assignments is $9-$12 per hour; an experienced copyeditor with specialized knowledge in a subject—e.g., scientific or technical—may be able to command a higher rate.

Content editing is an opportunity that writer/editor Elizabeth L. Dugger calls "the pearl of editing services." A content editor is responsible for analyzing and organizing a manuscript, determining what information should be added or deleted to improve and enhance the text. A content editing assignment is ordinarily offered to a freelancer only after he has worked with a publisher on several other projects and has earned the staff editor's trust. This freelance job pays very well compared to proofreading and copyediting assignments: $12-$50 per hour and up.

To gain the experience needed to become a regular proofreader or copyeditor for a major publishing house, the writer interested in freelance editing may begin with local proofreading jobs. Commercial printers and typesetting firms, for example, usually proofread the copy they've typeset to minimize the number of PEs (printer's errors) before returning it to the customer's proofreader. These firms, listed in the Yellow Pages under "Typesetting" (or those firms found under "Printing" that advertise typesetting services), often require part-time proofreading help. Schools, social service groups, government agencies and other community organizations that publish brochures, pamphlets and other printed materials are also likely to require proofreaders from time to time.

A solid résumé bearing editing or proofreading credits may lead to freelance editing assignments with major publishing firms. It is not uncommon for large publishing companies in New York, Boston and Chicago to work by mail on specialized books with freelance editors throughout the U.S. The freelancer who submits a résumé and engaging cover letter to a major publisher will probably receive back an editing test designed to measure background knowledge, ability to recognize and correct factual and grammatical errors, and familiarity with editing symbols. His performance on the test, as well as his specialized knowledge and areas of expertise, will determine whether the publishing house offers him a freelance editing assignment.

Freelance editing opportunities are regularly listed in the classified section of the trade publications *Editor & Publisher* and *Publishers Weekly*. Occasionally a freelancer may find an opportunity for a freelance editing position advertised in the classified portion of his local newspaper. A writer may use either of these avenues to advertise his own freelance editing services as well.

Besides providing additional income, freelance editing allows a writer to make contacts in the publishing field that may prove valuable in getting the writer's own work published. Some writers, however, feel that editing work saps energy from their own writing and seek out nonwriting-related employment. (*See: Copyeditor; Editor, content; Editors; Proofreading.*)

Additional information: *Jobs and Opportunities for Writers; National Writers Union Guide to Freelance Rates and Standard Practice.*

Editor. (*See: Contributing editor; Copyeditor; Editing; Editing, freelance; Editor, acquisitions; Editor, content; Editor, production; Editors; Magazine personnel.*)

Editor, acquisitions. An editor responsible for originating and/or acquiring new publishing projects. An acquisitions editor seeks out authors to write books based on ideas conceived by the editorial and marketing personnel. He also meets regularly with writers and literary agents who have presented book ideas to the company and who may likely contract with the company on future titles.

After a publisher accepts a book proposal, the acquisitions editor works out a contract with the author or agent, seeking—within the policy and monetary guidelines established by the company and with respect to the author's desires—a compromise acceptable to both parties. As the book idea is developed, the acquisitions editor works with the author to make the final product the most salable and attractive property possible. The exact duties of an acquisitions editor vary from company to company. In some, the emphasis is more on acquisition; in others, the acquisitions editor will edit as well, overseeing the book's progress from start to finish.

An acquistions editor working for a paperback publisher also deals with other publishing companies, negotiating reprint rights to some of their books.

Editor & Publisher (E&P). A weekly trade journal for the newspaper industry. Each issue includes industry news and articles on the editorial, advertising, production and business aspects of the newspaper field. Special annual sections of the journal are devoted to journalism awards and syndicates. E&P also publishes a *Yearbook*, listing details on each of the newspapers in the U.S., Canada and foreign countries, along with related information on associations, foreign correspondents, journalism schools, etc. Another of E&P's annual publications is its *Market Guide*, giving statistical information on the market areas served by the daily newspapers in the U.S. and Canada. The address of *Editor & Publisher* is 11 W. Nineteenth St., New York, NY 10011. (*See:* Editor & Publisher Syndicate Directory; *Journalism awards.*)

Editor & Publisher Syndicate Directory. This annual directory contains alphabetical listings of syndicates that provide columns, cartoons and comic strips to newspapers. Each listing includes the name and address of a syndicate, as well as one or more person to contact. The directory is cross-indexed by titles of features, the writers and artists who create them, and subject matter.

Writers who have an idea for a syndicated column should first check this directory (which is probably available in their local newspaper office or public library) to see what competition there is for their proposed subject matter. The Directory is published by *Editor & Publisher*, a trade magazine for newspapers, located at 11 W. Nineteenth St., New York, NY 10011.

Editor, content. Also called the *developmental* or *substantive editor*, the content editor is responsible for seeing that a book's completed manuscript remains true to its outline and fulfills the publisher's goals for the book. The content editor makes sure everything that should be included is, and that extraneous material is deleted. He evaluates the manuscript to determine whether material is presented in the best possible order and challenges the author on cloudy explanations, vague assumptions, faulty logic and potential legal problems. He also is concerned with making sure that the material is written and presented in the way it was envisioned: e.g., in formal or informal style, with a light or serious slant, anecdotally or straight to the point. Since the editor is the person who knows the book best, he is its leading advocate (and the author's) within the publishing house. The content editor usually is responsible as well for selecting and placing any illustrations that appear in the book. Some content editors may also acquire books. (*See: Copyeditor; Editor, acquisitions.*)

Editor, production. The production editor—sometimes called the *managing editor*—is a liaison between a publisher's editorial and production departments. He is usually responsible for conducting a manuscript through all phases of production to bound book—from copyediting through design, typesetting, and on through manufacture. The production editor assumes the complex task of coordinating editorial and production schedules, keeping a manuscript moving smoothly through the process with the fewest possible delays. The position of production editor is a difficult one: because he is seldom supervising just one book, the job requires that he juggle a number of schedules at once, coordinating several manuscripts simultaneously.

The job requires a general knowledge of the entire publishing process; the skill to assign, coordinate and supervise various freelance personnel; and the ability to work cooperatively with three departments—art, editorial and production—to ensure that a book is published on schedule. (*See: Book publishing jobs, editorial; Copyeditor; Editing, freelance; Editor, content.*)

Editorial ethics. Editorial ethics are guidelines pertaining to the business behavior expected by freelancers of the editors they deal with. Rooted in consideration and mutual respect, editorial ethics are standards for maintaining good writer-editor relationships. For instance, editorial ethics command that an editor will not rewrite a work without the author's permission, nor will he take one author's idea and assign it to another writer. Editorial ethics call for reimbursing a writer for time spent on an assigned story in the event that an editor cancels plans to use it, and reporting on submitted queries or manuscripts within a reasonable time.

Writers follow complementary ethical guidelines in their dealings with editors. The American Society of Journalists and Authors publishes a Code of Ethics and Fair Practices in its membership directory of freelancers. (See Figure 3.) Other professional organizations have similar codes of ethics for their membership. (*See: American Society of Journalists and Authors "Code of Ethics and Fair Practices"; Ethics for writers; Kill fee; Reporting time on manuscripts; Steal my idea?*)

Editorial Freelancers Association (EFA). This organization exists to advance professionalism, to exchange information and support, and to furnish benefits to its members. Activities include seminars and training workshops.

The EFA's 950 members work part time and full time in capacities such as editor, writer, indexer and proofreader.

The Association publishes a bimonthly newsletter and an annual membership directory. The newsletter contains news of past and future Association activities, features and tips related to freelancing, book reviews and classified advertising. The address of the EFA is 36 E. Twenty-third St., Room 9R, New York, NY 10159-2050.

Editorial rewriting. Editors usually make changes in submitted manuscripts for greater clarity, smoother flow or to accommodate space restrictions, but it is customary for them to send the altered manuscript or the galley proof to the author for approval. This practice avoids changes that obliterate points an author was trying to make. It also reflects the recognition that, because the author's byline is on the piece, he has the right to know how his work will appear in print.

A good editor does not rewrite for the sake of his own intellectual exercise: He strives for a clear, interesting and concise presentation of the author's ideas. (*See: Editorial ethics.*)

Editors. An editor's exact job description and title vary from publication to publishing house, depending on size and available personnel. Editors of small operations may easily do as much writing as they do editing. On the other hand, editing responsibilities on large publications are usually divided among several staffers.

There are many kinds of editing jobs in the publishing world. For example, copyeditors check manuscripts for grammatical details, factual errors and consistent writing style. Content editors are more concerned with clarifying ambiguities and correcting conceptual problems in a manuscript, as well as possible libel or other legal problems. Current rates for freelance content editors and copyeditors, some magazine editors, and in-house company publications editors are listed in the "How Much Should I Charge?" section of the annual *Writer's Market.*

Book publishing, too, offers freelance and editorial staff opportunities for editors. Acquisitions editors, for example, contact agents and scan magazines, newspapers and publishers' catalogs in search of ideas and possible authors to add to a publisher's list. Assistant editors may read manuscripts and write synopses and recommendations for action. (*See: Editing; Editorial ethics; Reporting time on manuscripts; Writer's guidelines.*)

Editors' filler services. These come in two forms: (1) a subscription to a camera-ready newsletter of editorial copy and cartoons, or (2) a newsletter detailing brief articles and photographs that can be requested for free use as filler. The latter are paid for by the client whose product or service is mentioned in the feature.

Filler services are offered by public relations firms that prepare the features and notify editors of their availability by periodically mailing a tabloid magazine filled with features and accompanying photographs, fillers, cartoons, puzzles and clip art. In the free versions, the editor requests certain features, indicates whether his publication is printed letterpress or offset, and specifies whether he wants mats or glossy proofs (with photographs newspaper-screened) for reproduction in his publication. Subjects may be recipes, health or medical advice, home maintenance tips or any other news or seasonal feature.

Some fillers include mention of a specific product. For example, a short feature "Prescription: Fun for

Sickbed Blues'' includes a drawing of a child in bed with his teddy bear playing at taking Teddy's temperature; the lead of the article includes this copy: "Toy Manufacturers of America, Inc. (TMA), the industry trade association, offers these suggestions for dealing with the special play problems of the bedridden child. ..." The article goes on not only to give advice about dealing with sick children, but also to make a plug for certain types of toys. For example, "Through play, a child may often act out (and thus relieve) fears. Dramatic play can be encouraged with doctor, nurse, or paramedic kits.''

Editors who would like to be put on the mailing list to receive notices of these free features can contact firms such as Derus Media Service, 500 N. Dearborn, Chicago, IL 60610 (features are available in Spanish as well as English); and North American Precis Syndicate, Inc., 201 E. Forty-second St., New York, NY 10017. Subscription fillers are available from Fillers for Publications, 7015 Prospect Place, N.E., Albuquerque, NM 87110. Call (505) 844-7636 for a sample packet. (*See: Clip art; Copyright-free art.*)

Editor-writer correspondence. Besides selling an editor on an article idea (the query letter) and submitting manuscripts (the cover letter), writers encounter other situations in which they must write an editor regarding their work.

Gary Turbak described some of the kinds of letters written to editors by freelancers in a *Writer's Digest* article. Besides query letters and cover letters (which are described in sepa-

rate entries in this book), another type of letter is written in response to an assignment or go-ahead (instructions to write a piece on speculation). This brief letter, the *confirmation of assignment/go-ahead,* simply lets the editor know that the writer does indeed plan to write the piece, acknowledges the editor's response to the query, and mentions a deadline, either by confirming one suggested by the editor or proposing a different one.

A brief letter is also in order when the writer discovers that he will not be able to meet an agreed-upon deadline. In this kind of letter, the *deadline postponement letter,* the writer merely informs the editor that he will need more time than he had anticipated and gives the editor the date that he can expect to receive the manuscript.

The *jog letter* serves to remind an editor (or jog his memory) about a submitted piece of work in a case in which a response from the editor is long overdue. In the jog letter, the writer is careful to omit evidence of any impatience or anger he may be feeling, and to convey a businesslike impression. He explains to the editor what has happened in the past regarding his manuscript and asks to be informed of the status of same. Turbak points out that the jog letter can also be used to inquire about query letters, photos and late payment.

The *demand letter* is the writer's recourse when more than one jog letter brings no response. The tone of this kind of letter is businesslike, but the writer is less tactful and more direct than in previous inquiries. Turbak suggests writing to others higher up in the organization after one demand letter to the editor brings no results.

Writers who have submitted material to a magazine on speculation and have been unable to get a reply from the editor after several jog inquiries should send one more certified letter indicating that, since the writer has not heard from the editor, the writer is formally *withdrawing his manuscript* from consideration and resubmitting another original elsewhere.

Sometimes a writer needs to explain in detail the kinds of rights he is selling, e.g., reprint rights. This is especially valuable when dealing with those who may not be familiar with the provisions of each kind of manuscript rights. The writer's *granting rights letter*, therefore, may be the only written evidence of which rights were sold. (*See: Cover letter; Go-ahead; Query.*)

Education for journalism. The classic educational debate among those in the field (who are, of course, future employers of today's students) concerns the value of a journalism degree as opposed to a liberal arts degree. Proponents of journalism degrees hold that concentration on writing skills and early exposure to the working world of the media are the foremost educational elements needed, while advocates of liberal arts degrees believe that general knowledge and basic composition skills are the ideal qualities of a beginning journalist. Schools that are accredited by the American Council on Education for Journalism (ACEJ) prepare their students for the varying expectations of employers in

that they require each student majoring in journalism to earn a specified number of credits outside the journalism department, thus exposing them both to journalistic practice and knowledge of other disciplines.

Education for writers. This can be seen as the total lifelong study and experiences that contribute to the development of a writer. Writers' educations may consist of formal university study, local creative writing courses, continuing education programs, weekend seminars, correspondence courses and countless informal lessons of living. Perhaps the only absolute of a writer's education is that it never ends.

Organized programs afford the writer opportunities to learn fundamental writing techniques, to polish style and to act on the insights of constructive criticism. They also teach discipline and perseverance. Writing classes or conferences may provide an opportunity for sharing experiences as well as instruction.

But out of the unstructured, casual learning situations that arise from the writer's being alert to life, also come the nuances of successful stories, articles and books. (*See: Associated Writing Programs; Continuing education; Correspondence courses for writers; Writing courses.*)

Educational Press Association of America (EDPRESS). Editors of education publications make up this six-hundred-member group, whose activities include editorial workshops and annual meetings. The Association publishes a monthly newsletter, an annual membership roster, *The*

Idea Book, The Book of Lists for the Education Editor, and other materials to aid the educational editor.

EDPRESS awards one Golden Lamp Award annually "to a publication which shows excellent and significant achievement in the field of educational journalism," and several other awards under the categories "Editorial," "Graphics" and "Graphics-Editorial." The competition is open to "publications, institutions, or individuals with paid-up ED-PRESS memberships." EDPRESS is at the Communications Department, Glassboro State College, Glassboro, NJ 08028.

e.g. An abbreviation for *exempli gratia,* a Latin term meaning "for example." *The Chicago Manual of Style* suggests that "general abbreviations such as *e.g., i.e.* and *etc.* are preferably confined to parenthetical references."

Words into Type advises "When other abbreviations are used freely in a work, it is acceptable to *introduce* a word or phrase with e.g." and cites this example: "In evaluating an IQ score several factors, e.g., socioeconomic level, must be considered."

800 numbers. Freelancers who want to find out if a company or institution they want to call long distance has a free "800" number can dial 1-800-555-1212 to reach the toll-free number information operator.

In searching for the toll-free number of a federal or state office that serves consumers, the writer may find useful "Direct Contacts for Consumers," a booklet published jointly by the U.S. government and the American Telephone and Tele-graph Company. This publication, which contains 150 listings, may be obtained free for a self-addressed postcard from the Consumer Information Center, 18 F St., N.W., Room G-142, Washington DC 20405.

Electronic journalism. This term refers to writing news programs, features, and documentaries for radio and TV. With the expansion of both cable and low-power TV stations, newly licensed by the Federal Communications Commission, potential exists for increased writing/reporting opportunities. Current references on the how-to's of the subjects can be located in the *Subject Guide to Books In Print* under categories such as "Journalism—Handbooks, Manuals, etc.," "Radio Journalism," "TV Broadcasting of News," "TV Production and Direction" and related topics.

Electronic mail. Also called e-mail, this is the method of sending messages via computers and modems to other users. When e-mail was first developed, only users of particular on-line services could transmit messages to each other. Now, via the Internet, messages can be sent from a user of America Online to a user of CompuServe. (*See: Internet; Online service; Snail mail.*)

Electronic publishing. The publishing of fiction and nonfiction—such as reference books—by electronic means. Electronic publishing could include—but isn't limited to—online services, computer disks and CD-ROMs.

Using hypertext, electronic books can contain even more information than meets the eye. In encyclopedias, for example, the information can be broken down into more manageable bits linked with the main text.

In the case of novels, plays or movies, the text of the work can be accompanied by interviews with the writer and other references that would be useful to the user. For example, on *The Crucible* compact disc, users can access the script as well as view a video clip of an interview with Arthur Miller and read remarks by the play's critics. (*See: Hypertext.*)

Electronic text. One of several terms (others are videotext, rotatext, teletext and intertext) that refer to the technology of electronic distribution of printed news and information via a TV screen. Dr. Ralph Lowenstein, Dean of the College of Journalism and Communications at the University of Florida at Gainesville, suggests that since this is a text-via-video medium, the word "videotext" is the most apt generic term.

The University of Florida is the first university in the nation to establish an electronic text center to experiment with this new technology and build an educational curriculum around it.

El-hi. A book-publishing term that refers to texts or other books suitable for supplementary reading both in elementary school and in high school. (*See: Stories in textbooks; Textbook publishing.*)

Ellipsis. An omission in a text. Ellipses can be made in composition, but such use is usually limited to poetry in which a word or two must be left out to keep the meter correct. More

often, ellipses are made in quotation for the sake of clarity and brevity; omissions up to an entire paragraph in length are permissible.

In quoting another work, ellipses must always be indicated by the use of *ellipsis points*: three dots for any omission within the body of a sentence, four dots for an omission including the period at the end of a sentence or anything longer than a sentence.

Here is a passage from Anthony Trollope's *Doctor Thorne*, first in its entirety, then as it might read with ellipses:

He felt rather sick at heart when Mr. Baker got up to propose the toast as soon as the servants were gone. The servants, that is, were gone officially; but they were there in a body, men and women, nurses, cooks, and ladies'-maids, coachmen, grooms, and footmen, standing in the two doorways to hear what Master Frank would say. The old housekeeper headed the maids at one door, standing boldly inside the room; and the butler controlled the men at the other, marshalling them back with a drawn corkscrew.

He felt rather sick at heart when Mr. Baker got up to propose the toast. . . . The servants . . . were gone officially; but they were there in a body. . . standing in the two doorways to hear what Master Frank would say. The old housekeeper headed the maids at one door. . . and the butler controlled the men at the other, marshalling them back with a drawn corkscrew.

The writer should refer to a good style book, such as *The Chicago Man-*

ual of Style, for more detailed information on ellipsis use.

Em. The square measurement of any size of type, so named because in conventional typefaces the capital M approximates that measure. For example, in twelve-point type an em is twelve points; in eight-point type, eight points. (There are twelve points to a *pica;* six picas to one inch.)

Editors, proofreaders and designers most frequently use the em to measure indents—paragraph indents, for instance, may be one, two, three (or more) ems wide, depending on the design; lists are indented by ems from the margin.

Dashes are referred to as *em-dashes* or *en-dashes,* depending on their width—an en-dash is half as wide as an em-dash.

Emoticon. Since online chatting forces us to communicate without the conveniences of gesture and inflection, it's fairly easy for sentences that were meant to be in fun to seem quite harsh. Emoticons are little symbols, made of combinations of keystrokes, that attempt to add a sort of virtual inflection. The most common is the "smiley" emoticon, :-), used to indicate that the prior sentence was said with a smile. (To see the smiley face, lean your head to the left.)

Emotion in writing. In fiction writing, an author elicits an emotional response from the reader through the situations in which he places the characters. Stories and novels not only relate what happens, they make the reader vicariously experience the events so that he can respond emotionally to them. The emotional responses of the characters also help convey emotions to the reader. Among the strongest emotions experienced by human beings (and therefore fictional characters) are the primary emotions of love, happiness, hope, compassion, courage, pain, hunger, hate, anger, grief, fear and greed. The secondary emotions, which are less powerful, include a sense of humor, loyalty, gratitude, pride, curiosity, self-pity, loneliness, jealousy, vanity, timidity, inferiority, envy, suspicion, revenge, guilt, shame and boredom. How the emotion is expressed varies with the type of fiction, but the ability to smoothly integrate an emotional quality into writing is characteristic of the successful short story writer or novelist. Beginning writers often neglect this aspect in their work.

The reader's empathy should be aroused in the first paragraph; from that point on, an emotional undertone should be present, according to writer Omer Henry. He suggests that although plot, character and theme are essential to a good story, emotion is the element that retains the reader's attention.

Emotion in writing is important in some types of nonfiction as well as in fiction. Here is an excerpt from a *Reader's Digest* "Drama in Real Life" piece about a mother and son caught in a flash flood:

Then Helen spotted a telephone pole about a yard away. "Grab that, Rowdy," she panted, "and hold tight! Whatever happens, hang on to that pole and don't let go!"

Helen herself was feeling very weak. Suddenly her torn left hand lost its grip on the fence. The current swiftly carried her away. There was time only to scream once more, "Stay where you are, Rowdy! Hold on, whatever you do!"

Horrified, the little boy saw his mother vanish into the dark, heard her receding screams.

"Stay where you are!" she had said. But Rowdy couldn't obey. He let go of the telephone pole and, spinning in the current, dog-paddled frantically after his mother.

"Mom!" he cried. "Mom, where are you?" But there was only darkness and the roar of the water rushing him along.

The writer should avoid confusing sentimentality, which tends to foster a one-dimensional, unrealistic view of life, with emotion. (*See: Empathy.*)

Empathy. The condition of being able to identify with another person's feelings. A writer must have empathy toward his characters to make them seem real to readers.

Author Colleen L. Reece evokes her own ability to empathize with her characters by recalling an experience in which she felt the same emotion she imagines the character would feel. Sometimes she instills in her characters emotions that were expressed by someone she knows and she can identify with. In Reece's technique, author and character usually do not face the same situation, but rather the same principle: Reece cites the examples of confronting prejudice and of being pressured to betray personal values.

Reece's philosophy shows her awareness of the need for empathy:

"Every character I create includes a small part of myself, no matter how minute. It may only be a passing thought, a fleeting moment, a quick flash of insight or temper. Yet it is that very part most needed to make those characters alive, real, lovable, or despicable." (*See: Emotion in writing.*)

Employment searches by writers. Writers seeking editorial or staff writing positions can refer to the trade magazines of specific writing fields such as *Advertising Age* and *Editor & Publisher* (for newspapers), which carry classified ads for writing and editorial opportunities. Most carry "situation wanted" ads as well.

In major publishing centers such as New York, Chicago or Los Angeles, specialized employment agencies exist to help writers and editors secure staff positions in their fields. They are listed under "Employment Agencies" in the yellow pages telephone directory.

The annual *Literary Market Place* lists agencies specializing in the placement of book publishing personnel.

In smaller cities, local and regional chapters of professional communications organizations such as the Public Relations Society of America or Women in Communications, Inc. are a good source of job leads.

Encyclopedia. An encyclopedia is a book or set of books containing alphabetically arranged articles/entries on numerous topics covering either many branches of knowledge or several aspects of one subject field. An encyclopedia's primary purpose is the clear, accurate presentation of facts. In addition, contemporary encyclopedias may use cross-references to help readers explore concepts further; they may use statistical charts and illustrations and art reproductions to enhance the text; they may include color photographs and striking visuals to establish a rapport with readers. Many American encyclopedias are designed for use as curriculum-related references. Freelance writers use them as reference tools, for checking historical facts, dates, etc.

Encyclopedias contain some of the same elements as dictionaries, textbooks, atlases and statistical manuals. General encyclopedias cover all important fields of knowledge and address lesser topics according to the needs and interests of the intended readers. There are currently more than thirty general encyclopedias published in the U.S. varying in reading level, number of pages and volumes. (The *Encyclopaedia Britannica* and *World Book Encyclopedia* are general works.) Special encyclopedias—often only one volume, rather than multivolume—confine their coverage to specific fields, subjects and viewpoints, e.g., the *Encyclopedia of Sports* and the *New Catholic Encyclopedia.*

Both general and specialized encyclopedias may contain entries written by specialists in a particular discipline or by staff writers. Specialists' articles are usually signed. Alphabetical arrangements of entries may be determined in at least two ways. Word-by-word arrangements place entries according to the first word in the title; for example, "On Wisconsin" would come before "onomatopoeia." The letter-by-letter method uses the complete title of the entry to determine its placement order; in this case, "onomatopoeia" would precede "On Wisconsin."

Encyclopedias are continually revised (representing freelance opportunities for writers and editors), and many publishers issue annual or quarterly supplements. As a tool of writers and readers, encyclopedias must be carefully examined. Their authoritativeness, accuracy, objectivity, clarity, style, quality, physical format and recency are important considerations prior to use or purchase. The American Library Association has published a guide, "Purchasing an Encyclopedia," which is available in most libraries.

Endings, story. There are many ways to end a short story, and even more ways to label different types of story endings. There are, however, certain elements required of a good story ending, regardless of the type of conclusion a writer chooses.

The ending of a story must, first of all, be satisfying to the reader. It honestly and fairly answers the question(s) the author posed at the beginning of the narrative. A good ending leaves the reader feeling that the story could have ended no other way.

Second, the ending must be logical: it must develop naturally from the characterization and events of the story. Even if the story solution is a surprise, the surprise must have been foreshadowed earlier in the story and not be dependent on some newly introduced character or amazing coincidence to provide the twist.

The ending of a story must be

consistent with the mood, atmosphere and subject matter of the piece. A light, humorous narrative about a young woman's adventures as she moves into her first apartment should not end with her brutal murder at the hands of a psychopathic killer. Similarly, the writer who creates a somber atmosphere throughout a piece should maintain that serious mood at the end; even though the conclusion may promise better days ahead, an abrupt shift from gray skies to blue may weaken the intended effect of the story.

A good ending *gives* the reader something, whether it be a surprise, an emotional charge, or an idea to reflect on—in other words, a good ending provokes a reaction from the reader. A story should end on an important note and not be allowed to ramble on or be dragged out to an anticlimax.

Finally, a story's conclusion should show that the viewpoint character has passed through an experience that has changed him somehow, as well as proved the theme of the story.

Every story ending should fulfill these fundamental requirements; within these basic rules however, a variety of approaches exist. In the *summary* ending, all the threads of a story are neatly tied up into a happy (or unhappy) ending. In the *reversal* ending, the protagonist undergoes a reversal of some character trait. The *twist* or *surprise* ending sometimes involves a gimmick. The *periscope* ending offers the reader a brief glimpse of what the future holds for the characters in a story, while the *reader's choice* leaves the reader to supply his own ending, once the problem has

been developed dramatically.

Fiction editors agree that a weak ending will inevitably ruin a story's chances of acceptance, despite a brilliant beginning, skillful characterization and a strong plot. The ending is the part of a story that will stay with the reader, the part that he will remember after he has closed the book or magazine. It is important that a writer spend as much time on the ending of a story as he does on the beginning and middle.

The ending of a story should probably be clear in a writer's mind before he sits down at the typewriter. Katherine Anne Porter once remarked, "If I didn't know the ending of a story, I wouldn't begin. I always write my last line, my last paragraphs, my last page first." (*See: Falling action; Plant; Plot; Surprise ending.*)

Entertainment columns. In small newspaper operations, all reviews (theater, music, cinema, dance, art, books, food, etc.) are sometimes written by one person. Because a small newspaper has limited space and a low budget, this job is likely to be given to a freelance writer. At a weekly or suburban paper, for example, pay may be only a byline to begin with, but such assignments offer the freelancer exposure and experience. Some writers prepare sample reviews to give the editor an example of their writing style, and request an opportunity to do some reviews on assignment. (*See: Arts review; Book review; Drama criticism; Restaurant review.*)

Epilogue. A section added at the end of some novels, long poems, plays and teleplays, often dealing with what happens to the characters after the actual conclusion of the story; it is not part of the plot. John Irving's epilogue to *The World According to Garp*, for example, briefly describes each of the characters' lives, until their deaths. These events all take place after Garp's death, which marks the end of the story. The climax/resolution takes place before the epilogue appears.

In a stage play, the epilogue can be a speech recited by an actor. In a teleplay, the epilogue, or *tag*, follows the climax and ties together any loose ends that may have been left. (*See: Television writing.*)

Epiphany. A term first used by Joyce to describe the abrupt revelation of an event's or thing's essential significance; also, a work or portion of a work in which such a revelation takes place. The concept of the epiphany grew fashionable in the 1960s and 1970s, when readers found epiphanies everywhere; it is considered more accurate, however, to restrict the term's use to Joyce's works. The fifteen stories that make up *Dubliners*, for example, all contain epiphanies.

Erotica. Any form of literature, art, film or photography dealing with the sexual aspects of love. Erotic content ranges from subtle sexual innuendo to explicit descriptions of sexual acts.

Erotica places sexual activity in context, giving the work a more literate feel. This treatment of sexuality makes erotic works increasingly popular with women. In fact, erotica is

sometimes called "pornography for women."

Publishers of erotica are listed in the book publishers subject index of *Writer's Market*. As with any other market, checking bookstores for recent titles serves as a valuable research tool.

(*See: Obscenity; Pornography.*)

Essay. A short, literary, nonfiction composition (usually prose) in which a writer develops a theme or expresses an idea.

Coined in 1580 to describe the personal reflections of the French writer Montaigne, this literary form survives in several types of articles in today's magazines and newspapers. It has been expanded to include descriptive, narrative, argumentative, satiric, historical and humorous pieces. Formal essays are generally serious, logically developed and intended to persuade or inform. Informal essays, whose topics and tones are practically boundless, are frequently known as personal, light and familiar essays. They are well-polished writings that tend to suggest much more than they actually say.

Essays are usually subjective—a revelation of the writer's own thoughts and feelings—but some more objective versions are used in some newspapers and magazines. In his book *Articles and Features*, Roy Paul Nelson describes the information essay—an extension of the news story, in which the writer is a detached reporter "teaching" his audience with facts—and the interpretive essay, which uses evidence and facts to stress the why's of an issue and offer new perspectives on it.

A number of magazines solicit opinion essays on topics of interest to their readers, and others use inspirational essays that deal (without being preachy) with uplifting personal experiences. The humorous essay is usually light and witty and treats as subject matter the trials and irritations common to the readers of the magazine to which it is submitted.

Publications listed in the "General Interest" section of *Writer's Market* often solicit essay material.

Establishing shot. A camera shot that affords a view of a large area; it is often used at the beginning of a film or TV program to help set the scene. When used in a script, the term is typed in all caps. (*See: Television script terms.*)

Establishing song. In a musical, a song that presents the setting or the general context for the story. It can perform its function in a *production number*, which uses a large group of performers, or a *soft opening*, a quiet song often sung solo. "Magic to Do," from *Pippin*, is a production number; "Try to Remember," from *The Fantasticks*, is a soft opening. (*See: Musical.*)

et al. Abbreviation for *et alii*, which is Latin for "and others." It is used in footnotes to refer to a work by more than three authors; however, it is always preceded by the name of the author listed first on the published work. It is typed in lower-case letters (et al.) in a manuscript.

Ethics for writers. A code of conscientious professional behavior for writers. Though ethics by their nature are subject to interpretation and translation and writers by *their* nature are diverse, complex personalities, certain rudimentary standards reflecting the ideals of the profession do exist. They are not laws, but guidelines, followed for the sake of professional and personal integrity, dealing with writers' actions toward their readers and editors.

The code of ethics relating to readership is based on truth. It takes effect when an idea for a novel, an article or even a filler is born. It dictates that a writer know his subject. It necessitates that he track down accurate information and complete the homework needed to produce a credible piece of fiction or nonfiction that is his own and not plagiarized from others. He doesn't mix fact and fiction. In following this ethical code, the nonfiction writer investigates opposing views and checks story corroborations. He honors interviewees' requests for anonymity and does not quote information given "off the record." The fiction writer narrates from a point of view appropriate for his theme. He strives to create a worthy literary work for his intended audience.

In writers' professional behavior toward editors, the bulk of the standards involve consideration and regard. A writer submits neatly typed material; the act of submitting a piece verifies its authenticity, if nonfiction, and confirms complete fabrication, if fiction. He sends manuscripts appropriate for a given market, having previously studied its needs. He encloses sufficient postage and an envelope for return of a manuscript or a query reply. If given an assignment, he is honest about his expenses, meets his deadline or notifies his editor in advance of reasons for possible delay. If he fails to complete a book manuscript through his own fault, he returns the advance or has the sum deducted from his royalties on other books. (*See: Conflict of interest; Editorial ethics; Press trip; Simultaneous submission.*)

Ethnic fiction. Stories and novels whose central characters are black, Native American, Italian-American, Jewish, Appalachian or members of some other specific cultural group. Ethnic fiction usually deals with a protagonist caught between two conflicting ways of life: mainstream American culture and his ethnic heritage. Except for black and Jewish writers—who can draw on a large body of work in their respective traditions and now often write in experimental forms—ethnic fiction tends to be conventional in form; the ground it breaks is in subject matter.

It is difficult for nonwhite ethnic writers to find a commercial publisher, since publishers feel that ethnic concerns tend not to be the concerns of the general American book-buying and reading public. There are exceptions, of course—Toni Morrison's works have achieved very respectable sales. For the most part, though, the action in ethnic fiction is with small and independent presses and literary/little magazines, many of which have a regional or cultural focus. In addition to the not-for-profit and low-profit publishers, though, commercial ethnic magazines such as *Ebony, Essence, Hadassah Magazine* and *The Italian Times* accept ethnic fiction.

eWorld. Apple Computer's online service, currently services computer users on the Macintosh and Windows operating systems. eWorld offers a smooth, easily negotiated interface, with ample opportunities for recreation and research. At the time of this writing, *Writer's Digest* magazine operates Writer's Digest Forum on eWorld, offering regular conferences, online writer's groups and more. For more information about eWorld or to obtain eWorld installation software, call (800) 775-4556. (*See: Electronic mail; Internet; Online service.*)

Exhibit. In publishing, *exhibit* has two meanings. Most commonly, it means a display at a book industry convention, but it can also refer to charts or illustrations used in the appendix of a book.

Expenses (editorial reimbursement). In most cases, writers are reimbursed by publications for costs incurred in completing an article assigned to them. Though many magazines pick up the tab for story-related expenses, a writer should get approval and verification before assuming that he will be reimbursed. An editor's willingness to pay for travel expenses, for example, may depend on an editorial budget and the importance of the writing project to the magazine. Writers should keep all receipts for reimbursement or tax deduction purposes.

In the case of expenses run up in writing a book, the writer receives an advance against royalties to help finance the project. Writers are expected to cover the costs of travel, extensive research, long-distance interviews, photocopying, artwork production, secretarial help, etc., out of this advance. However, a writer may sometimes be able to make arrangements with his publisher (if he lives in the same city, for example) to get photocopying done, use the WATS line, etc., to help defray some of these expenses. Occasionally, depending on the project and the expected costs, a publisher will agree to create a budget, separate from the royalty advance, to cover research or other expenses. This probably happens most often in the case of artwork (the publisher might ask the author to supply rough drawings but convert them into reproduction copy at the publisher's expense). The publisher may also pay all or some of the permissions fees for reproducing photos or artwork.

Experimental fiction. Setting and strong characterization are basic elements of experimental fiction. This form depends largely on the revelation of a character's inner being that elicits an emotional response from the reader. Helen Hinckley Jones, writer and writing instructor, says of the experimental short story: "This isn't so much a story of *doing* as a story of *being.*"

Other prominent characteristics of experimental fiction are style, structure, symbol and narrative technique. Experimental fiction can be unplotted, although the absence of a plot is not a necessary feature; when a plot is used, however, it is subordinate to the other, aforementioned elements.

What is experimental in one age can become cliché in the next; in its day, *Moby Dick* was an experimental

work that virtually no one understood. Some of the most important experimental writers of the past few decades are Alain Robbes-Grillet, John Barth and Thomas Pynchon; among the influential experimentalists today are writers Jorge Luis Borges, Don DeLillo, Gabriel Garcia Marquez, Joseph McElroy and Manuel Puig.

Except for the most important writers, who are published in prestige editions, experimental fiction is published primarily in university quarterlies and in little magazines. (*See: Mainstream fiction.*)

"Experts"—how to find them. Writers sometimes need to contact authorities for verification, explanation and update of research collected in writing an article or book. Public and university libraries often have comprehensive works suggesting individuals as subject-matter experts. Helpful sources include: *American Men and Women of Science* and the *Directory of American Scholars*, a four-volume set listing authorities by their expertise in the fields of history, English, languages, philosophy, religion and law. A master *Biographical Index* records individuals appearing in the many Marquis "Who's Who" publications. In addition, hundreds of reference directories, such as Wasserman's *Encyclopedia of Business Information Sources*, are listed in the *Directory of Directories. Speakers and Lecturers: How to Find Them* has a useful subject cross-index of topics on which these people could be contacted.

Other library materials writers may use in pursuit of authorities include general and specific periodical indexes (e.g., the *Reader's Guide to Pe-*

riodical Literature and *Psychological Abstracts*, respectively) where names of authors of recently published articles, who could be written in care of the publication, may be found. Writers may also refer to *A Writer's Guide to Research*, which provides the names of contact people, addresses and telephone numbers of various information-dispensing centers in government, industry, education and the arts.

Local authorities may be identified by contacting schools, libraries, newspapers and chambers of commerce that often compile lists of referral and resource people within their own community. Businesses listed in the Yellow Pages of the telephone directory may also be sources of local "experts."

Writers contacting experts usually enclose a photocopy of whatever statement, theory or research finding they need verification or updating on, with a cover letter asking the expert to respond at his convenience, in an enclosed stamped envelope addressed to the writer. Normally no payment is involved, since the expert wants to be sure any statement attributed to him is accurate and current.

In the case of specialized nonfiction books, the publisher may absorb the cost of having the manuscript vetted (checked for factual accuracy) by an outside expert. If not, the author may be required to pay this cost, which could vary from around fifty to several hundred dollars—depending on the complexity of the book, whether the author knows a local expert he can trust with the job, and other factors. (*See: Directories.*)

Exposé. An exposé is a revelation of documented facts intended to expose wrongdoing, injustice or foul play. Honest, legitimate exposés appear in newspapers and magazines and in book forms as products of careful investigative reporting. They are contrasted with the sensational stories in "gossip" publications.

Exposés are public disclosures that take on many shapes. They may be personality sketches, accounts of company practices or reports of government waste. They sometimes grow out of a writer's own experience or awareness of contradictions surrounding a subject or situation. They are usually written in straightforward, objective fashion. But they may also be successfully treated in a light, sarcastic or even cynical way. In fact, exposés of this type may have a better chance of reaching a large audience than do the hard-hitting accounts. Some editors may be reluctant to endorse a highly discrediting piece for fear of the unfavorable impact it could have on readership and advertisers.

Exposés have long served to influence social reform and public policy. To do so, they must be fairly written and free of libel and malicious intent. They must attribute controversial comments to at least loosely defined sources. Exposé writers often seek help from government regulatory agencies (through the provisions of the Freedom of Information Act), chambers of commerce and professional societies in verifying facts and tracking down statistics. The National Better Business Bureau, for example, is a valuable checkpoint in unearthing material for exposés dealing with products, services and companies.

Because of the inflammatory nature of some exposé material, writers must be ready to defend critical pieces (both to readers and editors) with unconditional evidence. Depending on the nature of the exposé, they may choose (for business or personal safety reasons) to withhold their identity from the public by using a pseudonym. Editors are generally cooperative about pseudonyms if the exposé is timely and well-documented. Exposés currently in demand include reports of consumer fraud.

Two well-known American exposés are Upton Sinclair's *The Jungle*, about the meat-packing industry in Chicago, and Woodward and Bernstein's probe of the Watergate affair, *All the President's Men*. (*See: Investigative reporting; Magazine article, types of.*)

Exposition. The technique of communicating information—in nonfiction writing, by explaining something to the reader in a news story or magazine article; in fiction, by skillfully relating details about events, characters or situations that have taken place before a story started and that the audience must know to understand the story.

Exposition can be presented in fiction through narration, dialogue or action. Writers skilled at this technique insert exposition subtly, so that the reader or viewer doesn't recognize it as exposition.

Exterior. In a motion picture or TV script, this term indicates an outdoor scene; it is followed by more specific information about the location, sometimes describing in detail how it looks. Typed in all caps in a script, *exterior* is abbreviated *ext.* (*See: Television script terms.*)

Fable. A story written in either prose or verse that intends to teach a lesson or a truth about living. Fables are similar to parables in that both teach lessons. However, fables often use personified animals while parables use human beings. The major character in a fable discovers a universal truth after undergoing a single experience; this truth, or *moral,* is usually presented at the end of the story, in the form of a platitude rather than as an implicit theme. The fable writer, or fabulist, intends to impress the moral upon the reader's memory. "Don't count your chickens before they're hatched" is the moral of Aesop's fable "The Milkmaid and Her Pail."

Fables existed before the printed word as folktales that were recounted orally. Hundreds of fables have been attributed to the Greek slave Aesop, who lived between 620 and 560 B.C. Two hundred of his tales were gathered in about 320 B.C. to make up the earliest known collection. During the medieval period, Latin translations of Aesop's fables were used as textbooks in schools. "The Crow and the Pitcher," "The Lion and the Mouse," "The Hare and the Tortoise" and "The Town Mouse and the Country Mouse" are some of Aesop's fables. Other ancient fable collections include *The Panchatantra* and *The Jatakas,* both from India. *The Panchatantra* was written about 200 B.C. Structured in verse, these stories are much more elaborate than Aesop's are. *The Jata-kas,* a huge collection of stories about the reincarnation of Buddha, dates at least as far back as the fifth century A.D.

Jean de La Fontaine, a seventeenth-century Frenchman, was the master of the French fable. His tales, written in verse, include "The Fox and the Crow," "The Grasshopper and the Ant" and "The Frog Who Would Be an Ox."

Adaptations of fables are published today as single stories, such as "The Monkey and the Crocodile," by Paul Galdone, and as modern versions of traditional stories, such as "The Black Sheep," by Jean Merrill. Some authors have adapted collections of fables, as shown in Louis Untermeyer's *Aesop's Fables,* intended for young children; other authors, such as James Thurber, have created *Fables For Our Time.* (*See: Folktale; Parable; Proverb.*)

Fact sheet. An outline used by an announcer during ad-libbed broadcast commercials.

Faction. The term for works that are presented as fiction but that use actual facts, events and persons in their story and plot lines. Fictional characters are often incorporated as well, which separates the "factional" novel from the nonfiction novel. (In the latter, the documentary facts, characters *and* plot are based on real events.)

The roman á clef ("novel with a

key'') is a form of faction in which famous people and events are used but not heavily disguised.

The novels by Arthur Hailey about the hotel business, international airports, and the automobile business (*Hotel, Airport, Wheels,* etc.) were often called ''faction'' by his publisher. Another novel that incorporated historical figures into the story line was E.L. Doctorow's *Billy Bathgate.*

Facts on File. (*See: Periodicals, indexes to; Research aids/techniques.*)

Fade in. An editing direction for motion pictures or TV, used to indicate that the image begins all in one color and the scene gradually comes up full. Used at the beginning of most screenplays, this direction is typed in all caps. (*See: Television script terms.*)

Fade out. An editing direction for motion pictures or TV, used to indicate that the scene fades away to black. This direction is typed in all caps. (*See: Television script terms.*)

Fair comment. Some authors of what might otherwise be libelous comments have a defense against lawsuit under the *fair comment privilege.* Fair comment requires the following criteria: (1) The libelous comment must clearly be an opinion, not a statement of fact. (2) The opinion must be fair. (3) There must be no malice. (4) The opinion must rest on facts.

The fair comment defense is a concern of writers of columns, reviews, letters to the editor and other articles of a critical nature.

The average citizen can sue for li-

bel a person he feels has damaged his reputation. A film reviewer, on the other hand, who writes that a certain director has produced less than his best work in a certain film, is usually protected under the fair comment privilege from a lawsuit for libel. (*See: Libel.*)

Fair use. The amount of copyrighted material that may be quoted—especially for the purposes of criticism, comment, news reporting, teaching or research—without infringing a copyright. Fair use is usually determined by these four factors: (1) the purpose and character of the use—for example, commercial or not-for-profit educational; (2) the nature of the copyrighted work; (3) the amount used in proportion to the copyrighted work as a whole; and (4) the effect on the market value of the copyrighted work.

A book reviewer, for example, may quote a passage from a novel to illustrate what he is criticizing; or a teacher may reprint a poem from a book, under certain conditions, to discuss its merits and/or faults with his class. Teachers and writers may wish to write for a free copy of ''Reproduction of Copyrighted Works by Educators and Librarians,'' Circular R21, from the Copyright Office, Library of Congress, Washington, DC 20559, which contains the ''Agreement on Guidelines for Classroom Copying. . .'' among other guidelines on fair use.

No specific number of words, lines or notes can safely be taken without permission, although writers and editors have established some ''rules of thumb'' that, until they are challenged in court, serve as guidelines. For example, quoting four lines from a 200-line poem is not expected to require permission, whereas four lines from an eight-line poem would. Quoting 100-250 words from a trade book without permission seems a common practice, whereas university presses may allow up to 500 words quoted without permission. Acknowledging the source of the copyrighted material does not substitute for obtaining permission when the material quoted goes beyond the fair use guidelines. (*See: Copyright; Permissions.*)

Fair use of broadcast materials. Guidelines have been established for off-air recording of broadcasts for educational purposes by not-for-profit institutions. The guidelines define *broadcast programs* as "TV programs transmitted by TV stations for reception by the general public without charge."

Basic limitations are: (1) the recorded program may be retained by the institution for no more than forty-five days after recording; (2) the program may be used only once by individual teachers during the first ten school days in the forty-five-day retention period; (3) the remaining thirty-five days is for teacher evaluation purposes only; and (4) the off-air recording must include the copyright notice on the program. The complete guidelines were published in the October 14, 1981 *Congressional Record*, pp. E4750-E4752. (*See: Copyright.*)

Fairy tale. A genre of children's fiction characterized by magic, personified animals and objects, and imaginary beings such as wizards, fairies, ogres, gnomes and witches. A fairy tale can be written as a traditional story, such as *Cinderella*, popularized by Charles Perrault in his 1697 collection, *Contes de ma Mère l'Oye* ("Mother Goose Tales"); a variation on the traditional tale, such as *Nibble Nibble Mousekin: A Tale of Hansel and Gretel*, by Joan W. Anglund; or an original, contemporary story, such as *Mary Poppins*, by Pamela L. Travers.

The structure of a fairy tale is similar to that of the short story in that it has a beginning, a middle that rises to a climax, and a conclusion in which the conflict is resolved. But fairy tales, unlike most contemporary stories, are often begun and ended with statements from a narrator; e.g., "Long ago and far away . . ." to begin and "And now the joy began in earnest. I wish you had been there, too."

Many fairy tales contain maxims, themes or religious messages, which have endured for centuries. Characters are often stereotypical: They clearly embody good or evil.

A storytelling feeling is evident in classic fairy-tale style, because many of these stories were recited for generations before being written down; even the published versions are characterized by naturalistic dialogue and economy in description. Verse is an element of some fairy tales.

Classic fairy tale anthologies include Hans Christian Andersen's *Fairy Tales*, and the early collection of fairy tales by Jacob and Wilhelm Grimm; *Kinder- und Hausmarchen* (*Chilren's and Household Tales*). Contemporary versions of some classic fairy tales are *The Blue Fairy Book*, by Andrew Lange, and *The Brocaded Slipper*, by Lynette Vuong (a collection of five Vietnamese counterparts of Western fairy tales such as *Cinderella, Thumbelina,* etc.).

The use of fairy tales in juvenile magazines (and which type if used) varies by publication. *Writer's Market* and *Children's Writer's & Illustrator's Market* listings provide editors' guidelines regarding fairy tales. (*See: Fantasy in children's literature; Folktale.*)

Falling action. In literature—especially drama—the part of the story that takes place after the climax. The falling action usually consists of a *reversal,* which indicates a change in the characters' situation, and a *resolution,* or unraveling of plot complications. The latter is also known as the *dénouement.* (*See: Dénouement; Rising action.*)

False plant. Information that has nothing to do with the conclusion or resolution of a conflict in a short story or novel. Usually found in mystery stories, the false plant's purpose is to throw the reader off the track; it is often referred to as a "red herring." A false plant, for example, might be the introduction of a character who seems to have a good motive and the means and opportunity for murder—even though he turns out not to be the real murderer. Erle Stanley Gardner's Perry Mason novels made frequent use of false plants to challenge the reader.

Dangling plants—information introduced and then never referred to again in the story—are annoying to both editors and readers. A satisfactory false plant is brought to a conclusion before the story ends. Although the information may be misleading, it is nevertheless adequately explained somewhere in the story. (*See: Plant; Plot; Red herring.*)

Fan magazine writing. Colorful portrayals of the lives of motion picture, TV and music personalities are found in fan magazines. Fan magazine writing, geared for a readership of teenagers and young adult women, depicts stars as "real" people with universal experiences, both triumphant and dismal.

Writing for fan magazines may fall into one of two categories: the exclusive and the angled story. *Exclusives* usually involve personal interviews with stars, and therefore are generally written by magazine staffers or correspondents. *Angled* stories, on the other hand, may be submitted by freelancers who hit on a timely new slant for an article about a currently popular star.

Because of the volatile lives that many celebrities lead, fan magazine writers often concentrate on aspects of stars' lives not likely to change quickly. They write of celebrities' long-term marriages, children, health and religious experiences. Usually running 1,500-3,000 words, angled stories are filled with quotes and anecdotes available from news clipping and library files. The actual story line in angled pieces is almost secondary to grabbing the reader's interest with a catchy title and showing him yet one more glimpse of a star's personal life.

Successful fan magazine writing comes from knowing the movie magazine field. Publications such as *Variety, People Weekly, Rolling Stone* and *US* give writers reliable information about which stars are currently "hot."

Fan magazine markets and their specific submission requirements and payment rates are listed in the Entertainment and Music sections of *Writer's Market.*

Fantasy in children's literature.

If fantasy is introduced in a children's story, it must be on a separate plane from reality, according to Claudia Lewis, educator and author of *Writing for Young Children.* She points out that the two worlds may be juxtaposed, as when a character awakens from a dream, but that one world may not be evidenced in the other—e.g., a character's bringing back a material possession from a dream or a fantasy world is unacceptable to most editors. In some stories, such as A.A. Milne's *Winnie the Pooh*, reality and fantasy coexist but only seem to be in conflict with each other. In Milne's story, while Christopher Robin appears to be a real boy, the fact that he lives alone in a treehouse helps the reader realize that Christopher is partially fantastic—and so he is believable when conversing with animals.

In some juvenile stories, the author can shift to a fantasy setting credibly if he transports the characters near the start of the piece, before readers are accustomed to the realistic scene.

Lewis contends that fantasy is ineffective when an author violates the reader's sense of logic: She gives the example of a personified train whose lights fail because of its emotional state, but then are repaired mechanically by an engineer.

Freelancers submitting fantasy to children's magazine editors should research each editor's own preferences and prejudices by reading specific requirements in *Writer's Market* and *Children's Writer's & Illustrator's Market.*

Farm writing.

Emphasizing informative articles dealing with the business of farming, farm writing reflects the many changes in the industry resulting from automation, scientific research and the trend toward larger farms. "Down home" farm tales of the early 1900s have been replaced with business management and profitability articles intended for farming entrepreneurs.

Most successful farm writers have at least a general understanding of agricultural terms. They frequently contact local agricultural colleges and land-grant universities to learn about particular farm commodities, crops and breeds of livestock. Armed with that knowledge, they are better able to focus and specialize their writing for a unique farm readership.

Knowing the farm audience and potential markets is perhaps the most crucial element in writing successful farm material. The readership is generally people twenty-five to fifty-five years old with college backgrounds and/or extension course work in some aspect of agriculture, managing a farm yielding a six-figure income. This clientele reads farm magazines for technical advice and for information about industrial suppliers, agribusiness organizations and pending farm legislation.

The writing reflects a farm viewpoint (not an urban one) and translates technical and business data into clear, readable prose substantiated with research and interviews.

In addition, there are some opportunities for feature articles dealing with rural life, health care and transportation in general interest and farm-life magazines. *Writer's Market* lists publications according to their farm specialty—such as "Crops and Soil Management" and "Dairy Farming"—to assist writers in querying magazines with appropriate material.

Fax (facsimile transmission). An increasingly popular mode of communication, the fax machine is used to transmit documents over the telephone lines. The use of fax devices rose from seventy thousand in 1983 to 1,500,000 in 1988. As with any communication, there are standards of etiquette that should be maintained. Always include a cover sheet with your name, telephone number and fax number. If the transmission of a document doesn't print out clearly or the receiver of the document has further questions, he can contact you.

The National Fax Directory provides fax numbers for more than 160,000 of the nation's most important companies and organizations.

Feature. The newspaper term for a piece of nonfiction intended to involve, teach or amuse the reader by giving him information of human interest rather than news. Features may use some of the conventions of fiction, including plot, symbolism, character and dialogue. They are colorful pieces that deal with real events, innovations, trends, issues and processes, placing an emphasis on the people involved.

Feature writing is not concerned so much with formula (as in the inverted pyramid structure of "hard" news writing) as it is interested in impact. The gamut of subject matter and writing style employed by feature writers is nearly endless, as "feature" becomes an umbrella term for many literary structures. Personality sketches, narratives, interviews, essays, exposés, how-to's, columns, miniature anthologies and reviews may all be considered features.

Ideas for writing features come from having a keen news sense, an awareness of human interests and a healthy curiosity. A successful feature story's coverage must be suited to its news value. Its tone and slant must be appropriate to the article's intended effect. For example, features that grow out of a slumping economy reflect the anxiety and despair of the individuals who are most affected.

Besides local newspapers as potential outlets for feature writing, the annual *Writer's Market* lists thousands of magazine markets for freelance articles. (*See: Article.*)

Federal Communications Commission (FCC). A U.S. government agency that regulates privately owned radio and TV stations, and telephone and telegraph operations. Established by the Communications Act of 1934, the Commission is composed of four members and one chairman who are appointed by the President of the U.S. and serve a seven-year term.

The FCC has the power to issue, revoke and alter licenses. A license is granted to a broadcaster on the basis of "public interest, convenience or necessity."

Some requirements of broadcasters, according to FCC regulations, are that call letters must be announced, sponsors must be identified and equal time to political parties must be given.

Federal Information Center Program, General Services Administration. Writers seeking information or "experts" in virtually any subject area can contact the Federal Information Center Program of the General Services Administration, a primary source of assistance for individuals with questions or problems related to the federal government. Experienced and knowledgeable about the wide range of services provided by the hundreds of departments, agencies and programs of the federal government, the numerous laws and regulations it administers, and the multitude of publications and periodicals available, the FIC staffs can either answer a question within minutes or refer the caller to specific agencies, departments or individuals considered authorities in a particular field.

Federal Information Centers are listed under the heading "U.S. Government" in the white pages of the telephone directory. (*See: Census Bureau, Department of Commerce; Library of Congress.*)

Fees. Fees for one-time editorial/writing jobs vary according to many factors, including the client, the reputation and experience of the writer, and the geographic area. The list of suggested fees provided in "How Much Should I Charge?" in *Writer's*

Market can guide the writer in establishing fees. The article also includes advice on choosing jobs and setting fees. (*See: Book publishing economics; Full-time freelancing, economics of.*)

Additional information: *Jobs and Opportunities for Writers; Jobs for Writers; National Writers Guide to Freelance Rates and Standard Practice.*

Feet. (*See: Verse.*)

Fellowships. (*See: Scholarships, fellowships, internships.*)

ff. Abbreviation for *folios.* It appears as lower case letters (ff) in indexes and footnotes after the first page number of the subject being referenced, when the subject is discussed on a considerable number of pages that are consecutive or in proximity. The abbreviation *ff.* connotes "and the following."

Fiction. This term refers to literary work created in the writer's imagination and designed to entertain readers. Although it is a work of imagination, it may incorporate large amounts of factual material, and in many genres, e.g., the historical novel and many modern suspense-thrillers, the appeal of the story resides as much in the factual background as in the imaginative narrative. The term *fiction* is generally applied to novels and short stories, but its ingredients are found in other genres, including poetry, drama, film, folklore and fairy tale. The earliest known *written* fiction, some say, is the Egyptian story "The Two Brothers," which dates from around 3200 B.C.

Fiction is an illusion of reality woven from concrete sensations and pertinent observations of the human experience. It is usually built on a character searching for a solution to a problem. The fiction writer's story, presented from a specific viewpoint, grows out of an appropriate setting where believable characters and significant, complicating events are developed through vivid narration and incisive dialogue; the suspense and action of fiction is directed toward the resolution of the initiating problem. Though novels and short stories employ constructions unique to themselves and frequently differ in length, depth and impact, they share these common elements that distinguish them as fictional works. Although formats change, the art of storytelling never seems to go out of vogue.

There are many molds for fiction writing, but traditionally, the writer plots a main character against at least one of three adversaries: nature, another character or characters or himself. Science fiction, westerns, mysteries, erotica—all works of fiction—are fashioned from the writer's creativity.

Mainstream, or commercial, fiction uses conventional storytelling devices, such as exposition, mood and a series of conflicts leading to a crisis and finally a climax. It may also consist of a story in which characterization may overshadow plot and the story "problem" pivots on the unusual.

Conversely, experimental fiction is more interested in the form and structure of the work as a literary composition and less concerned with developing a dramatic story line. Experimental fiction writers concentrate on literary style, narrative technique and symbolism to achieve a unified work.

Though fiction currently represents about 10 percent of the title output of the commercial book publishing world, the potential market for stories and novels is growing with the proliferation of small, independent publishing houses and literary/little magazines. In addition, specialized magazines continue to offer outlets for fiction material. *Novel & Short Story Writer's Market* is a reference book with up-to-date listings of fiction publishing markets, their terms and payment rates. It also carries articles on fiction writing composed by professionals in the art. (*See: Category fiction; Literary fiction vs. commercial fiction.*)

Fiction, indexes to. Writers who want to look up a specific short story or novel have several research sources available. Fictional works may be located through specialized indexes, which are either general or specific in category. Two standard indexes of general fiction are the *Fiction Catalog* and the *Short Story Index*. The *Fiction Catalog* lists both novels and anthologies of short stories, while the *Short Story Index* lists short stories that have appeared in anthologies—whether of a single author or several authors.

References to fiction in the detective and mystery categories are included in *A Catalogue of Crime*, arranged by author, title and series. The two-volume *Science Fiction and Fantasy Literature* leads the researcher to works of science fiction. Volume One is indexed by author, title, series and awards; Volume Two lists works by contemporary science fiction authors, through 1991. References in *Science Fiction Story Index* are listed by story title, but the book also has an index to authors. The *Science Fiction & Fantasy Book Review Index,* which lists book reviews of science fiction works and fantasy works, is indexed by author of the book and includes a title index.

Fiction terms. (*See: Adult fiction; Adventure story; Antagonist; Anticlimax; Antihero; Atmosphere; Character; Climax; Conflict; Crisis; Dark moment; Description; Dialogue; Emotion in writing; Empathy; Endings, story; Erotica; Ethnic fiction; Experimental fiction; Fairy tale; Fantasy in children's literature; First novels; First-person point of view; Flashback; Flashforward; Flat character; Foil; Folktale; Foreshadowing; Formula story; Gimmick; Gothic; Imagery; Interior monologue; Legend; Literary fiction vs. commercial fiction; Mainstream fiction; Motivation; Mystery story; Myth; Narrator; Nonfiction novel; Novel writing; Novelization; Novels for young people; Novels, marketing; Occult; Picaresque; Plot; Point of view; Popular fiction; Protagonist; Roman á clef; Romance novel; Romantic suspense novel; Round character; Scene; Science fiction; Second-level story; Setting; Short stories for young people; Short story; Short-short story; Stock character; Story line; Stream of consciousness; Subplot; Symbolism; Theme; Third-person viewpoint.*)

Fictional biography. The biography of a real person that goes beyond the events of a person's life by being fleshed out with imagined scenes and dialogue. The writer of fictional biographies strives to make it clear that the story is, indeed, fiction and not history.

Fictionalizing nonfiction material. This technique is used to disguise the identity of a quoted source in an article. Fictionalization is used as a means of protecting the source, the writer and the publication from lawsuits. In highly personalized or controversial accounts, the writer informs readers that the character/subject has been masked. He may use an alternate first name or a first name and last initial for identification. In addition, the writer may paraphrase one or more quotes to protect the anonymity of a source who uses a habitual expression. Another instance of fictionalization occurs when the writer inserts his own opinion by crediting it to a nondescript "observer" in the piece to avoid openly editorializing about an issue.

In addition to fictionalizing people, a writer may also use a generic rather than a specific name for a locale—e.g., "a small Midwestern farm town"—or a group—e.g., "a local fraternal organization" instead of the Rockford, Iowa, Rotary Club.

The great danger of fictionalizing nonfiction lies in jeopardizing the writer's and the article's or book's credibility. Therefore, a writer attempts to maintain a balance between attribution to "real" names and anonymous people. In any case, the editor should be informed about the writer's use of fictionalization and the reasons for it. (*See: Composite character; Faction; New Journalism; Nonfiction novel; Symbolic quote.*)

Fictitious names. When a work of fiction is based on a true incident, the author should give fictitious names to the characters, as well as change their occupations, the setting, etc., to avoid risking a lawsuit for invasion of privacy. The changes should be substantial enough that the real identity of the fictionalized character is not obvious. Author Gwen Davis Mitchell learned that lesson the hard way when she was sued by Dr. Paul Bindrim in connection with her novel *Touching*.

Fictitious names are also sometimes given to people mentioned in nonfiction articles (e.g., "Susan Smith—not her real name—is one of the more than fifty teenagers to appear before the County School Board in connection with . . .") to protect a source's privacy and/or to prevent the reporter/writer from losing a future source. (*See: Privacy, invasion of.*)

Figures of speech. Writing techniques that furnish the writer with a nonliteral means of conveying images. Figures of speech include hyperbole, irony, metaphor, metonymy, onomatopoeia, oxymoron, paradox, personification, simile, synecdoche and understatement.

When used effectively, figures of speech are appropriate to the characters and the setting of a story. A skillful writer uses them selectively and in moderation. (*See: Hyperbole; Imagery; Irony; Metaphor; Metonymy; Onomatopoeia; Oxymoron; Paradox; Personification; Simile; Synecdoche; Understatement.*)

Filler. A filler is a short, nonfiction item used by an editor to "fill" a column or page. The hallmark of filler material is its variety of subject matter. Fillers succeed more often because of their spontaneity than deep literary merit. They are informative morsels of writing that generate an instant reaction/rise from intended readers. They may be jokes, light verse, little-known historical facts, clever epigrams, word puzzles, helpful hints, crazy definitions—even distinctive photographs tied into the interests of a unique readership.

A popular filler with some editors is the humorous sign, such as this one mentioned in *Reader's Digest*: "Notice at Everglades National Park: 'Fishing in this area reserved for the birds.' " (Any issue of *Reader's Digest* carries a variety of fillers at the ends of articles.)

Ideas for fillers come from folklore and proverbs, from signs of a season and political shenanigans, from typographical errors and overheard conversations. Fillers may also be news clippings transformed into "newsbreaks"—short tidbits, not otherwise covered in a particular publication, but interesting for the acknowledgment of some technological breakthrough, medical advance or significant development.

Fillers appear in countless publications: newspapers, general- and special-interest magazines, and newsletters. Radio announcers and disc jockeys use them on their shows. Writers select potential filler markets according to the type of material they use and the characteristics of their readers/audience. Each filler is typed double-spaced, on an 8½" × 11" sheet of paper with the writer's name and address in the upper-left corner of the page. If the filler is a clipping, the publication name and date of issue is also included. *Writer's Market* lists hundreds of publications seeking fillers and specifies their individual payment schedules (usually a flat rate). (*See: Potboiler.*)

Film writing, nontheatrical. Certain public relations, industrial, scientific and documentary movies are produced for selected audiences rather than for use in commercial theaters. When the idea for a nontheatrical film is "sold" to a sponsor, the script is usually written in four stages. The first is a synopsis, a brief step-by-step outline of the plot and main action of the film. The second phase is the treatment, a fully developed narrative covering all the principal situations and some key passages of dialogue. The bulk of the research is done in writing the treatment; this is the key to a good script. Equipped with background information, the film writer uses his imagination and organizational skills to determine what will be covered, in how much detail, and in what order. From the treatment a first draft that breaks down the action into sequences and numbered scenes evolves. Finally, the screenplay, also known as the master *shooting script* or *scenario*, is written as a detailed, two-column shooting outline. Generally, all visuals, including scene description and camera directions, are grouped into one column, and all corresponding audio portions, including narration, music, sound effects and dialogue, are placed in the other. As literature, the script, like other manuscripts designed for the ear, does not usually stand too well on its own; rather, its merits lie in how effectively it serves as a blueprint for the multifaceted efforts involved in producing a film.

Film writing as a freelance venture is most often done for an inde-pendent sponsor such as the armed forces, various government agencies, boards of education or educators' associations or business and industry. Writers land film contracts by locating producers who are investigating particular market needs and using their own expertise and reputation to propose and "sell" an idea to a potential backer. Both producer and writer consult with a client, who outlines a purpose, budget and target audience.

Payments for nontheatrical film writing vary depending on the sponsor, but working for a production company currently yields the writer a percentage of the film's production cost. If, for example, production cost is $1,500 per release-minute, the writer would earn from $250 to $350 per requested scripted minute of film. *Writer's Market* lists rates for film writers in the audiovisual section of "How Much Should I Charge?" (*See: Audiovisual communication; Screenwriting.*)

Film writing, theatrical. (*See: Screenwriting.*)

Films. (*See: Screenwriting.*)

Financial writing. This category comprises articles related to business management, economics, finance, and case histories of successful businesses. Financial writing is one rib of the business-writing umbrella. It is clearly written and packed with verified facts, slanted for business professionals and other interested individuals. It may put the "human element" into business analysis; prepare reports for investment houses, managements, political decision makers; try to provide money-making ideas; or suggest profitable ventures for its readers.

The financial writer has a basic business "sense"—acquired through formal education, practical experience or informal study. Knowledge of the stock market is a common foundation; the writer then develops a financial specialty, since editors often look for writers who can add depth and focus to their work. A financial writing specialty may take any of several forms, including coverage of an industry (steel, oil), a profession (international business, banking), a discipline (accounting, investing, marketing), a category of investment items (precious gems, wines) or a geographical area (the Southwest, Canada). Writers keep current in their field by regularly reading industry publications, union newspapers, *The New York Times* and *The Wall Street Journal*. They gather accurate economic information from government offices, public relations agencies and professional societies associated with their writing specialty.

Financial writing appears in national and regional business magazines, newspapers and various trade magazines, where articles aim at informing readers about the state of their industry. Editors usually welcome technical articles on the latest developments in the field and case histories showing how successful members of the trade operate for efficiency and profit. *Writer's Market* lists specific outlets for financial writing in its "Business Management" and "Business and Finance" sections. (*See: Business writing.*)

First amendment. (*See: Freedom of the press.*)

First draft, revising and rewriting. The first draft of an article or story is the first typed version of the manuscript from beginning to end. No specific number of drafts can be said to result in a good manuscript; different writers complete their work by different methods. Some do several rewritten drafts of each manuscript, while others consider the first draft with minor revisions the final copy.

Although there are no set rules regarding manuscript revision, certain standard methods are widely used by writers. For example, it can be helpful to set aside the first draft for a day or more before rereading it, and to reread it in a different location from the one in which it was written. Rereading the drafts aloud to oneself or to another person can uncover slow or weak spots. Many writers have a tendency to reread the first draft, page by page, as it is written. This time-consuming method of revision is not as efficient as the alternate method suggested above, but some writers work best this way. Anyone who reads a page at a time should not forget at the end to go through the whole manuscript one more time. Focusing on one page at a time may result in small repetitions or contradictions from page to page; the writer needs to step back, figuratively, and look at everything all at once.

In editing his own work, much of an author's revision is accomplished through deletion and condensation. First, the author eliminates redundancies, irrelevancies, too-obvious statements, and unnecessary words and circumlocutions. Next, he assesses the logical order of the remaining elements of the work. Some writers, for example, color-code their first draft with a highlighting pen to emphasize the major elements of an article or story and to make sure the structure best serves the point they're trying to make. The author's next step is to add any necessary new information. Checking word choice should be the emphasis the next time he reads through; during this part of the revision, he looks for imprecise verbs and weak nouns needing too many modifiers. The final stage of revision finds the author concentrating on consistency of tense, verb agreement and other grammatical points, as well as punctuation and spelling.

Some changes needed in the first draft can be prevented by completing all necessary research before beginning to write.

Writers with word processors, of course, have several tools which make revision easier. (*See: Criticism of manuscript; Self-criticism.*)

First novels. While approximately five thousand novels are published each year, only one to two hundred on the average are by previously unpublished authors.

Although first novels represent only about 3 percent of the new books published annually, publishers still seek out the best prospects from the manuscripts they receive because the beginning novelist who shows promise today is likely to generate income with subsequent works.

In general, first novels receive little promotion and few reviews. Advances may range from only a few hundred dollars in the case of those publishers selling mainly to libraries, to a few thousand dollars. Since first novels are not promoted or reviewed, most don't yield enough income to pay back the advance to the publisher. The *median* print order on a first novel is forty-five hundred copies. More optimistic results for both author and publisher are possible with genre fiction—romance novels, science fiction, mysteries.

The beginning writer who intends to submit a novel for publication can consult publications that will direct him to publishers who handle first novels. *Novel & Short Story Writer's Market*, and *Writer's Market* list such publishers. *Booklist* and *Library Journal* review first novels. (*See: Book publishing economics; Booklist; Figure 17.*)

First-person point of view. The manner of writing that makes use of the pronoun ''I'' and thus lets the reader experience events through the viewpoint either of the main character in a piece of fiction or through the nonfiction writer himself. Writing from the ''I'' viewpoint has certain advantages. In the confession story, for example, designed for intense reader identification, the narrator can easily reveal her emotions: "I discovered that my husband was lying to me for the first time."

In nonfiction, personal experiences, inspiration, nostalgia and humor pieces often work best when told in the first person.

Writer's Market listings specify whether the editors prefer or prohibit first-person material. (*See: Point of view.*)

FIGURE 17

FIRST NOVELS

WHAT DOES ST. MARTIN'S PRESS LOOK FOR IN A FIRST NOVEL?

Ruth Cavin, St. Martin's Press

St. Martin's publishes a great deal of adult fiction, and it varies widely. (We don't publish juvenile or young adult fiction.) Our books can be literary or commercial novels, mysteries, Regencies, historicals, Westerns, women's novels, thrillers, comic novels, serious novels—just about any kind of fiction. Not many short story collections, but some; not much horror and science fiction, but some. The occasional horror or science fiction book is chosen on a book-by-book basis—if something really strikes an editor.

We read everything that comes in, but not all of everything. It's often easy to tell relatively early in a manuscript that it's not suitable for us. For example, it may be acceptably written but mundane and run-of-the-mill; or something I personally don't like, such as a psychic solution to a real mystery; or just plain bad writing ("the door to the bar yawned over his left shoulder").

We accept work directly from authors, including nonpublished authors. With agents, we are aware of our continuing relationships and we know that they have screened their properties before offering them to us, so they may get a little faster service. But eventually everything is looked at. It is best to address your submission to a particular editor; check the *Writer's Market* or *Literary Market Place* in your library.

Submissions pour in constantly, so we can be extremely choosy; the nothing-wrong-with-it-but-nothing-special-about-it-either manuscript goes back at once. The one that cries Take me! Publish me! has several things going for it. One is that the author has chosen to present the story with a fresh and uniquely personal approach. Two examples: *Bay of Sorrows* by Gaylord Fold or *Foxglove* by Mary Anne Kelly.

We need characters. Readers can't really care what is happening in a story if they can't believe in the people, if the characters don't speak and act like honest-to-God human beings. We need a sense of place and some detail that has meaning and isn't just tossed in. We need stories with conflict and motivation and an inner logic. (Plot problems, though, are the easiest to solve; it's two-dimensional characters and clunky writing that are virtually hopeless.) It doesn't matter what style the author's voice is in: long, complex sentences, or very laconic prose and dialogue. Two St. Martin's Press authors with divergent styles are Les Roberts and Laurie R. King.

In evaluating work submitted to us, we must do it from two points of view: is it a good book, well done, interesting and satisfying? And then, do we feel that enough people will want to buy it and read it to make it profitable for us and for the author? (Alas, sometimes the first condition is fulfilled but not the second.)

From a practical point of view, we more readily publish a first novel if it is a "category" novel—a mystery, a western, whatever. No matter how good a noncategory or "mainstream" novel might be, the public won't know anything

FIGURE 17 (CONTINUED)

about it unless we have felt justified in putting a large (and expensive) promotion effort behind it, or unless lightning strikes in the form of numerous rave reviews—the chances of which are very slim indeed. On the other hand, people who read mysteries don't have to know the author. They'll buy a mystery simply because that's what it is.

We are always looking for an author who has something to say and says it in a way that no one else quite does. This goes for serious literary works and for entertainments and commercial fiction as well. We don't expect future Nobel Prize winners with every submission; we do expect a well-crafted book on whatever level it might be.

Ruth Cavin is senior editor/associate publisher with the Thomas Dunne imprint at St. Martin's Press.

First-person short story. The fictional account of an event, told as if it really happened. The story may, and frequently does, have a basis in a personal experience; the fiction writer has the privilege of bending the truth; adding, combining or eliminating characters; and altering background and actual character traits. He exaggerates to build drama and suspense, and shapes the conclusion into what he thinks should have happened. He tells something of importance that—for better or for worse—has changed the character. The lesson—the character growth—may be subtle, but it is there.

First-person stories are used in every genre, from the confession to the detective, from the general to the literary. The writing style varies with each field.

Writers sometimes confuse the first-person short story with the *personal experience article.* (*See: First person, use in nonfiction; Magazine articles, types of; Personal experience.*)

First person, use in nonfiction. Although most magazine articles are written in the third person, a few article types lend themselves to narration in the first person. Many authors of personal experience, inspirational, nostalgia and humor pieces write in the first person for greater personal identification with the reader. Many of the listings in *Writer's Market*—such as those in the "Sports: Hunting and Fishing" category—specify whether the editors prefer or prohibit first-person material.

First printing vs. first edition. Writers sometimes confuse these two terms. There may be several printings of a first edition. But once a book is revised it becomes a second edition; it, too, may undergo several printings before it is revised again. The number of printings of a particular edition is usually shown on the copyright page.

First reader. The first person at a publishing house to read a book proposal or manuscript. Procedures vary widely from publisher to publisher, but usually an unsolicited, unagented manuscript (which most manuscripts are) is put in the *slush pile.* A junior editor or editorial assistant pulls a manuscript out of the pile, reads it and prepares a brief report summarizing the book, appraising its potential market and suitability for the publisher, and recommending either rejection or further consideration. A book recommended for consideration moves on to a more senior editor—sometimes, at a small house, the editor in chief. (*See: Book publisher reader's report; Figure 7; Slush pile.*)

First serial rights. (*See: Rights to manuscripts.*)

First vs. second serial rights. (*See: Rights to manuscripts.*)

First works, contests for. Publishing companies and other organizations offer contests exclusively for writers who have not yet been published in a particular genre. Such contests may be for novels, poetry or scholarly articles. The annual directories—*Writer's Market, Poet's Market* and *Novel & Short Story Writer's Market*, in their "Contests and Awards" chapter, and *Literary Market Place*, in its "Prize Contests Open" category—detail submission requirements and furnish the names and addresses a writer needs to enter these contests. (*See: Contests, writing.*)

Flashback. A fictive device in which a scene is interjected into the narration to relate events or situations that occurred prior to those just presented or before the work opened. It is relevant information adding to the reader's understanding of the story twists and characters' motivations: Flashbacks dip into the past to give meaning to the present. Because fiction often opens on a dramatic high note, a flashback may also be a necessary way of explaining how the story got to the opening point.

Flashback, to be effective, must be inserted into a story without interrupting its continuity and mood. Its association with the elements of the tale is organic, growing naturally out of the present action. In a short story, flashback may take the form of a one- or two-sentence glimpse into a character's memory. (For example: "The sparkling pearl on her finger took me back to the oceanside where we had scavenged for oysters.") In a novel, it could be a highly theatrical incident brought to the foreground by a conversation, action or emotional response by the character to some surrounding. It may take shape as a dream sequence or a character's reverie in response to a question about his past. In some cases, the flashback technique may compose much of the work itself, e.g., Tillie Olsen's novella *Tell Me a Riddle.*

Shorter fictional works (and especially children's literature) usually take fewer glances into the past, to avoid confusing the reader by frequent juggling of time sequences. In novels, however, flashbacks may be incorporated throughout the book into episodes that stir interest and provoke insight. In any case, the skill of using flashback rests in balancing the present with only those telling events of the past that give the story credence.

Flashforward. A fictive technique, generally employed at the end of a story or novel, that provides an inkling as to what will happen or how the characters will handle themselves in the future. The conclusion of *Gone with the Wind* uses flashforward, through the following lines of dialogue spoken by Scarlett: "I'll think of it all tomorrow, at Tara. I can stand it then. Tomorrow, I'll think of some way to get him back. After all, tomorrow is another day." (*See: False plant; Flashback; Plant.*)

Flat character. A flat character is a fictional person the writer has described with only one distinguishing trait; the flat character can be a major character in a short story or a minor character in a novel. Sometimes such a minor character does not participate significantly in the main plot and is just used as a foil. But if an editor has criticized a *main* character as "flat," the author should consider reconstructing the character in greater depth, with plausible motivations and a stronger change in his situation to produce a better semblance of reality. (*See: Foil; Round character.*)

Fog Index. This readability formula was designed by the late Robert Gunning, an American writer, editor and writing consultant. It is used to measure the level of reading skill that a reader needs to be able to understand a given piece of writing. Using this method, one considers length of sentences and of words to determine the complexity of a passage. A writer might wish to calculate the Fog Index of a publication he wants to write for, to see if his style conforms.

The Fog Index can be calculated in three steps. First, the average sentence length (the total number of words divided by the number of sentences) is determined. (Each complete thought, or *independent clause*, contained in a compound sentence is considered a separate sentence.) Then, the number of hard words is found: this step is accomplished by finding the number, per one hundred words, of words having at least three syllables. Proper names, compounds formed from short, easy words, and verb forms whose suffixes give them three syllables, should be omitted from this count (even though they may have three or more syllables).

The Fog Index of the passage is determined by adding the average sentence length to the percentage of hard words and multiplying that sum by .4. The resulting numeral represents the school grade level that corresponds to the reading skills necessary to understand the piece.

This entry, for example, contains 13.6 percent hard words; 18.6 words is its average sentence length. The sum of these two figures multiplied by .4 yields 12.8 as the Fog Index. (*See: Readability formulas.*)

Foil. In fiction, a foil is a contrasting person or thing that makes another seem better or more notable. Foils are often flat characters (the meek, understanding butler who worships his powerful master) or stock characters (the villain of a gothic romance). In the mystery, the foil usually plays a reversal role, appearing to be something he is not. (*See: Character; Flat character.*)

Folio. The most current use of *folio* is to mean page numbers, but it also designates a book's title, chapter titles and page numbers—or a magazine's or newspaper's name, date and page numbers—that run in the top or bottom margin of each page.

Folio also means a sheet of paper folded to form four book pages, or an outsized book format of any of several dimensions over a foot in height.

Folio is also the title of *The Magazine for Magazine Management*, published at 125 Elm St., New Canaan, CT 06840.

Folk music. Music inspired by the traditions, experiences and emotions of the people of a particular region, country, era, etc. It is usually written in ballad form.

Folktale. An anonymous, timeless and placeless tale that expresses the rituals, traditions and beliefs of common people. Charles Perrault's *Les Conte de ma Mère l'Oye* were among the first folktales published. There are many classifications of folktales: animal tales, magical stories, regional tradition, supernatural stories and pioneering superheroes. (*See: Fable; Fairy tale; Legend; Myth; Tall tale.*)

Food/recipe writing. This includes both articles and cookbooks giving recipes tested by the writer. Recipes, which can be either for one category of dishes or a variety of dishes grouped by category, are preceded by a short introduction about food. Articles are succinct and clear. They usually contain visual descriptions but are not so flooded with adjectives as to intimidate a novice cook. Titles, often snappy, are indicative of the content and scope of the pieces they accompany, e.g., "Master Meals With Your Microwave," "Easy Meals for Campers" and "Staying Healthy Without Meat." Typical elements of a piece containing recipes are nutritional values, an indication of the ease of preparation, and instructions on when and/or how to serve the dishes described.

Food articles and cookbooks contain recipes presented in any one of at least three ways. The *conventional-recipe-writing formula* lists all the ingredients and then in paragraph style explains the procedure. The *conventional-command pattern* differs only in that instead of paragraph format, it enumerates the sequence of steps required to prepare the dish. The *action-step-command method* of recipe writing retains the listed ingredients followed by a general procedural explanation (e.g., Mix liquids; stir in batter) that eliminates repeated mention of specific ingredients.

Regardless of the recipe presentation, each culinary formula contains the following basic information: title, yield (in portions or total quantity), ingredients, method of preparation, cooking times and temperatures, and pot or pan and utensil specifications.

Food articles that appear in national cooking and general interest magazines are usually written by staffers. (Some national magazines do accept recipe submissions.) But freelance food writing may be solicited by regional magazines, smaller circulation special-interest magazines and newspapers. In addition to standard articles about food, they may also feature pieces on recipe swapping, eating habits, etc. The "Food and Drink" section of *Writer's Market* and the freelancer's own local newspaper yield specific opportunities for submitting articles and/or tested recipes.

Some publishers specialize in cookbooks of American and foreign cuisine, or books aimed at those who prefer a particular style of food. Besides recipes, cookbooks may also contain articles on cooking trends and the food industry, and selected tips on the art. Writers with cookbook ideas or proposals are advised to contact first the publishers of the cookbooks that they themselves own and use.

Footnote. A citation of a reference source, or an explanation of text material, that is placed at the bottom of a page. The reader is directed to a footnote by a superscript number that is placed (like an asterisk) after the appropriate material in the text and before the footnote itself. Contrary to the style used in scholarly journals, magazine articles and trade books exclude footnotes that cite references. However, editors expect writers to keep records of their sources should a question arise on which the editor might like clarification. (*See: Bibliography.*)

Foreign agents. Most American literary agents work with agents abroad in selling authors' material. In cases in which two agents collaborate, the commission paid by the author is 20 percent, instead of the usual 10 percent afforded a single agent.

Authors who have no agent are represented in foreign sales by their publishers who are themselves represented by agents. *The International Literary Market Place* lists, country by country, the publishers and literary agents representing authors. Novels, nonfiction books and occasionally plays are the works most often sold abroad; few agents are interested in marketing shorter work such as articles and short stories.

Foreign markets. Foreign markets are potential buyers of literary works published in this country. Foreign markets include book publishers, book clubs, magazine editors and radio and TV producers. In some foreign countries, a book club may acquire the translation rights to a book, then sell the actual publication rights to a publisher in its country and language.

Practices surrounding the sale of books, magazine articles and scripts to foreign countries are not always standardized, and many variables affect the sale of foreign rights. In most cases, book translation costs are paid by the foreign publisher. However, the overall commission paid to agents for rights sold abroad is higher than for those negotiated at home. International book fairs annually bring publishers, editors, translators and agents together to buy and sell their goods.

It is important that authors' contracts specify who has the authority to contract with foreign publishers.

When a domestic publisher handles the sales negotiations overseas, the royalties are usually split, with 75 percent going to the author and 25 percent to the publisher. If the author's agent negotiates the sale, he frequently works through a foreign counterpart and each of them receives 10 percent. If an author owns all foreign rights to his work and sells these foreign rights independently, he earns *all* the royalties.

Royalty scales and advances against royalties vary among countries, with West Germany and England on the high end (an important title may bring 8 percent on the first five thousand copies sold, 10 percent on the next five thousand, and 12 percent on sales beyond that). Poorer and less literate countries frequently pay much less and may not report book sales figures regularly. Therefore, the author dealing with overseas markets attempts to secure as much advance as possible from foreign publishers. (Some publishers offer a flat rate.) In the case of specialized textbooks and other titles with limited marketability, an author may settle for an advance of only a few hundred dollars.

In addition to book sales, U.S.-published articles, short stories, plays and scripts may appear in foreign markets. *Reader's Digest,* for example, acquires world rights to any manuscript it buys, and its foreign editions often reuse the articles. Authors who sell only first North American serial rights to a U.S. magazine may sell their manuscripts abroad to publications accepting previously published material. Foreign magazines often have set fees for one-time publication of articles and stories.

A list of English-language foreign newspapers appears in *Editor & Publisher Yearbook,* and some English-language foreign magazine and book publishers are listed in *Writers' and Artists' Yearbook.*

Regarding the sales of writing for films, radio and TV, the Writers Guild of America (East and West) maintains liaisons with some foreign writers' guilds and gives assistance to authors negotiating contractual arrangements with foreign producers. The Guild is listed in this book.

Additional information: *International Literary Market Place.*

Foreign rights. Subsidiary rights to publish a work outside its country of origin. Foreign rights include translation rights, the right to publish a work in a particular country, or worldwide rights exclusive of the country of origin; the author/publisher contract specifies which rights a publisher buys and which rights the original author retains. Foreign rights are negotiated by the author's agent, if he has one; by his publisher, if he has no agent.

Foreshadowing. (*See: False plant; Plant.*)

Foreword. A brief commentary, included in a book's front matter, in which the author or another person remarks on the book's contents. A foreword is sometimes written by a well-known author or authority to add credibility and sales appeal to the work. Although the publisher often makes arrangements for the foreword to be written, the author's suggestions about experts in the book's particular subject field are usually welcome. (*See: Introduction; Preface.*)

Formal writing style. Formal writing style is characterized by complex sentence structure and a sophisticated vocabulary. Contractions are rarely used, and punctuation follows standard rules. In addition, formal style avoids slang and trendy phrases. It is used in professional journals, scholarly works and some textbooks; although a few writers using a formal style (such as Lord Chesterton and Winston Churchill) are widely read and enjoyed.

Formal style in magazine articles is less in demand than the more conversational, informal style. Examples of extremely formal writing can be found in legal and business documents; however, such documents are coming more and more under fire as consumers object to their obscurity. (*See: Informal writing style; Style.*)

Format. This term has four journalistic meanings. It can be a collective word referring to all the physical qualities of a book, magazine or newspaper, including shape, size, typeface, binding, paper quality and margin width. Furthermore, *format* can mean the amount of available space, to which the contents of a given page must be adapted (i.e., either reduced or enlarged). Also, it can refer to the internal structure of an article. In broadcasting, *format* concerns the makeup of a program for TV or radio.

Formula story. This term refers to a genre of fiction writing that uses a familiar theme treated in a predictable way. One of the oldest formula stories is "boy meets girl; boy loses girl; boy gets girl." "Relationship" formulas rely on such universal, emotional appeals. The "loyalty" formula, often used in heroic adventures, emphasizes cooperation and camaraderie in joint survival efforts; the "boy-into-man" formula depicts a young person's growth in responsibility and maturity in a crisis; and the "redemption" formula plots a protagonist struggling to recover his courage.

Formula stories may appear as westerns, commercially successful motion pictures or short stories in popular magazines. The challenge for writers is to find a fresh approach to these story patterns.

Foundations. Grants and fellowships from thousands of foundations represent sources of funding for writers in various fields. Funds are available to those engaged in fiction, poetry, journalism, playwriting and research. Some universities offer "writer-in-residence" fellowships, and writers' colonies such as Yaddo provide food and lodging for artists. The John Simon Guggenheim Fellowships are awarded to individuals engaged in advanced study and research adding to the educational, literary, artistic and scientific influence of the U.S. and promoting international understanding in all the arts.

Grant-getting is competitive, and authors who apply for funding often have work in progress or have published successfully in the past. Planning, perseverance and patience are the mainstays for writers seeking funds for their creative ventures. The publication *Grantsmanship: Money and How To Get It* advises individuals about how to find sources of grants, how to compose application letters and how to use grant directories. It also lists addresses and telephone numbers where information on grants can be obtained.

The *Foundation Directory*, updated annually, is available in most libraries. It provides specific information about existing grant opportunities. The directory is arranged geographically and indexes foundations by city, subject matter and names of donors, trustees and administrators. Entries covering more than 3,100 foundations in the U.S. include names, addresses, telephone numbers, purposes, activities and the grant application procedures for each foundation. In addition, the *Foundation Grants Index* summarizes grants of more than $10,000 made by over four hundred foundations, and the annual series of *Grant Guides* identifies $1,000 foundation grants in sixty-six subject areas. Both of these references are available from the Foundation Center, 79 Fifth Ave., New York, NY 10003. (*See: National Endowment for the Arts; Scholarships, fellowships, internships; Writers' colonies.*)

Frankfurt Book Fair. An annual international publishing exhibition. The Fair, held each October, is an important bargaining arena for both publishers and booksellers, as every year more than eight thousand exhibitors from more than ninety countries display more than 350,000 titles. Publishers meet other publishers, packagers and agents to negotiate foreign rights, translation rights and reprint rights. (Writers lacking an agent to arrange foreign sales of their work depend on their publishers to sell foreign rights at Frankfurt.) Booksellers look over new titles and buy quantities of books. Librarians, literary agents and writers also attend the fair to make contacts, buy or sell manuscripts and get an overview of the worldwide book market.

Generally the fair is a forum for exchanging information or discussing terms and granting options by handshake agreement. Formally contracted agreements follow.

Fraternal magazines. As monthly publications of service clubs and fraternal organizations, fraternal magazines publicize the ideals, objectives, products and activities of the sponsoring association. In addition, their editors seek manuscripts on a variety of general subjects, including case histories of successful members, community concerns and national/international issues, as well as topics of specific interest to members. To be successful, material must be researched, analyzed, and well written in the particular magazine's style (generally upbeat).

Fraternal publications usually solicit freelance nonfiction, photos and fillers, and occasionally solicit humor pieces. Specific requirements of the *Rotarian, Kiwanis Magazine, VFW Magazine* and others are listed in the "Associations" section of the annual *Writer's Market.*

Free photos. Freelance writers can often obtain free photographs from companies, associations and other organizations to accompany articles. When supplying such photographs, the source usually indicates, either on the back of the photographs or in an accompanying letter, the credit to accompany the illustration. (*See: Photographs accompanying manuscripts.*)

Free press vs. fair trial. A central concern both of jurists and journalists is the conflict between the right of a defendant to a fair trial and the right of the news media to press freedom. While journalists contend that they have the right to report on events and the public has the right to be informed, judges believe that publicity before and during a trial can preclude a fair trial by prejudicing jurors and potential jurors.

A judge who foresees a widely publicized trial has several options at his disposal to ensure just treatment of the defendant. A judge may order a *change of venue* (a move to a different locale), or he may postpone the trial. He may restrict the number of media representatives allowed in the courtroom or impose other courtroom rules regarding press coverage. In addition, those involved in the trial may be prohibited from speaking about the case outside of court, or the jury may be sequestered. Judges also have the right to impose gag orders, which prohibit those involved in a trial from informing the press.

Use of broadcasting and photographic equipment in the courtroom has been a similar source of confrontation between the press and the court. According to the Federal Rules of Criminal Procedure, cameras and broadcasting equipment may not be used in *federal courts*, except in the case of a ceremony. Despite the existence of Canon 3A(7), an American Bar Association guideline prohibiting cameras and other broadcasting equipment in the courtroom, thirty states permit cameras and microphones on a permanent or experimental basis.

The free press/fair trial controversy became apparent when the media published either excessive or prejudicial information during the trials or pretrial periods of the following individuals: Bruno Hauptmann, Sam Sheppard, Charles Manson and David Berkowitz. Coverage of these cases is detailed in books and articles on journalism law and journalism theory. (*See: Anonymity of sources; Freedom of the press; Shield laws.*)

Free verse. (*See: Verse.*)

Freedom of information. Laws granting the public access to records and meetings have been passed at federal and state levels. They are rooted in the belief that, since citizens can participate in the government, they have a right to be aware of its activities.

On the federal level, the Freedom of Information Act (FOIA) provides access to records, and the Government in the Sunshine Act requires some federal agencies to announce their meetings in advance and to open them to the public. With passage of the FOIA, the public's right to know was acknowledged, and the burden of justifying availability/secrecy was shifted from citizen to government.

In spite of the FOIA, some kinds of information can still be labeled confidential, including material concerning national security or foreign affairs; trade secrets; personnel or medical data, or other information involving privacy; law enforcement investigatory records (in some circumstances); and information forbidden from disclosure by other laws.

When information is requested from a federal agency, the agency has, under FOIA, ten working days from receipt of the request to respond. If the request is refused, the citizen has recourse by application to the agency's administration, then to the U.S. District Courts. In addition, the agency must inform the requestor of fees involved. A pamphlet that describes how the FOIA can be used is available for $3 from the Reporters Committee for Freedom of the Press, 1101 Wilson Blvd., Suite 1910, Arlington, VA 22209.

Most states have passed open meetings laws and/or open records laws, which vary regarding regulations and penalties.

Freedom of the press. The U.S. Constitution provides for freedom of the press through the First Amendment, which states: "Congress shall make no law . . . abridging the freedom of speech, or of the press. . . ."

Since the Bill of Rights was adopted, almost two hundred years ago, the American press has become increasingly complex. This complexity causes incidents in which conflicts of rights arise. In bringing about compromise in these cases, members of the judicial branch make decisions that sometimes result in qualifications to the First Amendment. The right of the media in courtrooms vs. the right of the defendant to a fair trial, for example, is a continuing legal problem that could not have been foreseen until the advent of electronic mass media.

Interpretations of the First Amendment differ. Some hold to the *absolutist theory*, which states that the amendment grants unconditional freedom (literally interpreting the phrase "Congress shall make no law"). However, since World War I, court cases have resulted in several formulations that determine the extent of protection granted by the amendment.

Cases that have posed conflicts regarding the First Amendment and that have been debated in the courts involve prior restraint (to prevent dissemination of news or commercials), libel, privacy, freedom of information, fair trial, reporters' privilege and obscenity. (*See: Free press vs. fair trial; Libel; Right of privacy.*)

Additional information: *Writer's Friendly Legal Guide.*

Freelance earnings. For financial reasons, most freelance writers begin their writing careers in the evenings and on weekends while simultaneously working for an employer at another job. Many writers are unsure about the point at which they'll be able to support themselves without a steady income from a second full-time or part-time job.

Some freelancers say one should be earning 75-100 percent of his regular gross salary as a freelancer before going full time. Others say that will only wear a person out and that the writer should take the plunge when he feels he has enough sales behind him and enough ideas to move ahead.

Each potential full-time freelancer must examine his own lifestyle and ability to produce salable material and decide accordingly. (*See: Full-time freelancing, economics of.*)

Freelance writer, origin of. The term *free lance* was used in the Middle Ages to refer to a knight or soldier who was paid for fighting and offered his services—i.e., his lance—to any available employer.

Today, *free lance* (also spelled as one word) has evolved into an adjective that describes an editor, writer, or any other full- or part-time self-employed person who works for a number of clients on a temporary or assignment basis.

Front matter. (*See: Book manuscript preparation and submission.*)

Frontispiece. The frontispiece of a book is a page immediately preceding, and usually opposite, the title page illustrating the book's major theme or subject. Frontispieces were used more frequently in the past.

Fulfillment house. A company that fulfills subscription orders for magazines or book orders for a publishing company. The masthead of a magazine frequently shows an address different from that of the editorial offices where subscription orders and changes of address should be sent. That address is usually for a fulfillment house specializing in maintaining magazine subscription lists and producing mailing labels and statistical reports for the circulation director and auditing organizations.

Other fulfillment houses specialize in processing book orders for publishers and book clubs.

Full shot. In motion pictures and TV, a camera direction indicating that the audience sees an entire subject or scene, as, for example, a whole person, or a room and all the people in it. It is typed in all caps. (*See: Television script terms.*)

Full-time freelancing, economics of. No one knows how many writers make their total income from freelance writing. The 1989 readership study of *Writer's Digest* magazine indicated that 7.9 percent of its 239,207 circulation were full-time freelance writers, but it is not known whether some also had other sources of income.

The American Society of Journalists and Authors (primarily magazine and book writers) estimated in 1990 that its members' median gross earnings from full-time freelancing were $26,000.

People who want to freelance full time must earn enough to equal a salaried position and an additional 25 percent to pay their own hospitalization, retirement funds and other fringe benefits normally provided by an employer.

Most writers who consider full-time freelancing build up experience and bylines over several years before attempting to support themselves entirely by freelancing. They also build a bank balance that they can fall back on in their first year or two as a new "business." After an initial period of writing on any subject that appeals to them and that they can sell to an editor, many writers develop a specialty (or two or three) so that editors will call on them with specific assignments. However, writers still originate the bulk of the ideas they sell. Full-time freelancers also try to obtain steady assignments that can guarantee some consistent income—such as editing a company publication on a monthly basis, or doing public relations or advertising for companies without a public relations or advertising agency. The majority of full-time writers are nonfiction writers, not fiction writers, because there are so many more markets for nonfiction. (*See: Specializing as a writer.*)

Additional information: *National Writers Union Guide to Freelance Rates & Standard Practice.*

Fund-raising. Writing for not-for-profit organizations in their continuing efforts to rouse interest and solicit money for new projects and ongoing programs can be a temporary source of income for the writer. Though sometimes less obvious than other markets, fund-raising projects are accessible to freelance writers who can effectively mix fact and emotion into an appeal message for a diverse audience.

The writer, as a publicity person for a fund-raising campaign, works with a campaign director who usually organizes the project and defines its purpose and scope. The writing involves researching the organization or cause, reading reports, interviewing staff and beneficiaries and getting close to the heart of the operations. The writing is designed to persuade a target audience to care enough to donate money to a particular cause. To this end, the fundraising writer prepares agendas and writes speeches, publicity releases, personal and formal letters, volunteers' manuals, posters and requests for foundation grants. He writes honestly and sincerely, keeping emotion and sentimentality under control. He writes campaign brochures that contain all the data and themes to be used in the effort, including captioned photographs that tell their own story.

Fund-raising writers may work for a variety of philanthropic organizations, including charities, hospitals, museums, colleges, churches and community groups. Specific organizations are listed in the yellow pages of the telephone directory under the heading "Social Service Organizations." Fund-raising organizations (listed as such in the yellow pages) may provide services to specific groups and offer opportunities for freelancers in search of experience. The United Fund is also a good source of information about local fund-raising efforts. In addition, the American Association of Fund-Raising Counsel, listed in the *Encyclopedia of Associations*, provides a list of national fund-raising firms and issues a fair-practice code for fund-raisers.

Writers usually charge a flat fee for a fund-raising campaign package that includes many of the kinds of writing described above. One writer's going rate for a complete campaign brochure taking twenty hours to research and thirty hours to write, have approved, laid out, and printed, is currently around $5,000. For the full-time professional fundraiser who both organizes *and* writes the entire campaign, the fee is usually much higher.

Additional information: *Jobs and Opportunities for Writers.*

Gag order. A rule imposed on the press in certain trials and on other people involved in the trial to protect the defendant's right to a fair trial. Gag orders vary from case to case, but generally they serve to prohibit lawyers, judges, law officers and others connected with a trial from revealing information to the press or the public. In each case, the judge bans from becoming public that information he deems harmful to the chance for an impartial trial.

Dr. Samuel Sheppard v. *Maxwell* was tried in the 1950s and appealed to the U.S. Supreme Court in 1966. Fraught with sensationalism and adverse publicity, press coverage of this case inspired a rash of gag orders in subsequent cases of the mid- and late-1960s.

The Dickinson Rule, established in a Baton Rouge, Louisiana, case in 1972, set a precedent for judges to follow. The case involved two reporters who violated a gag order by writing about a public hearing and were convicted for contempt of court. The judge's rationale for his decision to convict was that even though the gag order was unconstitutional in this case, the reporters were wrong in ignoring the gag order: They could have appealed it instead.

According to a 1976 case, *Nebraska Press Association* v. *Stuart*, a judge, to constitutionally justify issuing a gag order, must be able to prove that: (1) intense and widespread publicity will occur; (2) other measures at his disposal, such as change of venue, will not alleviate the problem of excessive publicity; and (3) the gag order will shield potential jurors from prejudicial information.

In 1968, the American Bar Association adopted the Reardon Report, entitled "Standards Relating to Fair Trial and Free Press." It furnishes guidelines regarding pretrial publicity and is aimed at lawyers, court personnel and law enforcement officers.

The story of William Farr, a California reporter who achieved notoriety in the mid 1970s for violating a gag order and later refusing to reveal his source, exemplifies the contemporary court/press clash on this issue. The gag order is one element of the issue "free press vs. fair trial," which is discussed in this book under that heading. (*See: Free press vs. fair trial; Freedom of the press.*)

Gag writing. A gag is usually a short, amusing statement intended to evoke a quick response. Gags supply the captions and ideas for cartoons. They may be casual one-liners, subtle remarks, obvious picture-situations without words or strung-out multipanel ideas. Techniques common to gag writing include the surprise ending ("He popped the big question all right—who do I think will win the National League Pennant?") and the reverse (a German shepherd walking a person).

Gag writers get their ideas from

FIGURE 18

GAG SUBMISSION SAMPLE

John Doe
1234 Maple St.
Anaheim CA 90007   409A

Supermarket. Man pushing loaded shopping cart for his wife, says to another man:

"I estimate the cost per mile to operate one of these things is around $300!"

---

the themes of other successful cartoons, from newspapers and from events in their surroundings, as well as from TV and books. They submit gags to an artist whose style they feel best matches the mood and theme of their ideas. A gag writer may submit ten to twenty ideas at one time, each single-spaced on 3″×5″ cards. He assigns a code number to the gag and puts that and his name and address on opposite corners of the front of the card containing the gag, so that all the information can be seen at once by the cartoonist. If the cartoonist accepts an idea, the gag writer shares in the cartoon's earnings. (*See: Comedy writing; Figure 18.*)

Galley proof. This term describes printed copy in its original typeset form. The type size and column width match the book's or article's format, but pages are not cut to size, and so copy appears on long, narrow sheets.

Galley proof was so named when type was composed by hand in a tray called a galley. Today, even though photocomposition is often the typesetting method, both the terms *galley proof* and *galley* refer to the long sheets of typeset copy used for proofreading.

A book editor sends galley proofs to the author for review and corrections. (*See: AA; Editorial rewriting.*)

Generalizations. Hasty generalizations in an article, the result of insufficient research on the writer's part, are a beginning writer's hazard. For most subjects, one expert's opinion or one sourcebook is not considered a broad enough basis for an article, because the writer and his readers must draw their conclusions after considering a range of viewpoints.

GEnie. An online service owned by General Electric that has more than 400,000 subscribers. Although it has included many other resources and features, at one time GEnie was considered a superior service only for online gaming. (*See: Electronic mail; Internet; Online service.*)

Genre. This term can refer either to a general classification of writing, such as the novel or the poem, or to the categories within those classifications, such as the problem novel, the roman à clef, the ode or the sonnet. The word *genre* is taken from the French and means *type* or *kind.*

Genre fiction is a term used in the publishing industry to describe commercial novels, such as mysteries, romances and science fiction.

Ghostwriting. Refers to the task of composing an article, story, report, book, speech or publication based on the views and insights of another person or organization who is named as or presumed to be the author. Ghostwriters write life stories for famous people who cannot write well or are too busy to take the time; they also write confession stories in the name of the narrator. Ghostwriters may also write books in a series created by another author. This is most common in genre fiction. The "Executioner" series of men's adventure novels, which appeard under the byline of Don Pendleton, is

one example. This arrangement is often referred to as *contract writing.* Ghostwriters get either no byline or perhaps an *as-told-to* or *with* credit, but generally they receive little public acknowledgment whether they are novice writers or established writers/editors. Nevertheless, they are recognized and respected for their ability to write in the voice of another person. Especially in nonfiction, they are also skilled in writing to the satisfaction of both editor and subject. A good speech or other ghostwritten piece should read exactly as if the other person had written it. The ghostwriter's personality/voice is completely hidden.

Freelancers around the country find many ghostwriting opportunities in the public and private sectors of their own states and towns. The domain for ghosted material is limited only by the extent of the writer's imagination. Business reports, inhouse publications, grant proposals, trade journal articles, editorials, newspaper columns and résumés may all be ghostwritten. The writer queries a potential client, demonstrates his proven abilities with written samples, and proposes a writing project designed to give the client favorable exposure. Some ghostwriters may choose to advertise in local newspapers and professional journals as writers providing "professional editorial assistance." They may offer their expertise as consultants, critiquing the writing of others, offering suggestions and reworking/refining materials.

Ghostwriters (especially those writing for prominent clients) often earn good incomes for their efforts, as money, not recognition, is usually their chief compensation. Rates range from $25 to $100 per hour or $200 per day plus expenses. Depending on the assignment, some ghostwriters establish a flat fee; ghostwriters working as consultants generally charge higher rates, as they are offering distilled information and concentrated advice. They may contact management consultants in the area to get an idea of the going rates. Ghosting a book about a company's history, for example, taking six months to complete, may currently bring its writer $13,000-$25,000; rates for commercially promoted books vary according to the publisher, the subject, the reputation of the ghostwriter and the book's marketability. (*See: As-told-to article or book; Collaboration; Ghostwriting speeches.*)

Ghostwriting speeches. Writers ghostwrite speeches for politicians, business executives, educators and community leaders who either cannot write well or don't have the time and/or discipline needed to turn out a good speech.

Markets for ghostwriting speeches are as close to home as a writer's own community. Chambers of commerce, large businesses and community organizations may know people who need speechwriters; local newspapers highlight town leaders and local business figures. The ghostwriter submits a query (writing samples and evidence of knowledge and interest in a subject), where possible delivering it in person, and attempts to establish a need for his writing services. He and the speaker establish a price for the assignment, including at least some percentage of cash in advance. Deadlines are set for a first draft, at

which time writer and client smooth over the speech's rough spots. The final draft is delivered to the speaker on time in some agreed-upon form (e.g., a typed manuscript, a $3'' \times 5''$-card outline). In whatever form, the completed speech is the property of the speaker, who may use it however and as often as he wishes.

Payments for speech ghostwriters vary according to the speaker, his needs and his prominence. National political figures pay $1,000 and more for a speech; local large business owners, sometimes $100 for a six-minute talk. *Writer's Market* lists the current rates for other clients in its "How Much Should I Charge?" section.

Gimmick. This term applies to a short, mystery-type story giving clues to help the reader solve a puzzle or uncover a secret before checking the solution, which is found on another page. Gimmick stories, usually running 500-1,000 words, appear in crossword-puzzle and some game books (e.g., the various Dell puzzle publications). They are written in regular short-story form up to the point of the climax, when the reader is asked an all-important question. The answer to the question is intrinsic to solving the "mystery."

There are at least three kinds of gimmick stories. The crux of the *fact gimmick* pivots on some verifiable common knowledge that the reader must have to unravel the story, e.g., understanding the writ of habeas corpus. The *seasonal gimmick* is based on a fact that ties in with a holiday or special occasion. (Seasonal gimmicks should be submitted to editors six to eight months before the tie-in date.) Another popular gimmick is the *detective story*, based on skillfully concealed clues that require no special knowledge to understand.

A gimmick may also refer to a physical object or phrase that causes the problem in a short story and then leads the major character to a solution. A family Bible may cause trouble between heirs, for example, and then hold the solution to the conflict.

To succeed, the gimmick story must be carefully constructed and free of contrived clues that strain a reader's credence. The most salable stories, according to one publisher, are those whose content and gimmicks are most believable.

Glossary. A glossary is a collection of alphabetically arranged terms in a special discipline, subject or area of interest and usage, accompanied by definitions. Many scientific and technical works include glossaries as appendices. Most books on specialized types of writing for newspapers, magazines, TV, radio, theater, film, etc., contain glossaries. Some glossaries are full-length works in themselves. For example, a work titled *Language of Journalism: A Glossary of Print Communication Terms*, by Ruth Kimball Kent, is a general compilation of terms used in the communications field.

Various professional organizations and interest groups often compose lists of terms related to their occupations. These glossaries often appear in trade magazines aimed at the same readership.

Go-ahead. In the magazine business, when a writer receives a *go-ahead*

from an editor, the latter has expressed interest in the writer's story idea and in reading the finished manuscript. However, a go-ahead is not an assignment: The writer receives no guarantee of publication or payment. (*See: Assignment, writing on; Editor/writer correspondence; On spec.*)

Gospel music. Begun as the spirituals sung by blacks working in the fields of the South, these emotional songs contrasted the hardships and temptations of daily life against the promise of a better afterlife. Eventually, gospel became the music of black church services and is recorded today by gospel singers such as Mahalia Jackson and The Staple Singers.

Country gospel music has its roots both in the traditional gospel music of the South and in the English and American folk hymns of the Appalachians, and is recorded by many popular country artists such as Tennessee Ernie Ford and Glenn Campbell.

Another type of gospel music, *contemporary gospel*, can many times be distinguished from Top Forty or easy-listening music only by its lyrical content, which must still carry a religious message. Popular contemporary gospel artists include Amy Grant and Kirk Franklin and the Family. All types of gospel music are enjoying more popularity than ever before, with many AM and FM radio stations thriving on a totally gospel format. For more information, contact the Gospel Music Association, 1205 Division St., Nashville, TN 37203, (615) 242-0303.

Gossip column. Gossip columns are probably best remembered from their heyday in the 1930s when Louella Parsons and Hedda Hopper wrote syndicated newspaper columns about the Hollywood stars of the day.

Most gossip columns today, such as those by Liz Smith and Marilyn Beck, are about political and entertainment celebrities and are still newspaper syndicated; but some columnists have gone "video" on TV news or magazine shows. There are some opportunities to establish local gossip columns with small newspapers; the successful gossip columnist is constantly wary, however, of material that may cause a lawsuit.

Gothic. This type of category fiction dates back to the late eighteenth and early nineteenth centuries. Contemporary gothic novels are characterized by atmospheric, historical settings and feature young, beautiful women who win the favor of handsome, brooding heroes—simultaneously dealing successfully with some life-threatening menace, either natural or supernatural. Gothics rely on mystery, peril, romantic relationships and a sense of foreboding for their strong, emotional effect on the reader. A classic early gothic novel is Emily Brontë's *Wuthering Heights*.

The gothic writer builds a series of credible, emotional crises for his ultimately triumphant heroine. Sex between the woman and her lover is implied rather than graphically detailed; the writer's descriptive talents are used instead to paint rich, desolate, gloomy settings in stark mansions and awesome castles. He composes slow-paced, intricate sketches

that create a sense of impending evil on every page. Book-length gothics (usually written in first person) are therefore long enough to accommodate lengthy descriptions; many run 65,000-90,000 words.

A variation of the traditional gothic work is the horror or Satanic tale. It concerns elements of the supernatural or parapsychology, such as witchcraft, the occult or ESP Since much remains unknown about these subjects, the writer is free to fully use his imagination. In works such as *Rosemary's Baby* or *The Exorcist*, these gothics penetrate the darker side of human existence, including mental disintegration. Interest in the occult and the power of the human mind periodically brings a resurgence in the market for this type of novel.

Though the popularity of the traditional gothic novel has often wavered throughout the years, there are nevertheless many faithful readers and publishers of this vividly escapist fiction. *Novel & Short Story Writer's Market* lists book and magazine publishers soliciting gothic material. (*See: Romance novel; Romantic suspense novel.*)

Government and the writer. As independent businesspeople, freelance writers are subject to certain local, state and federal regulations, some of which are less obvious than the income tax and social security laws. Writers establishing freelance businesses should check with their local city or village government to learn of any taxes, fees or licenses that may be required of them. For example, a writer who sells a self-published work could be required to obtain a vendor's license, charge sales tax on his book, and remit those taxes to the taxing authority on a periodic basis in the community or state in which he is selling. (*See: Retirement and the freelance writer; Taxes.*)

Government representatives, telephone numbers. Telephone numbers of U.S. legislators are listed in the *U.S. House of Representatives Telephone Directory* and the *U.S. Senate Telephone Directory.* These references are available in many large public libraries, and in all libraries that are regional depositories for government documents.

State legislators' telephone numbers may be obtained from the public information office, the legislative research office or the clerk of the legislature in the individual state. Telephone numbers for these offices, in turn, are listed in the *Book of the States* and the *State Legislative Leadership Committees and Staff* book available in most libraries.

Members of Congress from larger cities often maintain local offices, which can be found under the member's name in the white pages of the telephone book.

Grammar. Grammar is a series of statements that defines the basic structure of a language and how it works. A writer's goal (no matter what his genre or style) is to communicate precisely, logically, directly and clearly. To succeed, he must understand how to use the basic tool of his craft: language. The issue of grammar and correct usage has been a point of division between scholars and writers for many years.

Traditional grammarians in the eighteenth century relied on the fixed rules of Latin to frame the standards of the English language. They also tried to establish innovations of their own in attempts to improve the language, e.g., the "use of *shall* with the first person" rule. Their generally strict view of the "right" way to write came from analyzing formal written English. Their influence filtered down to classrooms, where the problem of applying formal rules to everyday English evolved.

In the 1930s, the structural (scientific) linguists began questioning the validity and consistency of some of the rules and definitions established by the traditionalists. They countered with studies of syntax (structure, form) and semantics (meaning) of language and concluded that language is not and cannot be permanently fixed, so long as it is used by individuals in a changing society. They espoused the general theme that a native speaker of the language could not make a mistake, because he was creating language as he spoke. The linguists concerned themselves more with spoken language than with written discourse.

Being practitioners of language, most writers find neither school of thought completely satisfactory. But by gleaning both viewpoints they can determine the meaning of "good grammar." They often come to believe that good English is not necessarily "correct" English; rather, it is appropriate English. The language of political discourse in a national affairs magazine is correctly formal; the language of an afternoon radio show may be correctly colloquial and spontaneous. Writers of various genres serve diverse and unique audiences. They use grammar dictated by their purpose, their message and their readers.

Indeed, some standards of usage in the name of direct, effective communication are necessary. Writers owe their readers and editors an understanding of parallel construction, the use of commas, the difference between *which* and *that*, the function of subject-verb agreement, the rules for forming possessives and plurals, the meaning of homonyms, and the many other "standards" that ensure clear writing. Whether he writes a business report or an advertising filler, the writer is responsible for the clarity and effectiveness of content.

Writers with solid foundations in English grammar and a sense of what is appropriate use reference tools as aids to better communication. Though the choice is a personal one, depending on the writer's needs and purposes, a few titles are worthy as companions to the essential dictionary. *The Elements of Style*, by William Strunk and E.B. White, is a concise summary of composition and word usage. Some editions of *Roget's Thesaurus* and Theodore Bernstein's *Reverse Dictionary* (a tool for finding words whose definitions are known) are especially valuable. Handbooks of modern English grammar and usage and manuals of style issued by universities and newspapers can be examined to see which might best serve the writer as a desk reference. (*See: Dictionary; Language and style, books on; Usage errors; Writing, books on.*)

Grants. (*See: Foundations; Grants, directories of; Scholarships, fellowships, internships; State arts councils.*)

Grants, directories of. Grants to writers, for certain projects and under certain terms, are available both from government and private sources. Several directories available in most large public libraries provide data on grants for the prospective applicant.

Grants and Awards Available to American Writers lists primarily those grants of at least $500 in value. The section "Grants and Awards," arranged alphabetically, carries listings that give brief descriptions of and amounts of awards. Also included in each listing are the kind of work that is considered, the eligibility specifications, an address where to apply, and whether a nomination is required. This directory is indexed by name of award and name of organization.

The *Annual Register of Grant Support* contains a section called "Literature," which lists information on grants (as well as fellowships, prizes and awards) available to writers; the section "Languages" lists awards available for translation of literature. Listings give data on prizes such as type, amount, frequency and eligibility, as well as number of applicants/contestants who previously applied, information on judges (of contests), deadlines, the person to contact, and an address to which inquiries may be sent. The directory's four indexes are categorized by subject, organizations/programs, geographic area and personnel.

Foundation Grants to Individuals, lists awards given to individual applicants (as opposed to organizations). Listings provide descriptions of the awards, including purposes, as well as financial information, application information and names of officers. The book is arranged in sections according to kinds of prizes, and its indexes are "Index of Grants by Subject," "Index of Grants Restricted by State," "Index of Company-Related Grants," "Index of Grants for Students at Specific Educational Institutions" and "Index of Foundations."

The Foundation Directory contains listings on grants from American nongovernmental sources, in a state-by-state arrangement. Each listing describes the foundation, amount of the grant, availability of scholarships, name of a person to contact and application information. In addition, the directory includes "Index of Foundations," "Index of Foundations by State and City," "Index of Donors, Trustees, and Administrators" and "Index of Fields of Interest."

In the *Directory of Research Grants,* writers may find the sections "Foreign Languages," "Grants for Canadians," "Humanities," "Media," "Poetry, Writing and Journalism," "Publishing Support" and "Theatre Arts" useful. The directory is indexed by name of grant, subject, organization and type of organization.

Gadney's Guide to 1800 International Contests, Festivals & Grants contains sections on writing and print journalism, film and broadcasting. In this directory, writers will find descriptions of awards, people to contact, entry fees and deadlines. This book contains an "Alphabetical Event/Sponsor/Award Index" and a "Subject/Category Index."

The National Directory of Grants and Aid to Individuals in the Arts, International, provides information on grants and the government, private organizations and associations that distribute them. Monetary prizes, awards and competitions are included in addition to grants. Age requirements and other limitations are indicated. Some categories in this directory are film, TV, radio, playwriting, poetry, fiction and photography.

The Grants Register is published every two years primarily for students at the graduate level or above. In addition to scholarships, fellowships and grants, it also includes exchange opportunities and other kinds of assistance from government agencies and international, national and private organizations. The subject index to "Creative and Applied Arts" will be the most useful to writers. (*See: Foundations; Scholarships, fellowships, internships.*)

Graphic novel. Novels that are similar to comic books in that they both contain comic-like drawings and captions. However, original graphic novels deal more with everyday events and issues, rather than with superheroes.

In addition, movies and novels can be *adapted* for graphic novels. Examples are The Walt Disney Company's *The Three Musketeers* and Anne Rice's *The Vampire Lestat.* The former was bound like a traditional comic book, whereas the latter was bound as an oversized book.

Greeting card writing. There are many categories of greeting cards, including alternative humor cards, inspirational cards, mechanical cards that feature pop-up or spring action, risqué cards, and soft-line cards that specialize in expressing personal feelings. Greeting card subject matter ranges from everyday, general wish and occasion cards (birthday, get well, graduation, wedding) to specialized cards (retirement, home purchase, dieting) to cards aimed at particular readers (boss, friend, grandfather).

Though many card companies have staff writers, opportunities do exist for freelancers. "Breaking in" rests with knowing what publishers want and need. Greeting card buyers (90 percent of whom are women) usually pick up a card because of its artwork and purchase it because of its words. To succeed, each kind of card must have a level of "sendability"; there must be a message appropriate for some occasion and suitable for a particular sender-receiver relationship. Inspirational cards, for example, rely on serious, contemplative verse composed in perfect rhyme and meter and filled with concrete images. Humor, on the other hand, depends heavily on the structure of the message. Puns, implied swearing, gift gags, jokes on age and slams all have their places. Humor cards often reward the receiver with the unexpected—an unpredictable punch line, a double entendre or other surprise. Though verse is still popular in greeting cards, new verse forms and upbeat ways of sending traditional messages are essential elements for success. Personal relationship cards (currently an expanding market) usually rely on succinct prose, figurative imagery and/or parallel construction outside and inside the card.

Writers discover market needs by studying greeting cards—their style, variety and format. In addition, they may request tipsheets or market letters outlining specific needs of publishers and requirements for freelance submissions. The National Association of Greeting Card Publishers, 1350 New York Ave., N.W., Suite 615, Washington, DC 20005, issues a list of publishers' specifications for freelance material.

Writers submit greeting card ideas on $3'' \times 5''$ or $4'' \times 6''$ cards in "batches" of ten or fifteen. The verse, prose message or idea is typed or printed in the center of the card with the author's name and address on the back, along with an identification number for the idea. For humorous card ideas, authors may submit dummies with rough designs or clip art that helps get across the message, or just a typed description of the card idea. Once an author establishes himself in the greeting card industry, some publishers may offer him specific writing assignments.

Payment rates vary: The fee for a card idea may be from $50 to $200; an artwork and idea package could earn more. Some greeting card publishers also solicit calendar, postcard and novelty ideas, too. The annual *Writer's Market* lists publishers' submission requirements and current needs. (*See: Figure 19.*)

Guarantee. A term that has several different meanings in publishing. It could mean a fee that a magazine publisher agrees to pay for an assigned article, or one that a book club or paperback house agrees to pay the author and publisher as a

FIGURE 19

GREETING CARD SUBMISSION SAMPLES

Typewritten Form

```
                                          Birthday Age 50


(Pg. 1)    Don't worry about turning 50.
           You can still lead
           a full and exciting life!


(Pg. 3)    But you better hurry.

           Happy Birthday
```

Dummied Card Form

Dad, I walked ten miles
barefoot in the snow
to get you this
Father's Day card!

Which is all
the more amazing
when you consider
that Father's Day
is in June.

Have a Terrific Day!

Label for the Back of Each

Writer's name
Address

Code number for identifying card

guaranteed (nonreturnable) advance against royalties for reprint rights. It also appears in book contracts, indicating the author's guarantee that he is the sole author and originator of the material in the book manuscript, and the publisher's agreement that he will publish the book, distribute it, and sell it in certain territories.

Guide to Literary Agents. This annual directory contains more than four hundred listings of agents who handle nonfiction books, novels, scripts, textbooks, juvenile books and plays. More than just straight listings, articles within discuss how to find the appropriate agent, how to have a successful relationship with that agent, and the Association of Authors' Representatives' canon of ethics.

Writers can also find listings of professional organizations, titles of recommended books and publications and a glossary in the "Resources" section.

The Guild of International Songwriters & Composers. The Guild, formed in 1936, now has more than twelve thousand members who come from around the world. Members are amateur and professional songwriters, musicians, record companies and music publishers. As well as giving members advice and services relating to the music industry, this organization provides contract and royalty information, a free copyright service and *Songwriting and Composing Magazine*. Membership fees are £40 for members outside the U.K. and £28 for members in the country. The offices are located at Sovereign House, 12 Trewartha Rd., Praa Sands, Penzance, Cornwall TR20 9ST, England.

Guidebook writing. Cities of adequate size and with significant historical backgrounds usually produce guidebooks for sale in local bookstores. Writers can either obtain assignments for these books from organizations that produce them (such as historical societies, printing companies, tourism bureaus and chambers of commerce), or they can write them independently and submit the manuscripts to local printers or publishing companies.

Guidebook writing can be compared to newspaper reporting because the writer finds knowledgeable people as sources and gathers information from them. People who may be able to contribute to guidebooks can be found at chambers of commerce, visitors' bureaus, newspaper offices, libraries, archives and churches; these same people may be able to refer the writer to other people whose knowledge he can tap. Guidebook writers sometimes use library resources to obtain background information on subjects they are unfamiliar with.

Guidebook writers are reviewers in that their material is somewhat opinionated, but balanced: They don't omit particular sites or establishments from a guide merely because of their unfavorable impressions.

Since a guidebook is read more often by residents than by tourists, it must report on the out-of-the-way and less prominent establishments in an area, as well as on the best-known ones. Although the extent of coverage varies from book to book (just as each city is individual in character), most guidebooks cover all the following general subject areas: restaurants, shops, bars, sports, the arts, history, annual events (in calendar form) and places for sightseeing. A good, functional index is an essential component of a guidebook. (*See: Restaurant review; Travel writing.*)

Haiku. A Japanese verse form in which the first line of a poem contains five syllables; the second, seven syllables; and the third, five syllables. Rhythmic and metrical patterns are not determined by the haiku form but are left to the poet to include if desired.

Following is an example of the haiku:

Empty fields of snow.
Already sparrows nesting
In the tractor tire
                              M.D. Mastroianni
Modern Haiku

Characteristics of the haiku's content include allusions, comparisons and references to nature. Traditionally, poems in this form are left untitled; however, some translators have chosen to attach titles to them. An index entry referring to an untitled haiku usually consists of the first line of the poem, set in quotation marks.

Journals of haiku, such as *Brussels Sprout* and *Modern Haiku,* consider freelance submissions of this verse form, as do general poetry magazines, literary/little magazines and other types of consumer magazines. *Poet's Market* and *Writer's Market* listings indicate which magazines solicit the haiku. (*See: Verse.*)

Half title. The page of a book that includes only the book's title; it excludes the subtitle, the name of the author and other information. A right-hand page that precedes the full title page, the half title is usually the first of a book's printed pages. Other names for half title are *bastard title* and *pretitle.*

Handwriting. Editors will not accept handwritten material from writers. All submissions must be neatly typed on good bond paper or output from a computer; during the editing process, however, most editors will accept short handwritten corrections. (*See: Author's alteration clause; Manuscript preparation and submission.*)

Hiatus. A period of time, usually from five to thirteen weeks, in which a program or spot under contract leaves the air; programs on hiatus are given a specific date on which they will recommence broadcasting.

Historical article. (*See: Magazine article, types of.*)

Historical fiction. A fictional story set in a recognizable period of history. As well as telling the stories of ordinary people's lives, historical fiction may involve political or social events of the time. (*See: Historical research; Historical writing.*)

Historical research. Both fiction and nonfiction require research for historical accuracy. Including actual persons, events, backgrounds and settings adds credibility and realism to historical writing.

Editors expect writers to provide accurate as well as readable manuscripts. If a writer's error is pointed out by the reader of a magazine or book, the writer may lose future assignments with that editor or publisher. (*See: Historical writing.*)

Historical writing. This category encompasses an assortment of forms, from profound scholarly articles and books to fillers. *Writer's Market* devotes a section to magazines specializing in history, but by far the larger market for historical nonfiction lies in general-interest consumer and trade magazines. While many editors indicate their disinterest in "routine historical pieces," almost any editor will buy a well-written historical piece related to the magazine's content—provided it's slanted properly and is fresh and lively in its approach.

In book publishing, more than one thousand titles in nonfiction history are produced each year. Publishers seeking historical fiction indicate their needs in *Novel & Short Story Writer's Market*.

Suggestions for researching, writing and marketing historical pieces are found in *A Guide to Writing History*, by Doris Ricker Marston; and *Researching, Writing, and Publishing Local History* (published by the American Association for State and Local History). (*See: Historical research.*)

Hold. In a TV or motion picture script, *hold* means the camera should hesitate or "freeze" while focusing on one character to emphasize his reaction to what is happening. The term is typed in all caps. (*See: Television script terms.*)

Home office. (*See: Taxes; Work space.*)

Honorarium. A payment for a manuscript, consisting of a (usually) insignificant amount of money and/or contributor's copies. Honoraria are used almost exclusively by literary/little magazines.

Hook. This term is used in two media to describe essentially the same technique. In a TV script, a *hook* is an event or comment that is placed at the end of an act just before a commercial break, and is intended to hold the audience's attention. *Hook* also refers to an opening scene in a film that piques the viewer's curiosity about the rest of the story. A successful hook ensures that viewers will return to watch the next act. According to screenwriter J. Michael Straczynksi, the hooks in a dramatic program often contain action—a thug blackjacking the hero—while those in comedy programs are usually verbal—a teenager announcing she's been asked to the prom by the class goon.

As used by magazine writers, *hook* indicates the kind of opening paragraph needed to draw the reader into the article or story that follows. (*See: Television writing.*)

Horizontal publication. This term usually applies to a publication for employees in similar jobs within specific trades or professions, i.e., a magazine for salespeople or purchasing agents, regardless of industry. *Sales and Marketing Management* is an example of a horizontal magazine. (*See: Vertical publication.*)

Horror. Howard Phillips (H.P.) Lovecraft, generally acknowledged to be the master of the horror tale in the twentieth century and the most important American writer of this genre since Edgar Allan Poe, maintained that "The oldest and strongest emotion of mankind is fear, and the oldest and strongest kind of fear is fear of the unknown. These facts few psychologists will dispute, and their admitted truth must establish for all time the genuineness and dignity of the weirdly horrible tales as a literary form."

Lovecraft distinguishes horror literature from fiction based entirely on physical fear and the merely gruesome. "The true weird tale has something more than secret murder, bloody bones or a sheeted form clanking chains according to rule. A certain atmosphere of breathless and unexplainable dread of outer, unknown forces must be present; there must be a hint, expressed with a seriousness and portentousness becoming its subject, of that most terrible concept of the human brain—a malign and particular suspension or defeat of the fixed laws of Nature which are our only safeguards against the assaults of chaos and the daemons of unplumbed space." It is that *atmosphere*—the creation of a particular sensation or emotional level—that, according to Lovecraft, is the most important element in the creation of horror literature.

The earliest predecessor of the modern horror genre was the gothic romance novel of the eighteenth century. The nineteenth century produced classic works of horror fiction such as Robert Louis Stevenson's *The Strange Case of Dr. Jekyll and Mr. Hyde* and Guy de Maupassant's *The Horla.*

The nineteenth century also marked the emergence of Edgar Allan Poe, whose work set a new standard of realism in the history of literary horror and had a profound impact on the mainstream of macabre writing.

Early twentieth-century writers of note include Lovecraft, Arthur Machen (*The Great God Pan*), and Algernon Blackwood (*The Willows*). Contemporary writers enjoying considerable success in the horror fiction genre include Stephen King (*Rose Madder, Four Past Midnight, Needful Things*), Robert Bloch (*Psycho, Night of the Ripper*), Peter Straub (*Houses Without Doors, Julia, The Throat*), and Charles L. Grant (*The Black Carousel, In a Dark Dream, In the Fog*) and Dean Koontz (*The Bad Place, The Door to December, Dragon Tears*).

Writers can research current trends in the genre by studying anthologies such as Charles L. Grant's *Shadows*, Kirby McCaulley's *Dark Forces*, and *The Year's Best Horror Stories*, edited by Karl Edward Wagner.

Markets for short horror fiction include several men's magazines (such as *Playboy* and smaller, dedicated publications like *Pulphouse, Weirdbook* and *Worlds of Fantasy and Horror*. Pay rates range from a very low ¼-½ cent per word among the little magazines to as much as $800-$1,000 per story for the major men's publications. Many major publishing companies have published novels with horror/supernatural themes, including Avon Books, Ballantine Books, Dell Publishing, Leisure Books, Doubleday and Viking Press. Other magazine and book publishers soliciting horror fiction—a category that includes supernatural horror as well as psychological terror themes—are listed in *Novel & Short Writer's Market.* (*See: Gothic; Romance novel.*)

Horror Writers Association. (Formerly Horror Writers of America.) An organization with more than five hundred members in two classes: active members, professional writers who have sold work; and affiliate members, professionals in the genre other than writers and those interested in horror.

HWA awards the Bram Stoker Award for Superior Achievement annually. It publishes a bimonthly newsletter and a membership directory. For information, write 5 Solitare Court, Gaithersburg, MD 20878-4123, or e-mail lawrence@clark.net or horrors@aol.com.

How-to articles and books. The how-to article or book offers the reader a description of how something can be accomplished. It is information plus advice. The writer must be able to convey his knowledge clearly and effectively so the reader will know exactly how to proceed.

Many writers consider the how-to market inexhaustible. Newspaper and magazine editors in nearly every subject area are always interested in how-to articles or fillers that have some element of novelty or immediacy. Many editors require accompanying photographs or illustrations, particularly for craft and hobby how-to pieces for which visual representations of instructions are necessary, e.g., "How to Build an Electric Car" or "How to Make and Sell Pine Cone Christmas Ornaments."

The increase of how-to books on the market over the past few years has been remarkable, and their popularity is expected to continue. *The Jump Into Life: Moving Beyond Fear* and *The Way of the Journal: A Journal Therapy Workbook for Healing* are just two of many self-help books (which are essentially how-to's) that reached the best-seller lists. Successful how-to book writers are those who are able to spot an impending trend and get their books out at the peak of public interest.

The Huenefeld Report. A newsletter published every other Monday for small book publishing companies (trade, textbook or mail-order and both commercial and not-for-profit types). Its editorial content is aimed at managerial personnel in book firms. Its publishing address is Box U, Bedford, MA 01730.

Human interest. Refers to emotional appeal in articles. The human interest element is an essential part of all feature writing, adding flavor and depth to the basic information conveyed in the article. A human interest or feature story, as opposed to an objective straight news story, is designed to appeal to readers' emotions. Typical human interest elements include people (a grandmother returning to school for her college degree), animals (a singing dog, a pony that drinks beer), universal desires (love, money, fame) and fears (death, inflation, rumor of war).

Human interest features involving local people and events can be sold to daily and some weekly newspapers. Human interest elements, such as anecdotes or accounts of personal experiences, can support ideas in magazine articles as firmly as facts or statistics. (*See: Feature.*)

Humor. Anything written, spoken or acted out that causes amusement. Based on incongruity, humor consists primarily of the recognition and expression of peculiarities, oddities and absurdities in a situation or action. There are two categories of humor: subject-matter humor (something funny by itself) and literary humor (something funny in the phrasing). The former depends on the writer being able to recognize the humorous thing or event and then report it clearly; the latter relies on the means by which the object or event is described, and is often based on the element of surprise.

Humor lies in the angle or point of view from which a writer approaches a subject. The writer may use one or more of the following devices to create humor: irony, exaggeration, parody, understatement, pun, double entendre, malapropism, manufactured words, spoonerism, pairing of unlike elements, and fancy and imagination.

Editors are interested in humor in both fiction and nonfiction. In addition to all-humor pieces, they sometimes look for some humor in articles that treat serious subjects. The spectrum of publications interested in humorous material is broad, but requirements differ greatly. Like any type of article, humorous pieces must be carefully slanted to the publication's readership and editorial needs.

Writers and editors agree that humor is often the most difficult type of writing to do. It is difficult to market, as well, because what is funny to one editor may not amuse another. Humor pieces are sold on the basis of the finished manuscript rather than a query. (*See: Irony; Parody; Satire; Spoonerism.*)

Humorous article. (*See: Magazine article, types of.*)

Hyperbole. An exaggeration that is so extreme as to render the writer's meaning clearer than it would be in literal form. Hyperbole is used to characterize in the following statement: "Mary changed her mind as often as she inhaled." Other functions hyperbole can serve are to describe someone or something ("His voice was so loud that our relatives on the other side of town called to ask what was going on.") and to establish a mood. (*See: Figures of speech; Imagery.*)

Hyperlink. An electronic mechanism that allows users of the Internet to connect to related pages or articles within the World Wide Web. The user can set off the hyperlink by clicking either on a button or a highlighted word. (*See: Hypertext; World Wide Web.*)

Hypertext. A type of computerized information organization system characterized by its three-dimensional "links" to more information. At first this system was used to organize pre-writing notes for fiction or nonfiction—the electronic version of 3″ × 5″ notecards. Each item of information was placed on a "card" with links to other, related cards, even those in different "stacks."

Hypertext is most visible today in finished writing products—like those that appear on CD-ROMs. In an electronic encyclopedia entry, for example, users can read the main text, and then, by way of clicking on highlighted words, can jump to additional information that is either more in-depth or just a simple definition. (*See: CD-ROM; Hyperlink; World Wide Web.*)

I.D./station I.D. Identification of a radio or TV station, consisting of channel or call letters, or both; the Federal Communications Commission requires it to be broadcast at certain intervals.

i.e. An abbreviation for *id est,* Latin for "that is to say" or "namely." The phrase is used to clarify a point, as in this example: "The directions read, 'Enclose a #10 (i.e., business-sized) self-addressed, stamped envelope with your submission.' "

ibid. An abbreviation for the Latin word *ibidem,* which means "in the same place." It is used in footnotes, with a page number or numbers, to indicate that the same source was cited in the immediately preceding footnote. It replaces all duplicate bibliographic information except page numbers. In a footnote, *ibid* is typed with an initial cap; however, publisher's preferences vary regarding italicizing and use of a comma after this abbreviation. (*See: Op. cit./ loc. cit.*)

Ideas, where to get them. Article and story ideas are everywhere. The writer must simply learn to recognize them.

The writer learns to recognize ideas through a number of sources: observation (using the five senses to become aware of people's ideas and concerns); experience (the writer's own or someone else's); reading newspapers (news stories, editorials, classified ads, columns and features), magazines (expanding on a published article or concentrating on just one aspect of it), books, theses and other printed matter; going to movies; watching TV and listening to the radio; and traveling.

The successful writer constantly analyzes what is going on around him to determine what interests people and why. He seeks ideas that either directly or indirectly appeal to his readers' self-interest and focuses on topics directed toward his readers' basic drives: hunger and thirst, sleep, sexual gratification, etc.

A salable article or story idea must be narrow in focus and specific enough to encourage reader identification. The writer must develop an idea with both depth and significance as he conducts the research and does the writing. Whenever possible the idea should be tied to a news peg or to an impending event or trend. The idea should also be developed with a specific market or audience in mind and slanted toward that market's editorial requirements and readership. (*See: Peg; Slanting; Theme.*)

Idiom. A way of using or constructing language so that the meaning is peculiar to a language or to a singular expression. *Idiom* can also refer to a dialect used by a people, or to the jargon of a trade or profession. An example of an idiom in English is "a horse of a different color," meaning a different matter altogether.

Often, an idiom cannot be translated from one language to another while retaining its original meaning; therefore, an idiom in English may not initially be comprehensible to a foreign person learning English.

Brewer's Dictionary of Phrase & Fable, the *Dictionary of American Regional English* and the *Dictionary of Idioms and Their Origin* explain English-language idioms. (*See: Dialect;* Dictionary of American Regional English.)

Illustration. Although photographs can be used to illustrate a book or an article, the mass media reserve the term "illustration" for art produced with a pen or brush rather than with a camera. Illustrations include pencil, chalk or ink drawings; oil, acrylic, designer-color or watercolor paintings; maps, charts, graphs and tables; and collages.

In printing, illustrations fall into two broad classes: *line* illustrations and *halftones.* A line illustration, the simplest type of illustration and most inexpensive to reproduce, is a drawing composed entirely of solid black areas or lines on a white background.

Halftones, such as photographs, paintings and pencil drawings with shading, contain various gradations of tones and require more complex forms of reproduction. Magazine or book publishers must have original photographs to reproduce from. They cannot use clippings of photographs that appeared in newspapers or other magazines, since screening an already screened photograph produces a moire pattern.

Magazine editors most often use illustrations for short stories and photographs for articles. Nonfiction pieces sometimes are best served by illustrations, however. A how-to piece may be illustrated with diagrams; a travel article may benefit from a map; an article about new-model cars may be accompanied by a graph comparing prices and options.

Editors generally make their own decisions about and arrangements for illustrations once an article is accepted. If the writer is capable of producing professional quality artwork to accompany the manuscript, he should submit samples with the story or article for the editor's consideration. When black-and-white photographs are being offered, it is preferable to send contact sheets so that the editor has a range of samples to choose from. Color should always be submitted in transparency (slide), not color print form. If the writer is not an accomplished artist, he may want to offer suggestions for illustrations—an idea for a cartoon, chart or graph. Such attention to the visual appearance of an article or story may improve the chance of a sale.

Illustrations are also an important element in many nonfiction books. From a production standpoint, illustrations are often the primary feature that distinguishes nonfiction books from novels and makes them more costly.

The amount of responsibility a writer must assume for book illustrations varies according to publisher. In some cases—such as children's picture books—the author will have little or nothing to do with the artwork; the publisher submits the manuscript to an in-house art director, who engages a freelance artist to do the illustrations. In other cases, depending on the type of book, illustrations are primarily the responsibility of the author, who must provide the artwork or rough sketches or recommend sources. In either case, the author's responsibility regarding illustrations should be clearly defined in the book contract.

Imagery. Imagery is description that clarifies for the reader a sensory experience, an action, a thing, a place or an idea. To create imagery, the writer chooses words so carefully that the reader feels he is experiencing a situation or a sensation.

Imagery can be literal or figurative. Literal meaning is directly conveyed through the words as they stand; in using figurative imagery, the writer speaks indirectly to stir the reader's imagination.

Both fiction and nonfiction writers use this device. The following paragraph, from Walker Percy's novel *The Second Coming*, contains both literal and figurative imagery:

Down, down he crawled, letting himself feet first down a rockslide, first prone then supine because he needed the flashlight. There was no way, he figured, to go wrong going down. He wished for a miner's head lamp and, thinking of it, seemed to catch a whiff of acetylene. The slide leveled gradually and entered a crawl. Dry rock gave way to wet clay. The crawl was longer than he remembered, a good hundred yards.

There were places where the ceiling came so close to the floor that he had to turn his head sideways like a baby getting through a pelvis. Progress could only be made by a slow scissors kick and rowing with his elbows. Once he got stuck. The mountain pressed on his back.

The next example, also a combination of literal and figurative imagery, is from a nonfiction piece, "A Sense of Where You Are," by John McPhee:

Then he began another series of expandingly difficult jump shots, and one jumper after another went cleanly through the basket with so few exceptions that the crowd began to murmur. Then he started to perform whirling reverse moves before another cadence of almost steadily accurate jump shots, and the murmur increased. Then he began to sweep hook shots into the air. He moved in a semicircle around the court. First with his right hand, then with his left, he tried seven of these long, graceful shots—the most difficult ones in the orthodoxy of basketball—and ambidextrously made them all.

Figurative imagery is discussed further under separate entries, headed by the respective names of the figures of speech. (*See: Figures of speech; Hyperbole; Irony; Metaphor; Metonymy; Onomatopoeia; Paradox; Personification; Simile.*)

Immediacy. Immediacy—the element of contemporary life—is important in today's magazine articles. Writers who rely only on experiences or events of years ago lose sales, because most modern readers are more interested in current events. Despite the fact that some popular TV series, some nonfiction books and many genre novels have been based on historical themes, immediacy is usually necessary in popular magazine article writing.

Imprint. The term for a publisher's line of books of a particular type; an editor may have an imprint (consisting of his own name) as well. An imprint can appear on a book spine either separately or in combination with the publisher's name. Such labels help categorize books for dealers and educators. Tor is an imprint of St. Martin's Press. HarperPerennial is an imprint of HarperCollins Publishers, Inc.

Imprints of individual publishers are listed in Section Two of *Literary Market Place* and in the *Publishers* volume of *Books in Print.*

In medias res. This Latin term, meaning "into the midst of things," refers to the literary device of beginning a narrative at a dramatic point in a story well along in the sequence of events to immediately capture reader interest.

A traditional convention of epic poetry, this literary technique is also used in novels, short stories, drama and narrative poetry. When an author begins his story in medias res, he usually employs a flashback or series of flashbacks to explain preceding events. (*See: Flashback; Narrative hook; Plot; Story.*)

Incident. Applied to the short story, the term *incident* has the same meaning it does in reality: It is a happening of *minor* consequence. In fiction, a *series* of logically connected incidents form the plot. The difference between an *incident* and a *story* is that a *single* incident in itself involves no character change, while a story always involves some kind of change in the central character. However, the result of a series of incidents in the story can bring about the change in the central character's thinking. (*See: Character change; Consequence, a sense of; Story.*)

Income of a freelance writer. (*See: Full-time freelancing, economics of.*)

Incomes, writing, sources of statistics on. A would-be writer can consult several sources to learn about writers' incomes. Unions such as the Newspaper Guild and the Writers Guild of America are able to provide such information regarding staff writing jobs with newspapers, radio/TV and films.

The entry "Full-time freelancing, economics of" in this book cites the average annual income for magazine and book authors. As a basis for setting one-time fees for freelance projects, the writer should consult the section "How Much Should I Charge?" in the current edition of *Writer's Market*, and the book *National Writers Union Guide to Freelance Rates and Standard Practice.*

Average salaries to be expected in writing-related fields can be located in government publications, e.g., the *Occupational Outlook Handbook.* Similarly, *The Vertical File Index* in most public libraries leads the researcher to pamphlets on specific careers. (*See: Book publishing economics; Full-time freelancing, economics of.*)

Incorporating yourself as a writer. Depending on a full-time freelance writer's level of income, there may be certain advantages to incorporating his freelance business. The writer should consult an accountant or an attorney before doing so.

Independent Literary Agents Association, Inc. (ILAA). A national organization composed of literary agencies that merged with the Society of Authors' Representatives (SAR) in 1991 to form the Association of Authors' Representatives (AAR). (*See: Association of Authors' Representatives.*)

Independent producer. Independent producers, as self-employed entrepreneurs, assemble scripts, actors, directors and financing for their film concepts.

Many film and TV screenwriters work for independent producers. Writers interested in approaching one with a film project usually do so through an agent. (*See: Screenwriting.*)

Index. An alphabetical listing (with page numbers) of the most important topics in a book, appearing at the end of the volume. An index may also be a directory of published material in periodicals, such as *The New York Times Index* or the *Readers' Guide to Periodical Literature.* (*See: Book indexing; Periodicals, indexes to.*)

Indexing. Indexing is a skill that requires attention to detail and a penchant for orderliness. An index renders a book more useful to readers and more popular with librarians.

The basic procedures of indexing consist of reading the book to be-come acquainted with its contents; rereading the book while noting each key word or phrase and page number(s); sorting, alphabetizing and editing the entries; and checking the page numbers against those in the book. The indexer is also responsible for proofreading index galleys and page proofs. Hypertext card files and other software programs make indexing by computer a practical alternative to hand-written and -sorted $3'' \times 5''$ cards.

Major categories of index entries are personal names, other proper names (e.g., organizations), subjects and ideas. In preparing entries, research may be necessary, since an index must give the full names of well-known people (even when the book does not) and must cross-reference words that are synonymous with some entries, when it is suspected that readers might look under one of two words for the same topic. Also, the indexer may need to consult with the author where "ideas" entries are concerned: He must ascertain that his conception corresponds to the author's.

Indexes are constructed by one of two systems of alphabetization: the word-by-word method and the letter-by-letter (or all through) method. Using word-by-word, the indexer considers only the first word (or the first unit before a space, such as a hyphenated word) as a unit for alphabetization purposes. In the letter-by-letter system, however, all letters that precede the first punctuation mark, regardless of the number of words, are considered to be one unit. For example, the subjects "bookkeeping" and "book manuscript" would appear in two different alphabetical orders, depending on which system was used. Alphabetizing word-by-word, the indexer would place "book manuscript" first, since *b-o-o-k* makes up the first unit before a space. However, the letter-by-letter system would place "bookkeeping" first of the two words because *b-o-o-k-k* comes before *b-o-o-k-m* (disregarding the space in "book manuscript") in the alphabet.

A person interested in becoming an indexer can instruct himself by reading manuals and stylebooks such as *The Chicago Manual of Style*; but it is unusual to acquire indexing jobs without practical indexing experience. Scholarly organizations and local groups may be outlets for beginners' volunteer indexing work. Local printers may be a source of freelance job opportunities. (*See: American Society of Indexers; Book indexing; Hypertex; Index.*)

Indirect quote. An indirect quote is information paraphrased by the writer; that is, information quoted in substance rather than verbatim. For example: *Mary Heaton Vorse once said that the art of writing is the art of applying the seat of the pants to the seat of the chair.* Although such remarks aren't enclosed in quotation marks, indirect quotes are usually attributed to an identified source. An indirect quote may be rewritten to shorten it, improve the grammar or make it more precise, but such revision must not distort or misrepresent the original intent of the remarks being paraphrased. (*See: Attribution; Quotes.*)

Informal writing style. Widely accepted in magazine articles and newspaper features or columns today, informal style is a generally relaxed manner of writing that creates an almost conversational rapport between reader and writer. Informal writing style is characterized by colloquialisms, humor and the occasional use of parenthetical material. To achieve an informal style, writers make use of contractions (*he's* instead of *he is*; *they're* instead of *they are*), first- and second-person point of view and occasional sentence fragments.

An informal writing style, while relaxed, doesn't permit bad grammar, imprecise words and phrases or misspellings. In her discussion of style in *Write on Target*, Connie Emerson notes: "One thing is certain. Whatever style you adopt for a particular article, you cannot afford to ignore the elements of good writing. Just because an editor likes fifty-six-word statements doesn't mean your modifiers can dangle or that you're free to disregard punctuation. Singular verbs with plural nouns . . . won't do the job even if your article is loaded with the kind of picturesque writing the editor adores." (*See: Formal writing style; Style.*)

Information superhighway. A buzzword that attempts to use an analogy of the highway system to describe the broad array of electronic and online services and technologies. This term, coined by Alvin Toffler, is most often used when talking about the Internet and its connections to private, public, government, corporate and educational institution computer users.

The Freedom Forum Media Studies Center at Columbia University in

New York presented a study in late 1994 on the term *information superhighway*, its various meanings, media coverage and implications. Some of those interviewed for that study consider the highway analogy inadequate and suggest instead interlocking spider webs or a gigantic human brain with cross-linked neural pathways.

Nevertheless, the highway analogy continues and has adapted other related words and phrases to describe knowledge (or lack thereof) about the Internet and other online forums: *wrong exits, wrong turns, gridlock, bottlenecks, roadblocks, roadkill, billboards,* etc. (*See: Internet; Online service.*)

Informational article. (*See: Magazine article, types of.*)

Infringement of copyright. Violation of a right granted by law to a copyright owner. With some exceptions, the owner of a copyright possesses exclusive rights to reproduce his work; create works derived from the original; sell, rent or otherwise distribute copies of his creation; and perform or display his work in public.

The law provides for certain kinds of use of copyrighted work by others. For example, under certain circumstances libraries and archives may reproduce copyrighted work, and teachers and students may perform or display copyrighted work. In addition, individuals are permitted to sell or display a single copy of a work. Broadcasters have the right to issue secondary transmissions in some instances and to make one copy of a program (except motion pictures and similar works) that they have been granted the right to broadcast.

When a person has been found guilty of copyright infringement, the plaintiff can recover *actual damages*—which compensate for loss or harm done to himself, his property or his rights—or *statutory damages,* the amount of which is determined by a judge within the range specified by the law. The court is permitted by law to award recovery of attorney's fees under certain circumstances as well. Where it can be proved that a person has infringed a copyright willfully and for commercial advantage or private financial gain, the infringer is subject to imprisonment in addition to fines and forfeiture of the material. (*See: Copyright; Fair use.*)

Inner monologue (or inner dialogue). (*See: Interior monologue.*)

Inspiration. For a writer, *inspiration* refers to a stimulus compelling creation or expression.

Psychologists Stanley Rosner and Lawrence Abt, whose book *The Creative Experience* is the result of interviews they had with creative people in science as well as the arts, reported that:

... there is widespread recognition of the significant place occupied by intuition, unconscious promptings and inexplicable insights, and the sudden awareness of relationships. ... The repeated references in our own interviews to 'I don't know where the idea came from,' and 'It just came to mind,' attest to functions in operation beyond the level of consciousness.

While most writers welcome spurts of inspiration, they don't depend on outside stimuli to accomplish their work. Successful writers realize that the difference between a writer and a would-be writer lies in knowing that inspiration is another word for hard work.

Successful writers work every day whether they feel like writing or not. Clair Rees, author of *Profitable Part-Time/Full-Time Freelancing*, explains: "The one quality dividing real professionals from most would-be writers is discipline. If you can write only when the muse is smiling you're not likely to get far in the profession. Manuscripts are sold by people who have the grit to sit at the typewriter—and stay there—until an assignment is finished and ready for mailing. Waiting until you're 'in the mood' to write is a luxury the professional freelancer simply can't afford." (*See: Ideas, where to get them.*)

Inspirational article. (*See: Magazine article, types of.*)

Inspirational writing. Inspirational writing generally incorporates a personal philosophy that the reader might adapt to his own life. Drawing on their own experience or the experience of others, writers of inspirational material strive to create an animating effect on readers, stimulating or impelling them to some action or viewpoint.

Almost any form of writing may be inspirational in tone: articles, books, gospel music, poetry, fillers, curriculum materials, games and puzzles, TV and film scripts and theological and scholarly material. An inspirational article, for example, recounts what an individual, group or community did to make something bet-

ter. How the residents of a town worked together to solve a problem or how an individual overcame a narrow-minded prejudice are two examples of inspirational themes. Other inspirational pieces may deal with attributes such as faith, determination, perseverance and patience.

A logical extension of the inspirational piece is the religious article that offers the reader a guide to developing courage, strength and fortitude through faith. Religious inspirational pieces, sometimes called devotionals, are often first-person stories of how the writer applied religious faith in coping with his day-to-day problems, or biographical-personality sketches of religious figures or admirable individuals.

Religious magazines such as *Guideposts* and *PLUS* offer the biggest market for inspirational articles, but many general-interest and juvenile magazines publish inspirational material with both religious and nonreligious themes. *Reader's Digest* regularly includes articles of an inspirational nature, for example.

Most inspirational articles are based on a narrative structure. The key to writing the inspirational piece lies in describing the facts honestly and well, creating an emotional impact but avoiding preachiness. Although the inspirational article may be written entirely from the writer's own experience, many inspirational pieces can benefit from research before writing. (*See: Personal experience; Religious writing.*)

Instant book. A book on a topical or newsworthy subject that appeals to a wide audience. Often issued in paperback, this type of book is published and placed on newsstands as soon as possible after the event has occurred, regardless of the publisher's usual production schedules. Among the first was Bantam's book on the Warren Commission Report on the Kennedy assassination.

Other names for the instant book are *extra* and *quickie.*

Insurance, authors' liability. The insurance policies of some publishers extend to provide liability coverage to authors who sign contracts with them. This type of coverage developed in the early 1980s.

Before such insurance was available to authors, book contracts contained warranty clauses requiring the author to pay all the publisher's expense and legal fees in the case of lawsuits brought about by the book, even if the publisher won the case.

Amounts of deductibles vary, as do arrangements regarding the party responsible for paying the deductible. If the author and the publisher split the deductible, that will be stipulated in the author/publisher agreement *and* the individual policy.

Media/Professional Insurance and Employers Reinsurance Corp. supply most of these liability policies. Standard policies include coverage for libel, invasion of privacy and infringement of intellectual property rights. To obtain coverage from an underwriter like Media/Professional or ERC, authors and publishers must work through a licensed insurance agent or broker. (*See: Libel.*)

Insurance programs. Since freelance writers lack the fringe benefit of company-sponsored insurance pro-

grams, they are responsible for securing personal insurance for themselves. Some professional writers' organizations offer coverage to members at group rates. For example, the American Society of Journalists and Authors, Inc., offers access to group health insurance, and the Society of Professional Journalists, Sigma Delta Chi, offers its members insurance plans covering life, health and accidental death and dismemberment. Other specialized writers' groups may have similar insurance programs. (*See: Retirement and the freelance writer.*)

Intercollegiate Broadcasting System (IBS). An association of broadcast stations at schools, colleges and universities. Its services to member stations include providing program services; representing the members before government, industrial and educational institutions; conducting surveys among stations; and providing information services (predominantly for member stations).

Its address is P.O. Box 592, Vails Gate, NY 12584.

Interior. In a motion picture or TV script, this term indicates an indoor scene; it is followed by more specific information about the location, sometimes describing it in detail. Typed in all caps, *interior* is abbreviated *int.* (*See: Television script terms.*)

Interior monologue. This technique of relating the thoughts inside a character's head is used to add immediacy, naturalness and simplicity to works of fiction. It also provides added character identification for the reader.

Not to be mistaken for random thoughts of stream-of-consciousness writing, interior monologue is coherent and organized—just as spoken dialogue is.

To help convey true naturalness, the author can insert interior monologue into an interrupted dialogue, or vice versa. In such instances, the dialogue or interior monologue—whichever interrupts—is enclosed in parentheses, and both the interruption and the interrupted part of the work are followed by ellipsis points.

The interior monologue, being a thought represented in words, is either italicized, enclosed in quotation marks or simply started with a capital letter. Here's an example from James Joyce's *A Portrait of the Artist As a Young Man*:

"You know," he said, "you can ask that riddle another way."

"Can you?" said Stephen.

"The same riddle," he said. "Do you know the other way to ask it?"

"No," said Stephen.

"Can you not think of the other way?" he said.

"No," said Stephen.

He looked at Stephen over the bedclothes as he spoke. Then he lay back on the pillow and said: "There is another way but I won't tell you what it is."

Why did he not tell it? His father, who kept the racehorses, must be a magistrate too like Saurin's father and Nasty Roche's father. He thought of his own father, of how he sang songs while his mother played and of how he always gave him a shilling when he asked for sixpence and he felt sorry for him that he was not a magistrate like the other boys' fathers. Then why was he sent to that place with them?

To use interior monologue, a writer must first understand it; a method for absorbing the technique is to read examples of it, then practice creating original examples. Interior monologue appears in various works of Eugene O'Neill and William Faulkner. (*See: Stream of consciousness.*)

Interlibrary loan. Public and college libraries that don't have a book a writer would like to use for research can sometimes borrow it from another library. The cost to the writer can vary from merely the postage to mail the book to and from the other library to an interlibrary loan fee of perhaps $5-$10. The lending department of the library can advise what kind of fees and waiting time are involved.

International Association of Business Communicators (IABC). This organization has 12,500 members who are writers, editors, audiovisual specialists, and managers of communication and public relations programs for profit and not-for-profit organizations worldwide. IABC is active in education and research; other activities of the organization include an annual international conference, seminars, video teleconferences, an accreditation program, and a placement service hotline open to members. In the accreditation program, members submit portfolios of their work—brochures, publications, speeches, videotapes or any other forms of business communication—and request an application for an examination, a four-and-a-half-hour oral and written test by which candidates are judged by an accreditation board appointed by the IABC president.

IABC convenes annually. Its headquarters are at 1 Hallidie Plaza, Suite 600, San Francisco, CA 94102.

International Center of Photography (ICP). "The ICP was established in 1974 to collect, preserve and exhibit the best photography has to offer, teach photography at all levels, and provide a forum for the exchange of ideas and information in the field of photography." The center's six thousand members range from those who enjoy looking at photographs to those who make photographs professionally. ICP presents exhibitions in New York and "approximately seventy-five venues around the world." Members receive free admission to these exhibitions in New York, discounts on the more than three hundred courses, lectures and seminars offered by ICP's education department and a subscription to the *Program Guide*—a quarterly journal describing classes, lectures, exhibitions and special events. Membership fees range from $25 for a Senior Individual to $2,500 for a Benefactor patron. The more costly memberships entitle the individual to special benefits from ICP. For more information, contact ICP at 1130 Fifth Ave., New York, NY 10128.

International Communications Industries Association. (formerly National Audiovisual Association). The 1,113 members of ICIA work in the audio-visual field as dealers, manufacturers, producers and suppliers of audiovisual, video and microcomputer products. Within the organization are a number of councils, including those covering industry and business, materials, nontheatrical film distributors and audiovisual equipment manufacturers. They bestow awards for innovative use of audiovisuals, industry contributions and advancing media use.

The Association publishes the monthly *Communications Industries Report*, and the annual *Directory of Video, Computer and Audiovisual Products*. The association is at 3150 Spring St., Fairfax, VA 22031.

International copyright. Refers to copyright protection in all countries that subscribe to various treaties, such as the Berne Union or Universal Copyright Convention (UCC). A U.S. author may obtain protection in countries that are party to the UCC by placing a copyright notice on the title page of his work or the page immediately following. In this case, the copyright symbol—©—must be used rather than the word *copyright* or an abbreviation of it, either of which is permitted under U.S. law. No copyright notice is required for works protected under the Berne Union. A work protected by the UCC must be registered with the U.S. Copyright Office for its author to have the right to file an infringement suit in the U.S. Berne Convention works that have a country of origin other than the U.S. are exempt from the requirement of registration before any lawsuit for infringement can proceed.

The Association of American Publishers operates the International Copyright Information Center as a service to writers. Contact the ICIC, % AAP, 1718 Connecticut Ave., Washington, DC 20009.

International copyright convention. According to the Copyright Office of the Library of Congress, there is no such thing as an international copyright that will automatically protect an author's writings throughout the entire world. "Protection against unauthorized use in a particular country depends basically on the laws of that country," the Copyright Office explains. "However, most countries do offer protection to foreign works under certain conditions, and these conditions have been greatly simplified by international copyright treaties and conventions."

There are two major international copyright conventions: the Berne Convention for the Protection of Literary and Artistic Works (commonly called the Berne Union), and the Universal Copyright Convention (UCC). The U.S. is a member of both. Although these two conventions differ in some respects, the fundamental principle of *national treatment* is common to both. Under this provision, a participating country is required to give the same protection to foreign works that meet Convention requirements as it gives to its own domestic works.

In addition to the two major international copyright conventions, there is also a series of seven Pan-American Conventions—regional agreements that govern to some extent copyright relations in the Western Hemisphere. Moreover, certain countries have adopted bilateral treaties that grant copyright reciprocity between two nations; others have laws granting protection to foreign works under certain conditions without regard to any international conventions or treaties. "In all of these cases," the Library of Congress Copyright Office advises, "the extent of protection and the requirements for securing copyright vary from country to country. An author who wishes to copyright his work in a particular country should first find out the extent of protection for foreign works in that country by contacting that country's embassy or a law library. If possible, he should do this before his work is published anywhere, since protection may often depend on the facts existing at the time of first publication." (*See: Piracy.*)

Additional information: *The ABC of Copyright.*

International Literary Market Place (ILMP). A directory of book publishers, agents, book clubs and others in the book industry located in countries besides the U.S. and Canada. ILMP lists more than ten thousand publishers and seventy-five hundred other organizations; content is categorized by country. (*See:* Literary Market Place.)

International Platform Association. This professional organization is dedicated to public speaking and performing; its membership includes actors, lecturers, business and professional people, politicians, musicians, artists, writers, booking agents and program chairpeople.

The group engages in workshops and annual critique sessions. Activi-

FIGURE 20

INTERNATIONAL POSTAL REPLY COUPONS

UNION POSTALE
UNIVERSELLE

COUPON-RÉPONSE   C 22
INTERNATIONAL

Ce coupon est échangeable dans tous les pays de l'Union postale universelle contre un ou plusieurs timbres-poste représentant l'affranchissement minimal d'une lettre ordinaire, expédiée à l'étranger par voie de surface.

Empreinte de contrôle du pays d'origine	Prix de vente (indication facultative)	Timbre du bureau qui effectue l'échange
	95 cents	

This coupon is exchangeable in any country of the Universal Postal Union for one or more postage stamps representing the minimum postage for an unregistered letter sent by surface to a foreign country. Can be purchased from your local postmaster to include with queries or manuscripts sent abroad.

ties aim to educate members, improve their skills and broaden their range of contacts. The organization's publication, *Art Group Newsletter,* is published quarterly. Awards (named after the association's famous members) are presented at the annual convention held in August in Washington, DC. Among these are the Daniel Webster Award, the Winston Churchill Award, the Theodore Roosevelt Award, the Mark Twain Award and the Lowell Thomas Award.

The association's headquarters are at P.O. Box 250, Winnetka, IL 60093.

International Reply Coupons. Material submitted to foreign publications and publishers, including the expanding Canadian market, requires International Reply Coupons to cover the cost of return postage. One of these coupons is exchangeable in any other country for a stamp or stamps representing the international postage on a single-rate, surface-mailed letter. The number of International Reply Coupons required is determined by the weight of the manuscript at the post office, where the coupons may be purchased.

Writers who deal regularly with

certain foreign markets find it less expensive to arrange to buy foreign stamps from the country's postal service than to use International Reply Coupons. A country's foreign embassy office in Washington, DC, whose address is available at any local library, can provide the writer with information regarding the postal rates for first-class or airmail service from foreign countries to the U.S., and the address to which orders for stamps may be sent. (*See: Figure 20.*)

International research sources. *The Europa World Year Book*, a two-volume set that furnishes information about international organizations and various countries of the world, is a useful reference for writers needing foreign research sources. It covers organizations, giving facts about their activities, financial structures and functions. A writer/researcher, for example, could find statistics on the Japanese fishing industry, the address of the Swiss National Bank or the name of the Director General of the British Tourist Authority.

Entries on each country include an introductory survey and cover topics such as government (including political parties), the judicial system and religions. In addition, each section describing a country contains a directory section, which provides names, addresses and other data on media organizations, finance, industry, tourism, universities and colleges, atomic energy and transport.

The *Year Book* contains an index of international organizations and an index of countries and territories.

International Trademark Association. A trade organization that supports registered trademarks and promotes their proper usage. Among the ITA's educational programs are its Trademark Checklist and its Trademark Hotline. The checklist includes some four thousand trademarks correctly spelled and their correct generic terms. This packet is available for $10 (1133 Avenue of the Americas, New York, NY 10036-6710). The Hotline answers questions of spelling and proper use, and is open weekdays from 2 P.M. to 5 P.M., Eastern Standard Time. Call (212) 768-9887. (*See: Trademark.*)

International Women's Writing Guild (IWWG). Established in 1976, this organization is a network for the personal and professional empowerment of women through writing. IWWG engenders and supports the joyful camaraderie that comes from shared interests of the women's writing community.

The Guild is open to any woman, regardless of portfolio. Women of all ages, backgrounds and ethnicities make up the membership. IWWG offers workshops on every kind of writing, and members publish close to one hundred books annually, many in major publishing houses.

The IWWG directs an annual week-long conference in August at Skidmore College, Saratoga Springs, New York. For information, write Hannelore Hahn, Executive Director, IWWG, P.O. Box 810, Gracie Station, New York, NY 10028.

Internaut. Internet user. (*See: Internet.*)

Internet. A network of computers designed by the U.S. government in the late 1960s as a redundant communications system that could survive nuclear or other war. Since then, the Internet has become a decentralized global web of computer sites that makes electronic mail between every type of computer possible. In addition, users can access information and documents from other computers.

Current users include universities, nonprofit organizations, businesses and governments. More than twenty million people have access to the Internet. Some commercial on-line services are now offering access.

Originally, information was available only as text. However, the development of the World Wide Web on the Internet has allowed users to link text with graphics, video and sound. (*See: Electronic mail; Information superhighway; Online service; World Wide Web.*)

Internships. A period of time in which a person gets hands-on experience in a chosen field and is sometimes paid. Journalism students, for example, may elect to work for a newspaper, magazine or publishing company for a semester or a summer. There is generally no commitment on the part of the employer or the employee after the agreed-upon time period.

The American Society of Magazine Editors sponsors an internship program every year, drawing students from across the country to its members' publications in New York City, Washington, DC, and other cities. One source to find available internships is Peterson's Guides' an-

nually updated *Internships: On-the-Job Training Opportunities for Students and Adults.* The *Subject Guide to Books in Print* also lists recently published sources on this topic. (*See: Scholarships, fellowships, internships.*)

Interview. The interview is a research method in which the writer talks with a primary source. The interview may be the foundation on which a personality profile is constructed, or it may be one means of gathering information for an article on a subject the interviewee is familiar with.

The first, and perhaps most difficult, step is to arrange an interview with a subject. Your options for arranging the interview are either to contact the subject directly yourself by phone or mail, or—if the subject is a public figure or celebrity—to work with the subject's assistant, agent, manager, publicist, etc. Although subjects may sometimes hesitate to be interviewed, most people are flattered to be asked about themselves and their jobs.

After gaining an appointment with his subject, a writer must do advance research in two areas: biographical and subject interest. A profile writer should bring to the interview a thorough knowledge of the interviewee's background—date of birth, real name (in the case of actors), hometown, education, current job responsibilities, etc.—gleaned from *Who's Who* listings and a review of any published magazine or newspaper articles about the individual. Other sources of background facts are friends, relatives and professional associates (such as press agents) of the interviewee. In addition, the writer must acquaint himself as thoroughly as possible with the subject area(s) he intends to talk about with the interviewee—politics, nuclear energy, Hollywood, baseball, etc.—by reading and talking with authorities in the field. Based on this knowledge, the writer will be able to prepare incisive questions before the interview, and interpret answers (checking with other sources on new information) and raise additional questions during the interview.

A writer interviewing for the purpose of gathering information need not do exhaustive research, but he should have some background knowledge of the topic, know the interviewee's official title and be aware of the interviewee's status in his field.

A good interview most often depends on *how* the subject is approached. Whether for a personality piece or merely for fact gathering, the interview is above all a personal situation, an exchange between two or more people. Curiosity, warmth and intelligence are all valuable assets to an interviewer, and a natural, conversational manner will usually yield good results. Sometimes gentle prodding and a firmer tone may be necessary to prompt more significant responses from a reluctant interviewee, but badgering usually results in a defensive, close-mouthed subject and an aborted interview. The writer is advised to save controversial questions until the end of the interview; then, if the subject refuses to respond, the writer still has the bulk of the information he needs.

An interviewer probably should start out with two or three set ques-tions firmly in mind. To avoid routine responses and monosyllabic answers such as "Yes" and "No," the interviewer must ask open-ended questions that give the subject the opportunity to elaborate. And in addition to *listening* to what the subject says, the interviewer must constantly *observe*. Details about the subject—the way he talks, uses his hands, dresses—the setting and the atmosphere are all important elements in creating a personality profile. As the respondent talks, the interviewer should also listen for possible anecdotes and flush these out as he recognizes them.

How you record the interview is a matter of preference. Some interviewers prefer to take written notes only, while others rely on the tape recorder to record the words so their notes can capture the environment and write down follow-up questions. In his book, *The Writer's Complete Guide to Conducting Interviews*, Michael Schumacher discusses the advantages and disadvantages of using a tape recorder. Keep in mind, though, that the subject may not be completely comfortable with a tape recorder around. However, interviews on controversial topics or with controversial people should always be taped and the tapes filed.

Fact gathering through interviews can be difficult on controversial subjects. In hard news or investigative reporting, the writer can accomplish his task without antagonizing his sources by drawing upon several people and taking bits of information from each one. This is a technique used by writer George McMillan, who believes that with this method, no single source feels uncomfortable about having revealed the whole story.

One interview with a subject may not be enough to write an article, so the interviewer should make an attempt at the close of the session to keep the door open for follow-up interviews, perhaps saying something like "If I have any additional questions, may I call you?" (*See: Attribution; Indirect quote; Off the record; Profile; Quotes; Tape recorder.*)

Interview article. (*See: Magazine article, types of.*)

Introduction. An introduction is the preliminary material leading into the main part of an essay, article, book, etc. The introduction to a book, for example, is a formal preliminary statement or guide to the volume, written by the author or editor to precede the main text. A book introduction may also be a foreword written by someone other than the author to introduce the author and his work to the reader. Here, for example, is the first paragraph of the introduction by John Buchanan-Brown to the Revised Centenary Edition of *Brewer's Dictionary of Phrase and Fable*, edited by Ivor H. Evans:

A reference book which has flourished for over a hundred years is clearly something exceptional. Its original compiler needs to hit upon not so much a new area of information of wide and permanent interest as a way of presenting that material and of providing access to it which satisfies and attracts generation after generation of readers. Equally such a compiler needs to place his book with publishers sensitive to changing tastes and aware of the need periodically to give the work that face-lift needed to attract fresh generations of readers to the mass of information within.

The introduction may be part of the front matter or presented as the first part of the text. (*See: Lead; Manuscript preparation and submission.*)

Inverted pyramid. A style of journalistic writing in which the major points of a news story appear in the first sentence or paragraph and the details are elaborated in descending order of importance.

Developed after the Civil War in response to the needs of the growing AP news service, the inverted pyramid replaced the double-ended story form that was based on a chronological order of events. The double-ended story was so called because reporters from the battlefield telegraphed a brief summary of a story before following it with a detailed version. In case the detailed story was delayed through problems with the telegraph service, the newspaper editor still had the summary, which gave the highlights.

Because the AP served newspapers all over the country, each of which did not always allot the same amount of space to a story, the inverted pyramid structure was designed. It begins with a summary lead giving the who, what, when, where, why and how details, followed by the most important element of the story regardless of the chronological order in which it occurred. The remaining facts are recorded in order of importance, with the least important details tapering off at the bottom of the pyramid structure.

The inverted pyramid form facilitates editing, since it can easily be cut at the end of any paragraph after the summary lead. The most important elements of the story remain, regardless of where the story is cut.

Investigative reporting. Investigative reporting, sometimes called *muckraking* or *exposé writing*, has been part of American journalistic tradition since the early eighteenth century. Investigative reporting is aimed at revealing facts that some person, business or government agency is trying to keep secret. The investigative reporter goes beyond the official version of an event or circumstance, examining critically every record, statement or opinion offered by an official source. Investigative reporting is popularly envisioned as involving clandestine meetings with off-the-record sources and threats from the underworld; in fact, it is most often based on patient, painstaking research and scrutiny of public documents.

Paul N. Williams, author of *Investigative Reporting and Editing*, describes investigative reporting as an intellectual process that requires gathering and sorting ideas, building patterns, analyzing options and making decisions based on logic rather than emotion.

Investigative reporter David Kraslow characterizes investigative reporting as "high-risk" journalism involving a great deal of time, money, pressure and personal integrity from the investigative journalist.

Newspaper and magazine editors are often reluctant to assign investi-gative pieces to staff or freelance writers because of the time and financial commitment an investigative piece requires, and because of the potential lawsuit that may result from such an article. (*See: Figure 21.*)

Additional information: *Investigative Reporting and Editing.*

Irony. A figure of speech in which the intended meaning of a word or statement is the opposite of its literal meaning. For example, Peter De Vries, author of *Let Me Count the Ways* and many other books, once said, "I love being a writer. What I can't stand is the paperwork."

What is stated ironically need not always be precisely the *opposite* of what is suggested, however. Irony may assert somewhat less than it suggests by the use of understatement; for instance, author Fran Lebowitz once remarked, "Having been unpopular in high school is not just cause for book publication." In addition to understatement, irony may be achieved through the use of devices such as hyperbole, sarcasm and satire.

A particular type of irony, *Socratic irony*, is named for Socrates, the fifth-century-B.C. Athenian philosopher who often feigned ignorance in a discussion with a view toward later defeating his conversational opponent. Socratic irony is a technique that involves adopting another's point of view to reveal that person's weakness and eventually to ridicule him. (*See: Dramatic irony; Hyperbole; Satire.*)

Irregular Serials and Annuals. This reference work, in most libraries, provides information on proceedings, yearbooks, handbooks, annual re-

FIGURE 21

INVESTIGATIVE REPORTING

Steve Weinberg, Investigative Reporters & Editors

*E*very year, a major newspaper or magazine proclaims the serious illness of investigative journalism in America, intimating that death may be near.

Hogwash. Investigative journalism in American newspapers such as *The Washington Post* and magazines such as *Mother Jones* has never been more pervasive, has never been of higher quality, than today. Investigative journalism in the broadcast media—at the networks and local stations like WCCO-TV/Minneapolis—is slightly less pervasive, but is in no danger of drying up.

There is some hard evidence. From my perch at Investigative Reporters and Editors (a national organization based at the University of Missouri School of Journalism in Columbia), I have watched enrollment double and triple in classes that teach the skills to the generation of journalists who will fill the shoes of the middle-aged and old pros doing such a good job right now. During the early 1970s, Watergate seemed to be the impetus attracting young journalists to look for corruption. In 1995, journalistic models are everywhere.

Most investigative journalism is drudgery—finding and reading government documents, convincing reluctant sources to give you a few minutes by showing them you already know a great deal about the subject, trying to organize mounds of material into a compelling saga, and writing, rewriting, rewriting again. But it is important drudgery. Only by showing readers the forest (such as a troubled state court system) instead of individual trees (such as one botched trial) can journalists hope to make systemic changes in American society. With investigative reporting now institutionalized in many newsrooms, readers are beginning to see the forest more often, realizing that change is possible, and demanding that change at the local, state and federal levels. Any good journalist is expected to be an investigative reporter or editor, even if he doesn't have that particular title. Many journalists have mastered computer-assisted reporting, allowing them to analyze complicated data kept in electronic form by government agencies. Computer-assisted reporting allows journalists to uncover wrongdoing in a few months that never would have been attempted in past decades because the gathering and analysis of information would have taken years.

The increase in the quality and quantity of investigative journalism has come despite bureaucratic, journalistic and legal obstacles. Those include federal government noncompliance with the Freedom of Information Act, harassment of journalists through meritless privacy and libel lawsuits brought by the rich and powerful, and refusal by the business sector to be held accountable for the problems it causes society. One obstacle has been erected by pseudo-journalists working for tabloid television programs, radio talk shows and sensationalist publications sold largely in supermarket check-out lines. By emphasizing titillation over serious investigation, those pseudo-journalists have discouraged knowledgeable sources from cooperating with legitimate newsgatherers. Many knowledgeable sources now refuse to talk because they are afraid their words will be used irresponsibly. Other knowledgeable sources are refusing to talk unless paid for their information.

continued on next page

FIGURE 21 (CONTINUED)

Fortunately, investigative journalists everywhere have learned the skills to get over, under or around such obstacles. The main element has been persistence, including use of the courts to shake loose documents. During the 1990s, watch for the continued growth of in-depth, quality journalism in local media and in national publications. In past decades, too many so-called journalists practiced stenography more often than true reporting. It is more and more evident that the era of "repeating not reporting" is in decline. Hooray for that.

Steve Weinberg, former executive director of Investigative Reporters & Editors, edits the organization's bimonthly magazine, the *IRE Journal*. He is the author of, among other books, *Telling the Untold Story: How Investigative Reporters Are Changing the Craft of Biography* and *The Reporter's Handbook: An Investigator's Guide to Documents and Techniques.*

views and other publications that a writer might be seeking for research purposes. The directory is set up alphabetically by subject matter so that if, for example, a writer is working in the area of public health, he can locate publications on the subject, not only from the U.S., but from foreign countries. Entries give the publisher's name and address, indexing or abstracting services in which the periodical is listed and other details.

ISBN. This acronym stands for International Standard Book Number. ISBN is a tool of the International Standard Book Numbering Agency and is used both for ordering and cataloging purposes. It consists of the prefix ISBN, followed by a series of ten digits separated by hyphens in this manner: ISBN 0-670-38744-4. The first digit is a geographic identifier, the second group of digits is a publisher identifier, the third group is a title identifier, and the fourth is a computer code verifying the correctness of the ISBN number.

The ISBN assigned to a book title is never reassigned, even if the title goes out of print. Separate ISBNs are assigned to the various formats in which a title may be published: paper, cloth, multimedia cassette, etc. In addition, revised editions of a book require new ISBNs. In general, an ISBN is not required. However, distributors and most bookstores will not stock books without it.

A book's unique identification number is printed on the reverse side of its title page or at the foot of the title page itself. It may also appear at the right foot of the outside book cover and the back of the book jacket. In the case of a paperback, the ISBN also appears on the book's spine.

Sometimes appearing with the ISBN is a UPC symbol (also called a bar code), which contains a series of identification and price bars and is necessary for a book to be sold in chain bookstores. Publishers and self-published authors can apply for a bar code at the same time as the ISBN and request a form for an ISBN from BOOKLAND/EAN at the address below.

Books published in foreign countries carry ISBNs with country identifiers necessary for validation.

ISBNs are assigned to book publishers who apply to the ISBN, 121 Chanlon Rd., New Providence, New Jersey 07974, for a unique ISBN Publisher Identifier. Upon application and payment of a service fee, publishers receive logbooks containing enough numbers for one hundred, five hundred or one thousand books. Individuals may purchase single numbers. (*See: ISSN.*)

ISSN. This acronym stands for International Standard Serial Number. ISSN is a tool of the National Serials Data Program of the Library of Congress. It uniquely identifies a periodical title regardless of the language or country in which it is published. It consists of eight digits displayed with the prefix ISSN in this way: ISSN 1432-2981.

Libraries, publishers and the U.S. Postal Service all use the ISSN system as an aid to ordering, communication and regulation.

The ISSN is printed on every issue of a serial, preferably at the top corner of the cover or in the area of the publication's masthead. If a serial changes its title, it is assigned a new ISSN.

Assignment of an ISSN is free upon receipt of a completed application form and a suitable representation of the publication at the office of the National Serials Data Program of the Library of Congress, Washing-

ton, DC 20540. Telephone requests for ISSNs may be made when publication deadlines are a factor. Requests for an ISSN for an already-published serial should include copies of the cover, title page and masthead. Prepublication requests should be accompanied by an artist's conception of the same identifying parts of the serial. (*See: ISBN.*)

Ital. An abbreviation for *italicize* used by proofreaders and editors to indicate that a word or words should be italicized. Written in the margin of a galley or page proof, *ital.* accompanies the proofreading symbol of a straight line under the word/words needing to be italicized. (*See: Proofreaders' marks/symbols.*)

Italics. Any type style in which letters slope to the right. Underlining is a standard way to denote italics in a manuscript to emphasize words or parts of words; indicate the titles of periodicals, books, films, plays and works of art; and to mark foreign words and phrases that have not officially become part of our language by being listed in the front part of the dictionary.

Although the use of italics to emphasize words is occasionally necessary, extensive use of the technique can weaken a piece of writing. Emphasis is best expressed by selecting precise words and constructing sentences carefully.

The cursive script of a typewriter or cursive/italic font on a computer is not an appropriate typeface in which to submit an entire manuscript.

Jargon. Words used primarily by members of a particular social, professional or other group. For example, medical jargon—words that are used to describe anatomy, disorders and various diagnostic, laboratory or other procedures—is generally unfamiliar to laypeople. Similarly, writers' jargon includes words and abbreviations such as *kill fee*, *on spec* and *SASE*. Like any dialect, jargon evolves within a subgroup of a larger culture to aid communication about the subgroup's specialized needs; the problem with jargon arises when members of the subgroup, in speaking with (or writing for) the general public, either consciously or unconsciously use jargon to confuse, exclude or exploit the nonmember—as when a doctor, for instance, neglects to explain a painful or risky treatment to a patient in terms he can grasp.

Writers should use jargon judiciously—always defining or making clear from the context what a word or phrase means—to add color and verisimilitude to their writing. By taking pains to translate jargon, writers serve their readers by helping them understand language they otherwise would not, but may have need to. By neglecting to explain unfamiliar words and terms, or using jargon unnecessarily, the language of the piece will come off as pretentious. Sometimes a writer's chief duty in covering a story characterized by bureaucratese and obfuscation—the nuclear incident at Three Mile Island, for example—is to cut through the jargon to find out what really happened.

In writing for a specialized market—a highbrow art journal, for instance—a writer will have to use jargon if he is to be taken seriously, but that doesn't mean that his prose cannot be readable. Clumsy or insecure writers use jargon to obscure the fact that they're not sure what they're talking about, or that they have nothing substantial to say; but jargon is not the primary cause of poor writing.

Additional information: *The Book of Jargon.*

Jazz. A musical style that evolved from Ragtime and served as dance music in the early twentieth century. It has now evolved into a highly improvisational music form indigenous to America and popular throughout the world.

Jingle. A jingle can be contained in a broadcast advertisement in two ways: A short jingle can alternate with a voice and background music, or the entire commercial can consist of a song whose words provide all the needed information. Most often, a combination of these two approaches is used, with stanzas of musical verse surrounding instrumental interludes that accompany readings of the script.

Music for jingles is unique, ear-catching and sometimes repetitive.

In creating lyrics, the writer should avoid crowding many ideas into the message and should consider the facility with which the words can be sung.

The freelance writer who submits jingle material on speculation may send tape-recorded music either to an advertising agency or to a music production house that furnishes agencies with new material. As in other fields of writing, the established jingle writer will find it easier to obtain jobs than the novice, but any writer will find it difficult to market a jingle unless he is very familiar with an agency's philosophy and the workings of a particular advertising campaign. Each campaign requires a long period of careful planning, and a jingle presented at the last minute is unlikely to fit the campaign's strategy.

Submissions should contain about six jingles of thirty to sixty seconds in length, without lead space between each piece; one jingle should fade out and another fade in simultaneously. Individual agencies differ in the form of tape they use: *Songwriter's Market* listings outline preferences as to kinds of tape, as well as other agency requirements. When the writer does get an assignment, it may specify that the agency needs lyrics only, music only or both lyrics and music for a jingle. Whether working on assignment or on speculation, the jingle writer first submits a tape of his work in a simple form that includes both melody and lyrics.

Jingle writers are paid by the job. Most agencies license advertising rights from the jingle composer. Purchasing all rights to a composi-tion, which is sometimes attempted by agencies, is a frowned-upon practice. For a local or regional commercial a writer might be paid $1,000 or more; for a jingle that is part of a national campaign, a writer might be paid $5,000 or more.

Jobs for writers. While the media, book publishing firms and other businesses provide full-time writing-related positions, many writing and editorial jobs needed by these organizations are adaptable to full- or part-time work at home. Living in the same area as a book publisher who has a rush freelance job is a distinct advantage. In some types of work, however, the freelancer need not even live in the same town as the employer. Copyediting, indexing, proofreading, résumé-writing, column-writing, newspaper stringing, book reviewing and educational grant proposal writing are jobs that are typically performed by freelancers. The booklet *Jobs and Opportunities for Writers* published by Writer's Digest Books guides the freelancer with descriptions and how-to-apply information about writing-related jobs for freelancers. (*See: Careers in writing* and other entries titled with job names or job titles, e.g., *Advertising copywriters; Book publishing jobs, editorial; Book publishing jobs, publicity.*)

Jobs in advertising. (*See: Figure 22.*)

Joint contract. A joint contract is a legal agreement between a publisher and two or more authors, establishing provisions for the division of royalties the book generates. For example, if the two authors of *Extra Cash for Women*—Susan Gillenwater

FIGURE 22

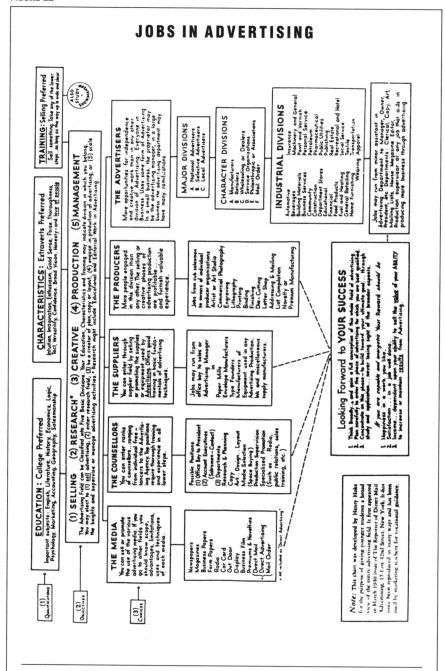

JOBS IN ADVERTISING

Reprinted by permission of The Report of Direct Mail Advertising *(now* Direct Marketing *magazine), 224 Seventh St., Garden City, NY 11531, (516) 746-6700.*

and Virginia Dennis—contributed equally to that book, their contract would call for a fifty-fifty split of the royalties. Other books' royalty divisions could be different depending on each author's contribution. (*See: Book contract.*)

Journal. A writer's journal is a record of thoughts, impressions, observations and story ideas. It is a convenient place to store ideas that may often be useful in the future, and that if not written down, could be easily forgotten.

Joan Didion, in the essay "On Keeping a Notebook," called the journal "something private, . . . bits of the mind's string too short to use, an indiscriminate and erratic assemblage with meaning only for its maker."

Besides serving as a storehouse of ideas, a journal gives the writer a nonthreatening atmosphere in which to experiment with new forms. Also, keeping a journal helps a writer become disciplined to write every day.

Creating works of literature is not the purpose of a journal. In fact, journal entries are often made without regard to grammar, spelling, logic or clarity (although the meaning of entries is clear to the writer). Similarly, content can be as mundane as the writer's reaction to a rejection slip, or his subjective observations about a long-term project (such as publishing a novel).

Some books that can be helpful in comprehending the reasons for keeping journals, as well as providing some exercises are *One to One: Self-Understanding Through Journal Writing*, by Christina Baldwin; *Jour-*

naling for Joy: Writing Your Way to Personal Growth and Freedom, by Joyce Chapman; *Discovering the Writer Within*, by Bruce Ballenger and Barry Lane; and *The New Diary*, by Tristine Rainer.

Journal and magazine, difference between. A journal and a magazine, though similar in format, differ in that a journal is usually published by and for a professional group, such as medical doctors or microbiologists, and a magazine is intended for a more general readership. One exception to the nomenclature is a group of magazines called *trade journals*, which are published for workers in various industries, such as *American Printer and Lithographer*.

Journal articles are usually contributions by members of the profession that make up its readership; manuscripts are not usually sought from writers outside the profession.

By contrast, magazines appeal to either a general-interest audience or to consumers or businesspeople with special interests; most do actively seek manuscripts from freelance writers.

Journalism awards. *Editor & Publisher*, a weekly trade magazine for the newspaper industry, publishes an annual "Journalism Awards" issue the last week of December; a separate pull-out section covers awards for professional journalists such as reporters, columnists and photographers, and student scholarships and fellowships. (*See:* Editor & Publisher.)

Journalism Educator. This is a professional journal aimed at educators in colleges and universities. Articles deal with research findings and proposals concerning teaching techniques, curriculum, technology and students. In addition, the journal reports news about faculty members, journalism schools and professional organizations. *Journalism Educator* is published quarterly by the Association for Education in Journalism and Mass Communication. The subscription office is at the College of Journalism, University of South Carolina, Columbia, SC 29208; editorial office is at the School of Journalism, University of Tennessee, Knoxville, TN 37916.

Writers who are interested in journalism teaching as a part-time occupation may find it a source of helpful observations as well as a potential market for their own comments.

Journalism Quarterly. This is a professional journal that publishes articles on original research in journalism and mass communication. The journal includes articles on historical research, reports of technological developments and book reviews. It is published by the Association for Education in Journalism and Mass Communication. Writers who are part-time journalism teachers may find each issue's reviews of books and articles on mass communication a helpful resource.

Business and subscription offices are at the University of South Carolina, 6021 College St., Columbia, SC 29208; the editorial office is at the School of Journalism, Ohio University, Athens, OH 45701.

Journalistic ethics. The media have established codes of ethics for jour-

nalists to follow to maintain themselves as respectable and trustworthy institutions in the eyes of the public. However, unlike the medical and legal professions, journalists have not formed a policing body to enforce their codes; conformance must stem from the individual's conscience, and be debated by related agencies such as critical journals, press councils, individual publications and the ombudsman system.

Codes of ethics have been drawn up by journalism organizations, groups of writers in specialties, and newspapers. Two such codes are the Code of Ethics of the Society of Professional Journalists, Sigma Delta Chi; and the Associated Press Managing Editors Code of Ethics.

Reporters, writers and editors face ethical problems regardless of whether codes exist. Such questions arise because journalists must serve the public's right to know while maintaining the privacy of people involved in the news. They must preserve the trust of sources while presenting accurate accounts to their audience. And they cannot allow personal interests—in business or politics, for example—to cloud their unbiased presentation of an issue.

One issue that journalists deal with is whether to accept press trips or other gifts from a source and risk losing their objectivity. Another ethical question for the media is raised by reporters who pose as people in other professions to obtain information (in exposé stories, for example). Sometimes a newsperson is faced with a conflict of interest when a personal or business interest clashes with his professional obligation to serve the public. (This issue is detailed in the entry "Conflict of interest.") And although fabrication of quotes and facts along with plagiarism have not yet been abolished from the profession, they are two practices considered absolutely unethical by virtually all journalists.

A reporter's taking part in a story on which he reports—such as trying to negotiate with a terrorist in a hostage situation—presents another kind of ethical dilemma. In addition, interfering in a person's private life (i.e., the subject of a story) can be unethical when the private facts reported have no bearing on the story in question, or when publishing certain facts does more harm to the subject than it benefits the public.

The media also have the obligation to conform to their local community's norms regarding obscene or shocking words and graphic descriptions of crime or accidents. Being fair is another duty: The reporter should present all sides of a controversy and viewpoints of opposing sides when one person is accused by another.

Revealing the name of a source when anonymity has been requested can lose the reporter future access to that source as well as violate a trust; on the other hand, some newspeople believe that, to preclude instances of fabrication, reporters should be required to reveal sources to their editors.

Often, names of juvenile criminal suspects are withheld from the public out of concern for the future of the accused. Names of victims of some types of crime, especially rape, are also withheld from publication or broadcast.

The freelance writer must confront ethical situations that are peculiar to his field. For example, he must decide whether to inform interviewees that he is writing on speculation. Will the articles being done for one magazine help that magazine in its competition with another magazine for which the freelancer is also doing work? The same kind of conflict can arise in book publishing. Publishers' contracts, in fact, specify that authors cannot write books for other publishers that would substantially compete with the works being contracted for. And when holding another job, he faces the problem of whether his freelance work interferes with his full-time work. (*See: Conflict of interest; Ombudsman, newspaper; Plagiarism; Press trip; Right of privacy; Shield laws.*)

Junket. (*See: Press trip.*)

Juvenile biography. A narrative account of a person's life, written for young people. Juvenile biographies differ from adult biographies in the writer's approach to the subject. They portray the subject as an understandable human being who is the lead actor in a story. The achievements of the hero are the reason for the biography. For example, *The Value of Determination: The Story of Helen Keller*, by Ann D. Johnson, is a juvenile biography.

Characteristics of successful juvenile biographies for readers aged six to twelve include simple, lucid writing; much dialogue and action; and few descriptive passages. Successful biographies for teenagers depict both good and bad characteristics of the subject without editorializing, and deal with themes of adult life at a level that can be grasped by adolescents.

Although publishers have varing requirements, the average biography length for readers aged five to seven years is 1,000 words; eight to twelve years, 10,000-25,000 words; and thirteen years to adult, more than 30,000 words. (*See: Biography.*)

Juveniles, writing for. This includes works (both fiction and nonfiction) intended for an audience usually between the ages of two and sixteen. Writing for children is a specialized art that's harder than it looks. The language must be appropriate for the age of the reader, the subject matter must be of interest to the target age group, the opening of the work must be vivid enough to capture the reader's attention and the writing throughout must be action-oriented to keep it.

The successful writer knows his young audience well. Story ideas begin with a strong character and meaningful, directed action. The use of suspense and the interplay of human relationships are two features of effective juvenile fiction. Books and stories are told almost exclusively from a single viewpoint (in first or third person), as this technique helps to establish and sustain a sense of reader identity.

Nonfiction for young people takes the form of educational articles, biographies, how-to's, verse and puzzles. There are very few subjects that cannot be successfully presented to children if the writing is clear, accurate and tuned into a young person's frame of reference.

Categories of children's books are usually divided in this way: (1) picture and storybooks (ages two to nine). These are books read to and with children. They have a minimal amount of text (up to 1,000 words) and achieve their impact mainly through pictures; (2) easy-to-read books (ages seven to nine). These books are read by children themselves. The stories have a definite plot or message and run from 2,000 to 10,000 words; (3) "middle-age" children's books (ages eight to twelve). These books are read by the largest cluster of young readers, those interested in just about everything—today, tomorrow, yesterday, people, animals, humor. The texts range from 20,000-40,000 words, and in the case of nonfiction subjects may include pictures/illustrations; (4) young adult books (ages twelve to sixteen). These books (50,000-60,000 words) include category novels—adventure, sports, career, mysteries and romance.

In addition to book publishers, potential markets for juvenile writing include young people's magazines (more than one hundred in the U.S.), children's story papers, and religious publications. *Writer's Market, Children's Writer's & Illustrator's Market* and *Novel & Short Story Writer's Market* outline details for submitting manuscripts.

Payment for magazine submissions is either by the word or at a flat rate for a certain manuscript length. In the case of books, writers generally get the standard book royalty. Heavily illustrated books, such as picture books, usually call for a royalty split between author and artist. (*See: Children's theater; Juvenile biography; Plays for young actors.*)

Kappa Tau Alpha. An honorary fraternity composed of more than thirty-five thousand people in all aspects of journalism. The Frank Luther Mott-Kappa Tau Alpha Research in Journalism Award is presented annually by this association for a book incorporating the best research in journalism or communication. Top advisor and Top Scholar awards are also given, along with a monetary award for the best student paper entered in the Association for Education in Journalism and Mass Communication contest.

Kappa Tau Alpha convenes annually at a meeting held jointly with the Association for Education in Journalism and Mass Commuication. The address of this organization is 107 Sondra Ave., Columbia, MO 65202.

Kill. This is a publishing term used to refer to the deletion of part or all of an article or book. (*See: Kill fee.*)

Kill fee. A fee paid to a writer who has worked on an assignment that, for some reason, is not published. For example, the editor of a city magazine assigns a writer a 3,500-word article on a local political figure. The next issue of the area's regional magazine carries an in-depth article on the same politician, and the city magazine editor decides his publication's article would be too repetitive. The city magazine editor informs the writer, who has already researched and written the story, that the article will not be published after all. The writer then receives a percentage— from 20-50 percent—of the initially agreed-upon price for the manuscript, depending on the publication's policy.

Terms of the kill fee should be established when the assignment is accepted. If an editor fails to mention a kill fee, the writer should inquire whether such an arrangement is possible. The writer does not ordinarily receive a kill fee unless mention of it is included in the original assignment.

Kill fees are not common. Many magazines do not offer kill fees at all; others offer them only to professional writers with established writing credits. Writer and editor Art Spikol explains: "Look at it from the magazine's point of view: they end up paying . . . for nothing. The writer, at least, can resell the story elsewhere. . . ."

After receiving the kill fee, the writer may submit the article to other markets for a possible sale. Kill fees are offered to writers *on assignment* only; they do not apply to unsolicited manuscripts submitted on speculation. (*See: Assignment, writing on; Fees; On spec.*)

Kirkus Reviews. This well-respected biweekly publication furnishes its subscribers with book reviews two months in advance of the books' publication dates; about forty-five hundred titles are reviewed annually. Novelists, university professors and experts on various topics who work on the *Kirkus Reviews* staff review both fiction and nonfiction, as well as books for children and young adults. Some self-published books are also reviewed by this service.

Subscribers to *Kirkus Reviews* include librarians, book publishers, producers, magazine and newspaper editors, agents, booksellers and individuals who want advance evaluations of forthcoming books.

The advantages to the writer of having a favorable review in *Kirkus Reviews* are a possibly wider library sale and promotion material for the dust jacket; the book may also be called to the attention of a producer or other potential subsidiary rights buyer.

The address of this publication is 200 Park Ave. S., New York, NY 10003.

l.c. An abbreviation for *lower case* used by proofreaders and editors to indicate that a letter or letters printed as capitals should be lower-case letters. Written in the margin of a galley or page proof, it accompanies the proofreading symbol of a slanted line (/) drawn through the erroneous letter.

Language and style, books on. A well-known guide to writing and editing style is *The Chicago Manual of Style*, by the University of Chicago Press. *The New York Times, The Washington Post* and the *Los Angeles Times* have all produced guides for newspaper writers, as have both the AP and UPI wire services.

An excellent summary of the elementary rules of word usages, principles of composition, and words and expressions commonly misused is *The Elements of Style*, by William Strunk Jr., and E.B. White.

American Usage and Style: The Consensus, by Roy Copperud, compares differing opinions on usage in well-known works such as Fowler's *A Dictionary of Modern English Usage* and *Webster's Third New International*, the *American Heritage*, and *Random House* dictionaries.

Latin American writers. Since the early 1960s, a torrent of extraordinary literature has come out of Latin America in a literary renaissance. Much of today's most influential fiction is Latin American, and no writer or student of literature can afford to ignore it.

The two dominant themes of Latin American literature are man against nature and man against man; stories are often set against a hostile—even dangerous—environment. A recurrent symbol is that of the labyrinth: the labyrinth of rivers, of jungle, of relationships, of crowded towns, of time. Themes are often bound up with historical events and the political and social persecution that result from a history filled with political instability, corruption and social inequality. The widest-read authors are renowned as stylists; their prose (and their plots) tend to be dense and convoluted. "Magic-realism," a term applied to the work of Gabriel García Márquez and José Donoso, is a style of grotesque (and frequently hilarious) fantasy so richly detailed that it seems real.

The most important fiction writers include Argentinians Jorge Luis Borges (1899-1986) and Julio Cortázar (1914-1984); Colombian Gabriel García Márquez, winner of the 1982 Nobel Prize, whose *One Hundred Years of Solitude* is one of the most important Latin American works; Guatemalan Miguel Ángel Asturias (1899-1974), winner of the 1967 Nobel Prize; Mexican Carlos Fuentes; Peruvian Mario Vargas Llosa; and Brazilians Machado de Assis (1839-1908) and Jorge Amado. Great Latin American poets include Chileans

Pablo Neruda (1904-1973) and Gabriela Mistral (1889-1957), who won Nobel Prizes in 1971 and 1945, respectively; Peruvian Cesar Vallejo (1892-1938); and Mexican Octavio Paz. Contemporary authors Laura Esquivel (*Like Water for Chocolate*) and Chile's Isabel Allende (*Paula*) bring women's voices into the wealth of Latin American literature.

Additional information: *The Eye of the Heart* and *Into the Mainstream.*

Law related to writing. (*See: Advertising, copyrighted; Censorship, literary; Copyright; Free press vs. fair trial; Freedom of the press; Lawyers, where to find; Libel; Model release; Shield laws; Volunteer Lawyers for the Arts.*)

Lawyers, where to find. The *Martindale-Hubbell Law Directory* is an annual sourcebook published in several volumes and available in most large city public libraries or county law libraries. Information in listings varies according to whether the listee subscribes, but every listing includes the lawyer's name, year of birth, college attended, law school attended and the legal firm he or she is associated with.

Listings in this directory are gathered from the U.S., possessions of the U.S., Canada and fifty-three foreign countries. They are arranged alphabetically by geographic areas.

In addition, the directory contains information on law associations, public-interest law firms, legal aid offices, public defender offices and American Bar Association committees. The directory also contains a law digest, which summarizes the laws of each state in the U.S., the U.S. federal government, Puerto Rico, the Virgin Islands and fifty-three foreign countries. Summaries can be found under specific categories of law, such as garnishment, wills and divorce; these categories are, in turn, listed under geographic headings. A topical index is included.

The Directory also contains digests of the U.S. Copyright Law, the U.S. Patent Law and the U.S. Trademark Law.

Many city bar associations also maintain a lawyer's referral service. Through this service, a writer can obtain consultation for a nominal fee. For example, Cincinnati lawyers may charge no more than $20 per half hour. If the writer wishes to engage the attorney, they then discuss what the attorney's fee would be. Bar associations are usually listed in the white pages of the phone book under the name of the city or county in which they're located. (*See: Volunteer Lawyers for the Arts.*)

Lead. This journalistic term applies to a short summary that serves as the introduction to a news story, magazine article or other copy. Also known as an opening, introduction or narrative hook, the lead is a paragraph or series of paragraphs carefully constructed to capture and hold reader interest.

An effective lead is generally acknowledged to be vital in selling a manuscript—fiction or nonfiction—to an editor. The first few paragraphs of an article or story must impress an editor and encourage him to read on.

The writer should look for lead ideas during the research and preparation phase of the writing project. He cannot assume that the reader is as interested in the subject as he is; rather, the writer must *create* interest by promising that the article or story will deliver something—new information, entertainment, a chance to look behind the scenes of some project or event, or some other ''reward'' that will encourage the reader to finish the piece. To stimulate reader interest, the lead should appeal to basic human needs and emotions and give the reader a reason to care about the information contained in the article or story.

Depending on the publication he's writing for, a writer may choose to open his article with an anecdote, a shocking or startling statement, a quote, a question, a comparison, a generalization, straight narrative, pure information, an enigmatic description, a teasing statement or a summary of the information contained in the entire article. Some leads to avoid are definitions, background information and generic labels. These have become cliché and often tell the reader nothing.

Certain openings work best in particular publications; e.g., the pure information paragraph and the summary statement make good leads for articles in professional or trade journals, while the anecdotal lead is common to general-interest magazines such as *Reader's Digest.* The narrative lead is perhaps the most popular, certainly in works of fiction and often in articles and features.

While the lead of the traditional news story must be brief and to the point—packing the who, what, when, where, why and how into the first one or two sentences—the lead of an article or feature may develop more gradually.

Lead sheet. In music publishing, a song's written form. It includes melody, chords and lyrics, along with the songwriter's name, address and telephone number. Lead sheets can also be written as chord charts with lyrics. (*See: Lyric sheet; Lyrics; Musical; Songwriting.*)

Lead time. The time at which a manuscript must be on an editor's desk before scheduled publication. In the case of a magazine this could vary from two to six months in connection with seasonal material. In the case of a book, the date by which the manuscript must arrive is indicated in the book contract. Publication usually occurs nine to twelve months after the arrival of a satisfactory manuscript.

Leading (pronounced ledding). The amount of white space between lines of type on a typeset page. Type that is ten points and has two additional points of leading (or white space) between each line would be called *ten on twelve* or written as 10/12. The word *leading* comes from the pieces of lead that were inserted on a page of metal type for spacing purposes.

League of Canadian Poets. Founded in 1966, this organization of four hundred Canadian poets strives to advance poetry in Canada, as well as promote the professional interests of its members. The League holds an annual general meeting in June and publishes a bimonthly newsletter; *Museletter,* a biannual literary magazine; *Who's Who in Canadian Poets;*

Poetry Markets for Canadians; and the bimonthly *Poetry Spoken Here Network,* which lists readings and events across Canada. The League also sponsors a National Poetry Contest, open only to Canadians, and presents The Gerald Lampert Memorial Award for the best first book of poetry and The Pat Lawther Memorial Award for the best book of poetry by a Canadian woman. For more information, write to the LC-Pat, 54 Wolseley St., Third Floor, Toronto, Ontario M5T 1A5, Canada.

Lecture agencies. These firms secure speaking engagements for their clients, who may be political figures, celebrities, well-known authors or experts on specialized subjects. Some well-known authors are represented by firms such as American Program Bureau, 36 Crafts St., Newton, MA 02158. Other companies, such as Success Leaders Speakers Service, P.O. Box 1400, Roswell, GA 30077, is a speakers bureau that concentrates on lecturers who speak at management conferences, sales seminars and business conventions.

Lecture agencies seek out some writers as potential speakers; some writers are recommended to them. Some writers send in background data on their books' successes, reviews of or features about their speaking appearances, and solicit lecture engagements. A moderately successful writer could command $1,000-$5,000 in lecture fees.

For their work in promoting their clients as speakers, lecture bureaus receive a commission (usually 30 percent) on the speaker's fee. (*See: International Platform Association; National Speakers Association; Speakers and lecturers.*)

Lecturing techniques. Writers are often called upon to speak before groups on subjects they have written about, or on some aspect of writing. For the freelance writer, lecturing can provide work that varies from, yet relates to, his day-to-day routine and that at the same time brings him extra income both from the lecture itself and increased book sales. Topics writers are frequently asked to speak on include their latest book, contemporary novelists or poets, children's literature, how to freelance for profit and how to write for film and TV.

A good lecturer is in tune with the audience he plans to address: He takes a different approach speaking to a group of college students than when appearing before the ladies' auxiliary of a conservative fraternal organization. However, the speaker can bring any kind of audience into closer contact with him and his material by involving them—by asking for a show of hands on some aspect of the talk, injecting questions into the speech or distributing handouts relative to the lecture material. Eye contact with individuals in the audience also adds to a speech's effectiveness.

A speaker must be conscious of the impression projected by his physical appearance: Clothing, jewelry, hairstyle, posture and facial expression all contribute to the audience's response. The speaker's voice is an important tool that, through intonation, can show either enthusiasm and conviction or boredom.

A speaker can rehearse his talk in

person (at the location where he plans to speak or elsewhere), in his mind or on tape. Professionals believe a speech is better spoken from an organized set of ideas in the speaker's mind or from notes, than read from a prepared text. As a courtesy to the audience and the sponsor of the speech, the speaker should limit the length of his presentation to the agreed-upon amount of time.

After the speech, the speaker can give the program's sponsor an evaluation form to receive comments— and names of groups to which he would recommend the speaker. The lecturer can evaluate himself by listening to a tape of the speech. (*See: Ghostwriting speeches; Speakers and lecturers.*)

Legend. A story handed down from one generation to the next, often of particular importance to a specific culture or nationality. The truth of a legend, as well as its author, is usually unknown; however, legends are frequently accepted as historically true by those in the culture with which the story is concerned.

A legend is distinguished from a myth by its major character, which is a human; a myth's protagonist is a god. (Originally, *legend* referred to a story about a saint.)

Some legends published recently include *The Legend of Snowshoes* (Holt & Co.) and *King of the Birds* (Crowell). (*See: Folktale; Myth.*)

Legitimate drama. This refers to plays professionally produced on the stage, as distinguished from drama presented in motion pictures or on radio and TV.

The phrase once described the body of plays, Shakespearean and other, characterized by critical acclaim for theatrical or literary merit. The scope of legitimate drama has been broadened in the U.S. to describe any drama—including farce and melodrama—produced on the stage. (*See: Theater.*)

Letterhead. (*See: Stationery.*)

Letters. These sometimes interesting research documents cannot be used without permission of the author or his heirs, even though they may have been addressed to the person who wants to quote from them. Under copyright law, letters are considered the intellectual property of the creator, and while the physical piece of paper may be owned by the receiver, the thoughts and ideas expressed in the letter are the property of the sender.

A writer, for example, who finds a fascinating series of letters addressed to his great-grandmother from his great-grandfather who served in the Civil War, and who wanted to quote from this correspondence in his own book about that war, would be required to clear permission with the heirs of the great-grandfather, if there were others besides himself.

A writer who wants to publish a book of letters from a famous person to his contemporaries would similarly have to write not only to the persons who received the letters, but to the famous person himself, or his estate if deceased.

Unpublished letters, no matter how old, gained copyright protection under the copyright law on January 1, 1978, as long as there is an heir or someone else capable of owning the copyright in the letters. Anyone who has the right to claim copyright on unpublished letters or other personal manuscripts may register his claim with the Copyright Office if the work has not been registered previously.

Letters to the editor. Letters-to-the-editor columns, found in newspapers and magazines, furnish beginning writers with opportunities for exposure. Although there is rarely cash remuneration for the letter writer except in the case of "Op-Ed Page" contributions to newspapers and a few magazines that pay for letters, having work chosen for publication does give the writer confidence in his skill, and a published sample of his writing. (*See: Op-Ed page.*)

Libel. Libel is a form of defamation, or injury to a person's name or reputation. Written or published defamation is called *libel*; spoken defamation is known as *slander*.

In the U.S., each state and the District of Columbia has its own libel law. The Supreme Court made no decisions on this issue until the 1964 *New York Times v. Sullivan* case, which widened press freedom by devising the actual malice rule. This rule states that, in a libel action begun by a public official, the public official cannot be successful unless he proves actual malice, which can be manifest in the publisher's/writer's knowledge that the material is false or in his "reckless disregard" of whether it is false. *New York Times v. Sullivan,* then, represents the first time that First Amendment principles were applied to libel.

The three prerequisites to a libel suit are defamation, identification and publication. Defamation is harm done to someone's reputation through the printed or spoken word; it connotes lying. Second, the defamation must be clearly applicable, in the mind of a third party, to the plaintiff, who must prove that the defamation refers to himself; identification can be proven through a nickname, a pseudonym or circumstances, as well as by the plaintiff's actual name. Finally, to be considered libel the defamation must be published. Publication consists of the printing, posting or circulating of the material, and the subsequent reading of it by someone else.

Defenses against libel include truth, consent and fair comment. In some cases, the writer may not wish to rely on truth as a defense, even though the alleged libelous statement is true, because to do so would force him to reveal a confidential source. (Truth should not be confused with accuracy, which is not a defense. For example, a statement that has been accurately reported, but that is false, may not be defensible in every case.)

Consent, referring to the consent of the person about whom the alleged libel was committed, is another defense to a libel suit. The rationale of this provision is that anyone who consents to having material about himself published risks the possibility of being defamed by the publication. Consent may be either explicit, implied or apparent, from the allegedly libeled person's actions or words.

Third, fair comment is considered a defense when a reporter or critic has commented on a person, spectacle or performance that has been presented to the public. However, proof of malice can eliminate fair comment as a defense.

A retraction or correction made by a publication, though not a defense to a libel suit, can reduce the amount of damages imposed on a publisher who loses a lawsuit. For example, in some states, the plaintiff may recover only special damages if a retraction has been published.

A person who wins a libel suit may collect damages of one or more of the following types: special damages, compensatory damages and punitive damages. Special damages relate to material losses, such as that of a job or business. Compensatory damages are paid for intangible losses such as emotional upset or harm to one's reputation. Punitive damages are imposed for malicious or careless behavior on the part of the publisher. Punitive damages are not frequently allowed, but when they are allowed, it is usually in addition to another kind of damage.

One successful libel suit involved the late Paul ("Bear") Bryant, and *The Saturday Evening Post.* Bryant accused the magazine of libeling him by reporting that he had attempted to fix a football game. Damages received by Bryant totaled more than $3 million.

Another suit, dealing with fiction, was brought against novelist Gwen Davis Mitchell and Doubleday & Co., Inc. The plaintiff, Paul Bindrim, contended that Mitchell's novel *Touching* libeled him through the portrayal of a character who was based on him. He was awarded $75,000 in damages.

Through privileges, the law exempts public officials and journalists from libel suits, under certain conditions. Absolute privilege is granted to public officials such as presidents and governors; they are exempted from any libel suit that may result from statements they make when acting in an official capacity. The qualified privilege granted to journalists permits them to report statements that are absolutely privileged (e.g., in a speech by a governor) without being subject to suit. Conditions of the qualified privilege are that the report be fair and accurate and that the writer not be maliciously motivated.

An advertisement can be the basis for a libel suit, but a headline, standing alone, normally cannot. A headline usually must be considered along with the article or broadcast it accompanies. Cartoons are subject to libel suits: An editorial cartoon that was published in the Victoria (British Columbia) *Times* brought $3,500 in damages to William Vander Zalm, cabinet minister. The cartoon, which depicted Vander Zalm pulling out flies' wings, was judged to show him as being cruel and sadistic.

Libel insurance, which can be obtained from large insurance companies, is more easily available to publishers than to freelance writers. However, a writer can sometimes get insurance on a single book for which he has secured a contract, and a few book publishers include their authors in their libel insurance coverage.

Because the law of libel, like other laws, is constantly evolving and changes are sometimes determined by individual cases, the best way to stay abreast of this issue is to read reports of cases and developments in journalism and writing trade journals. (*See: Insurance, authors' liability.*)

Libel Defense Resource Center (LDRC). This organization acts as an information source for attorneys and defendants in libel cases and invasion-of-privacy cases. It continually researches cases at the state and federal levels, and makes information available via a brief, pleading and information bank; a quarterly bulletin; and statistics concerning the incidence and costs of litigation. Annually, the LDRC makes available two fifty-state surveys: the Media Privacy and Related Law survey in June and the Media Libel Law survey in October.

Established in 1980, LDRC is supported by about 260 associations, firms and individuals who represent various areas of the communications industry, including the Authors League of America and the Reporters Committee for Freedom of the Press.

LDRC can assist writers in finding defense attorneys, but it does not maintain a defense fund or a formal referral service.

The address of the Libel Defense Resource Center is 404 Park Ave. S., Sixteenth Floor, New York, NY 10016. (*See: Lawyers, where to find; Volunteer Lawyers for the Arts.*)

Librarians. A librarian can be a valuable asset to the writer; he is more familiar with the library's collection than the writer is, and is aware of new sources of information the writer-researcher may not have

heard about. A writer can often save research time and effort simply by asking the librarian whether there are any new sources in his field of interest. The librarian can also direct the library user to special collections or departments the latter may be unaware of.

Many libraries have computerized databases that can locate books in other libraries when the work isn't in their collection. Many also have computerized bibliographic services, and if a writer has a specific subject on which he wants to search out newspaper or magazine articles, he can obtain computer search time. (*See: Research aids/techniques; Research sources, directories of.*)

Libraries, information on. The *American Library Directory* covers public, college, military, medical, vocational, institutional, law, religious and special libraries in Canada, the U.S. and U.S.-administered regions. Listings include address, telephone number, number of volumes, income and expenditures, and information on personnel, microforms and special collections.

Listings of American and Canadian special libraries can be found in the *Directory of Special Libraries.* Volume 1 lists the libraries alphabetically by name, but writers seeking specialized research will find the Subject Index most useful. Volume 2 contains one index of libraries by geographic region, and another of library personnel.

The Bowker Annual Library & Book Trade Almanac is an anthology of articles about the field of library science, book publishing and the information industry. Some of the book's topics of interest to writers are technological developments, library statistics surveys, prices of U.S.- and foreign-published materials, education and salaries of library personnel, and projections on library jobs.

The one-volume *ALA World Encyclopedia of Library and Information Services* contains information on ideas, history and prominent people in library science. *Library Literature* lists library science periodicals, refers readers to publications and films of interest to librarians, and informs the reader about library trends, issues, prominent people in the field, research and the history of librarianship.

Library classification systems. The Dewey Decimal System and the Library of Congress System are used by libraries to aid users in locating volumes.

The Dewey Decimal System, devised in 1876 and still used by most public libraries, was named for its originator, Melvil Dewey, an American librarian. Dewey was also founder of the *Library Journal* and co-founder of the American Library Association.

The Library of Congress System was established in 1897 when the Library decided it needed a more flexible system for its extensive holdings. Many college libraries use the Library of Congress system.

Directories showing the many subcategories under each main classification are available in any library (along with a subject cross-reference) so that the writer can look up what call numbers he might like to browse in if the library has open stacks. (*See: Figure 23.*)

Library of Congress. Writers outside the Washington, DC area can also use the many information and research services offered by the Library of Congress, the world's largest library. Primarily a reference library, the Library of Congress describes the services it makes available to the public in two publications, *Information for Readers* and *Services to the Nation*, both of which are available free of charge from the Library of Congress, National Reference Service, Washington, DC 20540.

Although the primary purpose of the Library of Congress is to provide Congress with the information that body requires to serve the nation, other services are offered by its various departments, each of which has a special intent. The one division not directly accessible to the public is the Congressional Research Service (CRS), whose eight hundred researchers work for Congress alone.

The Telephone Reference, Correspondence, and Bibliography Section will respond to telephone or mail inquiries by referring questions to the appropriate reference division. In response to written requests, the general reference room will suggest bibliographies. (Bibliographies of scholarly depth must be obtained from the appropriate reference librarian, however.)

The Library's Prints and Photographs Division houses more than ten million pictures, posters, drawings, negatives and motion pictures, all dealing with some aspect of American history or life. The writer who makes a personal visit to this division will find assistance in locating the pictures he needs or will receive a recommendation for a picture re-

FIGURE 23

LIBRARY OF CONGRESS SYSTEMS

*F*or browsing in open stacks at libraries using either the Dewey Decimal System or the Library of Congress cataloging method, here are selected references:

SUBJECT	LIBRARY CLASSIFICATION	DEWEY DECIMAL
Agriculture	S	630
Arts, Fine	N	700
Bibliography	Z	010
Biography	CT	920
Education	L	370
General Works (encyclopedias, etc.)	A	000
Geography	G	910
History, America	E	973
History, Outside America	D	900
Language	P	400
Law	K	340
Literature	P	800
Medicine	R	610
Military Science	U	355
Music	M	780
Naval Science	V	359
Philosophy	B	100
Political Science	J	320
Religion	BL-BX	200
Science	Q	500
Social Sciences	H	300
Technology	T	600

searcher who will—for a fee—hunt out the required photos. Those pictures selected can be duplicated and mailed to the writer; a list of fees and appropriate forms may be obtained from Photoduplicating Services at the Library of Congress. (These fees and forms apply to any other reference materials an individual may want to receive copies of.)

The Science and Technology Division can provide the writer with information about current scientific and technical resources that may not be available in a local library. The reference section of this division also publishes *Tracer Bullets*, a series of guides that provide bibliographies for certain scientific subjects. The freelancer can request a list of those *Tracer Bullets* already published and then order the ones in which he is interested. There is no charge for this service.

Library of Congress catalog card number. This number, assigned to a book by the Library of Congress, is used by librarians for classification and ordering purposes. The number is usually printed on the book's copyright page. The catalog number appears as two digits followed by a hyphen and five more digits (90-38471, for example) and sometimes has *CIP* typed below it. Established publishers can also get preassigned numbers, which appear as six characters following the *PN* prefix (PN 141.W75).

A publisher may apply for such a number either before or after a book has been published. For a book that has not yet been published, the publisher first submits an application to the Library's Cataloging in Publication (CIP) Division. Later, he sends an advance complimentary copy of the published book. At this stage, the Library determines whether the book will be kept in its collections, and, if it chooses the book, prepares suitable catalog cards.

To obtain a Library of Congress catalog card number for a published book, the publisher submits a copy of the book, along with a letter asking whether the book will be chosen for Library of Congress use and what the assigned catalog card number will be.

According to the Library of Congress, the Cataloging in Publication Program "benefits publishers because the cataloging records for Cataloging in Publication titles are entered onto Library of Congress MARC computer tapes, which alert librarians to forthcoming publications and enable them to select and order new publications promptly and accurately." Since Cataloging in Publication data are printed in the books themselves, libraries pay lower cataloging costs and readers have access to the books sooner.

The production or editorial department of a publishing house generally applies for the Library of Congress number on the author's behalf, but if an author self-publishes the book he must apply for the number himself by writing Cataloging in Publication Program, Library of Congress, Washington, DC 20540.

Library of Congress Photoduplication Service. A division of the Library of Congress that provides photocopies, photographs, and microfilm reproductions of research material to libraries, organizations and individuals. According to the Library, this service "will generally make photoduplicates of materials in its collections available for research use. . . . Certain restricted material cannot be copied."

To request photoduplicates, the researcher sends either a purchase requisition or an order form—both available from the Library of Congress—or a letter. Work on an order is sometimes completed in a matter of days, but larger orders may take two months. The Service's "Conditions of Order" statement lists charges for each type of duplication. Sample costs are: $.50 per photocopy of text and line material (subject to a minimum charge per order of $10); a photostat print from unbound material (up to 17½″×17½″ image size) or from bound volumes, $15. Orders of $20 or less carry a mailing fee of $3.50; $20.01-$50 adds $8.50; $50.01-$150 adds $13.50.

Above $150, the fee is 8 percent of the total.

All duplicates made by the Library of Congress comply with the copyright law; the recipient of the material is responsible for its fair use. The Library points out: "Written permission from the copyright owner or payment of a royalty fee may be required."

The mailing address is Photoduplication Service, Library of Congress, Washington, DC 20540; the telephone number is (202) 707-5640. (*See: Copyright; Fair use; Library of Congress.*)

Library reprint (scholarly reprint). (*See: Reprint.*)

Library use. In addition to using a public library, the freelancer may decide to take advantage of the services of a university library. These libraries are likely to be accessible even to freelance writers who are not students. Most university libraries are open on Sundays and have longer Friday and Saturday night hours than public libraries; a writer who lives near a university can usually take advantage of its research facilities when the local public library is closed.

It is suggested that a writer who wishes to use a university library explain his purpose to the librarian and ask about checking out books.

There are also many specialized libraries. Freelance writers researching a certain topic can find sources in the *Directory of Special Libraries,* which has a subject cross-index, as does *Who's Who in Special Libraries,* published by the Special Libraries Association. (*See: Librarians; Librar-ies, information on; Library classification systems.*)

Light verse. Light verse is intended to entertain, amuse or please readers. Characterized by brevity (seldom more than ten lines long, four lines being most popular) and conventional rhyme and meter, light verse is usually distinguished by its wit and subtlety and perfection of form rather than by depth or genuine literary significance. It makes use of humor, wit and/or satire, and often contains a "twist" gimmick—a paradoxical or ironic turn to a word, a rhyme or a common expression.

Subject matter for light verse is virtually unlimited; in many cases, the most ordinary topic—one focusing on a common experience shared by a large number of people—underlies the most salable verse. Here is an example by John Engle Jr.:

Two Fevers
This bright romantic rush of spring
I cannot tolerate,
Especially when flowers and trees
Begin to pollinate.

Though I've spring fever in my heart,
Hay fever's in my head;
And everytime I try to kiss,
I have to sneeze instead.

Markets for light verse include *Good Housekeeping, Golf Digest, California Bicyclist,* some religious publications and certain greeting card publishers. Payment may run anywhere from a high $5 per line among the major magazines to $.25 per line among the smaller publications. The average rate is $1-$2 per line. *Poet's Market* lists editorial requirements and pay rates for light verse markets.

Material should be submitted— one typewritten verse per page—in batches of three to five. Don't send more unless the guidelines indicate the editors want that many. A self-addressed, stamped envelope should be included with the submission. (*See:* Poet's Market; *Verse.*)

Limerick. A kind of light verse constructed in five lines, the first, second, and fifth of which are in trimeter, and the third and fourth in dimeter. The rhyme scheme of a limerick is usually AABBA, although the following example, by Edward Lear, is a slight variation:

A flea and a fly in a flue
Were imprisoned, so what could
they do?
Said the flea, "Let us fly!"
Said the fly, "Let us flee!"
So they flew through a flaw in the
flue.

One school of thought contends that the limerick originated in Ireland, where the people improvised this form at social functions. However, others trace the limerick to the work of Shakespeare, who included it, in imperfect form, in *Othello* and *King Lear*. Limericks became popular after publication of the work of Edward Lear, who wrote the *Book of Nonsense* (1846) and *More Nonsense* (1872).

The subject matter of the limerick varies widely, but the limerick is always humorous in tone. (*See: Verse.*)

Line of poetry, a. Lines in poetry are measured in vertical, rather than horizontal, space. A line can be one word or a dozen or more. Most mag-

azines pay poets by the line: The same fee is paid for each line, regardless of length. Some, however, pay a flat fee for a poem.

The example below, by John D. Engle Jr., contains sixteen lines of poetry, each of which is a different length. The fifth line, even though it contains only a letter and a hyphen, is still regarded as a line in this case.

Suggestion

Juggle
the alphabet
of being.
Break
a-
part
the patterned
syllables.
Fling
them
against the dark,
and watch them
write themselves
in stars
on the blackboard
of the night.

from *Modern Odyssey*,
Copyright 1980

The poet must use logic when dividing his work into lines: It is obvious to an editor when a poet has tried to take advantage of the pay-by-the-line policy. The humorous verse below, by John D. Engle Jr., exemplifies such cunning taken to the extreme:

Practical Poet

Dear
Editor,
here's

a
poem
of
mine,
inspired
by
all
that
is
divine.

Will
you
please
pay
me
by
the
line.
From *Laugh Lightly*
Copyright 1974
The Golden Quill Press

(*See: Poetry; Verse.*)

Line printer proofs. For editorial functions such as proofreading, some phototypesetting systems can produce inexpensive computer-printed proofs on ordinary computer paper. Line printer type is a plain typewriter type instead of a typeface; the line printer types out the words that have been typeset, indicating variations from the basic text—bold or italic type, bigger or smaller type sizes or spacing—in numbered codes that the computer or an editor familiar with the system can interpret. After proofreaders' and other editorial corrections and the author's alterations are entered into the computer, it can produce *hard type*, which is the actual typeset text, printed photographically on light-sensitive paper, as it will appear in the book or magazine.

A line printer system saves a publisher money in two ways: It is very easy to enter a file and correct and revise text *before* the typeset stage, and it minimizes consumption of expensive photopaper and developing chemicals.

Liner notes. Copy by a staff or freelance writer describing the song and the artist performing on a record. Freelancers with special knowledge of, or contacts with, a recording artist may secure a freelance liner copy assignment from the record company producing the album.

Literary awards. (*See: American Book Awards; Nobel Prize for Literature; Pulitzer Prizes.*)

Literary critic. A reviewer hired by a newspaper, syndicate or radio or TV network to appraise new books, plays, films or other literary work and express his opinion of it. (*See: Criticism of manuscript.*)

Literary executor. A person designated by an author to be an adviser, on the author's death, for his unpublished manuscripts—whether to release any of those manuscripts for publication posthumously. The executor of the author's estate ensures that his heirs receive the royalties from his already-published material.

Literary fiction vs. commercial fiction. To the writer of literary, or serious, fiction, style and technique are often as important as subject matter. Although some literary writers, such as Saul Bellow, have become financially successful, mass readership is usually not the primary expectation of authors of serious fiction.

Commercial fiction, however, is written with the intent of reaching as wide an audience as possible. Some commercial writers take advantage of social trends to which they can connect the subject matter of their work. Similarly, they note the types of fiction that a majority of the public enjoys reading. Commercial fiction is sometimes called *genre fiction* because books of this type often fall into categories, such as western, gothic, romance, historical, mystery and horror. Jude Deveraux and Stephen King, with millions of copies of their books in print, are examples of successful commercial fiction writers.

In 1994, approximately 3,121 hardcover and trade paperback novels—both new books and new editions of earlier works—were published. Many of these are mainstream serious fiction, but hardcover young adult "career" novels and other less serious works are also included in the count.

In 1994, approximately 2,298 new and revised editions of mass market paperback novels were also printed. Many of these are popular romances, westerns, mysteries, etc., but the figure also includes paperback reprints of literary works that hit the best-seller list. (*See: Avant-garde; Experimental fiction; Mainstream fiction.*)

Literary journal. Writers should note that there is a marked distinction between a little/literary magazine and a literary journal. Literary journals, such as *Kenyon Review* or *Yale Review*, are scholarly magazines most often connected with and financed by a university or foundation. They publish articles on national issues, politics, art, music, international relations or scholarly research in addition to fiction and poetry. Some literary journals include very little imaginative literature; their strength lies in criticism rather than creativity. While these journals may offer payment, they usually accept little freelance material, relying instead on academic contributors or writers sought out by the editor. Prestige is high, but competition is extremely keen for publication in literary journals. (*See: Little/literary magazine.*)

Literary Market Place (LMP). An annual directory covering eighty-two areas of book publishing. This book is used mainly by those in the book industry, but it can be useful to authors, librarians, broadcast personnel, job-seekers and academics. A book author, for example, who wants to look up names of publishers to whom his regional book might appeal could use its geographic cross-reference.

The eight major divisions of LMP are Book Publishers; Editorial Services and Agents; Advertising, Marketing and Publicity; Book Manufacturing; Sales and Distribution; Services and Suppliers; Associations, Events, Courses and Awards; and Books and Magazines for the Trade. Grouped under these eight divisions are the eighty-two sections, each of which represents a different aspect of the book industry.

In addition, the directory includes a section called "Industry Yellow Pages," which lists personnel and firms listed in its other sections. This section also serves as an index by listing the section number in which the organization appears in the directory. For instance, writers trying to track down an editor who has moved from one publishing company to another can use this index to find out the editor's current firm.

Listings in LMP include names, addresses, phone and fax numbers, names of personnel and other descriptive data on organizations. For example, a publisher's listing in the section "U.S. Book Publishers" contains some or all of the following information: names of editorial, sales, promotion, rights and permissions personnel; subjects of specialization; its advertising agency; distributors; number of titles published during the previous year; ISBN publisher's prefix; and foreign representatives.

Published by R.R. Bowker Company, this directory is available in most libraries.

Little theater. These are community theater groups of amateur performers who produce plays for local audiences. They secure the plays they perform from play-leasing companies from whom they buy copies of the script and to whom they pay royalties for the rights to perform the play. How much royalty they pay depends on the name and popularity of the author and his work. A percentage of such playscript sales and performance royalties is paid to the playwright by the play-leasing company. Little theater groups are an excellent source of working knowledge about playwriting for the author himself. After he has served his own apprenticeship with a company—perhaps as a stagehand or publicity

director—he may wish to approach the group about their producing one of his original plays. Getting such a local production can be an invaluable aid to the new playwright to see what parts of his script do or don't "work" in actual performance.

Little/literary magazine. This term is applied to a noncommercial publication of limited circulation (five thousand or fewer) that is usually literary or political in nature, and often unorthodox and experimental in its approach to prose and poetry. Its audience is composed mainly of other writers, editors and students of literature.

Little magazines are traditionally the place where quality writers—the men and women who are interested in literary excellence—publish their poetry, fiction and other creative work. Many fine writers—T.S. Eliot, William Faulkner, Flannery O'Connor, John Gardner and Joyce Carol Oates among them—made their reputations initially in little magazines.

Little magazines are financed by people whose ideal is to present an intelligent and sophisticated writing platform of new and avant-garde forms that may go unpublished in the larger commercial magazines. Editors of little/literary magazines need not compromise their ideals with popular taste because they do not rely on the general public for support.

On the other hand, little magazines are often underfinanced. The editors/publishers of the small literary magazines do not expect to make a profit from their publications; in fact, they seldom break even. For this reason, many literary magazines are short-lived.

Little magazines may develop around a specific theme or describe themselves as "eclectic"—willing to look at any manuscript of quality regardless of subject, theme or form. Publications may also have a particular regional, cultural or intellectual focus.

The literaries offer little incentive to the money-oriented writer. Payment is low or nonexistent; most authors receive only contributor's copies of the issue in which their work appears, or perhaps a year's subscription to the magazine. Once published in a literary, however, the writer will have the satisfaction of reaching dedicated, interested readers—and occasionally even editors of major magazines and publishing houses who scout small magazines for talent.

Although words in fixed, published forms are automatically copyrighted, writers are cautioned that some of the little/literary magazines are not copyrighted. Publication in such magazines doesn't mean the writer's work will enter the public domain; but just to be safe, the author's copyright credit line should appear with his poem, story or article. Details on editorial requirements are outlined in *Writer's Market* and *Novel & Short Story Writer's Market*. (*See: Literary journal.*)

Local color. A term referring to writing in which descriptions of a particular geographic region are prominent. Writers who use local color incorporate speech patterns, descriptions of dress and social customs, as well as characteristic scenery, into their fiction or nonfiction. This element is evident in the work of contemporary writers like Jimmy Breslin and John Gardner. "Color" is also used to mean any highly descriptive newspaper writing in which the reader's senses are evoked.

Logline. A scriptwriting term that refers to a boiled-down description of a TV or movie script. It consists of two or three concise sentences.

Logo. A trademark design, often incorporating the name of the publisher or publication it belongs to. Some well-known examples are the mountain for Tor Books; and the flaming torch for HarperCollins. (*See: Colophon.*)

"Long arm" law. A type of state law that renders people outside the state who conduct various types of activities in the state subject to the jurisdiction of the state's courts. A writer can in some cases use a long arm law to file suit in his own state for a payment that has been withheld by a publisher in a different state. Not all states have the same long arm statute: The writer can find out from an attorney what type of long arm statute exists in his own state. (*See: Complaints against publishers.*)

Long form. A TV program of more than one hour in length. (*See: Television script terms.*)

Lyric sheet. A song's lyrics typed out on paper, usually single-spaced with double spacing between verses. The lyric sheet should be typed neatly and include the writer's name, address and telephone number at the bottom. It is submitted by a song-writer with his demo tape to a music publisher or record company. (*See: Lead sheet; Lyrics; Songwriting.*)

Lyrics. The words to a song.

Although some lyrics read like a poem, this quality is not necessarily essential to a good set of lyrics.

Successful lyrics are those that combine, both in feeling and rhythmic pattern, with the music they accompany—e.g., normally stressed syllables should not be changed to fit the stressed musical beats. In the same vein, it is better to end a line with a vowel sound than a consonant, because a vowel ending is not as abrupt and can be sustained by the singer if he desires.

The length of a typical song does not allow for wordiness; every word should contribute to the meaning. The lyrics should state their point as soon as possible. Similarly, the title of a song—which should be repeated often throughout the set of lyrics—should reflect its main idea. A line of lyric is best when it can stand alone as a complete thought and is void of conjunctions such as *and, but* and *so.* Positive ideas are more effective than negative ones. The names given to characters in a song are more likely to contribute to successful lyrics when they are not out of the ordinary; however, a lyricist should feel free to use an unusual name to convey a particular image.

Some lyricists compose their own music to fit their words; others collaborate with another person. A beginning lyricist should not expect the music industry to locate a composer to write music for the words he submits; the only acceptable procedure is for the songwriter either to write his own music or to work with a collaborator before the piece is submitted to a music publisher.

Lyrics, like other forms of writing, are subject to lawsuits when they defame a person. Therefore, when basing his lyrics on a real event, the lyricist should be careful to change the names of the people involved. (*See: Songwriting.*)

Magazine, alternative. A publication directed toward individuals whose lifestyles and/ or cultural, political or literary values differ from current "establishment" values. Alternative magazines cover a wide range of special interests and provide a forum for expressing unconventional or minority ideas and views that wouldn't necessarily be published in the commercial or popular press.

Many alternative publications are "little" magazines that do not pay except in contributor's copies. The writer will also find, however, a number of well-established, well-paying markets among the alternative magazines, such as *Mother Jones, High Times* and *The Mother Earth News.* Editorial requirements for alternative magazines are listed annually in *Writer's Market.* (*See: Alternative Weekly; Little/ literary magazine.*)

Magazine article, types of. Articles fall into many categories, some of which have been established by repeated use and others that defy labeling. A writer need not be ruled by classifications each time he begins a new piece: Achieving the effect he desires outweighs constructing the article to fit a certain category.

Designated types of articles can be useful, however, in communication between writer and editor. Following are brief descriptions of some of the article types consistently bought by editors.

The *informational article* is meant to familiarize the reader with a topic of interest to him. It primarily contains facts, such as the article "School Nurse Emergency: Are Kids at Risk?" which appeared in *Parenting.*

The *how-to article* is a demonstration or explanation of how to accomplish something, e.g., "Making Tea," which appeared in *Saveur.* A subcategory of the how-to is the self-improvement article, which is sometimes called a "you" article because of the likely use of *you* in its title. Illustrations are an integral part of many how-to articles.

A *service article* is about a consumer product or service; it outlines the characteristics of several of the same type of commodity. Articles advising the consumer of points to consider and problems to avoid in a purchase are also called service articles. Samples of such articles might be a round-up on the types of paint to use on lawn furniture or a guide to selecting and buying a used car. One typical *Glamour* service article was titled "10 Critical Mistakes Your Doctor Could Be Making."

A piece in which the writer recounts an ordeal, process or event he has undergone is a *personal experience article.* It inspires, educates or entertains the reader. "The Spa and Me," published in *Shape,* is an article of this type.

Another kind of article, the *inter-*

view article, is based primarily on an interview with one person. Interview articles take one of three forms: the *question-and-answer format*; the *success article*, which outlines a person's rise to success; or the *profile*, which sometimes contains subjective observations by the writer as well as direct quotes from the interviewee. This third type can be biographical, professional or ideological in emphasis. "In the Beginning . . ."—a piece about Larry Gelbart—published in *Writer's Digest*, is an interview article.

The *think article* involves an analysis of facts, events or trends as the writer perceives them. The writer must present informed opinion and draw conclusions that are intended to persuade the reader. Think articles commonly appear in quality magazines and on newspaper op-ed pages. *Harper's* published "Gilding the News," a think article that analyzes the journalistic methods and practices of the media and the audience response they provoke.

In the *historical article*, different aspects of historical events can be covered in a light manner for popular magazines, or through in-depth research for scholarly publications. "Evolution of the Delta/Mississippi River Levee System," which was published in *Delta Scene*, is a historical article.

The *travel article* can pertain to any place in the world, but—like other kinds of articles—it must have a specific focus. "Fantasy Islands for Families," printed in *Child*, falls into this category.

Published in both consumer and trade magazines, the *product article* is intended to serve readers. Since editors are wary of publishing articles

that seem to be free advertising, they impose rigid guidelines on the product article; one such article is "Gun Journal Test: Remington's Model Four & Model Six," published in *Gun Journal*.

In those infrequent circumstances in which a freelance writer is at the scene of an event and newspaper reporters are absent, the result could be a newspaper *spot-news article*. This kind of story can also be written in an in-depth form as a background article for a magazine or a Sunday supplement. The spot-news article "He Was Dead," about the trial of convict-writer Jack Abbott, ran in the "Nation" section of *Time*.

The *exposé article* is the result of the writer's intensive research and investigation. It often includes an element of shock that is substantiated with fact, and its subject is often corruption in business or government, or a similar issue. The most famous exposé in the last twenty-five years was the series of articles concerning the Watergate scandal, written by two reporters for *The Washington Post*, Bob Woodward and Carl Bernstein, in the early 1970s.

A *seasonal article* is written about a holiday, season of the year or timely observance. This kind of article must be submitted months in advance of the anticipated publication date. "Suddenly It's Spring!," which appeared in *National Wildlife*, detailed the events of the short-lived spring of northern New England.

The *inspirational article* often concerns the successful efforts of an individual or group to improve a situation that affected them. Through it, the writer passes along a philosophy that the reader (ideally) is able to adopt. This kind of article sometimes has a religious theme. "Getting Along with Aging Parents," which appeared in *Home Life*, is an example of the inspirational article.

The *humorous article*, one of the most difficult kinds to write, can be a source of generous financial reward for the writer. Most successful humorists have attained their status only after years of experience. In a humorous article titled "Motormouth," which appeared in *Parents*, the writer described the incessant talking of her ten-year-old son.

Being aware of the article categories helps the writer structure his work and accommodate the needs of editors. (*See: Exposé; Historical writing; How-to articles and books; Humor; Inspirational writing; Interview; Nostalgia; Round-up article; Seasonal material; Travel writing.*)

Magazine editor salaries. (*See: Figure 24.*)

Magazine editorial contract. Magazines that work with freelancers generally use two types of contracts: one that spells out the terms of an assignment, and one that details the terms of purchasing an article whether it was assigned or unsolicited.

An assignment contract can include the name of the writer, the title or topic of the article, length, deadline, payment, rights and kill fee.

A contract to buy a piece usually calls for the author's name, address, social security number; title of article; amount to be paid; biographical information and rights being purchased.

A copy of "PEN Standards for Magazine and Periodical Assignments" is available free, for a self-addressed, stamped envelope from PEN American Center, 568 Broadway, New York, NY 10012.

Magazine Index. (*See: Periodicals, indexes to.*)

Magazine Industry Newsletter. (*See: Media Industry Newsletter [MIN].*)

Magazine personnel. A magazine staff consists of editorial, advertising, production, circulation and administrative departments. The magazine's revenue from circulation and advertising determines the number of employees.

Although most magazine jobs that involve writing are found in editorial departments, being employed in another department occasionally leads to an editorial position. News-oriented magazines hire staff writers; but many magazines depend on freelance writers for most articles.

Positions on magazines' editorial staffs vary, as do the duties and titles associated with each one. The top-ranking person, usually called the editor, editor in chief or editorial director, is responsible for generating ideas, advance planning, offering final criticism of each issue's content and supervising the publication. Positions next in line may be called executive editor or managing editor. Junior editors are responsible for reviewing unsolicited manuscripts for possible publication and senior editors for rewriting submitted material. Copyeditors (or copyreaders) polish spelling, style, syntax and punctuation. A researcher gathers information and checks facts in com-

FIGURE 24

MAGAZINE EDITOR SALARIES

Responsible for editorial direction and content, including art, text and cover of one or more magazines.

AVERAGE SALARIES		*% INCREASE FROM 1993 TO 1994*
All respondents	$52,800	15%
Consumer	$55,400	21%
Business	$49,700	7.8%
Top one-third	$87,400	
Middle one-third	$56,300	
Bottom one-third	$43,100	

	AVERAGE	*AVERAGE BUSINESS*	*AVERAGE CONSUMER*
RESPONSIBLE FOR:			
One magazine	$51,860	$54,749	$48,728
More than one magazine	55,598	56,873	53,493
BY NUMBER OF EMPLOYEES SUPERVISED:			
None/One	$34,149	$35,005	$32,736
2-4	44,990	45,133	44,737
5 or more	67,556	80,253	58,547
BY CIRCULATION:			
Up to 19,999	$58,853	$61,982	$33,000
20,000-49,999	54,388	59,644	46,108
50,000-99,999	44,244	41,066	46,300
100,000-499,999	53,283	56,763	48,022
500,000 or more	*	*	*
BY FREQUENCY:			
Weekly/biweekly	$59,622	*	*
Monthly	59,515	$65,538	$50,066
Other	42,679	39,148	45,896
BY TOTAL PAGES PRODUCED ANNUALLY:			
Up to 499	$37,873	$39,826	$34,237
500-999	56,906	67,325	47,352
1,000-1,499	47,683	*	*
1,500-2,999	*	*	*
3,000 or more	*	*	*

* Not enough information supplied to report results. Reprinted from the August 1, 1994 issue of FOLIO: The Magazine of Magazine Management. *© 1994 Cowles Business Media.*

pleted manuscripts; some magazines hire reporter-researchers, who interview, gather facts and present their material to staff writers to be turned into articles. Editorial assistants handle correspondence, proofreading, typing and other miscellaneous tasks.

A contributing editor is a freelance writer whose material is used so frequently that he is listed on the masthead and/or given space to work at the magazine's offices.

A significant number of staff-written articles are published in magazines; the authors of these may be listed on the masthead as staff writers, or be among the various editors on the magazine staff.

Departments other than editorial sometimes use the services of writers. Promotion managers hire writers to turn out advertising copy for the magazine, circulation directors need assistance in writing direct-mail packages for potential or renewing subscribers, and public relations practitioners hire writers to compose press releases and do other publicity-related writing. (*See: Contributing editor; Copyeditor; Figure 25; Masthead, how to read.*)

Magazine Publishers Association (MPA).

An organization of approximately two hundred magazine publishers who produce more than nine hundred magazines. Members' magazines may be of categories other than consumer, but they must be published at least four times per year.

MPA maintains an office in Washington, DC, that stays abreast of legislation and Postal Service affairs. The Association's Circulation Marketing Department informs members on magazine circulation marketing matters. Also, MPA operates a library of materials on the magazine business. The Association holds an annual management conference in the fall.

Awards presented by this organization are the Henry Johnson Fisher Award, to a magazine executive who has made a significant contribution to magazine publishing; and the Stephen E. Kelly Award (of $100,000), to the advertising agency that has produced the best magazine print advertisement of a given year.

MPA's thirty committees include Advertising Marketing, Circulation Marketing, Education, Government Affairs, Postal and Alternative Delivery, Publishing Management, and Transportation. The MPA can be reached at 919 Third Ave., New York, NY 10022.

Magazine publishers, multiple.

The term *multiple* (or *chain*) *magazine publishers* is often applied to companies that publish several magazines. They may all be allied in subject matter, such as Weider Publications (health and fitness) or House of White Birches (crafts); or they may be a variety of publications in different trade or technical areas, such as those owned by the Chilton Company (automotive, electronics, instruments, etc.).

Writers who submit manuscripts to a multiple publisher should not assume that a rejection from one editor is a rejection from other editors at magazines owned by the same company; the manuscript can be resubmitted to another editor at the same company.

Writer's Market listings give individual editors' names as well as publications' company affiliations.

A list of the multiple holdings of various magazine publishers appears in *Standard Rate and Data Service* directories of consumer, farm and business publications, available in most libraries.

Magazine revenues, costs, profits.

(*See: Figure 26.*)

FIGURE 25

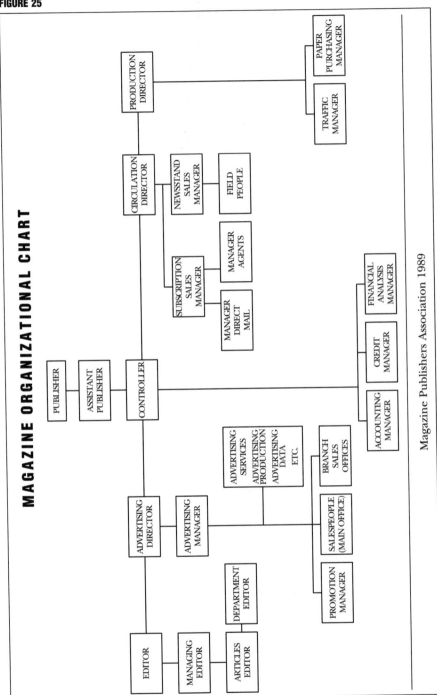

MAGAZINE ORGANIZATIONAL CHART

Magazine Publishers Association 1989

FIGURE 26

MAGAZINE REVENUES/COSTS/PROFITS

	PERCENTAGES OF TOTAL REVENUE
	1993
TOTAL NUMBER OF MAGAZINES REPORTING	213
REVENUE (in millions)	
Net advertising revenues	44.94
Gross subscription revenues	40.28
List rental revenues	0.79
Gross single copy revenues	13.99
Total magazine revenues	100.00%
EXPENSES	
Advertising	
Selling costs	6.06
Research and promotion costs	3.30
Total advertising expenses	9.36%
Subscription	
Commissions to subscription agencies	8.86
Other subscription promotion costs	9.03
First class postage costs	1.38
Third class postage	2.26
Fulfillment costs	2.42
Total subscription expenses	23.95%
Single copy	
Commissions on single copy sales	6.61
Other single copy promotion costs	0.83
Total single copy expenses	7.44%
Editorial costs	10.13%
Production	
Paper costs	10.56
Printing and bindery costs	10.71
Total production expenses	21.27%
Distribution	
Second/controlled class postage costs	6.86
Other subscription distribution costs	0.79
Single copy distribution costs	0.58
Total distribution expenses	8.23%
Administrative and other costs	7.86
Total magazine costs	88.24%
Operating profit	11.76%

Magazine Publishers Association 1994

Magazine, starting a new. When starting a new magazine, a publisher's first consideration is to ascertain that an audience for his ideas exists; then he must locate that audience. Costs for printing and delivering the product are other factors that must be considered. In addition, the publisher must determine whether income to cover his costs and profit will be generated solely from subscribers and newsstand sales or from a combination of circulation and advertising revenue.

In figuring the economics of a new magazine, a publisher can consult a printer for bids, a postmaster about postage, and an advertising letter shop regarding costs of reaching prospective customers by direct mail.

A magazine publisher budgets on a yearly basis, first estimating his total income (with the aid of the circulation and advertising managers), then setting aside a percentage of that estimated amount for federal taxes and net profit. Third, he allocates the remainder of the estimated income to each of the five departments—which typically are production, editorial, advertising, circulation and administration—for further development of the magazine.

A new major magazine requires the investment of millions and several years' effort before turning a profit. If the magazine publisher is a lone person performing all the functions of a "little" magazine's staff, then his estimates of revenue and expenses are even more crucial to the success of the publication.

Magazines, classes of. Magazines can be divided into three major groups according to content and audience. *Consumer magazines,* read by the general public, include both slick mass circulation publications such as *Reader's Digest* and secondary magazines geared toward smaller, specialized groups of readers, such as *The Kiwanis Magazine* or the literary magazines.

Trade journals are specialized publications aimed at people employed in a particular profession or trade. *Advertising Age, Nation's Business, Billboard* and *Progressive Farmer* are examples in this category. Some trade journals are published for people in a certain occupation, regardless of the industry—such as *Sales Manager's Bulletin*—while others seek readership among all people in various occupations within a single industry—such as *Ceramic Industry.*

Company publications, also called *house organs,* are issued by corporations and institutions. The audience of a company publication can be internal (employees and dealers), external (stockholders and the public), or both these groups. Two such publications are *Caterpillar World* and *P&G World.* Each class of magazine is discussed further under a separate heading in this book. (*See: Company publication; Little/literary magazine; Major magazine; Secondary magazine; Trade journal.*)

Magazines, defunct. When a magazine goes out of business, the manuscripts to which it has bought rights are still the literary property of the magazine, and as such can be transferred to someone who buys and/or renames the magazine.

When a writer has sold material to a magazine that dies before the piece is published, the writer must be certain that the publication rights he sold to the magazine revert to him before attempting to resell the work to another market. If the writer has sold all rights to the material, he may not resell it without arranging with the purchaser (if he can be located) to reacquire rights. (*See: Paid for but not published; Rights to manuscripts.*)

Magazines, reviews of. While writers' magazines and *Writer's Market* describe the editorial requirements of magazines from the freelance writer's point of view, other publications such as *The Whole Earth Catalog* periodically carry minireviews of new and/or outstanding publications that give the writer insight into current editorial content. Some newspaper syndicates also publish columns that highlight (panning or praising) selected articles from current magazines. The directory *Magazines for Libraries*, edited by Bill Katz and Linda S. Katz, contains descriptions and evaluations of most of the major magazines carried by public, school and college libraries; and Katz's column "Magazines" appears in every issue of *Library Journal*.

With the explosion of homegrown, self-produced zines, publications have begun to review and recommend the best (or most bizarre) of the bunch. *Might* magazine reviews zines, and *Factsheet 5*, subtitled "the definitive guide to the zine revolution" fills its pages with information on these personalized magazines.

Mail/delivery services. Over land, a writer has the option of shipping a manuscript either through the U.S. Postal Service or by private carrier.

Via the Postal Service, manuscripts can be sent either first class or fourth class; fourth class features a special low book or manuscript rate. First-class mail is guaranteed faster delivery than fourth-class mail, but it is, of course, more costly; in addition, first class does not apply to parcels weighing more than twelve ounces. (Anyone who wishes a piece of mail weighing more than that to receive first-class handling should send it *priority mail*, same as first-class mail handling.) Any package, whether first or fourth class, can be insured against loss or damage for a small fee. (Some writers and photojournalists insure their manuscripts/photos for the amount of money it would cost to have them retyped or reprinted.)

Another service the Postal Service offers is *Express Mail*, which can, in some instances, deliver letters and packages in less than a day. Express Mail delivery service is offered in some foreign countries as well as in many large cities in the U.S.; the cost of sending an Express Mail item includes insurance.

When it is necessary to send a letter with a manuscript, it may either be packed inside the box or attached to the outside of the package. When a writer wants a record of receipt of his letter or manuscript, he can send it *registered mail* or *certified mail* and request that a signed receipt be returned to him; registered mail, however, receives more careful handling en route, and is, therefore, sometimes slower in delivery. Both registered mail and certified mail are hand-delivered—i.e., they must be signed for, not dropped into a mailbox.

Mail sent *special delivery* receives better treatment and faster delivery than first-class mail; any class of mail, except Express Mail delivery services, is eligible for this option. Special delivery items are delivered every day, including Sundays and holidays, but are not required to be hand-delivered.

Besides the address and return address, certain instructions should be indicated on the outside of a piece of mail. Special delivery mail should be labeled with a sticker available from a post office; priority mail must be marked as such on all sides of a piece. The phrase "return postage guaranteed" printed below the return address ensures that the writer will recover his manuscript for a fee in the event that the letter or package is undeliverable. (If special-fourth-class manuscript mail does not carry this marking, it probably will *not* be returned to the sender if for some reason the addressee cannot be located.) A final technicality decrees that a package may not be marked "do not bend" unless it contains stiffeners.

An alternative to the Postal Service for heavier manuscript packages is United Parcel Service (UPS); in some cases, UPS is cheaper than the government service. The sender is charged according to the weight of his package and the distance it will be transported; insurance is included in this cost. A fuel surcharge is added to the bill—as is a fee for the optional service of having the package picked up. UPS parcels must be signed for, so there is a record of delivery.

FedEx is another nationwide delivery company; using this service, it is possible to have a package reach its destination the day after it is sent. Other national delivery services, such as the Special Delivery Express and DHL Worldwide Express, are listed in the yellow pages, as are local firms.

Writers may also submit material via fax or electronic mail. Check with the publication for electronic submission guidelines, and make sure it's OK to fax before you do.

Additional information: *National ZIP Code and Post Office Directory.*)

Mail-order publishing. A method of marketing books direct to the consumer through the mail. In this type of publishing, the projected sales and number of interested consumers are greater than those in conventional publishing.

Mail-order publishing is a concept initiated about twenty-five years ago. Publishers reach a considerably larger number of potential buyers with this approach than by distributing books only to bookstores, since not all the consumers who receive direct-mail packages are people who would seek books for themselves. Mailing lists for these sales efforts are obtained through various means— the publisher's own mail-order customer list, and lists rented from publishers of similar books or from organizations whose members have a known interest in the type of book being offered.

Typical categories of books marketed by mail are self-help, self-education and literary classics. Unlike book club arrangements, mail-order purchases do not commit the buyer to purchasing a certain number of books.

A writer whose book is sold by mail order receives a different royalty from that of traditionally marketed books—in some cases only half the rate as for the same type of book sold through conventional outlets.

Mainstream fiction. Fiction that transcends popular novel categories—mystery, romance or science fiction—is called mainstream fiction. Using conventional methods, this kind of fiction tells stories about people and their conflicts but with greater depth of characterization, background, etc., than the more narrowly focused genre novels. It is not, however, experimental in style as are more avant-garde works. Some examples of contemporary mainstream fiction would be the work of James Michener, John Updike and Joyce Carol Oates. The term is sometimes used interchangeably with *serious* or *contemporary fiction.*

Major magazine. This type of mass circulation consumer magazine is characterized by slick paper stock, a healthy advertising/editorial ratio, and good pay rates for writers.

A writer who markets work to a major magazine like *Woman's Day* or *Playboy* faces steep competition, mainly from established professionals; however, some beginning writers break into this field every year.

Sale of an article or short story to a major magazine could earn the writer $300-$3,500. (*See: Magazines, classes of; Secondary magazine.*)

Make-good. Compensation that a station pays to a sponsor when a commercial has been canceled or broadcast with errors. More often, it refers to a rescheduled spot that was missed by the station at its scheduled time.

Manuscript length, average. (*See: Figure 27.*)

Manuscript preparation and submission. Manuscript drafts submitted to publishers should be typed as neatly as possible, double-spaced, on 8½″×11″ white bond paper—and only on one side of the page. (The writer should be sure to keep a photocopy for his files.) Margins, including those at the top and bottom, should measure 1¼″-1½″. In addition to these general rules, certain manuscripts—such as plays or film scripts—are prepared according to specific guidelines. (See entries on those topics in this book.)

The first page of an article or short story manuscript contains the author's legal name, address and phone number in the upper left corner. If the writer chooses to include the approximate number of words (rounded up to the nearest hundred), rights for sale and a copyright line, he places them in the upper right corner. A copyright line is not required on a manuscript for copyright protection, but if it does appear, it should read "Copyright (or ©) 1995 Jane Doe." About one-third of the way down the page the work's title and author's byline (either a pen name or legal name) are double-spaced and centered. The text begins four to six lines after the byline. Succeeding pages carry only the

FIGURE 27

MANUSCRIPT LENGTH, AVERAGE

*T*he following table provides average word counts for each of the basic forms of writing; it gives the beginning writer the usual expected length of most manuscripts. When submitting work to magazines, though, the writer should adhere to the editor's requirements, which may be more specific than the average word count. *Writer's Market* lists individual editors' preferences as to word length.

HOW LONG IS A . . . ?

	Average Words
Short-short story	250–1,500
Short story	1,500–10,000
Novella/novelette	30,000–50,000
Novel—hardcover	60,000 words and up
Paperback original	60,000–80,000
Children's picture book	150–1,500
Juvenile book	15,000–60,000
Nonfiction book	20,000–200,000
TV script: ½-hour	25–40 double-spaced typewritten pages
TV script: 1-hour	55–70 double-spaced typewritten pages
Play: one-act	20–30 minutes playing time
	20–30 double-spaced typewritten pages
Play: three-act	1½-2 hours playing time
	90–120 double-spaced typewritten pages
Movie scenario	1½-2 hours playing time
	120–250 double-spaced typewritten pages
Radio feature copy	1 minute = 15 double-spaced lines
	3 minutes = 2 pages
Poem	2 lines and up (most mags prefer 4-16 lines)
Query letter	1 full-page, single-spaced
Speech	250 words = 2 minutes
	12–15 pages = ½ hour

EDITORIAL NOTE: The average full double-spaced typewritten page contains 250 words of pica typewriter type.

author's last name, abbreviated title and page number in the top left corner.

Articles, stories and poems of fewer than five pages may be folded and mailed in #10 envelopes, while longer pieces require 9″ × 12″ or 10″ × 13″ envelopes and are left unfolded.

Scripts for TV, motion pictures and plays must be submitted in binders, while greeting card verses and cartoon gag lines should be typed on 3″ × 5″ or 4″ × 6″ sheets of white paper or card stock. Writers submitting poetry should type only one poem per page. Editors specify in *Writer's Market* and *Poet's Market* the maxi-

FIGURE 28

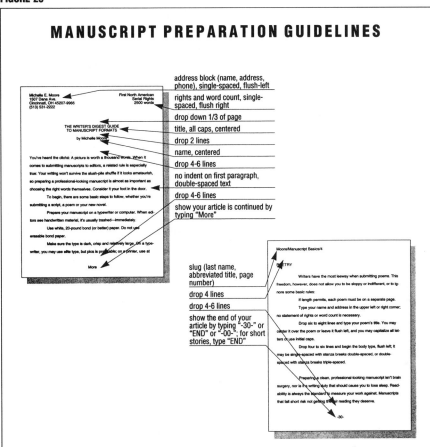

If the author uses a pseudonym, it should be placed on the title page only in the byline position; the author's real name must always appear in the top left corner of the title page— for manuscript mailing and payment purposes.

Reprinted from The Basics of Getting Started in Writing, *Copyright 1994, Writer's Digest.*

mum number of poems that may be submitted at one time to their magazines.

With any submission, the author should enclose a self-addressed, stamped envelope with proper postage for the return of his work. (*See: Book manuscript preparation and sub-*

mission; Figure 28; Reporting time on manuscripts; SASE.)

Market research. Writers can earn extra income and improve their interviewing skills by working in market research. Many private companies, as well as the government, conduct polls and surveys for which they hire outgoing, diplomatic, patient and intelligent persons. These interviewers work either as employees or as independent contractors. The latter arrangement leaves the interviewer responsible for deducting his own income tax (and self-employment tax, if he earns more than $433.13 per year).

Market researchers may conduct interviews on the street, in shopping centers, at home or at an office (by telephone), or throughout an entire state or region. They solicit people's views on social issues, politics or consumer products. Depending on length and type of report, the researcher may be paid a flat fee—such as $10 per report—or by the hour, averaging $15-$30 per hour.

The writer who becomes involved in market research must avoid using his subjects or their answers as material for his own writing, since the information gathered belongs to the employer. In addition, a private company is likely to dismiss him, and the government to fine him, for doing so.

Names and addresses of market research companies are listed in the *International Directory of Marketing Research Houses and Services.* (*See: Self-publishing.*)

Market, studying the. The successful freelancer spends a considerable amount of time determining not only the exact editorial needs of various magazines, but which magazines are directed at which audiences—since a magazine's content directly reflects its readers' tastes.

Every page of a magazine can tell an alert freelancer something about the kinds of articles the editors are looking for—and what his own chances are for making a sale to them. The articles themselves clue the writer in to a publication's style and tone; the advertisements tell about the readers' lifestyles; the masthead and contents pages reveal whether a magazine is primarily staff- or freelance-written; the cover blurbs show what articles appeal to readers the most.

David A. Fryxell, freelancer and *Writer's Digest* columnist, suggests looking at a magazine's table of contents to see whether a description of your article would fit there. "At its best, a contents page is the purest representation of a magazine's personality," he says. "These contents pages contain the distilled essence of how the editor sees the articles and how he or she wishes the readers to perceive the contents."

Sample copies of some magazines are available from their publishers free or for a small fee. The writer may also be able to borrow copies of trade journals from companies that subscribe to them; the library and the newsstand are other places to obtain copies of periodicals to study.

In addition, *Writer's Market* can help a writer study the market: It summarizes publications' various editorial requirements and taboos, including the availability of writer's guidelines.

Simple awareness of popular interests and trends is also valuable; it can keep a writer's thoughts synchronized with readers' (and therefore magazines') needs. (*See:* Writer's Market.)

Mass-market paperbacks vs. trade books. These two categories of books differ in sales outlets, audience and press run. Mass-market paperbacks are sold by supermarkets, drugstores, airports, newsstands and chain bookstores. They are directed toward an extremely large audience, so their subject matter tends to be nonspecialized or of wide appeal. A typical press run for this category will vary depending on the type of book and whether it's an original or a bestseller reprint. Print orders can range from as little as twenty-five thousand to a million or more. Mass-market fiction accounts for about half of all the fiction that is published.

Trade books, on the other hand, are sold at chain bookstores, college bookstores and department stores. Subject matter of this kind of book frequently concerns a special interest, such as jobs in the arts or holistic health care; the format can be either hardcover or paperback. Trade books are directed toward the layperson rather than the professional. A printing of ten thousand is common for a trade book except for fiction, where forty-five hundred would be the median print order.

Masthead, how to read. The masthead of a magazine, usually located on the editorial page, lists members of the magazine's staff, editorial and advertising office locations, company officers, subscription rates and related publishing information.

Freelancers pay particular attention to a magazine's masthead in analyzing that publication as a potential market for their work, since the masthead indicates the name of the magazine's current editor and, in some cases, the editor to whom freelance submissions should be sent. Whenever possible, the writer should avoid addressing a manuscript merely to "The Editor"; the masthead of a recent issue will provide the writer with the correct spelling of a specific editor's name and title.

The masthead also reveals something about the staff structure of the publication. If there are many layers of associate editors, department editors, assistant editors, writers, researchers or editorial assistants, chances are the magazine is written almost entirely by staff members. If very few staff members are listed, however, the publication probably depends on freelancers for at least some of its material. Comparing the names of staff members with article bylines on the contents page gives the writer an idea of how many and what types of articles are staff-written, and how many pieces are apparently the work of freelancers. (Many magazine editors and staff writers may pen several pieces for the same issue, writing under assumed names; the writer can't assume that all non-staff bylines are freelance pieces.)

A magazine's masthead often includes the names of contributing editors—freelancers who write regularly for that publication. This information helps in determining a certain article idea's chances for acceptance by that publication: If one of the contributing editors is a specialist in a particular field—fashion, for instance—a writer's chances of selling a fashion article to that magazine may be considerably less than to a magazine that doesn't have a fashion expert on call.

The masthead will sometimes list

the magazine's editorial requirements and offer special instructions to writers concerning freelance submissions.

Media Industry Newsletter (MIN). An eight-page weekly newsletter that reports on topics of interest to top advertising management in communications media such as newspapers, magazines, TV, radio and cable. Its content includes material on magazine start-ups, advertisement selling, advertising rates and media personalities.

This publication was formerly called *Magazine Industry Newsletter*. More information can be obtained from the offices of the *Media Industry Newsletter*, which are located at 305 Madison Ave., Suite 4417, New York, NY 10165.

Media ownership. The takeover of some publishers by other media organizations or other businesses has brought both criticism and favorable responses.

Some newspaper theorists point to lack of competition, which can result from "one newspaper" cities as well as cross-media ownership of newspapers and broadcasting stations. Both threaten the principle of providing for the public a variety of ideas and viewpoints from which to form their own opinions. Another peril of media concentration, according to critics, is the potential for news management. Conglomerates also have been criticized because they present the possibility for conflict of interest between the parent company and the media organizations. Results of various studies have upheld both sides of the media ownership issue.

Two major advantages of book publishing conglomerates, according to Dean R. Koontz, are the advanced marketing techniques and the additional capital with which businesses have furnished the publishing world. Koontz's book *How to Write Best-Selling Fiction* contains his rebuttals to ten criticisms of conglomerate ownership in the book industry. (*See: Conglomerates—book publishers; Magazine publishers, multiple.*)

Additional information: *How to Write Best-Selling Fiction; Who Owns the Media?*

Media personnel directories. (*See: Directories.*)

Media reviewers. Publications (both national, such as the *Columbia Journalism Review*, and regional, such as the *St. Louis Journalism Review*) critique media institutions, personalities or trends. (*See: Ombudsman, newspaper.*)

Medical writing. A writer working in this field is immersed in two fields at once: writing and medicine. He must stay abreast of the continuous developments of medical science by reading the journals and other publications read by health practitioners. In preparing the material, the writer must pay scrupulous attention to detail, since inaccuracies could mislead the public or perhaps even cause serious harm to a patient. Because drawn-out research processes can delay stories, the medical writer must also have patience. Because of the technical nature of the field, preparation for interviews about medicine often requires much time and concentration. Some universities now offer courses specifically for the science and medical writer; however, a writer can enter this specialty with a good background in the natural sciences and an understanding of medical jargon.

The freelance writer finds abundant opportunities in the medical field. Jobs include work on clinical papers, scientific exhibit brochures, physician's brochures, special report reviews, clinical abstracts, manuals/ guides, medical movie scripts and medical textbooks. In addition, medical products companies seek freelancers to write speeches, package inserts and pharmaceutical advertisements. Individual researchers employ freelancers to help write/ edit books and articles. Their needs are sometimes announced in the classified sections of professional journals; writers may advertise their availability for this work in the same manner. Medical writers seeking staff positions may find openings on large daily newspapers.

The writer can take precautions to ensure that his finished piece is as accurate as possible by taping the interview, verifying quotes with the interviewee, and mailing (or reading over the phone) a copy of the finished manuscript to the interviewee for deletions or changes.

Professional organizations of interest to medical writers are the American Medical Writers Association, 9650 Rockville Pike, Bethesda, MD 20814; and the National Association of Science Writers, P.O. Box 294, Greenlawn, NY 11740. (*See: Science writing.*)

Memoir. A memoir is an author's commentary on his life, his experiences and the times. It usually focuses attention on personalities and events that the author feels have significantly influenced his life. A memoir often details one phase of the writer's life rather than the whole of it (e.g., the memoirs of a President during his term of office). (*See: Biography.*)

Metaphor. A figurative comparison that usually uses some forms of the word *is*, although a verb is not absolutely essential to a metaphor. It is generally considered a strengthened simile (and doesn't use the words *like* or *as*). "He's nothing but a bag of wind" or "She's a doll" exemplify this technique.

The mixed metaphor, which is an inconsistent image, should be avoided, e.g., "Publicity is a two-edged sword, somebody said once, and it can get you into hot water."

Metaphors must be used with caution. Too many, too close together, can obscure rather than clarify meaning. (*See: Figures of speech; Imagery; Simile.*)

Meter. (*See: Verse.*)

Metonymy. The figure of speech that substitutes the name of one thing for the name of another. With this technique, the substituted name is associated with the original by a common quality or function, as when "Pollyanna" refers to a person who is excessively optimistic, or "the White House" refers to the President. Metonymy can be used for quick characterization. (*See: Figures of speech; Irony.*)

Microform. Any of several forms used to store greatly reduced photographic images of legal documents, books, newspapers or other periodicals in a stable, convenient-to-handle medium. A microform can only be read by using a special device to project the images on a reading screen; each microform requires a different device to light and magnify the images it holds.

The primary kinds of microforms used in libraries include: *microfilm*, a long strip of photographic film wound on a reel, which is most often used to store newspapers and magazines; *microfiche*, a 3″ × 5″ or 4″ × 6″ sheet of film; and *microcard*, a 3″ × 5″ or 4″ × 6″ opaque card onto which a sheet of photographic film holding images is laminated. A microcard is somewhat more difficult to read than the other forms.

Microsoft Network. An Internet online service for users of Windows 95. It looks and acts just like the Windows program, making it easier for Windows users to operate. "Content communities" cover subjects including arts and entertainment; news and weather; business and finance; sports, health and fitness; science and technology; computers and software; community and public affairs; and home and family. Users also have access to bulletin boards, e-mail and chat groups. Many other services are available, some for a fee. (*See: Electronic mail; Internet; Online service.*)

Mid-list books. Those titles on a publisher's list that are neither highly promotable books the publisher thinks will hit the best-seller lists, nor scholarly or literary works the publisher feels deserve publication but that he expects will have limited sales. A mid-list novel, for example, is usually mainstream fiction by a new or unknown writer that is not expected to be a blockbuster and is not a category novel—such as a mystery or science fiction—for which there is a well-defined market. Whether fiction or nonfiction, mid-list books' promotion budgets are usually small. Nevertheless, they offer the freelance writer an entrée to the reading public and an opportunity to build a following.

Misspelled words. (*See: Figure 29.*)

Model release. A model release is a form signed by a model or other subject of a photograph (or the subject's legal guardian if the subject is a minor). It authorizes the photographer's use of the photograph for business ("trade") as well as editorial purposes.

Legally, without the subject's consent, a photographer may not display or publish a photo featuring a person for any purpose other than to educate or inform. If a photograph is to be used for any advertising or display purposes, a model release is often necessary for objects (buildings, signs, etc.), as well as for people who appear in it. Writers should remember that a book jacket is considered advertising.

In the majority of cases in which the photographer has obtained a signed model release, he is legally protected. However, if the photograph is not used in the manner contemplated by the release—e.g., if the subject appears in an altered form,

FIGURE 29

50 FREQUENTLY
MISSPELLED WORDS

*E*ditorial Experts, Inc. has analyzed a number of spelling tests and they find that the fifty words below are among the most frequently misspelled. Not included are words that are troublesome pairs with similar spellings but different meaning—affect/effect, capital/capitol. (Reprinted from *The New York Public Library Writer's Guide to Style and Usage.* Copyright © 1994 Editorial Experts, Inc., 66 Canal Center Plaza, Suite 200, Alexandria, VA 22314-1538.)

accommodate	forcible	occasion
acknowledgment	foreword	occurrence
argument	grammar	perseverance
auxiliary	harass	personnel
commitment	hygiene	prerogative
connoisseur	hypocrisy	privilege
conscience	idiosyncrasy	proceed
consensus	inadvertent	queue
deductible	indispensable	rhythm
defendant	inoculate	sacrilegious
definitely	jewelry	separate
dependent	judgment	supersede
desiccate	liaison	threshold
embarrass	license	transferable
existence	lightning	weird
exorbitant	millennium	withhold
fluorescent	miniscule	

or if the subject is presented in an embarrassing light and has not given legal consent for such a variation—the photographer would have little protection if a lawsuit should occur. The release is not valid if it is obtained by coercion or fraud.

Suggested contents of a model release are a generalized description of all the ways the photograph may be used (e.g., in advertising and editorial media, both print and electronic), and the date the release is signed. Some model releases mention compensation. It is preferable to pay some consideration for a model release, but compensation is not necessary for the release to be valid—only *consent* is. Model releases

can be composed by the photographer and printed or typed, or forms can be purchased from firms advertising in photography journals. (*See: Figure 30; Illustration.*)

Money, illustration of. The federal government places restrictions on the practice of printing illustrations of money in newspapers, magazines, books, etc. An illustration may not represent a bill at its actual size: it must be either reduced to less than three-fourths or enlarged to more than 1½ times the piece of currency's actual size. Reproducing color pictures of paper money is also prohibited; illustrations of money must be in black and white.

FIGURE 30

PHOTOGRAPHER'S MODEL RELEASE

Roll Nos _____   Subject _____

Place _____   Date _____

I, the undersigned, do hereby grant to (PHOTOGRAPHER), and to his employees or assigns, permission to use, in any manner whatsoever, photographs made this date and place, and further described below. Such use to include, but not be limited to: publication, display, advertising, editorial illustration, resale, etc.

These photographs include images of:

Myself (Print full name) _____

Minor children (Print child's name, age and relationship to signer)

_____

Property, including pets (Identify by address or other description)

_____

Signature (I am over 21 years of age)

_____

Mailing Address _____

_____

Witness: Signature _____

Address _____

_____

Reprinted from Photographer's Market 1990, *Copyright © 1989 by Writer's Digest Books.*

The government also specifies the kinds of written material with which illustrations of money can be used. According to the Treasury Department, "To be permissible an illustration must be accompanied by numismatic, educational, historical or newsworthy information relating directly to the item that is illustrated. Illustrations used primarily for decorative or eye-catching purposes are not permissible." Time, Inc. won a lawsuit challenging these various restrictions.

While editors more than writers need be aware of these restrictions, writers' illustration ideas for their articles might be affected by these regulations.

Similar restrictions are on the illustration of U.S. and foreign postage stamps, government securities, White House press passes, etc.

Monologue. (*See: Comedy writing; Soliloquy.*)

Mosaic. A graphics-based Internet reader and navigation tool developed by the National Center for Supercomputing Applications. This program allows users to point and click their way to the information they want. (*See: Internet.*)

Motif. An idea, theme, image or subject that recurs throughout a work, closely allied to the main theme. For example, the Broadway hit *Mass Appeal,* a play about the friendship between a middle-aged parish priest and a young seminarian, has an underlying motif of priest as actor—an idea not directly stated in the dialogue, but made obvious through staging. Many motifs appear in a single complex work.

Motion picture script. A motion picture script, or *screenplay*, is often written from an outline and a treatment, as is a TV script. The screenwriter commonly divides his story into three acts (although the number can vary—TV movies, for instance, consist of six acts of equal length), of which the first and third usually consume one-fourth of the film's total time, and the second occupies one-half the time. The first act presents a conflict and the action's rise to crisis; the second act complicates the problem, leaving the protagonist in a quandary that is resolved in the third act. Each act is divided into *scenes,* each of which must be numbered in the writer's final draft.

Screenplays can range from 100 to 250 pages in length, although 120 is the preferred length; one page of script is generally equal to one minute of time on film.

Structurally, screenplays can be written in a *shot-by-shot sequence* or in *master shots.* When writing shot-by-shot, the writer begins each scene with a scene indication, then proceeds to divide that scene into individual camera shots and angles; but the master scene script is less complicated and usually preferred. Here, as before, the scene begins with a scene indication, followed by a narrative description of the action, without specifications about how that action is to be photographed. Either format contains description of the action, dialogue or a combination of both, depending upon what's happening in that scene.

Although screenplays can vary considerably in the degree of their complexity and readability (as opposed to the readability of the pre-screenplay treatment), it might be wise to bear in mind the caution of scriptwriter John Gregory Dunne, who reminds writers that because it is a form in which words are secondary to potential images, a screenplay is usually difficult to read; the better a script reads, the better it is to be suspicious of the script. (*See: Screenwriting; Television script; Treatment; Writers Guild of America.*)

Additional information: *Successful Scriptwriting.*

Motion picture script terms. (*See: Television script terms.*)

Motivation. Every believable character in fiction is motivated by a desire to satisfy a basic human need—such as for food, shelter or love. Planning motivation for characters aids the writer both in plot construction and characterization.

Experiences in a character's past,

for example, can be the factors that drive him to fulfill his need, thus motivating the action in a story. Physical or psychological characteristics (or a combination of the two) can also be the catalyst for a character's motivations. A physical handicap to be overcome is an obvious example of such motivation, but other physical traits can influence motivation as well.

Character traits can also motivate a character. Distasteful qualities such as greed and vengefulness are usually given only to villains, because a central character with an offensive trait loses reader sympathy. On the other hand, the major character is usually motivated by a sympathetic or positive trait or emotion such as love, altruism, or physical or spiritual survival. (However, even a character motivated by an admirable cause cannot be presented as perfect: As a human being, he must possess flaws of personality or character.)

To be believable, any action taken by a character—regardless of motivation—must be both rational and in keeping with the situation. For example, a medical student might decide to go into research to find a cure for the disease that killed his father (the motivation being the desire to save other families pain and grief). If, on the other hand, this character's decision was based on his reading an article about an epidemic, his motivation would be too weak, and therefore unbelievable.

Taking a psychology course that covers different theories of human needs can heighten the writer's understanding of motivation. (*See: Backstory; Characterization.*)

Movies from books. (*See: Tie-in.*)

ms. The abbreviation for *manuscript*—as well as *mss.*, for *manuscripts*—used widely by writers and editors.

Multiple contract. A kind of book contract by which the publisher agrees to publish, and the author agrees to have published, two or more consecutive books by the author. (*See: Book contract; Option clause.*)

Multiple sales. By offering a magazine "one-time rights only" to his material, a freelance writer can often generate additional revenue by selling the same article or story to a number of noncompeting publications. Newspapers in different geographical locations are particularly likely markets for multiple sales. In uncopyrighted newspapers, the author should be sure his copyright notice appears with the piece to prevent innocent infringement.

Magazines with different readerships—including many regional magazines, house organs, trade journals, religious publications and Sunday supplements—also buy one-time rights to material. (*Writer's Market* lists editors' requirements on rights.)

Most of the top-paying slick magazines prefer to buy First North American Serial Rights, which prohibits the writer from selling the same article or story elsewhere simultaneously. Even if the nonfiction writer must sell all rights to an article, however, he is free to create "spin-offs" from the finished piece; i.e., he can rework his original material—including information he wasn't able to use in the final draft of the article—into a second or third completely rewritten article slanted to any number of noncompeting publications.

In the same way, a fiction writer may offer one-time rights to a short story; once that story is published, he may resubmit the piece to a noncompeting magazine with the offer of second rights. Religious magazines, in particular, often buy second rights to short stories.

The writer may also be able to get more mileage out of his work by selling reprints to specialized magazines on occasion. *Reader's Digest*, for example, buys previously published material, as do some religious and secondary publications.

In pursuing multiple sales, the writer must exercise care in retaining second rights to his article. "One-time rights only" should be clearly indicated in the upper right corner of the first page of the manuscript. In purchasing one-time rights, the magazine or newspaper agrees to publish the material once; after publication, rights to the piece revert to the author. When the writer does make subsequent sales, he should inform the editors of where the same article previously appeared. (*See: Rights to manuscripts; Simultaneous submission.*)

Multiple submissions. (*See: Simultaneous submission.*)

The Music Industry. In the U.S., the music industry has three major hubs: New York, Nashville and Los Angeles. Those are the cities where most record companies, producers, publishers, managers, songwriters and performers can be found (although regional music scenes occasionally heat up in cities like Minneapolis, Chicago and Seattle).

Besides the artists and the record companies, which sign on the performers and market their work, other players are A&R *representatives* who are responsible for finding new talent and anticipating trends; the *producer* who is responsible for helping develop and fine-tune the artist's work; and the *publisher*—a songwriter's advocate—who attempts to find commercially profitable uses for the songs he represents.

Additional information: *Songwriter's Market*, which lists music publishers, record companies, producers and managers, and the *Recording Industry Sourcebook*, an annual directory published by Ascona Group, Inc., that lists record companies, music publishers, producers and managers.

Music types. Categories of music are described in this book under headings: A/C (adult contemporary), classical music, country music, folk music, gospel music, jazz, new age music, ragtime, rap, reggae, rhythm and blues (R&B) and rock.

Musical. A stage production in which songs are used to reinforce the major points of the story being acted out. The three major elements of a musical usually are song, dance and dialogue.

Though a writer working in this form cooperates with a variety of theater personnel during production, the writing phase of the project is done in close collaboration with a composer and a lyricist. The writer, or *librettist*, who in most cases is also a playwright, creates dialogue in collaboration with the composer and the lyricist, who compose the songs. (Where someone multitalented is involved, it takes only two people, or perhaps just one person, to write a musical.) The librettist's product is the musical's *libretto*, or *book*, which contains action, character, situation, setting, dance, dialogue and plot. Often, the book has been completed before the songs are inserted.

A musical's songs, known as *show songs*, are of the popular rather than the classical variety. The types of songs used in musicals are named for their functions: the *establishing song*, the *opening song*, the *reprise*, the *relief song* and the *comment song*.

To copyright their work, authors of musicals should request Form PA (for a work of the performing arts) from the Register of Copyrights, Library of Congress, Washington, DC 20559.

Broadway music royalties are usually 6 percent of the weekly gross split between bookwriter, lyricist and composer. (*See: Comment song;* Dramatists Sourcebook*; Establishing song; Opening song; Relief song; Reprise.*)

Mystery story. A form of narration in which one or more elements remain unknown or unexplained until the end of the story. The modern mystery story contains elements of the serious novel: a convincing account of a character's struggle with various physical and psychological obstacles in an effort to achieve his goal, good characterization and sound motivation. Publishers of mystery stories often look for one or more of these twelve categories—as described by *Mystery Writer's Marketplace and Sourcebook*:

In an *amateur sleuth*, the main char-acter does the detection, but isn't a professional private investigator or police detective.

Two detectives work together in a *bickering team* or *cohort mystery* series. The crime is the main focus, but the relationship—be it marriage or friendship—is also developed in the series.

A *caper* is a crime story usually told from the viewpoint of the perpetrator. The tone may be lighthearted and the crime is often theft rather than murder.

A murder mystery set in a small English or New England town that features an amateur sleuth is called a *cozy* or *English cozy*. The "detective" is usually a genteel old lady or gentleman.

A *gothic mystery* is one with a dark and brooding tone. Usually set at an old estate, a gothic contains elements of romantic suspense.

A story that features a streetwise and hardened detective is a *hard-boiled detective* story. Often a male, this character type was popularized in the 1940s and 1950s.

More serious than a caper, a *heist* focuses on solving the theft, as well as on the planning and execution of the theft.

A mystery involving a family member's murder is a *malice domestic*.

A *police procedural* is a mystery featuring a police detective or officer who uses standard professional police practices to solve the crime.

In a *romantic suspense*, strong elements of romance appear, usually between the detective and the victim or the detective and the suspect.

Nonfiction about real murders and serial killings is *true crime*. Truman Capote is credited with beginning this genre with *In Cold Blood*.

The focus is on discovering the identity of the murderer in a *whodunit*. (*See: Romantic suspense novel; True crime.*)

Additional information: *Mystery Writer's Marketplace and Sourcebook.*

Mystery Writer's Marketplace and Sourcebook.

A semiannual book that combines both writing how-to and market listings for the mystery writer. Sections of the book include "Trends in Crime Fiction," "Writing the Mystery" and "The Markets." Market listings include addresses, contacts, terms and tips for novel, short story and foreign publishers.

Other sections are "The Sources," which includes magazines, organizations, conventions and bookstores for mystery writers; and "For Your Reference," which includes books of interest to mystery writers, as well as a look at a real private investigator's day.

Mystery Writers of America, Inc.

This organization of twenty-five hundred members is "dedicated to the proposition that the detective story is the noblest sport of man." The membership includes published writers, novice writers and people in writing-related fields, such as publishers, editors and agents. Its motto is "Crime Does Not Pay—Enough!"

Annual activities include a convention, presentation of the Edgar Allan Poe and Raven Awards, and publication of an anthology of members' work. A newsletter, *The Third Degree,* is issued monthly.

The headquarters of this organization is at 17 E. Forty-seventh St., Sixth Floor, New York, NY 10017.

Myth.

A traditional story, usually involving gods or other supernatural beings, that attempts to explain the workings of the natural or spiritual world or to rationalize the perils of human existence. Myths are common to all cultures and sometimes parallel each other—for instance, all cultures have a series of creation myths, many of which involve a great flood.

Over thousands of years, myths evolve from a simple way of bringing order to a mysterious universe into (in literate societies) a highly developed literature that no longer carries the force of belief, but that does carry the weight of a civilization's intellectual and artistic development. Philosophers, writers, artists—even scientists—use the familiar figures and events of mythology as symbols to express their ideas in a vivid way. Anyone familiar with Greek mythology, for example, will not have to read too extensively into Freud to be able to grasp the basic concept of what he termed the "Oedipus complex."

Until the nineteenth century, Western readers studied only Greek, Roman, and—to a lesser degree—Norse myths; scholars next began working through ancient Oriental and Middle Eastern mythic literatures; today, scarcely a culture anywhere has not had its myths transcribed and analyzed. (*See: Legend.*)

Additional information: *The Intellectual Adventure of Ancient Man; The Golden Bough; The Sacred and the Profane.*

n. Following a page number in an index, this abbreviation indicates that that page includes a footnote on the indexed item.

N.B. (nota bene). Latin for "note well." A writer may use the abbreviation *N.B.* to advise the reader to take note of a particular point or reference in his material, as in this example, "The market listing read: 'We are particularly interested in stories and articles with Christmas themes. (N.B. Submit seasonal material three to six months in advance.)'"

Names, using real. A writer who wishes to use the real name of a person in a fictional piece, with or without a quotation from that person, must obtain permission from that person, regardless of whether the material is favorable or unfavorable. Permission is a defense in an invasion-of-privacy suit as long as the material is within the scope of the permission. If the person is a public figure, of course, and what the person has said is a matter of public record, no permission is necessary; nor is permission necessary in most states if the person is dead and the manuscript does not invade the privacy of living descendants.

Trade names and brand names may be used in a story without permission *if* they are not mentioned in a derogatory context. Trade names should be capitalized unless they are not capitalized as used. (*See: Trade name; Trademark.*)

Narration. Narration is a manner of writing in which the author tells what happened. Fiction may be narrated either from the viewpoint of the author's persona or another character. In connecting the series of events in a story, narration can incorporate other fictional elements, such as description, exposition and dialogue. (*See: First-person point of view; Third-person point of view.*)

Narrative hook. A literary device used at the beginning of a story or a novel for the purpose of arousing a reader's curiosity and encouraging him to read further. A narrative hook may take any number of forms—a startling quotation, a mention of murder or disaster, a vivid description of a fascinating character.

Anything that stimulates a reader's curiosity and promises action to come makes an effective hook; but it should be accomplished in approximately the first two hundred words. Other than that, there are no rules.

Compare the narrative hooks of two classic novels: *Moby Dick*'s "Call me Ishmael" and the opening paragraph of *A Tale of Two Cities*:

It was the best of times, it was the worst of times, it was the age of wisdom, it was the age of foolishness, it was the epoch of belief, it was the epoch of incredulity, it was the season of Light, it was the season of Darkness, it was the spring of hope, it was the winter of despair, we had everything before us, we had nothing before us, we were all going direct to Heaven, we were all going direct the other way—in short, the period was so far like the present period, that some of its noisiest authorities insisted on its being received, for good or for evil, in the superlative degree of comparison only.

The two hooks have nothing in common except that each is a single sentence—yet no one who has read either one can forget it.

Narrator. The one who tells a story. In fiction, the narrator of a story is most often referred to as the *viewpoint character*, i.e., one who carries the emotional focus of the story. The narrator may be either someone involved in the action of the story, or the author himself. Generally, however, the narrator is not the author's own voice, but the voice of a character created by the author to tell the story.

Narrators are sometimes found in dramatic works and films, usually as characters within the play or motion picture. In Tennessee Williams's drama *The Glass Menagerie*, for example, one of the characters, Tom Wingfield, narrates the introduction and the conclusion of the play; and some of Woody Allen's motion pictures use the technique of narrator-turned-character. (*See: Viewpoint.*)

National Academy of Songwriters. This twenty-two-year-old nonprofit organization educates and protects song-writers. Anyone may become a general member; songwriters with at least one song commercially released are eligible for professional membership; and songwriters with a "significant, recognized body of work" may become Gold members.

The NAS offers all its members services including access to attorneys at reduced fees, a song registration service, a toll-free hotline for song-writing-related questions, workshops and song evaluations. Members also receive *Song Talk* magazine and *Song-Line*, the NAS monthly newsletter. The NAS awards an annual lifetime achievement award to "the song-writer/artist who has left an enduring mark on the songwriting landscape." The headquarters are located at 6381 Hollywood Blvd., Suite 780, Hollywood, CA 90028.

National Association of Black Journalists. An organization of twenty-three hundred black journalists working in every phase of print and broadcast journalism as writers and reporters, publishers, managers and owners of newspapers, magazines, radio and TV stations, wire services and cable outlets.

The association's objectives include "strengthening ties among African-American journalists; becoming an exemplary group of professionals that honors excellence and outstanding achievements by African-American journalists and coverage of the African-American community; expanding media job opportunities for African-American journalists and assisting in job recruiting activities; working with high schools and colleges to identify and encourage African-American students to become journalists.''

NABJ offers four short courses in broadcast and print at historically black colleges, and awards scholarships and internships as well as annual awards. Since 1975, more than $500,000 in scholarships and $200,000 in internships have been awarded to more than 340 college students.

NABJ publishes a journal ten times a year. For more information, write the NABJ at P.O. Box 4222, Reston, VA 22090.

National Association of Science Writers (NASW). Members of this professional organization are writers and editors who prepare scientific information for the layperson.

Activities of the NASW include competitions and an annual joint meeting with the American Association for the Advancement of Science. NASW gives annual awards and distributes a *Guide to Careers in Science Writing* (single copies free for #10 SASE). The group also publishes a newsletter and the book *Communicating Science News* ($3 prepaid per copy). The address of the organization is P.O. Box 294, Greenlawn, NY 11740.

National Association of State Textbook Administrators. The objectives of this association are to foster a spirit of mutual helpfulness among textbook administrators; to arrange for continuing study and review of textbooks to develop stronger, more serviceable texts; to authorize surveys, tests and studies to benefit text adoption committees; and to find the best component products for textbook production.

The Association meets semiannually with the Association of American Publishers and the Book Manufacturers Institute to discuss and approve (or disapprove) textbook specifications. Contact recording secretary Barbara Wood at 350 N.E. Thirteenth St., Apt. 307, Salem, OR 97301 for information.

National Book Awards. (*See: American Book Awards.*)

National Book Critics Circle (NBCC). This organization, made up of book critics and book review editors, exists to raise the standards of book reviewing and book criticism and to foster public appreciation of literature and book criticism. It meets annually, presents awards annually, and publishes the *NBCC Journal* quarterly. The NBCC can be reached % Philadelphia Inquirer, 400 N. Broad St., Philadelphia, PA 19103.

National Endowment for the Arts (NEA). The National Endowment for the Arts is an independent agency of the federal government, created in 1965 to encourage and assist the nation's cultural resources. The major goals of the NEA are to promote the creative development of the nation's finest talent, to strengthen and support cultural organizations, to further the availability of the arts to Americans and to preserve the cultural heritage of the U.S.

The NEA allocates grants to eligible arts and cultural organizations; awards fellowships to qualified individuals in the arts; sponsors the National Endowment Fellowship Program for arts administrators; and publishes a number of newsletters, pamphlets and directories on the arts. Additional information about the goals and services of this organization, as well as the specific grants and fellowships of interest to writers, may be obtained from the Public Information Office, National Endowment for the Arts, Nancy Hanks Center, 1100 Pennsylvania Ave., N.W., Washington, DC 20506.

National Federation of Press Women, Inc. (NFPW). This association is made up of almost thirty-five hundred people who work in all communications fields, either full time or as freelancers. Its activities include an annual communications contest, educational workshops and youth projects. The NFPW operates a speakers bureau, grants journalism scholarships and annually presents an award to a woman of accomplishment. *Agenda*, a newsletter, is published monthly, and a convention is held each June. The National Federation of Press Women can be reached at 4510 W. Eighty-ninth St., Prairy Village, KS 66207.

National League of American Pen Women (NLAPW). This association five thousand professional women comprises three divisions: art, letters and music. Proof of professional work (i.e., in the case of writers, proof of sale of three original works—or one in the case of a book-length manuscript—within the last five years) is required for membership. Its activities include art exhibits, contests in the arts, seminars and a biennial convention. The NLAPW operates biographical archives and a three-thousand-volume library, and grants scholarships. It publishes a roster

every other year, and *The Pen Woman* magazine six times a year. The NLAPW is at 1300 Seventeenth St., N.W., Washington, DC 20036-1973.

National Magazine Awards. This annual program for editorial excellence is sponsored by the American Society of Magazine Editors (ASME) with a grant from the Magazine Publishers Association, and administered by the Columbia University Graduate School of Journalism. Entrants, which are nominated by magazines published in the U.S., are magazines rather than individual writers.

The contest is divided into the following eleven categories of editorial content and presentation: personal service, special interest, feature writing, public interest, photography, fiction, reporting, essays and criticism, single-topic issue, design and general excellence. In some categories, an entry may be a single article or a series, while in others—fiction, for example—contest guidelines specify the number of pieces required in an entry.

Each magazine that wins a National Magazine Award receives a plaque, a reproduction of the stabile ''Elephant'' by Alexander Calder, and an inscription of its name on a tablet on display at the Columbia University School of Journalism. Also, editors whose magazines win awards, writers whose articles win awards, and magazines that are chosen as finalists all receive certificates.

More information on the National Magazine Awards may be obtained from the American Society of Magazine Editors, 919 Third Ave., New York, NY 10022.

National Panhellenic Editors' Conference (NPEC). An organization made up of twenty-six editors of magazines of the National Panhellenic Conference, an association of "women's fraternities." NPEC stages workshops at its biennial conventions.

Contact the NPEC % Lisa Elliott, 3330 Founders Rd., Indianapolis, IN 46268.

National Press Club (NPC). This is a private social and professional organization of reporters, writers and others employed in news-editorial capacities by media organizations. It publishes the *Record* forty-eight times per year, presents awards, and sponsors a speakers bureau. The headquarters of NPC is at the National Press Building, 529 Fourteenth St., N.W., Washington, DC 20045.

National Speakers Association (NSA). Composed of approximately thirty-five hundred professional speakers, semiprofessional speakers and people interested in the field, this organization strives to make the speaking profession more visible to the public. It also serves as a learning and communication medium for speakers and those who'd like to speak—such as writers who are also lecturers. NSA sponsors a Mentor/Mentee Program through which less experienced speakers can meet with experienced professionals. Although its annual membership directory is used by organizations seeking speakers, the NSA does not perform referral or booking functions.

Activities of NSA include an annual convention, awards presentations and workshops. In addition to the membership directory, the association publishes *The Professional Speaker* magazine.

NSA's headquarters are at 1500 S. Priest Dr., Tempe, AZ 85281. (*See: International Platform Association; Lecturing techniques.*)

National Union Catalog. This index represents the works cataloged by the libraries contributing to its cooperative cataloging program; it refers the user to published materials, such as books, pamphlets, atlases and periodicals, cataloged by the Library of Congress and about eleven hundred other libraries participating in the National Union Catalog reporting program.

The *Catalog* is arranged by author or, in cases of title entry, by title. Each entry includes all available cataloging data. All titles represented by Library of Congress printed cards without mention of a contributing library are held by the Library of Congress. Entries supplied by participating libraries indicate the first library to report holding an item; additional location reports are published in the *National Union Catalog Register of Additional Locations.* By using these two catalogs the user can identify at least one location for all materials reported in the *Catalog.*

The *Catalog* is regularly printed in nine monthly issues, three quarterly cumulations, and in annual and quinquennial (five-year) cumulations. The *National Union Catalog Pre-1956 Imprints* (754 volumes) makes available in book form the total *National Union Catalog* maintained on cards by the Library of Congress since 1901. (*See: Interlibrary loan.*)

National University Continuing Education Association. Founded in 1915, the Association boasts a membership of about two thousand. It was founded to serve institutions of higher learning, with active extension and continuing education programs. NUCEA sponsors nontraditional degree programs and programs covering subjects such as women's studies, marketing, community development and service, and museum studies.

Publications include a monthly newsletter; a biennial *Guide to Independent Study Through Correspondence Instruction*; and the triennial *Continuing Higher Education Review*. An annual convention is held in April. The address is One Dupont Circle, Suite 615, Washington, DC 20036.

National Writers Association (NWA). The National Writers Association has two categories of members: professional members, who have either been published in national magazines, had a book published on a royalty basis, or had a stageplay, screenplay or teleplay produced; and associate members who have a serious interest in writing. The NWA operates a two-thousand-volume library and sponsors contests as well as a home study magazine writing course. It distributes to its members research reports on various aspects of writing, copyright, etc. Its publications include *Authorship, Flash Market News, NWA Newsletter* and *Freelancer's Market*. Conferences are held yearly. The address of the National Writers Association is 1450 S. Havana, Suite 424, Aurora, CO 80012.

National Writers Union. Founded in 1983, the Union has more than four thousand members. It is a union for writers, journalists, authors, poets, and technical and public relations writers who are not represented by an existing union. It engages in collective bargaining and provides other services for members such as grievance handling and health insurance. The Union works to raise rates and improve treatment of freelance writers by magazine and book publishers. It holds conferences on legal, economic, trade and craft issues affecting writers. The Union publishes the quarterly *American Writer*. Its address is 873 Broadway, Suite 203, New York, NY 10003.

National Writing Project. This association of more than 166 writing programs for teachers comprises writing centers patterned after the Bay Area Writing Project of the University of California, Berkeley. The programs are collectively referred to as the National Writing Project Network.

Individual programs were instituted primarily by universities and are located throughout the U.S., in Canada and in Europe. More information on the National Writing Project may be obtained from the National Writing Project, 615 University Hall, #1040, University of California, Berkeley, CA 94720-1040. (*See: Bay Area Writing Project.*)

NBC. (*See: Broadcast networks.*)

Nebula Awards. These are annual awards presented to science fiction writers by the Science-fiction and Fantasy Writers of America (SFFWA) in each of four categories: best novel

(40,000 words or more), best novella (17,500-40,000 words), best novelette, (7,500-17,500 words) and best short story (fewer than 7,500 words). Winners are chosen by members of SFFWA but are not required to be members themselves to enter the competition. Works of science fiction or fantasy are eligible as long as they have been published by a trade book publisher or in a nationally circulated magazine. Each recipient is presented a trophy.

Members of the annual World Science Fiction Convention also vote for winners of Hugo Awards (named after Hugo Gernsback). (*See: Science-fiction and Fantasy Writers of America.*)

Negotiating with editors. Any agreement between a writer and a publisher is open to negotiation. The writer may ask for better terms than are offered; the acquiring editor may agree to the request, decline it or suggest a compromise. In the end, it is the writer's choice to accept or decline an editor's offer. Once the writer agrees to an offer, however, it is unprofessional to seek changes later. Beginning writers should realize that editors are more likely to negotiate terms with established writers and writers the editors have worked with previously.

Typically, magazine contract negotiations focus on pay rates, time of payment and rights purchased. Book contract negotiations typically focus on advance and royalty payments, subsidiary rights handling and payments, future book options and book promotion. (*See: Book contract.*)

Net receipts. The amount of money a book publisher receives on the sale of a book after bookseller's discounts, special sales discounts and returned copies. Some authors' book royalties are figured on a percentage of net receipts rather than retail price of the book.

Netiquette. A term for appropriate behavior on online services or the Internet. This type of electronic '' 'net etiquette'' resembles the norms of politeness: Don't waste others' time; don't make lame arguments; use proper spelling. In most cases, a fellow user will usually point out any transgressions. (*See: Internet; Online service.*)

Neustadt International Prize for Literature. Established in 1969, the Neustadt International Prize for Literature was endowed by, and named for, a family of Oklahoma industrialists. It is presented to a poet, fiction writer or dramatist for outstanding achievement. Candidates for the prize do not apply, but must be nominated by members of an international jury, which changes for each award. The judging is based solely on literary merit; any writer in any language is eligible, but a representative sample of his work must be available in either English or French.

The prize, which consists of $40,000 and an eagle feather cast in silver, is awarded biennially at the University of Oklahoma.

Inquiries should be addressed to World Literature Today, 110 Monnet Hall, Norman, OK 73019.

New age music. A type of "mood music" that emerged in the mid-1980s as a reaction against vocalism and the loudness of pop and rock. Artists use traditional instruments but, in some cases, the sounds of nature make up whole albums. Some nicknames for this type of music include "Yuppie Muzak" and "wallpaper for the ears." Current artists include Enya, Yanni and Vangelis.

New Journalism. A style of writing that emerged in the 1960s. Also known as "interior" or "personal journalism," "documentary narrative," and "parajournalism," the term New Journalism is attached to the work of a group of writers that includes Tom Wolfe, Truman Capote, Jimmy Breslin, Gay Talese, Gloria Steinem, Hunter S. Thompson, Norman Mailer and a host of others with equally divergent writing styles. *In Cold Blood*, Truman Capote's 1966 book described by its author as a "nonfiction novel," is generally considered to be the forerunner of the New Journalism movement.

Tom Wolfe, one of the most successful of the new journalists, defines the style this way: "I think the New Journalism is the use by people writing nonfiction of techniques which heretofore had been thought of as confined to the novel or short story, to create in one form both the kind of objective reality of journalism and the subjective reality that people have always gone to the novel for." Wolfe describes these techniques as scenic construction, full use of dialogue, interior monologue and the recording of details such as gestures, habits, manners, style of clothing, eating and traveling—everything, Wolfe explains, generally symbolic of people's everyday lives.

It is the use of interior monologue—describing a subject's inner thoughts and feelings in a nonfiction piece—that has become one of the most controversial devices employed by the New Journalist; a journalist, it is argued, cannot possibly observe or listen to the inner thoughts of another person. Yet Wolfe, Talese and other New Journalists have effectively written about what they thought an article's subject was thinking at a certain time.

A second criticism of New Journalism is that it is too personal, too subjective; the writer becomes more important than the person or event he is writing about. At the hands of less talented writers, the intrusion of the personal results in rambling, unedited, "off-the-top-of-the-head" pieces that fail to capture reader interest or identification. For the skilled New Journalist who is able to manage it effectively, however, the personal imprint is what appeals most to some readers.

Many writers mistakenly believe that the New Journalism demands less discipline than articles written in a conventional style. The most successful New Journalists, however, are those who are using the techniques of basic news and feature writing as well as experimenting with innovative forms. Gay Talese says of New Journalism: "This form cannot succeed . . . unless the old style of reporting precedes it . . . the constant interviewing of your subject or subjects, getting to know everything you can about this person."

Because of its emphasis on subjectivity, using the New Journalism style in writing news stories is more loudly criticized than using a personal journalism approach in creating magazine articles and newspaper features.

The magazine and feature story writer has never been tied to the strict formula and premium on objectivity required of a straight news story; the devices that characterize New Journalism have, according to many journalists, been long used in various forms by writers throughout the years—Ernest Hemingway, Lillian Ross, Daniel Defoe and H.L. Mencken among them. (*See: Fictionalizing nonfiction material; Objective writing.*)

New product release. This press release is sent out to inform the media of a new product or service. It consists of a brief descriptive text sometimes accompanied by a 5″ × 7″ glossy photograph. This kind of writing calls for an informal style: contractions, colloquialisms and humor are used. Since brevity is necessary, each word is important. The textual part of a new product release package informs the reader of the name, the potential uses and users, the function, the advantages and the cost of the product, as well as where consumers may obtain it. At the end of the product information, the writer gives a name for the editor to contact for more information regarding the product and the time required by the manufacturer for delivery.

The new product release mailing list typically contains names of two hundred periodicals. (The writer should try to obtain the name of an editor of a specific department of the magazine as well.) *Writer's Market* lists trade journals and consumer magazines that may be candidates for new product releases. Other sources include *Editor & Publisher International Yearbook* (for newspapers) and *Oxbridge Directory of Magazines.* With each release, the writer inserts a return postcard or envelope—in case the editor wants more information or will indicate when he'll run the release—and cardboard to protect the photo in the mail.

A freelance writer may have the opportunity to write such releases for a small company or for an individual who does not regularly engage an advertising agency, and who wants to publicize a new product in appropriate trade journals or consumer magazines. This represents a source of freelance work that can often be found in the writer's own community.

Reading advertisements for small companies' products and advertising in newspaper classifieds are means for the new product release newcomer to find clients. A writer who has done this kind of work previously may be able to depend on referrals to obtain new clients. (*See: Figure 31.*)

John Newbery Medal. Established in 1922, this award is presented annually by the American Library Association for the best book written for American children. The award, a bronze medal, was named for John Newbery, an eighteenth-century British bookseller, who originated the idea of publishing books for children. The award almost invariably increases sales for the award-winning book—especially among schools and libraries.

News release. (*See: Publicity writing.*)

Newsbreak. A newsworthy event or item as described in a newspaper or

FIGURE 31

NEW PRODUCT RELEASE SAMPLE

For further information:

GENERAL MILLS, INC.
Pam Becker
FOR RELEASE   P.O. Box 1113
May, 1989   Minneapolis, MN 55440
(612)540-2470

GREAT TASTE, MORE OAT BRAN DISTINGUISH

NEW BETTY CROCKER OAT BRAN MUFFIN

A convenient new muffin mix from Betty Crocker brings together a much sought-after combination: the goodness of oat bran and great taste.

More oat bran than the other leading mix, Betty Crocker Oat Bran Muffin Mix with Streusel provides eight grams of oat bran in each muffin. Oat bran is the first item on the package ingredient list. In addition, Betty Crocker's muffin is made with vegetable shortening; no animal or tropical oils are used in the mix.

A cholesterol-free variation using egg whites or cholesterol-free egg product and skim milk is included on the package. Stir-in recipes on the side panel allow consumers to create easy flavor variations of the basic oat bran muffin, such as Blueberry, Raisin-Spice, Apple-Cinnamon, Zesty Orange, and Hearty Nut.

Because oat bran has very little taste, developing a good-tasting oat bran muffin has been a goal of General Mills. The combination of the oat bran muffin with the crunchy sweetness of a brown sugar streusel topping is a delicious way to add wholesome oat bran to your diet.

"Muffins are a convenient way of adding oat bran to our diets," explained David Ward, product manager. "Consumers generally recognize muffins as a healthier alternative for breakfast than sweet rolls and many other breakfast foods. We feel our introduction of Oat Bran Muffins with Streusel into the market will be offering consumers a product with the attributes that they've been looking for," he said.

-30-

Reprinted with the permission of General Mills, Inc.

news broadcast. Magazine editors also use the term to refer to a news item as it affects their particular readership. For example, a clipping about the opening of a new shoe store might be a newsbreak filler item of interest to a trade journal in the shoe industry. Some editors also use the word *newsbreak* to mean funny typographical errors.

Newsletters. A small publication featuring brief articles, usually dealing with a single subject.

Newsletters, which vary in size, shape and complexity, are circulated by businesses, not-for-profit organizations, and other groups of people sharing a common interest—a suburban community, for instance, or a softball league. A freelancer can enter the specialty of newsletter production either by replacing the editor of an existing newsletter or by proposing that a newsletter be published where none exists.

A newsletter writer gets story ideas from local newspapers, and from officers, employees and volunteers at the organization. A notice placed in the newsletter itself may also result in story leads.

Newsletter production for local clients furnishes the freelance writer-editor with a dependable income source and leaves time to spare for other writing pursuits.

Duties involved in the newsletter production process are research (including interviews), writing, rewriting, meetings with the client, taking or obtaining photographs or other artwork, preparing material to be typeset, delivering material to and picking it up from the typesetter, and proofreading (the galleys and

blueprint). The freelancer who produces a newsletter must schedule time for each of these steps, recognizing that some of them require cooperation with the client or the printer. In addition, the first issue that the freelancer works on requires *start-up time*, or time for him to become acquainted with the organization and his contacts within it.

Not all freelancers take on the responsibility of the entire production process: some—engaged by the organization or its printer—only write copy, for example.

Most fees for newsletter work are charged on a flat rate per number of pages, with an hourly fee used as a base. Work for a not-for-profit organization brings a slightly lower fee than that done for a business.

When proposing a newsletter to a potential client, the writer should take samples of newsletters produced by other organizations, as well as tearsheets and other credentials of his own. Producing a trial newsletter is a way that writer and client can work together on a "let's see" basis before committing themselves.

Additional information: *Editing Your Newsletter.*

Newspaper ads for small businesses, writing. Small businesses that can't afford to contract with an advertising agency are likely prospects for freelancers who can write advertisements to appear in local daily and weekly newspapers. Freelancer Fred Drewes, for instance, hit upon a particular type of advertisement that sold well, was easily produced and for which he faced little competition: single-column "article/ads" that various businesses could place in appropriate sections of the paper. A feature titled "Calling All Home-makers," for example, paid for by a furniture outlet, would appear on the lifestyle page and contain interesting facts related to furniture—along with a brief sales message that concluded with the store's address, telephone number and business hours. A small photo of the proprietor and his byline usually appeared in the ad/article. Drewes ghosted for ten such clients over a period of eight months—"The Home Front," "Your Car Needs Our Care," etc.—charged $10 per weekly insertion of the advertisement and cleared $100 per week.

Drewes believed that locale had something to do with his success selling his article/ads, that small towns and cities whose population was 8,000-25,000 provided little in the way of advertising or writing facilities, and so businesspeople were eager to take advantage of his services. He recommended beginning with neighborhood and hometown businesses and gradually moving further afield as clippings accumulated.

Drewes's success demonstrates the fertility of the small-town market, where the number of potential accounts and low-key way of doing business make up for lower rates of pay. Writers who live in small towns or rural areas can earn a respectable income serving local businesses. (*See: Business writing.*)

Additional information: *Writing for Money.*

Newspaper Fund, Dow Jones. Established by the publishers of *The Wall Street Journal* in 1958 to encourage careers in journalism. Produces informational surveys of journalism graduates and job opportunities, internship programs, etc. The address is P.O. Box 300, Princeton, NJ 08543.

The Newspaper Guild, AFL-CIO. This union, primarily composed of newspaper employees in news and business departments, bargains contracts with publishing companies that establish working conditions and minimum rates of pay. Following is a sample of minimum weekly rates provided for starting reporters under Newspaper Guild contracts in effect December 1, 1994: $1,215.25, *The New York Times*; $529.14, *Detroit Free Press*; $400.18, *The Sacramento Bee*; $456.19, *The Denver Post*; $566.79, *Plain Dealer* (Cleveland); $184, *Battle Creek Enquirer* (Michigan).

Newspaper indexes. (*See: Periodicals, indexes to.*)

Newspaper Organizational Chart. (*See: Figure 32.*)

Newspaper readability. Although neither The Newspaper Fund nor the American Newspaper Publishers Association (ANPA) has any national statistics on the reading levels for which newspaper copy is written, one paper, the Worcester (Massachusetts) *Evening Gazette*, commissioned a readability study of its news and feature pages. As reported in the newspaper trade magazine, *Editor & Publisher*, the paper discovered that article readability varied from the fourth- and fifth-grade levels to that of college sophomore. By departments, some scores ranged as follows (the numbers represent the school

FIGURE 32

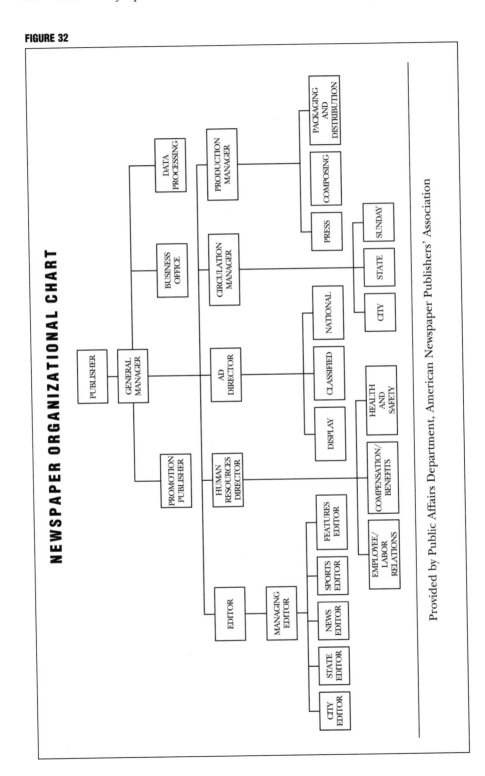

NEWSPAPER ORGANIZATIONAL CHART

Provided by Public Affairs Department, American Newspaper Publishers' Association grade reading level needed to understand the text): local news, 11.1; business news, 10.3; arts and entertainment, 9.7; family today features, 8.3; sports news, 6.6. The average score for the entire newspaper was 9.2. (*See: Fog Index; Readability formulas.*)

Newspaper reporting. A staff reporter on a newspaper works either as a beat reporter, who regularly gathers news from the same sources—such as police court or city council—or a general assignment reporter, who is given an individual assignment for each event or story he covers. On large papers, reporters may develop specialties covering developments in business, education, medicine or science.

To be successful as a reporter, a person must question, observe and adapt to different persons and situations. Good reporters have a "nose for news" as well; they discover subjects suitable for news stories, then research them. A good reporter must be competitive, persistent, willing to dig for details and able to produce under pressure.

In a 1981 survey of American newspaper reporters and editors, reporters named variety, autonomy, creativity and learning as advantages to their work. Favorable aspects of their jobs noted by reporters include ego satisfaction, the opportunity to work outside an office, having the status of an "insider," feeling that they accomplished something every day and working as a detached observer.

The same respondents pointed to lack of time, too little communication with and direction from editors, low pay and bad hours as frustrating aspects of their work.

Some newspaper editors prefer to hire reporters with liberal arts degrees; others prefer journalism degrees. The increasing numbers of journalism school graduates in relation to available jobs has made the market highly competitive for newcomers.

It is common for reporters to begin their careers on small newspapers, where there are more opportunities, then move to larger ones. (*See: Newspapers, daily—writers for; Newspapers, weekly—writers for.*)

Newspapers, back issues. Some small as well as most large newspapers usually keep clips of back issues in a *morgue*, or library, in which material is arranged by subject. Writers can usually gain access to these references by contacting the newspaper's librarian. In addition, a local library will likely hold back issues of that community's newspaper. Some large public libraries house back issues of major national newspapers on microform.

Newspapers, daily—writers for. A daily is issued each morning or afternoon or both; some papers do not publish on Sundays. Most of the well-known daily newspapers are published in large cities and offer staff and freelance opportunities to writers and editors. Whether a small city paper comes out daily is determined by its own budget and the population of the surrounding area.

Perhaps the most evident advantage that a daily newsperson has over a weekly newsperson is a higher income, often thanks to newspaper unions, whose power is strongest in large cities. (Median starting salary on a daily is about $390 per week; less on weeklies.) Another advantage to the large-staffed dailies is that employees can usually depend on more regular hours, although any newspaper worker should be prepared for unexpected assignments, since his work depends on happenings in his surroundings.

The opportunity to specialize in politics or education or other subjects is more readily available to daily newspaper workers, since dailies' staffs are larger than those of small-town and suburban papers. The editorial budgets of major newspapers afford the reporter on a large-city daily more opportunities for investigative work; weekly newspaper reporters seldom receive investigative assignments. But by the same token, a writer or editor who takes his first job on a daily may miss out on the comprehensive learning opportunity available to his weekly newspaper counterpart, who is likely to be assigned to tasks in various departments.

In recent years, many American dailies have been bought by newspaper chains; this phenomenon has both beneficial and harmful effects. While it strengthens the newspaper financially, some experts believe that the predominance of chains weakens and eventually destroys independent papers, thus repressing the traditional spirit of editorial competition. (*See: Conflict of interest; Newspapers, weekly—writers for.*)

Additional information: *Opportunities in Journalism Careers.*

Newspapers, directories of. Two directories, set up geographically, are the *Editor & Publisher International Year Book* and the *Gale Directory of Publications*. *E&P Year Book* lists foreign as well as U.S. newspapers; Gale's lists only U.S. and Canadian magazines. Writers seeking the names and addresses of publications and their editors in a specific locale will find both these directories in most public libraries, or in the editor's office at their local newspaper. (*See: Periodicals, directories of; Periodicals, indexes to.*)

Newspapers, weekly—writers for. The more than eight thousand newspapers in this country that are published in rural areas, small towns and suburbs are referred to by the collective term *weekly*, even though some of them (a minority) are actually published at larger or smaller intervals than a week. Most weeklies are the size of a standard newspaper, while others use tabloid format or an irregular paper size. Similarly, generalizations regarding page count cannot be made: Some weeklies comprise eight pages, and others run more than one hundred. The most common days of issuance are Thursday and Friday.

Because a journalist hired to work on a weekly is expected to perform a mélange of duties, this type of work is excellent training for those who aspire to staff positions at large-city dailies. Specifically, a reporter is likely to find himself editing, rewriting, proofreading, writing editorials and headlines, designing pages and taking photographs. Some editorial staff members even function periodically in the paper's advertising department.

This variety of duties is rarely performed in a forty-hour work week: A staff member typically works as many as seventy hours per week. In addition, he is paid less than a large-city journalist of comparable background. The absence of unions in most small-town newspaper operations is a contributing factor to this situation.

Advantages of small-town newspaper work include the opportunity for bylined features to build a portfolio. Although salaries are lower in rural areas than in cities, so is the cost of living. Some reporters use weeklies as stepping-stones to more sophisticated jobs in journalism, while others discover that the advantages of small-town life and newspaper work are satisfying in themselves. (*See: Conflict of interest; Newsweekly.*)

Additional information: *Opportunities in Journalism.*

Newsweekly. A weekly magazine, such as *Time* or *Newsweek*, that covers national and international news in greater depth than daily newspapers. This term occasionally refers to alternative weeklies. (*See: Alternative weekly.*)

Nobel Prize for Literature. Endowed by Alfred Bernhard Nobel, this award is one of the most highly valued and respected of literary prizes. It is presented annually to an author, on the basis of all his work, by the Swedish Academy of Literature in Stockholm. The recipient, according to Nobel's will, is the person "who shall have produced in the field of literature the most distinguished work of

an idealistic tendency." Authors do not apply for this award; a winner is chosen by the Swedish Academy of Literature from nominations provided by the Swedish Academy and other academies, previous winners, professors of languages and of the history of literature, and presidents of authors' organizations.

American writers who have won the Nobel Prize include: Sinclair Lewis, 1930; Eugene O'Neill, 1936; Pearl S. Buck, 1938; William Faulkner, 1949; Ernest Hemingway, 1954; John Steinbeck, 1962; Saul Bellow, 1976; Isaac Bashevis Singer, 1978; Joseph Brodsky, 1987; and Toni Morrison, 1993.

The prize itself consists of a gold medal and a substantial sum of money. Nobel also endowed prizes for physics, chemistry, medicine and peace.

Nom de plume. A French phrase that means "pen name." (*See: Pen name.*)

Non sequitur. Latin for "it does not follow." A *non sequitur* is a false argument or conclusion, an illogical inference that does not follow from the previous statements. The phrase is often used as a noun in English, as in this example: "To presume that your story is no good because the *Atlantic Monthly* rejected it is a *non sequitur.*"

Nonfiction books, marketing. The key to effective book marketing is research: research into the competition, research into finding the right publisher, and just enough research into the book's subject itself to put together a compelling proposal.

The first marketing step for the

writer with a book idea is to identify the book's audience; this will not only help the writer choose appropriate publishers to query (and bolster his sales argument), but also make the actual writing easier as he keeps his audience in mind. Research in the *Subject Guide to Books in Print* (at the library) and in bookstores will help him determine how much competition his book will have; he may find it advisable to find a new slant on the subject or even drop the project altogether.

After firming up the book's subject and slant, the writer should research the topic itself until he feels he knows enough to assemble a detailed chapter-by-chapter outline—generally, a paragraph summarizing the information contained in each chapter.

The writer then selects a publisher. *Literary Market Place* lists U.S. publishers alphabetically, with cross-indexes; by field of activity, e.g., mail-order or textbooks; by subject matter; and by geographic area. *Writer's Market* contains more detailed information on the editorial requirements of U.S. and Canadian publishers. The writer should also look at publishers' imprints on books they see on library shelves and in bookstores; check recent issues of *Publishers Weekly* and best-seller lists to see which publishers are producing which kinds of books. Once the writer selects a publisher (or publishers), he writes a query letter briefly describing the book, identifying its audience, discussing the competition, and stating his credentials to write the book—including practical, professional and/or academic experience in the field. The writer must be able to tell the prospective editor/publisher how the proposed book differs from others that have been written on the same topic; what is new in the book; or how this interpretation improves upon those of the past. He then puts together a *book proposal*—the letter, outline and a sample chapter—packages it neatly (*always* enclosing a self-addressed, stamped envelope), and mails the bundle to the proper editor at the prospective publishing house.

A busy publisher can take weeks or even months to reply, so the writer may wish to send proposals to several publishers at once. This practice is called *multiple submission* and is perfectly acceptable as long as (1) that publisher's *Writer's Market* entry okays it and (2) the author advises each editor that the book is being considered elsewhere. Multiple submission decreases total waiting time dramatically, increases the chances of a timely book being accepted and published while the topic is hot, and sometimes permits the author to choose the best deal from among competing publishers. (*See: Book manuscript preparation and submission; Synopsis.*)

Nonfiction novel. A work in which real events and people are written in novel form, but are not camouflaged, as they are in the *roman à clef*. In the nonfiction novel, reality is presented imaginatively; the writer imposes a novelistic structure on the actual events, keying sections of narrative around moments that are seen (in retrospect) as symbolic. In this way, he creates a coherence that the actual story might not have had. *The Executioner's Song*, by Norman

Mailer, and *In Cold Blood,* by Truman Capote, are notable examples of the nonfiction novel. (*See: Faction; New Journalism; Roman à clef; True crime.*)

Nonfiction sales to movies. Books and articles based on actual events can be the foundations for sales to TV (for movies, docudramas, miniseries and specials) or the motion picture industry. For example, the TV movie *Guardian Angels* appeared originally as an article in the *New York Daily News;* the Broadway and Hollywood musical *The Best Little Whorehouse in Texas* was based on an article in *Playboy.* Ted Schwarz, an author of nonfiction books who has sold material to TV, documents at least one case in which a writer sold material to TV on the basis of a "strong title and a brief description of plot and characters," but the usual procedure, he says, is to submit a title, a brief description of the story and an outline. Notes and other research materials used by the writer in covering the story can also encourage sales, as they can point out other aspects of the story that might have been left out of the article or book but that might be suitable for a motion picture.

According to Schwarz, the TV industry abides by the "*TV Guide* rule," which states that a major criterion for a successful movie idea is that it be able to attract a large audience by means of its title and a three-line description such as those appearing in *TV Guide.*

Selling material to the motion picture or TV industry must be accomplished through an agent. If a freelance writer or a staff writer thinks he has a possible film subject, an agreement between the writer and the major subject or subjects of the story (assuming they're not in the public domain) is also essential, since it prevents a movie production company or another writer from undertaking the same project at the same time. Such an agreement stipulates the ratio of the split of income between the writer, the subject and the agent, as well as the length of time that the writer has exclusive access to the subject as source and any documents relating to the story. The agreement should be either written or examined by an attorney. It is signed by all parties involved, in the presence of witnesses. It is suggested that scripts, treatments and outlines be registered with the Writers Guild of America, West.

The freelance writer who intends to sell nonfiction material to Hollywood must ascertain that he still owns the appropriate rights and has not sold them to a publication. In the case of a newspaper or magazine staff writer, the TV and film rights usually belong to the publisher from the beginning, but the writer is sometimes awarded all or part of the income from the movie sale that results from his article or series. (*See: Agents, TV; Screenwriting; Television markets; Television writing.*)

Nostalgia. Derived from the Greek words meaning "return home" and "pain," *nostalgia* refers to a longing to return in thought or in fact to one's home, to a former time in one's life or to one's family and friends. Nostalgia writing is a wistful examination of people, customs, items or incidents from the past; it is personal and emotional in contrast to historical writing, which is objective and factual.

As a category of writing, nostalgia describes a type of personal experience article intended to evoke from the reader an emotional response approximating the feeling the writer recalls. The most effective nostalgia pieces are written about subjects that have universal appeal; they focus on commonly shared experiences that transcend geographical location, age, sex and economic and social background.

Some types of nostalgia pieces described by Connie Emerson in her book, *Write on Target,* include *personal reminiscence articles, whatever-happened-to* or *do-you-remember-when* pieces; *celebrity reminiscence roundups,* consisting of personal recollections centered around one theme (e.g., "My first job" or "My most embarrassing moment"); and *historical nostalgia* (e.g., a music magazine may feature a piece on rock-and-roll stars of the 1950s).

Another type of nostalgia piece is the *quiz,* which is usually introduced with a paragraph of prose and continues with a series of questions related to nostalgic aspects of days gone by. Questions usually deal with personalities, literature, sports, TV shows, etc., of a certain decade; other nostalgia quizzes may be of the psychological variety (e.g., "Did You Have a Happy Childhood?").

The last type of nostalgia piece Emerson outlines is the antinostalgia article, which satirizes the nostalgia craze and offers proof that "the good old days" were not actually all that good.

Dozens of markets for nostalgia are listed annually in *Writer's Market.*

Many religious publications use reminiscences. General-interest magazines such as *The Atlantic Monthly, Capper's Weekly, Good Housekeeping* and *Reader's Digest* publish nostalgia, as do automotive, retirement and city and regional publications. Several of the food-and-drink, sports, antiques and music magazines carry an occasional nostalgia piece. Moreover, many of the magazines that don't buy nostalgia as a distinct article type do accept articles and short stories that include nostalgic elements or themes. As with any type of article, the writer must carefully study the editorial requirements of the market to which he is submitting a nostalgic piece.

Notable Books. A list published annually by the American Library Association. The roster of fifty books represents those works deemed significant by virtue of the knowledge and pleasure they afford to adult readers. The list is compiled by a panel of library professionals and without the influence of publishing companies.

Note-taking. Writers use three basic methods to accomplish the rapid note-taking that is necessary during interviews.

Shorthand is a fast and convenient means of taking notes, especially when a tape recorder is unavailable; however, it is a skill that requires training and practice. Through experience, some writers have devised their own systems of shorthand or abbreviation. The tape recorder can be an invaluable aid to note-taking in interviews. (*See: Tape recorder.*)

Novel & Short Story Writer's Market. An annual directory of about nineteen hundred listings describing commercial and literary outlets for fiction writers. The directory includes twenty-four chapters of practical, "how-to" fiction writing and marketing instruction, featuring articles and book/magazine excerpts on the craft and technique of novel and short story writing. Its sections dealing with fiction markets are "Literary & Small Circulation Magazines," "Commercial Periodicals," "Small Press" and "Commercial Publishers." Listings in each section include names, addresses and telephone numbers of fiction publishers; name of a person to contact; types of fiction the publisher deals in; and information on how to submit material.

Other listings in the directory are included in the sections "Contests and Awards," "Retreats and Colonies" and "Conferences and Workshops."

Novel writing. The structure of a novel resembles that of a short story in that it consists of a series of conflicts and temporary victories, then reaches a climax wherein the major conflict is either resolved or accepted as unsolvable. A dénouement is sometimes added at the end.

The novelist uses four devices in creating his work. *Scenes of movement,* the counterpart of the narrative used in nonfiction, present word pictures that show characters in action. *Characterization* involves lending believability to characters; it can be accomplished through description (physical and/or psychological), dialogue or thoughts of the character being described, dialogue of other characters and scenes of movement. A *plot* consists of a problem, subsequent actions of characters relative to the problem, and the outcome of the situation that the original problem created. Finally, *dialogue* between characters should be believable, but it cannot be so detailed as to bore the reader; it should be condensed into the most important and most interesting lines of a seemingly real-life conversation. To seem real, a character's speech must be suitable for his personality, occupation, education and other characteristics.

The novel allows the writer more time for characterization and plot development than the short story does. The novelist also has the liberty of changing viewpoint by switching the story's narrators, a technique that the short story writer can rarely employ successfully.

In conceiving novels, different writers use different starting points: Some begin with a character; others begin with a theme; still others invent a situation or plot twist.

Many writers believe that designing an idea outline is the first step in writing a novel. Such an outline includes general conceptions of plot, theme, characters, viewpoint and the emotions to be conveyed to the reader. Most idea outlines are about three to six pages long. Detailed plot synopses could run ten to thirty pages. Research, which can consume from one-tenth to one-third the total time spent creating the novel, is undertaken next to add credibility to the book and to cultivate the writer's imagination. After completing the bulk of the research, the novelist begins writing a first draft. Methods for this stage of novel-writing vary with the individual. (*See: Characterization; Climax; Conflict; Dénouement; First draft, revising and rewriting; Plot.*)

Novelette. This is a short novel averaging 30,000-50,000 words. Also called *novellas*, they are sometimes published as separate units by small press publishers. *Billy Budd* and *The Old Man and the Sea* are examples of this genre. (*See: Novel writing.*)

Novelization. Creating novels from popular movies is a specialty of some writers. The novels they write— referred to as movie "tie-ins"—are produced by paperback book publishers that have bought the adaptation rights from the original screenwriter or copyright holder. (*See: Tie-in.*)

Novella. A relatively short work of prose fiction comparable in length to a long short story or novelette, approximately 30,000-50,000 words. *Novella* is an Italian term that means "a story." (*See: Novel writing; Novelette; Short story.*)

Novels for young people. Books written for children (excluding picture books) are divided into two groups according to the ages of the readers: novels written for children younger than twelve years of age and those written for children older than twelve years of age. The main character in a children's novel should be no younger than the age group of the book's intended audience; however, the character *can* be a year or two older than the novel's oldest reader.

Novels for teenagers revolve around characters aged fourteen to seventeen who are involved in more complex plots and show more depth than those characters in novels for the under-twelve group. Also, novels for the older group employ a more sophisticated writing style, vocabulary, subject matter and general treatment.

In writing a novel for children older than twelve, the author should remember that his work will be read predominantly by young teenagers, since older teenagers are likely to read fiction written for an adult audience. Therefore, the plot and the situations of the characters should be identifiable to the child of junior high school age.

Reading children's novels is an important step toward understanding their audiences. A public librarian or school librarian can be an invaluable guide to an author's study. (*See:* Children's Writer's & Illustrator's Market; *Juveniles, writing for.*)

Novels, marketing. An important marketing tool is knowing which types of books are published by which houses. A publisher of mainstream fiction, for example, would reject a category novel simply because it would be incongruous with the rest of his line of books. Book publishers' listings in *Novel & Short Story Writer's Market* indicate the kinds of novels sought by each company. Reading catalogs of publishers' releases is another way to become familiar with their products. Many publishers send their catalogs free to writers on request. Or the author can refer to the *Publisher's Trade List Annual*—a collection of most publishers' current catalogs available at public libraries. Writers can also make note of novels in bookstores and libraries, jotting down the names of publishers whose works seem most compatible with their own.

As the first contact from new authors, most publishing houses prefer to receive either a query letter or an outline and three sample chapters of the book; however, some request that a complete manuscript be submitted at this stage. *Novel & Short Story Writer's Market* listings provide details on the preferences of individual book publishers. (*See: Book contract; Book manuscript preparation and submission; First novels.*)

NPR. (*See: Broadcast networks.*)

Number of writers, statistics on. The number of freelance writers has not been accurately determined by any survey, probably because of the difficulty in doing so. A 1980 Public Opinion Poll conducted for the American Council for the Arts indicated 22 percent of U.S. adults write creatively as a hobby or sideline. Figures compiled on writers by the Census Bureau represent mostly full-time staff writers (such as newspaper reporters) and only those full-time freelance writers who have so declared themselves.

Professional organizations for writers are another source of statistics, but their figures are limited to their own membership.

Numbers, how to show in manuscripts. Most style manuals state the preference that numbers from one to ten be represented as words, and numbers higher than ten be represented as numerals. However, when producing books containing money figures, statistics or scientific data, some editors forgo these style rules and use numerals throughout the text to promote readability.

Objective writing. Writing that reveals little or nothing of the personality, thoughts or feelings of the writer. Objective writing focuses on external things and events, presenting reality as it is—or as it appears to be—unaffected by the personal reflections, sentiments or emotions of the writer. Newswriting is an example of nonfiction objective writing.

Henry Fielding, Anthony Trollope and Ernest Hemingway strove for objectivity in much of their work. Saul Bellow is considered by some critics to be an objective fiction writer. The objective viewpoint is not as popular in fiction, however, since readers tend to want to identify emotionally with the characters and material in stories. (*See: New Journalism; Objectivity; Subjective writing.*)

Objectivity. A journalistic ethic requiring a reporter to present a complete, accurate and undistorted account of any news event he covers, and to keep his newswriting free from personal opinion or prejudice.

The ethic of objectivity was developed during the first half of the twentieth century, largely because of the growing influence of the wire services. Until then, news had been deliberately slanted according to the biases of the newspaper that carried it, but the AP and other wire services found it impossible to prepare a news story to fit the slant of each of their clients. This, coupled with the public's growing dissatisfaction with biased news, led to the development of the "straight news" story and the separation of fact and opinion.

By the beginning of World War I, the straight news story had become the standard form of reporting. When it was discovered that the American people had little understanding about the causes of war, however, a glaring deficiency of the facts-only form was made apparent. During the next two decades, as American life became more complex with the coming of the New Deal and the advent of the cold war, the larger newspapers realized that it was necessary to *interpret* news as well as report it.

The growth of interpretive reporting was slow, however. Journalists were afraid to jeopardize the separation of fact and opinion, and saw interpretive reporting as being subjective rather than objective. Interpretive reporting, which is prevalent today, *is* considered to be objective reporting: Interpretive reporting *explains* the facts; it does not judge or advocate, as does editorial opinion.

The ethic of objectivity has been criticized in recent years as an unattainable ideal. Journalist Bill Moyers was quoted in *Newsweek* as saying, ". . . of all the myths of journalism, objectivity is the greatest." Every account is somehow influenced by the reporter's personal judgment, his own powers of observation and consciousness: Merely deciding which facts to include in a story and which facts to leave out prohibits complete objectivity.

Many individuals in the newsgathering and reporting field contend nonetheless that, if journalists strive for an objective presentation of the news, the result should approach the ideal. Daniel R. Williamson, in his book *Newsgathering*, outlines the five basic precepts journalists observe in attempting to present an objective account:

(1) *impartiality*. A news story must contain all viewpoints—presented with reasonably equal balance—if it involves controversy.

(2) *absence of conflict of interest*. A reporter involved with causes or organizations may be vulnerable to suspicion of partiality.

(3) *opportunity of denial*. A reporter is required to give an individual about whom he is making a damaging allegation a chance to deny or refute that allegation.

(4) *absence of cronyism*. This breach of ethics occurs when personal relationships—such as those between a reporter and his news sources—influence news coverage.

(5) *avoidance of vengeance*. A reporter should not use his access to the media to report unfairly on individuals he personally does not like.

While these observances are not required of the freelance nonfiction writer as they are of newspaper or broadcast journalists, the ethic of objectivity nevertheless provides an effective guideline in all nonfiction writing. (*See: Conflict of interest; New Journalism; Press trip; Subjective writing.*)

Obscenity. Often used incorrectly as a synonym for pornography, obscenity has an alterable legal meaning, depending on evolving court rulings. The decision in *Miller v. California* states that obscenity is determined by (a) whether "the average person, applying contemporary standards, would find that the work, taken as a whole, appeals to the prurient interest . . . (b) whether the work depicts or describes, in a patently offensive way, sexual conduct specifically defined as prohibited by the applicable state law, and (c) whether the work, taken as a whole, lacks serious literary, artistic, political or scientific value."

In addition, by this ruling, local standards replaced national standards as the criteria for judging whether a work is obscene. An example is the 1990 prosecution of the rap group 2 Live Crew in Broward County, Florida. Their album *As Nasty As They Wanna Be* was deemed obscene and the group was arrested for performing songs from that album in concert. They were later acquitted of obscenity charges. (*See: Censorship, literary; Freedom of the press; Pornography.*)

Occult. *Occult* refers to supernatural phenomena. Occult subjects include ghosts, E.S.P., astrology, demoniac possession and witchcraft. Typical markets for occult writing are astrological and psychic publications, and some confession magazines. Nonoccult publications as well may be interested in a documented supernatural story slanted to their readership. For example, a theater magazine may accept a piece on theatrical ghosts; an animal magazine may be interested in an article about a ghostly cat. The supernatural often plays a part in gothic romance novels.

Certain book publishers listed in *Writer's Market* express interest in the occult as a subject for a longer work of either fiction or nonfiction. (*See: Gothic.*)

Off the record. When information is said by an interviewee to be "off the record," he expects the writer to keep it confidential and exclude it from his story.

If the writer does incorporate off-the-record material into his story, he risks losing future opportunities to interview the same source; however, the reporter's responsibility to accurately inform his readers must also be taken into consideration. The decision he makes is more often an ethical than a legal one.

Some reporters attribute off-the-record information to "informed sources" rather than to a specific person. Other writers have alleviated the off-the-record problem by setting guidelines with the source at the outset of the interview: e.g., both may decide that the interviewee will indicate, during the course of the interview, which comments are off the record. Or the writer may grant the interviewee the right to turn off the tape recorder before making an off-the-record remark.

One writer, using a direct approach, informs his subject at the start of the interview that no information he receives will be considered off the record. His intention is

to have the subject refrain from revealing any information he doesn't want to see in print; or to avoid having his hands tied by a source who tells him something off the record (perhaps something he already knows) with the idea that this manner of disclosing the information to the reporter will prevent him from printing it.

If a source is crucial to the story but is reluctant to consent to an interview for attribution, the writer may decide on a "background" discussion—similar to White House briefings without attribution. The goal is to get a better understanding of the topic from an authoritative source who feels the subject is too sensitive to permit the use of his name, or who wants to send up a trial balloon on a controversial subject.

For example, writer John Behrens believes a number of sources fear political, social and financial backlash if they comment on contemporary issues. It's especially true among middle-management business and government officers, he believes. Behrens describes an instance of backgrounding as follows:

I may do a major business story on taxes and tax shelters and I want a comment from a regional IRS official. The source knows he has the knowledge and the right to comment but he fears repercussions. He is willing to discuss the questions and offer examples as well as his interpretations. These may vary from official positions. I can always get the departmental stance but his unofficial explanations give me a better idea of how I can use materials I've already acquired. Furthermore, I've got examples to better illustrate parts of the story thanks to his background session.

The problem for both beginning and professional writers these days is the caution of knowledgeable people—doctors, lawyers, engineers and others—about being interviewed for attribution. Quasi-investigative techniques are sometimes necessary. To prepare a piece on Camp David, a publicly funded recreation area for U.S. presidents, Behrens had to undertake a letter-writing campaign to members of Congress to persuade Carter Administration officials to provide basic information. Finally, several government officers offered "leads" and background as long as he promised not to use their names.

Investigative reporters use methods that can be applied in some freelance writing assignments, Behrens contends in his book, *Typewriter Guerrillas*, in which prize-winning reporters describe their techniques. (*See: Attribution.*)

Offprint. (*See: Reprint.*)

Off-screen. A term used in TV and motion picture scripts to indicate a sound or voice heard, but not seen, by the audience. (*See: Television script terms.*)

Ombudsman, newspaper. A newspaper ombudsman, usually a veteran reporter or editor, serves as an external spokesperson for the public and an internal critic for the newspaper. According to guidelines adopted in 1982 by the Organization of Newspaper Ombudsmen (ONO), the ombudsman's duties are to: (1) repre-

sent the reader who has complaints, suggestions, questions or compliments; (2) investigate all complaints and recommend corrective action when warranted; (3) alert the newspaper to all complaints; (4) serve as an in-house critic; (5) make speeches or write to the public about the newspaper's policies, attitudes and operations; and (6) defend the newspaper publicly or privately when warranted.

To perform those functions, ombudsmen write newspaper columns, give speeches, circulate memoranda within the staff, and distribute questionnaires to persons mentioned in news stories.

The editorial independence of the ombudsman is a subject of debate in the newspaper field. Some believe that the person in this position should be exempt from contributing editorially to the newspaper for which he works, to preserve his neutrality in serving the interests of both the newspaper and the public; others point to the prohibitive expense of hiring a full-time ombudsman.

Use of the ombudsman in the United States came into existence only recently, the first newspaper ombudsman program having been established in 1967.

On spec. An editor may respond to a writer's query letter by offering to look at the proposed article "on speculation"; that is, the editor expresses interest in the article idea and agrees to consider the finished piece for publication. In his response, the editor will usually indicate desired word count and terms of payment if the article is accepted.

However, the editor is under no obligation to buy the finished manuscript.

For this reason, many full-time freelancers write only on assignment, with a firm commitment from an editor to purchase the article. However, the writer who is not well established enough to write only on assignment will find that an invitation to submit an article on spec generally means that the editor is interested in the idea and will buy the finished manuscript—if it is submitted within a reasonable length of time and meets editorial specifications. (*See: Assignment, writing on; Query.*)

One-act play. This form of drama, also called a *one-act* or *one-acter*, takes from twenty-five to sixty minutes to perform. Its time limitation restricts the content of the play: The plot must be kept simple, extraneous elements must be excluded and no more than one set should be staged. However, a one-act play must include a complete story and theme and solid characterization.

One-act plays are published more often for high school, college and amateur use than for commercial production, although theaters such as the Actors Theatre of Louisville sometimes stage them. *Writer's Market* lists play publishers and play producers, and *Dramatists Sourcebook* lists competitions that consider one-act plays. (*See: Dinner theater; Dramatic convention; Dramatis personae; Plays for young actors; Playwriting.*)

Online service. A commercial organization that allows computer users—with the appropriate hard- and soft-ware—to hook up with a modem to a central computer. These services include—but aren't limited to—America Online, CompuServe, Delphi, eWorld and Prodigy. Some of the features include archived periodicals, connection with the Internet, downloadable libraries of software, e-mail capabilities, news, shopping services and travel services. Users can also leave posted responses on bulletin boards and interact with other subscribers in real-time. (*See: Electronic mail; Internet.*)

Onomatopoeia. A word whose sound represents a physical sound. Deliberate use of such words is most frequent in poetry, but occurs in prose—and in common speech—as well. *Plop, click* and *sizzle* are onomatopoeic words. (*See: Figures of speech; Imagery.*)

op. cit./loc. cit. These two Latin abbreviations are used in footnotes to indicate that a source has been previously documented in that list of notes. *Op. cit.* stands for *opere citato*, meaning "in the work cited"; and *loc. cit.* stands for *loco citato*, which means "in the place cited."

These abbreviations are preceded by the author's name and sometimes followed by a page number. However, when footnotes contain references to more than one book by the same author, *op. cit.* and *loc. cit.* may not be used to refer to that author's work. (*See: Ibid.*)

Op-Ed page. The page opposite the editorial page of a newspaper, used for columns and opinion articles. Some pieces may be staff-written, while others may be written by freelancers. Harrison E. Salisbury of *The New York Times,* who created the Op-Ed page, points out in his introduction to *The Indignant Years*:

The Seventies ushered in an age of skepticism. Not one institution of American society escaped reexamination . . . Nothing in society was too profound or too trivial to be put under the magnifying glass of critical analysis. It was into this era that the Op-Ed page of *The New York Times* was born, a child of its times, a calculated effort to meet what was perceived as one of the great needs of our times, a place where men and women could express themselves on what was closest to their hearts, strongest in their passions, most fiercely in their principles. The criteria for Op-Ed could not have been more simple: to have something challenging to say and to say it with eloquence.

Salisbury goes on to explain:

That was and is the cornerstone of Op-Ed. It gave more emphasis to the right since one of my precepts was not to repeat or reinforce the liberal views already expressed by *Times* columnists and *Times* editorials. We sought out the Walt and Eugene Rostows, the Bundys, the right-wing Republicans. We gave everyone a platform, the more diverse the better. . . .

We solicited contributions all over the world from high and low and read every contribution submitted—soon they came in by the hundreds. They run thousands a year now. Every one used was paid for—not much, usually about $150 for 750 words—but paid. The innovation caught on like wildfire. *The Washington Post* was so eager to imitate us they started theirs three days before ours, having learned our start-up date. And there is not a paper in the country of any consequence which does not have an Op-Ed these days. And of course it brought in Op opinions to *Time* and *Newsweek,* to the networks and elsewhere.

Not all newspapers publish opinion essays from freelancers, and many do not pay for the material they do publish. Those that do solicit opinion pieces are listed in *Writer's Market.* To these newspapers the freelancer submits a titled, well-written essay, unfolded in a manila envelope and accompanied by a self-addressed, stamped envelope, to the ''Op-Ed Editor'' or ''Viewpoint Editor'' of the paper. (*See: Opinion essay.*)

Open-end transcription. A syndicated radio program in which time has been left at both beginning and end for the station to insert local commercials.

Opening song. In a musical, the song that usually begins an act. It has an establishing function, but also serves to incite the audience's interest. ''Tradition,'' from *Fiddler on the Roof,* falls into this category. (*See: Musical.*)

Operetta. (*See: Musical.*)

Opinion essay. A short article—usually fewer than 1,000 words—in which the author offers his personal commentary on some event, condition or situation about which he has a special knowledge or interest.

Newspapers publish this kind of article on their Op-Ed pages. A variety of magazines—alternative, child care, general-interest, health and women's—use it as well. Publications that seek opinion essays from writers are listed in *Writer's Market.* (*See: Essay; Op-Ed page.*)

Opinion poll interviewing. (*See: Market research.*)

Option clause. A clause often found in author-publisher book contracts that grants the publisher the right to publish the author's next book. The option clause is sometimes called the *right of first refusal* because it allows the publisher first crack at the author's next book, which the publisher may or may not decide to take on. In other words, this type of clause ordinarily binds the author rather than the publisher.

For this reason, the option clause might be better deleted from many contracts. As agent Georges Borchardt notes in *Writer's Friendly Legal Guide,* if a publisher does a terrible job publishing an author's first book, why should the author subject his second book to the same fate? Borchardt explains the dangers of the option clause:

Some option clauses state that the publisher may acquire your next book on the same terms as your first; some state that the publisher need not make up his mind until several months after he has published book number one. Both of these stipulations should be avoided. The option to contract for your next book should be on terms to be agreed upon within a stated period of time,

and if it is a work of nonfiction the option should be exercised on the basis of a synopsis, within a month of submission . . . If the publisher and author cannot agree within the stated period of time, the option should expire.

Borchardt's counsel is important. When a specific time period within which a publisher must make a decision is not defined in the clause, the publisher may wait to determine how well the first book sells before making a decision. While the publisher prolongs the moment of decision, the author is not free to submit his book proposal elsewhere.

The Authors Guild says, ''The best way to deal with an option clause is to delete it from the publisher's contract form.'' (*See: Book contract.*)

Additional information: *A Writer's Guide to Book Publishing.*

Organizing article/book material. Different writers approach the organization process in different ways, and their systems range from complex arrangements of systematically classified index cards to casual groupings of related notes. One professional writer uses a coding system of colored pencils for related research materials. Another writes short segments of the article he's working on immediately following each interview. Many professional writers favor the cut-and-paste method to reorganize their first draft for smoother transitions. In many cases, the way a writer organizes his research material depends entirely on the type of article or book he's writing; organizational methods may change from one project to the next.

No matter what method a writer uses, organization of research is essential. Editors will often reject a well-researched manuscript because a writer did not take the time to organize the information collected.

As vital as the organization process is, however, overemphasizing its importance may be dangerous. As writer Dickson Hartwell explains in *A Treasury of Tips for Writers*, "Just as the tendency to over-research is a sign of a lack of confidence in one's own ability to get started with the actual writing, so is a predilection to over-organize."

During the organization process, the writer should select the essential information that relates to the theme or peg of the piece and file away any tangential information that, while not necessary to this particular project, might be useful for other books or articles. The writer should spend enough time organizing this essential material to be thoroughly familiar with the information, notes, anecdotes, etc., that he intends to use, and then determine some type of order or outline in which to present that material. When the first draft is completed, the writer can refer to this outline to make sure the manuscript covers all the intended points. (*See: First draft, revising and rewriting; Outline; Research aids/techniques.*)

Originality. The quality of being creative, inventive or out of the ordinary. This characteristic is difficult to define precisely in relation to writing. As one editor remarked in a *Writer's Digest* article, "If you could pinpoint the exact nature of origi-

nality, it wouldn't be original any more." As elusive as it may be to define, however, originality in articles, stories and books is precisely the quality editors are constantly searching for.

Given that there are virtually no new ideas under the sun, originality in writing becomes largely a matter of clothing a worn subject in a new approach. Few article topics and story themes have not been done before, but the creative writer faces— and meets—the challenge of expressing those topics and themes in an individual way, giving fresh insight to an idea to make it *seem* as if the subject hadn't been done before.

In respect to copyright law, the term *originality* does not refer to literary skill, artistic value or uniqueness; rather, it means that the work is created by the author and not originated by someone else. (*See: Creativity; Plagiarism.*)

Oscar Awards. The Oscar Awards are presented annually by the Academy of Motion Picture Arts and Sciences. The fifteen categories of awards represent various skills involved in film production; additional awards for general contributions to the motion picture industry exist, but are not necessarily presented yearly.

Writing for film is recognized by two awards: Best Screenplay Written Directly for the Screen, and Best Screenplay Based on Material from Another Medium.

Music for film is judged in two categories: Best Original Score and Best Original Song.

Outcue. The last words in the copy for a radio ad. Often, all spots for the same account employ the same outcue, e.g., the address or slogan of the sponsor. Air talent listens for the outcue as a signal to come on-air with whatever is scheduled to follow.

Outdoor Writers Association of America, Inc. (OWAA). Established in 1927, the Outdoor Writers Association of America is a not-for-profit professional and educational organization comprising newspaper and magazine writers, editors, photographers, broadcasters, artists, cinematographers and lecturers engaged in the dissemination of information on outdoor sports—hunting, boating, fishing, camping, etc.—and on the conservation of natural resources. In addition to conducting an annual conference, the organization publishes a monthly newsletter containing market coverage, writers' opinions, news of writers in the field, and craft improvement articles. Members are required to publish a specified quantity of paid material annually. Membership applicants must be sponsored by an active OWAA member. The address of the Association is 2017 Cato Ave., Suite 101, State College, PA 16801-2768.

Outline. An outline is a general description indicating only the main features of an article, story, book, speech or other project. It is a means of organizing material in which the order and general relationship of ideas are expressed so as to reveal a work's intention.

For a nonfiction writer, an outline serves as a plan or guide that provides a solid basis for the development of his article. Depending on a writer's preference and ability to organize, the outline may take various forms: It may be written out or merely a mental arrangement of facts; it may be a formal, detailed organization of ideas, or a brief collection of key words or statements indicating the progression of a piece. Whatever form the outline takes, it enables writers to organize their material and focus their attention on the subject of the article. Although important in providing a framework for an article, an outline should always be flexible enough to accommodate new ideas that develop from a writer's research and actual writing.

The nonfiction book author also uses an outline in preparing a book proposal. This more in-depth outline features chapter-by-chapter highlights in the order in which they'll appear in the book. This outline, together with one or two sample chapters and a specialized cover letter introducing the book's subject and explaining its salability, make up the book proposal an author submits to a publisher.

Fiction writers also use outlines to sketch out their plots in advance of the actual writing. Again, these plot outlines vary widely in the amount of detail their authors put into them. The only constant is that an author should never feel constrained by his outline; when he begins the actual writing, the author shouldn't ignore the new directions the story or characters may seem to move in. (*See: Nonfiction books, marketing.*)

Out-of-print books, how to find. The Manhattan Yellow Pages, available in libraries, lists bookstores that handle out-of-print books in the section "Book Dealers—Used & Rare." In addition, the annual *American Book Trade Directory*, in the section "Retailers & Antiquarians in the United States & Canada," lists this type of bookstore by state and city. Some book search services advertise in the back pages of *The New York Times Book Review* and other publications that cater to book lovers.

The section "Micropublishers" in *Literary Market Place* lists publishers of microfilm and similar materials, some of which contain out-of-print books and papers. Specific microforms are listed in *Guide to Microforms in Print* and *Micropublishers' Trade List Annual*.

Overseas Press Club of America (OPC).

The 515 members of the OPC are correspondents, reporters, editors, photographers, freelance writers and book authors. They work over-seas, have worked overseas in the past, or have worked in the news media for at least three consecutive years.

The organization presents several annual awards for reporting and photography concerning events overseas or foreign affairs. OPC members have access to various press clubs around the world.

Some of the organization's committees are Book Publishing, Foreign Journalists Liaison and Freedom of the Press. OPC publishes the monthly *Overseas Press Club Bulletin* and the annual *Dateline*, which contains articles by outstanding journalists. The OPC's address is 320 E. Forty-second St., New York, NY 10017.

Oxymoron.

A Greek word meaning "acutely silly," oxymoron names a figure of speech that combines contradictions, like *jumbo shrimp* and *thunderous silence.*

Pace. Tempo, or rate of progression. This term, which applies to both fiction and nonfiction works, refers to a written work's effect on the reader through the text's rate of movement.

A writer creates a slow pace by using substantial amounts of narration, description and digression. Action, dialogue and a series of incidents following in rapid succession quicken the pace. A writer varies pace to accommodate different moods and action in his writing, alternating between a rapid tempo and a more relaxed one, depending on the material and the effect the writer wishes to produce.

Pace is a feature of filmed or staged as well as printed material: The swift pace of an action-packed detective drama, for instance, contrasts with the leisurely exploration of a nature subject in a TV documentary.

Pad. To lengthen an article or book by adding text or detailed material related in a peripheral way, such as appendices, tables and lists. The latter may be desired by some book publishers to add reference material to a book, especially the type that in revised editions could be changed without affecting the pagination of the rest of the text; however, magazine editors generally reject articles padded with superfluous information that adds no significant value to a specifically focused manuscript.

Page proof. A reproduction copy of typeset matter after division into page form and before actual printing. On a page proof, galley corrections have been made, and line art illustrations, notes and display type (chapter heads, ornaments, and occasionally subheads) will usually appear in their proper positions.

Page proofs are carefully examined and read by the publishing house's proofreader as a final check. Depending on the nature of the book and the production schedule that has been set for it, an author may or may not see page proofs of his book.

Since editorial and design changes at the page proof stage are costly, time-consuming and likely to delay production of the book, trade book authors generally must have a specific provision to see page proofs written into their contracts, and must pay for any author's alterations required at this stage. (*See: Author's alteration clause; Galley proof.*)

Page rate. The method by which some magazines pay writers, as opposed to a per-word rate or a flat fee. In this sense, a *page* refers to a printed page rather than a manuscript page.

Paid for but not published. A magazine may sometimes accept and pay for an article that for one reason or another never reaches print. In many cases, a paid-for piece is never published because editorial policy changes; in other cases, a magazine's editor moves to another publication and the editor who replaces him doesn't like the piece.

A writer anxious to know if and when his purchased story or article will appear in print may send a polite inquiry to the editor who bought the piece. If this action does not prove satisfactory, the writer may follow up with a letter advising the publication of the guidelines for reclaiming rights to an unpublished manuscript established by the American Society of Journalists & Authors, Inc., and requesting the editor's consideration of same. According to these guidelines, if after one year the article or story has not appeared in print, all rights to the manuscript should return to the author, who may submit it elsewhere for publication. The author should be permitted to retain the original fee paid for the manuscript. (*See: Kill fee; Magazines, defunct; Rights to manuscripts.*)

Pamphlets. (*See:* Vertical File Index, The.)

Pan. To swing a motion picture camera from left to right or from right to left, without moving the camera base, to show a broad view of a location or scene. The direction is given as *pan right* or *pan left*. *Whip* indicates a rapid pan. The directions are typed in all caps in a script. (*See: Television script terms.*)

Paperback originals. (*See: Mass-market paperbacks vs. trade books; Paperbacks, history of; Trade paperback.*)

Paperbacks, history of. The first paperback novel, *Malaeska: The Indian Wife of The White Hunter*, was published in June, 1860. The 128-page book, written by Ann Sophia Winterbotham Stephens, a widely respected hardcover novelist of her day, was published by Irwin P. Beadle and Company and sold for $.10.

The first "dime novel," as it came to be called, was an immediate success; a print order of sixty thousand for *Malaeska* sold out within two months. Other publishers followed suit with paperbacks of their own. Dime novels came to enjoy tremendous popularity, creating a reading habit among those who previously could not afford to buy books.

As the competition increased, however, the literary level fell. Dime novels eventually gave way to the larger "pulp" magazine format.

Paperbound originals attempted a comeback in the 1930s, but failed to capture reader interest; the failure did, however, encourage Robert de Graff to initiate in 1939 his Pocket Book line of $.25 reprints of popular hardcover books, thus establishing the foundation for the entire modern paperback book industry.

In the next several decades, the success of paperback reprints stimulated keen competition among publishing houses. Pocket, Bantam, Signet and other publishers vied for the best books in every category—mystery, western, suspense, romance, etc. The shortage of good books by well-known authors created an economic suicide situation: to get the book he wanted, a publisher was forced to pay more than he would earn. The reprint line quickly became saturated with "loss leaders"—books offered at a loss by publishers to get rack space and attract customers to their entire line of books.

Although it was obvious that paperbound publishers would have to change their source of supply, it was magazine publisher Roscoe Fawcett who made the first move. When his line of original paperbacks—Gold Medal Books—debuted in 1950, they paved the way for the paperback originals industry that is still growing today.

In *A Writer's Guide to Book Publishing*, Richard Balkin discusses trends in the paperback book industry. Today, says Balkin, most of the mass-market houses are either owned by conglomerates or are subdivisions of hardcover houses. Many hardcover houses have trade paperback lines, as do most of the mass-market publishers. All major mass-market publishers have established their own hardcover imprints, or are affiliated in one way or another with a hardcover house (Avon's parent company, for example, also owns Hearst Books and William Morrow).

Balkin reports that in the last ten years or so, mass-market publishers such as Avon, Dell, Warner and Ballantine have increased their output of paperback originals, which ranges from 40-50 percent of their lists. Several reasons account for the increase of original titles, Balkin says: the increasing price of hardcover books and subsequent consumer reluctance to buy them; a decreasing reluctance on the part of critics to review paperbacks; a greater consumption of paperbacks as high school and college texts; and the frequently high prices and occasionally extravagant auctions for paperback reprint rights. Seven-figure advances paid by Bantam, for example, went to Tom Wolfe for *The Bonfire of the Vanities* and to Pat Conroy for *Prince of Tides*.

Other factors that have influenced the increasing number of original paperbacks include the need for more titles than hardcover houses can supply, and the fact that it is cheaper to commission a book for, say, $5,000 and control all rights, than to lease paperback rights only, for, say, $7,500 for only seven years.

The ongoing trend toward paperback originals is good news for novelists, particularly writers of "category" fiction, which is a growing area for the industry. The same is true, however, of nonfiction books with wide readership appeal. (*See: Category fiction; Mass-market paperbacks vs. trade books; Trade paperback.*)

Parable. A short narrative designed to teach some religious principle, moral lesson or universal truth. A parable is often an allegory in which each character in the story represents an abstract concept, such as obedience or honesty, that is illustrated through comparison with real-life events. Perhaps the most widely recognized parables are those told by Christ in the New Testament—the stories of the prodigal son and the good Samaritan are two examples. Parables often provide an excellent source of universal themes for all types of stories. (*See: Fable; Proverb.*)

Paradox. An apparently self-contradictory statement that actually contains truth. For example, Oscar

Wilde said, "Life is far too important a thing ever to talk seriously about." George Bernard Shaw once remarked, "The truth is the only thing that no one will believe."

Like wise sayings and quotable quotes, paradoxes come to an individual in a flash of inspiration. A writer ordinarily cannot sit down at his typewriter with the intention of creating a paradox; for this reason, paradoxes are found infrequently in most writing. (*See: Irony; Satire.*)

Parallelism. A principle of grammatical construction requiring elements or ideas similar in content and function, and of equal importance, to be expressed in similar form. This structural principle—known also as *parallel construction*—applies to all parts and units of speech, from words, phrases and clauses to sentences, paragraphs and whole units of composition.

Faulty parallel structure is a common problem for beginning writers, but even skillful writers occasionally have trouble with parallelism. Attention to parallel structure is essential to the construction of clear, effective sentences; it enables the reader to recognize immediately the coordinating elements and ideas in a composition.

The key to parallelism lies in using consistent verb tense, person, voice and grammatical structure to express coordinating elements and ideas. For instance, the writer should avoid shifting verb tenses, as in this example: "The ball *rolled* down the stairs and *bounces* on the landing." Since the verb in the first clause is past tense—*rolled*—the verb in the second clause should also be past tense. *Bounced,* not *bounces,* is correct.

Similarly, the writer should avoid shifting from second to third person or from active to passive voice within a sentence. Grammatical units such as clauses, infinitives and phrases should be kept parallel; an infinitive, for instance, should be followed by an infinitive of similar form and function. For example, "She liked *to read* books and *seeing* movies," is not parallel. The correct construction is, "She liked *to read* books and *to see* movies."

Parallelism also requires that a writer use articles and prepositions consistently. For example, "This project can be done in one, two or in three steps," should, according to the principles of parallel structure, be expressed as either "This project can be done in one, two or three steps," or "This project can be done in one, in two or in three steps."

Similarly, a writer should maintain consistent grammatical construction when using correlative expressions such as *both, and; not, but; not only, but also; either, or;* and similar phrases. "He is both a bore and dense," is an example of this type of faulty parallel construction. The sentence should read, "He is both boring and dense."

Absolute parallel structure is not always necessary. The primary concern is that the grammatical *functions* are parallel, even though the grammatical *forms* may not be. For instance, in the sentence, "He drove *recklessly* and *without regard for traffic signals*" both *recklessly* and *without regard for traffic signals* modify the verb *drove;* their grammatical functions are the same, and so the construction is parallel.

Parallel construction applies only to elements of *equal importance* in a sentence. The writer should avoid a series of words or phrases that seem to modify the same element but in fact do not. For instance, "Delia left, and she had a friend" is parallel in construction. The two clauses are not of equal importance, however, and the sentence should be expressed in this way: "Delia left with a friend."

Paraphrase. A paraphrase is a restatement of a quotation or text that is phrased in new words by the writer to make the original statement clearer or more succinct. Paraphrasing must not be used carelessly. In researching information for a book or article, for example, a writer may come across some interesting ideas that he would like to incorporate into his own material; to avoid plagiarizing the information, however, the writer must be certain to credit paraphrased words and ideas to their proper source.

Spoken remarks—made during an interview, for example—may also be paraphrased and attributed to the source as an indirect quote. Whenever paraphrasing, a writer must take care that his restatement of another's words and ideas—whether written or spoken—is accurate and true to the meaning of the original material. (*See: Attribution; Indirect quote; Plagiarism; Quotes.*)

Parody. A humorous, satirical imitation of a person, event, novel, story, poem, play, film or other subject. By following the style and substance of the original work, a parody may seek to ridicule, criticize or merely amuse without devaluing the original.

Since it involves by its very nature a certain amount of imitation of the original, parody often poses a special problem in the area of copyright law. The writer or other artist who attempts to parody some literary composition, film or other work risks copyright infringement in too closely imitating the copyrighted work of another. Protection from copyright infringement in regard to the creation of parodies is based on the concept of "fair use"; that is, permissible use of copyrighted material, which does not constitute infringement.

There are no clearly defined boundaries regarding how much a parodist may appropriate from an original copyrighted work. Recent court cases support the following basic guidelines: (1) a parodist may use only enough of the original material sufficient to cause a reader or viewer to "recall and conjure up" the original work on which the parody is based; (2) copying that is virtually complete or almost verbatim—even though it may contain grotesque, burlesque or parodic elements—is not protected under the "fair use" defense; (3) the copyrighted material itself must be the object of parody—and not merely used *within* a parody—to be protected under the fair use concept; (4) the use of copyrighted material should in no way confuse the public into believing the parody has any association with the original work; (5) the resulting work imitating the copyrighted material should not be in economic competition with the original.

Guideline (2), above, came about as a result of a 1958 case in which Jack Benny was sued regarding the film *Autolight*, a parody on the film *Gaslight*. The court denied Benny the fair use defense on the grounds that a substantial amount of material (in this case, dialogue) had been copied. Guideline (3) was reflected in the 1975 case *Walt Disney Productions v. Mature Pictures Corp.*, in which the latter used the "Mickey Mouse March" as background music for an erotic scene depicting sexual deviation. The court decided that copyright infringement had occurred and that parody was not a defense, because the "Mickey Mouse March," although used in the film, was not the subject of the parody.

These criteria apply also to the infringement of trademark registration. An individual is not protected under the fair use concept in parodying a trademark if the parodist's satire of the registered trademark (1) confuses the public, misrepresents a product or damages the value of the trademark; (2) attempts to cash in on the good name and trade of the trademark owner; or (3) is so similar to the original that it leads the public to believe that a distinctive product or service is being offered by the parodist.

Fair use and copyright infringement in regard to parody are often complicated legal areas. The writer who intends to imitate the copyrighted work of another for the purpose of creating parody should have a thorough understanding of the law of copyright and concept of fair use in order to avoid potential legal conflicts. The market for parody seems limited today to a few publications such as the more literary men's magazines, the *New Yorker* and *Mad*—the latter of which wants not prose submissions but descriptions of visuals that can illustrate them. Brief passages of parody also appear in drama, film and TV reviews. Some novelty books might also be considered parodies. (*See: Copyright; Fair use; Humor; Trademark.*)

Participation. The sharing of commercial time and costs for the same broadcast program by more than one sponsor.

Pay on publication. Many publications, particularly among the smaller markets, pay the freelancer for a manuscript only after the story or article has been published. This practice means the editor of a pay-on-publication magazine may accept a freelance submission and hold it indefinitely without ever printing it— and, thus, without ever paying the author. The passage of time or a change in editors may make the manuscript unusable. Also, because the pay-on-publication policy is characteristic of smaller markets that operate on tight budgets, the magazine may go out of business. Even if the piece is eventually published, it may be many months before the freelancer receives any money.

The pay-on-publication policy is strongly criticized by professional writers. Writer and editor Art Spikol comments: "Selling an article to a market that pays on publication is like selling a bed to somebody and not requiring payment until they actually sleep in it."

Although most books on writing caution freelancers to avoid pay-on-publication markets, they also acknowledge that these smaller magazines are often the easiest for beginners to break into. Writers are warned to protect themselves when dealing with pay-on-publication markets. "If you do place a manuscript with one of them," says Lois Duncan, author of *How to Write and Sell Your Personal Experiences*, "ask for a written guarantee that if publication and payment do not occur within a set time (six months seems appropriate to me), you will be allowed to withdraw the manuscript and submit it elsewhere." (*See: Full-time freelancing, economics of.*)

PBS. (*See: Broadcast networks.*)

PE (printer's error). A typesetting error; also called a *typo*. When an editor or proofreader goes through galleys clearing up typos, making last-minute revisions, incorporating the author's alterations, etc., he marks the typos *PE* to distinguish them from editorial changes. This is an accounting procedure: If copy is set by a firm independent of the publisher, the publisher will be charged only for editorial revisions and not for mistakes the typesetter has made. Another reason for keeping track of typos and revisions is that if an author has made more than the percentage of alterations his contract allows for, the typesetting cost will come out of his royalties.

Peg. The one angle of a subject on which a nonfiction writer develops his article. Most good article subjects suggest several pegs, and each of them can be developed into a separate, salable article slanted toward a particular market. For example, a writer who planned to write about vegetable gardening could use three different pegs for three different articles: how to use vegetable plants in a landscaping/decorative scheme; how to convert to the French intensive method of gardening for economy and self-sufficiency; and how to grow an easy-to-care-for vegetable garden indoors. The first article could be slanted toward a landscaping trade journal; the second, toward an alternative magazine; and the third, toward an apartment dweller's magazine. (*See: Slanting.*)

PEN American Center. Established in 1921, PEN is a world association of poets, playwrights, essayists, editors and novelists. The organization defines as its purpose "to promote and maintain friendship and intellectual cooperation among men and women of letters in all countries, in the interests of literature, the exchange of ideas, freedom of expression, and good will." PEN has more than twenty centers in Europe, Asia, Africa, Australia and the Americas. Membership is open to "all qualified writers, translators and editors who subscribe to the aims of International PEN." Membership is by invitation of the Admission Committee after nomination by a PEN member. To qualify for membership, an applicant must have "acknowledged achievement in the literary field, which is generally interpreted as the publication by a recognized publisher of two books of literary merit." The address of this organization is

568 Broadway, Suite 401, New York, NY 10012.

Pen name. Also known as a *pseudonym* or a *nom de plume*, a pen name is used by an author instead of his real name. Mark Twain was the pen name of Samuel L. Clemens; David Cornwell writes under the name John le Carré.

Whether a writer uses his own name or a pen name depends on a number of factors. The pen name might represent co-authors writing under one name. An author's own name may be unsuitable, either because it is too similar to that of an established writer, is difficult to pronounce, or is somehow ridiculous-sounding. In other cases, an author writing different types of material—children's picture books and romance novels, for example—may wish to maintain different literary identities for different literary pursuits. Very prolific writers often employ pen names if they produce several books a year or find themselves with duplicate bylines in the same issue of a magazine. Finally, a writer may choose to publish under a pen name merely to avoid recognition.

The freelancer writing under a pen name generally types his real name and address in the upper left corner of the first page of his manuscript. (His real name should also appear in the upper left corner of succeeding manuscript pages.) His pen name is typed as the byline under the title of his article or story. This indicates that the writer wishes his pen name to appear in print on the article or story; the editor will, however, pay the writer with a check made out to the author's real name.

If for some reason the writer wishes to conceal his identity from the editor to whom he submits his manuscript, he types his pen name in the upper left corner of the first page as well as in the byline position; his real name does not appear at all on the manuscript.

The writer using only a pen name and not his real name should notify his bank and local post office, advising them that he may be receiving checks and mail in that business name. He would also file his income tax return showing his pen name on Schedule C, for example, "John Smith doing business as (or dba) William Jones." (*See: Byline.*)

PEN Prison Writing Program. A division of PEN, the writers' organization, which sponsors an annual writing competition for writers in prison and provides sources of information on writing to prisoners. This information ranges from answers to commonly asked questions and referrals to other programs for prisoners to listings of magazines that accept prisoners' writing. The Center distributes some free publications and sometimes receives books and magazines that it also gives to prisons. (Writers who wish to donate used books to prisoners as a tax-deductible gift should contact PEN for further information.)

The Center's competition, the Writing Awards for Prisoners, offers nine awards annually: first-, second-, and third-place prizes in fiction, nonfiction and poetry categories. Entries are accepted until September 1; awards are presented in late spring. Winning pieces are published in *The Fortune News.* Contest requirements and other information on the Center's services may be obtained from PEN American Center, 568 Broadway, New York, NY 10012.

Performing right. One of the rights granted to a copyright owner under the copyright law. It stipulates that the person who owns the copyright to a work has the sole right to publicly perform, or to authorize public performance of, that work. According to the law, performing includes reciting, rendering, playing, dancing and acting. This can be accomplished, "either directly or by means of any device or process or, in the case of a motion picture or other audiovisual work, . . . (by showing) its images in any sequence or . . . (making) the sounds accompanying it audible."

To *perform publicly* a work is "to perform or display it at a place open to the public or at any place where a substantial number of persons outside of a normal circle of a family and its social acquaintances is gathered" or "to transmit or otherwise communicate a performance or display of the work . . . (publicly, as defined above) whether the members of the public capable of receiving the performance or display receive it in the same place or separate places and at the same time or at different times." The latter part of this definition refers to programs aired on closed-circuit TV, programs recorded for delayed broadcasting, and similar electronically produced programs.

Exceptions to the performing right include performance of a copyrighted work by students and teachers in not-for-profit schools and in governmental agencies, by people conducting/participating in religious services, and by those who perform works for the handicapped. All others must get permission from the copyright owner. (*See: Copyright.*)

Performing rights organizations. These organizations collect royalties on behalf of songwriters and publishers for work that is performed in clubs, on TV (including cable TV), on radio and on jukebox records. The three major American performing rights organizations are American Society of Composers, Authors and Publishers (ASCAP); Broadcast Music, Inc. (BMI); and SESAC, Inc. (SESAC formerly stood for Society of European Stage, Authors and Composers, but the title is no longer applicable.)

Performing rights organizations license broadcasters and other establishments where music is performed (such as nightclubs) by charging each licensee a fee. In the case of broadcasting stations, the fee is normally determined by a percentage of the adjusted gross income of the station. In the case of nonbroadcast licensees, the fee may be fixed in the terms of the capacity of the establishment, its entertainment budget and other factors. Methods of establishing how often music is performed—which differ from organization to organization—include surveying network or station music logs, and as SESAC does, examining charts in trade magazines.

To collect performance royalties, the songwriter must be affiliated with the same organization his publisher belongs to. Since music publishers commonly divide their various corporate affiliates among the different organizations, it is possible for an already-affiliated writer to work with the publisher he desires without changing organizations.

Both ASCAP and BMI divide performance royalties between publisher and writer, after having extracted a small percentage for overhead. On the other hand, SESAC divides 50 percent of its income between publisher and writer and retains the other half for its own purposes.

Addresses of the three major American performing rights groups are as follows: American Society of Composers, Authors and Publishers, 1 Lincoln Plaza, New York, NY 10023; Broadcast Music, Inc., 320 W. Fifty-seventh St., New York, NY 10019; and SESAC, Inc., 421 W. Fifty-fourth St., New York, NY 10019. (*See: Subsidiary rights.*)

Periodic sentence. A sentence that cannot be fully understood until it has been read completely. Also called a *suspended sentence*, the periodic sentence draws the reader along by withholding an essential element or idea until the end. For example: "Once the story action is outlined and the character description completed, I can begin to write the novel."

A writer uses periodic sentences to break up the monotony of the standard subject/verb/complement sentence pattern and to add variety to his writing. Since the reader must keep in mind the subordinate elements as he progresses toward the main idea, periodic sentences often require greater concentration to be understood and should be used sparingly.

Periodical. A publication issued at regularly recurring intervals of more than one day, but less than a year, is classified as a *periodical.* The term is applied primarily to magazines and journals; it does not ordinarily refer to newspapers. (*See: Periodicals, directories of; Periodicals, indexes to.*)

Periodicals, directories of. *Ulrich's International Periodicals Directory* and the *Standard Periodical Directory* are two references that categorize periodicals by subject matter. Two monthly directories, *Consumer Magazine and Agri-Media Source* and *Business Publication Rates and Data*, are also arranged by subject matter. They contain information such as advertising rates and production and circulation details, as well as a profile of usual editorial content of import primarily to people interested in advertising in magazines and journals.

Those periodicals that consistently buy freelance material from writers are detailed in *Writer's Market, Novel & Short Story Writer's Market, Children's Writer's & Illustrator's Market, Writer's Handbook* and a variety of volumes specializing in a particular genre or geographic area. These books typically give information on the publication's editorial focus, the types of material published, rates of pay, the length of time in which the editor will report on manuscripts, rights purchased and other details. Both consumer magazines and trade journals are categorized by subject.

Periodicals, indexes to. These directories and microfilms help writers do research by cataloging information published in magazine, newspaper or journal articles by title, subject, and author. Most are available at large public libraries or college libraries and many are available on CD-ROM for faster searches. Some general indexes to magazines are *Readers' Guide to Periodical Literature*; *The Magazine Index*; *Access: The Supplementary Index to Periodicals*; *Popular Periodical Index*; and *Abstracts of Popular Culture*. Two indexes to newspapers are *Facts on File* and *The New York Times Index*. *Ulrich's International Periodicals Directory* tells the reader if a magazine publishes its own index and which periodical indexes also carry it.

Indexes to publications for specialized fields include *Education Index*; *Business Periodical Index*; *Art Index*; *Periodical Indexes in the Social Sciences and Humanities*; *Abstracts and Indexes in Science and Technology: A Descriptive Guide*; and *Index Medicus*. (*See: Periodicals, directories of;* Readers' Guide to Periodical Literature.)

Permissions. Permissions involve granting either an author or a publisher the right to excerpt copyrighted material—a passage, page, chapter, short story or poem—for use within another work. For example, if a writer plans to copy an illustration or quote more than a few lines from a copyrighted work, he must get written permission to do so. Obtaining permission to quote or copy material is the responsibility of the author, not his publisher; many publishers do, however, have their own printed forms for authors to use. Since some copyright holders specify the exact form an author must use in giving credit, all permissions should be obtained before the manuscript is typeset.

Obtaining permission to excerpt material does not ordinarily involve a fee if the intended use is incidental—for example, if a novelist wishes to introduce a chapter with a passage from another writer's work, or the author of a nonfiction book quotes a paragraph from a reference volume written by an authority in the field. Although many requests of this type are considered "fair use," written permission is nevertheless solicited in many cases, just to be on the safe side.

In selecting material for an anthology or collection of critical essays, however, an author may be required to pay permission fees to various copyright holders; the same may be true of a translation, a book containing artwork or a reprint of a book no longer in print, if the material for these does not fall into the public domain.

"Many anthologies have extremely high permission costs," notes Richard Balkin, author of *A Writer's Guide to Book Publishing*. "An anthology of contemporary poetry or drama could cost upward to $15,000 in permissions alone. Every editor will consider these costs before making a decision, and they will definitely influence the final verdict on whether or not to sign up the book."

A publisher, says Balkin, usually allocates a permissions budget, pays the fees and then deducts the costs from the anthology editor's future royalties. "It is very important for the anthologist to make sure that the house is going to lay out the permissions costs and that this is stated clearly in the contract," Balkin advises.

Balkin reports that permission fees for magazine and journal articles generally run about $10 per page. Fees for other material vary considerably, depending on the particular publisher or copyright holder, as well as the current reputation or prestige of the author of the selection. (*See: Anthology; Fair use; Public domain; Quotes.*)

Personal experience. A writer's personal experience can provide the information for any number of articles, including personality profiles, opinion pieces and how-to articles. A wide variety of magazines also solicit the pure personal experience article—the true adventure or experience written as an article in the first person.

The effectiveness and marketability of the personal experience or "intimate" article depends primarily on the universality of its subject. What the author is writing about must be relevant or interesting to people besides himself; the story must be one with which his audience can identify. For this reason, successful personal experience articles often appeal directly to the reader's feelings and emotion.

An engaging style is also vital to the personal experience piece. The author must express honest feeling without sentimentality, and avoid sermonizing or taking too didactic a tone.

Like any type of article, the personal experience piece must be well organized. Insignificant details and tangential information must be ed-

ited out, and illustrative anecdotes should be woven into a tightly knit structure. The personal experience piece must have a clearly defined focus: The story must be shaped so as to make a definite point and result in a satisfying conclusion. And although the article may be based on the writer's own experience or opinion, supporting quotes from recognized authorities or significant statistics and other factual information can add strength and credibility to the piece.

A personal experience piece may take many forms: confession, nostalgia, opinion, controversy, humor, self-help, inspiration or commentary on current trends and lifestyles. It appears in general-interest magazines such as *Reader's Digest* and *The New York Times Magazine,* as well as in hundreds of other consumer and trade publications.

The primary element of a good personal experience piece is that it has something worthwhile to say. According to one writer, "unless your experience, your advice, your opinion is to some extent original, you'll have little to offer editors or readers." (*See: First-person short story.*)

Additional information: *Writing Articles From the Heart: How to Write & Sell Your Life Experiences.*

Personification. Personification is a figure of speech in which inanimate objects, abstractions, animals and ideas are attributed human form, characteristics or sensibilities. "The wind shrieked through the windows," and "The sauce bubbled over onto the burner, hissing for attention," are examples of personification.

Personification is frequently used as a literary device in poetry. The prose writer—both of fiction and nonfiction—also uses personification to strengthen the imagery of his article or story. (*See: Figures of speech; Imagery.*)

Persuasive writing. Sometimes called *argument*, this kind of writing tries to incite the reader to an action, such as buying, contributing or adopting a particular viewpoint. In a larger sense, almost all writing has to be persuasive, but advertising, publicity and propaganda exemplify persuasive writing in its more intense form.

The persuasive writer can achieve his purpose either through emotional appeal or logical appeal. For example, the magazine advertisement with the headline "The Advantages of Renting Office Furniture" appeals to the reader's logic, while the cruise ship ad headlined "All the Amenities of Home. (If You Happen to Live in Paradise.)" appeals to his emotions.

Fundraising appeals and solicitations of all types rely on persuasive writing to meet their goals. Writers may find some helpful books on the subject under the categories of "Persuasion (Psychology)" and "Persuasion (Rhetoric)" in the *Subject Guide to Books in Print.*

Photo CD. A recent development in photo technology and desktop publishing that allows for a four-color slide image or transparency to be digitally scanned onto a specially formatted compact disc. The image can then be placed into a desktop publishing program with overlay registrations marked.

This method saves the time and money that would be needed for traditional image preparation—as very little outside work is used.

Photo processing labs. If the writer who takes his own photographs is unable—because of lack of knowledge, equipment or time—to develop and print his own film, he must rely on a commercial photo processing lab.

Professional Photo Source, published annually by *Photo District News,* lists commercial photo processing labs and services. Professional photo developing labs also advertise regularly in photography magazines such as *Petersen's Photographic Magazine* and *Photo District News.* The writer/photographer will find photo processing labs located in his own community in the yellow pages under "Photo Finishing—Retail."

Photo release. (*See: Model release.*)

Photocopied manuscripts. In sympathy over increasing costs of typing services, paper and postage, and in response to improvements in photocopying quality, many editors who once insisted on seeing the original, good-bond copy of a manuscript now accept photocopied submissions from writers.

Photocopying a manuscript is primarily a convenience for an author, as well as a precautionary measure; if a manuscript is lost or damaged in the mail or misplaced at an editor's office, the writer has the original copy on file and need not take the time and expense of retyping the manuscript.

A photocopied manuscript

should be of excellent quality, as clean, neat and legible as the original. (*See: Simultaneous submission.*)

Photographer's model release. (*See: Model release.*)

Photographer-writer relationship. In some situations a writer chooses a photographer to take pictures to accompany the text of a book or article he is writing. Photographers who work with freelance writers play an important part in determining the salability of a manuscript.

Writers try to choose photographer-partners especially suited to their particular kinds of writing and the specific markets that buy their work. Local chapters of professional photographer associations, camera clubs and classified ads in local newspapers are sources for finding available photographers, as are college art departments (if they teach photography). The selection process involves the writer's examining the photographer's portfolio. He evaluates the subject matter, the quality and style of the work and how it relates to the type of writing he does.

The writer supplies his photographer-partner with a draft of the manuscript, or at least an outline of the main points, and works with him to determine ways to enhance the writing with visuals. Actual photographs are chosen from the contact sheets the photographer makes. Prints picked for publication are accompanied by photographer's model releases in those cases where the photographs may be used for other than editorial purposes. The writer should also get a brief statement signed by the photographer granting the use of a photograph(s) in conjunction with a specified manuscript to appear in a particular publication.

The photographer may be paid in one of two ways: (1) the writer and photographer can agree in advance on a flat fee for the shooting and prints, or a percentage of the total article price for the photographs; or (2) the writer can suggest (in advance) to the editor a qualified local professional photographer, with the editor making the photo selections from the contact sheet and paying the photographer directly. (*See: Photographs accompanying manuscripts; Photojournalism.*)

Photographic Society of America (PSA). This is the only photographic organization that "promotes the arts and sciences of photography through teaching, exhibitions and program services for all photographers, novice to advanced, amateur and professional, individuals and groups, in all branches of photography." PSA serves its members by sharing the accumulated knowledge of "generations of outstanding photographers" and information about the newest styles and techniques of photographers worldwide. Membership dues range from $25 to $40 depending on the age of the individual. The PSA can be contacted at 3000 United Founders Blvd., Suite 103, Oklahoma City, OK 73112-3940.

Photograph/picture sources. Writers may find leads for illustration materials in various directories, including *Stock Photo Desk Book*, published by the Photographic Arts Center, and the membership directory of the

Picture Agency Council of America. Also, *Photographer's Market* contains a section on stock photo agencies—companies that sell photos on a variety of subjects. Other sources include the various online networks and compact disc collections of photographs and clip art. (*See: Free photos; Photographer-writer relationship; Photographs accompanying manuscripts.*)

Photographs accompanying manuscripts. Many professional writers maintain that, for certain markets, a freelance article manuscript has a much better chance of selling when accompanied by a selection of high-quality photographs and presented to an editor as a complete package. In fact, some editors *require* pictures to accompany article submissions.

Ideally, a writer should be able to take his own pictures, and if he intends to illustrate his own article he must study the photo requirements of the market as thoroughly as he studies the editorial requirements—noting whether the magazine uses color, black and white or a combination of the two; determining the ratio of posed to unposed shots and horizontal to vertical pictures; and identifying the types of people, amount of action and related elements characteristic of the magazine's photographs. Some magazine editors supply editorial guidelines for photographers as well as for contributing writers.

If the writer is unwilling or unable to take his own photographs, he may either team up with a photographer or search for free or inexpensive photos. Government agencies, chambers of commerce, trade associations, travel bureaus and large businesses often maintain public information departments that supply writers and editors with photographs as well as facts in exchange for acknowledgment in the published photo credit. Private picture agencies may have thousands of good photos in stock, but one-time use may cost the writer up to several hundred dollars and involve additional research and security deposit fees. (Generally it is editors rather than writers who deal with private photo agencies.) The photo credits of published pictures will give the writer additional ideas for picture sources for the editor to contact.

Photographs should be fully captioned and protected by sheets of cardboard or fiberboard, with rubber bands binding the package together. It is important not to attach paper clips, which can damage prints.

Editors generally buy the manuscript and accompanying photos for a flat package rate, but some magazines pay extra for pictures. *Photographer's Market* and *Writer's Market* detail the specific photo policies of individual publications. (*See: Caption [cutline]; Illustration; Photographer-writer relationship; Photograph/picture sources.*)

Photographs, marketing. Freelance magazine writers have discovered that photographic skills can increase the size of their article checks. That often leads writer/photographers to seek primary markets for their photographs as well. Book publishers, calendar companies, advertising agencies, trade journals and newspapers represent the diversity of potential markets. Success rests in knowing the unique needs of the journal or company and being able to meet those needs with quality photographs. The annual *Photographer's Market* details where and how to sell photographs nationwide. It summarizes the business of photojournalism, including specific information on payment, copyrights, model releases and work-for-hire agreements.

Photography, legal and ethical aspects. (*See: Model release; Privacy, invasion of.*)

Photojournalism. The art of relating news or communicating the significant details of an event through photographs. The substance of photojournalism is the carefully composed or uniquely captured picture.

The newspaper photojournalist usually works with a reporter in covering an event. His job is to record on film some of the significant action of an event, so that the newspaper reader can tell a great deal about the story from one (or a few) pictures.

In the *photo essay* or *photo story*, the photographer is allotted more space in which to communicate; the photojournalist presents an event, a personality, a situation or a geographic area predominantly through photographs. A photo essay may contain captions and/or a copy block, but the photos are the element that attracts the reader and holds his attention. The photographer sometimes writes the copy, sometimes collaborates with a writer. In the layout process, the photographer works with a design editor to convey the right tone, using only photos that reflect his chosen theme.

Life magazine and the now-defunct *Look* magazine contain excellent examples of photo essays.

The term *photo essay* is used interchangeably with *photo story* and *picture story*, although the last term can be used to describe an event recorded in photographs but lacking the photo essay's unity of mood. (*See: Model release; Photograph/picture sources; Photographs accompanying manuscripts.*)

Picaresque. This term, derived from the Spanish word *pícaro* (rogue, knave), applies to novels or tales that relate, in a series of humorous or satiric episodes, the adventures of a rogue.

A typical picaresque novel tells the life story of a rascally but engaging hero or heroine who triumphs in one situation after another by his or her own wit and cunning; the hero's scampish but good-hearted ways are contrasted against a realistic background of middle-class life.

The picaresque novel form originated in Spain in the sixteenth century with the anonymous work *La vida de Lazarillo de Tormes* (*The Life of Larry Tormes*). Well-known picaresque novels include DeFoe's *Moll Flanders*, Twain's *Adventures of Huckleberry Finn*, Cervantes's *Don Quixote*, and Fielding's *Tom Jones*. A more recent work of fiction that may be considered picaresque is Erica Jong's *Fanny: Being the True History of the Adventures of Fanny Hackabout-Jones*.

Picture book. Written for children to read or have read to them, a picture book usually contains 150-1,500 words and 32-48 pages. (They can also have no words at all, or very few in a shorter book, even though a writer created the concept to be illustrated.)

The text of a picture book is well organized and carefully constructed, since its audience has little experience with literature. Because picture books are often read aloud and children have an instinctual fondness for rhythm, poetic techniques (e.g., alliteration, consonance, assonance and onomatopoeia) can enhance a picture book's story. Other techniques attractive to children are the repeated anecdote, used in *The Three Little Pigs*, and the refrain, used in *The Gingerbread Man*.

Vocabulary in this category of writing is simple, since the books are intended for children even if read by adults. Sentence construction is likewise uncomplicated; it often uses the active voice and mimics speech patterns. In general, the narrative of a picture book sounds appealing when read aloud.

As publishers usually choose the artist to illustrate a picture book, the author who has an artist in mind should secure approval from the publisher before asking the artist to proceed. To approach the publisher with the idea of collaboration, the author should submit one or two samples of art with the manuscript. (*See: Juveniles, writing for; Picture book submission techniques.*)

Additional information: *How to Write and Sell Children's Picture Books* and *Children's Writer's & Illustrator's Market*.

Picture book submission techniques.
The children's picture book author should first research likely markets for his work by checking *Children's*

Writer's & Illustrator's Market, and publishers' catalogs, if possible, before submitting a manuscript. In the picture book field, it's usually not necessary to query unless, in the course of research, the writer discovers that a particular publisher prefers this approach; instead, the writer should pay special attention to his proposal package. A picture book manuscript, although brief, is somewhat complex; it usually may be typed any of several ways according to what the manuscript seems most suited to and what the author is comfortable with.

The manuscript may be typed as any other manuscript would be, with illustration suggestions made separately at the end, or included in the cover letter. It also may be typed page for page as the writer envisions the book, with the illustration suggestions placed on a page following each manuscript page, or on the manuscript page itself. Or, if the writer feels confident doing so, he can make up a dummy of the book to accompany the plain typed manuscript, either sketching in the art ideas himself or just typing the descriptions separately from the text.

The cover letter accompanying the manuscript should be carefully written. It should be brief and professional, yet still friendly in its tone. Jean E. Karl, in *How to Write and Sell Children's Picture Books*, says the cover letter should "interest the reader who receives it, and not put that person off by overcleverness or cuteness. . . ." Karl recommends mentioning the title of the work being sent, a sentence or two about the material, and a brief summary of previous writing experience. If the author has no previous experience, the point should not be brought up. Simply thank the editor for his consideration. Olga Litowinsky, in *Writing and Publishing Books for Children in the 1990s,* suggests finding out something about the editor or the publisher's list and complimenting him. "Perhaps your friendly tone will result in a friendly answer."

One mistake many novice picture book authors make is assuming that art must accompany a manuscript. Art is not at all necessary; picture book editors are skilled at visualization, and may well have an artist in mind whose style fits the manuscript. In fact, art might be a hindrance to selling the book: Some publishers do not even want suggestions about art from the author, reasoning that art is the province of the artist.

What matters most in submitting a picture book manuscript is the originality of the idea and its appropriateness for the publisher: a publisher geared toward preschoolers will probably not accept a book for older children, no matter how wonderful it may be. Similarly, the exact length of a manuscript and the complexity of its vocabulary are secondary to the ideas; editor and writer can adjust those after discussion.

The only real taboo in picture book publishing is submitting finished artwork with the proposal: this is the unmistakable mark of an amateur—worse, an amateur who has not researched the field. The size, color and method of printing the art can only be determined after a book is budgeted and designed.

Piracy. The term describes the unauthorized use of copyrighted materi-als, such as books, recordings and films; copyrighted material reproduced or manufactured without permission of the copyright owner is pirated material. *Piracy* is currently applied primarily to the unauthorized reproduction of records, tapes and video cassettes, while the unauthorized use of literary material is called a pirated edition.

Because it is a violation of the exclusive right of copyright, the act of piracy is illegal in the U.S. and in the many other countries that subscribe to one of the international copyright conventions. (It may, however, be considered within the limits of the law in countries that are not members of such a convention.)

Despite its illegality, record, tape and film piracy is a practice widespread throughout the world. As a consequence, record, tape and film manufacturers have called for stiffer penalties and more serious legal sanctions for those found guilty of trafficking in pirated recordings and movies. The U.S. Congress passed a law in 1982 making piracy and counterfeiting a felony carrying penalties as high as $25,000 and five years in jail. (*See: Copyright; International copyright convention; Pirated edition; Plagiarism.*)

Pirated edition. This term refers to an unauthorized edition of a literary work, usually republished in another country without permission of the copyright owner.

Since the establishment of international copyright conventions during the late nineteenth and early twentieth centuries, pirated editions have become less common. However, pirated editions may still be found in those countries that do not subscribe to one of the international copyright conventions. (*See: International copyright convention; Piracy.*)

Pitch meeting. A meeting between a writer and a film or television producer during which the writer verbally outlines his idea for a script he proposes to write. A pitch meeting, writes Syd Field in *Selling a Screenplay*, is a performance. "And you have to be prepared. You have to present your material with passion, clarity and confidence."

When pitching a film, Field recommends knowing the story's structure well enough to explain its beginning, middle and end; having a couple ideas of who should play the lead; having examples of recent films that have the visual style of the film you're proposing; and having a lot of information about the characters.

When pitching ideas for existing TV series, concentrate on your story idea—the characters and settings are already well established. Producers will expect to hear three to eight story lines in a single meeting.

Plagiarism. Using or closely imitating another person's material without permission, acknowledgment or compensation, representing it as one's own work. Plagiarism is illegal when it involves infringement of copyright. Under copyright law, an individual found guilty of infringement of copyright is liable for either (1) actual damages suffered by the copyright owner as a result of the infringement, and any profits of the infringer that are attributable to the infringement; or (2) instead of ac-

tual damages and profits, statutory damages of a sum of not less than $250 nor more than $10,000, as the court considers just. Additional remedies for infringement are detailed in the copyright law.

Plagiarism may also occur legally—that is, without copyright infringement—when material in the public domain, noncopyrighted works, or works in which the copyright has expired are reprinted under claimed authorship of the plagiarist. While this type of plagiarism is not illegal, it is nevertheless unethical. A writer discovered to be a plagiarist of uncopyrighted works, while not liable under the law, will nonetheless establish an exceedingly bad reputation for himself as an author.

To avoid plagiarism, a writer should give full credit to his sources of information and obtain written permission from copyright owners to use their copyrighted material in his own work. (See: *Copyright; Fair use; Journalistic ethics; Paraphrase; Piracy; Public domain; Quotes.*)

Plant. Information woven into a work of fiction for the purpose of making incidents that occur later in the story consistent and believable. Any object, fact, person or condition a writer plans to use in the course of a short story or novel must be *planted* to make subsequent events related to the plant convincing.

In the second paragraph of *The Open Window*, for example, author Saki (H.H. Munro) plants the information that the main character, Framton Nuttel, has retired to the country to recuperate from a nervous disorder and knows no one in the village; as a result, the young woman in the story is able to frighten him out of his wits with a completely fabricated tale of ghosts tramping through the open window in the room.

The movie *Jaws* contains another example of effective planting. At the beginning of the film, the audience learns that the oceanfront town in which the action takes place depends almost entirely on the summer resort trade for its livelihood. That information becomes significant when, as the film progresses, the town's officials at first refuse to acknowledge the danger of a shark in the waters, and later refuse to close the beaches for fear the tourist trade will suffer.

In mystery stories, clues are said to be "planted." A plant in this sense can be the *absence* of information, as in Dorothy L. Sayers's *Five Red Herrings*, in which the contents of an artist's case are listed and it later develops that one color—white—is missing. The absence of white is the plant.

Plants are vital to story credibility; they rid a story of coincidence. Plants must, however, be introduced subtly rather than overtly. In *How to Write Best-Selling Fiction*, Dean R. Koontz discusses the dangers of heavy-handed planting. Although he is speaking primarily of novel writing here, his remarks apply to short stories as well:

Events in a story should never be foreshadowed by having the author speak directly to the reader. For example, *never* write a sentence like this one: "If only Becky could have known that Ralph would betray her on Wednesday, she would not have

told him her priceless secret at dinner on Tuesday evening." And here's a sentence that's even worse than that: "As she danced and laughed and drank champagne on New Year's Eve, little did Polly know that her life would be in ruins by the end of January." During the early stages of the novel's growth as an art form, authors thought it permissible to directly address their readers in the middle of a story, either to emphasize a thematic point or to crudely foreshadow upcoming plot developments. The modern reader is sophisticated and simply will not tolerate intrusions of that sort because they shatter the fragile illusion of reality that makes a story enjoyable.

The writer should also take care to plant only information that is necessary to the story action: Plants left dangling are annoying both to editors and readers, a principle perhaps best illustrated by Anton Chekhov's counsel to beginning playwrights: "If a gun is hanging on the wall in the first act, it must fire in the last." All plants introduced in a story should be brought to a conclusion that satisfies and convinces the reader. (*See: False plant; Plot.*)

Play format notes. (*See: Figure 33.*)

Play publishing and production. There are two ways to earn money with a play. The first way is to sell it to a play publisher, who has the organization for printing and selling playscripts, and for selling performing rights to drama groups. The publisher thoroughly knows his market—the many thousand small drama groups in

FIGURE 33

PLAY FORMAT NOTES
BY MARTHA MONIGLE

STYLE: Follow the New York style with character names (capitalized) at center of page. English style places those names to left margin.

PAPER: Use heavy bond, twenty pound preferred. No erasable or onionskin. White 8½″ × 11″ sheets; punch two holes to left and place script in simple binder with fasteners. One-acters may be submitted without holes to publishers.

TYPING: Pica preferred. Not elite or script form.

PAGE NUMBERING:

—FIRST PAGE (unnumbered) is "cover sheet" with title centered in caps; next spaces show if one or three acts; author's name and address.

—SECOND PAGE (unnumbered) has heading CHARACTERS (or CAST OF CHARACTERS) in caps. On separate lines below place character names, not caps. Age and identification may be placed beside each name.

—THIRD SHEET is numbered: I-1. Mark either at top or to right edge. Indicate each act by Roman numerals, pages by Arabic. Each of the three acts starts with page 1 to its end, as: I-1; II-1; III-1. In scene division, mark: II-2-15 for second scene in act II, page 15. Note that a new scene of an act requires a new page and heading.

—One typed sheet equals about a minute's playing time. One-acts average 15-20 pp. Full plays (two or three acts) run little more than two hours, or about 115-125 pp. Children's theater ranges from five-minute skits to full-length high school plays up to 69 minutes.

FORMAT: Single-space for speeches and stage directions but double-space between those units. Wide margins, 1″-1½″ on all sides.

—Dialog starts at left margin.

—Stage directions, always in parentheses, indented ten spaces. If brief and contained in character's speech, directions may be so enclosed in the dialog. Sometimes a directional word or phrase may be inserted between character name and speech. (See example below.)

—Capitalize character NAME at all times except when mentioned in dialog.

—Capitalize ENTRANCES and EXITS, which must be noted in script.

Note: Directions are written from actor's position; JOAN ENTERS L means "stage right" from audience view. State time and place.

OPENING PAGE EXAMPLE:

SUNDAY'S MYSTERY   *I-1*
ACT ONE

TIME: The present. Noon. Sunday.
PLACE: The Blairs' living room in Los Angeles.
AT RISE GEORGE is seated on couch with Sunday papers strewn about him. He wears pajamas and slippers. JOAN ENTERS L, annoyed at disorder. She is fully dressed. She picks up papers from the floor.

GEORGE

Why?

(JOAN continues to work)

JOAN

It's Sunday.

GEORGE

(groaning)

Oh, Joan! I bet Scott isn't nagged by his wife.

(EXIT JOAN in injured silence to kitchen)

PROPERTIES LISTING: Type list of properties or "props" on last page. Objects carried or used by actors in play, as newspapers above.

schools, churches, clubs, community centers, etc., all across the country—and he wants plays that will have wide, long-lasting appeal. He does not want material of narrow, local interest; he does not want topical subjects and references that will quickly make a play out-of-date.

The typical amateur drama group wants a play to have a catchy, comprehensible title, to be a comedy rather than a tragedy (though tragedy is not completely taboo), and to have more female than male roles. It does *not* want excessively large casts; over-elaborate, costly costumes; complicated, expensive sets; or controversial themes or language.

Publishers usually don't read untested scripts. Writers should get the play produced and send proof of production—photos, programs, reviews, etc.—with the script. Terms of payment vary somewhat from publisher to publisher. There is usually no advance on purchase; typical offers are 25-50 percent of the performance royalties collected by the publisher, and 5-10 percent of playbook sales receipts.

Payments may be higher for playwrights whose previous work has already succeeded in publication, but the beginner is not in a strong position to bargain. A published play that proves itself popular with audiences and drama groups may yield a flow of royalties for many years.

The other way for a dramatist to make money is by direct sale of performing rights to a theater company or play producer. Chances for such sales are better if the author can write about assigned subjects and make his script precisely fit the casting and financial resources of the customer.

For such commissioned work, terms are negotiable—usually some advance payment and, if the play succeeds, royalties on performances.

After the customer company has finished with the play, it can perhaps be sold—with some adaptation if necessary—to a publisher for general distribution. Play publishers and professional theaters that accept freelance material are listed in the "Scriptwriting" section of *Writer's Market*, which also lists playwriting contests and awards in the "Contests and Awards" section.

Information about other publishing opportunities and playwriting contests and awards can also be found in *The Dramatists Sourcebook*, published by the Theatre Communications Group, 355 Lexington Ave., New York, NY 10017. This reference guide also lists membership and service organizations, artists' colonies, fellowships and grants, and submission guidelines for more than one hundred professional theater companies nationwide, plus much additional information of interest to playwrights. (*See: Dinner theater; Dramatists Guild; One-act play; Play royalties; Theater.*)

Play royalties. If a "first-class" theater contracts to produce a playwright's script and that playwright is an active member of the Dramatists Guild, the playwright is eligible to use the Guild's Approved Production Contract for Dramatic Works as negotiated by the Guild with the League of American Theaters. It calls for a royalty to the playwright of 5 percent of the gross weekly box office receipts, going to 10 percent after recoupment of production expenses.

First class is a technical business designation that generally applies to a production presented in a large city, in a large theater, for an indefinite run. Stock, amateur, Equity-waiver, regional or LORT (League of Resident Theatres), or Off-Broadway theaters interested in producing a playwright's script usually negotiate royalty fees on an individual basis. These agreements may offer the playwright anywhere from a flat fee per performance to 5-20 percent of the gross box office receipts from the show's run. (*See: Dramatists Guild; Playwriting.*)

Plays for young actors. Dramas written to be performed by children to entertain other children and/or adults. This kind of drama differs from children's theater in that the latter is intended to be performed by adults, for children.

The key to writing successful plays for young actors is simplicity. Because the director and actors of these dramas are not usually experienced in the complexities of the theater, elements such as play concepts, staging, setting and costuming are flexible. Plays for children use the techniques of fiction writing and begin with an immediate drama. They are printed in playscript form with simple, appropriate stage directions, setting descriptions, etc.

Plays for young actors have children's interests and capabilities in mind. Elementary-age children, for example, usually perform for an audience of their peers. Children sometimes are given the opportunity to invent the play's dialogue and action for play outlines that are published in some trade publications for educators.

Dramas for very young children (ages four to six) usually take fewer than fifteen minutes to perform. Elementary and junior high school plays often run fifteen to twenty-five minutes. Their subject matter may be curriculum-related (historical events or literature being studied) or connected with the celebration of a holiday or special occasion. Scripts generally call for five to seven main characters, with parts divided equally between the two sexes, and a flexible number of minor characters, so as to involve as many young actors as possible.

Plays written for high school students are usually one- or three-act dramas performed for mixed audiences that run twenty-five to fifty minutes. Light comedies currently make up 90 percent of the plays published for high-school-age people; light romances, family living and maturing experiences are other subjects successfully handled by these actors. Girls at this age are often less self-conscious about acting than their male peers, so plays frequently contain more female than male parts. One-act plays may call for casts of six or nine; three-act plays, casts of ten to fifteen.

Formats for amateur plays vary; specification sheets are sometimes available from the editorial offices of play publishers. Other markets for children's plays include the professional education magazines and juvenile magazines that sometimes publish plays or play outlines in their issues. The drama outlines suggest a bare framework for a play; children themselves fill in the specifics and then act out the play they had a hand in writing.

Amateur plays for young actors may sometimes be bought outright, rather than on a royalty basis. (Payment ranges on the average from $50 to $500.) Specific markets are detailed in *Writer's Market*; buyers of musicals are listed in *Songwriter's Market*. (*See: Children's theater.*)

Playwriting. A play has the same basic requirements as a work of fiction: It must contain interesting characters presented in convincing conflict that is logically resolved by the end of the piece. A play must offer emotionally important dramatic action, expressed in effective dialogue. The dramatist's goal is to establish a link between the spectator and the stage, to involve the audience in the play's action and thus evoke an empathetic response from the playgoer.

Although there are many innovative ways to structure drama—one-actor shows, "choreopoems," plays consisting of one long act or of a series of interwoven vignettes—the majority of plays tend to fall into one of two formats: the one-act play, which is relatively uncomplicated to be satisfactorily resolved in twenty-thirty minutes; or the full-length play, which contains two or more acts (which may be further broken down into scenes) and can run up to 2½ hours.

The playwright's primary tool is dialogue: It is all-important, since theater is a spoken medium. The dramatist cannot rely on visuals to help make a point, as the screenwriter can (although clever staging can emphasize or counterpoint particular lines). Good stage dialogue is extremely difficult to write. It cannot exactly reproduce the rambling, disjointed sentences and phrases in which real-life people speak, yet it must sound realistic. Without seeming stilted, chatty or contrived, it must give the audience all the background information it needs to understand the characters' motivation. It must also be interesting; a playwright cannot afford to let his audience's attention lag.

Because drama is a live medium, the playwright should do all he can to make his work performable. The best way to learn about performing is to perform: In addition to attending plays and reading plays and theater criticism, the dramatist not already active in theater should join an amateur dramatics group and work in every possible aspect of it—acting, directing, constructing sets, collecting props, running lights, etc. Through a combination of play analysis and practical dramatic experience, the beginning playwright learns how to write dialogue that is easy to memorize and deliver; how to structure effective scenes; and how to develop character through dialogue. (He also learns what *not* to do.) He will learn, too, about the business end of the theater and make contacts within the local theater community. In this way he can either find a group to produce his plays or at least a number of actors willing to do readings that will help him revise and polish his work. (*See: Dinner theater; Dramatists Guild; One-act play; Play publishing and production; Play royalties; Theater.*)

Plot. The sequence in which an author arranges a series of carefully devised and interrelated incidents so as to form a logical pattern and achieve an intended effect. A *plot* can also be called the structure, backbone or framework of fiction. Essentially, it is a causal sequence of action that progresses through conflict to a climax and ends with a resolution.

The difference between a plot and a story has been explained by English novelist E.M. Forster: "We have defined a story as a narrative of events arranged in their time sequence. A plot is also a narrative of events, the emphasis falling on a causality. 'The King died and then the queen died' is a story. 'The King died, and then the queen died of grief' is a plot."

A sound, believable plot is essential to a salable story, although it may not be the strongest or most evident element. How much emphasis a writer puts on plot depends on his conception of the story and what he has to say. Writer and creative writing teacher R.V. Cassill has commented, "In some cases—and this is often true of first-rate contemporary work—the plot is so elaborately interwoven with the other threads of fiction that its presence is only detectable under a determined scrutiny. . . . When plot is properly integrated with the over-all scrutiny, it can be first among those elements that give the illusion of life to fiction." Plot is generally more important in genre fiction (romance, western, science fiction, etc.) than in serious literary fiction. (*See: Plant; Story.*)

Plug. An advertisement for a product, program or service; sometimes provided free by a radio station as a public service announcement (PSA).

Informally, a plug is a seemingly offhand mention of the product, program or service by a commentator or interview subject. An author is said to be "plugging his book" when he manages to work the title, publisher and toll-free order number into an interview.

Poetic license. Refers to the privilege claimed by a writer (poet, novelist, dramatist, essayist, etc.) to deviate from conventional form, established rules and perhaps even fact and logic to achieve a desired effect.

Writers, particularly poets, have claimed the "license" to invert word order, introduce archaisms, use—or overuse—figurative language, employ contractions such as *e'er* and *o'er* and otherwise depart from standards of ordinary speech. But such breaches of grammar, misuse of idiom, mispronunciation for the sake of rhyme, or similar devices are no longer accepted in serious verse.

Poetry. The oldest form of literature and the first to be put into written form. An extremely complex and subjective concept, poetry cannot be completely or precisely defined. It is generally agreed, however, that poetry as a literary form expresses, through extraordinary use of language and a highly developed artistic form, a unique and imaginative interpretation of a subject. Good poetry creates an emotional impact and aesthetic effect by appealing primarily to a reader's senses and emotions.

Poetry is often used as a synonym for *verse*. Although all poetry may be considered verse—speech or writing in metrical form—not all verse may be thought of as poetry. The distinction between the two lies in the profundity of thought and emotion. For example, "Mary had a little lamb, its fleece was white as snow," is both lyrical and metrical; it does not, however, represent the depth of thought, imagination and emotion that characterizes poetry.

Poetry is further distinguished as a literary form from *prose*—spoken or written expression that is not metrical. Poetry makes greater use of literary devices such as metaphor, simile, allusion, alliteration and onomatopoeia than does prose. The emphasis in poetry is on economy of language—as the poet compresses as much meaning as possible into the fewest possible words, the language is elevated to a unique artistic expression.

A more fundamental distinction between poetry and prose is that a writer may use prose to communicate information and ideas that, when expressed by a different arrangement of words, still convey the same basic message. In a poetic composition, however, the purpose of which is to create an emotional impact, words and ideas cannot be separated from form; the two are inextricably linked. Poet Judson Jerome explained in *The Poet's Handbook*: "Great poetry may contain great wisdom, but that is never the reason it is great poetry. It is not enough. It is the form, the shaping of the language, which makes poetry endure. It is not what it meant to the poet that is important; rather, it is the effect it has on an audience."

Although there are many kinds of poems—classified in part according to style, subject matter, form, intended effect or purpose, metrical pattern and viewpoint—there are three acknowledged major divisions in Western literature: narrative, dramatic and lyric. (*See: Poetry book publishing; Poetry, dramatic; Poetry, lyric; Poetry, marketing; Poetry, narrative; Verse.*)

Additional information: *Poet's Market; The Art and Craft of Poetry; The Poet's Handbook; The Writer's Manual.*

Poetry book publishing. Once a poet has had several poems published in quality magazines (those respected by the literary community), he usually considers publishing a collection of his poems. One of the most important factors in getting a first book accepted will be the list of credit lines from those magazines in which the poet's work was first published. Since the market for poetry is neither large nor profitable, even the poet with an impressive list of credits will have a difficult time finding a publisher, however. Publishers most receptive to a book of poetry are the small presses listed in *Writer's Market* and *The International Directory of Little Magazines and Small Presses.*

Another option is self-publishing, wherein the poet hires a printer to produce the book for him. The poet might get bids from several local typesetters and/or "instant" printers or contact some of the small poetry book printers that advertise in writers' magazines. Prices for such books could vary considerably depending on whether they were printed from camera-ready typewritten copy, or from typeset copy; the type of paper and binding; the page size; number of copies printed; etc.

A third route may be an arrangement with a cooperative publisher, in which the poet assumes part of the cost of publication. (Cooperative publishing is not to be confused with subsidy publishing.) (*See: Cooperative publishing; Poetry; Poetry, marketing; Subsidy publishing; Verse.*)

Additional information: *The Art and Craft of Poetry; Poet's Market; The Poet's Handbook.*

Poetry, dramatic. One of the three divisions of poetry in Western literature, dramatic poetry is the most immediate of the forms. A dramatic poem presents a story through dialogue and action rather than through exposition. Plays, dramatic monologues and dramatic lyrics written in verse—such as Shakespeare's plays in blank verse—are classified as dramatic poetry.

The dramatic monologue is perhaps the only popular form of dramatic poetry used by contemporary poets. T.S. Eliot's *The Love Song of J. Alfred Prufrock* is an example of dramatic monologue. (*See: Poetry; Poetry, lyric; Poetry, narrative; Verse.*)

Poetry, lyric. The most inclusive of the three major poetry divisions in Western literature. *Lyric* describes any relatively short poem that expresses the personal thoughts and feelings either of the poet himself or of the narrator-voice of the poem.

Most of the poetry published today is lyric. The term includes hymns, sonnets, songs, odes and elegies among its many forms. (*See: Poetry; Poetry, dramatic; Poetry, narrative; Verse.*)

Poetry, marketing. Generally speaking, poets do not make a living from their poetry. The few commercially successful poets—Rod McKuen and Ogden Nash, for example—are not usually taken seriously by the literary community. A poet must, however, find the audience and media appropriate to his talent and recognize that some verse is simply better suited than other verse for commercial markets: greeting card and poster publishers, church magazines and some women's publications, for example. And, as noted in *Writer's Market*, some commercially successful poets have syndicated newspaper columns or contracts with popular magazines; others combine their writing with singing or other performance.

The poet to whom literary esteem is more important than commercial success will probably get his start in the little/literary magazines. These publications are listed in *Poet's Market* and *The International Directory of Little Magazines and Small Presses.* Other good resources are university libraries and quality bookstores that devote a rack to poetry magazines. Hundreds of literary and little magazines are being published, some given exclusively to poetry and others that publish both poetry and prose. A poet must obtain sample copies (sample copies of literary and little magazines are rarely available free of charge) and study them carefully to determine which magazines are publishing the type of poetry he is writing.

In addition to studying the publications carefully, poets are advised by the editors of many poetry magazines to solicit opinions on their work from other poets before submitting poems for publication. The poet should not expect to receive criticism on his work from the editors of poetry magazines to which he submits material; nor should he send his poems to professional poets, requesting their opinions.

The most likely environment for a writer to find knowledgeable criticism and support is in a writers' group or workshop. The National Federation of State Poetry Societies (% Wanda Blaisdell, 2664 Shamrock, Ogden, UT 84403) may be able to advise a poet whether a chapter of his state poetry society meets in his area. A poet may also check his local library or nearby college or university for information about other writers' groups in the area.

Unless a specific magazine indicates otherwise, the general rules for submission of poetry are these: poems should be typed (usually double-spaced) on 8½″ × 11″ white paper, one poem to a page. The author's name and address should appear in the upper right corner of each page. The poet should keep a carbon or photocopy of each poem, and a careful record of where the material is submitted. Three to five pages of poetry should be included in the submission packet, along with a self-addressed, stamped envelope. Cover letters are not necessary, nor is an indication of line count. Proofread carefully, for the poem as submitted should be exactly as you would like to see it appear, down to the last comma and capital.

A poet seeking publication must act on his own behalf. Reputable literary agents do not handle poetry because there is so little money in it.

Poets should, therefore, be wary of so-called "agents" who, for a fee, agree to read their work and place it. Likewise, poets should learn to recognize the hundreds of "vanity" gimmicks and schemes designed to exploit beginning poets—the contests that require competitors to purchase the book in which the winning entries will be published in order to enter. For regular announcements of reputable contests and publishing opportunities in general, poets can look to *Writer's Digest* and *Poets & Writers*. (*See: Poetry; Poetry book publishing.*)

Additional information: *The Poet's Handbook.*

Poetry, narrative. One of the three major divisions of poetry in Western literature, *narrative* is probably the oldest type, with a long tradition in epic and ballad forms. The narrative poem tells a story, primarily through exposition or through a combination of narration and dialogue, as in the narratives of Robert Frost or Robert Browning. Book-length narrative poems called epics are tales of heroic events set against vast and exotic backgrounds. Well-known epics include the *Iliad*, the *Odyssey* and *Beowulf*. The form is not popular today. (*See: Poetry; Poetry, dramatic; Poetry, lyric; Verse.*)

Poetry Society of America. Founded in 1910, the Poetry Society of America's nearly two thousand members—poets and nonpoets alike—seek to raise the awareness of poetry, deepen the understanding of it and encourage more people to read, listen to and write poetry. To this end, the PSA presents a national series of readings including "Tributes in Libraries" and "Poetry in Public Places," mounts poetry on mass transit vehicles through "Poetry in Motion," and broadcasts an educational poetry series on public television.

The PSA also offers annual contests for poetry (many open to non-members), seminars and poetry festivals, and publishes the PSA newsletter. For more information about awards, programs and membership, send SASE to 15 Gramercy Park, New York, NY 10003.

Poets & Writers, Inc. This organization defines its purpose as, "to serve as an information clearinghouse and service organization for the nation's literary community." In addition to maintaining biographical archives on poets and fiction writers, Poets & Writers, Inc. provides a telephone information service to people seeking either answers to questions of a general literary nature or the current address of a poet or writer listed in its publication, *A Directory of American Poets and Fiction Writers.* The organization also publishes *Poets & Writers, Writer's Guide to Copyright, Author and Audience* and *Literary Agents,* as well as booklets on literary agents, copyright, literary bookstores and sponsors.

In addition to living poets and fiction writers whose work has been published in the U.S., *A Directory of American Poets and Fiction Writers* also lists writers who perform their work and who are available for lectures and readings. Writers who wish to be listed in the directory should contact the organization at 72 Spring St., New York, NY 10012, for publication requirements.

Poets laureate. In England, the court poet appointed for life by the prime minister to write poems celebrating official occasions. Ben Jonson was the first such, appointed in 1619.

A new U.S. poet laureate is named each year. Poets holding the title in the past include Rita Dove and Howard Nemerov. Poets laureate are also chosen by individual states; however, not every state names one. A state poet laureate may not necessarily be well known.

Poet's Market. An annual directory of about seventeen hundred listings describing commercial and literary outlets for poets. Its section dealing with poetry markets is "Publishers of Poetry." Listings in this section include names, addresses and telephone numbers of poetry publishers; name of a person to contact; types of poetry the publisher deals in; and information on how to submit material.

Other listings in the directory are included in the sections "Contests and Awards," "State and Provincial Grants," "Conferences and Workshops," "Writing Colonies," "Organizations Useful to Poets" and "Publications Useful to Poets."

The front material introduces the poet to the practical aspects of writing poetry, describing fundamentals such as workshops and networking, agents and book publication, self-publication, contests and anthologies, and the business of poetry writing.

Point of view (POV). In TV and motion pictures, a camera direction indicating that the audience sees the scene as if they were looking through the eyes of the actor in that scene. In a script, whether abbreviated or spelled out, this term is typed in all caps.

For fiction writers, the term speaks to the vantage point from which a story is presented. (*See: First-person point of view; Television script terms; Third-person point of view; Viewpoint.*)

Political campaign writing. A freelancer may find a part-time job or full-time career as a political campaign writer. Depending on the nature and extent of a candidate's campaign, a campaign writer's duties may include ghostwriting speeches, writing press releases, answering correspondence and perhaps even shaking hands and tacking up posters. In general, the larger the campaign, the greater the chances of two, three or several campaign writers being employed by a candidate. A writer will usually have more responsibility and more varied duties working for a candidate running for local office than for national office.

The primary function of a political campaign writer is to provide his candidate with a steady supply of facts, figures, ideas, words and phrases. Consequently, the job requires good research and writing skills. A newspaper background, particularly one with a focus on politics or public affairs, may be helpful.

A campaign writer's first task is to acquaint himself thoroughly with his candidate's background, personality, physical habits, speech characteristics and thinking processes to write speeches and prepare biographical and informational literature that effectively projects the candidate's image. The writer must also familiarize himself with the audience the candidate hopes to reach, and target his material to that audience.

There are several routes a freelancer might take to land an assignment as a political campaign writer. One is to contact his home state's Democratic or Republican Party headquarters. Another is to send a brief letter to the executive director of local party headquarters (listed in the white pages of the telephone book), outlining his qualifications and inquiring whether any candidates are in need of a freelance writer. A freelancer may personally seek out local elected officials and indicate his availability. He may also contact advertising agencies handling campaign publicity for political candidates, since these agencies often take on extra help during a campaign.

Financial terms are negotiated between the writer and candidate or the campaign manager. For the average freelancer, a fair rate in most locales will run a bit higher than the salary paid top-scale newspaper reporters. (According to Newspaper Guild figures, reporter salary ranges from $346 to $1,283 per week, depending on the city.) Freelancers negotiating for payment for their services are advised to avoid promises of future rewards in lieu of adequate salary; freelance campaign writing may, however, lead to an offer of a full-time position with the candidate. (*See: Ghostwriting speeches.*)

Pony. An informal word for materials used in place of the original work being studied in a literature course. Used especially to refer to literal translations of literary works in foreign languages, this term can also denote a synopsis, a set of notes and other supplements used in conjunction with a work of literature. Writers—especially those with teaching backgrounds—can obtain assignments from publishers of these study guides. (*See: Abridgment.*)

Popular fiction. Generally, a synonym for category or genre fiction; i.e., fiction intended to appeal to audiences for certain kinds of novels.

In *Writing Popular Fiction*, author Dean R. Koontz describes popular fiction as "those stories we can easily apply labels to—science fiction, fantasy, mystery, suspense, gothic, western, erotica." Popular, or category, fiction is defined as such primarily for the convenience of publishers, editors, reviewers and booksellers who must identify novels of different areas of interest for potential readers.

Popular fiction is distinguished from *mainstream fiction*, fiction that does not comfortably fit into the categories described above. Because mainstream fiction is generally written for a narrower, more intellectual audience, it has traditionally been regarded by educators and critics as being superior to popular fiction. As Koontz observes, however, many writers whose literary efforts have gained immortality—including Mark Twain and Edgar Allan Poe— have been category writers. In recent years, popular fiction writers such as Raymond Chandler, John D. MacDonald and Alistair MacLean have attained not only financial success but also considerable critical acclaim for their work. Koontz offers this advice for the writer who may not have considered the economic realities that govern the publishing industry: "Since genre fiction is more widely read than mainstream, the writer's market for category work is larger than for mainstream. Publishers, like any businessmen, operate within the law of supply and demand."

Koontz lists five elements required of genre novels, elements that don't always appear in mainstream fiction: (1) a strong plot; (2) a hero or heroine; (3) clear, believable motivation; (4) a great deal of action; and (5) a colorful background. (*See: Fiction; Mainstream fiction.*)

Additional information: *How to Write Best-Selling Fiction.*

Pornography. Literature, art, photographs or films characterized by substantial sexual content are sometimes classified as pornography. Though both pornography and erotica contain sexual content, pornography differs from erotica in its more graphic and explicit treatment of sex.

Men's magazines continue to be the strongest market for short pornographic fiction. Editorial needs vary widely, so study the publications carefully before submitting. Pay rates range from $100 to $2,000 (*Playboy, Penthouse* and *Hustler* are at the high end of the scale), with the average being $250-$300 for a story. (*See: Censorship, literary; Erotica; Obscenity.*)

Postage rates for writers, foreign. (*See: International Reply Coupons; Mail/delivery services;* Writer's Market *["Postage by the page"].*)

Postal Service. (*See: Mail/delivery services.*)

Potboiler. Something written expressly for the purpose of making money quickly. The term refers to writing projects a freelancer does to keep the pot boiling—in other words, to *eat*—while he works on major articles, stories or books.

Depending on the writer's facility and knowledge of the marketplace, a potboiler may run anywhere from a six-line how-to, to a 1,500-word short story, to a 65,000-word novel—any writing project, in other words, designed to bring in a quick check with minimum time and trouble. A practice that can be slanted to nearly any market the writer knows well, the secret of a successful potboiler lies in quantity and quick production: A project that eats up more time than it's worth isn't a practical potboiler.

Because they are usually penned in a hurry, few potboilers can boast of superior literary quality. Nevertheless, potboilers should be submitted as cleanly and professionally as any other material. (*See: Filler.*)

Preface. This term is applied to preliminary remarks written as an introduction to a book by its author or editor. A preface usually explains a book's subject, purpose and plan; it often contains acknowledgments of assistance in creating and publishing the book. Occasionally, a preface, as well as the foreword, will be written by another authority in the same field to lend extra credibility to the book. (*See: Foreword; Introduction.*)

Preferred time/prime time. Time of day when a large audience listens, or when the audience for a specific product is likely to listen to a broadcast. In radio, these are usually *morning drive* (5:30 A.M. to 9:00 A.M.) and *afternoon drive* (3:00 P.M. to 6:00 P.M.), when most drivers are on the road. TV prime time is usually 8 P.M. to 11 P.M.

Premise. A statement that an author makes through the events and outcome of a story. A premise is not necessarily a truth that is generally accepted; it is, however, true in relation to the story. For example, the premise of a short story may be "arrogance leads to loneliness," "arrogance leads to power" or any other statement that pairs a personality trait with a resulting situation. Though the reader might not agree with the premise of a story, he cannot deny that it is true within the boundaries of the specific story character's experience.

Every premise implies a character, a conflict and a resolution. The writer usually establishes a premise before writing a story, so that he can easily stay with one story line. For other writers, the premise grows out of the development of the characters in the writer's prestory planning. All aspects of a story should contribute to the author's original premise.

In TV, the writer seeking a scriptwriting assignment must "pitch" a story—present a premise orally—before he can obtain a contract to work up a treatment and/or final script. (*See: Pitch meeting; Television writing.*)

Prepublication review. Certain publications review forthcoming books well in advance of their official publication dates, using preliminary editions prepared from photocopies of final galley proofs. Such an advance notice is called a *prepublication review.*

Prepublication reviews appear primarily in three trade publications: *Publishers Weekly, Library Journal* and *Kirkus Reviews.* These publications, which are read by librarians, reviewers, bookstore and wholesale book buyers, and mass market and book club editors, can influence the success of a book by inducing potential subsidiary rights sales, as well as increasing library sales and bookstore orders.

Conversely, a poor review can dampen the enthusiasm and sales efforts of the publishing house. (*See: Kirkus Reviews; Review copy.*)

Presentation. A description of a proposed TV series an author gives to a producer. (*See: Pitch meeting; Television script terms.*)

Press card. Also known as a *press pass,* a press card is an identifying card carried by journalists that enables them to gain access to events, people or locations to cover a story for the newspaper or magazine with which they are affiliated.

Freelance writers, most of whom are not affiliated with a magazine or newspaper, do not have the credentials necessary to admit them to "for press only" events or places. To obtain a press pass, and thus gain entry to otherwise restricted areas, a freelance writer usually must ally himself with some specific newspaper, magazine or syndicate market. In some cases, presenting a letter of assignment from a magazine or book publisher indicating that he is working on a story may admit a freelancer to a "for press only" area or event. (*See: Business cards.*)

Press Encyclopedia, The World. A two-volume reference work that describes the print and electronic media establishments in approximately 180 countries. The entries are written so that the press can be understood in relationship to other elements of the individual societies, such as political systems, philosophies and economic systems.

The encyclopedia is arranged by country, and it contains a classification system by which the following subjects (further broken down into more than seventy topics) are covered: basic data (such as number of daily newspapers and literacy rate); size of the newspaper industry; economic framework; censorship and limitations on access to news sources; state-press relations; news agencies; and attitudes toward foreign media.

Press galleries. Galleries that overlook the House and Senate chambers where accredited members of the media may observe floor debate on legislation in Congress. Within the rooms entering into the galleries, reporters have the help of several staff members, who answer telephones, manage news conferences for members of Congress, issue press releases from committee hearings, and in general act as liaison between Congress and the press.

There is a gallery for members of the daily press; another for representatives from magazines; a radio and TV gallery; and a press photographer's gallery. Rules for eligibility are published in the Congressional

Directory and are concerned mainly with the fact that the applicant earns more than 50 percent of his income from a news-gathering organization and lives in the Washington, DC area.

Press release. (*See: Publicity writing.*)

Press trip. A press trip (sometimes referred to as a *junket*) is a trip furnished to a writer by a business that has an interest in a proposed article topic. For example, the public relations firm handling a new hotel may provide a newspaper travel editor with a free trip and accommodations in anticipation of receiving favorable mention in an article. While the greatest number of press trips are offered to travel writers and business writers, any journalist may receive this type of invitation.

A practice related to press trips is offering a writer gifts, such as meals or tickets to a cultural event.

A press trip can present the writer with an ethical dilemma in that his loyalty may be divided between his readers and the sponsor of his trip. Whether to accept an invitation is the writer's personal decision that may be made on the basis of what—if anything—he is expected to write regarding the sponsoring business; what percentage of the expenses are paid by the business; and the degree of objectivity the writer is able to retain.

This ethical question has led some magazine and newspaper travel editors to not accept articles that result from a press trip. Writers are often asked to sign a statement certifying their research was not assisted by sponsored trips or other freebies. Many travel writers argue this policy is unfair, since the publication may not cover all the writer's expenses.

A discussion of press trips appears in the Society of American Travel Writers Ethics Code. (*See: Journalistic ethics.*)

Prestige copy. A broadcasting term for copy that lacks a selling element but presents a favorable image of a company or product.

Pricing/selling. (*See: Negotiating with editors.*)

Primary listening area. The geographic area in which listeners receive consistently good reception from a radio station.

Primary source. A primary source is one that provides the writer with original, firsthand information. Primary research is based on the writer's own experience and observation; direct contact with other people (usually in an interview); or information gleaned from personal papers, correspondence, diaries or manuscripts written at the time or on the scene by the person or about the subject being studied. Because it is closest to the source, primary research is preferred over secondary research, which is based entirely on already-published material such as books, newspapers, magazines, and information available through computerized abstracting services. (*See: Secondary sources.*)

Print advertisement, rough. (*See: Figure 34.*)

FIGURE 34

PRINT ADVERTISEMENT, ROUGH

You Are Now Within 5¼ Inches Of Knowing It All.

NEXIS

Print ad rough reproduced courtesy of Northlich/Stolley/LaWarre Advertising, Cincinnati, Ohio

Privacy Act. In 1974, the U.S. Congress passed the Privacy Act, which gives individuals some control over the personal information the government compiles about them. Under the Privacy Act, an individual has the right to request his personal files, the right to sue the government for letting other individuals see his files, and the right either to have information in his file corrected or to enclose a personal statement regarding information the government refuses to change.

The Privacy Act is by no means all-inclusive. It applies only to files held by an agency under the executive branch of the federal government, and even then only to files that are primarily about the person who requests them and that are organized in a retrieval system. The Privacy Act does not apply to files held by the legislative or judicial branches, by state or local governments or by private organizations; to information about an individual contained in a file about some other person, event or organization; or to information not organized for easy retrieval.

A writer can, of course, use the Privacy Act to see *his* confidential files. But the writer may also run up against the Privacy Act when he is doing research and is not permitted access to government files containing confidential information about another person. (*See: Freedom of Information.*)

Privacy, invasion of. An individual's privacy is protected by various statutory and common laws from invasion by newspapers, TV, radio, magazines, books, pictures and motion pictures, advertising, creditors and wiretapping. The rights of public figures tend to be defined by law somewhat differently from private citizens'.

Generally, a person's right to privacy can be invaded in one of four ways:

1. *Intrusion.* Bruce W. Sanford in *Synopsis of the Law of Libel and the Right of Privacy*, notes, "this type of invasion of privacy . . . usually involves the wrongful use of tape recorders, microphones, cameras, and/or other electronic recording or eavesdropping devices to record a person's private activities." Privacy is invaded when the intrusion occurs; actual publication of information obtained is irrelevant to the claim of "intrusion." Reporters were found to have intrusively invaded the privacy of a physician when they posed as patients to enter his office and secretly take photographs and make recordings.

2. *Misappropriation.* The majority of states, either by common law or by statute, recognize as an invasion of privacy the use of a person's name, likeness or personality for advertising, trade or commercial purposes or for one's own use or benefit without that person's written consent. Exceptions occur when the material or subject is of general interest to the public, or when the subject is newsworthy. An individual won a case on the grounds of misappropriation when a Georgia court, in the case *Pavesich* v. *New England Life Insurance Co.*, ruled that the insurance company used the individual's name without consent in an endorsement. In contrast, a suit filed by Joe Namath, *Namath* v. *Time, Inc.* (1976), was declared not to invade his pri-

vacy. Namath's photograph and name were used by *Sports Illustrated* in an advertisement for the magazine. The athlete did not have a case for invasion of privacy because, according to the court, the photo had previously been published editorially by the magazine, it was newsworthy and it was used merely to convey the "nature, quality and content" of the magazine, not to endorse the magazine.

3. *Publicizing in a false light.* The publication of nondefamatory but untrue information about an individual, information which places him in a "false light" before the public and would be considered offensive or highly offensive to the average person, is considered an invasion of privacy. As established in the case of *Time, Inc.* v. *Hill* (1967), material, to be considered as presenting someone in a false light, must be published "with knowledge of falsity or reckless disregard for the truth." The Hill case involved *Life*'s report on a Broadway play, *The Desperate Hours*, which is based on the James Hill family's encounter as hostages. In the final decision (in this case, that of the U.S. Supreme Court), *Life* was considered to be within the law because no actual malice was shown.

4. *Public disclosure of private and embarrassing facts.* The publication of facts concerning an individual that, while they may be truthful, are private and embarrassing, constitutes an invasion of privacy. A news report or photograph of an event that takes place in *public*, however, is not an invasion of privacy. A well-known case in this area is *Cox Broadcasting* v. *Cohn* (1975), which concerned broadcasting the name of a rape victim. Although the victim was deceased, her father sued the TV station that had reported her name. He lost the case, however, because the victim's name was included in judicial records, which were open to the public. (*See: Libel; Right of privacy; Right of publicity.*)

Additional information: *Synopsis of the Law of Libel and the Right of Privacy.*

Privileged communication. Confidential communication that the law may not require the parties involved to disclose. Depending on the jurisdiction, privileged communication may apply to that between a husband and wife, lawyer and client, doctor and patient, religious counselor and believer, and, in some cases, journalist and news source. The right of journalists to protect their news sources has been sharply limited in a number of significant court cases, however, and some journalists have gone to jail for refusing to reveal their sources of information. The press continues to strive for legislation to protect news sources from disclosure.

The term also has a second meaning: it refers to the press's right to publish or broadcast a full, fair, impartial, and accurate report of legal or legislative proceedings, even though statements made in those proceedings are defamatory or libelous. For example, if a reporter reports statements made by witnesses during a trial that later turn out to be false and libelous, he may be permitted to defend such statements on the ground that they are conditionally privileged.

The defense of conditional privilege is lost, however, when it is "abused"; that is, when it can be shown that a statement was published or broadcast by the media even though the publisher or broadcaster knew the statement to be false or had serious doubts as to its truth. (*See: Libel; Shield laws.*)

Prizes, writing. The annual *Literary Market Place* lists prize contests for writers of poetry, short stories, scholarly articles, etc. Prizes for journalists, fiction and nonfiction writers, and film, video, and audio writers are detailed in some books described in the entry "contests, writing" in this book; some other contests and prizes are described in the entries "Nobel Prize for Literature," "Pulitzer Prizes" and other entries headed by prize names.

Prodigy. A commercial online service that began as a joint venture between IBM and Sears. It was first released in 1985 and acquired national access in 1990. It currently has more than one million subscribers. (*See: Electronic mail; Online service.*)

Product article. (*See: Magazine article, types of.*)

Professional Photographers of America, Inc. (PPA). PPA is the world's largest association for professional image-makers. The 114-year-old association provides educational opportunities for its fourteen thousand members, establishes standards of professional performance and promotes consumer awareness of professional photography. Members receive the *Professional Photographer*, which covers issues in the field rang-

ing from business to art. The PPA also publishes the subscription magazine *Photoelectronic Imaging*, which includes technical and product information. Basic membership is open to anyone. Full-time, professional photographers can get involved in PPA's continuing eduation programs. For more information, contact the organization at 57 Forsyth St., N.W., Suite 1600, Atlanta, GA 30303.

Professional vs. amateur. There is a widespread belief that the professional writer is wealthy and famous, lunches with New York City editors, and jets about the country interviewing celebrities and sports personalities and government officials. An amateur writer, it is likewise assumed, pecks out stories on a rusty old Remington at the kitchen table after the kids have gone to bed, has never met or spoken with an editor, and has no access to the exciting and stimulating subjects about which the professional writer writes.

In reality, the difference between a professional writer and an amateur lies not in the writing profession's external trappings but in the writer's own attitude toward his work. Flaws in grammar and word choice, lackluster style, sloppy plotting or research, poor organization and absence of focus in a manuscript are all marks of the amateur rather than the professional. The amateur writer takes a very subjective view toward his work. He is too easily satisfied with a project once it is finished and unwilling to change a single word. He fails to study the market to which he submits his work, and then attributes the inevitable rejection either to the market's blindness to the merits of his masterpiece or to his own failure as a writer.

A professional writer, on the other hand, recognizes that writing is a profession rather than a hobby. He is able, says Lois Duncan in *How to Write and Sell Your Personal Experiences*, to be objective. "He regards writing as a business," Duncan continues, "and his stories and articles and books as products he is offering for sale. If his commodity is rejected, he does not consider it an insult. He realizes that he has probably offered the wrong thing to the wrong person at the wrong time, chalks it up as a learning experience, and sends his material somewhere else. At the same time, he tries to figure out what *would* be right for that market that rejected him, so that next time he can offer something more in keeping with its needs."

It doesn't matter whether a writer lives in New York City or Newark or Newtonsville. It makes no difference how many New York editors he knows. The writer who works hard at his writing, studies the market and—specifically for that market—produces a polished manuscript that skillfully treats its subject is a professional writer. The writer who is not willing to work hard at his writing will remain an amateur.

Profile. The profile, or personality sketch, is an article—not a question-and-answer interview—whose main subject is a person who is for some reason noteworthy. Profile subjects may be entertainment or sports celebrities, people in the public eye or figures of notoriety; they may also be individuals who have interesting jobs, unusual hobbies or inspirational philosophies. Almost all magazines, both consumer and trade publications, carry personality profiles; some daily newspapers also buy profiles from freelancers.

When the profile writer chooses his subject he must determine (1) *why* that individual is noteworthy and (2) *to whom* he would be interesting (i.e., potential markets). The second step requires research: The writer reads previously published material about the subject; checks appropriate records (depending on the subject) such as Dun and Bradstreet reports and college transcripts; and conducts interviews with people who know the subject and can round out the information offered by the subject himself.

The profile writer then interviews the subject—usually more than once—to get a fuller view of him. The profile's success is often in proportion to the interviewer's skill: The writer should recognize effective anecdotes and provocative quotes; his questions should provoke responses that reveal the subject's opinions, aspirations, passions and peeves—responses with emotional content.

During the interview the writer should also be aware of how the subject talks, what he is wearing, what the surroundings are like—everything the writer observes that helps illuminate the subject enhances the profile.

The finished piece should not glorify the subject; rather, it attempts to create on paper a comprehensive picture of the individual's personality—warts and all. Although the profile may, depending on length, contain a certain amount of personal background information—hometown, early life, schools, marriage(s)—the focus of the article should be *current*—the individual is interesting because of what he does or is *today.*

The profile is built upon anecdotes, "appearance words" (which help the reader form a mental picture), and revealing quotes from the subject and the people who know him.

The term *profile* usually refers to a personality piece; however, some magazines "profile" places and events using the techniques described above. (*See: Interview.*)

Program log. A catalog of data (such as length, sponsor and time of day to be broadcast) on announcements, commercials, newscasts and most other material (other than music) that is broadcast. The Federal Communications Commission requires all radio stations to keep a program log.

Programmed instruction (PI). A kind of teaching that involves a stimulus, a response and a reward. It is modeled on the theories of behavioral psychologists, who invented it. Other names for programmed instruction include *self-paced instruction, individualized instruction* and *computer-assisted instruction.*

Programmed instruction can be taught through textbooks or computers. A small piece of information, called a frame, serves as a stimulus by requiring a response from the student. The student is then rewarded by being allowed to move on in the program, or told to review the ma-

terial if he responded incorrectly. A series of frames and responses, which can be structured in different ways, makes up a PI text.

When the writer has completed a PI text, he tests it on people who represent his intended audience. A ninety-ninety ratio, occurring when 90 percent of the students learn 90 percent of the material, is satisfactory: If the writer has not achieved it, he must rewrite the text until he does.

Textbook publishers and local businesses are markets for PI texts. However, this field is specialized, and some markets accept only writers with established reputations or with teaching experience. Publishers require sample frames and an outline of the program; businesses need to see samples of the writer's work. Rates paid and rights purchased by the publisher vary and are outlined in the individual contract. On specific assignments for industry, the writer usually turns over all rights to the company.

Promo. A radio or TV announcement that promotes one or more of the station's programs.

Promotion by author. Because no one knows a book's topic better than the author and no publisher can adequately promote *every* title on its list, a book author should consider promoting his book. This can be done on his own or in conjunction with his publisher.

Promotion can take the form of book signings, lectures, TV and radio broadcasts, queries to newspaper editors about reviews or features, classified ads, letters or sales pitches—either direct or indirect—at bookstores. When approaching newspaper editors and other publicity contacts, it is advantageous to apply the desired publicity to their needs; this can be accomplished by giving the newspaper editor a local angle for his feature, or pointing out the book's market slant to a bookstore manager. In any case, the author must consult with the publisher's publicists regarding promotion strategies to avoid duplication of effort.

The author should remember that, even though the publisher's marketing staff may promote the book, the author must personally finance the travel and other expenses of his independent promotional ventures. However, it is sometimes possible, through negotiation, for an author to obtain part of the total promotion cost from the publisher. (*See: Self-publishing.*)

Proofreader's marks/symbols. Many of the changes on manuscripts indicated by proofreaders are denoted by a standard set of symbols that are understood by typesetters and printers as well. (*See: Figure 35.*)

Proofreading. This term usually applies to the process of reading typeset copy (printer's proofs) to identify and correct errors in that copy. In *Freelance Jobs for Writers*, Elizabeth L. Dugger describes proofreading as "the painstaking, word-for-word, character-for-character comparison of typeset galley proofs against the original manuscript to see that nothing was omitted, added, or changed by the compositor, that words have been divided correctly at the ends of lines, and that the type specifications (specs) regarding typeface, style, and margins were followed." In some jobs, the proofreader may also be responsible (prior to typesetting) for checking the copy for spelling, grammar and style, as well as for doing the comparison work after copy is typeset.

In identifying and correcting errors in composed copy, the proofreader uses a fairly standard set of correction marks. (*See: Editing, freelance; Figure 35.*)

Propaganda. The deliberate dissemination of information or ideas intended to persuade people toward or away from a belief, action, individual, movement, nation, institution or organization. Propaganda may consist of opinions, facts, arguments, allegations or rumors presented by word of mouth or through printed and visual material, music, drama or any of the mass media. Certain acts such as demonstrations, assassinations and hijackings may also be perpetrated for propaganda purposes.

The term is derived from the Congregation for the Propagation of the Faith, a committee founded in the seventeenth century by Pope Gregory XV to propagate—that is, to spread—Christianity to foreign lands. It took on a negative connotation during World War II when falsified reports and opinion-influencing discussion came to be labeled propaganda.

Although propaganda can be used to promote both good and bad causes, it is generally disclaimed as being unfairly slanted. It is distinguished from education, which seeks to inform through reason. Often ap-

FIGURE 35

PROOFREADER'S MARKS

MARK	*EXPLANATION*	*(In margin)* *EXAMPLE* *(In Text)*
ℓ	Take out character indicated.	*ℓ* Your manuscript.
stet or...	Let it stay.	*stet* Your manuscript.
#	Put in space.	*#* Yourmanuscript.
⌒	Close up completely.	Writer's Di gest School.
tr	Transpose; change places.	*tr* Yuor manuscript.
caps or	Use capital letters.	*caps* Writer's digest school.
lc	Use lower-case letters.	*lc* Your Manuscript.
bf or	Use bold-face type.	*bf* Writer's Digest School. Writer's Digest School
ital or ___	Use italic type.	*ital* Writer's Digest
⌄	Put in apostrophe.	*⌄* Writers Digest School.
⊙	Put in period.	⊙ Your manuscript
*/	Put in comma.	*/ Your manuscript
:/	Put in colon.	:/ Your manuscript
;/	Put in semicolon.	;/ Writer's Digest School
"̇ "̇	Put in quotation marks.	*"̇ "̇* He said, Yes.
(?)	Question to author.	(?) *No hyphen OK* Free lance writer.
=/	Put in hyphen.	=/ Free lance writer.
!	Put in exclamation.	! This is great
?	Put in question mark.	? Are you starting
c/ɔ	Put in parenthesis.	(/) Your first rough draft.
¶	Start paragraph.	*¶* a writer. Learn to sell
‖	Even out lines	Writer's Digest and Writer's Digest School.
⊏	Move the line left	Your manuscript.
⊐	Move the line right	Your manuscript.
No ¶	No paragraph; run together	*NO ¶* a writer. There are more needed
out, sc	Something missing, see copy.	*out, sc* Writer's School.
spell out	Spell it out.	*spell out* Your ms.

pealing to desires, fears and prejudices, propaganda is criticized because it does not give fair and impartial consideration to opposing views. (*See: Censorship, literary; Persuasive writing.*)

Proposal/prospectus. A detailed plan of a proposed new enterprise, such as a new publication or a new company, that is used as selling material for that project. A prospectus usually involves a description of the contents and projected market for the proposal. It is often used in relation to textbook proposals and in proposals for foundation grants. (*See: Outline; Textbook publishing.*)

Prose. All spoken and written language that is not expressed in a regular rhythmic pattern. *Prose*, as distinguished from *poetry*, is the ordinary form of communication in words. The distinction between prose and poetry cannot always be clearly defined, however; there are often poetic elements in prose compositions, as well as prosaic poetry. Prose may be fiction or nonfiction. (*See: Poetry.*)

Prose poem. A style of writing constructed in prose form (sentences and paragraphs rather than lines), but possessing the dramatic language of poetry—imagery, rhythm, cadence, assonance, alliteration, etc. Karl Shapiro's *The Bourgeois Poet* is a volume of prose poems. Here is an excerpt:

Poems, flowers of language, if that's what you are, grow up in the air where books come true. And you, thin packet, let your seed fly, if you have any.

Protagonist. A protagonist is the central character of a story or play. Plot is created when this character faces a conflict, and if another character is the cause of the conflict, that character is called the *antagonist*.

Protagonist is often incorrectly used as a synonym for *hero*; similarly, *antagonist* is incorrectly used for *villain*. Actually, a hero is an admirable character, and a villain is one who embodies evil; regardless of the characters' personal qualities, the character who demands the most attention of readers is the protagonist, and the character who opposes him is the antagonist. (*See: Antagonist; Characterization.*)

Proverb. A short, familiar saying, usually of unknown or ancient origin, that expresses a useful thought, supposed truth or moral lesson. *Proverb* is synonymous with *adage, aphorism, apothegm, maxim, saying* and *saw*. Writers searching for ideas or universal themes for their work may develop an article, story or novel from a well-known proverb.

PSA. (*See: Public service announcement.*)

Pseudonym. A pseudonym is a fictitious name used to conceal the identity of an author. More generally, *pseudonym* is a term for any alias. (*See: Pen name.*)

Psychological novel. A narrative that emphasizes the mental and emotional aspects of its characters, focusing on motivations and mental activity rather than on exterior events. The psychological novelist is less concerned about relating *what* happened than about exploring *why* it happened. Although Shakespeare's *Hamlet*, James Joyce's *Ulysses*, and much of the work of Henry James may be considered psychological, the term is most often used to describe twentieth-century works that employ techniques such as interior monologue and stream of consciousness. Two psychological novels among those published in recent years are Judith Guest's *Ordinary Peo-*

ple and Mary Gordon's *The Company of Women.*

The label *psychological novel* is not necessarily an exclusive one. A work of science fiction, for example, may also be psychological. Contemporary mystery novels in particular are becoming more psychologically oriented. Unlike the straight crime puzzlers of the past, present-day mystery and crime fiction emphasize character motivation and analyze action— particularly criminal action—in terms of a character's psycho-history. The novels of Lawrence Sanders (*The First Deadly Sin, The Third Deadly Sin*) allow the reader to explore the inner mind of the main character— usually a murderer—and to tune in to his motivations, emotions and the forces affecting his decisions and actions. (*See: Interior monologue; Stream of consciousness.*)

Public domain. Material not protected by copyright, patent or trademark, and therefore available to the general public for use without fee, is said to be in the public domain. An author may use as he pleases, without obtaining permission, any material he finds in the public domain.

Certain types of material cannot be copyrighted and so fall immediately into the public domain. The facts in newsstories that appear in newspapers become part of the public domain once they are published. (Many features and columns appearing in the newspaper *are* copyrighted, however—as shown by the copyright symbol, year and copyright owner's name—and a writer must obtain permission from the author, newspaper or syndicate to use this material.) Most government publications are uncopyrighted and, therefore, in the public domain. Facts—well-established information—cannot be copyrighted. Jokes cannot be copyrighted. Ideas, titles and transcripts from public hearings cannot be copyrighted. All of these are in the public domain.

Current copyright law does not require work to carry a copyright notice to be protected. However, works published before March 1, 1989, *did* require that notice. In general, material immediately became part of the public domain when it was published in an uncopyrighted publication without a notice.

A copyrighted work may fall into the public domain once its copyright period runs out. Before January 1, 1978, copyright protection under the old law was for twenty-eight years and could be renewed just once for another twenty-eight years. Any copyrighted material more than fifty-six years old (except for material whose copyright expired from 1962 to 1977 and was renewed each year for one more year by Congress while it considered a new copyright bill) would now be in the public domain. Under the new law, copyright is for the author's life, plus fifty years. (*See: Copyright.*)

Public relations (PR) manager. This person is responsible for presenting and maintaining a favorable image of his company or institution before a public. People work in this capacity for hospitals, universities and other institutions; for private corporations; and for public relations firms, which represent and counsel a variety of clients. In business the title of the public relations manager may be

Director of Corporate Communications or Director of Marketing Communications, rather than Public Relations Director.

One important function the public relations manager performs is working with top management in forming the company's public relations policies. He also is up-to-date on trends in the field in which he works and with the activities of competing companies and organizations, as well as his own.

Community relations is a major concern of a public relations person whose company/institution is active in a small region, while media relations is a major concern for one who works for a national or international company/institution that seeks favorable national exposure through magazines and broadcast networks and through local media. In addition, presiding over employee, investor or government relations is a responsibility sometimes delegated to the public relations manager.

A public relations office communicates through newspaper features, press releases, brochures, open houses, newsletters, news conferences, direct mail, exhibits, speeches, commercials and public service announcements and seeks opportunities to send company or institution representatives to radio and TV talk shows, especially if they are nationally known and respected spokespeople.

Because the public relations manager either writes or approves of every communication that his company dispatches to publics, he must possess a command of language. He must also be well versed in photography and video since PR material must be striking enough to capture an editor's attention. Knowledge of design and printing principles helps, too.

A national professional public relations organization is the Public Relations Society of America, 33 Irving Place, Third Floor, New York, NY 10003, (212) 995-2230. (*See: Public service announcement; Publicity writing.*)

Additional information: *Professional's Guide to Publicity.*

Public Relations Society of America (PRSA). About sixteen thousand public relations professionals are members of this largest public relations society in the world. PRSA provides its members with networking opportunities as well as opportunities for professional development. Members attend chapter meetings and an annual convention. They also receive the monthly newspaper, *Tactics*, which covers current strategies in public relations, and the quarterly magazine, *Strategist*, which deals with other public relations issues. Yearly dues are $175 plus chapter dues. PRSA's headquarters are located at 33 Irving Place, Third Floor, New York, NY 10003.

Public service announcement (PSA). A public service announcement is a period of broadcast time given by a station to a community group, in accordance with the Federal Communications Commission stipulation requiring TV and radio stations to operate in the public interest. The publicist who seeks broadcast time for his organization must assess the needs of—and therefore the audiences of—available stations to find the ones most likely to comply with his request.

A public service announcement can take several forms. Straightforward announcements that inform the audience of an event are heard in station breaks, spot announcements and community calendars. News releases, telephone call-in talk show programs ("two-way radio"), editorials, features, panel discussions and interviews are longer broadcast items of which the public service announcement may be only a part; whatever form of public service announcement is written, economy of words and emphasis on facts are essential to good copy.

A public service announcement must be typed, double-spaced—no more than one on a page—with two-inch side margins on 8½″ × 11″ bond paper. Words should not be hyphenated at the ends of lines; the copy should contain no abbreviations. A paragraph should not end at the bottom of a page: continuing it on to the next page keeps broadcasters from mistaking the end of a paragraph for the end of the public service announcement. The publicist also inserts phonetic spellings of unfamiliar names and words.

While the actual announcement begins one-third of the way down the page, other information belongs at the top: the name, address and phone number of the organization, along with the publicist's name, should be typed in the upper left corner. The dates to broadcast the announcement go in the upper right corner; it is best to submit copy fifteen days before the first day it is intended to be broadcast.

One kind of public service announcement, the spot announcement, is programmed by time at radio and TV stations. The following word counts for radio serve as a guide to the public service announcement writer: twenty-five words can be read in ten seconds, fifty words in twenty seconds and 150 words in sixty seconds. In TV copy, which is read at a slower pace, twenty words can be read in ten seconds, forty words in twenty seconds and 125 words in sixty seconds. Public service announcements for TV, of course, should be accompanied by an appropriate visual in the slide or tape format preferred by the individual station. The longer the public service announcement, the more slides required, since a single slide makes for a dull, static spot; it's important to keep the TV station's needs in mind when assembling public service announcements. (*See: Figure 36.*)

Public Television. Some broadcast licenses are allocated by the Federal Communications Commission to provide educational programming to schools and the general public. The licenses are assigned to colleges and universities, state and local municipalities or community groups. Funding comes from government appropriations, foundation and corporate support and viewer contributions.

There are 345 public TV stations. They broadcast material that reinforces and enriches conventional classroom study; promotes public awareness of local, regional and national issues; and fosters cultural and artistic expression. Writers may find the programs featuring interviews

FIGURE 36

PUBLIC SERVICE ANNOUNCEMENT FOR TV

"CARING ABOUT TREES," INTRODUCING SPUNKY SQUIRREL

30 Seconds   16mm   5400 K   SOF

ANNCR: (V/O) "Trees are treasures."

MAN: (V/O) "Dani...come see what just landed."

DANI: (SYNCH) "It's a squirrel...It's Spunky Squirrel!"

SPUNKY: (SYNCH) "Any home in America can have healthy trees when you follow Spunky's five point check list."

ANNCR: (V/O) "Trees are treasures. People who care, care for them. To keep your trees a valuable part of your property...

write for a free brochure today."

EDITOR'S NOTE: Public Service Directors of TV stations remind local groups seeking airtime that it is important to have more than one piece of video (a slide) to support a ten-, twenty-, thirty- or sixty-second piece of copy. Only one slide makes for too static a spot, and it is useful to keep the needs of the TV station in mind when formulating a Public Service Announcement to ensure airtime.

with authors especially helpful.

The major source of programming is the Public Broadcasting Corporation, through five major affiliates: WNET, New York; WTTW, Chicago; WGBH, Boston; KQED, San Francisco; WQED, Pittsburgh; and WETA, Washington, DC. In addition, smaller stations and independent production groups—such as Children's Television Workshop and the Agency for Instructional Technology—produce and distribute programming to stations.

Depending on their size and budget, local educational TV stations may or may not produce original programming and/or only distribute programs originating elsewhere. Inquiries from scriptwriters should be directed to the program director at the local station.

Publicity writing. Publicists, who are either self-employed or staff members of public relations or advertising agencies, are engaged by companies, not-for-profit organizations, politicians, celebrities and others to write and send press releases (and sometimes photographs) to appropriate media about newsworthy products or events. A publicity writer combines the creativity of a magazine writer with the fact-finding ability of a newspaper reporter to emphasize the benefit of something or the good qualities of someone.

For a writer who intends to enter the publicity field, experience as a newspaper reporter is very helpful, since a knowledge of what is truly newsworthy—as opposed to puffery—can increase the success the publicist has in placing material in the media (which is publicity's ulti-

mate goal). Volunteer work with not-for-profit organizations can help a writer enter this field by giving him experience and contacts. Also, photography skills can be an asset to this type of career.

Simplicity is the key to writing the news release: Its style is direct and the message is concise; elaboration with adjectives is rare. According to publicist Thomas J. Rizzo, the *who, what, when, where* and *why* should be stated at the outset. He advises constructing the copy so that deleting the name of the client or cause would render the press release difficult to understand. At the same time, the release should be so constructed that it will be easy for an editor to run it as is, without any changes.

A press release is typed on $8\frac{1}{2}'' \times 11''$ white bond paper. Its format should be similar to Figure 37 or to the instructions that follow.

Copy for the print media is double-spaced; that for the broadcast media is triple-spaced. Side margins are $1\frac{1}{2}''$ each. In the upper right or left corner, the writer types the name, address and phone number of the contact person and sponsoring organization.

The final item to be placed in the upper right or left corner is the phrase *for immediate release*, typed in all caps along with the date the information is to be released. The writer indicates the city of origin and the date, either at the beginning or the end of the copy, and places either "-30-" or "# # #" at the end of the release. An entire press release rarely exceeds two pages.

Some experts advise creating a catchy or appropriate headline for a press release for a print medium, in

FIGURE 37

PRESS RELEASE SAMPLE

FOR IMMEDIATE RELEASE

FROM: Mayfield Senior Citizen's Center
3210 Apple Road
Cincinnati, Ohio 45209

CONTACT: Jane Doe
987-6543

Kathy White, a Cincinnati native, is the new director of the Mayfield Senior Citizen's Center, 3210 Apple Road. She replaces Abby Jones, who resigned to take a camp position in Michigan.

Ms. White has been with the Cincinnati Recreation Commission as an arts specialist at both the downtown and Eden Park Senior Centers. She is a graduate of the University of Cincinnati, in Theater Arts and Arts Administration.

One of Ms. White's first duties will be to coordinate Mayfield's "Old-Fashioned Arts and Crafts Fair." It will be held at the center Saturday, October 20, from 10:00 a.m. to 5:00 p.m. The public is invited.

\#

Reprinted by permission from The Publicity Handbook *of the Cincinnati Chapter of* Women in Communications, Inc.

---

case it happens to be suitable for the editor's needs. However, editors do accept press releases that lack headlines. (*See: Figure 37; Public service announcement.*)

Public's right to know. (*See: Freedom of information.*)

Publisher's catalog. A promotional booklet sent by a book publisher to bookstores, libraries and individuals. Such catalogs are commonly issued by hardcover publishers twice a year, in spring and fall; by paperback publishers more frequently. They inform consumers about the newest releases and other current titles, providing short summaries of the books' contents, authors and intended audiences.

A publisher's catalog is one

means of researching a company's editorial emphasis before submitting a manuscript to an editor there. In many cases, publishers send catalogs free for a request and a self-addressed, stamped envelope; *Writer's Market* listings furnish details on obtaining publishers' catalogs.

Publishers, music. (*See:* Songwriter's Market.)

Publisher's rep. A representative of the publisher who calls on bookstores, wholesalers, etc., to sell the new and backlist titles of the publisher. He may either be employed by the publisher (sometimes called "house reps") or be an independent entrepreneur representing several publishers and paid on a commission basis for books sold.

The term also refers to the representative of a magazine publisher who calls on magazine wholesalers to monitor the distribution of the magazine to appropriate outlets in the wholesalers' retail trading area.

Publisher's Trade List Annual. A multivolume set of directories available in most libraries containing publishers' current catalogs. Catalogs are listed alphabetically by publisher and show both the current and backlist titles of the company. It is most useful to writers researching book ideas to see what subjects have been treated most recently by publishers the author has in mind as prospective markets for his own book ideas.

Publishers Weekly (PW). A trade magazine covering current events in the publishing industry. Each issue contains an interview-profile of an au-

thor or other person influential in publishing, announcements of personnel changes and *Publishers Weekly's* own lists of paperback and hardcover best-sellers. The department "Forecasts" features brief reviews of soon-to-be-published fiction, nonfiction, how-to, paperback and children's books.

News in other categories is regularly reported under "Rights and Permissions," "Bookselling & Marketing," and "Calendar" (announcements of workshops, conferences, seminars and courses).

The two largest special issues of *Publishers Weekly* announcing forthcoming books are the fall announcement number in August and the spring announcement issue in January. A religious books issue is published twice a year (usually in February and September); a children's books issue, in February and July; the International/Frankfurt Book Fair issue, in September; and the ABA convention issue, in May. The annual summary, published in March, briefly reports on important events—such as prizes, awards and best-sellers—of the previous year.

Writers find *Publishers Weekly* useful in learning what books are planned for publication by which publishers. They can then evaluate their own ideas in relation to potential publishers. Most libraries subscribe to *Publishers Weekly*. The address is 249 W. Seventeenth St., New York, NY 10011.

Publishing, courses in. For the college student or other adult seeking a career in publishing, or the individual already employed in the publishing industry and interested in professional advancement or enrichment, a number of courses—both academic and professional—are offered by colleges and universities, publishing houses, industrial firms and professional organizations.

Several academic institutions offer credit and noncredit courses for both undergraduate and graduate students in various aspects of publishing: manuscript editing; printing, layout and design; graphics techniques; book promotion; copyrights and contracts; textbook publishing; publishing finance and accounting; and related subject areas. Three of the best known are the Radcliffe Publishing Procedures Course at Harvard, the Diploma Program in Book Publishing at New York University and the Stanford Professional publishing course at Stanford University. Professional programs, such as the one offered by Folio Magazine Publishing Corporation, include workshops, seminars and conferences in all areas of publishing. These programs are designed primarily for professionals in the field.

Literary Market Place lists courses for the book trade in its "Associations, Events, Courses & Awards" section. *Guide to Book Publishing Courses: Academic and Professional Programs* is another directory available in most public or college libraries that may be useful to writers seeking staff jobs with publishing companies. (*See: Continuing education.*)

Publishing house. The term originated with early publishing companies, many of which were family-operated enterprises. Today, *publishing house* is synonymous with *publishing company*.

Publishing party. This is an essentially social function given occasionally by a publishing house in honor of a recently published author. At a publishing party, the author, the author's agent, some of the publisher's employees, reviewers, trade journalists, representatives of radio and TV, and relatives and friends of the author gather for the primary purpose of celebrating the accomplished book. In addition, people interested in buying paperback rights or other subsidiary rights that have not already been sold are invited by the publisher.

The job of organizing a publishing party belongs to the publisher's publicist, who sometimes chooses a location connected in some way to the book. For example, a party in celebration of *Scruples* was held at a San Francisco store similar to the store in the novel. (*See: Autographing party.*)

Puff. A publicity release that praises an individual, product, service or organization. Because it does not involve objective presentation of information and generally has little or no news value, newspaper and magazine editors are not receptive to an article based solely on puff. One-sided, poorly researched pieces built only on information supplied by somebody's publicity department and that describe their subjects only in the most positive terms are not, according to many editors listed in *Writer's Market*, seriously considered for publication.

Book publishers, on the other hand, welcome puff as a tool for promoting book sales. Testimonials by well-known individuals that appear on the dust jacket of the book and attest to its quality are, in essence, puff. (*See: Blurb; Book promotion.*)

Pulitzer Prizes. The Pulitzer Prizes in Journalism, Letters, Drama and Music are a group of annual awards established in 1917 under the terms of the will of Joseph Pulitzer (1847-1911), a Hungarian-born newspaper owner and editor (the New York *World*) who is also remembered for endowing the Columbia University School of Journalism.

Designed for the "encouragement of public service, public morals, American literature, and the advancement of education," awards of $3,000 ($500 before 1942) are presented annually for distinguished work in U.S. newspapers, as well as for distinguished achievement in literature, drama and music by Americans. Included in the Letters Awards are those for fiction, biography, history, poetry and general nonfiction. In addition to the sixteen awards in journalism (including cartoon and photography awards), there are also three traveling fellowships for graduates of Columbia's Graduate School of Journalism.

Eligibility requirements and competition deadline information may be obtained by writing Secretary, The Pulitzer Prize Board, 702 Journalism, Columbia University, New York, NY 10027. (*See: Figure 38.*)

Pull back. An indication in a motion picture or TV script that the camera should move back from a particular scene for a wider view. In a script, the term is typed in all caps. (*See: Television script terms.*)

Pulp magazine. A popular magazine printed on coarse, low-quality paper stock and usually containing lurid or sensational articles and stories. Although the term historically connotes low standards of taste and literary quality, a great deal of good writing has been published in pulp magazines. The term is seldom used today.

Pulp magazines, or *pulps*, enjoyed success and popularity from the 1920s into the 1940s. They were inexpensive for publishers to produce (being printed on cheap paper, displaying little decoration, and representing a low-paying market for writers) as well as inexpensive for consumers to buy.

The first pulp magazine, *Argosy*, was introduced as such in 1896; it had existed since 1882 as a children's magazine, and when the publisher, Frank Munsey, changed its target audience to adults and its content to adventure stories, he began printing it on lower-quality pulp paper. Adventure was the only category offered by the earliest pulps, but later it was joined by love, detective, western and science fiction magazines with titles such as *Love Story, Detective Story, Western Story* and *Amazing Stories.*

Just after World War II, the pulp magazine business began to suffer noticeably when competition from paperback books and comic books became a serious threat. In addition, publishers had escalating production costs to contend with. During this period, some publishers ceased publication, others intensified their use of market research and national advertising, and another group of publishers converted their pulps to

FIGURE 38

PULITZER PRIZE WINNERS IN LITERATURE AND DRAMA: 1990–1995

FICTION

1990   Oscar Hijuelos, *The Mambo Kings Play Songs of Love*
1991   John Updike, *Rabbit at Rest*
1992   Jane Smiley, *A Thousand Acres*
1993   Robert Olen Butler, *A Good Scent From a Strange Mountain*
1994   E. Annie Proulx, *The Shipping News*
1995   Carol Shields, *The Stone Diaries*

GENERAL NONFICTION

1990   Dale Maharide and Michael Williamson, *And Their Children After Them*
1991   Bert Holldobler and Edward O. Wilson, *The Ants*
1992   Daniel Yergin, *The Prize: The Epic Quest for Oil Money and Power*
1993   Gary Wills, *Lincoln at Gettysburg: The Words that Remade America*
1994   David Remnick, *Lenin's Tomb: The Last Days of the Soviet Empire*
1995   Jonathan Weiner, *The Beak of the Finch: A Story of Evolution in Our Time*

POETRY

1990   Charles Simic, *The World Doesn't End*
1991   Mona Van Suyn, *Near Changes*
1992   James Tate, *Selected Poems*
1993   Louise Glück, *The Wild Iris*
1994   Yusef Komunyakaa, *Neon Vernacular*
1995   Philip Levine, *The Simple Truth*

DRAMA

1990   August Wilson, *The Piano Lesson*
1991   Neil Simon, *Lost in Yonkers*
1992   Robert Schenkkan, *The Kentucky Cycle*
1993   Tony Kushner, *Angels in America: Millennium Approaches*
1994   Edward Albee, *Three Tall Women*
1995   Horton Foote, *The Young Man From Atlanta*

BIOGRAPHY

1990   Sebastian de Grazia, *Machiavelli in Hell*
1991   Steven Naifeh and Gregory White Smith, *Jackson Pollock: An American Saga*
1992   Lewis B. Puller, Jr., *Fortunate Son: The Healing of a Vietnam Vet*
1993   David McCullough, *Truman*
1994   David L. Lewis, *W.E.B. Du Bois: A Biography of a Race, 1868-1919*
1995   Joan D. Hedrick, *Harriet Beecher Stowe: A Life*

HISTORY

1990   Stanley Karnow, *In Our Image: America's Empire in the Philippines*
1991   Laurel Thatcher Ulrich, *A Midwife'sTales: The Life of Martha Ballard, based on her diary 1785-1812*
1992   Mark E. Neely, Jr., *The Fate of Liberty: Abraham Lincoln and Civil Liberties*
1993   Gordon S. Woods, *The Radicalism of the American Revolution*
1994   No award
1995   Doris Kearns Goodwin, *No Ordinary Time*

slicks—thus establishing the men's general-interest magazine. (*See: Pulp writer; Women's slick magazine.*)

Additional information: *Magazines in the Twentieth Century.*

Pulp writer. Someone who writes for pulp magazines. The term traditionally referred to those who wrote for confession, western and other "pulp" (paper) magazines, but is seldom used today. Well-known writers whose work appeared early in pulp magazines include Edgar Rice Burroughs, A. Conan Doyle, Theodore Dreiser, Dashiell Hammett, Rudyard Kipling, Booth Tarkington and Edith Wharton.

Punch. In radio, emphasis placed on a particular line or on a commercial.

Puzzle writing. Writers interested in constructing and selling puzzles may choose from a variety of puzzle categories: straight crossword puzzles, topical crosswords, word-search puzzles (also called word-find and seek-a-word), fill-ins (known also as Kriss Krosses), anacrostics, acrostics, cryptograms, mazes, brain teasers and word games. Requirements vary considerably from magazine to magazine, so the puzzle writer is advised to request editorial specifications on puzzle submissions from the magazine to which he intends to send his material. One requirement that applies to all categories of puzzles and that is common to nearly all puzzle publishers is extreme accuracy: The puzzle writer must take special care to make certain the drawings, numberings, spellings and definitions are all correct before submitting the puzzle. Puzzle publishers ordinarily require that a list of the sources for each word in the puzzle accompany the submission.

A number of magazines publish nothing but puzzles. The best-known are those in the Dell Puzzle Publications group: *Dell Crossword Puzzles, Dell Word Search Puzzles, Official Crossword Puzzles* and others. Publishers who publish puzzles exclusively are listed in the "Puzzle" section of *Writer's Market.*

Puzzles are often considered to be filler material and are accepted as such by a wide variety of consumer, trade and company publications. Religious, juvenile, teen and young adult, and general-interest magazines in particular solicit puzzles of all types. Their requirements and typical rates of pay are listed in *Writer's Market.*

Puzzle writers who concentrate on crossword puzzles should be aware that published crossword diagrams—the arrangement of open squares and black spaces—are used over and over again, and are, in effect, in the public domain. Only the arrangement of words within the diagram can be copyrighted.

q.v. Abbreviation for the Latin phrase *quod vide* which translates to *which see*. This term most often appears in footnotes, encyclopedia entries and book reviews; it follows a reference to another work or entry that can be looked up. For instance, an encyclopedia article on airplanes might read, " . . . invented by Wilbur and Orville Wright, q.v.," meaning that the reader should then look up the encyclopedia entry for the Wrights if he wishes to know more about them.

Query. A query is a sales letter to an editor that is designed to interest him in an article or book idea. A query usually refers to nonfiction only, but could be a requirement for novel-length fiction as well, especially when a particular market is swamped with fiction submissions. The purpose of a query letter is twofold: it attempts to convince an editor that a proposed idea is good for his readership, and it tries to make him believe that the writer can turn out a well-written piece.

Though queries are as individual as the submissions they pertain to, there are general guidelines writers may use to structure their proposals. Knowing what to include and what to omit in a query may mean the difference between a sale and the slush pile. No query alone will sell a manuscript, but a bad one may prevent an editor from even considering an idea.

The lead paragraph of the article query letter, for example, may include an alluring but concise summary of the article's central idea and the style and viewpoint in which it will be written. Subsequent paragraphs may support the article's premise with facts, anecdotes and observations. The writer may also share some of his sources of information and describe briefly his qualifications (if they are relevant) for developing the idea. The query closing may be a straightforward request to do the article, and may specify a proposed length for the piece and a delivery date.

Another form of query, the outline query, begins with a lead in double-spaced type that might not be the exact wording to be used in the article, but that favorably represents the author's writing style. The balance of the outline query (typed single-spaced) provides the same information, examples and credentials as those described in the basic query.

Specific items to omit from a query letter include discussion of fees, the writer's opinion of the article idea's worth, and requests for advice. Editors read well-written, up-front queries that make their point succinctly.

In addition to content, there are technical aspects to submitting a successful query: keeping the letter to one single-spaced typed page, if possible; addressing the current editor by name; referring to the writer in the first person; enclosing a self-addressed, stamped envelope; and ensuring accuracy in spelling, grammar and writing mechanics. Samples of the writer's work and a list of credits may accompany a query letter. In addition, if the writer has tantalizing photographs that illustrate his story idea, he may enclose three or four of them with the letter.

Listings in *Writer's Market* often indicate whether an editor prefers a query letter or a complete manuscript. (*See: Figure 39.*)

Quill and Scroll Society (QSS). An international organization of high school students involved in journalism and creative writing. In a school that has established a Quill and Scroll Society chapter, the newspaper, the yearbook and the literary magazine are all eligible to induct members. Individual students, to become members, must be recommended by their schools.

The Society publishes a chapter manual, a stylebook and the quarterly magazine, *Quill & Scroll*. In addition, it publishes materials for students, teachers and school administrators, including booklets on effective editorial writing and managing publications, as well as a principal's guide.

QSS conducts research, presents scholarships and sponsors the National Writing Contest. Its headquarters are at the School of Journalism and Mass Communications, The University of Iowa, Iowa City, IA 52242.

Quotations, books of. Quotations can be helpful to a writer or lecturer who needs a succinct introduction to his material. They also can be used to lend authority to points made within a piece.

Books of quotations include *Bartlett's Familiar Quotations* (considered the classic work in this field), *The Dictionary of Biographical Quotation, Great Quotations, Great Quotes from African Americans; The International Thesaurus of Quotations, The Quotable Woman, A Treasury of Religious Quotaions* and *The Writer's Quotation Book*.

Quotations references are subdivided either by subject or by speaker/writer. Other titles can be found listed under "Quotations" in the *Subject Guide to Books In Print*.

Quotes. (*See Figure 40.*) This term can be used to refer either to the words enclosed in quotation marks or to the quotation marks themselves.

When quoting published material, the writer should be aware of the restrictions imposed by copyright law. Material in the public domain (e.g., government records or publications, works on which the copyright has expired) may be quoted without the publisher's permission, provided the source is given, but quoting of copyrighted material is subject to the copyright owner's approval. (The writer quoting from government publications, though, must be careful about whether the material originated with the government, since federal publications are exempt from copyright restrictions but sometimes incorporate copyrighted material.) The "fair use" provision of the copyright law, however, allows for the direct

FIGURE 39

QUERY LETTER SAMPLE

Ms. Bernadette Carr, Editor*
Weight Watcher's Magazine
149 Fifth Avenue
New York, NY 10011

Dear Ms. Carr:

It happens eventually in the closest of families. For years, you've been dining together at the appointed hour, sharing food, feelings, and conversation—then one day you ring the dinner bell, and nobody comes.

Or worse yet, they straggle in at different hours, all expecting nourishment without communication, and the one special hour of family sharing slowly dissolves into an evening marathon of exits and entrances. Tommy has a basketball game, Jill works evenings at McDonald's, your husband has racquetball court time, and you are left staring glumly at a four-pound roast beef for one.

My proposed article describes this phenomenon, which I call the "midlife meal crisis," in about 2,500 words. Titled "COPING WITH THE STAGGERED DINNER HOUR," the piece details the problem with various examples, and provides ways of circumventing the situation. It will cover aspects of keeping family togetherness intact; shopping, planning and cooking for staggered diners; coping with "no-shows"; and how to avoid being the kitchen slave while the troops come and go.

I have published many articles in SEVENTEEN MAGAZINE, and also write frequently for NEWSDAY, MIAMI HERALD, CHICAGO TRIBUNE and various other publications. I am including some published samples, and I'd be willing to do the proposed piece for you on spec, since we have never worked together before.

Thanks for your time and interest.

Very truly yours,

Judy Loveless
Judy Loveless

---

*The current editor-in-chief of *Weight Watchers* is Lee Haiken and the magazine is now at 360 Lexington Ave., Eleventh Floor, New York, NY 10017. This writer's letterhead, of course, carried her address and phone number.

FIGURE 40

QUOTES
Glen Evans

*T*he professional nonfiction writer makes use of three necessary techniques when doing an article or book: anecdote, quotation, and exposition. I'm concerned here with quotations, or quotes, as a fundamental tool in the arsenal of the serious writer.

Quotation marks indicate that the words the writer includes between them have been borrowed from someone else—an expert, an authority in a particular field, a celebrity. You must, however, learn to choose and use only those quotes that will make your article or book more exciting, more informative, less obscure.

Quotes are an effective way to present your story in human terms. They're especially good when they 1) describe the action more vividly or accurately than you could yourself; 2) answer questions about the speaker's personality; and 3) give a sense of immediacy and credibility to the story.

The best way I know to ensure accuracy when you're interviewing someone for information (whether in person or by telephone) is the tape recorder, that convenience you can buy for about $25.

I try to contact subjects beforehand, either in person, on the telephone, or in writing. I get their permission to either record or not as the interview is being scheduled.

When you contact a possible interviewee, you should include the following so he understands fully your mission: who you are, for whom you're doing the interview, the purpose of the interview, why you're asking that specific person and how you went about selecting him, and whether the interviewee has prepublication editing rights. (There are instances when the interview will be anonymous and confidential, without attribution.)

There's a suction-cup gadget you can use with your tape recorder by affixing it to your phone to record telephone conversations; it costs only $2–$3 at most Radio Shack retail stores. The same stores also have a recording device that hooks up and ties in the recorder and telephone and costs roughly $20. The latter is more permanent and also more reliable than the suction-cup device.

Always advise the telephone interviewee that you are recording the conversation for factual accuracy. Credibility depends upon factual correctness, completeness, and relevance—written, of course, with taste, fairness, and professionalism.

You can still edit, condense, and correct bad English. Just be true to what your interviewee is saying. Don't change his meaning. And, above all, don't use his comments out of context.

There are instances where you'll be interviewing a particular kind of person whose colorful speech is grammatically awkward. To provide readers with a credible picture of such a person, say a Brooklyn dockworker, retain his words and manner of speaking whenever possible. If he uses "ain't," so be it. If he says "Old Benny just bust out cryin'," let it stand. Select, reject, thin, even transpose the order of your quotes where it's necessary, but don't sacrifice color and realistic characterization simply for good English.

FIGURE 40 (CONTINUED)

The writer's duty, to the interviewee and to the reader, is to present the person being interviewed accurately. That's why writers like Studs Terkel and Oscar Lewis have been so successful with their oral histories.

To sum up, use a quote when you need the voice of authority or when someone's way of saying something is important to the clarity, color, or meaning of your story. Use a tape recorder when you want to be certain you've got that source's words down accurately. There is "sell" value in good, solid quotes.

A parting caveat: Back up your tape recording with note-taking. It's good insurance against the recorder malfunctioning or a tape breaking down.

Glen Evans is the author of nonfiction books such as *The Encyclopedia of Suicide* and numerous magazine articles. He is a past president of the American Society of Journalists and Authors.

quotation of short passages for criticism, teaching or research purposes.

There is no set number of words or sentences an author may quote from another's copyrighted work without permission. Traditionally, however, writers using only a few sentences from a long work have simply attributed the source of the material in their own manuscripts. (Since poems and songs are so short, permission must be requested before excerpting from them.)

When writing a publisher for permission to quote, it is courteous, as well as expedient, to include a self-addressed, stamped envelope for his reply.

Quotes from printed material must be reproduced exactly as they appear on the page. Words may be omitted with the use of ellipsis points—as long as the context is not changed—and incorrect spelling or usage may be acknowledged by placing *(sic)* after the word or phrase in question.

When quoting material from a live interview or speech, the writer faces the decision of whether to correct faulty grammar or insert words for the sake of logic. To avoid the risk of misquoting, the writer can either paraphrase the person's remarks (leaving out quotation marks) or tape the entire interview to ensure an accurate record of it. When using only some of the interview, the writer must be careful to avoid quoting out of context and misrepresenting the speaker's idea.

Quotations can add authority to an article, but the writer must learn to decide when a quote would enhance his work and when too many would detract from it. (*See: Attribution; Copyright; Fair Use; Libel; Plagiarism.*)

Radio commercials. Advertising copywriting for radio is concise and colorful. Using short phrases, it appeals to the senses of the listener through well-chosen adjectives and verbal images. Repetition, a conversational tone and a central theme are fundamental to successful copy.

Finished copy must meet certain format specifications. It must be typed, double-spaced, on a continuity form. This form also includes the references to music or sound effects to be used, the name of the client, the length of the commercial, and the first and last dates the commercial will be broadcast. The copywriter makes liberal use of punctuation: Dashes and commas indicate pauses; exclamation points and underlining, emphasis. Copy for the air never includes abbreviations. (A sample script appears in Figure 41.)

Before a spot is taped or read on the air, the writer times his work by reading it aloud. At this stage, he includes phonetic spellings—or any spellings that are more logical—for words that are difficult to pronounce. Commercials most often last either sixty seconds (which can accommodate 120-160 words) or thirty seconds (60-80 words).

Most of the necessary information is supplied by the client's account executive, but a writer may wish to consult the client's print ads, other printed information on the product, or the client himself. Dictionaries or handbooks of pronunciation are also helpful, especially with foreign words and proper names. (*See: Radio drama; Television commercials.*)

Radio copywriting. The key characteristics of a successful copywriter are organization and the ability to work quickly without losing creativity or imagination.

Copywriters work either full time or part time. Some begin working while still in college, although larger radio stations usually require a college degree and two years' experience in the radio field as prerequisites for filling the position. Smaller stations that do not require the full-time services of a copywriter will sometimes hire a person to perform a combination of tasks, e.g., copywriter-traffic (getting advertisements written, scheduled, delivered on time) and copywriter-producer.

An aspiring copywriter should take a résumé and copy samples to an interview. During the interview, it is not uncommon for the interviewer to ask the writer to create radio copy on the spot.

A freelance copywriter can earn from $20 to $100 per script or $200 to $400 per week at part-time copywriting depending on where they're located. (*See: Advertising copywriters; Radio drama.*)

Radio drama. Nearly dead in the U.S. since the advent of TV, radio drama

FIGURE 41

RADIO COMMERCIAL SCRIPT

Client <u>Delta Air Lines</u> Title <u>Bobsled</u> Spot No. <u>5729R</u>
Date <u>10/18/89</u> Job No. <u>DLASCHR92787</u> Type _____ Length <u>:60</u>

SFX: (Wind blowing, Coyote Howling)
Man: (Deadpan) Mildred?
Wife: (Obedient, Gladys Kravitz type)
Yes dear?
Man: Have you noticed anything unusual about this ski resort?
Wife: Like what?
Man: Like we're the only people here.
Wife: We are?
Man: And the ski slopes . . .
Wife: Yes?
Man: They're not sloped.
Wife: They're not?
Man: And the ski lift?
Wife: Uh-huh.
Man: You have to feed it to make it work.
SFX: (Cow moos)
Wife: Oh silly, that's not the ski lift . . . that's the free limo that picked us up at the airport.
Man: Mildred?
Wife: Yes dear.
Man: Didn't we agree to buy a Dream Vacation ski package from Delta?

Wife: Well, yes dear . . . but then I heard about this place. (Proudly) It's probably the best-kept secret in the Sierras.
Man: But I know why they kept it a secret, Mildred.
Wife: Ohhh . . .
Man: You see there's no snow anywhere . . .
Anncr: This winter, give your spirits a lift. Call Delta for a Dream Vacation Ski package to Utah, Colorado, New England, the Sierras, Canada, or Europe.
SFX: (Wind blowing)
Wife: Cheer up dear. Tomorrow we're going bobsledding.
Man: Mildred.
Wife: Yeah?
Man: Bob looks kind of old.
Wife: Yeah, I hope he can pull us both.
Man: Ohhh . . .
Singers: DELTA, WE LOVE TO FLY AND IT SHOWS.

is making something of a comeback, largely due to funding from arts councils, private foundations and interest in public broadcast circles. The leading domestic exponents are the CBS Mystery Theatre, the National Radio Theatre, and NPR (National Public Radio) Playhouse. In addition, religious broadcasters rely extensively on inspirational radio plays: The country's oldest continuing series are *Unshackled,* produced by the Pacific Garden Mission, and *Heartbeat Theatre,* produced by the Salvation Army.

While radio drama of the so-called Golden Age was almost exclusively commercial, the current burst of activity is virtually unlimited in subject matter, approach, tone, atmosphere and audience. It is particularly well suited to humor and expressionist fantasy. The medium itself offers both opportunities and limitations for a writer: Because the length of a production is usually only fifteen or thirty minutes, complexity of plot and depth of characters are limited; but within seconds, the radio dramatist can transport his characters to a distant area or a time in the future or past.

Radio is the most evocative of dramatic forms and arguably the most involving—hence the phrase "theater of the mind" so frequently applied to it. In a nonvisual form almost all key action must be relayed through the dialogue. Still, advanced electronics have enabled "sound texturing," i.e., the blend of dialogue, sound and music, to convey the total impression. Some writers see radio as an opportunity to pen uninterrupted discussions, but sophisticated novel-like plotting and rapid scene shifting have been tried successfully.

Because of the comparatively low expense of radio productions, producers have more leeway to experiment with new writers. Authors who have written for radio include Arthur Miller, Edward Albee, John Gardner, Arthur Kopit, David Mamet, Harold Pinter, Tom Stoppard, Samuel Beckett, Max Frisch, Bertholt Brecht, Friedrich Duerrenmatt and Eugene Ionesco. Seminal figures in U.S. radio drama writing are Norman Corwin, Arch Oboler, humorist Stan Freberg, and Lucille Fletcher, whose *Sorry Wrong Number* is to radio drama what *The Necklace* is to the short story.

Pay for dramatic radio scripts varies from as little as $75 to as much as $2,000, depending on length and buyer. (*See: Figure 42; Religious broadcasting; Soap opera, writing for; Unities.*)

Radio terms. (*See individual entries under the headings: Across the board; Adlib; Affiliate; Announcement; Availability list; Cart; Continuity; Co-op copy; Daybook; Donut; Double spotting; Down and under; Dub; Fact sheet; Federal Communications Commission; Hiatus; I.D./ station I.D.; Make-good; Open-end transcription; Outcue; Participation; Plug; Preferred time/prime time; Prestige copy; Primary listening area; Program log; Promo; Public service announcement; Punch; Remote pickup/remote; ROS; Saturation; Script; Service; Signature; Sound effects (SFX); Spec; Spot; Stand by; Start date/stop date; Station rep.; Tag; TFN; Time signal; Traffic; TWX; Up full.*)

Radio, writing for. (*See: Radio commercials; Radio copywriting; Radio drama.*)

Ragtime. A style of dance music of Negro origin characterized by syncopation. Coming into its own about 1910, this style of music was the forerunner of Jazz and Swing.

Raison d'être. French for "reason for existing" or "justification for existence."

The phrase may be used to describe the motivation, purpose or primary goal of literary characters. For instance, pursuing and killing the great white whale is Captain Ahab's raison d'être in *Moby Dick*. (*See: Motivation.*)

Rap. A style of black American popular music that originated in New York in the mid-1970s. Devoid of melody, rap contains rhymes performed to rhythmic accompaniment. This "chanted street poetry" contains lyrics heavy on social state-

FIGURE 42

RADIO DRAMA SCRIPT SAMPLE

RRT XMAS SHOW 12/1/89 (REV.)

(SFX: DOOR OPENING, FEET TROOPING OUT, DOOR CLOSING.)

(JOEY: ?)

T. BIX

AND SO, THE RIDERS ARE OFF ON THEIR MERRY WAY. ALL ACROSS TUMBLEWEED VALLEY THE SNOW IS FALLING, THE THERMOMETER IS DROPPING, AND SPIRITS ARE RISING. EVERYWHERE THE MILK OF HUMAN KINDNESS IS OVERFLOWING . . . EVERYWHERE, THAT IS, EXCEPT IN THE SMALL BACK ROOM OF THE DRYGULCH SALOON. HERE THERE ARE NO CANDLES IN THE WINDOW, NO WREATHS ON THE DOOR, NO FESTIVE TREE, NOR DECORATIONS OF ANY KIND . . . BECAUSE HERE IS THE LAIR OF A MAN NEVER KNOWN TO SIT STILL IN A ROOM, AND HIS NAME IS SLOCUM.

(SFX: ADDING MACHINE)

SLOCUM (TO HIMSELF)

(LAUGHS) NOT BAD . . . NOW LET'S SEE WHAT THE USED NINTENDOES WILL BRING IN.

(SFX: KNOCK ON DOOR)

CHARLIE. (THROUGH DOOR)

IT'S ME, BOSS!

SLOCUM (CALLING OUT)

C'MON IN, CHARLIE.

(SFX: DOOR OPENS, CHARLIE ENTERS, DOOR CLOSES.)

CHARLIE

MERRY CHRISTMAS, BOSS.

SLOCUM

CHRISTMAS, BAH! JUST ANOTHER EXCUSE TO PUT YOUR HAND IN SOMEBODY ELSE'S POCKET. HMM, MAYBE IT AIN'T SO BAD AFTER ALL. HA HA HA!

This radio script page was provided by the WVXU Network, producers of Riders' Radio Theater, and reprinted with permission from Mammoth Radio Pictures.

EDITOR'S NOTE: This script was prepared for a live performance. Most radio drama scripts use a format in which speakers' names are typed to the left, and dialogue is typed in caps and lower case, as in the radio commercial script sample.

ments. The first known rap group is Sugar Hill Gang. Another early group, Run D.M.C. is considered the epitome of the genre by some followers. Current artists include Dr. Dre, Warren G and Snoop Doggy Dogg.

Readability formulas. Readability formulas indicate the difficulty of written material according to the skill (by school grade level) needed to understand it. They are necessary because of the inconsistency between the percentage of people who have completed a given grade level and the reading ability of those same persons. For example, even though 75 percent of adults in the U.S. have graduated from high school, not all of them can read at twelfth-grade level. (It is estimated, in fact, that more than half cannot.) Further, a reader is apt to misunderstand—or even ignore—material that is too difficult. Popular magazines must maintain fairly low readability levels because their business depends on sales—which in turn depend on readability.

One readability standard, the Flesch formula, determines a passage's level of difficulty by the number of syllables per one hundred words and the average number of words per sentence. The Dale-Chall formula, which also considers the average number of words per sentence, incorporates a list of three thousand familiar words into the calculations. The percentage of words that do not appear on the list determines word familiarity. Factors used in the Farr-Jenkins-Paterson formula are the number, per one hundred words, of one-syllable words, and the average number of words per sentence. The Danielson-Bryon formula determines readability by counting spaces between words as well as characters per sentence.

The Cloze test is a standard that involves a reader in the actual testing process. For the test, every fifth word of a passage is deleted, and the reader is instructed to fill in the blanks left by those words. The writing is judged readable to the extent that the substituted words are accurate.

The Fog Index is another formula that uses word length and sentence length as variables, as described by its creator, Robert Gunning, in his book, *The Technique of Clear Writing*.

Gunning advised writers: "Use the (formula) as a guide after you have written, but not as a pattern before you write. Good writing must be alive; don't kill it with system." (*See: Easy Listening Formula; Fog Index*.)

Reader identification. This term is used primarily to describe the process by which a reader projects himself into a work of fiction, associating himself with the adventures, conflicts, desires, feelings and responses of the characters in the story. Damon Knight explains in *Creating Short Fiction*: "Identification with the central character is strongly desired by readers of commercial fiction. A woman reading a gothic romance wants to imagine herself as the heroine and live through the latter's perils vicariously. A man reading a western story wants to imagine himself tall in the saddle." Strong reader identification in fiction is achieved by providing the reader with strong, believable characters involved in a significant conflict in pursuit of a goal. Many commercial magazines that publish short fiction actually *require* that the protagonist and setting of a short story are such that the magazine's readers can easily identify with them.

Reader identification—through choice of subject matter—is important in nonfiction writing as well. Peggy Teeters, author of *How to Get Started in Writing*, says, "Keep reader identification in mind when you are writing; it will help you sell your manuscripts. Whenever the reader can nod his head and say, 'That's the way it was' or 'Hey, that's what happened to me!' you're on your way to a sale."

Reader (or first reader). (*See: Book publishing jobs, editorial; First readers*.)

Readers' Guide to Periodical Literature. An index to general-interest magazines, in which magazine contents are categorized by subject and author. The number of magazines indexed in this publication varies; currently it is 240.

The Readers' Guide is published monthly. Large libraries subscribe to it; small libraries, children's departments of libraries and school libraries may instead have the abridged version of this index available. Most libraries have *The Readers' Guide* on computer database for easy referencing.

The Readers' Guide has been published since 1901. (*See:* Abridged Readers' Guide to Periodical Literature; *Periodicals, directories of.*)

Real names, using. (*See: Names, using real.*)

Ream. From the Arabic word for bundle—*rizmah*—a ream is a quantity of paper, usually considered to be five hundred sheets. (Some paper manufacturers and printers designate 480 sheets as a ream.) The writer may find it more convenient and economical to buy paper by the ream from a stationery store rather than purchasing it in smaller quantities in college bookstores or variety stores.

Recordkeeping. Because a writer must attend to the business side as well as the artistic aspects of his work, business records are important. They prepare him for annual income tax filing (as well as possible audit), and keep for future reference data such as market information and the status of manuscripts. With this information documented, the writer can keep accurate track of sales, expenses, marketing efforts and other data the I.R.S. may require the writer to produce, if it challenges him. Records are also important for learning how long it takes to do certain kinds of jobs, what kinds of freelance work are most profitable, etc.

A filing system used by many article writers, for example, contains the following categories: *in process, current manuscripts out* and *business record*. The *in process* file comprises articles being written or queried on, and file folders containing notes to be used in writing the pieces.

Current manuscripts out lists the markets submitted to, postage spent, the article's title, date sent, and the date the article was either returned or sold.

An annual *business record* is kept on purchases of paper and supplies, postage, equipment upkeep, depreciation, illustrations and other costs, rent, telephone, electricity and transportation. Of course, receipts must be kept on all tax-deductible expenses.

Fiction writers keep similar files on work-in-progress.

To supplement a filing system, a writer can use a wall, desk or computer calendar with space for noting appointments, deadlines, telephone calls and work schedules. (*See: Query; Taxes.*)

Additional information: "Business of Writing," *Writer's Market; Guide to Record Retention Requirements.*

Recto page. A page appearing on the right side of a book. All numbered recto pages have odd numbers. (*See: Verso page.*)

Red herring. A false clue in a mystery designed to throw the reader off the track. (*See: False plant; Plant; Plot.*)

Redundancy. The use of more words or phrases than are necessary to communicate an idea; needless repetition.

Redundancy is a common problem in the work of beginning writers who believe such reiteration will produce greater emphasis. In other cases, writers express an idea in both positive and negative terms when only one statement is ordinarily needed to convey the message.

Stating an idea once, clearly and concisely, should suffice. In a long piece of writing, however, it is advisable to provide the reader with a summary at the end, highlighting the major points of the piece. (*See: Readability formulas; Tautology.*)

Reggae. A music form combining Jamaican calypso music with rock influences in a distinctive 4/4 repeating rhythm pattern. Lyrics in reggae are linked to social, economic and religious influences of the Jamaican and other black peoples.

Regional book publishing. Some book publishers market to a portion of the U.S. instead of to the entire country or world. Finding a regional publisher is an advantage for an author whose book idea appeals only to readers in a limited geographic area. *Literary Market Place* contains a section of book publishers arranged by geographic location.

Regional magazine. A category of magazine that covers a specific geographic region, such as an area of a country, a city or a state. Numerous regional magazines are in existence, and their editorial requirements vary.

Brian Vachon, author of *Writing for Regional Publications*, has categorized regionals into five groups. *Large city magazines* are concerned with either a city or a city's events and issues; they sometimes cover the surrounding area as well. Included are arts and restaurant reviews and accounts of muckraking and controversial articles. *Positive publications*, which can be either privately or government-owned, emphasize the favorable aspects of a region. The *newspaper insert*, or Sunday magazine, is able to offer the reader the most timely information. *Environmental magazines*, many of which are sponsored by government agencies or nature organizations, devote themselves to conservation and other natural-resource issues. *Guide and tour books* are the regional publications that reflect an evident sense of pride in an area. Their audiences are made up of tourists and visitors unfamiliar with the region a given book covers.

A regional magazine can confirm the positive emotions a reader has for his home, console a reader with nostalgic feelings for a former home, or inspire a person who hopes someday to live in the magazine's locale. Not all subscribers to a given regional publication live in the area the magazine covers; e.g., many people in the continental U.S. read *Alaska* magazine.

A beginning writer can acquire valuable experience working for a regional, and the successful freelancer is one who researches a magazine and shows an awareness of its needs in his query letter.

Some examples of regional magazines are *Yankee, New Hampshire Profiles, Los Angeles Magazine,* and *Charlotte.* Many publications belong to the City and Regional Magazine Association, which sponsors annual awards for editorial excellence.

Pay rates for writers are usually low; privately owned magazines with large circulations pay best. Individual listings in *Writer's Market* indicate specific dollar amounts. (*See: City magazine.*)

Rejection slip. The written communication from an editor informing the writer that his submitted work has not been accepted. The rejection slip can take any of several forms, including everything from a printed form on a $3'' \times 5''$ card to a personal letter. It is accompanied by the returned manuscript and sent in the self-addressed, stamped envelope (SASE) the writer included in the original submission.

Manuscripts are rejected for any number of reasons, which may have nothing to do with the value of the manuscript itself. The editor may have just bought something similar; he may have just assigned the idea to another writer; he may have published another story on or related to the topic too recently to take it on again. Few editors have the time to include these reasons—or detailed criticism if the article or story *is* faulty—so the writer should not expect more than a short printed note of rejection. If the editor does take the time to offer some comment, the writer can take note of the reason and apply it to his future writing or marketing efforts. And if the editor does add a hand-written note at the bottom of the rejection slip indicating a willingness to look at other ideas, the writer should take that encouragement literally.

It is important to remember that a rejection is only one editor's opinion regarding one submission. A rejection does not mean every editor will refuse the writer's work, or that this editor will not buy a different piece from the writer at some other time. A writer guards against rejection's sometimes debilitating sting by always keeping several works in the mail simultaneously. This way, all of the writer's hopes aren't carried in one submission. Also, as a writer researches and writes a piece, he should note additional appropriate markets beyond his first choice. This gives the writer a list of other places to send a rejected manuscript or idea. Some writers make it a habit to have the rejected work back in the mail within forty-eight hours of its return.

A writer need not give up after five, ten or even fifty rejections, as the story "I Can Climb Higher Than You," by Jesse Stuart, shows. It was rejected forty-seven times before being accepted; it then went on to win the title "Best Story of the Year" from one of the same magazines that had previously rejected it. (*See: Reporting time on manuscripts.*)

Relief song. A song in a musical that provides a tone that contrasts with that of the previous scene. A *respite,* one category of relief song, gives the audience a sense of relief from the tension caused by the story's events—"Gee, Officer Krupke!" in *West Side Story* interjects a comical tone into the tragic story. In contrast, a *novelty number* shoots energy into a placid series of events. "Once in Love with Amy" is a novelty number in *Where's Charley?* A third kind of relief song, the *interlude song*, is inserted between events, such as "Poor Professor Higgins" in *My Fair Lady.* (*See: Musical.*)

Religious broadcasting. Radio and TV programs, stations and networks that specialize in religious material offer opportunities for writers to use their skills in various capacities. In this field, staff positions are more abundant than freelance jobs. The writer who becomes involved in writing for the religious electronic media will most likely be paid less than one who writes for secular radio and TV, since many religious stations depend on listener contributions rather than commercial advertising for their operating funds. Staffs of religious stations are generally small; consequently, staff writers are sometimes called upon to perform various duties.

Staff positions at religious broadcast stations include reporter, script editor, announcer, assignment editor, newswriter, camera person, programming planner, continuity writer and advertising (or public service announcement) writer. Writers are hired for these jobs either on a full-time or part-time basis. At small Christian commercial stations, the norm is to employ no more than one full-time writer.

Freelance writers are most often used in religious broadcasting to create dramatic scripts for radio. Radio drama for this market is religious in theme and conforms to the goals and needs of the particular station that it is written for. Before submitting a script, the writer should become familiar with the nature of the program and should know what geographic area(s) it reaches.

The Christian Broadcasting Network, located in Virginia Beach, Virginia, produces religious drama in soap opera style. Other religious broadcasters include Moody Bible Institute, National Christian Network and the Bible Broadcasting Network. (*See: Religious writing.*)

Religious writing. The field of religion offers writers many opportunities to publish through periodicals, books and instructional materials.

More than three hundred major magazines in the U.S. emphasize religion. They can be grouped into the following categories: denominational, nondenominational, family, journals of opinion, magazines for church leaders, inspirational, official publications of national organizations and Christian comic and picture books. Examples of major religious magazines are *Catholic Digest, Christianity Today, Guideposts, Hadassah* and *Moody Monthly.*

The trend in this field is toward a human-interest tone. Today's editors look for articles of a practical nature that are less dogmatic than those of the past, and generally eschew articles that are preachy or saccharine. Controversial topics are now accepted in fiction and given in-depth treatment in articles. In spite of these changes, however, religious overtones are still present in the magazines.

A religion writer must know his readers thoroughly, because each market is specialized and holds sacred a common set of beliefs, values and taboos. It is important to become familiar with the publication as well; some small religious magazines have formats to be followed by the writer (e.g., number of typed characters per line) because they are limited in staff, time and money for manuscript preparation. Writers should be aware that not all the religious magazines are published solely for nationwide audiences. Some—especially publications for organization members—are published regionally as well.

Fees paid to writers by religious magazines are generally lower than those paid by other types of consumer magazines.

Trends in religious book publishing are reflected by the categories of books published, which in turn are influenced by factors such as Sunday school lessons. The semiannual religious book issues of *Publishers Weekly*—usually in February and September—are indicators of trends. Similarly, *Subject Guide to Books In Print* lists books in the religious field, under "Bible—Appreciation," "Christian Life," "Christianity—Psychology," "Faith," "God," "Jewish Religious Education" and "Jewish Theology."

Royalties in the religious publishing field may vary from the standard trade royalty of 5-15 percent of list price to 5-10 percent of the net receipts; and advances may be limited to a few hundred dollars at some smaller houses.

Publications used in Sunday schools and parochial schools make up an important segment of materials used for religious instruction. Although teacher's books, study books, workbooks, games and time lines all require writers, the freelance writer finds the most frequent opportunities in the church school take-home paper. This type of publication is a magazine or leaflet intended to reinforce a student's spiritual values during the week, between class meetings.

Materials for Jewish religious instruction include minicourses, games, songbooks, plays, teacher's manuals and task cards; freelancers may tailor their material to one of several age groups, from preschoolers to high school students. Educators in Catholic schools use religion-centered filmstrips, films, textbooks, duplicating books, pamphlets and trade journals. (*See: Audiovisual communication; Juveniles, writing for; Religious broadcasting.*)

Additional information: *Religious Publishing and Communications; Writer's Market.*

Remainder. In book publishing, remainders are copies of a book that are slow to sell. A remainder book company sometimes purchases leftover stock from the publisher at a considerably reduced price. In this situation, the author receives either a reduced royalty, or—if the publisher has sold the remainder stock at below manufacturing cost—no royalty. These arrangements are detailed in the author's book contract.

Remote pickup/remote. A program or commercial broadcast live from a site other than the studio.

Repetitive stress injury. Also known as *carpal tunnel syndrome.* A muscular disorder caused by compression of the median nerve as it runs through the carpal tunnel—a bracelet-like bone structure in the wrist. Triggered by repeated flexing or extending of the wrist, tendons in the carpal tunnel swell and pinch the nerve as it branches to the thumb and first three fingers. Symptoms include burning pain, decreased hand dexterity and, in some cases, paralysis. Treatments include rest, anti-inflammatory drugs and, occasionally, surgery. The syndrome is common among musicians, athletes, data processors and writers. In the early 1990s, the 185,000 reported cases of RSI accounted for more than half the number of occupational injuries in the U.S.

Reporting time on manuscripts.

Reporting time on manuscripts is commonly acknowledged to be six weeks to two months for magazines and two to three months for book publishers, but the writer should check *Writer's Market* or one of the specialized market books for specifics on individual publishers. For a reply from a literary agent, a writer should allow three weeks to two months; from a literary critic, three weeks for short pieces and two months for a book. If the usual reporting period passes with no reply, the writer should send a letter inquiring about the status of the manuscript; a self-addressed, stamped envelope should accompany the letter. The writer who receives no response at this stage should write again, advising that the manuscript submission has been withdrawn from consideration and that another copy is being submitted elsewhere.

Reprint.

A reprint is a part of a publication, such as an article or chapter, that has been reproduced for use as a separate publication. (This is not to be confused with updated printings of a book, which are also sometimes referred to as reprints.) Publishers offer reprints to their readers free or at minimal cost. Another term for reprint, which is used in literary and scholarly publications, is *offprint*. Scholarly reprint publishers may reprint entire books of narrow appeal (usually from university presses) in small, limited editions. Book publishers also sell reprint rights to other publishers, book clubs, etc. (*See: Transcripts of broadcasts.*)

Reprint rights.

This refers to the right granted by the copyright owner/author to a magazine to reprint an article, poem or story after it has already appeared in another publication. Reprint rights are also called second serial rights, especially when they refer to a portion of a book that is being sold to a magazine or newspaper for printing after the book is published. If the magazine rights were exercised before publication of the book, they would be first serial rights.

A magazine or newspaper editor would pay less for reprint rights to a piece than for rights to first-time use of original copy in his publication. Markets that will buy reprint rights indicate so in their listings in *Writer's Market.* (*See: Multiple sales; Rights to manuscripts.*)

Reprint, writer's fee for.

When a writer is approached by a magazine publisher who is interested in reprinting one of his published articles, the publisher may make a specific offer or ask the writer to set his own fee. In the latter case, the author usually sets a word rate or article flat fee, which equals a percentage (say, 25-50 percent) of the new publisher's pay rate for an original article as shown in *Writer's Market*. (*See: Self-syndication.*)

Reprise. In a musical, the recurrence of a song that has already been performed. In later uses of a song, the title and the melody remain unchanged, but the lyrics are sometimes altered.

A reprise is a scene in itself. It can advance the plot or explicate character in a short time. In either case, it enhances the story, and its recognition value is a major part of its effect on the audience. "Tonight," from *West Side Story*, is used as a reprise. (*See: Musical.*)

Research aids/techniques. In researching a subject, writers use a wide range of techniques in addition to approaching librarians and consulting traditional reference books. Books in the children's room of a public library, for example, can be helpful because they present material in simplified terms; thus, reading them can familiarize the writer/researcher with topics that are very technical or foreign to him. A special library, which houses material on one subject or a group of related subjects, is conducive to in-depth research, as it offers specialized books and librarians expert in the field.

A writer may find information resources outside the library as well. A home computer and modem allows access to dozens of online informa-

tion services, which house vast stores of reference materials previously only available in libraries. Posting information requests on online bulletin boards—discussion groups devoted to specific topics—can also draw facts and access to experts in that particular field.

Other sources of information include the public relations office of a business, university or museum for the most up-to-date and/or historical information on a topic, while a professional organization leads the researcher to well-respected practitioners for opinions. Similarly, bibliographic items, prefaces and introductions in books can provide the writer with names of people who may be helpful. (Their addresses, if not given in the books, may be listed in directories of specific professions or associations, or in telephone books.) Embassies in Washington, DC are helpful when gathering information about foreign countries. When the writer has located a primary source, he arranges to interview that person, either in person or by telephone.

A newspaper, in either the writer's home town or another city, is another valuable research source; a researcher can write the newspaper's librarian, a department editor or a specialty reporter, any of whom may be able to supply the telephone number of an expert on a subject the paper has written about. The mail survey, a questionnaire that serves as a simultaneous interview of several persons, can be another means of requesting information. Chambers of commerce provide a great deal of printed material, as does the federal government.

Radio and TV talk shows can also

furnish information for the writer. Some programs make transcripts or cassettes available, which the writer may need to validate his source with an editor.

Sometimes a writer can draw on his own experience for information: He may have traveled to the place with which his article is concerned, for example, or have played the sport he is writing about.

As another research tactic, the writer can simply advertise that he is researching a certain topic, choosing either a newspaper or a specialized magazine to reach possible sources. (*See: Database; Directories; Interview; Libraries, information on; Periodicals, indexes to; Primary source; Research services, freelance; Research sources, directories of; Secondary sources; Telephone usage, tactics on; Transcripts of broadcasts.*)

Research by correspondence. A writer may send a request for information to an authority in a field related to his article. This type of letter, which is specific and brief, is addressed to one person by name. The writer either encloses a self-addressed, stamped envelope or offers to reimburse the addressee for postage and photocopying costs. (Government agencies, however, absorb the cost of postage.) To those sources who provided assistance or information, writers sometimes send a short thank-you letter and copies of the finished article after it is published. (*See: Research aids/techniques.*)

Research note-taking. When gathering material from printed sources, writers take time to digest what they read and then note key ideas in their own words. This method gives them an understanding of the material that facilitates their work at the writing stage. (Any ideas that are exceptionally well phrased may, of course, be quoted verbatim, as long as the writer gives credit either in a footnote or in the text itself.)

During the note-taking process, it is essential that the writer take down page numbers, magazine issue numbers, titles of books, the name of the library he is using and other data, so that he can later supply an editor with his sources without a time-consuming search. Some writers prefer using $3'' \times 5''$ cards for these notes; others simply note the sources alongside their references in a notebook on each writing project. If the writer is doing a book, a more detailed bibliography on sources (book title, author, publisher, city of publication, copyright date, etc.) should be compiled as the research is being done. (*See: Interview; Tape recorder.*)

Research services, freelance. Various research jobs are available to freelancers interested in working for others, while writers who need help with their own research can seek out a freelancer for hire.

Freelancers interested in doing research work for others can query universities, public libraries and marketing research firms. University professors sometimes hire researchers from outside the university, while freelance authors can find university graduate students to aid *them* in research. Researchers can sometimes find announcements of freelance research job openings posted on a public library's employee bulletin board.

Places to list freelance research services are *Literary Market Place* and the classified section of *Publishers Weekly.* Rates of pay, which vary with experience, geographic area and nature of the work, range from $5 to $30 per hour; some fees for special jobs are higher.

To find work in genealogy, researchers place ads in the *Genealogical Helper* or inquire at a local library. The genealogical researcher earns from $25 per hour. Genealogists become certified by the Family History Library of the Church of Jesus Christ of Latter Day Saints, 35 Northwest Temple, Salt Lake City, UT 84150. (*See: Directories.*)

Research sources, directories of. Through libraries, writers have access to bibliographies of reference books and other kinds of research sources.

Two sources used regularly by reference librarians, for example, are Sheehy's *Guide to Reference Books* and the *American Reference Books Annual.*

Two books that can lead the writer to other sources are the *Directory of Directories* and the *Guide to American Directories,* which are either arranged by subject matter or have subject cross-indexes.

Writers who want to see what books are currently in print on certain subjects can refer to the *Subject Guide to Books In Print.* If they want to locate the publisher of a specific book whose title or author's name they know, they can refer to *Books In Print.*

If the writer is seeking specialized research material, he may want to refer to the *Research Center Directory* or the *Directory of Special Libraries.*

For research materials that may be in specialized forms, the writer can consult the *Subject Guide to Microforms in Print.* (*See: Celebrity addresses; Database; Periodicals, indexes to.*)

Residual rights. Rights that the copyright owner has retained; or rights that he has sold but may expect to re-own in the future, such as rights that have been transferred and may be returned to him under the copyright law after thirty-five years.

The term *residual rights* also refers to a particular kind of rights owned by performers. These rights provide for performers to be paid for use or sale of their recorded, taped or filmed work; the amount of payment is determined in the performer's contract or the union contract under which he works. For example, a TV producer contracts to use a commercial for a given number of weeks. After the first period has ended, he is given the option to use the commercial for another designated period, but from that point on, he must pay fees, called *residuals,* to the performers.

Resolution and reversal. (*See: Falling action.*)

Restarting your writing. There are several methods of restarting a writing project too lengthy to be completed in one session. Following are three standard practices; individual writers can, of course, invent other methods more personally suitable.

One technique is to stop in the middle of writing an idea or a sentence. At the start of the next writing session, the writer, having this idea in his mind, knows exactly how and where to pick up.

As another way to begin, some writers retype the last page typed in the previous session; this helps remind the writer of the mood and style of his piece.

A third method consists of destroying the last page typed in the previous session, then reconstructing and retyping it from memory. This technique sets the writer's mind, as well as his fingers, in motion.

Restaurant review. A critical account of the writer's experience at a restaurant, written for a newspaper or magazine. The restaurant review usually includes comments on food, service, atmosphere (including other patrons), menu and price.

To qualify for restaurant reviewing, a person must have an appreciation for food and its preparation, have dined out frequently and have an ability to write about food. Knowledge of food may come from professional experience in the food industry, experience preparing fine cuisine at home or study of books in the field. The unpublished reviewer should approach an editor with sample reviews and a letter explaining his interest in restaurant reviewing. (For this first impression, he might review a restaurant that is out of the way and that is not often reviewed.)

A general guide for payment is that the reviewer receives enough to double his dining expenses. Once the freelance reviewer is getting regular assignments from one publication, he is likely to be paid monthly, the payments being based on the average cost of his meals per month.

One way to minimize expenses,

and at the same time get the opportunity to sample several dishes from the menu, is to visit a restaurant with a group of friends or of associates in the food industry. (The latter group could add another dimension to the reviewer's own critical sense.)

An ideal situation for the reviewer is being seated where he will not be observed by the head waiter and where he has a comprehensive view of the room. No matter where his table is located, the reviewer should make it a point to sit with his back to the wall.

To be fair to a restaurant, the critic should visit it at least twice before writing a review. Similarly, good judgment and a keen sense of taste are needed during the meal, so the critic should not overindulge in alcohol.

Because restaurateurs in some cases threaten or take legal action when faced with unfavorable reviews, the reviewer should keep his notes so that he can later prove that his comments were based on the actual situation he encountered.

Writers interested in acquiring more background in the food field and restaurant reviewing should read the works of food writers in major food magazines such as *Gourmet* and *Bon Appetit*; and leading newspaper reviewers in *The New York Times*. (*See: Arts review.*)

Résumé writing, business of. A writer who creates résumés for others can establish a full- or part-time business at home. Earnings, which depend on the writer's geographic location, range from $25 to $500 per résumé.

Résumé writers obtain new clients through newspaper classified advertisements and referrals from clients.

The client schedules an appointment with the writer, at which time he is interviewed and/or asked to fill out a questionnaire. During the interview, the writer gathers information such as what field the client is in, what type of work he is interested in doing, what jobs he has held in the past (and at present), how much education he has, what his military background is (if any), and what his personal history entails (e.g., family, hobbies, memberships, address and telephone number). Based on the information gathered from the interview and/or questionnaire, the writer drafts the résumé, then proofreads the finished product and presents it to the client for a second look. Some writers deliver the finished résumés to the client. Writer Jan A. Noble, Sr., suggests charging a flat fee for all services involved in preparing a résumé.

Regarding the client's initial inquiry, Noble advises: "Tell (the client) that if he is dissatisfied with the résumé, you will refund his money in full. But don't promise anything but a professional résumé prepared confidentially. You can't guarantee that it will get him a job or that it will get him an interview with a particular employer."

A freelance résumé writer can sometimes associate with an employment agency by paying the agency a commission of 5-10 percent for every referral he obtains from them, and/or by making his business card available in the agency's office. Writers interested in working for another person can seek full- or part-time work at commercial résumé services, which advertise in the yellow pages. (*See: Résumés.*)

Résumés. Though all résumés contain the same basic information, they can be divided into categories on the basis of purpose. The *sequential résumé* lists all an employee's previous jobs and the duties performed in each, accompanied by the dates he began and left each, with the most recent job listed first. The *functional résumé*, especially beneficial to employees with little experience or with periods of unemployment, omits dates and details an employee's jobs in terms of accomplishment.

In the *skills résumé*, sections headed by names of skills—such as editing, proofreading and pasteup—that the applicant will bring to a new job, follow the applicant's name and address, which are placed first among the items. Following these two sections are "Education," "Experience," "Personal Background" and "Job Objective." The "Experience" section is where the applicant denotes specific companies or organizations for which he has worked.

The *creative résumé* breaks the rules of standard résumé form and appearance. For example, it could contain artwork, be printed on colored paper or be designed in the form of an advertisement. This type of résumé succeeds only in certain fields. Before using it, the writer should consider whether creativity is appropriate to the field in which he is seeking work.

Finally, the *curriculum vitae* is a kind of résumé that contains, along with the applicant's qualifications for a job, more details about his professional memberships, publications, etc., than does the conventional résumé used in business. It is used to apply for jobs in academe.

(*Curriculum vitae* is a Latin term meaning "the course of one's life or career.")

All résumés should begin with the employee's name, address and telephone number. (Including an alternate telephone number where a message can be taken gives the applicant the advantage of ensuring that the employers will be able to reach him.) Sometimes personal data, such as family situation, health status, height and weight, are included as well, if such information strengthens the job-seeker's candidacy.

Stating salary requirements on a résumé is detrimental, since it can decrease negotiating power at the interview stage. Similarly, names and addresses of references are better replaced by a strong letter of recommendation sent along with the résumé, or a statement that they are available on request.

Indicating a career or job objective is a practice that, though instituted recently, is becoming accepted as standard. The applicant includes this information (usually in a short phrase, such as "Reference librarian") below the heading "Objective" or "Employment Objective." This heading is placed after the applicant's personal data and before information on his work experience, which is followed by a description of his educational background. If the applicant would accept employment in any of several jobs, he may list all the jobs, in order of preference, under one of these two headings.

The applicant who is qualified to work in more than one field may wish to prepare a separate résumé for each field, according to "Merchandising Your Job Talents," a U.S.

Department of Labor publication. This tactic can also be helpful when the applicant will approach different kinds of institutions that seek different kinds of credentials. ("Merchandising Your Job Talents" is available in those public libraries that are depositories for U.S. Government publications. *(See: Figures 43 and 44; Résumé writing, business of.)*

Additional information: *Resume Writing: A Comprehensive, How-to-Do-It Guide; What Color Is Your Parachute?; Who's Hiring Who;* and *Martin's Magic Formula for Getting the Right Job.*

Retainer. A retainer is a working arrangement by which a writer is paid a fee at regular intervals but works for the client irregularly, on an as-needed basis. The client could be a business, a not-for-profit organization, a politician, a professional association or the sponsor of a special event.

With the guaranteed income of a retainer, the freelance writer can be discriminating in accepting writing assignments from other sources. (On the other hand, the writer on retainer is at the client's beck and call.) Retainers give the writer first-hand knowledge of certain businesses or organizations, which can sometimes be applied to freelance articles. The writer should, of course, be concerned about potential conflicts of interest in his other writing jobs.

Pay from a retainer client is usually received in monthly or semi-monthly installments, having been originally established as a flat fee for a set period of time, as outlined in a letter of agreement. Rates depend on the writer's ability and experience, and the field the client is in.

FIGURE 43

RÉSUMÉ: SKILLS

Shirlie Jane Doe

24 Mockingbird Terrace   Single—willing to
Cincinnati, Ohio 45331   travel and relocate

Telephone: (513)000-0000   Available immediately
or leave message 000-0000

JOB OBJECTIVE: Field of personnel (selection and recruit-
ment nontechnical personnel)

WORK EXPERIENCE: The Pyramid Manufacturing
Company
July 25, 1964 to   1234 XYZ Street
April 1, 1981   Finneytown Hill,
Cincinnati, Ohio 45201

Selected personnel for executive offices. Developed a training-grant program to guarantee an inflow of competent secretaries. Cost saving of $15,000 the first six months, increased savings thereafter.

Worked with our public relations department and local press on series of articles about our employees. Result: A sharp drop in turnover and an equally sharp rise in the number of job candidates. We ran no want ads during this period. Money saved from the advertising budget was used to implement the program mentioned above.

June 25, 1958 to   Acme Temporary Placements
July 25, 1964   5678 ABC Street
Cincinnati, Ohio 45201

Client sales. One of my clients was Pyramid. They negotiated with my employer when an opening developed in their personnel department.

EDUCATION: Walnut Hills High School, graduated 1954
University of Cincinnati, 1954-56
University of Miami, Coral Gables, Florida,
1956-1958 (B.A. in English)
University of Cincinnati Evening College
(personnel courses including tests and
measurements, techniques of interviewing,
and communications)

FIGURE 44

RÉSUMÉ: FUNCTIONAL

NAME: Smith, John David

ADDRESS: 606 Main Street, Big City, Maine 04330

TELEPHONE: (207)000-0000
　　　　　　　Message can be taken at (207)000-1111

JOB OBJECTIVE: If you're familiar with the employer's terminology, use it.

EDUCATION:　　　　　　　　Whichever of these two categories is
　　　　　　　　　　　　　　the more impressive should be listed
　　　　　　　　　　　　　　directly under the job objective.

WORK EXPERIENCE:　　　　　If you hold a degree, you won't need
　　　　　　　　　　　　　　to waste space on high school back-
　　　　　　　　　　　　　　ground; unless, of course, you were
　　　　　　　　　　　　　　valedictorian or class president.

SPECIAL SKILLS/ATTRIBUTES:

This is the section where your résumé should be different. Think about the job requirements and list those skills/attributes that show how to meet them.

Each item mentioned here won a job interview for the person who listed it:
• knowledge of a foreign language (tell which one)
• knowledge of sign language
• knowledge of procedures for federal grant requests
• knowledge of a computer language (tell which one)
• ability to type sixty words per minute
• knowledge of shorthand
• knowledge of cardiopulmonary resuscitation (CPR)
• ability to handle ⅔-axle vehicles
• willingness to travel or relocate
• have own transportation (One young man mentioned five years of accident-free driving and won a job.)

REFERENCES: If you decide to use them, be sure you include full addresses and phone numbers. Also, indicate that you have the permission of the person listed.

NOTE: Author Phyllis Martin reports that "The candidates I work with are outstandingly successful when they attach a letter of reference instead of listing references. My guess is that the employer responds favorably because this practice saves so much work for him or her."

The résumé examples on this page and the page that precedes it are reprinted by permission of the author, Phyllis Martin, from her book: *Martin's Magic Formula for Getting the Right Job,* published by St. Martin's Press. Copyright © 1987 by Phyllis Martin.

Retirement and the freelance writer. Unlike the employee, who is compensated by his employer, the full-time freelance writer must anticipate retirement and take the initiative in providing for it. The federal government has devised two plans for setting aside retirement funds for self-employed people.

Under the Keogh Act (the Self-Employed Individuals Tax Retirement Act) of 1962, a self-employed person is entitled to establish a retirement fund that is tax free until he withdraws it—presumably at retirement, when his tax bracket is lower. Specifically, this law allows for a writer to set aside as much as 20 percent of his net annual income, the maximum allowed being $30,000 per year, in an IRS-approved account. This savings is tax deductible for that year. Funds must remain in the account until the owner reaches age 59½; the owner must begin to draw on them when he reaches age 70½. In addition, he is not obligated to deposit money every year. Penalties for early withdrawal are the discontinuance of tax-free accumulation of interest and a tax penalty.

For people wishing to invest, various plans are available through banks, savings and loan associations, and other financial institutions. (*See: Social security.*)

Additional information: IRS Publication 334, Tax Guide for Small Business.

Returns. A term that refers to books that a bookstore was unable to sell and has sent back to the publisher. One type of arrangement between publisher and bookstore is that a bookstore may receive full credit on books that are returned during the first year after they were bought.

When returning paperback books, the wholesale distributor keeps the books' pages, which it sometimes sells as paper pulp, returning only the covers. When dealing with hardcover books, the bookstore returns the complete product. Many publishers also offer a "self-remaindering" program, whereby the bookstores clip a designated portion of the dust jacket or an inside page and mark the book down for sale in their stores. The clipped portions are then returned to the publisher in exchange for a small amount of credit.

The *reserve against returns* clause of an author's contract denotes that the publisher can estimate the amount of returns he expects on sales to bookstores and pay the author's royalties based on that estimate. Returns on a first novel, for example, could run as high as 50 percent. If more sales (fewer returns) are actually made, the publisher later pays the remaining royalties owed.

Reversion of rights. The writer should make certain that this clause (also called the *out-of-print, termination* or *discontinuance of manufacture* clause) is included in his book contract with a publisher. The reversion of rights clause should provide that, when the publisher allows the original hardback edition of a book to go out of print and declines to reprint the book within a reasonable time period, *all* rights—not just publication rights—revert to the author.

Conventional clauses require that the author, upon discovering the book to be out of print, write to the publisher, requesting that the book be reprinted. According to the suggested contract established by Poets & Writers, Inc., the publisher must then notify the author within sixty days of receipt of this request, indicating his intention to comply or not. This suggested contract states that the publisher will reprint the book within six months of this correspondence, "unless prevented from doing so by circumstances beyond his control." If the publisher does not respond at all to the author's request, or if he fails to reprint the book within the six months, all rights revert to the author, with the exception of those licenses (rights) previously granted by the publisher to another party. Other contracts may give the publisher longer than six months to reprint the book. It is important, however, to establish a deadline—whether it be six months, two years or whatever the author feels is reasonable.

It is often the author's responsibility to determine whether his book has gone out of print, since some publishers do not advise authors of this fact. Failure to receive a royalty statement may be the author's first clue that the book is no longer in print. The author should then write the editor or the president of the company, asking if the book has gone out of print and, if so, to cancel the contract and revert the rights to him. If the reply is that the book is "Temporarily Out of Stock," then a printing date should be expected from the publisher almost immediately. If the reply is that the book will not be reprinted, the author may wish to notify the publisher of an in-

terest in buying either the negatives, plates, or remaining copies of the book at the cost of manufacture or the remainder cost, since the reversion of rights or discontinuance of manufacture clause also normally offers the author the right to buy the negatives or plates of the book, as well as remaining copies of the bound book, at a discount.

An author should make certain to include a precise reversion of rights clause in his contract, since a reprinter may be interested in publishing the book at some point in the future. This would mean another advance and royalty for the author. There is also the possibility that an out-of-print book will be "rediscovered," as was the case with Kate Chopin's *The Awakening*, an 1889 novel that was revived in the late 1960s and early 1970s during the period of renewed interest in women's literature. *The Awakening,* once out of print, has been reprinted in several editions since 1972. (*See: Author's copies; Book contract; Poets & Writers, Inc.; Reprint; Rights to manuscripts.*)

Review copy. A free copy of a bound book, sent to newspapers, magazines, journals and syndicates that carry book reviews, and often to radio and TV programs that discuss books or interview authors. A publisher distributes review copies in the hope of securing the "free" publicity that good reviews stimulate.

Of course, this type of publicity is not really free; review copies subtract from the publisher's profit and they do not earn any royalties for the author. The number of review copies distributed is, therefore, usually limited to approximately 100-150 books. A smaller publisher may send out only twenty-five books to reviewers, particularly if the book has a very specialized interest; a major publisher, on the other hand, may distribute as many as five hundred review copies of an anticipated bestseller.

Publishers have their own lists of reviewing media to whom they regularly send review copies. They may supplement a general list with an individually selected roster of specialist newspapers, magazines, journals, etc., slanted toward the subject matter of the book. A publisher will often make use of an author's expertise, inviting him to suggest publications likely to review the book, as well as contacts in the book's subject field who may be willing to promote it.

Although an effective means of securing "free" publicity, getting a book reviewed is by no means an easy method of promotion. While there are a number of consumer review media, none but *The New York Times Book Review*—a Sunday supplement to *The New York Times*—and *The New York Review of Books* are devoted almost exclusively to reviewing new titles; even these media can review only a few thousand new books each year. Combining the number of book reviews that appear in major newspapers such as the *Chicago Tribune* and national magazines such as *Time, Harper's, Newsweek* and *The New Yorker*, as well as the many smaller newspapers, regional publications and journals that regularly review books, does not even come close to the total of more than 40,000 new books published each year. Conse-

quently, competition among publishing houses is keen for the little media space that is available for book reviews.

Of course, a review in a national publication may not necessarily work to a book's advantage. A less-than-enthusiastic discussion of the book can hurt sales rather than help them. (*See: Prepublication review; Promotion by author.*)

Revising and rewriting. (*See: First draft, revising and rewriting; Usage errors.*)

Rhyme. (*See: Verse.*)

Rhythm and blues (R&B). A popular music form stemming from the rhythms and emotional intensity of black music, rhythm and blues is also identified as *soul* music. It combines aspects of modern rock music for popular sounds.

Right of privacy. A legal right protecting a living individual's peace of mind, spirit, sensibilities and feelings, and allowing that person to live as he sees fit without his name, visage or activities becoming public property, unless he waives or relinquishes that right.

As a general rule, "public figures," corporations and public institutions have no right of privacy, nor can relatives of deceased individuals suffer invasion of their right of privacy from any grief or embarrassment caused by publicity concerning the deceased. (*See: Libel; Privacy, invasion of; Right of publicity.*)

Additional information: *Writer's Legal Companion; Synopsis of the Law of Libel and the Right of Privacy.*

Right of publicity. Many people in the public eye—entertainers, sports figures and other celebrities—object to the exploitation or *misappropriation* of their name, likeness or performance for pure advertising and commercial purposes without their consent, and the law supports their "right of publicity."

As a general rule, this right dies with the person, although some courts have enforced the rights of heirs of celebrities such as Elvis Presley and Humphrey Bogart to control the commercial exploitation of their celebrity relatives. (*See: Libel; Privacy, invasion of; Right of privacy.*)

Additional information: *Synopsis of the Law of Libel and the Right of Privacy.*

Rights for sale. (*See: Figure 45.*)

Rights license period. This term refers to the amount of time that a publisher owns the publishing rights to a particular book. In most cases, when an author signs a contract regarding a hardcover book, the publisher retains the publishing rights to the book for as long as the book stays in print. However, when the book goes out of print, the author may usually reobtain the rights by terminating the contract a certain number of months after the book goes out of print.

To publish a paperback version of a book, the paperback publisher licenses rights from a hardcover publisher. The *rights license period* for such a book is usually five years.

Rights to class assignments. Freelance writers who have been students in college classes where an assignment involves, for example, creating hypothetical advertising copy for a local company sometimes complain that their ideas and/or portions of their manuscripts have been appropriated by the instructor without proper credit and/or remuneration to the student. Ideas, of course, cannot be copyrighted, but there is an ethical as well as a legal question regarding misappropriation of another's literary property for one's own advantage.

One college faculty handbook addresses this question this way: "The right to assign work to students that may contribute to their own or to general knowledge, is accompanied by the obligation not to exploit them or to infringe upon their academic freedom, and to give full credit for work done by them." The American Association of University Professors's Statement on Professional Ethics reads in part: ". . . a teacher . . . avoids any exploitation of his students for his private advantage and acknowledges significant assistance from them."

One way freelance writers might forestall any intentional or unintentional misappropriation of their work is to use a copyright credit line (i.e., copyright/year/name) in the upper right corner of manuscripts where they think the problem might occur.

Rights to manuscripts. Rights are sold to editors and publishers in varying forms and degrees. An established writer usually has more power to negotiate than a novice does; nevertheless, any writer should try to avoid, in most instances, selling all rights to a piece of work. The kinds of rights

FIGURE 45

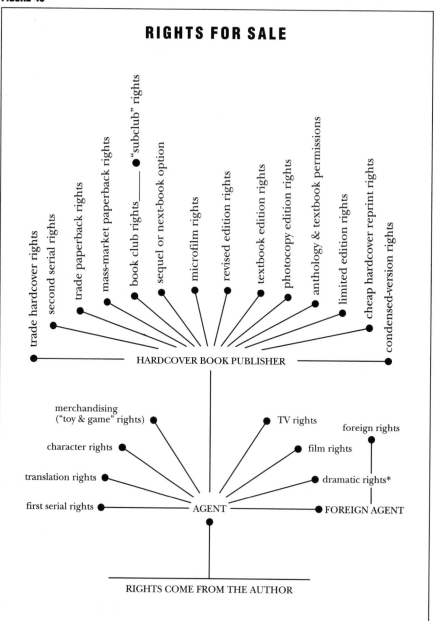

RIGHTS FOR SALE

- trade hardcover rights
- second serial rights
- trade paperback rights
- mass-market paperback rights
- book club rights
- ● "subclub" rights
- sequel or next-book option
- microfilm rights
- revised edition rights
- textbook edition rights
- photocopy edition rights
- anthology & textbook permissions
- limited edition rights
- cheap hardcover reprint rights
- condensed-version rights

HARDCOVER BOOK PUBLISHER

- merchandising ("toy & game" rights)
- character rights
- translation rights
- first serial rights

AGENT

- TV rights
- foreign rights
- film rights
- dramatic rights*
- FOREIGN AGENT

RIGHTS COME FROM THE AUTHOR

Reprinted from *Literary Agents, A Complete Guide*, published by Poets and Writers, Inc., 72 Spring St., New York, NY 10012. Copyright 1988 by Poets and Writers, Inc.
*Although dramatic rights were not included in the original chart, since they represent a right for sale by the author, they are included in this reprint.

most commonly sold to magazine editors are outlined below.

First serial rights are sold to periodicals (serials). Included in these rights is the agreement that the periodical will be the first publisher of the material. First serial rights can be restricted to include a particular area; e.g., modified versions are first North American serial rights and first U.S. serial rights.

Second serial (reprint) rights are rights sold to a newspaper or magazine with an article, story or poem that has previously been published in another periodical. An excerpt from a published book, regardless of whether it was previously published in a periodical, will also customarily be sold to a periodical with second serial (reprint) rights.

Foreign serial rights, rights sold to a market abroad, can be sold by a writer—provided he still has the rights. For example, if a writer has sold first U.S. serial rights to an American magazine, he is free to market the same piece in Europe; if, however, a U.S. publisher has purchased "first serial rights," without any geographical limiting phrase, the publisher may have foreign editions and be assuming he has ensured that he will be the first to publish it in any country in the world.

The term *syndication rights* refers to rights sold to a syndicate under the term "serial rights." A book published in installments in several newspapers, for example, would be placed under this category. If the newspaper installments appeared before the book's publication, the author would be syndicating first serial rights to the book; if the installments appeared after publication, he would be syndicating second serial rights.

Simultaneous rights are rights sold to two publishers (whose circulations do not compete) at the same time. The publisher who owns several magazines might also buy simultaneous rights to use the same piece in two or three of his publications. When a piece is being submitted to more than one publication simultaneously, it is best to advise the editors accordingly.

When an editor buys *all rights* to a piece, the writer loses his right to sell it to another publisher. A work-for-hire agreement is one that includes the writer's selling of all rights in addition to the copyright.

A writer can also sell rights to his work to other media, namely theater, TV and film. *Dramatic rights, TV rights* and *motion picture rights* are often offered at a percentage of the total price as an option to buy for a specific period of time. The property is then brought to the attention of people in the industry—actors, directors, studios or TV networks—for possible production.

The copyright law that took effect January 1, 1978, provides the creator of a piece of writing with all rights as soon as the work is complete. The creator may sell all or part of those rights, but the power to decide which belongs to him. (*See: Check contract; Copyright; Dramatic rights; Magazine editorial contract; Simultaneous submission; Subsidiary rights; Work made for hire.*)

Rising action. Although most often used relative to the plot structure of a play, the term *rising action* can also be useful in describing the plot structure of some works of fiction.

Rising action refers to the first stage of the plot that begins with the presentation of essential information through narration and dialogue (particularly information about what events have occurred before the action begins); rises through a complication (the protagonist encounters some conflict or opposing force); and peaks at the crisis or climax (the moment of highest intensity, when a decision must be made or an action taken to resolve the conflict). The events that occur from the moment of crisis until the end of the play or story are described as *falling action*. (*See: Climax; Crisis; Falling action; Plot.*)

Rock. Music form that originated in the 1950s as *rock and roll* and had evolved from a meshing of blues, gospel, jazz, folk and ragtime sounds. It was characterized by strong, driving rhythms played by small groups rather than the big bands of the previous era. The music was made popular by black entertainers such as Chuck Berry and Little Richard but soon was picked up by white performers such as Elvis Presley and Jerry Lee Lewis, among others. In the 1960s, rock was strongly influenced by British groups such as the Beatles and the Rolling Stones. In the 1970s, some rock music was typified by an emphasis on electrified instruments and became known as *heavy metal* or *acid rock* (because of its identification with the hallucinogen LSD or "acid"). In the late 1970s, *punk rock* originated in Britain with its high-energy sound and with lyrics and performers' attire and routines

aimed at making social statements about the era's lifestyles.

Rock music is continually evolving. To keep up with the changes in rock music, songwriters should listen to local radio stations that program popular rock singles and albums, and read trade/consumer magazines such as *Billboard, Cashbox* and *Rolling Stone,* as well as record and concert reviews in other magazines and in newspapers.

Roman à clef. The French term for "novel with a key." This type of novel incorporates real people and events into the story under the guise of fiction. Robert Penn Warren's *All the King's Men,* in which the character Willie Stark represents Huey Long, is a novel in this genre. (*See: Faction.*)

Romance novel. Also known as the *category romance,* the romance novel is a type of category fiction in which the love relationship between a man and a woman pervades the plot. The story is told from the viewpoint of the heroine, who meets a man (the hero), falls in love with him, encounters a conflict that hinders their relationship, then resolves the conflict. As opposed to many gothic romances, settings in these stories are contemporary; the characters are modern. Though marriage is not necessarily the outcome of the story, the ending is always happy.

Romance is the overriding element in this kind of story: The couple's relationship determines the plot and tone of the book. The theme of the novel is the woman's sexual awakening. Although she may not be a virgin, she has never before been so emotionally aroused. Despite all this emotion, however, characters and plot both must be well-developed and realistic: Contrived situations and flat characters are unacceptable.

Throughout a romance novel, the reader senses the sexual and emotional attraction between the heroine and hero. Lovemaking scenes, though sometimes detailed, are not generally too graphic, because more emphasis is placed on the sensual element than on physical action.

Romance novels fall into three distinct formats. The *sensual romance*, which is currently the best-selling type, is illustrated by the Silhouette Desire line. The emphasis in these plots is on the sensual tension between the hero and heroine, as well as the sizzling sexual scenes. The *spicy romance*, which includes Harlequin SuperRomances and Harlequin Presents is exemplified in stories in which married characters resolve (to a happy end) their problems; books in these lines consist of less sex and more story, compared to some other lines of romances. The *sweet romance*, which is on the wane at the moment, is published in Harlequin Romances, Silhouette Romances and Bantam's Loveswept. Many of the heroines in sweet romances are virgins, and the stories contain little if any sex.

The appeal of the romance reaches the teenaged market, as well, with romances highlighting relationships of sixteen-year-old contemporary heroines and their seventeen- to eighteen-year-old boyfriends. The stories concern the problems of growing up and the difficulties of romantic encounters in youth. Explicit sex and highly controversial issues such as abortion and unmarried pregnancy are not considered by editors of teenage romance novels.

Today's adult romance novel differs from its counterpart of the past in that it reflects society's increasing respect for women. "Bodice-rippers" and "rape sagas," though still being published in the historical romance field, are becoming less popular than category romances, as authors and readers increasingly subscribe to the values fostered by the women's movement. Some publishers now recommend in their guidelines that the heroine have a career; others are loosening the restrictions on the status of women deemed acceptable heroines.

Each publisher of romances has detailed, specific guidelines regarding his line. The publisher will stipulate, for example, whether the setting may be a foreign country or within the U.S., whether the heroine may engage in sex outside of marriage, whether marriage will occur at novel's end, and whether the heroine is in her twenties, thirties or another age group. In addition, publishers specify lengths for romances, which usually are from 50,000 to 60,000 words; books in some lines, however, are longer, such as Harlequin's Worldwide SuperRomances, which run about 85,000 words.

The romance writer's submission to a publisher includes a query letter, a synopsis and the first fifty pages of the novel, and a self-addressed, stamped envelope.

Yearly sales of romance novels represent one-fourth of mass-market softcover volumes. Most romance writers are women, but some male authors have broken into the market, many using female pseudonyms. *Novel & Short Story Writer's Market* lists publishers who solicit romance novels. Advances vary, but $3,000 could be an average for a new author, and royalty could be 6 percent and up on retail price.

The *Romantic Times* Book Lovers' Convention is an annual event for romance lovers. Writing workshops, publishers' hospitality suites and opportunities to meet agents are features of the event.

The Romance Writers of America is an organization dedicated to spreading the legitimacy of the romance novel and giving it recognition as a popular genre of adult fiction. Its members attend national and regional conferences for publishers, editors, readers, writers and agents.

One publication for and about romance readers/writers and the industry is: *Affaire de Coeur,* 1555 Washington Ave., Suite B, San Leandro, CA 94577. *Romantic Times* can be reached at 55 Bergen St., Brooklyn, NY 11201. (*See: Gothic; Romance Writers of America; Romantic suspense novel.*)

Romance Writers of America (RWA). This organization was established in 1979. Writers need not be published to join RWA, whose more than 7,700 members include individuals in foreign countries and more than 150 local chapters.

RWA strives to make romantic fiction a recognized genre, to increase interest in it, to support and encourage writers in their careers and to provide market information. The Golden Heart Award, presented annually, recognizes an RWA member who is an unpublished writer of romantic fiction. Rita Awards, presented annually, recognize the best in published romantic fiction. RWA publishes a bimonthly newspaper, *Romance Writers Report.* It holds an annual conference and regional conferences. Headquarters of the organization are at 13700 Veteran's Memorial Dr., Suite 315, Houston, TX 77014.

Romance Writer's Sourcebook. This directory shows romance writers where they can sell their manuscripts. The listings for markets in the U.S., Canada and Europe include names and addresses of the companies, interviews with the publishers or editors, and information on how to submit material.

Other sections of interest are ''The Romance Fiction Field,'' ''Craft and Technique,'' ''Markets for Novels,'' ''Markets for Short Fiction,'' ''Finding an Agent,'' ''Editors at Work'' and ''Resources.''

In ''Craft and Technique,'' writers are instructed in techniques of character development, dialogue and how to cross genres. In ''Editors at Work,'' excerpts from selected novels appear, as well as comments from the editor on why she chose that book. The section also contains interviews with authors who have recently published their first novels.

Writers can find descriptions of online services, organizations, conferences and workshops, awards and contests in ''Resources.''

Romantic suspense novel. The romantic suspense novel is a modern emergence of early gothic writing. This genre evolved in the 1950s with writers such as Mary Stewart and Victoria Holt; around 1960, romantic suspense novels began appearing in paperback.

Though the genre resembles the traditional gothic in that it pits an admirable heroine against some force of evil, it has distinctive characteristics of its own. Romantic suspense novels differ from the usual gothic form in tone, setting and character. Whereas gothic novels do not include sexually explicit scenes, romantic suspense novelists may choose to incorporate either sexually vivid passages or nonexplicit episodes. In addition, recent novels have not bound their heroines to bleak estates and gloomy mansions; rather, they have freed them to roam the world in either a historical or contemporary setting. Romantic suspense novels are not confined to a mystery angle in their plots; instead, they may emphasize the mounting anxiety of the heroine's confrontations with evil.

The genre is recognizable when contrasted with other writing. It is not a detective mystery story because the law (police) rarely gets involved in the action. It also differs from traditional "male" suspense novels because it moves more slowly and has more character interplay and psychological conflict than the fast-paced violence of suspense thrillers. Though romantic suspense novels have a small male readership, they are written mostly by women, for women.

The market for this escapist fiction is a potentially lucrative one for writers: The skillfully written work may sell 100,000 copies and more in softcover. Authors' advances and royalties may range from $1,500 for a short paperback to five figures for a novel by a well-established writer. Book publishers and magazines soliciting romantic suspense novels are listed in *Novel & Short Story Writer's Market.* (*See: Gothic; Romance novel.*)

ROS. Run of schedule. Refers to a commercial whose broadcast time is scheduled by the station rather than the sponsor.

Round character. A round character is a fictional person so specifically portrayed and described as to be recognizable and individually different from any other character in a novel, play or film. The protagonist and other main participants of a work are usually round characters: Their development is complex and tends to focus on their inner person (motivations, human traits, flaws, conflicts, distinctive qualities). Hamlet, for example, is a round character.

Minor, or flat, characters are generally less fully developed characters. (*See: Character; Flat character.*)

Round-up. In journalism, a news story or broadcast compiled from a number of sources or geographic areas. The term also refers to a short broadcast of the latest news.

Round-up article. A kind of article containing direct quotes on a subject from various notable people. The writer chooses a topic that is likely to bring opinionated or subjective responses during interviews, then rounds up the responses for the article. Examples of round-up articles are "The Nation's Five Top Football Coaches Pick the All-Time Greats" and "Three Up-and-Coming Starlets Talk About Beauty." Round-ups can be sold to a wide variety of magazines whenever a writer finds a topic of interest to a magazine's readership and a group of interviewees whose opinions that audience respects or is curious about.

Royalties. The author's share of a book's selling price. For instance, if the author receives a 10 percent royalty on a book that sells for $20, the author's royalty payment would be $2 per book sold. This percentage is agreed on in the publisher's contract with the author; royalty payments are made by the publisher to the writer on a regular schedule (also determined in the contract).

Usually the publisher pays the writer an *advance* against future royalties prior to publication. No other royalties are paid to the author until the publisher recoups the advance. Advances to first-time authors may be only a few thousand dollars or even nonexistent. Similarly, royalties vary, but the usual rate is 10 percent of the retail price on the first 5,000 copies, 12½ percent on the next 5,000 copies and 15 percent thereafter. (*See: Book contract; Royalty publishing.*)

Royalty auditing services. If his contract includes the right, an author may hire an auditing service to check a publisher's records when he believes that he is not being paid the agreed-upon amount in royalties. Underpayment of royalties by publishers has three major causes: clerical error, disputable interpretations

of contractual clauses by publishers, and overly high projections by publishers of the number of returns. (Most publishers' contracts contain a provision allowing the withholding of a percentage of royalties to cover the subsequent return of books previously ordered.)

An accountant engaged in such a situation reviews the publisher's records, which include billings, discount schedules, ledgers and inventory; interprets contracts; composes reports; and serves as a negotiator. Fees for these services range from $50 to $70 per hour. However, since royalty examinations in general have been known to cost from $2,500 to $25,000, only an author with sales sufficient to warrant such an audit usually engages an accounting firm. (*See: Book contract; Book publishing economics.*)

Royalty publishing. The method of publishing a book in which a publisher purchases a manuscript it thinks has a reasonable chance of selling enough copies to pay for its publication and turn a profit. As payment, the author receives a *royalty*— a percentage of the book's income— for every copy the publisher sells. (Royalties on textbooks and professional books are based on net receipts rather than the retail price.) The standard royalty rate for clothbound books is 10 percent of the retail price on the first 5,000 copies, 12½ percent on the next 5,000 and 15 percent on everything thereafter.

In most cases, the publisher gives the author an *advance* against royalties, which may be paid as a lump sum or in two or three separate payments upon delivery of various portions of the manuscript. Depending on the book, the author's reputation and the book's projected sales, the advance can range from as little as a few hundred to many thousands of dollars; once the accumulated royalties exceed the amount of the advance, the author receives royalty payments quarterly or semiannually on additional sales of the book.

Some authors who find it difficult to place their books with commercial publishers pursue alternative methods of publication. (*See: Book publishing economics; Co-publishing; Self-publishing; Small press; Subsidy publishing; Trade paperback.*)

Running gag. A situation or punch line repeated at intervals in a comic routine. Some famous comedians repeat a running gag throughout their careers—Jack Benny's radio routine, for example, in which Rochester would need a small amount of money for something and pinchpenny Benny would go to the base-

ment (unlocking noisily chained doors, etc., in the process) to get the money from his vault. (Because of his skillful and frequent use of the running gag, Benny has been called the master of this technique.)

A stand-up comic sometimes takes advantage of a joke that fails in front of an audience. During the same routine, each time a joke fails to elicit laughter, the comedian, as a running gag, explains the first unsuccessful joke. This variation is used by Bob Hope and Johnny Carson.

The classic example of the running gag was in the Broadway show, *Hellzapoppin*: A delivery boy appears from time to time with a plant, announcing, "Flower delivery for Mr. Abercrombie." Each time he tries to deliver the plant, it is larger and more awkward, until, at the end of the play, it is a tree in which the delivery boy sits in the lobby. As the theatergoers depart, they hear him announce, "Flower delivery for Mr. Abercrombie." (*See: Comedy writing.*)

Said, substitutes for, in dialogue.

In their attempt to use verbs of attribution some writers choose inappropriate verbs to substitute for *said*.

The key to using colorful verbs of attribution lies in refraining from overusing them. Although words such as *muttered, prompted, pleaded,* and *warned* can be used judiciously to clarify the emotional overtones of a scene, overuse of substitutes is often unnecessary; in a section of effective dialogue, the word *said* doesn't register in the mind of the reader. A fiction writer, through what his character says and does, has much better means of establishing character; in fact, unusual verbs of attribution tend to draw attention to the mechanics, and not the meaning, of a piece of dialogue.

Other pitfalls of dialogue writing are redundancy, as in "he asked, questioningly," and use of a verb when a modifier is needed, as in " 'Please come in,' he smiled," instead of " 'Please come in,' he said, smiling."

When a substitute for *said* interrupts the flow of reading or reasoning, it should be changed. *Said*, being the simplest word, is often the most effective. When the speaker of each statement is clear to the reader and the section of dialogue is fairly short, neither the word *said* nor a substitute is necessary.

St. Louis Journalism Review. (*See: Media reviewers.*)

Salvaging a manuscript.

For the writer who doesn't have a word processor and printer, or easy access to a photocopy machine, a manuscript that has been returned to an author wrinkled or crumpled may be salvaged from the time and expense of retyping by ironing the pages. A touch-up with the iron will also remove paper clip marks.

Freelance writer/teacher Elizabeth Allen offers the following directions for restoring wrinkled pages: "Get out your iron. If it is a steam iron, do not use water. Set it on Wash-and-Wear. Then iron each page of your manuscript. It will look as though you had just gotten it ready for its first flight." Other writers recommend that the page be ironed on the back rather than the front, so as not to smear the ink. (*See: Manuscript preparation and submission; Photocopied manuscripts.*)

Sarcasm.

This term applies to taunting, bitter remarks spoken or written with the intention of hurting another's feelings. Sarcasm involves a deliberate personal attack, and is usually expressed in a contemptuous manner. Sarcasm may make use of irony; i.e., saying one thing but meaning the opposite. Unlike true irony, however, sarcasm makes no attempt to disguise the real meaning beneath the apparent one. (*See: Humor; Irony; Satire.*)

SASE. This stands for "self-addressed, stamped envelope." An SASE is a necessary part of every submitted manuscript or query.

Satire. A literary technique that mocks a powerful or influential personality, institution, moral code or social trend, often using exaggeration and irony to point out the flaws and shortcomings of its target. While anger and contempt frequently underlie a work of satire, the satirist's most powerful tools are wit and humor, which pique the reader's or listener's sense of the ridiculous and thus undermine the subject—hence Mark Twain's statement that "against the assault of laughter nothing can stand." No matter how strongly the satirist feels about his subject, if he wishes to be effective he must remember to entertain his audience, not preach to it.

Satirists of ancient times include the Greek playwright Aristophanes and the Romans Juvenal and Horace. (Some experts classify all satire either as Juvenalian—meaning that it incorporates bitterness—or Horatian, which is more lighthearted mockery.) The seventeenth and eighteenth centuries produced the English satirists Pope, Dryden and Swift, and the French satirists Molière and Voltaire.

Among the best-known American satirists are Robert Benchley, James Thurber and S.J. Perelman. Cartoonist Garry Trudeau and newspaper columnist Art Buchwald are highly regarded contemporary political satirists; popular satirists of a more general nature are essayist Fran Lebowitz and *New York Times* columnist Russell Baker. Satiric essays appear in the *New Yorker, Esquire* and other comparatively "literary" magazines, while the *National Lampoon* and *Mad* magazine are wholly devoted to satire. (*See: Humor.*)

"Satisfactory" clause. A clause found in every publisher/author contract; it allows the publisher to reject a completed manuscript if it is not found to be "satisfactory." What constitutes "satisfactory" may be specified in detail, in general or not at all; since a writer who cannot deliver a satisfactory manuscript may be obligated to repay the publisher any advance he has received, the satisfactory clause is a topic of some concern to authors.

Sometimes a contract allows the publisher to reject a manuscript based on the condition of the market. For instance, if an author has contracted to write a book about Alpine wildflowers, but three other works on Alpine wildflowers are published between the time the author contracts for the book and the time he delivers the completed manuscript, the publisher can legally reject the manuscript, even if it is a superb work—*if* the market clause is present in the contract.

The Author's Guild has revised the satisfactory clause in its standard contract so as to shift the burden of proof of unacceptability to the publisher. The contract states objective criteria a manuscript must satisfy, rather than allowing a publisher's subjective judgment to determine acceptance or rejection ("The Author shall deliver a manuscript which, in style and content, is professionally competent and fit for publication"). This enables the author to sue a publisher he feels has unjustly rejected a contracted manuscript. Under the previous contract, an author's only legal recourse was to prove the publisher acted in "bad faith."

Saturation. Frequent, short-term use of broadcast advertising.

Scene. This term has several meanings. In its most comprehensive sense, *scene* means the place where some action or event occurs.

In drama, *scene* refers to a division within an act of a play, indicated by a change of locale, abrupt shift in time or the entrance or exit of a major character.

Similarly, a scene in a screenplay begins with a change in either time or place. Each scene serves to pass along essential information to the audience and is therefore an integral part of the story.

The term *scene* is also used by fiction writers to describe a unit of dramatic action in which a single point is made or a specific effect is achieved. A series of scenes arranged in a logical, dramatic sequence form a story.

In her book *How to Write Short Stories That Sell,* author Louise Boggess defines the essential elements of an effective scene. Each scene of a story, she says, should have a purpose: It should advance the story action by assisting or hindering the protagonist in the solution of his conflict. Second, each scene should take place within a definite time period and locale. The third essential element is character: The viewpoint character appears in all scenes, along with one or more minor char-

acters who produce the conflict action. Action—mental, physical or emotional—is another essential ingredient of a scene. Finally, the scene ends, according to Boggess, when the viewpoint character summarizes (in thoughts or dialogue) his choices for action and decides on one as a possible solution to his problem or conflict.

Blocking out the scenes before writing the story provides the means of combining plot summary and character development. (*See: Story.*)

Scholarships, fellowships, internships. Financial assistance is available to writers through scholarships and fellowships sponsored by governments, corporations and private foundations. These awards can be used for study, travel or a combination of the two; usually the purpose of the award is predetermined. By contrast, an internship is a temporary position, sometimes paid, that is offered by a corporation or not-for-profit organization. It is designed to afford the intern experience in and exposure to the career field of his choice, without a permanent commitment on the part of either employer or employee.

The National Endowment for the Arts, Nancy Hanks Center, 1100 Pennsylvania Ave., N.W., Washington, DC 20506, offers fellowships and residencies to published writers and organizations. Categories applicable to writers are the Literature Program, the Media Arts Program, the Music Program and the Theater Program.

In addition, information on scholarships, fellowships and grants, along with addresses of application offices, can be found in a number of directories, such as *The Grants Register*, a biennial book reporting on awards offered in the U.S. and abroad by governments and private organizations. *Study Abroad* provides information on fellowships and grants; listed are government programs, privately sponsored awards, teacher exchange programs and awards for women. Data on scholarships, fellowships, internships and grants are furnished in *Foundation Grants to Individuals*.

Another source for people seeking internship opportunities is Peterson's Guides, an annual directory listing primarily American internships and providing articles related to the practical aspects of interning.

The *Subject Guide to Books In Print* lists other recently published sources on these topics. (*See: Foundations; Grants, directories of.*)

Schools for writers. (*See: Associated Writing Programs; Correspondence courses for writers; National University Continuing Education Association.*)

Science fiction. Science fiction can be defined as literature involving elements of science and technology as a basis for conflict, or as the setting for a story. The science and technology are generally extrapolations of existing scientific fact, and most (though not all) science fiction stories take place in the future. There are other definitions of science fiction, and much disagreement in academic circles as to just what constitutes science fiction and what constitutes fantasy. This is because in some cases the line between science fiction and fantasy is virtually nonex-

istent. Despite the controversy, it is generally accepted that, to be science fiction, a story must have elements of science. Fantasy, on the other hand, rarely utilizes science, relying instead on magic, mythological and neo-mythological beings and devices, and outright invention for conflict and setting.

Some of the basic elements of science fiction have been in existence for thousands of years. There have always been fortune-tellers, prophets, clairvoyants and other extraordinary people who sought to foretell the future. The grand adventure in an exotic setting—a recurring story structure in science fiction—has been a literary theme almost as long as the desire to know the future. Tales of mythological gods and their involvement with humans are echoed by modern-day science fiction stories of encounters with alien beings. The heroic quest, occurring so often in all mythologies, is paralleled by stories of pioneering space explorers.

There is some disagreement about when the first true science fiction story was written, but most scholars feel that *True History*, written by a Greek, Lucian of Somosata, about 175 A.D., was the first real science fiction story. This tale dealt with a trip to the moon in a ship borne aloft by a great whirlwind.

The direct ancestor of modern science fiction is generally considered to be Mary Shelley's *Frankenstein: or, The Modern Prometheus* (1818). Over the next few decades, authors such as Poe, Stevenson and Verne expanded the field, developing what was known as the "scientific romance." H.G. Wells capped the development of the scientific romance and, in 1926, science fiction emerged as a distinct *genre* (under the name "scientifiction") with the publication of the first all-science fiction magazine, *Amazing Stories*.

The pulp magazine era was just beginning, and the explosion of markets for short stories in magazines helped science fiction gain a firm foothold in the American literary scene. The market for original paperback novels opened up in the 1950s. Major talents such as Robert A. Heinlein, Isaac Asimov and Arthur C. Clarke emerged during this period and brought the field to maturity. Under the influence of scores of writers and editors—as well as of films—science fiction has reached its current state of development.

Contemporary science fiction, while maintaining its focus on science and technology, is more concerned with the effects of science and technology on *people*. Since science is such an important factor in writing science fiction, accuracy with reference to scientific fact is important. Most of the science in science fiction is hypothesized from known facts, so, in addition to being firmly based in fact, the extrapolations must be consistent. Science fiction writers make their own rules for future settings, but the field requires consistency. For example, if a future is established in which mass transit is the *only* form of personal transportation, a character cannot be shown driving a personal vehicle just because it is convenient to the plot. In the same manner, in a setting derived from our own world, it would be inconsistent to introduce a human being who has reached the

stage of evolution in which it reproduces asexually.

Whatever the background, science fiction, as other forms of fiction, is dependent upon the "standard" elements of storytelling—plot, characterization, theme, motivation, etc.—for success. Many would-be science fiction writers miss this fact, and attempt to dazzle readers with gimmicks and gadgets, to no effect.

Beyond inconsistency and an overabundance of gadgetry in place of a good story, there are few taboos in science fiction. Anyone wishing to write science fiction should spend time reading both current and past work to gain insight into its distinct characteristics.

There are several subcategories of science fiction, including *dark fantasy, sociological SF, humorous SF, space opera, military SF, alternate history* and *cyberpunk*, each having its own peculiarities. Extensive reading in the field can aid the neophyte in identifying these subcategories, and is recommended for anyone wishing to write science fiction. *Locus Magazine* is considered the genre's bible. (Beginners should also note that editors and writers prefer the abbreviation *SF* to *SciFi* for their specialty genre.) (*See: Fantasy in children's literature; Myth.*)

Science Fiction Research Association (SFRA). This organization, established in 1970, exists to improve classroom teaching; to encourage and assist scholarship; and to evaluate and publicize new books and magazines dealing with fantastic literature and film, new teaching methods and materials.

Twenty-two countries are represented in SFRA's membership, which is composed of students, teachers, professors, librarians, futurologists, readers, authors, booksellers, editors, publishers and scholars. Academic affiliation is not a requirement for membership.

Members receive SFRA's annual membership directory, as well as the journals *Extrapolation* (quarterly), *Science-fiction Studies* (three times per year) and the *SFRA Review* (six times per year).

The Association's annual national meeting features authors of science fiction and fantasy, papers written by members, discussions and the presentation of awards: the Pilgrim Award for "outstanding contributions to science fiction and fantasy scholarship"; the Pioneer Award for best short essay of the year; and the Thomas D. Clareson Award for Service to Scholarship.

Membership information can be obtained by writing SFRA's Treasurer, Robert J. Ewald, at 552 W. Lincoln St., Findlay, OH 45840.

Science Fiction Writer's Marketplace and Sourcebook.

This semiannual writing and marketing companion for science fiction and fantasy writers features information on short story markets, book markets, literary agents, anthologies, conventions and workshops.

Other sections include "Science Fiction Trends," "Craft and Technique," "Editors at Work" and "Resources."

Science writing.

Specialization in publishing and increasing development of technology are two factors leading to expanding opportunities in science writing, both for freelancers and staff writers.

Opportunities exist for staff members on consumer magazines, trade and professional journals, newspapers, wire services and broadcast networks. Freelance science writers produce magazine and newspaper articles; books; press releases; and educational, industrial and public relations audiovisual materials. Technical journals such as *Journal of the American Medical Association* are written by researchers, but journalists are sometimes hired as editors on their staffs. Topics in the areas of family health, psychiatry and sexuality are generally sought by magazines read by women; editors tend to prefer women writers to cover these topics.

A college education may give a science writer an advantage in that he has been exposed to science as a field; he can thus decide whether to pursue it as a specialty. Some universities offer specialized courses in science writing that teach individuals the analytical skills demanded of today's science writers.

A writer who is unestablished in the scientific community or who lacks a specialty in science should be aware that many editors prefer articles written by scientists with writing skills rather than those written by general freelancers without scientific backgrounds.

Trends in the field of science take the form of an abundance of research being carried out on certain topics. A freelancer, using his marketing instincts, keeps abreast of such trends by scanning indexes to find subjects most written about in recent journals and magazines.

Media Resource Service, 1328 Broadway, Suite 300, New York, NY 10003, can refer writers to scientists in various fields. These experts can furnish technical information and opinions on scientific issues. The toll-free number of MRS is (800) 223-1730, or (212) 268-5279 in New York State. The Media Resource Service operates from 9 A.M. to 5 P.M. Eastern Standard Time, and an answering service is available outside those hours.

The National Association of Science Writers (P.O. Box 294, Greenlawn, NY 11740) considers applications of people who have been directly involved in the dissemination of scientific information for a minimum of two years. (*See: Medical writing.*)

Science-fiction Fantasy Writers of America (SFFWA).

Formerly the Science Fiction Writers of America, this organization was founded in 1965 by Damon Knight. More than eighteen hundred SF/Fantasy writers, artists, editors and allied professionals are members. The SFFWA has four categories of membership: Active, for published authors and their estates; Associate, for beginning writers with one professional publication; Affiliate, for allied professionals such as agents, editors, artists and publishers; and Institutional, for organizations such as schools and universities. All members receive the quarterly *Bulletin*, the annual membership directory, *The SFFWA Handbook* and copies of the model paperback and hardcover contracts. Active and Associate members also receive *The SFFWA Forum*, an in-house journal, six times a year. SFFWA supports a Grievance Committee, legal counsel, a Speaker's Bureau and a Circulating Book Plan, which offers members access to new hardcover books. Various committees monitor contracts and royalty statements, maintain contact with other writers' organizations, set standards for author/agent relationships, and help members deal with the strange world of science fiction conventions. SFFWA presents the Nebula Awards for the best SF or Fantasy short story, novelette, novella and novel of the year. Contact the SFFWA % Peter Dennis Pautz, Executive Secretary, 5 Winding Brook Dr., #1B, Guilderland, NY 12084. (*See: Nebula Awards.*)

Screenplay.
(*See: Motion picture script.*)

Screenwriting.
The writer who aspires to be a scriptwriter for movies or TV should live in Southern California, where most American movies and programs are produced, if he expects to make a steady living at it. Also—unlike writers for other media—he should consider a literary agent necessary: Producers often will not accept manuscripts otherwise, although in some cases they will look at scripts that have been preceded by a query and are accompanied by a standard release form. Besides providing access to studios and producers, the screenwriter's agent serves him by interpreting contracts and negotiating deals. Agents who are willing to work with previously unproduced screenwriters are listed in *Writer's Market Guide to Literary Agents* and in a brochure available through the Writers Guild of America, West.

The script market is not as clear-cut as the market for other kinds of writing. Not every script that's sold or optioned actually becomes a film—generally, of twenty to thirty purchased or optioned screenplays, only one is produced. To increase the chance of production, would-be screenwriters should read and study scripts to learn this specialized craft, in which prose is subordinate to the visual element.

Prominent producers caution novice screenwriters to avoid practices that mark them as amateurs. These include script covers that contain garish or poorly executed artwork (largely considered optional in the first place), a list of characters, ideas for casting (unless the script was written with a specific star in mind), submitting a story synopsis *with* the screenplay, an overabundance of camera directions not necessary to the telling of the story, the inclusion of apologetic notes, and putting the Writers Guild of America registration number on the cover page in an obvious way.

Legal protection for a script is crucial. It can be secured through registration with the Copyright Office and the Writers Guild of America, West, 7000 W. Third St., Los Angeles, CA 90048. (*See: Rights to manuscripts; Television writing.*)

Script. A group of pages that contain the written-out elements of a film, play, radio or TV program.

Script release form. (*See: Figure 46.*)

Script samples. Examples of copies of scripts of already produced movies and TV shows are sold by California companies. These firms often adver-

tise in the classified advertising pages of *Writer's Digest.*

Seasonal article. (*See: Magazine article, types of.*)

Seasonal jobs for writers. Freelance writers can find temporary or seasonal work for extra income. Such work is determined by overloads at corporations or by the temporary nature of certain projects.

Local, state and national political campaigns begin their activity as much as a year in advance, which is the same time writers should seek employment as speechwriters or as writers for printed promotional materials. A speechwriter's fee depends on the level of candidate he works for. A speech for a local political candidate may yield $250; for a statewide candidate, $375-$500; and for a national candidate, $1,000 or more. For other campaign public relations work, a writer can earn up to 10 percent of the campaign's budget.

Another area that uses seasonal writers for publicity material is fundraising for not-for-profit organizations such as social service agencies. A freelance writer working for this type of campaign would be likely to produce a campaign brochure, agendas for meetings, speeches, publicity releases, personal letters and form letters. A sample flat fee for work on a fund-raising brochure, which might represent fifty hours of work including research, writing, layout and printing supervision, is $5,000.

Corporations in all fields encounter a yearly surplus workload in the form of an annual report, a printed disclosure of financial activity. Work

FIGURE 46

SCRIPT RELEASE FORM

Gentlemen:

I am submitting to you herewith the following material (hereinafter referred to as "said material").

TITLE: _____

FORM OF MATERIAL

Synopsis	Screenplay	Radioplay
Treatment	Telescript	Other_____

PRINCIPAL CHARACTERS: _____

_____

BRIEF SUMMARY OF THEME OR PLOT: _____

_____

_____

_____

WGA REGISTRATION NO.: _____ NO. OF PAGES: _____

    1. I request that you read and evaluate said material, and you hereby agree to do so, and you agree to advise me of your decision with respect to the material.

    2. I warrant that I am the sole owner and author of said material, that I have the exclusive right and authority to submit the same to you upon the terms and conditions stated herein; and that all of the important features of said material are summarized herein. I will indemnify you of and from any and all claims, loss or liability that may be asserted against you or incurred by you, at any time, in connection with said material, or any use thereof.

    3. I agree that nothing in this agreement nor the fact of my submission of said material to you shall be deemed to place you in any different position than anyone else to whom I have not submitted said material.

    4. I understand that as a general rule you purchase literary properties through the established channels in the industry and not through a submission such as this. I recognize that you have access to and/or may create or have created literary materials and ideas that may be similar or identical to said material in theme, idea, plot, format, or other respects. I agree that I will not be entitled to any compensation because of the use by you of any such similar or identical material which may have been independently created by you or may have come to you from any other independent source. I understand that no confidential relationship is established by my submitting the material to you hereunder.

FIGURE 46 (CONTINUED)

5. You agree that if you use any legally protectible portion of said material, provided it has not been obtained by you from, or independently created by, another source, you will pay me an amount that is comparable to the compensation normally paid by you for similar material or an amount equal to the fair market value thereof as of the date of this agreement, whichever is greater. If we are unable to agree as to said amount, or in the event of any dispute concerning any alleged use of said material or with reference to this agreement, such dispute will be submitted to arbitration.

6. I have retained at least one copy of said material, and I hereby release you of and from any and all liability for loss, or damage to, the copies of said material submitted to you hereunder.

7. I enter into this agreement with the express understanding that you agree to read and evaluate said material in express reliance upon this agreement and my covenants, representatives, and warranties contained herein, and that in the absence of such an agreement, you would not read or evaluate said material.

8. I hereby state that I have read and understand this agreement and that no oral representatives of any kind have been made to me, and that this agreement states our entire understanding with reference to the subject matter hereof. Any modification or waiver of any of the provisions of this agreement must be made in writing and signed by both of us.

9. If more than one party signs this agreement as submittor, the reference to "I" or "me" through this agreement shall apply to each party jointly and severally.

Very truly yours,

_____   _____
Address   Signature

_____   _____
City and State   Print Name

_____
Telephone Number
                                    Accepted and Agreed to by

                                    _____
                                    Signature

EDITORIAL NOTE: Some production companies may have their own versions of this standard release form. In any case, whichever form you use, be sure to write the words RELEASE FORM ENCLOSED on the envelope containing your script to avoid having the package sent back unopened. Release form reprinted from *The Complete Book of Scriptwriting,* © 1982 by J. Michael Straczynski.

on an annual report is sometimes assigned to a freelancer, e.g., when the company's in-house staff is too small to handle the project. The production of these reports involves writing, layout, editing and proofreading skills. Graphic arts are also a part of annual reports, and the writer skilled in that area who can deliver a text-illustration package is more in demand as a freelancer. Hourly rates range from $25 to $50; writers working on a flat-fee basis earn $1,500 to $10,000, depending on the complexity of the report.

Freelance writers may also find seasonal work at publishing houses, which often hire extra help during the busier phases of their production cycles. Seasonal proofreading can be a steady source of income for a number of consecutive weeks. A proofreader earns $12-$20 per hour. Research for publishers pays $12-$20 per hour or more; it is sometimes done for a flat fee. Copy for a book dust jacket, while generally written in-house, can be assigned to a freelance writer; it would bring him $100-$600 per jacket for a job that includes writing copy for the front, back and inside covers. (*See: Seasonal material.*)

Additional information: *Jobs and Opportunities for Writers.*

Seasonal material. *Seasonal material* is the term used to describe an article, story, poem, greeting card or book that has a holiday or another timely observance as its theme. Holidays, anniversaries of historical events, national week-long observances and seasons of the year supply topics for freelance magazine and newspaper articles.

Writers who produce seasonal material need to plan their work around editors' schedules, which usually require seasonal articles from three to eight months in advance of the publication date. *Writer's Market* listings indicate individual editors' requirements for seasonal submissions. Another way to become familiar with editors' preferences is to record dates of acceptance—and dates of rejection for articles returned because they were submitted too late.

A writer who is more comfortable coordinating his work schedule with holidays instead of publishing schedules could write, for example, a Christmas story in December and file it until June, when he would retrieve it to revise and submit to a publication. Because rejected holiday stories and articles can be submitted the following year, it is best to avoid including timely elements such as current events.

For the writer who plans to do seasonal writing, a file of articles and pictures, categorized by month, can be a source of inspiration. Photos or other illustrations are equally as important to seasonal articles as they are to other magazine submissions.

Some references that indicate holidays and other special observances include the *World Almanac*; a compilation called *Chase's Calendar of Annual Events*, published by Contemporary Books, 2 Prudential Plaza, Suite 1200, Chicago, IL 60601; and brochures produced by state governments and the U.S. Government Printing Office, Washington, DC 20402. In addition, each issue of the *Standard Rate and Data Service Business Publications Directory* carries a page listing "Promotional Dates" (National Baby Week, Law Day, etc.) for the coming months.

Secondary magazine. A secondary magazine is one with relatively low circulation that is intended for an audience with a specialized interest. *Indiana Business* and *Pest Control* are examples of secondary magazines.

Secondary magazines are more receptive to the work of new writers than are the major magazines.

Knowledge of, interest in, or curiosity about a particular subject is a prerequisite for writing for secondary magazines. Hobbies and personal experiences are sometimes prime ideas for articles, while many other sources can provide background information for writers who lack knowledge of, but are interested in, a topic. Since many readers of secondary publications are extremely well versed in the subjects they cover, the writer who does not have a solid grounding in the subject he's writing about must do thorough research. (*See: Major magazine.*)

Secondary sales. Under the new copyright law, a writer is obligated to sell only one-time rights for his work to a publication unless he agrees otherwise in writing. Therefore, after selling first rights only to a publication, the writer may be able to locate additional magazines or newspapers with noncompeting circulations to make secondary sales and receive additional profit from the same manuscript.

An accepted means of informing an editor which rights are for sale is to indicate such rights in the upper right corner of the manuscript—

for example, "First North American Serial Rights Only."

When a previously published piece is submitted to a second publisher, the writer should inform the publisher of the publication history of his submission. (*See: Multiple sales; Rights to manuscripts; Simultaneous submission.*)

Secondary sources. In using only secondary sources, the writer runs the risk of his research being inaccurate, since he is depending on the work of other writers, whose work may contain misquotations, misinterpretation, printing and typographical errors, etc. However, secondary sources should not be ignored, because they can provide useful supporting information for an article, as long as they are verified for accuracy.

Primary sources, e.g., people interviewed in the research process, are necessary to write most articles, because a writer cannot usually construct an effective article solely from secondary sources. The writer also needs to check one person against another, as well as the written record. (*See: Primary source.*)

Second-level story. The *second-level story* deals with the inner lives of the characters—their psychological growth (and periods of regression), attainment of insights, realizations of universal truth. Psychologically speaking, the second-level story is where the *real* action takes place; in some fiction, in fact—the work of Henry James, for instance—there's next to no surface-level action at all.

The second-level story strengthens a piece by lending purpose to the series of incidents and credibility to the characters. It's what makes a story or novel more than just a good read; it makes the characters stick with the reader long after he's finished with it. The more skillfully the surface level and the second level are interwoven, the more valuable the work of fiction that results. (*See: Fiction.*)

Selection (or main selection). In book club offerings, a book given primary importance among all the books offered during one period. (*See: Alternate; Book clubs; Book club selection.*)

Self-criticism. Although necessary to the work of all writers, self-criticism can become a pitfall if it is overcome by perfectionism. When that happens, a writer tends not to write anything because he is afraid his work will be inadequate.

Self-criticism is frequently the basis for a writer's hypersensitivity to all criticism. In *The Writer's Survival Guide*, authors Jean and Veryl Rosenbaum explain: "Writers spend inordinate amounts of time deprecating their talent, questioning their abilities, and worrying about acceptance. One side effect of this perpetual self-criticism is that writers tend to bristle when others—critics or readers—comment unfavorably about their work, since it confirms their worst fears."

Writers who overindulge in self-criticism should remember: (1) though their work should be of quality, every piece of writing will not be a masterpiece; and (2) there is a point at which the writer must deliver responsibility for judgment to the editor. (*See: First draft, revising and rewriting.*)

Self-mailer. A commonly used type of direct-mail promotional piece containing all its parts on a single printed sheet. An envelope is not used with a self-mailer; instead, the sheet is folded and the address is placed on the outside. Sometimes a self-mailer contains a built-in reply form, with instructions to the consumer to clip, fold and staple it before returning.

Expenses for this form of direct-mail are relatively low because only one form is printed; stuffing, sealing and/or clasping of envelopes is not necessary; and the cost of postage is usually less than for a more elaborate mailing piece.

Self-publishing. Authors who do not sell their manuscripts to commercial publishers will generally follow one of two routes. *Subsidy publishing* (the author's paying a publisher to produce a book for him) is an investment with the prospect of little or no return. In a *self-publishing* arrangement, the author keeps all income derived from the book, but he pays for its manufacturing, production and marketing, the latter of which can be very expensive. The most important factor for an author to consider before self-publishing a book is whether he can earn enough from his own efforts in book sales to pay back his investment.

Self-published books are usually successful when there is a specific, easy-to-reach audience with the need for that particular book and when the author has a cost-efficient way to reach them. For example, an author who is regularly called upon to speak at regional and national conventions because he is knowledgeable about a certain topic has access to large groups of potential buyers of his book, without having to depend on costly direct-mail promotions or personal visits to innumerable bookstores to sell it. Self-publishing a book can sometimes lead to further distribution by a regular publishing company, if sales are encouraging.

Although a single proprietorship is often the most effective arrangement for the self-publisher, prospective associates who may be able to contribute financial support or publicity contacts should not be overlooked. Another option is to become part of a writers' cooperative, an organization composed of writers who contribute to the publication of other members' work as well as their own. Cooperatives are funded by grants, members' contributions and product sales. (*See: Sponsored books; Subsidy publishing.*)

Additional information: *Book Market; The Publish-It-Yourself Handbook; Publish It Yourself; The Self-Publishing Manual: How to Write, Print & Sell Your Own Book.*

Self-syndication. Self-syndication is the marketing of one's own columns or articles to newspapers and/or magazines. Self-syndication involves submitting completed pieces to editors and publishers (usually local to begin with), promoting and selling the column idea, establishing payment rates, billing the publications, securing a copyright (usually on an advance collection of columns), and earning 100 percent of the proceeds. Self-promoted newspaper columns are sometimes offered gratis to an editor to gain initial acceptance, after which publication the writer

may earn only $10-$20 per column from small papers, but larger papers may offer much more. Even though fees from any one newspaper may be small, when columns or features are sold to others in noncompeting circulation areas, proceeds build.

One device used by new column writers to build readership is to encourage questions or comments from readers; the editor can gauge reader interest in the topic by the amount of mail it generates at the paper. Another device is to offer some free booklet on a related topic (which the author has either prepared himself or obtained from an appropriate source) to encourage reader response.

Besides being one way "to get into print," self-syndication may be a route to eventually being acquired by an established national syndicate. (*See: Contributing editor; Syndicated column.*)

Sell copy. Copy written primarily to persuade the consumer to buy or do something. In book publishing, *sell copy* takes the form of subtitles and material on dust jacket flaps, such as blurbs and testimonials. In magazines, it is the cover copy enticing the newsstand buyer. In TV, it can be commercials for a product, promotion for an upcoming program, or a public service announcement for a social service agency.

In many fields of business, forms of sell copy include that used in advertising, promotion, speeches, radio continuity, public relations, sales letters, publicity releases and brochures. (*See: Advertising copywriters; Blurb; Business writing; Direct-mail advertising; Newspaper ads for small businesses, writing; Political campaign writing; Publicity writing; Radio copywriting; Speechwriting; Television commercials.*)

Semimonthly. Issued or occurring twice a month (i.e., every half-month). A *semimonthly* magazine, for example, is published twice a month. (*See: Bimonthly.*)

Semiweekly. Issued or occurring twice a week (i.e., every half-week). A *semiweekly* newspaper, for example, is published twice each week. (*See: Biweekly.*)

Sequel. A story connected with a previously written one by means of plot and/or characters. The sequel can continue the plot of the previous story (which is complete in itself, as well), or place the same characters in a different situation or adventure.

The writer of the original story owns exclusive rights to his characters, even when they are used in a later work by another. When a writer intends to write a sequel using the characters of another writer, he must secure permission from the original creator. In the case of a deceased writer, depending on the copyright date of the original work, permission should be sought from his estate.

An example: when Margaret Mitchell's two nephews, heirs to her estate, realized the copyright to *Gone With the Wind* would expire in the year 2011, and anyone could pick up the story where Mitchell left off, they asked the William Morris Agency to find an author to do the sequel. Of the twelve final candidates, Alexandra Ripley, author of four previous historical novels set in the South, was chosen, said Morris agent Robert Gottlieb, because "She had the right sensibility, an understanding of the essence of Southern culture and of Scarlett."

Serial comma/Harvard comma. A serial comma, also known as the Harvard comma, is one that is placed before the conjunction in a series of items in a sentence. The sentence, "The design is bold, bright, and colorful" uses a serial comma, although it would also be correct without a comma after the word *bright.*

Whether a serial comma is used is a matter of the style preference of each individual publication. *The Associated Press Stylebook* advises omitting the serial comma except when one of the elements of the series includes a conjunction, or when the elements of the series are complex, i.e., long phrases. The first exception can be seen in the following sentence: "They sat down to a meal of fruit, potatoes, peas, bread, and turkey and dressing." (If *dressing* were not included, the comma after *bread* would not be used, according to *The Associated Press Stylebook.*) The exception regarding long phrases is shown in the following sentence: "He acquired the writing assignment because he was willing to work quickly to meet the short deadline, he had written a convincing query letter, and he had published related material within the last two years."

The *Chicago Manual of Style*, the *U.S. Government Printing Office Style Manual* and *The Elements of Style* recommend using a comma before the conjunction in a series that contains three or more items. The punctuation in the following sentence is correct, according to their styles: "Olympic training requires skill, talent, and persistence."

Serial rights. (*See: Rights to manuscripts.*)

Series. A group of related articles or books covering the same subject or theme. Series for newspapers and for radio and TV news broadcasts—run in daily, weekly or even monthly installments—are written by staff writers or freelancers well known to the publication or station; magazine series are often written by contributing editors. Nonfiction books are sometimes serialized in periodicals and novels are occasionally serialized as well.

Newspaper and magazine series tend to be investigative or analytical pieces on controversial (even dangerous) subjects requiring much legwork from reporters; e.g., the Pulitzer-Prize-winning series, "Being Black in South Africa" written by David Zucchino of the *Philadelphia Enquirer*. Editors prefer to assign such large projects to staff people, often to a staff team as a built-in check and balance. Newspaper and magazine series thus are not a big freelance market—although when a freelancer having the right background, interests and contacts lands a series, it usually pays well.

Series fiction can be very lucrative, however—particularly series paperback novels. (*See: Series books.*)

Series books. A series of novels is a group of books in which the same character appears in different adventures or situations. Don Pendle-

ton has created a series of more than thirty books about the character Mack Bolan and his attempts to avenge the murder of his family; the series' novels include *Arizona Ambush* and *War Against the Mafia*. John D. MacDonald's series character, Travis McGee, is a detective who appears in the books *The Deep Blue Good-by* and *Bright Orange for the Shroud* (among others). A contemporary American suburbanite, Rabbit Angstrom, is the central character in John Updike's series, which includes *Rabbit Run*, *Rabbit Redux*, *Rabbit is Rich* and *Rabbit at Rest*.

Service. The practice of regularly contacting or calling on an advertiser to maintain his account.

Service article. (*See: Magazine article, types of.*)

Service mark. Similar conceptually to the term *trademark*, a service mark is a word, symbol, name or device used to identify the services (as opposed to a product) and advertising of an individual, corporation or other entity, and to distinguish those services or advertising from that of others. The slogans used by a dry-cleaning establishment to describe the services it provides for customers (e.g., "One-Hour Martinizing") are examples of service marks. Freelance writers may sometimes work with a client to develop the idea for a service mark. (*See: Trademark.*)

SESAC. (*See: Performing rights organizations.*)

Sestina. A form of lyric poetry composed of six six-line stanzas and one three-line envoi.

The sestina's pattern of repetition uses the words that end the lines in the first stanza. These words are used to end lines in the rest of the poem according to a set formula:

Stanza I 1-2-3-4-5-6
Stanza II 6-1-5-2-4-3
Stanza III 3-6-4-1-2-5
Stanza IV 5-3-2-6-1-4
Stanza V 4-5-1-3-6-2
Stanza VI 2-4-6-5-3-1

The envoi (or final stanza) not only repeats the terminal word, but uses repetition within the line. Line one places word 2 in the middle and word 5 at the end. Line two places word 4 in the middle and word 3 at the end. Line three has word 6 in the middle and word 1 at the end. (*See: Verse.*)

Setting. The time and location in which a story takes place. The term is used in connection with short stories, novels, plays, motion pictures and TV programs.

Although a particular setting can be the inspiration for or a powerful presence in a story, it cannot be the essence of it. Other elements, such as plot and characterization, are also necessary to a meaningful story.

Sexism in writing. Sexism in publishing is manifest in two forms: stereotyped roles and male-oriented words.

Stereotyped females, formerly prevalent in textbooks, are gradually being abolished from American book publishing.

Nouns and pronouns that disregard females are being replaced with more inclusive words or combinations of words. The terms *he or she,*

person, and others are gradually coming to replace other, sexist words. Because using two pronouns can be awkward, though, sexism can often be avoided by recasting passages in the plural and using the pronouns *they, them* and *their.*

One means by which both sexism and stereotyping are avoided is to use nonsexist descriptions of occupations, e.g., "newspaper men and women," "police," "fire fighters," "flight attendants." (See the Preface regarding the use of *he* in this book.)

SFX. (*See: Sound effects [SFX].*)

Shelf life. How long a hardcover or paperback book remains on the bookstore shelf or newsstand rack depends entirely on its salability. An original hardcover novel might last three months; a best-seller, two years or longer. A paperback original might have only five or ten days to reach its potential buyer, whereas a reprint of a best-seller might be available for several years. The competition from newly published books for shelf and rack space continually forces off books that have not been promoted, either formally or by word of mouth from satisfied buyers, and therefore don't sell.

Shield laws. Enacted to grant confidentiality in court proceedings between newspeople and their sources, shield laws have been adopted by more than half the states. Depending on the individual law, a reporter may be protected from revealing information only, or the information and the source; some shield laws permit confidentiality under certain circumstances only. Shield laws usually protect only newspeople, not free-lance writers; however, several states now include freelancers among those who are protected.

There is no federal shield law, but many journalists believe they are exempt from the obligation to reveal their sources on the basis of the First Amendment. Besides, they fear that revealing a source's name would break future contact with that source, thus infringing on the public's right to know. The court, on the other hand, holds that granting reporters immunity from revealing information when subpoenaed obstructs due process of the law and gives reporters special privileges as citizens.

Short stories for young people. Though the structure of a short story remains the same regardless of audience, the writer of stories for juvenile markets must consider features of particular appeal to the age group of his intended audience.

The needs of kindergarten-age readers require a simple plot and a story length of no more than 500 words. Older children, who read stories of from 800 to 1,000 words, need drama, action, a quick pace and a definite plot. Writers of short stories for teenagers must include plot, characterization, conflict, suspense and a satisfying solution; the story's situation should be in keeping with teenagers' interests and lifestyles, e.g., school, part-time work and interpersonal relationships.

In any children's short story, the main character is the same age as or older than the reader; he is never younger than the reader and is seldom an adult. The story's time span

should be confined to two days or less. Anthropomorphism (attributing human qualities to a nonhuman being or an inanimate object), a device some writers of stories for young children fall back on, is unacceptable to most editors.

Opportunities for marketing children's short stories exist at both secular and religious publications. *Writer's Market, Novel & Short Story Writer's Market* and *Children's Writer's & Illustrator's Market* direct the writer to magazines seeking short stories for children. (*See: Juveniles, writing for; Short story.*)

Short story. A piece of fiction that revolves around a character with a specific problem to solve. The method the author uses to help him solve his problem is the *plot*; the point the author wants to make (or to prove) in the story is the *theme*. An essential ingredient of a short story is the recognizable change—for better or worse—that occurs in the main character or in his situation as a result of having solved his problem (or having recognized his failure or inability to do so).

The short story usually ranges from 1,500 to 10,000 words—six to forty doubled-spaced, typewritten pages—in length. It contains only the number of characters and scenes necessary to its plot. (A common flaw in beginning writers' stories is including superfluous characters and scenes.) Similarly, the time span of the story is usually limited: One day or one week for the main action is common.

The short story has existed for thousands of years; one of the earliest known short story collections is

Tales of the Magicians, which originated in Egypt four to six thousand years ago. In the Middle Ages, the short story took the forms of the beast fable and the *exemplum*, which contained morals, and the *fabliau*, which was a bawdy tale written in verse.

Edgar Allan Poe was the first to establish rules for the short story: his concept values unities of mood, time, space and action, and stipulates that a story reach for only one effect—an effect determined in advance by the author, and reflected in all events of the story and every word of the composition.

Annual collections of contemporary short stories include: *Prize Stories, the O. Henry Awards*; *The Best American Short Stories*; and *The Pushcart Prize: Best of the Small Presses*.

Magazine markets for short stories include those in the literary/little, women's, men's, children's, religious, regional and science fiction categories, which are detailed both in *Writer's Market* and *Novel & Short Story Writer's Market*. (*See: Confession; Short stories for young people; Short-short story; Vignette.*)

Short-short story. A story of 1,500 words or less. While, as in a regular short story, the main character gains insight by responding to and learning from a situation, the short-short story is built on a theme rather than a complex plot. Its author conveys a bit of philosophy through his character's change of attitude, which results from his response to a situation. Though a change in attitude is evident at the end of every short-short story, it need not necessarily result in a brighter outlook on the part of the character. But the reader must infer, at the end of the story, that the character's new attitude—whether brighter or more gloomy—will be integrated into the character's philosophy.

The short-short story covers a brief period of time and has as few characters and scenes as possible; it must be effective without background, description or extra words, relying totally on characterization, conflict and resolution.

The axiom "don't tell the reader, show him" is especially appropriate to the short-short story, where it makes for economy of words as well as literary effect. Markets for short-short stories are listed in both *Writer's Market* and *Novel & Short Story Writer's Market*. (*See: Confession; Short story; Vignette.*)

Show don't tell. A common admonition from editors to beginning fiction writers who fail to use dialogue and action to reveal a character's emotions, relying instead solely on narration. It is the difference between actors acting out an event, and the lone playwright standing on a bare stage recounting the event to the audience. (*See: Emotion in writing.*)

sic. Latin for *thus* or *so*. Usually enclosed in brackets or parentheses, *sic* is inserted after a word, phrase or expression in a quoted passage to indicate that the word or phrase has been quoted exactly as it was written, even though it may seem strange or incorrect. Writers use *sic* to disclaim responsibility for errors in grammar, spelling, etc., that may appear in the material they are quoting verbatim. (*See: Quotes.*)

Sidebar. A short feature that accompanies a news story or magazine article. It elaborates on human interest aspects of the story, explains one important facet of the story in more depth, or provides additional factual information—such as a list of names and addresses—that would read awkwardly in the body of the article.

A sidebar is often given distinctive graphic treatment by being screened, boxed, bordered, or set in a different typeface from the main article. It is usually given a title separate from that of the main article.

Signature. A sound or piece of music used consistently with a particular radio program; very often synonymous with *theme.* Signature is also used in magazine and book publishing to refer to a group of pages printed at one time and folded into a unit—such as a sixteen-page signature.

Simile. A figure of speech based on comparison. In a simile, two things are compared to each other, generally using either the word *like* or the phrase *as . . . as.* The two things or person and thing being compared must be dissimilar in more ways than they are similar, since one purpose of the simile is to make the unfamiliar (e.g., a new character) immediately familiar to the reader. For example, the writer might use comparison to describe a new character in a story as Maugham did in *Of Human Bondage*: "She had large black eyes and her nose was slightly aquiline; in profile she had somewhat the look of a bird of prey. . . ."

In his description of a student's rented room, John Irving used this simile: "It was a cheerless place, as dry and as crowded as a dictionary. . . ." (*See: Figures of speech; Imagery; Metaphor.*)

Simultaneous submission. A manuscript submitted for consideration to more than one publishing company at the same time is known as a *simultaneous submission* or *multiple submission.* Once taboo, multiple submission has become a moderately common practice in publishing today for certain kinds of articles, for some book proposals, and for finished book manuscripts. Although many magazine editors listed in *Writer's Market* indicate that they will accept photocopied, previously published, or simultaneous submissions, some editors still prefer to see the original typed copy of a manuscript and to know that other magazines are not considering the same material at the same time. Major magazine markets that pay top prices expect to get an exclusive look at the ideas presented to them; simultaneous submissions should not be made there. Smaller magazines such as religious publications, company magazines, etc., which pay lower rates and whose readerships are unlikely to overlap with other magazines in the same field, are usually more willing to look at simultaneous submissions. A writer, therefore, may be able to sell one-time rights to the same story or article a dozen times.

It is usually more acceptable for the freelance magazine writer to submit multiple *queries*—particularly if the subject of the article is a timely one—than to ask the editor to read an entire article that the writer may end up withdrawing from consideration because he has sold it elsewhere.

The practice of submitting the outline and sample chapters of a book proposal to more than one publishing house at the same time has become more common in the past decade. An original cover letter, carefully typed and addressed to the appropriate editor, should accompany the photocopied outline and sample chapters for each submission.

Approximately half the book publishers listed in *Writer's Market* indicate that they will accept simultaneous submissions; many of them do, however, insist that the author advise them that the manuscript is a multiple submission, and some require that the author indicate the names of other publishers considering the material. (*See: Ethics for writers; Multiple sales; Photocopied manuscripts; Spin-off.*)

Sine qua non. Latin for *without which not.* The phrase is used to describe an absolutely indispensable condition or something essential. *The Dictionary of Literary Terms*, by Harry Shaw, offers this example: "Conflict is the *sine qua non* of every work of genuine fiction."

Slang. Words that are used colloquially but that have not been recognized as standard English. Although in most cases inappropriate for use in books because of its tendency to become outdated, slang can be used justifiably in a story to set the scene or to establish the dialect of a character. But even for these two effects,

slang becomes intrusive if used too frequently.

Slang words are usually acceptable for use in newspapers, magazines and other timely publications, and writers may use such media to stay abreast of changes in usage, new slang words and new idioms. (*See: Idiom; Language and style, books on.*)

Additional information: *Slang Dictionary.*

Slanting. Slanting refers to the writer's skill in aiming his articles (or stories) at a particular market. Successful writers spend as much time researching the markets as they do writing.

The object of market study, of which slanting is part, is to be able to sell a piece most directly and expediently. It is a simple process, involving five steps: (1) conceiving an idea; (2) checking the *Reader's Guide* to see what's already been published and by whom; (3) selecting from *Writer's Market* those magazines whose needs seem most suitable; (4) obtaining and studying three or four copies of each prospective market (e.g., magazine); and (5) writing the article or story with the editor's needs in mind.

Appropriate slanting can be achieved when the writer has learned, through studying magazines, factors such as the interests, occupations, socioeconomic status and psychological makeup of his prospective readers.

A writer can sometimes revise and partially rewrite an already-published article to give it a different slant, thereby adjusting it to suit the needs of a second magazine. For example, as former *Writer's Digest* nonfiction columnist Art Spikol points out, an article on stress tests could be sold to a wide variety of publications, depending on the approach. "Why Top Execs Get Stress Tests" might be the title of a piece sold to an in-flight magazine, while the same research material slanted toward sports magazines could be an article called "How a Stress Test Can Help Improve Your Game." (*See: Market, studying the.*)

Slice of life. A type of short story, novel, play or film that takes a strongly thematic approach, depending less on plot than on vivid detail in describing the setting and/or environment, and the environment's effect on characters involved in it. The slice of life emphasizes mood and atmosphere rather than action, and builds to an emotional peak through carefully selected detail, skillful characterization and naturalistic dialogue. Unlike a traditional work that has a beginning, middle and end, the slice of life is a seemingly unselective presentation of life as it is; a brief, illuminating look at a realistic rather than a constructed situation, revealed to the reader without comment or interpretation by the author.

A slice-of-life work is not without structure, however. It has some plot or plan to it, and, as in a conventional work, the viewpoint character undergoes a change, however slight it might be. The story makes a definite thematic point but comes to no conclusion. The reader does not know what came before the events of the story, nor does he know what lies ahead for the characters. As one writer notes, "The story ends and life goes on."

Little/literary magazines are more interested in slice-of-life material than are commercial markets, most of which require strongly plotted stories; and it is in little/literary magazines that the slice-of-life writer has the best chance of publishing. These magazines are listed in *Novel & Short Story Writer's Market* and *The International Directory of Little Magazines and Small Presses*.

Some examples of well-known slice-of-life works are the Alan Sillitoe novel *Saturday Night and Sunday Morning* (later made into an important film); the Elmer Rice play *Street Scene* (later adapted into an opera scored by Kurt Weill); and *Small Change*, a film by François Truffaut.

Slick. (*See: Major magazine.*)

Slugline. A newspaper reporter or wire editor places a slugline at the top of each section of copy on a story; it explains in a word or short phrase the story's subject. Also known as a slug, catchline, guide or guideline, a slugline serves to keep all copy on the same story together throughout production and printing.

Slush pile. This is a collective term for unsolicited material received by book publishers or magazine editors. Editor Elaine Stanton describes the term in this way: "What is slush, after all, but what is left after the snow has started to melt? And it is only natural that editors will choose first to read the 'snow' that is the substance known to them, authors they regularly work with, staff material, and material submitted by agents.''

In recent years, some book and magazine publishers have discontinued the departments that handled unsolicited manuscripts and announced in their *Writer's Market* listings that they would only accept submissions from agents. Some writers without agents have managed to circumvent this policy by directing an advance query to a specific editor's name and, when the idea has sufficient appeal, getting a go-ahead to submit the manuscript to the editor's personal attention.

Small press. A category of publishing in which firms generally operate on low budgets. Small press houses are independent organizations whose budgets depend on the publishers' personal funds, donations from authors and grants.

Small press works of fiction and poetry, which make up more than half the products turned out in this field, are of serious literary quality: Experimental fiction and ethnic fiction are characteristic of books published by the small press. Small press nonfiction tends to be concerned with social issues, political thought, and ideas not yet current among the general public.

Many small presses distribute review copies of their books to newspapers, special-interest magazines and little magazines and send annual catalogs to bookstores, libraries and individuals. Small press houses also place a small amount of advertising in the print media.

In working with a small press publisher, the writer plays a larger role in the publishing process than he does with a larger publishing house. He may take part in some or all of the editing, layout, graphic design, binding, printing, promotion and advertising.

The writer is not guaranteed an advance from a small press publisher, because the publisher's financial status often is precarious and depends largely on outside sources. Since this industry has not adopted a standard royalty as the commercial presses have, the writer should ascertain that terms for royalties and/or other forms of payment are spelled out in his contract. *Novel & Short Story Writer's Market*, in its "Small Press" section, contains advice on dealing with the small press.

Small press publishers can help self-publishing authors by offering advice through personal correspondence and publications, and by reviewing self-published books in small press magazines. *Small Press Review* is one such magazine; a monthly, it is devoted to reviews of small press works as well as other information about the field.

The Committee of Small Magazine Editors and Publishers (COSMEP) and the Council of Literary Magazines & Presses (CLMP) are two major organizations in the small press field. Members of COSMEP include self-publishers as well as those involved in the small press.

The International Directory of Little Magazines and Small Presses assists the writer in locating small press publishers. Along with names and addresses, the listings in the Directory furnish information on content, payment and reporting times. (*See: Little/literary magazine; Magazine, alternative; Self-publishing.*)

Snail mail. A term that—according to e-mail users—describes the traditional route of receiving correspondence: the U.S. Postal Service or other surface delivery systems. (*See: Electronic mail.*)

Soap opera, writing for. Soap opera has its roots in radio drama (originally sponsored by soap companies), in which dialogue is a fundamental factor. Even though TV is now the primary medium for "the soaps," skill in writing dialogue is still as important as the ability to construct plots and invent scenes with a prevailing emotional element.

Included in the staff of a soap opera are one or two head writers, who construct the show's *long-term projection* (also called the *book* or the *bible*), which is a narrative containing the story's plot and character development for shows to be produced during the following six months. A soap opera's two to four dialogue writers are hired by the head writers; they write the scenes from the head writer's week-by-week outline of the long-term projection. (Head writers earn six-figure incomes, out of which they pay their dialogue writers.)

Unlike a freelance writer, a soap opera staff writer works on a contractual basis. A thirteen-week period is the typical range of a contract. In addition, all writers for soap opera must belong to the Writers Guild of America.

The responsibilities of a soap opera writer are varied. Besides writing, he is expected to take part in casting characters; ascertain that each actor works the required number of days; stay abreast of the competition; and

be available for last-minute script changes.

Some head writers in soap opera have put forth this advice for the aspiring soap opera writer: Perfect your dialogue-writing skills; study TV writing or screenwriting, either formally or informally; and critically view the soap operas on TV. Those in the business point out that breaking in is much more difficult for a writer who lives outside New York or Hollywood, since many writers with industry connections live in those cities.

When actually writing to a producer, the writer should include a résumé, short tearsheets and a letter mentioning previously published dialogue. Unsolicited manuscripts are not accepted. (*See: Radio drama.*)

Social security. Social security refers to the U.S. government's tax-and-insurance system through which salaried and self-employed people can build a base for retirement income. A self-employed writer qualifies to make social security payments if he earns $400 or more per year and if he writes on a continuous basis. For every $630 earned annually, the writer gains a quarter of coverage— four quarters if he earned $2,520 or more in 1995. No one can earn more than four quarters in a year.

A writer may work both as an employee and as self-employed. He computes the tax on the employee earnings first and then figures the self-employed tax on the balance. But he does not pay a tax on earnings of more than $61,200, the social security taxable ceiling as of 1995.

A writer must reach insured status before he becomes eligible to receive social security benefits. The number of quarters of coverage based on his income determines his status.

A writer attains *currently insured* status when he has accumulated six quarters of coverage during the thirteen-quarter period immediately preceding the time of receiving benefits, i.e., retirement or disability, or death. His survivor or survivors receive death benefits.

A writer reaches status of *fully insured for life* when he has earned either forty quarters of coverage or a total ten-year income equivalent to the amount that would earn him four quarters coverage per year. He may earn these quarters consecutively or nonconsecutively.

The writer may draw full monthly retirement benefits at age sixty-five, or he may retire at sixty-two and receive smaller payments. The social security office computes an individual's monthly payment from his average earnings during his career.

Medicare, disability insurance, and survivor's insurance are other social security benefits available to the self-employed writer. To be eligible for any type of social security benefits, the writer must register with the social security office if he does not have a social security number. (*See: Retirement and the freelance writer.*)

Society for Collegiate Journalists (SCJ).

A fifteen-hundred member college journalism honorary society. SCJ sponsors an annual writing contest and presents the National Student Journalist of the Year award and the Edward E. McDonald National Chapter Award as well as the Medal of Merit, Certificate of Merit and Presidential Citations for contributions to college journalism.

The Society publishes *The Collegiate Journalist* annually and holds a biennial convention. The SCJ can be reached by contacting Dr. William Lawbaugh, at the Writing Center, Mt. Saint Mary's College, Emmitsburg, MD 21727.

Society for Technical Communication (STC).

This is an international association of people who are professionally or personally interested in technical communications; members include publishers, artists, scientists, writers, editors, engineers and educators. *Technical communication* refers to the conveyance of information on any subject—not just the obvious scientific or engineering topics—for which the user needs an explanation. Technical communication can be as simple as an instruction sheet for assembling a toy and as complicated as a computer program for a space shuttle. Awards are presented to members for audiovisuals and publications, art and on-line communications. STC presents scholarships and sponsors writing contests for high school students. Its annual conference is held in May. Headquarters are at 901 Stuart St., #304, Arlington, VA 22203.

Society of American Business Editors and Writers (SABEW).

This is an organization of twenty-two hundred editors, teachers and writers of business journalism. SABEW offers its members a résumé bank, so potential employers can have easy access to their qualifications; a 24-hour jobs hotline, with a recorded list of available jobs; and a CompuServe bulletin board, which contains organization news, job listings, selected articles from *The Business Journalist* and other reference materials. Members also receive a membership roster and *The Business Journalist,* SABEW's bimonthly newsletter. SABEW holds an annual convention and presents the distinguished achievement award to the business journalist who has made a lasting contribution to the profession. The organization recently created a contest to recognize overall excellence in newspaper business sections. Contact SABEW % Janine Latus-Musick, University of Missouri, School of Journalism, 76 Gannett Hall, Columbia, MO 65211.

Society of American Travel Writers (SATW). This organization is concerned with conservation, historic preservation and quality travel reporting. Members include writers, editors, photographers, broadcasters, travel film lecturers and public relations representatives. Annual awards are based on contributions to conservation, preservation and beautification. The address of the organization is 4101 Lake Boone Trail, Suite 201, Raleigh, NC 27607. (*See: Figure 47.*)

Society of Children's Book Writers and Illustrators (SCBWI). Formerly the Society of Children's Book Writers, this organization has about ten thousand members who are published or unpublished authors and illustrators of children's books. The SCBWI acts as a professional guild and offers workshops, conferences, meetings and critique groups throughout the country. Members receive the bi-monthly *SCBWI Bulletin,* which contains current information about the children's book publishing industry. The organization also presents grants for writers and illustrators, the Golden Kite Award for the published children's book, and the Magazine Merit Award. SCBWI is located at 22736 Vanowen St., Suite 106, West Hills, CA 91307.

Society of Magazine Writers. (*See: American Society of Journalists and Authors.*)

Society of Professional Journalists, Sigma Delta Chi (SPJ-SDX). This national organization has fourteen thousand members and three hundred active chapters. To become a professional member, an applicant must, at the time of application, be principally engaged in journalism (more than 50 percent of his working hours).

The society annually awards the Wells Memorial Key, the Distinguished Teaching in Journalism Award, Distinguished Service Awards in Journalism and Outstanding Graduate Citations. The Mark of Excellence Contest is another annual activity. SPJ-SDX publishes *The Quill,* a monthly magazine, as well as materials for the public. An annual meeting is held in the fall, and regional conferences take place every spring. The address of the organization is 16 S. Jackson St., Greencastle, IN 46135.

Soliloquy. A speech in which a character, either while alone, unaware of, or unconcerned with the presence of others, expresses his

FIGURE 47

SOCIETY OF AMERICAN TRAVEL WRITERS CODE OF ETHICS

CODE OF ETHICS

All members of the Society of American Travel Writers—Actives and Associates—subscribe to the highest standards of professionalism and, by accepting membership, agree to abide by the Code of Ethics of the Society.

The Code is comprised of Principles and Rules, and Procedures for enforcement.

The Principles represent the highest standards of conduct toward which all members should strive, and represent the overriding concepts from which the specific rules are derived.

The Rules are mandatory. They state the minimum level of conduct below which no member of SATW can fall without being subject to disciplinary action. The rules are uniformly applied to all members.

The Procedures set forth the process by which violators of the rules will be investigated and disciplined. Disciplinary action, which may be imposed by the Ethics Committee or the Executive Committee of SATW, may range from a reprimand to suspension or expulsion from membership in the Society.

PRINCIPLE I

SATW members are professional travel communicators and should always strive to maintain the highest professional standards.

Rules

1. Members shall not engage in plagiarism or infringement of the rights, including copyright, of others.
2. No member shall publish information about a destination about which he or she has no first-hand knowledge unless the member uses reliable sources of information.
3. No member shall misrepresent his or her SATW membership category or status.
4. No member shall falsely represent his or her credentials or work output as part of any SATW membership review or listing.
5. No member shall use the SATW name or insignia except to designate his or her membership, and no member may use official SATW stationery except for the conduct of official business of the Society.

6. Members shall not engage in conduct that embarrasses the Society or that will otherwise harm its reputation or professionalism.

PRINCIPLE II

SATW members should conduct business in a professional manner.

Rules

1. No member shall knowingly sell rights that he or she does not own.
2. No member shall permit his or her byline to appear as sole author on work not produced by him or her, nor shall a member be listed as co-author of a work to which he or she has not contributed.
3. When photographs or editorial materials have been furnished by others, a member shall so advise the publisher.
4. No member shall deliberately misrepresent his or her participation in a press trip in order to secure an editorial assignment.
5. Associate members shall not accept nor pay money for acquiring new accounts, except for proposal fees, and shall not offer cash or any other form of payment to editors or writers in exchange for editorial coverage purporting to be objective unbiased reporting of information.

PRINCIPLE III

SATW members should maintain the highest standards of professionalism on press trips.

Rules

1. No member shall deliberately misrepresent the status of an assignment in order to secure participation in a press trip.
2. All assistants accompanying a member on a press trip shall be fully qualified assistants; all others accompanying a member must be identified as guests. The participation of guests on press trips is subject to the restrictions of the host and at no time shall a guest attend in place of a member.
3. A member shall personally pay for all services required by that member that are personal, or over and above the services voluntarily provided by the host.

PRINCIPLE IV

SATW members should avoid all conflicts of interest.

FIGURE 47 (CONTINUED)

SOCIETY OF AMERICAN TRAVEL WRITERS
CODE OF ETHICS

Rules
1. No member shall accept payment or courtesies in exchange for an agreement to produce favorable material about a travel destination, service or supplier that is contrary to his or her own professional appraisal.
2. Members who are or have been employed by or associated with a travel destination, service firm or supplier shall disclose that fact to all potential editors and/or publishers prior to accepting an assignment relating to that destination or involving that service firm or supplier.

PROCEDURES

As provided in the Procedures section below, the Society shall discipline members found guilty of violations of the SATW Ethics Code, as well as for conduct detrimental to the best interests of the Society.
1. Complaints of suspected violations of any rule of the SATW Code of Ethics must be made in writing, signed by the complainant(s), and sent to the Society's Executive Director at the Society's headquarters office.
2. The Executive Director will immediately forward copies of the complaint to the members of the Society's Ethics Committee and the President.
3. The Ethics committee will promptly investigate all complaints forwarded to it and, within 60 days, shall determine if the complaint shall be dismissed, investigated further, or set for a hearing.
4. If the complaint is dismissed, the Ethics Committee will notify the complainant(s) and the President of the committee's decision, which shall be final.
5. If the Ethics Committee determines that the complaint should be investigated further, the committee shall notify the member of the complaint and by whom it was made, and advise him or her of the right to present evidence relating to the complaint. The Ethics Committee may interview by telephone, by mail, or in person, either members or others who have information relevant to the complaint.

6. If the Ethics Committee determines after further investigation that a violation has occurred for which a reprimand is appropriate, the committee shall prepare a written report detailing its finding of the facts, the nature of the misconduct so established, and the form of the reprimand imposed; a copy of the report will be sent to the charged party, the complainant(s), and the President. The decision of the Ethics Committee shall be final unless appealed by the charged party to the Executive Committee within 60 days of the decision; the request for an appeal must be made within that time frame by certified mail to the President at the Society's headquarters office.
7. If the Ethics Committee determines after further investigation that a violation has occurred for which suspension or expulsion from membership may be appropriate, the Ethics Committee shall hold a hearing by telephone conference call or at a location mutually convenient for all parties. Notice shall be given to the charged party, the complainant(s), and the President at least 60 days prior to the date set for the hearing. The charged party may appear with counsel at his or her own expense. The Chairman of the Ethics Committee shall preside over the hearing, which shall be conducted in an informal manner, with or without the presence of SATW's legal counsel. At the option of the charged party, a hearing may be waived and the complaint resolved by documents submitted in response by both the charged party and the complainant(s). After the conclusion of the hearing, the full committee shall decide by four-fifths vote to suspend or expel the charged member. The decision of the Ethics Committee shall be final unless appealed by the charged party to the Executive Committee within 60 days of notice of the decision; the request for an appeal must be made within that time frame by certified mail to the President at the Society's headquarters office.

FIGURE 47 (CONTINUED)

SOCIETY OF AMERICAN TRAVEL WRITERS
CODE OF ETHICS

8. Upon any appeal filed by a charged party subject to reprimand, suspension or expulsion, the Executive Committee shall hold a hearing by telephone conference call or at the next regularly scheduled meeting of the Board of Directors. The charged party may appear at the appeal hearing with counsel at his or her own expense. The President shall preside over the appeal hearing, which shall be conducted in an informal manner, with or without the presence of SATW's legal counsel. At the option of the charged party, an appeal hearing may be waived and the appeal resolved by documents submitted in response by both the charged party and the complainant. After the conclusion of the hearing, the full committee shall decide by four-fifths vote (with the President not voting) to uphold or reverse the decision of the Ethics Committee.

9. All proceedings of the Ethics Committee and all appeal proceedings of the Executive Committee shall be held in closed sessions, unless open sessions are requested by the charged party. All evidence submitted to either committee shall be maintained in the strictest of confidence.

10. A suspension may be imposed for any definite period of time. At the conclusion of the suspension period, no formal action is required for reinstatement of membership. A member who is expelled cannot be reinstated or reapply for membership.

thoughts aloud. This convention, most often found in drama, is used to reveal a character's innermost thoughts and feelings, or to provide the audience with necessary information. An important convention in Elizabethan drama, some of the best-known soliloquies are found in Shakespearean tragedies such as *Hamlet, Macbeth* and *Othello.* During the nineteenth century, when theater artists were determined to create the illusion of reality on stage, soliloquies were virtually eliminated from plays; the convention has been revived in the twentieth century, however, by dramatists such as Eugene O'Neill, Thornton Wilder, Tennessee Williams, Edward Albee and Samuel Beckett.

A soliloquy differs from an *aside,* an artificial device rarely used today, which are words spoken aloud by a character that are audible to the audience but presumably not to the other characters onstage. The soliloquy may be considered a *monologue,* although the latter term is usually reserved for an extended speech— in a narrative as well as a drama— delivered by one character and heard but not interrupted by others present. (*See: Monologue.*)

Song lead sheet. (*See: Figure 48.*)

Song lyric sheet. (*See: Figure 49.*)

The Songwriters Guild of America. Made up of both published and aspiring songwriters, this association, formed in 1931, provides a number of services to its members: Royalty Collection Plan, the Audit Program, the Catalogue Administration Program and the Copyright Renewal Service, a group medical and life insurance plan, contract review,

FIGURE 48

SONG LEAD SHEET

FIGURE 49

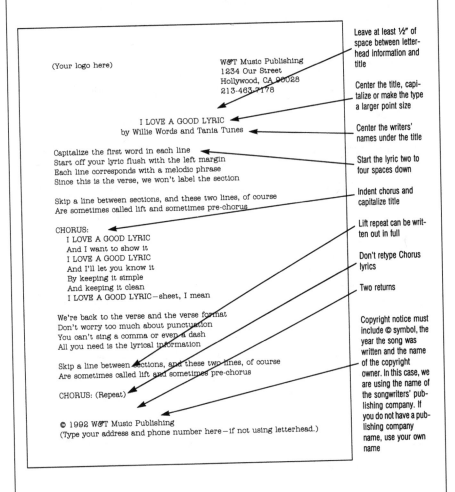

SONG LYRIC SHEET

(Your logo here)   W&T Music Publishing
1234 Our Street
Hollywood, CA 90028
213-463-7178

Leave at least ½″ of space between letterhead information and title

I LOVE A GOOD LYRIC
by Willie Words and Tania Tunes

Center the title, capitalize or make the type a larger point size

Center the writers' names under the title

Capitalize the first word in each line
Start off your lyric flush with the left margin
Each line corresponds with a melodic phrase
Since this is the verse, we won't label the section

Start the lyric two to four spaces down

Skip a line between sections, and these two lines, of course
Are sometimes called lift and sometimes pre-chorus

Indent chorus and capitalize title

CHORUS:
    I LOVE A GOOD LYRIC
    And I want to show it
    I LOVE A GOOD LYRIC
    And I'll let you know it
    By keeping it simple
    And keeping it clean
    I LOVE A GOOD LYRIC—sheet, I mean

Lift repeat can be written out in full

Don't retype Chorus lyrics

Two returns

We're back to the verse and the verse format
Don't worry too much about punctuation
You can't sing a comma or even a dash
All you need is the lyrical information

Skip a line between sections, and these two lines, of course
Are sometimes called lift and sometimes pre-chorus

CHORUS: (Repeat)

© 1992 W&T Music Publishing
(Type your address and phone number here—if not using letterhead.)

Copyright notice must include © symbol, the year the song was written and the name of the copyright owner. In this case, we are using the name of the songwriters' publishing company. If you do not have a publishing company name, use your own name

Reproduced from *The Songwriter's Market Guide to Song & Demo Submission Formats* ©1994.

estates administration, and the foundation for music scholarships and workshops. It publishes a periodic newsletter.

The former names of the Guild were the Songwriters Protective Association, and then the American Guild of Authors and Composers. Currently it is The Songwriters Guild of America. The Guild meets annually. Its headquarters are at 1500 Harbor Blvd., Weehawken, NJ 07087. The West Coast branch is at 6430 Sunset Blvd., Suite 317, Hollywood, CA 90028. The Nashville branch is at 1222 Sixteenth Ave. S., Nashville, TN 37203.

Songwriter's Market. An annual directory describing commercial outlets for songwriters' compositions. Its sections dealing with markets for songwriters are "Music Publishers," "Record Companies," "Music Print Publishers," "Record Producers" and "Play Producers & Publishers." Listings in these sections include names, addresses and telephone numbers of the companies; name of a person to contact; types of music the companies deal in; and information on how to submit material.

Other listings in the directory are included in the sections "Managers & Booking Agents," "Contests & Awards," "Organizations," "Advertising, AV and Commercial Music Firms," "Fine Arts," "Publications of Interest" and "Workshops." "Insider Report" articles which appear throughout the book, are profiles of noted songwriters and others in the music business.

Songwriter's Market also introduces the songwriter to the practical aspects of the music industry, describing fundamentals such as payment, copyright and recordkeeping; furnishing advice on how to submit material; and providing words of caution about the unethical side of the music business.

Songwriting. New York City, Nashville and Los Angeles are the three music publishing and recording centers in the U.S. To approach a music producer or publisher in any of these cities, a songwriter must have both a typewritten lyric sheet and a professionally produced demo tape; sometimes a lead sheet is required as well.

If a writer is presenting to a publisher, a good general rule is: when making a demo of a ballad, a piano/voice or piano/guitar version is sufficient. When making a demo of a rock or rhythm-and-blues tune, the writer should always indicate the rhythm when it is an intrinsic part of the song.

It is also helpful to the writer if, before this stage, his music has been played locally—for example, on radio or by a local group. Such exposure helps prove that the music is marketable.

The Songwriters Guild of America has devised a songwriter's contract that is used by some of their members; it includes provision for a fair-deal royalty and the return of the material to the writer if the publisher fails to achieve commercial release within the designated period. Some publishers use different contracts, but the Songwriters Guild reviews other contracts free for its members. Some music publishers who do work under the Songwriters Guild contract indicate that fact in their *Songwriter's Market* listings.

The Copyright Law of 1909 provided for the payment of royalties on sheet music and records as well as for public performance rights, but it was only with the Copyright Law of 1976 (effective 1978) that jukebox performance royalties were established.

Mechanical royalties in 1995 for the sale of records and tapes were $.66 per song, maximum, split between songwriter and publisher less reasonable publisher's expenses. Royalties on sheet music range from 3-8 percent; performance royalties vary widely depending on the vehicle and frequency of performance, etc. (*See: A&R [artists' and repertoire] representative; Figures 48 and 49; Lead sheet; Liner notes; Lyric sheet; Lyrics; Musical; Performing rights organizations; The Songwriters Guild of America.*)

Sonnet. A poem of fixed form that originated during the Renaissance and is still widely used. The word *sonnet* is derived from the Latin word for "song" and, ultimately, "sound."

Most sonnets contain fourteen lines of pentameter (usually iambic). Most are rhymed according to one of various schemes or patterns, though there is wide variation in modern usage. The Italian form, developed by Petrarch and Dante, introduces an idea in an *octave*, or eight-line section, made up of two *quatrains*, or four-line units; it concludes with a *sestet*, or six-line section, made up of two *tercets*, or three-line units. The *scheme*, in which repeated letters indicate the line endings that rhyme with one another, is *abba abba* in the octave. There are many patterns for the sestet, such as *cde cde* or *cdc ede*.

The English form, developed especially by Shakespeare (hence sometimes called the "Shakespearean sonnet"), rhymes *abab cdcd efef gg*.

Sonnets tend to be unified in thought, the whole poem developing a single idea—but this, in practice, is no more true of the sonnet than of other short poems. A series of related sonnets is sometimes called a "sonnet sequence." Petrarch and Dante wrote sonnet sequences in Italian, and Sir Philip Sidney's sonnet sequence, *Astrophel and Stella*, introduced the practice in English. Most of the great poets in English have written sonnets; some of the major practitioners, besides those mentioned above, are Milton, Wordsworth, Yeats, Frost and Cummings. (*See: Verse.*)

Sound effects (SFX). Sounds to be broadcast; produced by either taping the actual sounds or creating sounds with other materials, e.g., crumpling paper close to the microphone to simulate the crackling of fire.

sp. An abbreviation for *spell out* used by proofreaders and editors to indicate that an abbreviation or number should be spelled out. Written in the margin of a galley or page proof, *sp.* accompanies the proofreading symbol of a circle around the number or abbreviation. (*See: Proofreader's marks/symbols.*)

Space advertising. Units of *space*—such as one column, two columns, one page, or a double-page spread—are purchased by advertisers from newspapers and magazines. In contrast, advertising placed on TV or radio is purchased in units of *time*, such as thirty seconds or one minute. (*See: Advertising copywriters; Radio commercials; Television commercials.*)

Spacing of manuscripts. Editors at magazines and newspapers expect manuscripts submitted by freelancers to be double-spaced. Exceptions are made for poetry, which is sometimes single-spaced, with double spacing between stanzas.

Speakers and lecturers. Writers should not overlook the numerous opportunities to speak on their area of expertise: writing. Such appearances bring both direct lecture income and indirect income through increased sales of the author's books. Freelance writers can secure speaking engagements through local schools and colleges, as well as through various agencies.

The *Directory of Personal Image Consultants* catalogs speechwriters; listings in the biennial directory include specialty, credentials, number of staff members, teaching methods, fees and principal clients. Individuals and corporations throughout the U.S. are represented. The directory also lists consultants in speech, dress, personal public relations and motivation; information can be obtained from Image Industry Publications, 10 Bay St. Landing, Suite 7F, Staten Island, NY 10301. (*See: International Platform Association; Lecture agencies; National Speakers Association.*)

Spec. Shortened form of *speculative.* Refers to a radio spot written in an attempt to obtain a particular client's account. (*See: On spec.*)

Special sales. Any sale made by a publisher to a type of outlet that he usually does not deal with. The term *special sales* is a relative one, having a different meaning for each publisher. A premium book, or a book sold to an organization that distributes or sells it, is one kind of a special sale, as is a book sold to a convention on a topic of interest to the attendees.

Depending on quantity, books sold as special sales may yield higher-than-usual discounts for the organizations that buy them, as well as lower-than-usual royalties for their authors. (*See: Sponsored books.*)

Specializing as a writer. The beginning writer usually writes on a variety of topics until he becomes known to editors. This gives him the opportunity to find a topic that interests him enough to specialize in.

The specialist, after writing many articles and/or books, will find that both editors and the public associate his name with his subject. Because of this, he sometimes finds assignments easier to obtain and manuscripts easier to sell.

Speechwriting. This involves the same kind of research as writing an article, with one valuable addition: Much of the work in writing a successful speech rests in getting to know the speaker himself. By talking with a client, the writer learns his opinions, biases, frames of reference, sense of humor, personality, and natural style of speaking. This information is bolstered by seeking out written verifications of the client's opinion (as in the voting records and position papers of politicians) and tracking down hard facts (as in the annual reports and records of companies). In his search for background information, the speechwriter uses available resources in government offices and agencies, libraries, universities and communities. In the case of prominent political figures, the League of Women Voters, the Library of Congress, and the various arms of political parties are valuable contacts.

After knowing the speaker and understanding his unique needs for a speech, the writer tailors his words to a specific audience in a unique setting. The speech may be given formally or informally; it may be presented to the speaker's colleagues or his constituents; it may be designed to inform or persuade; it may be heard by a crowd of five hundred or a gathering of fifty. As does a magazine article, a speech projects a definite message (theme) with an appropriate beginning, middle and end. It is written in a style appropriate to its audience. A businessperson's speech is generally filled with elements of reason, logic and the language of business; it often deals with the speaker's business, commercial ventures in general, or a mixture of civic and business interests. A politician's speech, on the other hand, might cover any one of a spectrum of topics presented with verve and emotion.

Whatever the speech topic and purpose, whoever the speaker, the speechwriter composes a message mainly for an audience's ear. The writing is clear, concrete, simple, precise; the theme must be easily recognizable. Prose for speakers differs from prose for readers in several ways: Speech sentences are shorter and contain more imperative, interrogative and exclamatory phrases; they may include slang, sentence fragments and contractions; they are concerned with the sounds of words and the rhythms and repetitions of the language. (*See: Ghostwriting speeches.*)

Spelling mistakes. (*See: Misspelled words.*)

Spin-off. The recycling of a book or article, part of a book or article, or research material compiled for a book or article. Spin-offs include multiple sales to noncompeting markets, squeezing a second (or third) article out of research conducted for a different piece, or even selling reprints of a published article to a company or organization having a special interest in its subject.

Writers spin off their work in many ways. Magazine writers may make a point of doing copious research instead of just enough, or may specialize in articles appealing to a wide audience to sell to regional publications around the country. Book authors learn to shape chapters for easy condensation, query large-type or foreign publishers, or pursue lecturing or teaching careers on the side.

Sponsored books. Books that are financed by a company, association, institution, foundation or other group to serve its interests in some direct or indirect way. Sponsored books are written by either a freelance writer, an expert in a particular field or a company employee. For example, a state arts or humanities council (or both) might finance a book dealing with some aspect of state history; a large glassware manufacturer might underwrite a book about art glass; some other firm might wish to commemorate a business anniversary or offer consumer information on a selected topic. The firm or organization would use the book as part of a public relations or marketing campaign. Sponsored books distributed at no cost or at a discount cost are known as *premium books.*

A writer might conceive of a book idea after reading about an event involving a company, association or region. He would then approach a trade publisher or a publisher specializing in sponsored books, with an outline and a prospective company or organization that might benefit from the book.

The writer's fee for a sponsored book varies widely, and is not necessarily proportionate to the amount of writing produced. In general, however, this field of writing pays well. The book sponsor usually offers the writer a flat fee for the entire project; sometimes a royalty is included, especially if the book is likely to have a long life. (Royalties vary, and are different from those paid by trade book publishers. A minimum royalty might be 5 percent of the book's cost, in bulk, to the sponsor.) The writer's fee must be negotiated on the basis of the individual project; variables include the writer's name and reputation, and the amount of time allotted for the book. (*See: Copublishing; Self-publishing; Small press; Subsidy publishing.*)

Additional information: *How You Can Make $25,000 a Year Writing.*

Sponsored magazines. Some publishers, such as Whittle Communications, have created magazines whose editorial content is sponsored by a single advertiser. These magazines may be targeted to specific markets such as doctor's offices or collegiate audiences.

Spoonerism. Named for W.A. Spooner, an English clergyman and warden of New College, Oxford, who frequently made such slips, *spoonerism* describes a transposition of the initial or some other sounds of two or more words. "Let me sew you to a sheet" (for "Let me show you to a seat") and "a well-boiled icicle" (for "a well-oiled bicycle") are examples of spoonerisms. A spoonerism may be a witty turn of phrase or an accidental slip of the tongue.

Sportswriting. Today's sportswriting covers more sports, more categories within each sport, and a wider range of sports-related subjects than that of previous eras. Women's, high school and college sports are given newspaper space; participant sports such as hunting and fishing have separate columns; and "minor" sports such as swimming and track are attracting more attention from editors. For this reason, the aspiring sportswriter benefits by learning about as many sports as possible.

A good sportswriter has enthusiasm for sports in general, as well as the ability to avoid the clichés that tend to become rampant in this field in the work of less-skilled writers. Good writing is essential since a sportswriter's work must have entertainment value. In addition, accuracy is crucial in a sports write-up, since its audience pays close attention to facts.

In covering competitions, the sportswriter will find athletic directors and publicity directors helpful contacts. Similarly, fanatical fans can be valuable assistants in that their records on high school and college sports are often more extensive than those kept by the schools themselves.

Beginning sports reporters who work on small newspapers are often assigned other duties and non-sports stories as well. On large newspapers, sportswriting is unique among specialties in that the beginning reporter motivated toward it can often cover sports without previous general-assignment experience. However, a novice's assignments consist of high school and community group games, while coverage of college and professional events is usually reserved for more experienced sportswriters.

Spot. A radio or TV commercial; sometimes refers to advertising time sold separately, without regard to programming. A spot may also be a public service announcement.

Spot-news article. (*See: Magazine article, types of.*)

Stable. A collective term used to describe those authors whose work is regularly produced or run by one publishing house or publication.

Staff writer. Positions for writers exist both in print and broadcast media organizations.

Most writers on the staffs of large magazines have obtained their positions as the result of previous experience, either as freelance writers for magazines or in the newspaper field.

At smaller magazines, which rely on freelancers for most of the articles, the editor doubles as the staff writer. A magazine staff writer's duties can include writing original articles the magazine preferred to do itself rather than assign to a freelancer; and/or writing headlines, captions for illustrations, editorials, contents page copy and sometimes promotional material for the circulation manager.

Staff writing positions in broadcasting are also obtained through previous journalistic experience, in the case of radio and TV news departments; or after successful freelance assignments, for TV sitcoms and comedy/variety shows. (*See: Stringer.*)

Stage directions. In *Playwriting: The Structure of Action*, playwright and academic professor Sam Smiley describes the purpose and principles of stage directions:

The major, overall function of stage directions is to provide essential information to the production people about how they should present the play visually and vocally. Stage directions include *all* words other than the dialogue. It is crucial for the dramatist to compose directions for the theatre artist rather than for a reading public. Poor directions usually result from an author's ignorance of what they should be or his confusion about to whom they should be directed. The guiding principles for stage directions are: (1) Only necessary stage directions should be admitted. (2) They describe physical actions that take the place of dialogue. (3) They indicate the proper

Standard Directory of Advertisers **411**

reading of a word or a speech when the dialogue does not suffice. (4) They suggest pauses and other considerations of timing. (5) They explain specific matters about visual elements of production, such as scenery, properties, and lighting. A playwright should strive, however, to avoid stage directions and work the necessary bits of information into the dialogue.

In addition to the principles of necessity and clarity, Smiley notes that stage directions should not tell the director, designers and actors how to do their jobs by imposing interpretations and limitations that have not been woven into the dialogue.

Smiley describes three main types of directions: introductory, environmental and character. Introductory directions such as the character list, indication of time and place and a description of the setting precede the beginning of the dialogue. Environmental directions, which include specifications about time, space, light, temperature and physical objects, may appear in the introductory material or throughout the play. Character references state or qualify what the characters do and say.

Stage directions should be simply stated, Smiley says. Brief, declarative sentences, or sentence fragments, are most functional. It is better, according to Smiley, to indicate an action such as laughing as a stage direction—(He laughs.)—rather than use the words *ha ha* in the dialogue. All character entrances and exits should be noted in the stage directions.

Stage directions in the script are enclosed in parentheses. Instructions are typed in upper- and lower-case letters, with the exception of character names, which are always in caps. For example: (HANK moves to the bar and pours a drink. He hands it to EMILY.)

"Adroit stage directions are vital," Smiley explains, "and a playwright should exercise artistry in their composition." (*See: Playwriting.*)

Stand by. In broadcasting, refers to backup copy to be used in an emergency. As a verb, *stand by* is a signal to radio personnel that they are about to go on the air.

Standard Directory of Advertisers. An annual directory of twenty-six thousand corporations that advertise nationally or regionally. The classified edition, in which listings are arranged by the companies' products, and the geographic edition, in which listings are arranged by state and city, are published in January. Each edition contains a trade name list, an alphabetical index and a classifications index.

The following data are included in the listings: name, address and telephone number of the company; names of personnel; products of the company; advertising agency engaged by the company; advertising budget; month of the year in which annual advertising budget is devised; amount of sales; media through which the company advertises; scope of product distribution (such as national or regional); and number of employees.

Supplements are published in April and October. The *Directory* is also called the Advertiser Red Book.

(*See:* Standard Directory of Advertising Agencies.)

Standard Directory of Advertising Agencies. This directory, also known as the Agency Red Book, lists more than nine thousand U.S. and foreign advertising agencies. Included in the listings are the names, addresses and telephone numbers of the main and branch offices; names of managers and account executives; clients; number of employees; year of the company's establishment; memberships; and annual billing broken down by medium—magazines, newspapers, radio, TV, direct mail.

The *Directory* is published in January and July, and is supplemented in April and October. It contains a geographical index, and a special market index that lists agencies specializing in advertising directed toward specific groups, such as blacks, Hispanics, the medical field and the resort industry. (*See:* Standard Directory of Advertisers.)

Standard Rate and Data Service. This publishing company issues directories that contain advertising-related data on various media. One volume covers consumer and farm magazines; another, business magazines. Other directories are for newspapers, direct mail, TV and radio. In the magazine and business directories, each listing contains a summary of the editorial content that writers may find useful. Listings in the newspaper directory point out special sections of newspapers, which may offer freelance opportunities; the radio directory lists information on audience and programming, which may be of use to the freelance advertising copywriter; the direct-mail directory catalogs various mailing lists that might assist writers in research. These volumes are available in local libraries.

Stanza. (*See: Verse.*)

Start date/stop date. In radio advertising, the first and last dates a commercial should be run; usually indicated on both the copy and the cart.

State arts councils. Operated by state governments, state arts councils distribute grants to writers and artists. In most cases, however, grants are made to organizations rather than to individuals, so a writer interested in applying for state grants should make his initial overtures to a school, college or other potential sponsor. Poets and fiction writers, for example, are eligible for both short- and long-term residencies in the "Artists in the Schools and Community" programs sponsored by some state arts councils. They teach writing and read their work in the sponsoring schools, which are usually expected to provide matching funds to the amount granted by the arts council.

An arts council is usually located in each state capital. Addresses of state arts councils are available through the arts departments of public libraries.

State government publications. State travel offices and economic development offices can provide writers with material that can be useful in research. Travel writers, for example, can obtain free glossy black-and-white photographs and descriptive information on tourist attractions in each state; business writers can obtain statistics and forecast information about the state's leading ustries from the economic development offices. Most of these offices are located in state capitals; their telephone numbers, and sometimes their addresses, can be found in the white pages of the capital city's telephone book.

Some world almanacs include the addresses of the State Chambers of Commerce, along with general information about each state, in their annual editions. *The Directory of State Chamber of Commerce and Association of Commerce and Industry Executives*, available from the Chamber of Commerce of the U.S., 1615 H St., N.W., Washington, DC 20062, (800) 638-6582, lists all the state chambers. (*See: U.S. government publications.*)

Station rep. A person or company that sells radio or TV advertising time to potential sponsors, usually national, sometimes regional in scope.

Stationery. A supply of stationery that includes printed letterhead and business cards is an integral part of the freelance writing business, especially for the nonfiction writer. Printed stationery conveys the image of a writer who is serious and responsible. It is especially valuable to a writer whose name is yet unfamiliar to editors.

Computers make the generation of professional-looking stationery easy. Simply design a letterhead with your name, address and phone number, and print pages when necessary.

A clean look is best. Avoid fancy fonts and unnecessary illustrations.

You may want to list your areas of specialization, but avoid pigeonholing yourself. Simply listing *writer* is adequate.

Business cards also enhance the writer's professional image; they may be handed to interviewees or posted on bulletin boards at locations where a writer's services could be advertised.

Statistics. Statistics are facts or numerical data tabulated in a way to give information about a specific subject in condensed form. Statistical information is used in articles to emphasize a point or to support an argument on an issue. A reference containing statistics on various American institutions is the annual *Statistical Abstract of the United States.* Published by the U.S. Department of Commerce, the book is a compilation of tables and graphs reflecting social, economic and political activity in the U.S. A bibliography of state statistical abstracts is also contained in this publication.

Other sources of statistics are one-volume almanacs such as the *Information Please Almanac.* (*See: Background information, books of; Database.*)

Additional information: *How to Lie with Statistics.*

Status quo. Latin for *state in which.* The expression is used in English to mean "the existing condition," "the existing state of affairs" or "things as they are."

Steal my idea? Beginning writers often express concern about having a manuscript rejected while its idea is stolen by the same editor, who supposedly assigns it to another writer. Actually, editorial piracy—conscious or unconscious—is so rare among reputable publishers that it need not worry writers.

The question of piracy often arises when a writer sees his idea published in a magazine shortly after his submission was rejected by the same publication. However, the assumption that an idea has been stolen is usually incorrect: The published article was, in most cases, assigned and/or bought months earlier than the rejected one was submitted.

An idea in itself is not copyrightable; only the writer's particular presentation and structuring of information is.

Smart freelancers will concentrate on generating as many ideas as possible instead of worrying about editorial theft. (*See: Copyright; Editorial ethics.*)

Stereotype. Stereotypical characters—simple stock types that are instantly recognizable—are a major flaw in many writers' work. The brainless, buxom blonde; the black kid who's a whiz on the basketball court and the dance floor; the bloodless, myopic, absentminded professor have all been written about over and over again.

Stereotypical characters arise from laziness, condescension or a lack of imagination.

As Damon Knight writes in *Creating Short Fiction*: "Resist the impulse to stereotype your characters according to their occupations or their media images. The reader can do that himself; why should he pay you to do it? Let's say your character is a police sergeant with almost twenty years' experience. He need not be a wrestling fan, a beer drinker, or a Republican. He may be a Marxist and a Transcendental Meditation student who breeds dahlias and has a child bride. Give your characters credit for being as complex and interesting as you are, and give them a little slack. Listen to what your unconscious has to say about them; find out what *they* want to do." (*See: Stock character.*)

stet. Latin for *let it stand*. Editors and proofreaders place the word *stet*, encircled, in the margin of a manuscript to indicate that a marked change or deletion should be ignored, and the copy typeset in its original form. (*See: Proofreader's marks/symbols.*)

Stock character. This familiar figure-type traditionally appears in certain kinds of writing. For example, stock characters such as villains and heroes are regularly on hand in melodramas and category fiction. Stock characters include the rich socialite, the confidante and the evil authority figure.

The use of too many stock characters leads to their becoming merely cliché figures who contribute little to the strength of a work. It can also reinforce the bad habit of lazy characterization in the writer. (*See: Character; Cliché; Foil; Round character.*)

Stock response. Certain stimuli in works of art and literature may produce stereotyped or predictable reactions from readers and spectators. Traditionally, authors and filmmakers have relied heavily on the stock response; audiences have been conditioned to applaud heroes, jeer at villains and thrill at the bad guys' getting shot.

Since a stock response may interfere with or prevent a more appropriate and less conditioned response from an audience, conventional exploitation of the stock response has fallen out of favor in recent decades. Genuine literary artists now attempt to avert stock responses by shaping their material carefully so as to produce more individual responses.

Stock situation. A conventional pattern, incident or situation common in fiction and literature. For example, "boy meets girl, boy loses girl, boy gets girl" is a stock situation. Mistaken identity, the love triangle and quest for revenge are all recurring patterns in literature. Stock situations sometimes fail to rise above the level of stereotype because they lack fresh, original treatment; others become contemporary classics when the author makes the situation plausible through believable characters, convincing motivation and a suspenseful plot. The film *Breaking Away*, for instance, is a fairly typical story of initiation, but because of the freshness and fullness of its characters, it charmed critics and moviegoers alike. (*See: Formula story; Stock character.*)

Stories in textbooks. Most stories are reprinted from books or magazines, but some textbook publishers buy individual stories for reading texts directly from freelance writers. It is important to query a publisher before submitting a manuscript because some publishers use no freelance work, and there is usually a seven-

year interval between revisions of existing textbooks when new material *is* needed; if the writer has not queried first, his chances of submitting unneeded—and ignored—material are great.

Reading textbooks are planned in series, each of which is divided into grade levels. In some series, upper grades develop material introduced in earlier grades; in others, each grade level is given a separate study unit.

Peculiarities of textbook writing include vocabulary limitations in material for young children and space limitations that can cause a story to be drastically cut during the publishing process. Nor will a writer necessarily receive a byline accompanying his work: Some publishers list all writers' names at the beginning of a textbook instead of giving individual bylines.

Writers should read several textbooks and research individual publishers' needs before submitting to understand today's standards and practices.

Story. A story is a narrative told orally or written, either in prose or verse. It is designed to interest, amuse, entertain or inform an audience of readers or listeners. It involves its audience emotionally, encouraging them to care what happens to the characters.

A problem common to beginning writers is the inability to distinguish between a story and an incident. A story differs from an incident in that it possesses a quality of completeness: A character moves through a conflict to a conclusion, never completely the same at the end of the action as he was at the beginning. It is this change, for better or worse, that makes a story.

A further distinction exists between story and plot. A story is the sequence in which events occur as part of a happening; a plot is the sequence in which the author arranges or dramatizes those events. A murder mystery, for example, may be based on the following events: a man and woman engaged in an adulterous affair scheme to murder the man's wife; they drug her with a lethal dose of sleeping pills one evening and rig up a fake suicide note; an astute detective uncovers the crime and eventually brings them to justice. That is the *story*—the chronological sequence in which the events occurred. The author may decide the story would be told more effectively, however, if it began with the wife's death and ended with the uncovering of the affair and the murder. This sequence of events is the *plot*.

Robert Louis Stevenson, noted storyteller and novelist, had this to say about creating a story:

There are only three ways of writing a story: You may take a plot and fit characters to it; or you may take a character and choose incidents and situations to develop it; or you may take a certain atmosphere and get action and persons to express and realize it.

(*See: Plot.*)

Story analysts. Full- or part-time readers employed by film studios to read scripts submitted by agents, producers, stars and freelancers. They report to the studio's story editor.

Story rejection terms. Some editors explain their reasons for rejecting manuscripts when they send rejection slips to writers, although they are not obligated to. Following are editors' elaborations on common reasons given for rejecting short stories.

When a story is *too sentimental*, it exaggerates the emotional appeal with which the author tries to capture the reader. Sometimes, too, characters are portrayed as being overwhelmingly good; the author neglects to present at least some undesirable traits to make the characters seem human, not superficial.

The story that *lacks a theme* will usually be rejected. The plot of a story must tie in with a theme or—as in most confession stories—a lesson.

A story that contains a *melodramatic plot* is replete with magnification of events and emotions. When a plot is *contrived*, it depends on circumstance or coincidence for its resolution, and is therefore not believable.

An editor may remark that a story contains *wooden characters*. In that case, he means that the characters seem unnatural. Woodenness is often created through dialogue, so a fiction writer needs an awareness of natural speech patterns and of the peculiarities and skill levels in speech of persons at various ages. The term *characterless characters* refers to characters that have no unique qualities and so elicit no empathy from readers. They are essentially stock characters.

An editor's comment that the writer is *telling, not showing*, points to his overuse of narration and insufficient use of scenes and dialogue that would bring the story to life. On the other hand, a story that is rejected on the basis of its *purple prose* contains overstated, flowery language.

When rejecting a confession story, an editor might comment on a *passive narrator*, ruled more by outside circumstances than by his own will. An *unsympathetic narrator* is also a basis for rejecting a confession. This type of character embodies a prominent undesirable quality, so the reader is repelled by, rather than drawn to, him. (*See: Article rejection terms; Description; Dialogue; Narration; Show don't tell; Stock character.*)

Storyboard, magazine. A mechanical that shows the layout of a magazine's pages. It allows editors to see the flow of articles and advertisements. It's at this stage that editors can spot and solve layout and design problems.

Storyboard, TV. The layout for a TV commercial. Sometimes called a *board*, it is made up of pairs of frames that show both the video and audio parts of the broadcast. The upper frame—usually in the shape of a TV screen—displays a scene, while the smaller, lower frame supplies a verbal description of the scene and indicates the announcer's and actors' spoken parts.

A storyboard is produced in more than one stage, since it is subject to approval by agency executives and the client. Its final form may be a flat, paper-and-cardboard sheet, a cardboard accordion shape, a book, a filmstrip or a little movie.

In a good storyboard, the visual element outweighs the verbal (copy), and both elements are related, i.e., what is shown corresponds with what the announcer says, as when words are superimposed on the image. (Superimpositions are effective in commercials because of their power to reinforce an oral message.) A variety of camera distances and angles—the majority of shots being close-ups—and a minimum of characters and scenes also contribute to a successful TV advertisement.

Advertising executive Maxine Paetro advises the job-hunting copywriter not to include too many storyboards in a portfolio, because of the difficulty in reading them as compared with the ease of reading a printed advertisement. "If you load up your book [portfolio] too heavily with boards, you may find half your book will go unseen," she cautions, in *How to Put Your Book Together and Get a Job in Advertising.* (*See: Figure 50; Television commercials.*)

Stream of consciousness. The writing technique in which prose is intended to imitate real-life thought processes, i.e., it presents a character's thoughts and sensations exactly as they pass through his mind; the author does not distinguish between levels of consciousness, but runs complex and apparently random (but actually carefully plotted) patterns of memories, images and fantasies one after another. Works of James Joyce, Virginia Woolf, Dorothy Richardson and William Faulkner contain stream-of-consciousness writing. (*See: Interior monologue.*)

Stress (poetry). (*See: Verse.*)

Stringer. A writer who submits material to a magazine, newspaper, wire service or TV station from a specific

FIGURE 50

STORYBOARD FOR A TELEVISION COMMERCIAL

VIDEO: Open on two men as they walk on center camera. First man has a huge nerf sledge hammer in his hand. Second man follows him on stage rather reluctanly.

VIDEO: Man with hammer stops and talks to camera.

AUDIO: MAN: If you're like most people, you probably don't think much about most parts of your body until they start to bother you. Like take your nose.

VIDEO: A shot in the stomach.

AUDIO: And few things are as painful as a stomach ache.

VIDEO: Guy now doubled over.

AUDIO: How lucky he is to live here in Nashville. Because he can call Health Match, Nashville Memorial's free physician referral service. Why they'll fix him up with a doctor in no time.

TV advertising storyboard reprinted courtesy Northlich/Stolley/LaWarre Advertising, Cincinnati, Ohio.

FIGURE 50 (CONTINUED)

geographical location. He is distinguished from a staff writer because he works away from the home office. Some magazines call such writers stringers, others call them correspondents. They are part-time contributors, not full-time employees. They may be paid by the assignment or at an hourly rate.

Stringers function as reporters with assignments to be researched, written and sent in to the publication. Spot news is usually telephoned to the home office and "written up" there. Occasionally the stringer is assigned to do initial research and set up local interviews for a staff writer who writes the actual story. In addition to their assigned obligations, stringers are on the alert to advise editors of local developments that might deserve wider coverage. They may submit feature articles as well. A stringer has deadlines to keep and may or may not have a byline.

Stringers apply for work on local weeklies and broadcast media, city dailies, and nationally news-oriented trade publications. Trade magazines that are produced by small staffs rely heavily on the input of qualified writers nationwide who have a working knowledge of a particular technical specialty. Some consumer magazines also use stringers, however, sometimes listing them on the masthead by city or region. Independent stringers may work for more than one noncompeting newspaper or magazine. Payment is usually by the column-inch in newspapers, by flat fee for magazines.

Stringers are also used by TV and radio stations; they film or tape as well as write stories. Most of the opportunities are in the feature story area; most of the work can be found in medium-sized cities. Work is submitted on speculation to either the news director or the assignment editor.

The term *stringer* originated from the practice of measuring a stringer's typeset copy in a galley tray in the days when newspapers were set in hot metal, and the lines of type were tied together with string.

Strophe. (*See: Verse.*)

Style. Style is an elusive concept, one that defies precise definition. E.B. White had this to say on the subject: "There is no satisfactory explanation of style, no infallible guide to good writing, no assurance that a person who thinks clearly will be able to write clearly, no key that unlocks the door, no inflexible rules by which the young writer may shape his course."

Every writer, whether he creates fiction or nonfiction, poetry or drama, catalogs or textbooks, displays an individual style that involves not only his method of presentation, but also his very expression of ideas. Writing style can be developed, through the practice of writing and the comprehension and mastery of grammatical techniques.

Three criteria can determine the effectiveness of writing style: naturalness from the writer's viewpoint, acceptability from the reader's viewpoint, and appropriateness to the content of the piece.

Good writing style is a quality that evolves, refining itself with practice. (*See: Formal writing style; Informal writing style; Language and style, books on; Slang.*)

Style book. All magazines, newspapers and book publishing houses have style books that outline their rules regarding such elements as specialized spellings, language parameters and phraseology. For example, one magazine's style may allow foul language that another magazine would edit out. *The Chicago Manual of Style* is one of the most widely used style books, especially by magazines. Newspapers make use of *The Associated Press Stylebook and Libel Manual.* (*See: Language and style, books on.*)

Style sheet. Many book publishing houses issue a set of guidelines on style to help authors prepare their manuscripts according to the particular preferences of the individual publishing house. Style sheets usually refer to physical style—e.g., handling of numbers, hyphenation, references to gender—rather than literary style, although there are exceptions. Some publishers of paperback romances, for instance, issue very specific guidelines to plot, setting and so on—down to the heroine's age and appearance.

Subhead. This publishing term is used two ways. *Subheads* are brief explanatory headlines that appear periodically in the main body of the text. They are used both in magazine articles and within book chapters.

Another kind of subhead—usually called a subtitle—is a secondary explanation of a book's or article's main title; it is placed below the title.

Subject Guide to Books In Print. An annual directory listing books in print according to subject categories corresponding to those of the Library of Congress. Listings, which are alphabetized under each category according to author's last name, also provide information such as title, name of publisher or distributor, publication date, price, indication of illustrations, Library of Congress number and ISBN.

Subject Guide to Books In Print is printed in more than one volume; the last volume of each annual series contains an alphabetical listing of abbreviations of publishers and distributors, with addresses.

Subjective writing. Writing characterized by the personal, reflective involvement of the author. Based on the writer's own experiences or on his reactions to the experiences of others, subjective writing centers on the expression of personal thoughts, impulses and feelings. A subjective writer asserts his own personality in his writing and reveals something of his life or his views to the reader. (The objective writer avoids any such intrusion of his own background or opinions in his writing.)

Almost any type of writing can be subjective. Autobiographies are, naturally, almost entirely subjective; much contemporary poetry, such as the work of Dylan Thomas and Robert Lowell, is subjective; Virginia Woolf's novels and essays and John Dos Passos's poems, plays and novels are particularly subjective.

An author's material is described as subjective only if the ideas and emotions expressed by him or his characters are his own ideas and emotions, representative of his own personality. Seldom is the *I* narrator of a first-person novel the voice of the author; more often than not, that *I* is a character created by the author to tell the story. Someone reading a contemporary women's novel, for example, should not assume that, because the *I* narrator of the story has an abortion, the author of the book is revealing that she herself has had an abortion and takes a positive stand on the subject. All writing is to a certain extent inevitably subjective, but a reader should not assume that the events of a novel or the emotions revealed in a poem are necessarily autobiographical.

One danger in subjective writing is that the author becomes so self-reflective that much of what he has to say is of little importance to the reader. Even the subjective writer must write about matters that interest many people, not just himself—topics with which his reader can identify. As is true of all material written to be read, the purpose of subjective writing is to communicate. Personal introspection and unfocused rambling that cannot be generalized to a larger population than the author himself will not usually result in readable writing or effective communication. (*See: Objective writing; Personal experience.*)

Submission of manuscripts. (*See: Manuscript preparation and submission.*)

Subplot. A minor or secondary plot in a play or work of fiction that may highlight or contrast the principal plot. In Lawrence Sander's novel *The First Deadly Sin*, for example, the main plot involves a police detective's pursuit of a mass murderer; a subplot running throughout the narrative deals with the illness and hospitalization of the police detective's wife, and its effect on his personal and professional life. (*See: Plot.*)

Subscription books. A type of book that is marketed as a group, usually by direct mail, but sometimes in retail stores. Encyclopedias, general reference books, atlases, dictionaries and literary classics can fall under this category. The various Time-Life series, sold by direct mail, are examples.

Subsidiary rights. A term that usually refers to rights to a book other than book publication rights. Subsidiary rights include dramatic, radio, TV, motion picture, foreign and serial rights.

Profits from subsidiary rights are divided between author and publisher. The actual terms of those divisions—i.e., which party has the right to sell them and who receives what percentage of the earnings—is spelled out in the contract for the sale of the manuscript. The Authors Guild has established guidelines for negotiating division of subsidiary rights. It advises that the author receive at least 80 percent of the earnings on a British edition, 75 percent on foreign editions, 50 percent on paperback and book club sales, and 90 percent on movie and TV sales.

Even though terms are agreed on in the contract, the author's income depends on the success of the publisher or agent in selling the various subsidiary rights. (*See: Book contract; Rights to manuscripts.*)

Subsidy publishing. A publishing venture that is financed entirely by the author. The subsidy publisher profits on every book he produces, while the author takes the financial risk. Reviews are hard to obtain on subsidy-published books, and for most books published by this method, it is estimated that only one of ten authors recoups his investment. On the other hand, people who can afford the cost of production have the satisfaction of seeing their ideas, opinions or information set forth in a permanent form to share with others.

A major factor that distinguishes subsidy publishing from self-publishing is that in the subsidy business, ownership and distribution of the book belong to the publisher, while in self-publishing, they belong to the author.

Before entering into a subsidy publishing agreement, an author should determine the policies of the publisher. The *Writer's Digest* reprint "Does it pay to pay to have it published?" (available for a self-addressed, stamped envelope, from Writer's Digest Books, 1507 Dana Ave., Cincinnati, OH 45207) enumerates basic questions that should be addressed to a subsidy publisher.

Although a subsidy publisher usually pays the author's copyright fee, the book should be copyrighted in the author's name. Similarly, the author should retain all rights to his work. The agreement should provide for a royalty greater than that paid by a trade publisher, the latter of which is 10-15 percent of the retail price.

Some advantages of subsidy publishing are short production time, little chance of rejection and royalties that are tax free until the author recovers his original investment.

Subsidy publishers advertise in newspapers and magazines and will discuss details during in-person interviews with authors in various cities their salespeople visit.

In the age of desktop publishing, in which many freelancers have the electronic capabilities to produce their own high-quality books, subsidy publishing is no longer the only alternative to commercial publishing. (*See: Desktop publishing; Self-publishing.*)

Sunday magazine. Formerly known as a Sunday supplement, this is a category of magazine that is inserted in a Sunday newspaper. Material published in a Sunday magazine is timely and of regional focus. It often deals with news-related subjects, although its longer production lead time—sometimes six weeks before publication—makes it unsuitable for fast-breaking news.

One purpose of the Sunday magazine is to provide in-depth material that usually cannot be accommodated by the newspaper itself. What was formerly a hard news story, for example, is sometimes recapitulated with additional information, interviews and interpretive analysis, and written as a feature for publication in a Sunday magazine.

Features published in Sunday magazines usually require more research than those published in the newspaper. Investigative articles, articles of opinion, how-to articles, round-up articles and personality profiles are other categories sought by many Sunday magazine editors. Although there are exceptions, the writer submitting material to these magazines generally should avoid history and fiction.

Since editors depend on freelance writers for most Sunday magazine articles, the category represents a market with numerous opportunities; the frequency of publication indicates the quantity of material required. In addition, these publications are generally receptive to the work of new writers.

Earnings in the Sunday magazine category are relatively low; very few local publications pay as much as $150 minimum per article. Nationally distributed magazines, however, such as *Parade*, pay $2,500 for 800-1,500 words.

Sunday supplement. (*See: Sunday magazine.*)

Super. Abbreviation for *superimpose.* In TV and motion pictures, titles are often superimposed over scenes. Sometimes one picture is superimposed over another. In TV advertising, a slogan or other message is sometimes superimposed over a shot. (*See: Storyboard, TV; Television script terms.*)

Surprise ending. A sudden and unexpected twist in the action at the end of a narrative—usually a short story. A surprise ending differs from a *trick ending* in that information making the surprise ending logical and satisfying to the reader is planted early in the story. Editors do not like surprise endings in which, for example, the main character turns out to be a dog. O. Henry (William Sidney Porter) and Saki (H.H. Munro) are noted for their mastery of the surprise ending. Stories featuring the surprise or twist ending are often found in *Alfred Hitchcock's Mystery Magazine.* (*See: Plant; Trick ending.*)

Suspense. Suspense is the element of both fiction and some nonfiction that makes the reader uncertain about the outcome. While most obvious in mystery stories such as those published in *Ellery Queen's Mystery Magazine* or *Alfred Hitchcock's Mystery Magazine*, suspense is present in all good fiction.

Suspense can be created through almost any element of a story, including the title, characters, plot, time restrictions and word choice. For example, if the plot involves the hero trying to reach an intended victim before a bomb is set to explode, the author has used time restriction as a suspense device.

Another means for creating suspense is to use the *objective viewpoint* in which the story is told, not through the mind and feelings of a major character, but only by what he says and does. That character may have some secret that affects the outcome of the story, but since the author never tells us what the character thinks—or remembers—but only what he says and does in the present, the viewpoint adds to the suspense.

The reader may also be tantalized as an *impending event* is gradually unfolded.

Just as readers will remain loyal to a writer who offers well-constructed, suspenseful plots, they are likely—as are editors—to reject one who resorts to trickery. A trick ending, for example, introduces a solution in the form of a character or a piece of information that has not been alluded to before.

Suspension of disbelief. The mind of the reader, viewer or listener willingly effects a suspension of disbelief when the author's successful rendition of a fictional character or event seems "real" to the reader. This process allows the reader or audience member to accept the imaginative aspects in a work of fiction, poetry or drama.

Ben Jonson made the first allusion to this concept, when he wrote, in *Discoveries*: "To many things a man should owe but a temporary belief, and suspension of his own judgment." Coleridge, in *Biographica Literaria*, described this idea as "that willing suspension of disbelief for the moment, which constitutes poetic faith."

Symbolic quote. A statement in an article that is put in quotation marks, but is not a specific quote from one single person; instead, a symbolic quote is a composite of ideas expressed by several people in different interviews. For example, a quote that is a composite of several different quotes from middle management executives of Midwestern companies may be attributed to a single middle management executive with a Midwestern company.

Symbolic quotes are used to avoid repetitive quotes from similar people, and to let one symbolic representative of similar sources be the spokesperson; however, some writers and editors consider use of the symbolic quote to be somewhat unethical. When a writer submits an article containing symbolic quotes, the editor must be notified, since he may have a policy of using quotes only from specific individuals.

A symbolic quote is distinguished from a *paraphrased quote* in that the latter is a restatement of another person's words or ideas that remains true to the intent of the original. (*See: Composite character; Paraphrase.*)

Sympathy. The act of or capacity for understanding or sharing the feelings of others; the expression of pity or compassion. Sympathy—a "feeling with"—is often confused with *empathy*, the ability to project one's personality *into* someone else and feel with that other person on a personal and deeply involved basis.

Sympathy is an important element in writing. It is that feeling that a writer strives, through skillful characterization, to evoke from readers. A reader who doesn't care what happens to the characters in a story will most likely put down the book or turn to another piece in a magazine. To engage the reader's capacities for identification and sympathy, then, a writer must create characters the reader can care about. (Developing in-depth profiles of a story's characters before they start to write is one way some writers achieve this.) When the reader experiences concern, admiration, sorrow, approval, pity or compassion for a character, the writer has succeeded in creating a sympathetic character.

To create engaging characters, an author must himself be sympathetic and understanding, both toward his characters and toward the human condition in general. In *Writing the Novel*, Lawrence Block explains, "A first principle of characterization may seem fairly obvious, but I think it's worth stating. Characters are most effective when they are so drawn that the author can identify with them, sympathize with them, care about them, and enjoy their company." Hallie and Whit Burnett concur with Block in their *The Fiction Writer's Handbook*: "A writer without sympathy or understanding for his characters or for the human condition would have difficulty arousing emotional response in any reader."

A sympathetic character does not have to be a "good" person. Skilled writers present morally reprehensible characters sympathetically by illustrating the factors that made a character develop a certain way. When attempting this, however, writers should give their character at least one redeeming trait. (*See: Characterization; Reader identification.*)

Syndicated column. A syndicated column is a piece of writing sold simultaneously to different newspapers or magazines by a business concern (syndicate), usually for a commission on the sale price. (Some syndicates pay writers a salary or buy material outright.) Syndicated columns are promoted and sold to publications that pay for them according to the size of their circulation. The syndicate's commission is usually 40-60 percent of the net proceeds of the column (gross receipts less the cost of salespeople, promotion, mailing, etc.). Writers of nationally syndicated columns may earn $50,000 or more a year; most syndicated columnists earn much less.

Because syndicates' primary customers are newspapers, material submitted for syndication must be clearly and succinctly written. Popular syndicate material includes how-to articles and personality pieces about entertainers and sportspeople.

In addition to columns, national syndicates may also handle features, puzzles, news, cartoons and photographs. Some syndicates are interested only in certain specialties, e.g., education features, financial analyses, articles of interest to women. *Writer's Market* lists topics, submission requirements and syndicate outlets for more than fifty syndicates around the country. The *Syndicate Directory* of *Editor & Publisher* magazine (11 W. Nineteenth St., New York, NY 10011) tells which syndicates handle current syndicated columns and classifies all syndicated columns by subject matter, so a writer can see what the existing competition for a new column idea is. (*See: Self-syndication.*)

Additional information: *The Road to Syndication.*

Syndicates. (*See: Syndicated column.*)

Synecdoche. A figure of speech that substitutes a part for the whole or a whole for the part. For example, in "The pen is mightier than the sword," *pen* substitutes *discourse* and *sword* substitutes *warfare.*

Synonym. A word having the same or nearly the same meaning as another word in the same language. For example, *gratitude* is a synonym for *thankfulness*; *cranky* is a synonym for *ornery*. A word or expression recognized as another name for something—such as *Ma Bell* for the Bell

Telephone System—can also be described as a synonym.

Using synonyms to express the same ideas or subjects in a more effective, interesting way is one device a writer employs to add variety to his work. Since two words are seldom identical in meaning, however, a writer must choose synonyms carefully. Although the denotative meaning—i.e., the dictionary definitions—of two words may be similar, the connotative meanings—those implied or associated—may be entirely different. Some individuals may say a man who lifts weights for four hours every day is a physical fitness *fanatic*; the man may huffily reply that he is a physical fitness *enthusiast*. In other words, two words may mean basically the same thing, and yet have very different implications. (*See: Thesaurus.*)

Synonym finder. (*See: Thesaurus.*)

Synopsis. A statement giving a brief, general review or condensation of a topic or subject. It is most frequently used to describe the plot summary of a story, novel or play.

A synopsis also forms part of a book proposal that an author submits to a publisher. A proposal generally consists of a comprehensive summary of the contents of the proposed book (the synopsis), along with two or three sample chapters and an outline detailing chapter-by-chapter highlights of the work. (*See: Book manuscript preparation and submission.*)

Syntax. The arrangement and grammatical relations of words, phrases and clauses in a sentence. Although the word is often used as a synonym for *grammar*, syntax is actually a branch of the science of grammar. (*See: Grammar.*)

Table of contents. A listing at the beginning of a book or magazine, indicating chapter, article or story titles and their corresponding page numbers. A table of contents can also include brief descriptions of each article, or titles of the sections, as well as the chapters, of a book.

An integral part of the front matter of any published book, a table of contents is also a necessary accompaniment to an author's proposal to a potential publisher on a nonfiction book idea. The writer should submit to the publisher a proposed table of contents that contains at least a one-paragraph description of each chapter. This provides the publisher with a concise and convenient way to evaluate the book's contents.

Tabloid. A weekly newspaper printed on paper that is half the size of a standard newspaper, and characterized by its emphasis on emotional impact. In addition to regular newsstand sales, they are also sold at the checkout counters of some supermarkets.

In general, stories printed in tabloids concentrate on unusual angles of more popular news stories. Their lively tone is evidenced by the inviting leads and upbeat, sometimes surprise, endings.

Subject matter covered in most tabloids includes celebrities, consumer issues, unusual human interest, self-help, strange phenomena, handicapped people and developments in medicine. In addition, news features—articles elaborating on one phase of a recent news event—are prominent in tabloids.

A freelance writer who sells to a tabloid will earn varying rates, depending on the size of the publication. Fees range from less than $50 to more than $1,000.

Taboos. Writers may wonder whether there are still taboos, or subjects undesirable to editors, in the magazine world. Such restrictions do indeed exist: One example is shown by the field of religious magazines, whose taboos correspond with those in the religious groups they represent. In addition, any given juvenile magazine is almost certainly a market in which taboos exist. In general, magazines in this category reject subject matter that is too mature for their readers.

Other types of magazines have limitations as to acceptable material, which may or may not be associated with societal taboos. Generally, such taboos are derived out of the political and economic interests of a publication's readers. For example, a strongly environmentalist magazine would never accept an article arguing that economic need warrants draining and building on the nation's remaining coastal marshlands—nor would a construction publication publish an article advocating legislation to freeze coastal development.

Even though taboos exist in some markets, writers of many years of experience should remember that as standards change with time, so do taboos. Some religious magazines, for example, now publish material dealing with homosexuality, theological questions, and challenges of hierarchy; in the past, such topics would have been unacceptable.

The easiest way for writers to avoid violating editors' restrictions is to check the listings in *Writer's Market* and write for sample copies and editorial guidelines. (*See: Confession; Juveniles, writing for; Religious writing; Short stories for young people.*)

Tag. A bit of information the announcer adds to the end of a previously taped radio commercial; it consists of information such as the sponsor's name, address and business hours.

Tag (character tag). A descriptive technique that helps to quickly identify a character throughout a story. Tags are not character traits but project the specific outer person with unique gestures, speech patterns or other background details. These vivid identification labels are effective when used consistently in the characterization of a subject; they can even make flat characters appear round. They often project a character as positive or negative: A negative tag may blind the major character to another character's trait, or a positive tag can hide the negative traits of supporting characters. Tags can make readers either sympathize with or dislike a charac-

ter. Tags are most successful when they are neither too obvious nor too disguised.

Writers have many kinds of tags with which to build character identification. A *name tag* depends on the connotation of a name, e.g., Bobby Jo as a Southerner. An *action tag* refers to the peculiar body movements of a character—a limp, a way of frowning when thinking. A *speech tag* consists of a character's unique voice quality, word choice, inflection or delivery. *Background tags* identify a character by age, education, social status or religion, e.g., a Harvard scholar, an orthodox Hindu. *Sensory tags* are used to create images in the reader's mind, e.g., a highly perfumed woman. *Mental tags* show how a character thinks, such as calmly or bizarrely.

Writers can also tag characters by using figures of speech to describe them, e.g., a voice as soothing as nails across a blackboard. (*See: Characterization.*)

Talent. Although superior talent is perceived by most critics and editors to be an inborn quality, other personal factors play a role in determining a successful writing career. Many published writers are proof that people with limited talent can develop the writing skills needed to please readers. On the other hand, a talented writer who lacks energy and/or persistence may not publish as much material as a writer with less talent whose ambition effects his success.

Talk shows. A TV or radio talk show appearance presents the writer with an opportunity to reach large audiences in his marketing efforts. Self-help and business topics are most desired by talk shows. If your book is designed to help readers improve their health, finances or romantic lives, you'll have an easier time getting on a show. Appearing on a broadcast medium can be an overwhelming experience for the initiate. Author Raymond Hull has outlined some strategies for making broadcast interviews run smoothly:

Before the program, the writer can prepare himself in several ways. Watching/listening to the program can teach him about the interviewer's techniques and the program's format—e.g., whether there is a group of guests or only one. For an interview in another city, proper scheduling is crucial. The writer should be sure that he arrives in town with ample time to spare and that he arrives at the station one-half hour before the program begins. (Staying in the city for a day after the interview can result in other promotion opportunities.) It is also important that the writer learn about the program's audience, so that he is prepared to discuss his book in a way most interesting to that particular group.

Personal preparation involves dress, voice and self-confidence. For TV, a white shirt or blouse is inappropriate for best camera effect; a blue one is most suitable. A low-pitched voice—which can be acquired through practice with a tape recorder—is the most pleasing to the ear. A course in public speaking may help give the writer the self-confidence necessary for a TV appearance.

It is advisable to take a copy of the book being promoted to the interview: the copy sent by the publisher (in the case where the publisher has arranged the interview) could have been lost. During the interview, the writer may also mention the book's title a few times, in suitable contexts.

The writer should be aware that he may be on camera whether or not he is speaking. Similarly, at the end of the program, the show may remain on the air for some seconds even after the conversation has stopped. In radio interviews, the writer must remember to verbalize all his responses: a shake or nod of the head communicates nothing in this medium!

After the program, the staff and crew should receive the courtesy of a thank-you.

(*See: Promotion by author.*)

Talking book. (*See: Blind writers' resources; Books, tapes of.*)

Tall tale. A type of folktale originating on the American frontier. In these stories, the physical attributes, capabilities and exploits of characters are wildly exaggerated for comic effect. John Henry is a phenomenally strong railroad man and Paul Bunyan is a gargantuan logger, for instance. Washington Irving and Mark Twain are two of many American writers who incorporated tall tales in their fiction. More recently, writer and storyteller Rick Sowash compiled the fabulous tales of Cy Gatton, a late-nineteenth-century storyteller, in *Ripsnorting Whoppers*. (*See: Folktale.*)

Tape recorder. This tool is useful to the writer during interviews, since it accurately and completely records the subject's responses, enabling the interviewer to concentrate on his subject, his surroundings and new questions he may want to ask.

Tape recorders can be purchased in a range of sizes and in many degrees of quality. The pocket-sized ones are preferred by many writers because they are inconspicuous: They tend not to intimidate the interviewee. Using a high-quality tape recorder reduces the risk of malfunction—and thus of distractions—during interviews. The interviewer should always test the recorder in advance of any interview, and use fresh batteries for each interview.

Beware of external noise as well. If you're interviewing in a restaurant, for example, you may find your tape contains the noise of silverware clattering and conversations from other tables. Taped interviews work best in a quiet setting, such as an office.

An inexpensive accessory to the tape recorder, the telephone jack, is used to tape telephone interviews. Most states have laws regulating the taping of telephone conversations. It's best to inform your subject that he is being taped.

When a writer fails to get a personal or telephone interview with the subject, he may suggest a taped one. The author makes a list of questions he wants answered and sends the tape with the questions (also included on the tape) to the person, along with a self-addressed, stamped package for its return. (*See: Tape recordings, reference file of.*)

Tape recordings, reference file of. Interview tapes containing material on controversial subjects should be retained in case of a lawsuit arising from the article. Subject to rules of admissibility, a tape recording can come to the writer's defense since it may prove what was said during the interview.

When the possibility of a lawsuit exists, the writer should check the state's statute of limitations, which might apply to his article (depending on where it is published, the type of claim against the article, etc.). (*See: Interview; Recordkeeping.*)

Target audience. The group of readers toward which a magazine or book is directed. It is characterized by similarities in age, education, income, values, interests, needs and other such characteristics.

The salability of a piece of writing can be determined by the needs or wants of its intended audience and the skill with which the writer fulfills those needs or wants.

In the magazine field, the audience's needs are assessed by the editor, and the writer's chances of finding an audience here are greater, since there are thousands of established magazines with clearly defined target readerships. If a writer was planning an article on single-parent families, for example, he would decide on an audience to which it should be directed, then study magazines to find one aimed at his target audience. In this case, a women's magazine, a magazine on parenting or a religious magazine would likely be suitable.

Similarly, before a book is written, the professional writer has researched the existence of a need and the size of his proposed audience and uses that information when approaching a publisher.

Writer's Market listings provide descriptions of publications' audiences. (*See: Writer's guidelines.*)

Taste. The ability to perceive and appreciate that which is harmonious, appropriate or beautiful, particularly in literature, art or decorum. Although certain standards of good and bad taste are established in any society, what is considered appropriate is often a subjective matter, subject to frequent change. Some critics believe that taste can be improved by studying and analyzing excellent examples of art and literature; many artists and writers, however, contend that taste is a limiting concept that stifles imagination and self-expression.

Although taste may well be a matter of subjectivity, the writer who intends to sell his work to consumer and trade magazines, or to most publishing houses, is obliged to stay within the realm of what is generally considered "good taste." For example, some satirical magazines' idea of humor would not be considered good taste by most other magazine editors. In general, magazine editors consider bathroom humor, cartoons ridiculing religion, ethnic jokes, jokes that demean women, and humor about handicapped people in poor taste.

Writers who feel confined by society's standards of appropriateness may have more success submitting their work to alternative publications such as the ones listed in *Writer's Market* and *The International Directory of Little Magazines and Small Presses.*

Tautology. Unnecessary repetition of the same idea in different words, without the addition of meaning or clarity. Tautologies such as "free giveaway" and "advance reservation" are frequently found in spoken and written expression. The careful, concise writer ruthlessly edits redundancy from his work.

Taxes. All writers who earn a profit, i.e., whose earnings are greater than their expenses, must pay federal income tax. Those with incomes of $400 or more after deductions are required to pay social security tax and to submit a self-employment form, Schedule SE, in addition to the Form 1040 and Schedule C tax forms.

A part-time freelance writer cannot claim losses as deductions unless he has earned a profit in three of five consecutive years. A writer earning less profit is considered to be a hobbyist rather than in business.

The writer should be aware of all aspects of his business that are tax-deductible and should keep detailed records, especially receipts, to prove his claims. Some deductible items are classes, including those taken as research or as refreshers in technique (but not as preparation for writing); mileage for travel; and dues of professional organizations. Writing supplies and expenses such as paper and postage are also deductible, as are the purchase, repair, maintenance and depreciation of writing or writing-related equipment such as typewriters, tape recorders and cameras.

A writer may deduct expenses for the room in his house in which he works, but only if he writes regularly and uses the room solely for freelance writing.

Depending on where the writer lives, he may be required to pay state or city business taxes as well as income tax. Information on local taxes is available from individual state or city tax offices. Since tax laws are subject to frequent amendment, it is best to obtain instructions each year from a local tax office. (*See: Figures 51 and 52; Recordkeeping; Retirement and the freelance writer; Social security; Travel.*)

Teachers & Writers Collaborative, Inc. This not-for-profit organization sponsors a program of creative arts education through which writers, painters, dancers, filmmakers and musicians are brought into classrooms. The Collaborative's original emphasis was on language arts, and it has established three assumptions concerning the teaching of language. They are: (1) "Children who are allowed to develop their own language naturally, without the imposition of artificial standards of grading, usage, and without arbitrary limits on subject matter, are encouraged to expand the boundaries of their own language"; (2) "Grammar and spelling develop as a result of an attachment to language and literature, not vice versa. Teaching these skills before children feel they are relevant stifles their interest in language"; and (3) "Children who write their own literature and read other children's are more likely to view all literature as an effort to deal with experiences in creative ways,

whatever that experience may be."

The Teachers & Writers Collaborative publishes *Teachers & Writers Magazine* six times per year. The magazine's content consists of teaching ideas, news digests, interviews, book reviews, letters, editorials, features and excerpts from the diaries kept by artists who participate in the program. Student work and contributions from others are also published. Its address is 5 Union Square, W., New York, NY 10003.

Teaching writing. Teaching can involve the writer with various age groups and with all types of writing. In preparing for classes, he often learns new material; and in teaching others, *his* analytical, organizational and communicative skills are expanded.

One way to become involved in teaching is to apply for a position with a creative writing program sponsored by some elementary and secondary schools. Teaching certification may be required, especially if students receive academic credit for the course. Some schools, however, offer enrichment courses for which no credit is given. Generally, teachers of enrichment courses do not need certification. Payment for a teaching writer is approximately $25-$35 per hour, although the exact rate is determined by the aspects of the particular program.

A variation of these programs are writer-in-residence programs, which are known by different titles in each state. Funds are provided by state arts councils, individual schools and/or the National Endowment for the Arts; information is available from state arts councils, whose

FIGURE 51

WRITER'S TAX RECORDS

FREELANCE OFFICE EXPENSE   1989

DATE	ITEM	COST
5/3	oceanography books	39.64
5/6	photocopies	.60
5/17	computer power surge strip	31.60
5/20	business envelopes	.57
5/20	" letterheads	5.28
6/3	library parking	1.75
6/3	" photocopies	.40
6/4	magazine subscription	21.80
6/12	aviation books	13.46
6/14	priority mail to publisher	2.40
7/14	university library parking	1.00
7/14	library photocopies	1.20
8/10	white out / pen / stapler	3.80
8/12	business envelopes	1.30
8/12	letterheads	5.39
8/15	2 phys. diskettes - computer	11.58
8/16	Freelance postage stamps	25.00
8/18	computer lessons	136.74
8/25	Prevention ms. phone calls	8.22
8/31	science museum	2.00

Business Travel Expense record kept separately by trip date

Accurate recordkeeping is a must for all freelancers. Many word-processing programs contain a spread sheet function, or you can keep credit card receipts and post smaller cash purchases in a ledger like the above, with back-up receipts.

FIGURE 52

WRITER'S TAX FORM

SCHEDULE C **(Form 1040)** Department of the Treasury Internal Revenue Service (O)	**Profit or Loss From Business** (Sole Proprietorship) ▶ **Partnerships, joint ventures, etc., must file Form 1065.** ▶ **Attach to Form 1040 or Form 1041.** ▶ **See Instructions for Schedule C (Form 1040).**	OMB No. 1545-0074 **1994** Attachment Sequence No. **09**

Name of proprietor	Social security number (SSN)

A	Principal business or profession, including product or service (see page C-1)	**B** Enter principal business code (see page C-6) ▶
C	Business name. If no separate business name, leave blank.	**D** Employer ID number (EIN), if any

E Business address (including suite or room no.) ▶ ....
City, town or post office, state, and ZIP code

F Accounting method: **(1)** ☐ Cash **(2)** ☐ Accrual **(3)** ☐ Other (specify) ▶ ....

G Method(s) used to
value closing inventory: **(1)** ☐ Cost **(2)** ☐ Lower of cost or market **(3)** ☐ Other (attach explanation) **(4)** ☐ Does not apply (if checked, skip line H) | Yes | No

H Was there any change in determining quantities, costs, or valuations between opening and closing inventory? If "Yes," attach
explanation . . . .

I Did you "materially participate" in the operation of this business during 1994? If "No," see page C-2 for limit on losses. . .

J If you started or acquired this business during 1994, check here . . . . ▶ ☐

Part I   Income

1	Gross receipts or sales. **Caution:** *If this income was reported to you on Form W-2 and the "Statutory employee" box on that form was checked, see page C-2 and check here* . . . . . . ▶ ☐	**1**	
2	Returns and allowances	**2**	
3	Subtract line 2 from line 1	**3**	
4	Cost of goods sold (from line 40 on page 2)	**4**	
5	**Gross profit.** Subtract line 4 from line 3	**5**	
6	Other income, including Federal and state gasoline or fuel tax credit or refund (see page C-2) . .	**6**	
7	**Gross income.** Add lines 5 and 6 . . . . ▶	**7**	

Part II   Expenses. Enter expenses for business use of your home **only** on line 30.

8	Advertising	**8**		**19**	Pension and profit-sharing plans	**19**	
9	Bad debts from sales or services (see page C-3) . .	**9**		**20**	Rent or lease (see page C-4):		
				a	Vehicles, machinery, and equipment .	**20a**	
10	Car and truck expenses (see page C-3)	**10**		**b**	Other business property . .	**20b**	
11	Commissions and fees. . .	**11**		**21**	Repairs and maintenance . .	**21**	
12	Depletion	**12**		**22**	Supplies (not included in Part III) .	**22**	
13	Depreciation and section 179 expense deduction (not included in Part III) (see page C-3) . .	**13**		**23**	Taxes and licenses	**23**	
				24	Travel, meals, and entertainment:		
14	Employee benefit programs (other than on line 19) . . .	**14**		**a**	Travel	**24a**	
15	Insurance (other than health) .	**15**		**b**	Meals and entertainment .		
16	Interest:			**c**	Enter 50% of line 24b subject to limitations (see page C-4) .		
a	Mortgage (paid to banks, etc.) .	**16a**					
b	Other	**16b**		**d**	Subtract line 24c from line 24b .	**24d**	
17	Legal and professional services	**17**		**25**	Utilities	**25**	
				26	Wages (less employment credits) .	**26**	
18	Office expense	**18**		**27**	Other expenses (from line 46 on page 2)	**27**	

28	**Total expenses** before expenses for business use of home. Add lines 8 through 27 in columns. ▶	**28**	
29	Tentative profit (loss). Subtract line 28 from line 7	**29**	
30	Expenses for business use of your home. Attach **Form 8829**	**30**	
31	**Net profit or (loss).** Subtract line 30 from line 29. • If a profit, enter on **Form 1040, line 12,** and ALSO on **Schedule SE, line 2** (statutory employees, see page C-5). Estates and trusts, enter on Form 1041, line 3. • If a loss, you MUST go on to line 32.	**31**	

32 If you have a loss, check the box that describes your investment in this activity (see page C-5).
• If you checked 32a, enter the loss on **Form 1040, line 12,** and ALSO on **Schedule SE, line 2** (statutory employees, see page C-5). Estates and trusts, enter on Form 1041, line 3.
• If you checked 32b, you MUST attach **Form 6198.**

32a ☐ All investment is at risk.
32b ☐ Some investment is not at risk.

For Paperwork Reduction Act Notice, see Form 1040 instructions.   Cat. No. 11334P   Schedule C (Form 1040) 1994

FIGURE 52 (CONTINUED)

Schedule C (Form 1040) 1994   Page **2**

Part III   **Cost of Goods Sold** (see page C-5)

33	Inventory at beginning of year. If different from last year's closing inventory, attach explanation . .	**33**
34	Purchases less cost of items withdrawn for personal use	**34**
35	Cost of labor. Do not include salary paid to yourself	**35**
36	Materials and supplies	**36**
37	Other costs	**37**
38	Add lines 33 through 37	**38**
39	Inventory at end of year	**39**
40	**Cost of goods sold.** Subtract line 39 from line 38. Enter the result here and on page 1, line 4 . .	**40**

Part IV   **Information on Your Vehicle.** Complete this part **ONLY** if you are claiming car or truck expenses on line 10 and are not required to file Form 4562 for this business. See the instructions for line 13 on page C-3 to find out if you must file.

41   When did you place your vehicle in service for business purposes? (month, day, year) ▶ ..../......./..... .

42   Of the total number of miles you drove your vehicle during 1994, enter the number of miles you used your vehicle for:

a   Business ....   b   Commuting   c   Other ....

43   Do you (or your spouse) have another vehicle available for personal use? . . . . ☐ **Yes**   ☐ **No**

44   Was your vehicle available for use during off-duty hours? . . . . ☐ **Yes**   ☐ **No**

45a   Do you have evidence to support your deduction? . . . . ☐ **Yes**   ☐ **No**
   b   If "Yes," is the evidence written? . . . . ☐ **Yes**   ☐ **No**

Part V   **Other Expenses.** List below business expenses not included on lines 8–26 or line 30.

....		
....		
....		
....		
....		
....		
....		
....		
....		
46 **Total other expenses.** Enter here and on page 1, line 27	**46**	

✪ *Printed on recycled paper*   ☆ U.S. GPO: 1994-375-198

Schedule C-EZ is also available from the IRS. You may use the EZ form if you had gross receipts of $25,000 or less; had business expenses of $2,000 or less; use cash accounting; did not have any inventory; did not have a net loss; had only one business as sole proprietor; had no employees; are not required to file Form 4562, Depreciation and Amortization; do not deduct business expenses for business use of your home; and you do not have prior year unallowed passive activity losses from this business.

addresses can be obtained from the local public library.

High schools offer writers work teaching journalism. A part-time job pays from $15 to $70 per hour. Certification is required for teaching high school journalism; a writer with a college degree may be eligible for a provisional certificate or for enrollment in additional courses leading to a teaching certificate.

Independent teaching is another option for writers. Students of the independent teacher are most often a mixture of adults and teenagers. A newspaper photo and press release, along with signs posted in the community, make up one kind of self-promotion campaign. A conference room rented from a business can serve as a classroom, and student fees can be based on comparable course fees at a local college (published in the course catalog). Many courses founded by an independent writer are sponsored by educational institutions, such as the adult education departments of high schools or school districts. In such cases, the instructor's sponsor furnishes facilities, publicity and a salary.

Tearsheet. A tearsheet is a sample of writing in its published form, cut from the newspaper or magazine in which it appeared. If the tearsheet does not include the title and date of the publication, the writer should add that information. (*See: Clip.*)

Teaser. The opening scene of a teleplay. Its action is designed to intrigue the audience so that it will watch the following scenes. Other words for *teaser* are *hook* and *prologue.* (*See: Television script terms.*)

Technical writing. Though the term refers to instructions or descriptions on any subject matter, it is being used to mean writing for the fields of engineering, government, industry and science.

Various types of organizations hire technical writers: corporations, university researchers, advertising agencies, newspapers and government and private organizations that carry on research in the physical and social sciences.

Private companies, particularly those that conduct research and manufacture parts and equipment for specific customers, represent the largest market for jobs in technical writing. The private company engages a technical writer who, working closely with engineers, first produces a technical proposal that aims to sell the product, and then provides periodic progress reports detailing the work for the customer. Finally, the writer produces a handbook and an instruction manual to accompany the finished product. A writer may specialize in one of these phases of the job, or he may participate in all three.

An experienced technical writer earns $20,000-$50,000 per year. Writers can expect to start around $15,000 with a bachelor's degree; higher with a more technical degree; or $35-$75 per hour, depending upon the complexity of the job. The yellow pages, under the headings "Employment Contractors—Temporary Help" and "Technical Manual Preparation Service," lists sources of temporary employment. (*See: Society for Technical Communication.*)

Techno-thriller. This genre utilizes many of the same elements as the thriller, with one major difference. In techno-thrillers, technology becomes a major character. In Tom Clancy's *The Hunt for Red October,* specific functions of the submarine become crucial to plot development.

Telephone area code map. (*See: Figure 53.*)

Telephone usage, tactics on. The telephone can aid a writer both in conducting present business and in acquiring new projects.

The writer who spends a great deal of time doing long-distance telephone interviews may benefit from installing a WATS line (Wide Area Telecommunications Service) or contracting with a private long-distance discount service such as MCI or Sprint. In addition, telephone tape-recording attachments are available so that a writer can tape a telephone interview. Taping a telephone call is not illegal as long as it is not being taped for an illegal purpose. The writer should ask the interviewee when the conversation begins if he may record for factual accuracy; the subject's agreement on the tape is his backup.

Another business technique related to the telephone is the use of an electronic answering service. This device allows an associate to reach the writer on his first attempt. Call waiting also prevents the writer from losing calls from prospective clients that may come in when he is on the phone.

In querying editors about possible assignments, the writer should use the telephone judiciously. Most editors prefer query letters to telephone calls, except in cases of urgent timeliness.

Teleplay. The script for a TV program or a made-for-TV movie. (*See: Television script terms.*)

Teletext. (*See: Electronic text.*)

Television and Radio, Museum of. A museum located in New York City that contains cassette recordings of radio and TV programs. The collection represents the U.S. and foreign countries, and contains material produced during the past sixty years. Writers who live within commuting distance of Manhattan may find the archives useful in communicating the flavor of a certain time in visual and audio form, as opposed to a backdated newspaper account.

In the Museum's library, a card catalog indexed by title, subject, date, network, cast members and production staff gives users access to cassette tapes. The tapes are viewed at consoles on videocassette players; they are not lent by the library. Tapes are available for an hour at a time and are distributed on a first-come, first-served basis.

Museum visitors may also view programs in the MB Theater and the Videothèque, which screen programs and stage exhibits for large groups.

In addition, the Museum maintains a reference library of books and periodicals, a collection of twenty-four hundred radio scripts, and the NBC Radio archives, which hold recordings of radio programs.

The Museum of Television and

FIGURE 53

Area code map reprinted courtesy The American Telephone and Telegraph Company.

Radio is at 25 W. Fifty-second St., New York, NY 10019.

Television commercials. The work of the TV copywriter involves duties besides writing, because jobs in this field often overlap among departments. Sometimes one person plays the combination role of writer-producer. The writer may be called upon to work along with the account executive, assessing the client's needs and studying the intended consumers of the product, who will make up the commercial's audience. With the producer, the writer may help choose the technical crew and actors for the commercial, and supervise wardrobe selection.

The copywriter spends several hours each week—along with other agency personnel—meeting with clients to discuss their needs, their past successes and failures and their marketing problems. At a large advertising agency, the copywriter may spend only fifteen minutes per week in actual writing.

Though this type of work differs from that of most writers, the TV copywriter possesses certain specialized skills. He must be able to think in visual terms and to create a theme that will both entertain the audience and sell a product in a very short time.

One advertising director suggests that the writer ask himself three questions about any TV commercial he produces: (1) Does the commercial make clear what the product or service is? (2) Does it show how the product or service is different or better from others? and (3) Is the tone of the commercial compatible with where the consumer is, in relation to the need for the product?

A writer interested in working in this field should write to an agency, submitting a résumé and requesting an appointment to show his writing samples, and discuss his commercial ideas for the agency's clients. (*See:* Standard Directory of Advertising Agencies; *Storyboard, TV.*)

Television, jobs in. Staff positions in TV are numerous and varied. Most are in four major areas: production, news, engineering and public relations. Production jobs include floor directing, camera operation, lighting, switching, directing and set construction. Newswriting, reporting, editing and photography are duties performed by people in a TV station's news department. Engineering work comprises electronics maintenance, mechanical maintenance and master control operation. Public relations practitioners are responsible for duties such as writing press releases and producing public service announcements.

Freelance TV opportunities are outlined in the booklet *Jobs and Opportunities For Writers.* (*See: Television station organization chart.*)

Television markets. Freelance writers find markets for their work in the TV series, the made-for-TV movie, the documentary, the soap opera, etc. A limited number of freelance jobs are also available for TV advertising copywriters.

Selling material to TV is difficult for the writer who lives outside the two centers of the industry, New York and Los Angeles. Another complicating factor is that a writer usually needs an agent to be able to sell his work to a TV market. A list of TV agents to whom writers may submit teleplay scripts appears in *Writer's Market* and the *Guide to Literary Agents*.

Once he has made a sale, the writer can join the Writers Guild of America, which negotiates contract terms with producers. (*See: Documentary; Screenwriting; Soap opera, writing for; Writers Guild of America*.)

Television program material release form. (*See: Figure 54.*)

Television script. The TV writer usually delivers a script to a producer one step at a time, developing it from premise to outline to script.

The *premise* is the idea for a story. It contains the basic plot, i.e., a beginning, a middle and an end; but it does not describe the story's elements in detail. It is often delivered verbally to the producer.

The outline, also called the *treatment* or the *story*, represents a great amount of effort on the writer's part. At the outline stage, he writes a narrative of the story, filling in details of plot, characterization and emotional impact, but usually omitting dialogue. (The character's statements are written in, however, in narrative form, e.g., "John tells Jane to get out.") The outline may include camera directions.

A *format* for a series of one-hour TV programs may range from one to eighty pages, containing a narrative description of what the series will be about, the leading characters and several typical plots.

The *script*, or *teleplay*, for the individual show consists of dialogue, camera directions and stage direc-

tions. The plot of a teleplay is structured much like that of a novel or short story, except that it necessarily emphasizes action rather than reflection on the part of characters, and it usually ends at the climax. Other elements peculiar to the teleplay are the *prologue* (also called the *teaser* or *hook*), which is the first scene of the drama; and the *tag*, an epilogue in the form of a brief scene sometimes appended to the end of the drama to tie together loose story ends. (*See: Figure 55.*)

Television script terms. Definitions of these terms are listed at their alphabetical locations in this book: angle; backstory; beat; close shot; close-up; cut to; dissolve; establishing shot; exterior; fade in; fade out; full shot; hold; interior; long form; off-screen; pan; point of view; presentation; pull back; scene; super; teaser; teleplay; treatment; two shot; voice-over; wide angle.

Television station organization chart. (*See: Figure 56.*)

Television writing. Like screenwriters, TV writers should live in Southern California or New York City, since it is difficult to keep abreast of changes in TV series without living in the area where they are produced. Writers attempting to break into TV, however, face considerable financial risk by moving to New York or Los Angeles without a sale, an agent or industry contact.

Writers Guild rules prohibit a member writer's actually writing a script without a contract guaranteeing compensation, but writers who aspire to breaking into the field must

FIGURE 54

TELEVISION PROGRAM MATERIAL RELEASE FORM

———————————————— , 19 ————

Title and/or Theme of Material Submitted Hereunder: ————————————

————————————————————————————————————

Gentlemen:

I am today submitting to you certain program material, the title and/or theme of which is indicated above (which material is hereinafter referred to as the "program material"), upon the following express understanding and conditions.

1. I acknowledge that I have requested permission to disclose to you and to carry on certain discussions and negotiations with you in connection with such program material.

2. I agree that I am voluntarily disclosing such program material to you at my request. I understand that you shall have no obligation to me in any respect whatsoever with regard to such material until each of us has executed a written agreement, which by its terms and provisions will be the only contract between us.

3. I agree that any discussions we may have with respect to such program material shall not constitute any agreement expressed or implied as to the purchase or use of any of such program material which I am hereby disclosing to you either orally or in writing.

4. If such material submitted hereunder is not new or novel, or was not originated by me, or has not been reduced to concrete form, or if because other persons including your employees have heretofore submitted or hereafter submit similar or identical program material which you have the right to use, then I agree that you shall not be liable to me for the use of such program material and you shall not be obligated in any respect whatsoever to compensate me for such use by you.

5. I further agree that if you hereafter produce or distribute a TV program or programs based upon the same general idea, theme, or situation, and/or having the same setting or background and/or taking place in the same geographical area or period of history as the said program material, then, unless you have substantially copied the expression and development of such idea, theme or situation, including the characters and story line thereof, as herewith or hereafter submitted to you by me in writing, you shall have no obligation or liability to me of any kind or character by reason of the production or distribution of such program(s), nor shall you be obligated to compensate me in connection therewith.

6. You agree that if you use any legally protectible portion of said program, provided it has not been obtained by you from, or independently created by, another source, you will pay me an amount that is comparable to the compensation normally paid by you for similar material or an amount equal to the fair market value thereof as of the date of this agreement, whichever is greater.

I acknowledge that but for my agreement to the above terms and conditions, you would not accede to my request to receive and consider the said program material that I am submitting to you herewith.

Very truly yours,

————————————————————

————————————————————

————————————————————

This release form reprinted by permission of the author from *The Complete Book of Scriptwriting* © 1982 by J. Michael Straczynski.

FIGURE 55

TELEVISION SCRIPT SAMPLE

TED
(puts hamster in cage)
Are you?

6   CLOSE—LIZ
presses her lips together as a wave of pain hits her. He starts toward her.

TED
(continuing)
Something wrong?

She forces a smile, shakes her head. He continues looking at her questioningly. A beat. Then he lets it pass.

TED
(continuing)
You know what you need? Hot sun . . . warm beach . . .

LIZ
(wanly; dreamily)
M-m-m- . . .

TED
Listen, I've got a week coming next month. I'd be glad to pick up an extra plane ticket . . . Did you ever see the water off Ladego Beach, Jamaica . . . it's so blue and clear . . .

7   FAVORING LIZ
taking off her white jacket, looking into the reflection of her drawn face in a small mirror perched on a shelf, she wearily pushes some strands of hair away from her forehead.

TED
(continuing; watching her)
You haven't heard a word I said . . .

She looks across at him.

TED
(continuing; unhappily)
Tell me something, hun—what have these hamsters got that I haven't got . . . ?

There are one- and two-column TV scripts for teleplays. The two-column format presents both the video and audio (the sights and the sounds) of a teleplay separately—one in each column of the page. A script written in the one-column format, on the other hand, alternates descriptions of video and audio. Most directors prefer the one-column format, since it leaves them room to make notes and indicate camera changes as they see fit.

This excerpt reprinted by permission of the authors from *The Writer's Digest Guide to Manuscript Formats* ©1987 by Dian Dincin Buchman and Seli Groves.

FIGURE 56

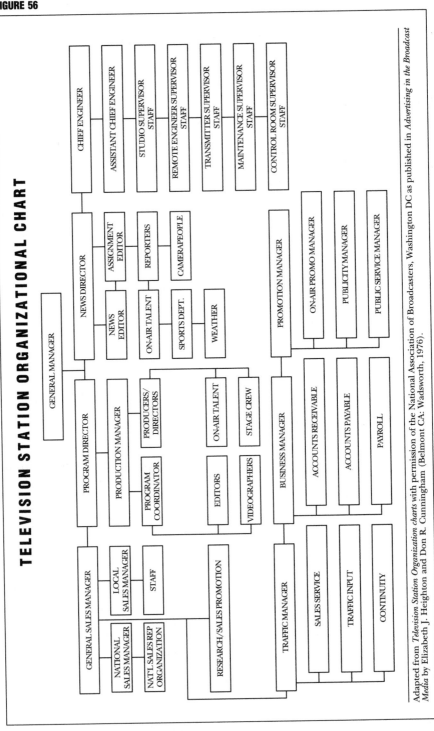

TELEVISION STATION ORGANIZATIONAL CHART

GENERAL MANAGER

CHIEF ENGINEER
- ASSISTANT CHIEF ENGINEER
- STUDIO SUPERVISOR / STAFF
- REMOTE ENGINEER SUPERVISOR / STAFF
- TRANSMITTER SUPERVISOR / STAFF
- MAINTENANCE SUPERVISOR / STAFF
- CONTROL ROOM SUPERVISOR / STAFF

NEWS DIRECTOR
- ASSIGNMENT EDITOR
- NEWS EDITOR
- ON-AIR TALENT
  - REPORTERS
  - CAMERAPEOPLE
- SPORTS DEPT.
- WEATHER

PROMOTION MANAGER
- ON-AIR PROMO MANAGER
- PUBLICITY MANAGER
- PUBLIC SERVICE MANAGER

PROGRAM DIRECTOR
- PRODUCTION MANAGER
  - PROGRAM COORDINATOR
  - PRODUCERS/ DIRECTORS
  - EDITORS
  - ON-AIR TALENT
  - VIDEOGRAPHERS
  - STAGE CREW

BUSINESS MANAGER
- ACCOUNTS RECEIVABLE
- ACCOUNTS PAYABLE
- PAYROLL

GENERAL SALES MANAGER
- NATIONAL SALES MANAGER
- LOCAL SALES MANAGER
- NAT'L SALES REP ORGANIZATION
- STAFF
- RESEARCH/SALES PROMOTION

TRAFFIC MANAGER
- SALES SERVICE
- TRAFFIC INPUT
- CONTINUITY

Adapted from *Television Station Organization charts* with permission of the National Association of Broadcasters, Washington DC as published in *Advertising in the Broadcast Media* by Elizabeth J. Heighton and Don R. Cunningham (Belmont CA: Wadsworth, 1976).

usually do so by writing entire scripts on speculation—without an assignment or guarantee of production. The unknown freelancer presents prospective agents with a completed script, rather than a mere idea, a plot synopsis or a treatment because he must demonstrate that he can write a produceable script.

Before a would-be writer heads to Hollywood—or even *writes* to Hollywood—he should be thoroughly familiar with the peculiarities of TV scriptwriting. He must be able to neatly structure a script around commercial breaks, and write convincing characters for series that have been created by other writers. He should understand production limitations and confine an episode's action to a series' standard sets; he must also be able to figure out what subject matter is taboo for a particular series.

Most teleplays are bought in the early spring of each year, although the introduction of the two-season year has created a year-round need for TV scripts. To sell his work, a TV writer should have an agent. Experts advise the aspiring scriptwriter to proceed by writing a teleplay on speculation and mailing it to an agent.

A booklet containing TV writers' minimum rates, which are established by the Writers Guild of America, is available for a small fee from Writers Guild of America West, 7000 W. Third St., Los Angeles, CA 90048.

Protection for a TV script can be secured either through Writers Guild of America registration (registrants need not be members) or Copyright Office registration. (*See: Audiovisual communication; Figures 61 and 62; Screenwriting; Soap opera, writing for; Television commercials; Television script; Writers Guild of America.*)

Additional information: *The TV Scriptwriter's Handbook.*

Tempo. (*See: Pace.*)

Testimonial. An endorsement of a product intended to induce others to buy that product. Testimonials often appear on the dust jackets of books, recommending those works to potential buyers. These endorsements may be from celebrities, recognized authorities in the subject field, other well-known authors, or sometimes individuals who are not well known at all, but who represent satisfied readers of the book.

A publisher's publicity department generally takes care of soliciting testimonials from individuals—including other authors—whose names and/or remarks they feel will stimulate sales of the book. An author may suggest to his publisher the names of celebrities or authorities he believes will respond favorably to his book. The writer who intends to publish his own book may attempt to gather endorsements for his book while it is still in the manuscript stage; these testimonials can then be incorporated on the dust jacket (or cover, if the book is paperback) when the book is printed. (*See: Blurb.*)

Textbook publishing. A writer who writes a textbook has the best chance of having it published if he has teaching experience in the field he covers, knowledge of current research and the ability to write clearly.

First, the writer must determine

what other books have been written on the topic. Such research involves analysis of topic coverage, noting organization, problems and examples, and style.

Next, the writer must test the book's teaching capacity. A publisher needs to know whether a book is effective in practice. If the writer is a teacher, he tests his book by using it (or the completed sections) in a classroom and giving it to other teachers to use.

Finally, a writer submits a *prospectus*: the writer's résumé, title, synopsis of the contents, a description of the competition, and an indication of the proposed audience and market for the book. Also included are the estimated length of the book; a description of the number and kinds of illustrations; what copyrighted material will be used; and a statement of how much of the manuscript has been written, along with an estimate of time needed to complete the manuscript. The prospectus also includes an outline of the manuscript and the parts of the actual text that have been tested. With the prospectus, a writer should send a short letter informing the publisher of the subject matter and grade level of his book.

Textbook publishers sometimes research the market themselves, by questionnaires, visits to teachers, market reports and attendance at teachers' conferences, for example. In such a case, an editor devises a plan for a textbook and chooses an author, who then writes the book.

Each state has criteria by which it chooses books to be used in its schools. Also, textbooks written for elementary school use are often part of a series, so the writer in this field should be prepared to work on books for several grade levels.

Royalties for elementary school and secondary school textbooks range from 3-5 percent of the publisher's net receipts; those for college-level texts range from 10-15 percent.

A press run of printed and bound textbooks is usually five to ten thousand copies. In some cases, more books are printed but are left unbound until needed. (*See: College Textbook Publishers, largest; Stories in textbooks.*)

TFN. " 'Til further notice''; sometimes used on commercial copy instead of a final broadcast date.

Theater. Many markets are open-minded about the work of new playwrights. Local groups and clubs perform children's plays and church-related plays. Most high schools and colleges stage dramatic productions at least once a year; schools with flourishing drama departments may produce a dozen. Some communities have drama groups, made up of talented amateurs and/or former professionals, that may be receptive to new material. The dinner theater, another locally based market, is an outlet for playwrights who produce light entertainment. No matter which local market, however, getting produced is often easier for the playwright who has been involved with the group in another capacity, e.g., as a stagehand or actor.

The more ambitious new playwright, however, can approach a regional professional equity theater, such as Actors Theatre of Louisville or Chicago's Goodman Theatre, that solicits new plays and whose productions often reach Broadway; he can also approach an off-Broadway theater such as the Manhattan Theatre Club, or a play publisher. The "Scriptwriting" section of *Writer's Market* details the guidelines for theaters and publishers around the country.

Plays that are produced on Broadway earn the playwright royalties, which are based on weekly box office receipts. The Dramatists Guild and the League of American Theatres and Producers, Inc., have established the following royalty system for the playwright's earnings: 5 percent of the gross weekly box office receipts pre-recoupment, 10 percent of the same post-recoupment. (*See: Children's theater; Playwriting.*)

Theme. The theme of a story is the point a writer wishes to make. It poses a question, a human problem. The plot is the series of events that proves or disproves that point. The plot is like the trunk and branches of a story; the theme is the carefully hidden roots. The theme should never be obvious, but without it, a story is trivial.

A theme may be as simple as "Honesty is the best policy" or as complex as the violence in the work of Joyce Carol Oates. Oates says, "I have been aware for many years of the precariousness of our life in America." This precariousness is her theme.

In the religious writing field, the theme is often the power of prayer. In stories for children and young adults it frequently deals with character development. Charles Dickens wrote of child exploitation in *Oliver Twist* and *David Copperfield; All Quiet on the Western Front* and *The Deer Hunter* tell of the ugliness and tragedy of war.

A theme is a natural, unobtrusive part of a story. The writer starts with an idea; as his story develops, it is influenced by his own philosophy or his observation of the human condition. This is his theme, the quality that brings with it a sense of values and drama.

Thesaurus. A reference book listing synonyms and antonyms. Some thesauri arrange words alphabetically, while others group them according to subject. Using a thesaurus helps the writer find the exact words he needs to convey a meaning or image.

Peter Mark Roget first published, in 1852, his *Thesaurus of English Words and Phrases Classified and Arranged so as to Facilitate the Expression of Ideas and Assist in Literary Composition*—and many subsequent editions and variations have followed. A current edition reminds writers that "In a dictionary you start with a word and look for its meaning. In *Roget's International Thesaurus*, you start with your idea and find the words to express it."

Think article. (*See: Magazine article, types of.*)

Third-person point of view. In this method of narration, the author follows *only* what the main character sees, hears, feels and thinks. This helps foster strong reader identification with the main character. While dialogue is in the first person, the narration by the author is told in third person.

30. This symbol is typed at the end of a newspaper story to denote the end of that piece of copy. The origin of this practice is unknown, although several stories attempt to explain it.

The most popular story places the origin of *30* in the Civil War period when news was transmitted by telegraph. The first message sent to a press association in the U.S. contained thirty words, and so its sender, as was the practice, indicated this with the number *30* at the end. The *30* was retained for all telegraphed news, and eventually, for news stories in general.

Other theories reported in William Metz's *Newswriting: From Lead to "30,"* maintain that *30* evolved from the symbol *XXX*, which was placed at the end of the very early, handwritten news items. The symbol, interpreted as a Roman numeral, became, naturally, *30*.

Still others have related the origin of *30* to an early typesetting practice that used the symbol to indicate the end of a line; the original Associated Press quota of 30 items per newspaper per day; and a reporter who added his name, Thirtee, to the end of a telegraphed message, which was changed by the telegrapher to *30*. Some magazine writers use the symbol *30* to indicate the end of an article; others use three number marks (i.e., # # #); still others simply type *The End*.

Thor Power Tool Ruling. An I.R.S. rule that resulted from the 1979 case *I.R.S. v. Thor Power Tool Co.* This rule limits the extent to which businesses can reduce the value of their inventoried goods to lessen the amount of tax they pay on profits. In book publishing, the only inventoried goods permitted to be counted as losses are books that have been remaindered or destroyed.

The major consequences of Thor for the writer are that: Books are remaindered sooner so their exposure to the public is more limited; and publishers are less willing to take chances on risky books.

Thriller. A film, novel or play intended to arouse feelings of excitement or suspense. Works in this genre are highly sensational, usually focusing on illegal activities, international espionage, sex and violence. A thriller is often a detective story in which the forces of good are pitted against the forces of evil in a kill-or-be-killed situation. Ken Follett (*Eye of the Needle, The Key to Rebecca*) and Frederick Forsyth (*The Day of the Jackal, The Odessa File*) have written a number of successful novels in this genre. Alfred Hitchcock directed countless film thrillers, including the classic *Psycho*. (*See: Suspense; Techno-thriller.*)

Tie-in. This term refers to a work issued in two or more media—for example, a motion picture and a paperback or hardcover book based on that motion picture, or a TV miniseries and a book based on that miniseries. This merchandising venture is designed to stimulate sales of the work in both media by strategic timing of issuance and joint promotion. In recent years, product tie-ins have become common. Movies such as

Jurassic Park, The Lion King and the Batman series inspire toys and games that help enhance interest in the films. (*See: Novelization.*)

Time advertising. (*See: Radio commercials; Space advertising.*)

Time signal. In radio, the combination of a ten-second commercial from a sponsor or the station's call letters with an announcement of the time of day.

Timeliness. In article writing, the timeliness of a story can make it necessary for the writer to bypass the customary query letter and telephone an editor about his piece. For example, a writer who gains access to a celebrity who will only be visiting his town for one day will need a no or a yes from his editor right away.

Editors require that seasonal articles be submitted months ahead of their intended publication date; their preferences in lead time generally range from three to six months. (These lead times refer to magazines.) (*See: Lead time; Seasonal material.*)

Title page. A page at the beginning of a book that carries the work's full title (including subtitle), the author's or editor's name, the publisher's name, and any other publishing information required by the author-publisher contract or desired by the publisher. There may also be various credits such as the name of a translator, photographer or illustrator on the title page. Sometimes a quotation or illustration appears on this page. (*See: Half-title.*)

Titles. Although every title is the result of creative effort, inventing one is not necessarily purely inspiration. There are patterns to follow (usually based on successful titles) and literary devices to incorporate; both of these approaches can help the writer express a title effectively.

Suggested devices to use in creating effective titles are alliteration, superlatives, mysticism, negativism, interrogative words, prepositional phrases, and quotations, either from another literary work or from the work being titled.

The important elements of good titles are clarity and suspense. The title should give the reader a direct indication of the work's content or plot, but should not, in the case of fiction, reveal too much of the story. Other functions of a title are to entice potential readers, to instill curiosity, to give an indication of what type of book or story a work is, to set the tone for the piece and to clarify a theme. Book titles, especially, are chosen for sales appeal as well as clarity. Book titles are often short so they can be printed in larger type, making them visible from farther away in a bookstore and making them easier to read when the jacket is reproduced in small scale in ads or shown on TV.

The writer should remember that a title usually influences an editor, either consciously or unconsciously; in that sense, creating an effective title is part of the writer's sales effort. However, an editor who buys a manuscript has the right to change a title; the writer may or may not be informed of a change.

Tone. The tone of a piece of writing is set by the author's attitude toward his characters or subjects; he chooses words and literary techniques to create the atmosphere he wants. For example, is the effect to be achieved sombre, playful, ironic, intimate, or some other attitude? Whereas a speaker can partly indicate tone by changes in voice or manner, the writer must rely on language and literary devices alone.

Tony Awards. These awards for accomplishment in the Broadway theater are presented annually by the League of American Theatres and Producers, Inc., under the official name the Antoinette Perry Awards. Each winner receives an embossed silver medallion. Various categories of theater work are recognized; awards applicable to writers are Best Play and Best Musical. The address of the League of American Theatres and Producers, Inc., is 226 W. Forty-seventh St., New York, NY 10036.

Tools, writing. In the past, a writer needed only a sharp pencil and a ream of paper. Today, an investment in electronic equipment is more worthwhile.

Most writers consider a computer basic equipment. Word-processing software makes originating and revising copy easier, while personal finance software allows writers to keep more detailed records of business expenses.

As electronic submission of manuscripts becomes more prevalent, modems become more necessary. As well, a modem allows access to on-line services and other research sources.

The freelancer may also consider a fax machine for quick communication with editors, but he should keep in mind that unsolicited faxes are rarely welcomed.

Topical. This adjective is applied to subjects of current interest. Topical subjects are often called "hot" topics. As public interests wax and wane, so do related hot topics. Writers try to stay abreast of topical subjects by reading as widely as possible.

The subjects a writer chooses for nonfiction books and articles should always be timely—i.e., of contemporary interest. There is a danger in a too-topical idea, however, both in book proposals and article ideas. In *A Writer's Guide to Book Publishing*, Richard Balkin says that while there is always room for the serious, carefully researched, well-written book that has permanent value, many writers make the mistake of submitting proposals for books whose subjects are one to three years out of date. He explains:

Certain subjects of topical interest become popular for a year or two. Then they either become permanent features, such as ecology, maintaining a long life; or they abruptly fade into obscurity. The publisher, during the period of intense interest, receives scores of proposals from authors who attempt to jump on this bandwagon, though many of these are hastily conceived proposals (often for anthologies and reprints) that arrive too late to be of real interest. In the past few years back-to-the-land, the occult, women's studies, pollution and counter-culture have been subject areas heading the fad list. While such topics may deserve the consumer and publishing attention they get, the average publisher can be overcontracted in those fields by the time the topic is nationally popular, or feel that the wave has crested.

(*See: Ideas, where to get them; Timeliness.*)

Tour de force. French for *feat of strength, skill or virtuosity*. The phrase is sometimes used to describe an exceptional achievement by an author. The phrase also applies to an artful technique in dealing with a difficult situation in writing.

tr. An abbreviation for *transpose* used by proofreaders and editors to indicate that two letters or words should change places. Written in the margin of a galley or page proof, *tr* accompanies the proofreading symbol of a line curving over the first letter/word and under the second letter/word (resembling a backward and sideways *S*). (*See: Proofreader's marks/symbols.*)

Trade books. Trade books are so called because they are distributed principally through retail trade bookstores and libraries, as distinguished from books sold through subscription series, and other means of reaching consumers directly. Trade books include novels, nonfiction and children's books. (*See: Trade paperback.*)

Trade discount. A discount in the sale of trade books granted to a bookseller by a publisher. The range of American trade discounts on quantity orders is considered 40-50 percent, but each publisher has an individual discount schedule—a chart showing the percentage of discount per number of books ordered.

Trade journal. A magazine or tabloid published for people in a certain business or profession. Roundup articles on opinions or products, information on new developments, ideas, tips, how-to articles, and convention reports are the kinds of material usually found in trade journals.

The beginning freelance writer will find a good starting point in the trade journals, since they represent a field with less competition than the consumer magazines. Also, since some editors have fewer writers to work with, they usually offer help and advice to the writers to whom they assign articles. Although trade journals pay less than consumer publications, they furnish the novice with experience and exposure while he develops his skill.

Trade journals, also called *trade publications*, can be categorized in different ways according to different functions. A vertical trade journal is published for all ranks and departments of the same industry (e.g., the apparel industry), while a horizontal trade journal is aimed at people in the same job who may or may not be employed in the same industry (e.g., salespeople). Some trade journals are company publications, read by employees and/or stockholders; others are independently published, and financed by advertising. In addition, these periodicals can be classified according to the fields they cover. Industrial publications include articles on manufacturing; merchandising publications, retailing; and professional journals, new developments in medicine, education and other areas.

Consistent buyers of material for trade journals are listed in *Writer's Market.*

Trade list. A catalog listing all of a publisher's books in print; one means of advertising for a publisher. Besides titles, a trade list includes content descriptions of the newest books, plus prices and details on ordering both new and backlist titles. Trade lists are produced either annually or semiannually; many appear in the *Publisher's Trade List Annual. (See:* Publisher's Trade List Annual.)

Trade name. A name by which a person, corporation or business entity is known. A legal question frequently asked by writers is whether a pen name or pseudonym can be considered a trade name. Usage is the key factor in this situation. As use is made of the name and the name begins to take on meaning and gain recognition value among the general public, the writer acquires a *property interest* in the name. The greater and more extensive the use made by the writer publishing under the name, the greater and more easily available the protection is by state and federal laws preventing unfair competition. One writer may not, for example, pass off his own work as the work of a well-known and successful writer by using that famous writer's name, or even a name very similar to it that may confuse the general public or lead them to believe that it is the work of the famous author. Nor may a writer use as a major character in his own work a char-

acter that has, over time, become identified in the public mind with another author who created the character.

Trade paperback. Published either as an original or as a reprint of a hardcover book, a trade paperback is distributed through bookstores—as opposed to the mass-market paperback, which is smaller sized and is distributed through newsstand racks in drugstores, airports, supermarkets, etc., in addition to bookstore outlets.

Authors' royalties on trade paperbacks vary by publisher but may range from 6-7½ percent.

Trade publisher. (*See: Trade books.*)

Trademark. The Lanham Act of 1946 defines a trademark as "any word, name, symbol, or device or any combination thereof, adopted and used by a manufacturer or merchant to identify his goods and distinguish them from those manufactured or sold by others." The Trademark Law Revision Act of 1988 took effect November 1989. Under this law, trademark applications may be based on either use of the mark in commerce or the applicant's bona fide intention to use the mark in commerce. This "intent to use" provision puts the U.S. in line with the rest of the world, as the majority of other countries do not require use before registration and none, other than the Philippines, requires use before application for registration.

A trademark is distinguished from a *service mark*, which identifies *services* provided by a merchant, and from a *trade name*, which, in a general sense, is a name, title or designation under which a person, corporation or other entity operates or does business. All three terms—*trademark, service mark* and *trade name*—apply to symbols protected by law to prevent unfair competition practices.

Federal registration of trademarks and service marks is accomplished through the U.S. Patent and Trademark Office, Washington, DC 20231, which will provide an application and information on request. The duration of trademark registration is twenty years, as is the renewal period.

The notice of trademark registration is either the symbol ®, the phrase "Registered in U.S. Patent and Trademark Office," or the abbreviation of the same, "Reg. U.S. Pat. and Tm. Off." It is preferred that a form of the notice follow the trademark word or symbol each time it is used.

There are several advantages to federal registration of trademark provided under the Lanham Act of 1946. These include the right to subsequently register the trademark in many foreign countries; the right to sue for infringement of the mark in the federal courts; constructive notice of appropriation to the entire country; the right to stop importation of foreign goods carrying infringing marks; a broader scope of what is registerable than is found in many state courts; and a broader and more meaningful range of remedies than is found in many state registration systems. But there is an important limitation of federal registration under the Lanham Act: Trade names are not registerable as they are under most state statutes.

Failure to police usage can result in a trademark's becoming a generic word—the name of some product or service totally lacking in distinctive character, and therefore not eligible to be registered as a trademark. The terms *aspirin* and *cellophane,* for example, were once valid trademarks that have lost their distinctive character and thus their claim to trademark rights.

For this reason, many manufacturers insist that trademarks used in the media—newspapers, books, magazines, etc.—be capitalized. If a short story writer says of a character, "Jack ordered a Coke from the waitress," "Coke," which is a trademark, should be capitalized. The same with Marlboro cigarettes, Dexter shoes and the like. The term *Xerox,* often used as a generic term for *photocopy,* is actually a valid trademark and should be capitalized in written work. (*See: Copyright; Figure 57; Service mark; Trade name.*)

Traffic. The department of a radio station that is responsible for programming and scheduling.

Transcripts of broadcasts. A TV or radio program can be a research source for the writer, and a transcript is a permanent record he can refer to as many times as necessary. Both private and public broadcasting networks offer transcripts of programs, primarily those of a news or documentary nature. Sometimes a fee is charged.

Journal Graphics provides written and videotaped transcripts of news broadcasts for ABC, CNN, PBS and NPR. Written transcripts cost from $10 to $17 if they are sent by regular

FIGURE 57

CHART OF RELATIONSHIPS AMONG PATENTS, TRADEMARKS, AND COPYRIGHTS*

TYPE OF PROTECTION	FUNCTIONAL PATENT	DESIGN PATENT	COPYRIGHT	TRADEMARK-SERVICE MARK
What is protected?	Functional features of process, machine, naufactured item, or composition of matter.	Ornamental designs for article of manufacturer	Works fixed in tangible medium of expression, e.g., literary, musical, pictorial, and motion picture words.	Words, names, symbols, or devices.
Criteria for protection	New and "nonobvious"	New and "nonobvious"	Originality	Used to identify and distinguish goods or services
How obtain rights?	Granted only by federal government (U.S. Patent & Trademark Office)	Granted only by federal government (U.S. Patent & Trademark Office)	Federal rights automatic upon creation. To maximize rights: publication with notice and registration of claim with Register of Copyrights.	Common law: adoption & use (sometimes secondary meaning required) Federal or state registration: application and compliance with statutes.
Lifetime?	Seventeen years from date of federal grant or twenty years for more money	Fourteen years from date of federal grant	Post 1/1/78 works: life of author plus sixty years.	Common law: as long as properly used as a mark. Federal regulation: Ten years (if formalities complied with) renewable for ten-year periods.
Test of infringement?	Making, using, or selling in U.S. devices embodying the claimed invention?	Designs look alike to eye of ordinary observer?	Substantial portion copied? Similarity?	Likelihood of confusion, mistake, or deception?

* CAVEAT: This chart is obviously an over-simplified comparison of Patents, Trademarks and Copyrights. Each of the words used above is a term of legal art and the subject of extensive litigation. The chart is intended only for a very basic analysis.

Reproduced with permission from Trademarks and Unfair Competition *by J. Thomas McCarthy, 2d ed. 1984. Copyright © 1984 The Lawyers Co-operative Publishing Company.*

mail. Call (212) 227-7323 to place an order.

Transcripts of news broadcasts on NBC and CBS cost from $6 to $10 and can be ordered by calling (800) 777-TEXT.

Writers should remember that transcripts of copyrighted programs are subject to copyright laws; therefore, quoting substantial amounts of material from a transcript requires written permission from the original copyright owner or the network, as the case may be. (*See: Broadcast networks.*)

Transition. A passage in a work of literature or a film that leads from one section to another.

In nonfiction, a transition serves to give the article cohesiveness and logic. It can link either sentences, paragraphs or sections, and is often accomplished by inserting words or phrases into a sentence or paragraph to connect it smoothly to the preceding one. Sometimes, an effective transition is achieved by merely adding one word.

The key to a good nonfiction transition is unobtrusiveness, i.e., inserting the transition in such a mechanical and contextual way that it does not distract the reader. Notice the following transition, from an article on billiards: "there is still the time-honored bugaboo: a talent at pool is the sign of a misspent youth.

"Actually, the game has a tradition, if not respectability, behind it."

The word *actually* implies a contradiction to the idea of a "misspent youth" expressed in the first sentence. The statement that the game has a "respectability" further supports the counterargument. The second sentence serves as a logical transition to a discussion of the history of the game.

Transitions in fiction lead the reader from character to character, from place to place, or from present to future (or past). The writer can mention a possible action in one paragraph and begin describing its actuality in the next. Another means of bridging gaps of time is to connect time's passage with a character's corresponding emotions. With this method, however, the transition, i.e., the emotional response, must be related to a significant element of the story. By the same token, the mere passage of time does not justify the author's outlining of all "events" in a character's life; only those relevant to the plot should be mentioned. Here, for example, is a brief transition describing a lapse of five months and the character's emotional relationship to the time gap. "She was heartbroken the first month, furious the second, elaborately indifferent the third; and she was in her second month of determination to forget him, when he walked into her office and said 'Hi' as if he'd never been away."

To move from character to character, the writer need only instill thoughts about one character into the mind of another, then move on to the subject of the thoughts. For transitions from scene to scene, the double-jump (the use of four spaces rather than the usual double space) is often an effective technique. To maintain reader interest, though, the writer must allude to forthcoming action before the break.

Transitions are also used in the audio and visual media, where they take on different forms. Television, theater and films use sound effects, lighting, music and camera techniques as linking devices, while radio drama typically includes transitions of music, sound effects and periods of silence.

Translating of languages. Writers with proficiency in one or more foreign languages can profit from translation work, in either commercial or literary form.

Markets for commercial translation include scientific researchers, patent attorneys, international corporations, publishing companies and government.

In translating literature, a writer must secure permission from the copyright owner, usually through his publisher. Short works may be completed before submission to a potential publisher, while book inquiries should include two translated chapters, a synopsis, a résumé and a letter informing the publisher that the translator has permission from the original author to complete the project.

A new translator who is not yet established may want to work through an agent. Experienced translators, on the other hand, advertise their services through means such as the yellow pages and direct mail. Rates average $50-$100 per thousand words. Professional organizations, both local and national, can provide association with other translators. A national organization is the American Translators Association, 1735 Jefferson Davis Highway, Arlington, VA 22202. Information on their Translator's Model Contract is available for a self-addressed, stamped envelope from PEN American Center, 568 Broadway, New York, NY 10012.

Translation rights. One of the subsidiary rights of the owner of a copyright, such as a book author. Sales of these rights to foreign publishers are made either by the author's agent or his publisher on the author's behalf. Contacts are made either with foreign agents or the foreign publishers themselves, frequently at international gatherings such as the Frankfurt Book Fair. Industry standard royalty percentages are 7 percent of the retail hardcover price on the first 10,000 copies, 8 percent on the next 10,000 and 10 percent thereafter. The Authors Guild recommends that the author's share of these royalties be 75 percent (of the 7 percent, 8 percent or 10 percent) on foreign editions, and 80 percent on British editions, but some publishers split fifty-fifty with the author. Paperback royalties are usually lower.

A publisher that decides to produce its own translated edition for a foreign language market pays the translation fee and splits the royalties between original author and translator at an agreed-upon rate. The translator's royalty is a percentage (usually 15-20 percent) of the original author's royalties.

Travel. Travel expenses related to the writing business may be deducted from federal income tax. It is necessary to save receipts that verify transactions and to keep records of expenditures throughout the year.

Tax-deductible items include courses and trips for research and conferences. However, a writer may deduct costs of only those educational functions of a refresher-course kind; the cost of a course taken to become a writer is not tax-deductible.

Transportation cost may be figured either in terms of mileage or operating expenses of the writer's car. The IRS allows a deduction of $.29 per mile across the board. Automobile operating expenses for gasoline, oil, tires, maintenance and depreciation may be deducted if the $.29 per mile is not taken. (The total yearly cost of these needs may be deducted if the writer uses his car solely for business; otherwise it is prorated according to the percentage of the car's use for business.)

Other tax-deductible expenses of travel are those for food and lodging. (*See: Recordkeeping; Taxes.*)

Travel article. (*See: Magazine article, types of.*)

Travel Journalists Guild (TJG). This organization is made up of seventy-five professional freelance travel writers, photographers and filmmakers. It was established in 1980, with Bern Keating as founding president. To be eligible for membership, a writer must submit samples of published or produced work.

It is a member of the Council of Writers Organizations. Information about the TJG can be obtained by writing Executive Secretary, Travel Journalists Guild, P.O. Box 10643, Chicago, IL 60610. (*See: Council of Writers Organizations.*)

Travel writing. The travel article has two basic objectives: to inform the reader by way of facts and to en-lighten him by way of impressions. The travel writer must be perceptive enough to look beyond landmarks and scenery (although both are important) to the less conspicuous elements of his trip, such as people, customs and atmosphere.

Although the travel writer takes a considerable amount of notes during his actual travels, there is often preliminary research to be done before he leaves. Information can be obtained from travel bureaus, chambers of commerce, books, magazines, other travelers, and newspapers in the town of destination. In addition, querying editors and informing them of the travel destination can help the writer in focusing his research, since it is possible that editors will make suggestions when making assignments.

The travel writer should be prepared either to take photographs or to collaborate with a photographer, because photographs are an essential part of most travel pieces.

A travel article can be written in any of a variety of styles. The *quality* article displays a sophisticated writing style that includes imagery. The *special-interest* article relates the trip to another of the readers' interest, e.g., sports. The *Me-and-Joe* piece is written in narrative form and includes dialogue and other fictive techniques. The *mile-by-mile* article resembles a log and mentions each activity along the route and at the destination.

Markets for travel articles include magazines for women, men, families, sports enthusiasts, outdoorsmen and organization members. Often one trip results in a group of articles, each of which is given a different peg, for noncompeting magazines. *Writer's Market* lists many categories of potential markets; payment is denoted in the individual listings.

An organization that promotes travel writing is the Society of American Travel Writers, 4101 Lake Boone Trail, Suite 201, Raleigh, NC 27607. (*See: Travel Journalists Guild.*)

Travelwriter Marketletter. A monthly newsletter for writers who specialize in travel writing. It includes the following sections: "Trips" (descriptions of trips and tours sponsored by cities, states, regions and airlines for writers); "Marketwatch" (data on publications, including editorial needs); "Books" (brief reviews of books on travel writing and writing in general); and "Freelancers Achievements" (news of publication and other travel writers' accomplishments).

Travelwriter Marketletter is available both as a ten-page printed publication and through NewsNet, a computer database. Its publication address is The Waldorf-Astoria, Suite 1850, New York, NY 10022.

Treatment. The narrative, sometimes containing key dialogue, that the scriptwriter writes as a preliminary to the script. The treatment is also called the *outline* or the *story*. (*See: Television script terms.*)

Trick ending. Although many editors use this term synonymously with *surprise ending* or *twist ending*, other editors consider a trick ending to be one that is illogical and unsatisfying, or that brings about a story's resolution by means of incredible coinci-

dence. (*See: Deus ex machina; Endings, story; Surprise ending.*)

Trilogy. This term, from the greek *trilogia*, originally referred to a series of three tragedies performed at the festival of Dionysus in ancient Greece. Now any group of three dramatic or literary works, individually complete but related in subject or theme, is called a trilogy.

Perhaps the best-known contemporary literary trilogy is Tolkien's *Lord of the Rings* series: *Fellowship of the Ring, The Two Towers* and *Return of the King.* (*See: Sequel.*)

Triteness. Words or phrases that have lost freshness, originality and effectiveness because of overuse. *Cliché* and *hackneyed language* are two other terms used to describe triteness. Triteness also denotes overdone article and story themes. Learning what is trite and what is not comes from wide reading habits and comparing the work of quality writers with mediocre ones.

Sometimes, however, a cliché or well-known slogan can be twisted to produce a fresh, original thought. For example, "He who laughs last has no sense of humor," or "It's not whether you win or lose, it's how you place the blame." (*See: Cliché.*)

True Crime. A nonfiction genre based on factual re-creation of a crime, usually murder. In his book *How to Write and Sell True Crime*, Gary Provost placed true crime "somewhere between a novel, which nobody takes seriously, and a newspaper story, which everybody takes seriously."

A successful true crime book tells a true story using real people and events. But true crime is not straight reportage. In fact, the writing of such books has more in common with a thriller or action/adventure novel. The writer must pay careful attention not only to the way he structures his account of the crime, but to the details he includes in order to give the reader a reason to turn the pages.

The true crime book blends novelistic and journalistic styles of writing. The novelistic style brings literary devices to the story, while the journalistic style brings information. A successful combination of the two results in scenes that move well and interest the readers, yet still contain factual information readers need to accurately follow the narrative.

When using these two styles together, conflict arises over creative license. While a novelist creates his story out of whole cloth, a true crime writer must put existing pieces together to create an interesting story. When some of those pieces are missing—forgotten dialogue, for example—the writer must use creative license. Of course, the writer should never alter facts he knows, or invent anything that would change the course of events. To fill in these gaps, the writer must rely on his knowledge of the people and places involved and make educated guesses.

Writer's Market lists magazines that buy short true crime stories under "Detective/Crime." Though many crime story magazines have regular staff writers, freelancers may provide accounts of intriguing crimes committed close to their homes. A detailed query letter on the case should precede any manuscript submission.

Magazines that buy true crime stories usually try to buy all rights to them. To find publishers of true crime books, study published true crime books at your local bookstore. (*See: Nonfiction novel.*)

Additional information: *How to Write and Sell True Crime.*

Truth as a defense against libel. (*See: Libel.*)

Twist ending. (*See: Surprise ending.*)

Two shot. A TV or motion picture scene in which the camera shows two characters. A *three shot* would show three characters. These terms are typed in all caps when used in a script. (*See: Television script terms.*)

TWX. A teletype machine or a message from a teletype machine.

Typewriter. The advent of the computer has rendered the typewriter obsolete. Many writers still compose on typewriters, but the ease with which computers can aid in recordkeeping, revision and creation make them essential equipment.

Typing services. A writer can learn of available typists (and current charges) through classified advertisements in writer's magazines such as *Writer's Digest* and from bulletin boards at local colleges. Also, writers sometimes place their own classifieds in local newspapers, seeking typing services.

Before contracting a typing service, be sure that details concerning turnaround time, type style and payment of delivery fees are discussed. (*See: Recordkeeping; Taxes.*)

u.c. An abbreviation for *upper case* used by proofreaders and editors to indicate that a letter or letters printed as lower case should be capitalized. Written in the margin of a galley or page proof, *u.c.* accompanies the proofreading symbol of three lines under the letter. (*See: Cap; Proofreader's marks/symbols.*)

Unabridged. Not shortened or condensed. *Unabridged* is a label often applied to a dictionary that represents the most comprehensive, definitive edition in a series by the same publisher. Unabridged dictionaries are large, usually containing more than 250,000 entries. (*See: Dictionary.*)

Unauthorized biography. An account of a person's life written without his cooperation or, in the case of a deceased person, without the cooperation of his estate or heirs. Subjects of unauthorized biographies have ranged from movie and TV personalities to rock stars, sports heroes and political figures. Timing and immediacy are important factors in marketing such a work.

Some celebrities have claimed that they alone have the right to write their own biographies. While the courts have not upheld that opinion, the late James Cagney once succeeded in having the acknowledgment page of a book about him show that it was an unauthorized bi-

ography. (*See: Biography; Figure 58.*)

Unconscious. Those mental processes existing or operating just outside awareness. The unconscious can influence a writer's life and work in a number of ways.

In their book, *The Writer's Survival Guide*, therapists Jean and Veryl Rosenbaum describe the unconscious part of the mind as an invisible tape recorder imprinted with all the emotions and events of childhood. "The unconscious retains the forgotten, profoundly affecting conscious decisions, feelings, and choices," say the Rosenbaums. "The positive facet of the unconscious stimulates creative thought and works silently on problem solving."

Damon Knight, author of *Creating Short Fiction*, echoes the Rosenbaums' conviction. Knight encourages writers to "collaborate" with their unconscious minds:

Now writing, like any art (and also very much like creative science and invention), is a thing you can't do without the close collaboration of the two parts of the mind. When you think about a creative problem, or even when you think something as simple as "I wish I had an idea for a story," you are sending a message to the unconscious. The return message may be in the form of a sudden realization, or an image, or some tantalizing ghost of an idea. It may

FIGURE 58

UNAUTHORIZED BIOGRAPHY
Ted Schwarz

*U*nauthorized biographies are almost always about public figures, including those who have become known as the result of a crime (e.g., hotel magnate and convicted tax cheat Leona Helmsley, convicted insider trader Ivan Boesky, etc.) or those who gained fame for unusual actions (e.g., World War II hero Audie Murphy). Interesting people totally unknown to the general public are usually considered private individuals, even when married to someone famous. Writing about them without their permission may be considered invasion of privacy, a situation that seldom arises with politicians, entertainers, and others who are obvious public figures.

Unauthorized biographies require careful documentation of facts. Interviews should be tape recorded when at all possible. A writer should use only virgin tape, carefully recording and noting the subject, time, date, and location of the interview on the cassette. Never record on a cassette that has been previously used. A writer's notes are considered valid as proof of what was said during an interview, but a notebook, containing the same information as the tape, will not be as impressive as a recording.

Obtain copies of all public records that may be important. These may include court proceedings involving the subject, arrest records, birth certificate, marriage and divorce proceedings, property purchases, etc. Military records are public information available from the specific branches of the armed services in Washington, D.C. Some FBI and other government records can be obtained using the Freedom of Information Act.

Fairness to your subject is critical. The August, 1989 ruling concerning the libel case of *David Price v. Viking Penguin, Inc. and Peter Matthiessen* showed that bias *can* be expressed by individuals quoted in a book provided there is equal opportunity for all sides. Ideally there should be interviews with the subject or official representative of the subject's estate, letting him present a personal viewpoint. This is not possible with most unauthorized biographies, requiring you to find people familiar with the situations discussed who can provide balance. If no balance is provided, you must be certain that you can prove your allegations.

For example, when trying to write about singer Frank Sinatra, many sources were hostile to him and he refused to give interviews. By checking old newspaper reviews of his performances, I was able to find other entertainers, stage hands, and casino managers with whom he worked. People such as comedian Joey Bishop, located through Screen Actors Guild, were able to provide positive anecdotes.

The statement by someone who claims to be present at an event may not always be adequate documentation. An allegation of an illicit rendezvous at a hotel between your subject and your source will require you to prove that your subject was registered and present in the hotel at the time that your source was there, and, ideally, that there were witnesses to both. Copies of credit card receipts, travel agency itineraries, personal diary notations by one or more individuals present, and similar items all will help.

FIGURE 58 (CONTINUED)

Positive information is equally important. When doing interviews, ask questions such as, "What was the funniest experience you remember with the subject? The nicest? The most surprising? The most different from the way the public often perceives him?" These often bring forth good things about people whose character might otherwise come through as mostly negative.

Multiple, unrelated sources of the same information generally provide safe documentation. If both friends and enemies of the subject tell essentially the same story, you can feel comfortable using it. Some writers use a minimum of three unrelated sources. Others feel four or more are safer. The important point is to be certain all sides are covered so there is what is known as an "absence of malice," even when the final results may reflect negatively on your subject. You may be guilty of libel if it can be shown that you intended to stress the bad side of a subject, then failed to seek information that might show a different side to his character. However, if you can show that you have tried to be objective, even a highly uncomplimentary biography of a public figure usually will not be libelous because there was no malice on your part. This absence of malice is also some protection if you accidentally make a mistake and present negative information that, despite your efforts to check for accuracy, ultimately proves untrue.

Be aware that your objectivity may result in unexpected criticism of you. Many people want their heroes to be perfect, not flawed humans. Reverend Ralph Abernathy's autobiography mentions the womanizing of Dr. Martin Luther King, Jr., a statement confirmed by Dr. King's colleagues. Rev. Abernathy was severely chastised for being objective about a man who, despite personal weakness, led the nation in the repudiation of what, for generations, had been legalized discrimination against a large segment of the American public. The author was attacked because the book was objective.

Ted Schwarz is the author, co-author, or "ghost" of approximately sixty books, including *The Hillside Strangler, DeLorean,* and *Kept Women.*

come weeks or months later, even years.

(*See: Interior monologue; Stream of consciousness; Writer's block.*)

Additional information: *The Writer's Survival Guide; Creating Short Fiction.*

Uncopyrighted publications. Some magazines and newspapers do not claim copyright in their publications. The writer who submits material to such a periodical should request that his article, story or poem appear with a copyright notice (©, the year, the owner's name). While the copyright notice is no longer mandatory since March, 1989, when the U.S. joined the Berne Union, it is still useful to show ownership and to rebut claims of innocent infringement. (*See: Copyright.*)

Understatement. A device in which a writer uses deliberate restraint in expressing his idea. In understating, a writer phrases his remark less strongly than would be expected, or communicates the idea in negative terms. A critic for a Hearst newspaper, for example, who was assigned to write a review of Hearst friend Marion Davies's latest film, is reported to have closed his review this way: "Marion Davies was never better."

Context is important in making sure the reader realizes an idea is being understated. (*See: Humor.*)

Unfinished manuscripts, how to resume work on. (*See: Restarting your writing.*)

United Press International (UPI). One of the two major wire services in the U.S., United Press International (UPI) is a privately owned commercial news agency established in 1958 in a merger of United Press and International News Service. From its forty foreign bureaus and more than 100 domestic bureaus located throughout the U.S., UPI gathers, prepares and distributes local, national and international news and photographs to newspapers and radio stations that pay for the service.

The headquarters of UPI are at 220 E. Forty-second St., New York, NY 10017. (*See: Associated Press; Wire services, jobs in.*)

U.S. government as a resource. The U.S. government can be a valuable information source on almost any conceivable subject. The U.S. Government Printing Office issues thousands of publications covering a legion of topics; in addition, a number of government bureaus and agencies can provide the freelancer with, or refer him to, sources of facts and data, experts in a subject field, bibliographic material, and answers to

specific questions. Call information for the phone number of a specific agency located in Washington, DC. (*See: Census Bureau, Department of Commerce; Database; Federal Information Center Program, General Services Administration; Library of Congress;* United States Government Manual; *U.S. government publications.*)

United States Government Manual. An annual directory published by the U.S. National Archives and Records Service, the *United States Government Manual* provides comprehensive information on the agencies, divisions and members of the legislative, judicial and executive branches of the U.S. government. It includes all departments, agencies and boards, and is indexed by name, subject and agency. A valuable reference volume for writers seeking government experts in specific subject areas, the *Manual* is available for purchase from the Superintendent of Documents at the U.S. Printing Office, Washington, DC 20402. (*See: U.S. government publications.*)

U.S. government publications. A writer has various means of access to these publications, which can be valuable sources for article and book research.

The writer's source of information is the *Catalog of United States Government Publications,* issued quarterly and incorporating approximately one thousand new and popular backlist publications listed by author, title and subject. Some public and college libraries serve as depositories from which the actual publications may be borrowed. A "List of Depository Libraries" may be obtained by writing the Superintendent of Documents, U.S. Government Printing Office, Washington, DC 20402.

In addition, the Government Printing Office has several bookstores throughout the country from which publications may be purchased. Writers can also write for a free copy of the *Consumer Information Catalog*, a list of pamphlets and booklets available from the Documents Distribution Center, U.S. Government Printing Office, Pueblo, CO 81009. (*See: Database; U.S. government as a resource;* United States Government Manual.)

U.S. government, writing for. The Office of Personnel Management, Roosevelt Federal Bldg., 1900 E. St. N.W., Washington, DC 20415, is the agency of the federal government responsible for the recruiting, examining, training and promoting of federal workers. The federal government employs 1,940 people classified as writer/editors.

Entry-level positions of editorial clerk or editorial assistant are required to edit for basic grammar and structural clarity, verify references, prepare publication formats and proofread. Applicants for these positions must have some experience and may be required to take appropriate tests. Positions as writers and editors at higher levels are evaluated on their education, experience and training in relation to the specific duties of the position.

The Office of Personnel Management has five regional offices around the U.S. where applicants may inquire about writing-related positions. The writer should call the Federal Information center in his state to find out whether there is an OPM regional office in his area.

In addition to writing-related job opportunities with the federal government in Washington, the OPM regional offices may also be able to advise about regional opportunities.

Unities. In establishing principles of dramatic composition, Renaissance critics drew on Aristotle's observations of the three unities that were incorporated into dramatic works: unity of *time*, unity of *place* and unity of *action*. The unity of time limited a play's fictional time span to one day; the unity of place limited its physical setting to one place. Similarly, only one plot per drama was permitted by the principle of unity of action.

The unities are rarely followed by today's writers of plays in English. However, the time limitations imposed by radio drama make unity of action necessary. (*See: Radio drama.*)

Universality. This is an important element for writers to consider, since articles and stories intended for sale to magazines must have wide appeal. Some beginning writers have experiences that are intensely interesting to themselves and their families, but that, when written up as magazine articles, for example, lack the universal human-interest quality required to sell them.

University press. A publisher directly or indirectly associated with a university. University presses traditionally have specialized in scholarly works of no interest to the commercial press, but many such presses now regularly publish quality books of wider appeal. State university presses, in particular, now publish books about the state or geographic area in which the institution is located.

Many university presses publish fiction and poetry of high literary merit, especially by regional writers, that might not be published commercially. Some of these books, however, have achieved respectable sales. Many publishers look to university presses to find authors who might be ready for wider distribution.

Unsolicited manuscript. An unsolicited manuscript is a book, article, story or poem submitted by a writer without the publisher's having requested it. Publishers are under no legal obligation to be responsible for unsolicited manuscripts, so the writer should always consult the listings in *Writer's Market* to make sure a publisher is willing to look at unsolicited manuscripts. The writer should always include a self-addressed, stamped envelope when submitting an unsolicited manuscript. (*See: Slush pile.*)

Up and out. In radio advertising, a direction to increase the volume of music or sound effects, then fade it out.

Up full. In radio advertising, a direction to increase the volume of music or sound effects to the maximum.

USA Today. A national newspaper established by the Gannett Company in September 1982. Although *USA Today* has its own staff and draws on the resources of the many newspapers in the Gannett chain, the publication uses freelance material to some extent.

The individual sections of the paper to whose managing editors queries should be sent are, News, Money, Sports, and Life. *USA Today*'s address is 1000 Wilson Blvd., Arlington VA 22229.

Usage errors. (*See: Figure 59.*)

FIGURE 59

50 COMMON USAGE ERRORS

*T*he Associated Press's Writing and Editing Committee prepared the following list primarily for newspaper writers, but magazine article and other writers will find some good reminders here, too. Most are examples of word usage. Some are spelling problems. Some are grammatical rules. The committee, headed by Wallace Allen, *Minneapolis Tribune,* published this list in 1974, but the bulk of it was assembled and written over several years by Dick Reid, an assistant managing editor of the *Minneapolis Tribune,* in *Tribune* staff memos as Common Flaws, Ltd.

1. AFFECT, EFFECT
Generally, *affect* is the verb; *effect* is the noun. "The letter did not *affect* the outcome." "The letter had a significant *effect.*" BUT *effect* is also a verb meaning to bring about. Thus: "It is almost impossible to *effect* change."

2. AFTERWARD, AFTERWARDS
Use *afterward.* The dictionary allows use of *afterwards* only as a second form.
   The same thinking applies to *toward* and *towards.* Use *toward.*

3. ALL RIGHT
That's the way to spell it. The dictionary may list *alright* as a legitimate word, but it is not acceptable in standard usage, says Random House.

4. ALLUDE, ELUDE
You *allude* to (or mention) a book. You *elude* (or escape) a pursuer.

5. ANNUAL
Don't use *first* with it. If it's the first time, it can't be annual.

6. AVERSE, ADVERSE
If you don't like something, you are *averse* (or opposed) to it. *Adverse* is an adjective: *adverse* (bad) weather, *adverse* conditions.

7. BLOCK, BLOC
A *bloc* is a coalition of people or a group with the same purpose or goal. Don't call it a *block,* which has some forty dictionary definitions.

8. COMPOSE, COMPRISE
Remember that the parts *compose* the whole and the whole *comprises* the parts. You *compose* things by putting them together. Once the parts are put together, the object *comprises* the parts.

9. COUPLE OF
You need the *of.* It's never "a couple tomatoes."

10. DEMOLISH, DESTROY
They mean to do away with *completely.* You can't partially demolish or destroy something, nor is there any need to say *totally* destroyed.

11. DIFFERENT FROM
Things and people are different *from* each other. Don't write that they are different *than* each other.

12. DROWN
Don't say someone *was drowned* unless an assailant held the victim's head under water. Just say the victim *drowned.*

13. DUE TO, OWING TO, BECAUSE OF
We prefer the last.
   Wrong: The game was canceled *due to* rain.
   Stilted: *Owing to* rain, the game was canceled.
   Right: The game was canceled *because of* rain.

14. ECOLOGY, ENVIRONMENT
They are not synonymous. *Ecology* is the study of the relationship between

FIGURE 59 (CONTINUED)

organisms and their *environment.*
Right: The laboratory is studying the *ecology* of man and the desert.
Right: There is much interest in animal *ecology* these days.
Wrong: Even so simple an undertaking as maintaining a lawn affects *ecology.*
Right: Even so simple an undertaking as maintaining a lawn affects our *environment.*

15. EITHER
It means one or the other, not both.
Wrong: There were lions on *either* side of the door.
Right: There were lions on *each* side of the door.

16. FLIERS, FLYERS
Airmen are *fliers.* Handbills are *flyers.*

17. FLOUT, FLAUNT
They aren't the same words; they mean completely different things and they're very commonly confused. *Flout* means to mock, to scoff or to show disdain for. *Flaunt* means to display ostentatiously.

18. FUNERAL SERVICE
A redundant expression. A funeral *is* a service.

19. HEAD UP
People don't *head up* committees. They *head* them.

20. HOPEFULLY
One of the most commonly misused words, in spite of what the dictionary may say. *Hopefully* should describe the way the subject *feels.*
For instance:
Hopefully, I shall present the plan to the president. (This means I will be hopeful when I do it.)
But it is something else again when you attribute hope to a nonperson.

You may write: Hopefully, the war will end soon. This means you hope the war will end soon, but it is not what you are writing. What you mean is: I hope the war will end soon.

21. IMPLY AND INFER
The speaker *implies.* The hearer *infers.*

22. IN ADVANCE OF, PRIOR TO
Use *before;* it sounds more natural.

23. IT'S, ITS.
Its is the possessive; *it's* is the contraction of *it is.*
Wrong: What is *it's* name?
Right: What is *its* name? *Its* name is Fido.
Right: *It's* the first time he's scored tonight.
Right: *It's* my coat.

24. LAY, LIE
Lay is the action word; *lie* is the state of being.
Wrong: The body will *lay* in state until Wednesday.
Right: The body will *lie* in state until Wednesday.
Right: The prosecutor tried to *lay* the blame on him.
However, the past tense of *lie* is *lay.*
Right: The body *lay* in state from Tuesday until Wednesday.
Wrong: The body *laid* in state from Tuesday until Wednesday.
The past participle and the plain past tense of *lay* is *laid.*
Right: He *laid* the pencil on the pad.
Right: He *had laid* the pencil on the pad.
Right: The hen *laid* an egg.

25. LEAVE, LET
Leave alone means to depart from or cause to be in solitude. *Let alone* means to be undisturbed.

FIGURE 59 (CONTINUED)

Wrong: The man had pulled a gun on her, but Mr. Jones intervened and talked him into *leaving her alone.*
Right: The man had pulled a gun on her, but Mr. Jones intervened and talked him into *letting her alone.*
Right: When I entered the room I saw that Jim and Mary were sleeping so I decided to *leave them alone.*

26. LESS, FEWER
If you can separate items in the quantities being compared, use *fewer.* If not, use *less.*
Wrong: The Rams are inferior to the Vikings because they have *less* good linemen.
Right: The Rams are inferior to the Vikings because they have *fewer* good linemen.
Right: The Rams are inferior to the Vikings because they have *less* experience.

27. LIKE, AS
Don't use *like* for *as* or *as if.* In general, use *like* to compare with nouns and pronouns; use *as* when comparing with phrases and clauses that contain a verb.
Wrong: Jim blocks the linebacker *like* he should.
Right: Jim blocks the linebacker *as* he should.
Right: Jim blocks *like* a pro.

28. MARSHALL, MARSHAL
Generally, the first form is correct only when the word is a proper noun: John *Marshall.* The second form is the verb form: Marilyn will *marshal* her forces.
The second form is the one to use for a title: *Fire Marshal* Stan Anderson, *Field Marshal* Erwin Rommel.

29. MEAN, AVERAGE, MEDIAN
Use *mean* as synonymous with *average.* Each word refers to the sum of all components divided by the number of components. *Median* is the number that has as many components above it as below it.

30. NOUNS
There's a growing trend toward using them as verbs. Resist it. *Host, headquarters* and *author,* for instance, are nouns, even though the dictionary may acknowledge they can be used as verbs. If you do, you'll come up with a monstrosity like: "Headquartered at his country home, John Doe hosted a party to celebrate the book he had authored."

31. ORAL, VERBAL
Use *oral* when use of the mouth is central to the thought; the word emphasizes the idea of human utterance. *Verbal* may apply to spoken or written words; it connotes the process of reducing ideas to writing. Usually, it's a *verbal* contract, not an *oral* one, if it's in writing.

32. OVER, MORE THAN
They aren't interchangeable. *Over* refers to spatial relationships: The plane flew *over* the city. *More than* is used with figures: In the crowd were *more than* 1,000 fans.

33. PARALLEL CONSTRUCTION
Thoughts in series in the same sentence require parallel construction.
Wrong: The union delivered demands for an increase of 10 percent in wages and to cut the workweek to thirty hours.
Right: The union delivered demands for an increase of 10 percent

FIGURE 59 (CONTINUED)

in wages and for a *reduction* in the workweek to thirty hours.

34. PEDDLE, PEDAL

When selling something, you *peddle* it. When riding a bicycle or similar form of locomotion, you *pedal* it.

35. PRETENSE, PRETEXT

They're different, but it's a tough distinction. A *pretext* is that which is put forward to conceal a truth: He was discharged for tardiness, but this was only a *pretext* for general incompetence.

A *pretense* is a "false show"; a more overt act intended to conceal personal feelings: My profuse compliments were all pretense.

36. PRINCIPLE, PRINCIPAL

A guiding rule or basic truth is a *principle*. The first, dominant or leading thing is *principal*. *Principle* is a noun; *principal* may be a noun or an adjective.

Right: It's the *principle* of the thing.
Right: Liberty and justice are two *principles* on which our nation is founded.
Right: Hitting and fielding are the *principal* activities in baseball.
Right: Robert Jamieson is the school *principal.*

37. REDUNDANCIES

To avoid: Easter Sunday. Make it *Easter.* Incumbent Congressman. *Congressman.* Owns his own home. *Owns his home.* The company will close down. *The company will close.* Jones, Smith, Johnson and Reid were all convicted. *Jones, Smith, Johnson and Reid were convicted.* Jewish rabbi. Just *rabbi.* 8:00 p.m. tonight. All you need is *8:00 tonight* or *8:00 p.m. today.* During the winter months. *During the winter.* Both Reid and Jones were denied pardons. *Reid*

and Jones were denied pardons. I am currently tired. *I am tired.* Autopsy to determine the cause of death. *Autopsy.*

38. REFUTE

The word connotes success in argument and almost always implies an editorial judgment.

Wrong: Father Bury *refuted* the arguments of the pro-abortion faction.
Right: Father Bury responded to the arguments of the pro-abortion faction.

39. RELUCTANT, RETICENT

If he doesn't want to act, he is *reluctant.* If he doesn't want to speak, he is *reticent.*

40. SAY, SAID

The most serviceable words in the journalist's language are the forms of the verb *to say.* Let a person *say* something, rather than declare or admit or point out. And never let him grin, smile, frown or giggle something.

41. SLANG

Don't try to use "with-it" slang. Usually a term is on the way out by the time we get it in print.

Wrong: The police cleared the demonstrators with a sunrise *bust.*

42. SPELLING

It's basic. If reporters can't spell and copy editors can't spell, we're in trouble. Some ripe ones for the top of your list.

It's *consensus*, not concensus. It's *restaurateur*, not restauranteur. It's *dietitian*, not dietician.

43. TEMPERATURES

They may get higher or lower, but they don't get warmer or cooler.

FIGURE 59 (CONTINUED)

44. THAT, WHICH
That tends to restrict the reader's thought and direct it the way you want it to go; *which* is nonrestrictive, introducing a bit of subsidiary information.

For instance:

The lawnmower that is in the garage needs sharpening. (Meaning: We have more than one lawnmower. The one in the garage needs sharpening.)

The lawnmower, which is in the garage, needs sharpening. (Meaning: Our lawnmower needs sharpening. It's in the garage.)

Note that *which* clauses take commas, signaling they are not essential to the meaning of the sentence.

Editorial Note: Although some prominent grammarians advocate, for the sake of clarity, using only *that* to introduce restrictive clauses, they concede that some writers, not incorrectly, use *which* in that type of clause. For an extensive discussion of the subject, see *A Dictionary of Modern English Usage,* by H.W. Fowler, or *Modern American Usage,* by Wilson Follett.

45. UNDER WAY
Not underway. But don't say something got under way. Say it *started* or *began.*

46. UNIQUE
Something that is unique is the only one of its kind. It can't be very unique or quite unique or somewhat unique or rather unique. Don't use it unless you really mean unique.

47. UP
Don't use it as a verb.

Wrong: The manager said he would *up* the price next week.

Right: The manager said he would *raise* the price next week.

48. WHO, WHOM
A tough one, but generally you're safe to use *whom* to refer to someone who has been the object of an action. *Who* is the word when the somebody has been the actor:

A nineteen-year-old woman, to *whom* the room was rented, left the window open.

A nineteen-year-old woman, *who* rented the room, left the window open.

49. WHO'S, WHOSE
Though it incorporates an apostrophe, *who's* is not a possessive. It's a contraction for *who is. Whose* is the possessive.

Wrong: I don't know *who's* coat it is.

Right: I don't know *whose* coat it is.

Right: Find out *who's* there.

50. WOULD
Be careful about using *would* when constructing a conditional past tense.

Wrong: If Soderholm *would not have had* an injured foot, Thompson wouldn't have been in the lineup.

Right: If Soderholm *had not had* an injured foot, Thompson wouldn't have been in the lineup.

Vanity press. (*See: Subsidy publishing.*)

Variety. This is both a weekly and daily newspaper that reports on entertainment industries; its coverage is international. *Variety* publishes news about TV, cable TV, motion pictures, radio, records, nightclubs, auditoriums, theater and notable individuals in entertainment. It is also beginning to cover new media such as CD-ROMs and the Internet.

A comedy writer who wants to reach a performer (and potential client) can sometimes find in *Variety* the address of the club or resort at which that person will be appearing.

Variety has fifteen international bureaus; it is published by Variety, Inc., 249 W. Seventeenth St., New York, NY 10011.

Verbal, oral. These words are often incorrectly considered synonymous. *Verbal* applies to *all* words, spoken or written, in which thought or feeling is expressed. *Oral*, which means uttered by mouth, describes only that which is *spoken*.

The confusion regarding correct use of these two terms is complicated in part by the seemingly contradictory case of *verbal agreement*, a term that means oral agreement—agreement expressed only in speech and not in writing.

The writer achieves clarity by using the word *oral* rather than *verbal* to mean spoken language.

Verbatim. A term that means "in exactly the same words," or "corresponding word for word to the original source or text."

The term is often used in relation to direct quotations, those that record another person's remarks verbatim—i.e., word for word, exactly as the remarks were spoken or written. (*See: Plagiarism; Quotes.*)

Verbiage. Wordiness; an overabundance of words in written or spoken expression. The word has a negative connotation, often implying communication that is meaningless and insincere. (*See: Pad.*)

Verification of quotes, facts. This is important to a writer's credibility—and to other aspects of his reputation, since misquoting in some instances leads to libel suits; in others, to a loss of confidence in the reporter on the part of a source or an editor.

Many novice writers erroneously accept unquestioningly all material they read in their article sources, e.g., newspapers and magazines. Instead of relying on another writer who may be in error, the writer should verify quoted statements with the people who made them, and facts with additional sources. In investigative research, of course, verification of facts is essential; after information is learned firsthand, other people or sources should be consulted.

This kind of checking and cross-checking helps the reporter or researcher learn important information, clarify contradictory statements, and discover errors that have crept into already-published material. (*See: Interview; Libel.*)

Verisimilitude. Having the appearance or semblance of truth or fact; likelihood; probability. A writer attempts to achieve the quality of verisimilitude in his work through such skillful selection of narration and dialogue that the reader will be caught up in the work as representative of "real life."

Vernacular. Language native to the people of a particular country or locality. *Vernacular* applies to the natural pattern of speech used daily by people in a certain geographical area, and is distinguished from more formal language used primarily in schools and in literature. For example, the sentence structure of a "Pennsylvania Dutchman" speaking English—"Throw the horse over the fence some hay"—is an example of vernacular.

A work written in the native language of a particular country or locality is described as "in the vernacular." Editors prefer just enough use of such language to give the flavor without being hard to read when overused. The word is also applied to vocabulary peculiar to a particular trade or profession. (*See: Dialect;* Dictionary of American Regional English.)

Vers libre. (*See: Verse.*)

Verse. The late Judson Jerome, former *Writer's Digest* poetry columnist,

analyzes the various forms of verse as follows:

Verse is writing that uses lines. Any writing, good or bad, poetic or prosaic, that is broken into consciously determined line units is verse.

Free verse, also called *vers libre,* is that in which the length of the lines is not measured by a specific number of units.

Thus any piece
of writing that is broken into lines of irregular length may be
called free verse, whether
it advertises nylons, records Samson's celebration of light,
or explains prosody dryly
as this.

Before this century most verse, free or otherwise, began each line with a capital letter. Most of the line breaks in free verse occur at the end of grammatical phrases, so the line break constitutes a kind of punctuation. Free verse can be analyzed into metrical units (explained below), though there is no set number of such units per line. Some free verse poets use line breaks to divide individual words, sometimes putting single letters or groups of letters on a line for special effects:

is that you &
i are more than you
& i(be
ca
us
e It's we)

                              e.e. cummings

Metered verse is that in which the length of the lines is measured by an arbitrary number of units. The language is made to fit some predetermined design of the poet. Some poets, for example, have written on adding-machine tape to impose an arbitrary limit on the number of spaces and characters in a line. Any such measure can be used to meter poetry, as:

This writin
g has ten let
ters per lin
e but varies
in the numbe
r of spaces.

Syllabic verse is the simplest, common type of metered verse. Line length is determined by the number of syllables, as:

Each of these lines has
five syllables. Some-
times that requires di-
viding the end words.

Accentual verse is that in which line length is determined by the number of stresses, regardless of the number of syllables, as:

*An*glo *Sax*ons *sang* their *mead* songs
in *lines* of *four* emphatic *feet*
with no *fixed pat*tern im*posed* on the *num*ber
of *light syll*ables, nor *set* po*si*tions—
but the *first* or *second stress* in the *line*
had to al*lit*erate with the *heavy beat*
in the *third* po*si*tion, *start*ing the *sec*ond half.

As in this example, there is some unavoidable ambiguity about which syllables should receive stresses; in the last line, *half* might as readily be stressed as *second*. Writers of accentual verse have to work at keeping

the rhythm strong so as not to lose control of stress placement.

Accentual syllabic verse is the most common—and most complex—form of metered verse in English. Certain fixed combinations of number of syllables and placement of accent are called *feet*. Line length is then determined by the number of feet in a line. For example, the combination of one unaccented syllable and a following accented syllable is called an *iamb*. A line with five feet, most of them iambs, is called a line of *iambic pentameter*, as:

a LA de DAH ap PROACH to
verse will DRIVE
the COM mon READ er SCREAM
ing UP the WALL

Such a rigid pattern of alternating stresses is almost impossible—and quite tedious—to maintain. In practice, almost every "iambic" line has one or more variations.

Feet common in English and American poetry are the following: (u = unaccented syllable; / = accented syllable)

iamb (u/)
the HILL is GREEN and STEEP
trochee (/u)
STEEP and GREEN is YONder HILL side
spondee (//)
STEEP GREEN YON HILL
anapest (uu/)
o ver THERE is a HILL that is SHIM mer ing GREEN
dactyl (/uu)
GREEN is the SHIM mer of HILLS at this AL ti tude

Another foot, the *pyrrhic*, consists of two unaccented syllables—and cannot be used except as a substitute for other kinds of feet, usually iambs:

> i SIGH in the en CHANT ment of her EYES;
> one SYLL a ble is ALL she SAID to me.

Rising meter refers to iambs, anapests and spondees—which end with accents. *Falling meter* refers to trochees and dactyls. If a line of rising meter ends with an unaccented syllable (or sometimes two) after the final foot, those syllables are called *hypermetrical*. Endings with unaccented syllables are called *feminine*; those are *masculine* that end with stress.

Verse paragraphs function much as paragraphs function in prose; they are indicated on the page simply by spaces between groups of lines or initial indentation. A long poem such as *Paradise Lost* is broken into verse paragraphs, and a short poem such as *Mending Wall* may be a single verse paragraph.

Strophe is another word for *verse paragraph*, particularly for those units that seem to turn away from the subject matter to introduce a new mood or new dimension of thought.

Stanza is a group of lines more formally determined than verse paragraphs or strophes. (The stanza is to the verse paragraph or strophe as metered verse is to free verse.) Stanzas usually have a fairly fixed pattern, or formula, in which lines of the same length are repeated in the same sequence, often reinforced by rhyme patterns.

A poem is a group or groups of lines. In addition, however, there are some traditional formulae for whole poems, such as the sonnet, a fourteen-line poem in iambic pentameter, usually with one of several traditional rhyme schemes.

Fixed forms, thus, are traditional designs for whole poems. The most common fixed forms in English poetry are *sonnets, sestinas, villanelles, haiku* and *limericks* (see their separate entries in this book), but there are many other fixed forms deriving from other languages.

Verso page. A page appearing on the left side of a book. All numbered verso pages have even numbers. (*See: Recto page.*)

Vertical File Index, The. The Vertical File Index provides information on pamphlets, including title, author, address and cost. It is published monthly, except August, by the H.W. Wilson Company. Listings are categorized by both title and subject.

This reference is usually available in the reference departments of medium-sized or large libraries, and often provides writers/researchers with additional sources of information not available in a card catalog or periodical index.

Vertical publication. This term refers to a publication directed at the entire spectrum of a specific industry, such as *Apparel Industry Magazine*, which may be read by design, manufacturing, sales, finance, management or training personnel within the garment industry. (*See: Horizontal publication; Trade journal.*)

Vet. A term used by editors when referring to the procedure of submitting a book manuscript to an outside expert for review before publication. A manuscript is usually vetted at the publisher's expense, although some authors may use the same procedure themselves before submitting their final draft to the publisher. What the author pays to have a manuscript vetted depends on the relationship of the vetter to the author, the vetter's interest in the book (whether he may possibly contribute a foreword to it), and other factors.

Videlicet. (*See: Viz.*)

Video display terminal (VDT). A computer terminal containing a screen on which text and graphics appear. (A computer *terminal* consists of a keyboard and a screen.) The screen, similar to a TV screen, is a cathode ray tube (CRT), a term sometimes used interchangeably with VDT.

Other names for the VDT are *editing terminal, layout terminal, word processing terminal, video-editing terminal, video-layout terminal* and *videotext terminal.*

Videotape. Magnetic tape on which both picture and sound are recorded electronically. Unlike film photography—the alternate means of storing moving pictorial information—videotape recording does not depend on chemical development: It is capable of immediate replay.

Videotape is a medium through which lucrative opportunities are available to people with appropriate skills. A writer who can operate a video camera or who can collaborate with a videotape artist can produce materials for education, training, entertainment, business and advertis-

ing. Many reality-based TV shows use videotape, both to save money and to add image realism.

The Association of Independent Video and Filmmakers, Inc. (AIVF) is a not-for-profit trade association open to such producers, directors and technicians. Its headquarters are at 625 Broadway, Ninth Floor, New York, NY 10012.

Writer's Market, Photographer's Market and *Artist's Market* list details on videotape markets for freelancers. (*See: Audiovisual communication.*)

Videotext. (*See: Electronic text.*)

Viewpoint. This term refers to the mind of the character through which the reader is told a story. There are several kinds of viewpoint, labeled according to the characteristics of the viewpoint itself and the storyteller with whom the viewpoint originates.

Objective viewpoint is used when the narrator relates facts but avoids emotion. *Subjective viewpoint*, the type most used in fiction, incorporates a character's thoughts and emotions into the storytelling. The reader thus shares in the character's emotional life.

A short story can be told in the first person through the mind of either a major or a minor character; the latter viewpoint is useful as a technique if there is a minor character—but no major character—who is present in every scene. It can also be used if the major character is difficult for the reader to identify with. Most short stories, however, use the technique of single-major-character viewpoint.

Longer works of fiction are able

to use forms of viewpoint that can reveal the thoughts of more than one character to the reader. Using the *omniscient viewpoint*, an author can relate the perceptions of any of his characters or detach himself from them to serve as narrator. The *detached viewpoint*, on the other hand, lets the reader sense that he is watching the story as it unfolds; the author gives decriptions and impressions, but never through the perception of a character.

The *multiple-character viewpoint* is used to tell a story from the perspectives of different characters, one at a time. Unlike works using the omniscient viewpoint, this viewpoint stays with one character for a considerable length—for example, a chapter in a novel. This technique is useful when the story must, but the characters are unable to, make an extreme change of scene. (*See: First-person point of view; Third-person point of view.*)

Vignette. A short piece of writing intended to convey an image of, or cast illumination on, a scene, a character or a situation. Characteristics of the vignette are exactness of phrase construction and a poignant tone.

In TV, a vignette is a brief (five seconds to thirty seconds) incident shown to illustrate a point or principle. It often borders on melodrama. (*See: Slice of life.*)

Villanelle. A form of lyric poetry written in tercets (three-line stanzas) with a closing quatrain (four-line stanza) characterized by two refrain lines.

These lines appear as one and three in the first stanza, and alternate as line three in suceeding stanzas. In the final stanza, the refrain lines are lines three and four. (*See: Verse.*)

vis-à-vis. French for *face to face*. The term is most often used as a preposition, meaning *in relation to, compared with,* or *in regard to.* For example: The Senator's position vis-à-vis the nuclear energy bill was indefinite.

It may be used as an adjective to describe people facing each other, as on opposite sides of a dining table. It can also be used as a noun to mean "one who is opposite or opposing" (e.g., a person of equal rank, position, etc.).

viz. An abbreviation of *videlicet,* a Latin word meaning "that is to say." *Viz.* is an expression used primarily in formal English to mean "namely." It's seldom used in contemporary writing. (*See: i.e.*)

Voice-over. A TV/motion picture term referring to the use of a person's voice when that person or character does not appear in the scene being shown. Documentaries often use voice-overs. When used in a script, this term is typed in all caps, or abbreviated as *VO*. (*See: Television script terms.*)

Volunteer Lawyers for the Arts. This nationwide organization of lawyers offers free legal services to people in the creative arts, including writers, on matters related to practicing art. Eligibility for these services is determined by the writer's income; in some cases, even though writers qualify for free legal services, they are responsible for paying court costs.

For information on free legal aid, or to locate branches in other cities, writers should contact one of the following: California Lawyers for the Arts, Fort Mason Center Building C, Room 255, San Francisco, CA 94123, (415) 775-7200; Lawyers for the Creative Arts, 213 W. Institute, Suite 411, Chicago, IL 60610, (312) 944-2787; or Volunteer Lawyers for the Arts, 1 E. Fifty-third St., New York, NY 10022, (212) 319-2787. For legal advice from VLA, call their Lawline at (212) 319-2910.

Washington Independent Writers (WIW). A twenty-two hundred member organization of writers in the Washington, DC area. It acts as a medium for the exchange of information, ideas and knowledge, and the encouragement of professionalism and fairness.

WIW publishes a newsletter, a membership directory and other professional publications. It offers a job-listing service as well as monthly seminars, workshops and some small genre discussion groups. It belongs to the Council of Writers Organizations. Headquarters address of WIW is 220 Woodward Bldg., Washington, DC 20005. (*See: Council of Writers Organizations.*)

Western Writers of America (WWA). The WWA is made up of freelance writers who specialize in western fiction or nonfiction of many forms, including books, short pieces, scripts and juvenile material. The Saddleman Award and the Spur Awards are granted by this organization, as well as the annual Owen Wister Award for "lifelong contributions to the history and legends of the American west." The WWA publishes a bimonthly, *Roundup*, and convenes annually. Contact James Crutchfield, Secretary/Treasurer, at 1012 Fair St., Franklin, TN 37064.

Wide angle. In TV and film, a term that refers to a scene shot from a distance or with a wide-angle lens to show the audience an all-encompassing view. *Wide angle* is typed in all caps in a script. (*See: Television script terms.*)

Widow. A typeset line considerably short of the standard copy width, standing by itself at the top of a column or page. Unsightly widows—those less than two-thirds or half the standard line measure—are typically fixed in the editing process.

Wills. Authors have special, professionally related considerations to make when drawing up their wills.

Under the copyright law effective in 1978, a literary work is protected for the duration of the author's life plus the succeeding fifty years. An author's will can specify who owns the copyright and who is to receive the royalties earned by his work subsequent to his death.

Another point that may be made in an author's will is a requirement that a particular unpublished work or works not be published posthumously. (*See: Lawyers, where to find.*)

Wire services, jobs in. Jobs available at the wire services are primarily those in news reporting and photography. The major wire services have branches throughout the world. (*See: Associated Press; United Press International.*)

Women in Communications, Inc. (WICI).

Women in Communications, Inc., is a professional organization for women and men in all fields of communications. Its twelve thousand members work in advertising, communications education, film, magazines, newspapers, photojournalism, public relations, publishing, radio, technical writing and TV. There are eighty-six campus chapters and eighty professional chapters in addition to members-at-large.

WICI's purposes are to unite members for the purpose of promoting the advancement of women in all fields of communications; to work for the First Amendment rights and responsibilities of communicators; to recognize distinguished professional achievements; and to promote high professional standards throughout the communications industry. The Clarion Awards competition is sponsored annually to recognize excellence in all areas of communications.

The organization publishes a national magapaper, *The Professional Communicator*, ten times per year; and a national directory of professional members biennially. A national professional conference is held annually.

The national headquarters address is 2101 Wilson Blvd., Suite 417, Arlington, VA 22201.

Women writers.

The major problem women writers (and would-be women writers) have suffered throughout history is lack of opportunity to write. Women traditionally have not been allowed—either by custom or necessity—to be educated; and while it is not essential to be highly educated to write, it is essential to be literate. There have always been exceptions—the Greek lyric poet Sappho, the mystical essayist Teresa of Avila, the seventeenth-century American poet Anne Bradstreet—but for the most part, writing was not considered seemly activity for wives and mothers; the most literate women were usually courtesans, nuns, aristocrats or daughters of intellectuals who believed women should be educated.

It was only with the growing popularity of the novel in the nineteenth century (as general literacy increased) that women achieved significant influence in any literary genre; even then, however, the novel was considered a disreputable and inferior form, beneath those practiced by men of letters, who wrote essays and poetry. But Mary Shelley, Charlotte and Emily Brontë (who first published under male pseudonyms), George Sand (born Amandine Aurore Lucie Dupin) and George Eliot (Mary Ann Evans) are some of the most important literary figures of the century.

In studying women writers, it is necessary to remember the distinction between writing and being published: Many women who wrote are lost to history. Emily Dickinson, for instance, published a comparative few poems during her lifetime, but took pains to ensure that her poems would all survive and be published. It is very likely that many fine women writers did not take such pains. Today academicians pore through nineteenth-century periodicals, diaries and letters for evidence of literary endeavor, but materials older than that are seldom available.

Additional information: *The Madwoman in the Attic: The Woman Writer and the Nineteenth-Century Literary Imagination; Silences.*

Women's National Book Association (WNBA). The WNBA includes men as well as women. Its members, who work in all occupations allied to the publishing industry, include publishers, authors, editors, librarians, booksellers, literary agents, designers, educators, critics, administrative personnel and individuals engaged in book production, marketing, finance, subsidiary rights, etc.

The Association maintains its archives at Columbia University. It publishes the magazine *The Bookwoman* three times per year. A WNBA board meeting is held annually.

The WNBA presents the biennial Women's National Book Association Award (formerly called the Constance Lindsay Skinner Award) to "a distinguished living bookwoman for her extraordinary contribution to the world of books and through books to the society in which we live." Its Lucile Michaels Pannell Award is for "the most effective bookstore program bringing books and children together."

WNBA chapters are located in Binghamton, New York; Boston; Detroit; Los Angeles; Atlanta; Dallas; Nashville; San Francisco; and Washington, DC. The Women's National Book Association can be reached at 160 Fifth Ave., New York, NY 10010.

Women's slick magazine. This type of magazine is characterized by quality paper, four-color graphics, national advertising and well-known writers.

The nonfiction editorial content deals with various topics related to women's interests: careers; marriage, family, sex, psychology, personal care, interpersonal relationships and time management.

A decreasing number of women's slick magazines publish fiction, as well. Generally, editors seek fiction aimed at readers aged twenty-one to thirty-four, and avoid stories set in the past, stories told from the viewpoint of a child or an elderly person, slice-of-life pieces, and plots concerned with topical matters.

At present, the women's slicks pay $1 per word and up for articles. (*See: Confession.*)

Word count. Magazine writers usually indicate on page one of manuscripts the approximate number of words contained in the piece. Total number of words can be estimated with the procedure outlined here. First, every word (including *a, an* and *the*) on the first full three pages of the manuscript is counted, and the average number of words on those pages is calculated. Then, the average, representing the estimated number of words per page, is multiplied by the total number of pages in the manuscript. Finally, the total word count is rounded to the nearest hundred (e.g., 3,500, not 3,463 words) and typed in the upper right corner of page one. Most word processing software has a word-count feature.

Word processor. Previously defined as a specialized computer—really a glorified typewriter—this term now refers to software that allows writers to process copy more efficiently on their computers.

There are a variety of programs on the market, but most allow the user to move copy, check spelling, conduct searches through the entire files and count words. (*See: WYSIWYG.*)

Work made for hire. This term, often called simply *work-for-hire*, designates work prepared either by an employee as part of his ordinary full-time job responsibilities, or by an individual specifically contracted to produce a particular work under written agreement with an employer. A Supreme Court decision in the case of *CCNV* v. *Reid* concluded that Congress provides two distinct means for classifying created works as work-for-hire. The first concerns work created by employees within the scope of their employment in which copyright belongs to the employer. The second section of the law requires that three conditions must exist to designate a work-for-hire. The work must be "specially ordered or commissioned," both parties must sign a written document in which they "expressly agree" that the work is a work-for-hire, and the work must be "for use as a contribution to a collective work, as part of a motion picture or other audiovisual work, as a translation, as a supplementary work, as a compilation, as an instructional text, or as a test, as answer material for a test, or as an atlas."

When a piece is considered a work made for hire, the person who assigns the work owns the rights to it permanently. This should not be confused with an agreement that stipulates that "all rights" will be purchased, with no mention of the term "work made for hire." In the case of a sale of "all rights," the writer or his heirs may regain the rights after thirty-five years by following the termination procedure delineated in the copyright law.

Even the duration of the copyright in a work made for hire is different from other works. It lasts for seventy-five years from the year of its first publication, or one hundred years from its creation. On all other works, the copyright is good for life of the last surviving author plus fifty years.

The most important thing for a freelance writer to remember is that unless there is an express written agreement, signed by both parties, that the work is "made for hire," the work does not fall into that category. Even where the entire copyright is assigned by the author, he can get it back eventually. But once a work is legally designated a work made for hire, an employment relationship is deemed to exist, and the employer is considered the author for all time, no matter who wrote the piece. (*See: Figure 60.*)

Work space. Although a complete room used only for writing is the ideal arrangement, it's impractical for many. However, writers should have a particular place, used consistently and regularly, reserved for writing. This place can be a desk, a garage, a portion of a room or simply a table. (*See: Camera; Tape recorder; Taxes; Tools, writing.*)

Working Press of the Nation. This is a five-volume set of annual directories published by the National Research Bureau, Inc. It lists organizations

FIGURE 60

WORK MADE FOR HIRE: ASJA POSITION
ANNOUNCED APRIL 28, 1978

It has long been the established practice for responsible periodicals, in commissioning articles by freelance writers, to purchase only one-time publication rights—commonly known as "first North American rights"—to such articles, the author retaining all other rights exclusively and all revenues received from the subsequent sale of other rights reverting to the author.

This practice is affirmed by the Code of Ethics and Fair Practices of the American Society of Journalists and Authors (ASJA), the national organization of independent nonfiction writers. The philosophy underlying this tradition has been further reaffirmed by the Copyright Law of 1976, which took effect in January of 1978 and states explicitly that copyright is vested in the author of a work and commences at the moment of creation of that work. "Copyright" is, literally, the "right to copy"—i.e., to publish in any form; that right is the author's, transferable only by written agreement and only to the degree, and under the terms, specified by such agreement.

It has come to the attention of the ASJA that certain periodical publishers have recently sought to circumvent the clear intent of the law by requiring independent writers, as a condition of article assignment, to sign so-called "all rights transferred" or "work-made-for-hire" agreements. "All rights transferred" signifies that the author, the recognized copyright owner, transfers that ownership—and the right to all future revenues that may accrue therefrom—to the publisher. A "work-made-for-hire" agreement specifically relegates the independent writer, so far as the article under consideration is concerned, to the status of an employee and creates a mythical—but nonetheless presumably legally binding—relationship in which the author agrees to function as a hired hand, while the publisher assumes the mantle of "creator" of the work, with all the rights of ownership vested in the creator under the law.

Both types of agreement clearly presume that the work being produced has an inherent value beyond one-time publication. Both the law and the ASJA Code of Ethics recognize that presumption, and it is the intent of both documents that the transfer of any rights beyond one-time publication take place only as the result of negotiation that assigns a monetary value to each such specific right a publisher seeks to acquire. Both types of agreement described above deny the author's basic role as owner and creator and seek to wrest from the writer, even before the work has been produced, all future interest in revenues that may derive from that work.

This effort, subverting the intent of the law and contrary to ethical publishing trade practices, is condemned by the American Society of Journalists and Authors. The demand for blanket assignment of all future right and interest in an article or other creative work simply *will not be met* by responsible independent writers. Publishers who persist in issuing such inequitable agreements in connection with commissioned works will find that they have done so at the certain risk of losing a healthy flow of superior professional material. The result, for those periodicals, is likely to be a sharp and inevitable decline in editorial quality—an erosion and debasement of the standards on which periodicals must rely in order to attract readers and maintain their own reputations.

and personnel in various media, providing information such as names, titles, addresses and telephone numbers of personnel in the industry. Directory titles are as follows: Volume One, *Newspaper Services Directory*; Volume Two, *Magazine and Editorial Directory*; Volume Three, *TV and Radio Directory*; Volume Four, *Feature Writer, Photographer and Syndicate Directory*; and Volume Five, *Internal Publications Directory*.

Volume Four of this series can be of special interest, since it is the directory that lists freelance writers. Included in each listing are the writer's name, his home address, areas in which he specializes and magazines in which he has had material published. The possibility of assignments resulting from editors' referring to the directory is one advantage of being included.

Freelance feature writers interested in being listed in *Working Press of the Nation* should write to the National Research Bureau, 310 S. Michigan Ave., Suite 1150, Chicago, IL 60604. At present, listings are free of charge.

Working Press of the Nation is available in most large libraries. (*See: Directories.*)

World Intellectual Property Organization (WIPO).

This is an agency of the United Nations that is devoted to the protection of intellectual property, which comprises industrial property such as rights in inventions, and copyright in creations in the arts.

WIPO is especially active in providing technical assistance requested by developing countries. Writers seeking information about the copyright laws in a particular foreign country may be able to get advice on their question from the Public Information Officer of WIPO, whose address is 34 chemin des Colombettes, 1211 Geneva 20, Switzerland.

World Wide Web (WWW).

A hypertext network within the Internet developed by researchers in Geneva, Switzerland. This interface allows publishers to link text, graphics, video and sound. The WWW comprises "home pages" or "sites," where publishers provide hypertext links that allow users to click a button to get related information within the site, or at another site. (*See: Hypertext; Internet.*)

The Writer.

This monthly magazine, established in 1887, has an audience of freelance writers. Its content, largely instructional, relates to the work of the writer of traditional literary forms—short story, poem, article, novel, etc.

The Writer's editorial and subscription offices are at 120 Boylston St., Boston, MA 02116. (*See:* Writer's Digest.)

Writers, biographical directories of.

Directories that furnish biographical material on authors can be useful to a writer in researching nonfiction or in gathering lecture material.

Contemporary Authors is a series of 106 volumes, begun in 1962, of nontechnical book authors published by commercial publishers or university presses.

The biennial *Writers Directory* contains more than fifteen thousand descriptions of fiction and nonfiction writers from various countries, all of whom have published at least one book in English. The *Directory's* "Index to Writing Categories," a cross-reference section, groups the writers listed according to kind of writing (e.g., children's nonfiction) or subject matter (e.g., medicine/health).

Among directories dealing with authors of childrens' books are *Twentieth Century Children's Writers* and *Something About the Author*. Other directories of specialized writers include the *Contemporary Writers Series: Contemporary Poets* (Volume I), *Contemporary Novelists* (Volume II), *Contemporary Dramatists* (Volume III), and *Contemporary Literary Critics* (Volume IV). Revised every five years, the series lists living writers who write in English. The *National Playwrights Directory* contains approximately five hundred entries of living American playwrights—arranged alphabetically by author's last name—and an index of plays.

Creative Canada is a series of references to visual artists, musicians and performing artists, as well as writers, not all of whom are living. Another Canadian directory is *The Writer's Union of Canada: A Directory of Members*. Its three hundred members write in categories such as literary fiction, political commentary, bestsellers, travel, humor, cookbooks, memoirs and children's books. (*See: Biographical references; Directories, writer-related;* Working Press of the Nation.)

Writer's block. A state that may be manifested by a dearth of ideas, self-dissatisfaction or an inability to organize.

One step toward conquering writer's block is to acknowledge the fact that it comes from within the self.

Performing work-related tasks, such as reading, tidying one's desk, corresponding with other writers or speaking before a local organization, can help the writer during a period of block. Also, buying a new piece of equipment or a reference book may raise spirits.

Causes of writer's block vary. For many writers, block results from fear that their writing isn't any good, and that once it's in print *other* people will see it and realize it's no good. In other writers, it results from fear of disapproval. Many professional freelancers claim that the best cure for block is when bills come due.

Writers' clubs. A writers' club is an informal group established for mutual guidance and encouragement. Activities include reporting sessions, which compel each member to recount his accomplishments, and manuscript critiques, which are designed to provide the writers with honest evaluation and advice. These planned discussions often digress to other writing-related ones, such as discussions on how or where to sell a particular piece or how to overcome a case of writer's block. Sometimes a club invites a prominent local writer to speak to the group.

One of the major aims of writers' clubs is to instill motivation and enthusiasm in members through interaction with other professionals.

Beginning in 1982, the National Writers Association, 1450 S. Havana, Suite 424, Aurora, CO 80012, began publication of a *Directory of Local Writers' Organizations*. Latest publication date and price can be obtained by writing the National Writers Association. (*See: Writers' organizations.*)

Writers' colonies. Writers' colonies offer writers and other artists (painters, sculptors, composers) a place to work and think. Each colony presents its residents a unique writing environment—from the stateliness of a mansion surrounded by gardens to the informality of a community-type arrangement that invites writers' families. Writers' colonies may encourage interaction among their residents, or they may represent a sanctuary for the creative process. Two of the oldest colonies are the MacDowell Colony in Peterborough, NH, and Yaddo in Saratoga Springs, NY.

Some of the colonies offer free room and board; others request their residents prepare meals and buy their own groceries. Voluntary contributions are often encouraged. Lengths of stay vary. Some colonies take beginners; others do not.

Applications for admission to most writers' colonies include submitting writing samples and recommendations from former residents or other appropriate people. Addresses and other information about specific writers' colonies are sometimes available from Poets and Writers, Inc., 72 Spring St., New York, NY 10012. (*See:* Poet's Market; *Scholarships, fellowships, internships.*)

Writers' conferences. Organized learning/writing experiences. Writers' conferences around the country offer varied settings, purposes and formats to meet the specific needs of writers. They may range from one-day seminars to month-long assemblies. Some are highly focused both in theme and enrollment, e.g., Writing Workshop for People over 57; Experimental Writers' Workshop. Others are broad in extent and renowned by reputation, e.g., Bread Loaf Writers' Conference.

Some writers' conferences hold contests or offer private critiques of manuscripts submitted prior to the conference opening. Some may be lecture-oriented; others offer numerous question-answer opportunities. Some provide writers with the option of consulting privately with a publishing professional during the conference.

A list of conferences held nationwide appears in the May issue of *Writer's Digest* and in the annual *Literary Market Place.*

Writer's Digest. Established in 1920, this is the largest circulation national monthly magazine aimed at freelance writers. The magazine emphasizes guidance in three major areas: the kinds of manuscripts bought; how to write them; and where to sell them. Articles cover a wide spectrum of writing-related subjects: techniques for writing stories, articles, novels, nonfiction books, audiovisual materials, speeches—any writing for which a freelancer is used. Regular columns in the magazine cover fiction, nonfiction, poetry, scriptwriting, electronic writing and monthly market listings that tell what publishing firms are in search of material and writers. The publication carries interviews with well-known writers, information on subjects involving legal matters and material on the business of writing. *Writer's Digest* is located at 1507 Dana Ave., Cincinnati, OH 45207.

Writer's guidelines. A printed reference sheet supplied to writers by editors. It describes a magazine's purpose and audience, and outlines specifications for submitting material. In writer's guidelines, the editor indicates specific word lengths for material; categories and topics needed; need for, and policy on, photographs; and, sometimes, rates of pay. Some book publishers—such as those with romance novel imprints—also have writer's guidelines pointing up the specific restrictions of heroine's age, plot structure, etc. The object of writer's guidelines is to provide for smooth dealings between writer and editor, and to guide the writer in selling his material by detailing the publisher's needs and requirements. (*See: Style sheet.*)

Writers Guild of America. A labor union representing professional writers in motion pictures, TV and radio. Like any other labor union, its chief purpose is to ensure the protection and well-being of its members through the processes of collective bargaining under the National Labor Relations Act of the United States. The Guild was founded in 1954 as the result of an amalgamation of the Screenwriters Guild, the Radio Writers Guild and the TV Writers Group.

For administrative purposes only, the union is divided by the Mississippi River into the Writers Guild of America, East, and the Writers Guild of America, West. In all other respects it is a single union, jointly holding national agreements with producing organizations. A National Council, made up of members of East and West, meets semiannually in New York and Los Angeles. Annual meetings of the membership are held simultaneously in New York and Los Angeles each September.

The Guild presents annual awards for outstanding achievement in writing in the areas of its jurisdiction. Each Guild publishes its own monthly newsletter; jointly they publish a directory of members. Each also has a registration service for manuscripts.

Membership in the Guild can be acquired only by the sale of literary material to, or employment for, writing services in motion pictures, TV and radio. At WGA, West, there is an initiation fee of $8,500, with basic dues of $25 per quarter, and an assessment of 1½ percent of a writer's gross earnings in any of the fields of jurisdiction, also payable quarterly. Fees for WGA, East, are $1,000 initiation, and annual dues of $50 plus 1¾ percent of gross earnings.

A booklet listing the Guild's minimum rates for scripts of various lengths is available from either Guild for $3.55, which includes postage, plus applicable sales tax for residents of New York and California. WGA, East, also publishes a booklet, "Professional Writer's Teleplay/Screenplay Format," for about $4.28, which includes postage, plus applicable sales tax. A certified check, or a money order made out to "Writers Guild of America" should accompany any order.

Writers Guild of America, West, is at 7000 W. Third St., Los Angeles, CA 90048. Writers Guild of America, East, is at 555 W. Fifty-seventh St., Room 1230, New York, NY 10019.

(*See: Writers Guild Script Registration Service.*)

Writers Guild rates: screenplay. (*See: Figure 61.*)

Writers Guild rates: television. (*See: Figure 62.*)

Writers Guild Script Registration Service. Since a writer's rights under the law begin when a work is completed, the Writers Guild of America has formed a registration service to verify the completion date and identity of formats, outlines, synopses, storylines or scripts for theatrical films, TV and radio. (Book manuscripts, plays, music, lyrics, illustrations and legal documents are not eligible for registration with the Guild.) Some agents and producers will not accept a script unless it has been registered with the Guild; this minimizes the charges of story theft that are bound to be made in industries so barraged with material that ideas often overlap.

A writer does not have to belong to the Guild to register his work. To do so, he must send an 8½″ × 11″ unbound copy of the manuscript to the registration service, along with his registration fee ($10 for Guild members, $22 for nonmembers for scripts up to 150 pages; $23 for members, $32 for nonmembers for scripts between 150 and 350 pages; and $57 for scripts 350 pages and up). The manuscript is sealed, dated, given a registration number and filed; a receipt is sent back to the author, who then is responsible for inscribing the registration number on his copies of the manuscript. The Guild keeps the manuscript on file for ten years, at which time the work will be de-stroyed, unless the author renews the registration by repaying the registration fee.

The mailing address of the registration service is Writers Guild of America, West, 7000 W. Third St., Los Angeles, CA 90048. (*See: Copyright.*)

Writers, how many. Figures on file with the Bureau of Labor Statistics in 1995 showed that 112,000 people listed their occupation as "author" 72,000 listed themselves as "technical writers" and 267,000 listed their occupations as "reporters and editors."

These figures do not include the part-time and freelance writers and the hobbyists who only occasionally submit a poem or other short manuscript to a newspaper or magazine. (*See: Full-time freelancing, economics of.*)

Writer's Market. This annual directory from Writer's Digest Books lists four thousand freelance writing markets in the U.S. and Canada, including book publishers; company, trade and consumer magazines; syndicates; film, TV, theatrical and audiovisual producers; and greeting card publishers. *Writer's Market* also lists contests and awards, organizations of interest and publications of interest. Individual entries are revised yearly.

Writer's Market listings provide a market's address(es); phone number; names of editorial personnel; circulation, distribution and format; readership (or audience) profile; pay rates, manuscript lengths and seasonal deadlines; rights purchased; kill fees; types of work the

FIGURE 61

WRITERS GUILD RATES: SCREENPLAY
WGA 1995 THEATRICAL AND TELEVISION BASIC AGREEMENT
THEATRICAL COMPENSATION

Employment, Flat Deals*	First Period Effective 5/2/95—5/1/96	
	LOW BUDGET	*HIGH BUDGET*
A. Original screenplay, including treatment	$39,452	$74,002
Installments:		
Delivery of original treatment	17,877	29,603
Delivery of first draft screenplay	15,538	29,603
Delivery of final draft screenplay	6,037	14,796
B. Non-original screenplay, including treatment	34,528	64,207
Installments:		
Delivery of treatment	12,946	19,736
Delivery of first draft screenplay	15,538	29,603
Delivery of final draft screenplay	6,044	14,868
C. Original screenplay, excluding treatment/ sale of original screenplay	26,512	54,266
Installments for employment:		
Delivery of first draft screenplay	20,475	39,470
Delivery of final draft screenplay	6,037	14,796
D. Non-original screenplay, excluding treatment/sale of non-original screenplay	21,575	44,399
Installments for employment:		
Delivery of first draft screenplay	15,538	29,603
Delivery of final draft screenplay	6,037	14,796
E. Additional compensation for story included in screenplay	4,937	9,867
F. Story or treatment	12,946	19,736
G. Original treatment	17,877	29,603
H. First draft screenplay, with or without option for final draft screenplay		
First draft screenplay	15,538	29,603
Final draft screenplay	10,355	19,736
I. Rewrite of screenplay	12,946	19,736
J. Polish of screenplay	6,476	9,867

* The Minimum Basic Agreement provides for a discount with respect to employment on a flat deal basis of a writer who has not been previously employed under a Guild MBA in TV, theatrical films, or dramatic radio, subject to an adjustment to full minimum if a photoplay is produced utilizing writer's material.

FIGURE 62

WRITERS GUILD RATES: TELEVISION

WGA 1995 Theatrical and Television Basic Agreement
Television Compensation (continued)

Network Prime Time (ABC, CBS, NBC and Fox)

Applicable Minimums	*Effective 5/2/95–5/1/96*	*Effective 5/2/96–5/1/97*	*Effective 5/2/97–5/1/98*

Length of program: 45 minutes or less (but more than 30 minutes)

Story*	$ 7,188	$ 7,368/7,404	$ 7,552/ 7,589/ 7,626
Teleplay	11,854	12,150/12,210	12,454/12,515/12,576

Installments:

*First draft — 60% of agreed compensation but not less than 90% of minimum

Final draft — Balance of agreed compensation

Story & Teleplay	18,015	18,465/18,555	18,927/19,019/19,112

Installments:

*Story — 30% of agreed compensation

First draft teleplay — 40% of agreed compensation or the difference between the Story Installment and 90% of the minimum, whichever is greater

Final draft teleplay — Balance of agreed compensation

Length of program: 60 minutes or less (but more than 45 minutes)

Story*	$ 9,169	$ 9,398/ 9,444	$ 9,633/ 9,680/ 9,727
Teleplay	15,120	15,498/15,574	15,665/15,863/16,041

Installments:

*First Draft — 60% of agreed compensation but not less than 90% of minimum

Final Draft — Balance of agreed compensation

Story & Teleplay	22,984	23,559/23,674	24,148/24,266/24,384

Installments:

*Story — 30% of agreed compensation

First draft teleplay — 40% of agreed compensation or the difference between the Story Installment and 90% of the minimum, whichever is greater

Final draft teleplay — Balance of agreed compensation

---

* On pilots only, the writer is to be paid 10% of the first installment (as an advance against such first installment) upon commencement of services. The applicable minimum for a pilot story or teleplay is 150% of the applicable minimum set forth above.

editors are looking for; and tips from the editors on how to break in. In addition to the listings, up-front chapters deal with the business of freelancing, including manuscript preparation, recordkeeping and what rights to sell. A regular feature is "How Much Should I Charge?," which lists rates of pay for different kinds of writing and writing-related work. Other pages show current postal rates, and reproduce sample query letters. It's available in bookstores, libraries and from Writer's Digest Books, 1507 Dana Ave., Cincinnati, OH 45207.

Writers' organizations. Writers' organizations exist for two reasons: professional advancement and sociability. Large organizations (Writers Guild, Authors League, American Society of Journalists and Authors) are concerned mainly with the economic advancement of the writer. National and local clubs offer writers the camaraderie of other writers, by mail or in person. Many of the leading professional writers' groups are described in individual entries in this book.

Writers' organizations and associations are also described in the *Encyclopedia of Associations*, available in most libraries. (*See: Writers' clubs.*)

Writers' unions. Trade organizations that, through negotiations, enhance the writer's power in dealing with publishers or producers.

Countries in which writers have formed unions include England, Canada, Sweden, Denmark, Norway and West Germany. These foreign unions have sometimes succeeded in obtaining fairer treatment from pub-

lishers by collectively refusing to submit work to them; compelling publishers to deliver payment of advances or royalties; raising royalty payments; instituting fair payment procedures, such as paying for rewrites; and establishing a means of payment for use of books in libraries.

In the U.S., The Newspaper Guild has successfully negotiated salary rates for reporters and copyeditors, and the Writers Guild of America negotiates with producers for film and TV fees. The National Writers Union was adopted at the American Writers Congress in October 1981. (*See: National Writers Union.*)

Writer's Yearbook. Subtitled "The year's best writing on writing," this annual magazine is published by *Writer's Digest* and sold at bookstores and newsstands January through March. Issues contain the editorial requirements of the top one hundred magazine markets, ranked by the *WD* editors. Interviews with bestselling authors and articles on fiction and nonfiction technique are also included as are essays and a year-in-review feature. The publication is also available by mail from *Writer's Digest*, 1507 Dana Ave., Cincinnati, OH 45207.

Writing, books on. Books for freelance writers fall into several broad categories. They may be general works designed to help improve writing style, or biographies of well-known writers intended to inspire. How-to books offer information, for example, on the techniques of writing magazine articles, interviewing, or getting credible motivations for story characters. Specialized works explain how to write and sell children's picture books, TV scripts or greeting cards.

Most nonfiction books on writing are listed in the *Subject Guide to Books In Print*, under the following general categories: "Authorship—Handbooks, Manuals, etc.," "Authors and Publishers," "Journalism—Handbooks, Manuals, etc.," "Reporters and Reporting" and "Writing," and under specific headings such as "Advertising Copy," "Fiction—Authorship," "Medical Writing," "Authorship—Juvenile Literature," "Moving Picture Authorship" and "Playwriting." The *Subject Guide* is in any library.

The most prolific publisher of books for writers is Writer's Digest Books, Cincinnati, Ohio.

Writing courses. Courses of organized study are available to freelance writers, poets, playwrights, novelists and others wishing to further their expertise in a particular field of writing. The ideal writing courses are taught by instructors who are also professional writers. Instructors may teach literary skills and reader consciousness; and they may function as editors who critique the publishability of student writing.

Writing courses are offered by many colleges and universities around the country. They are available both through degree programs on campus and home study. Some proprietary schools also offer home study courses in writing. (*See: Associated Writing Programs; Correspondence courses for writers.*)

Writing, the discipline of. Writing is a skill acquired through education but developed largely through practice. Like the Olympic swimmer, the well-trained writer achieves success through consistent effort exerted over a period of time. While a good liberal arts education is almost a given, the writer must continue to analyze his writing, compare it to the work of talented contemporaries and strive to improve his style.

The key to developing writing skills is discipline, which is shown by daily writing: The practicing writer composes something each day, even if one day's writing consists only of an entry in a journal.

Observation skills are also necessary to good writing: The writer must be adept at extracting ideas for articles and books from his everyday experiences and surroundings. (*See: Journal; Note-taking.*)

Writing instruction on film, tape, cassette, record. The films and recordings departments of many public libraries have collections of well-known authors reading their works and/or discussing the techniques of their writing. Some publishers of curriculum materials for schools also sell home study tapes for adults on grammar, interviewing, speed reading, memory development, etc. A librarian may have such companies' catalogs available.

Writing schools, home study. (*See: Correspondence courses for writers.*)

WYSIWYG. This acronym stands for "what you see is what you get." This applies to most word-processing software—the monitor displays an exact replication of what the printer will output.

Xenophobia. The fear of, or hatred toward, foreigners or strangers. Since an unwillingness to appreciate or to become familiar with cultures other than his own only narrows a writer's viewpoint, xenophobic authors tend to be quickly relegated to literary obscurity.

Xenophobia as a theme does occur in various literatures; it is important, for instance, in American ethnic fiction, since ethnic Americans can be objects of xenophobia.

Yearbooks, encyclopedia. These references, which report both on general news and highlights of a given year, can be useful in researching articles summarizing the events of a previous year; nostalgia writers and fiction writers use older editions for reference. Yearbooks are usually published in February or March of the year following the one being covered. *Writer's Digest* magazine publishes an annual each January titled *Writer's Yearbook*, which features "the year's best writing on writing."

For more immediately available information, newspaper indexes and *Facts on File* can be consulted. (*See: Background information, books of;* Writer's Yearbook.)

Yellow journalism. A newspaper style that emerged in the late 1800s. It is characterized by sensational accounts of crime and scandalous events, and by stories about crusades undertaken by "average" people. Newspapers of this genre introduced the banner head (a large, bold headline that occupies the entire width of the page), the Sunday supplement and liberal use of photographs and illustrations.

The best-known practitioners of yellow journalism were New York *World* owner Joseph Pulitzer and New York *Journal* owner William Randolph Hearst, who, during the late 1890s, battled for the largest newspaper readership. One tactic in this circulation war was each publisher's luring of staff members from the competing paper to his own. The comic strip the *Yellow Kid* and its creator, Richard Outcault, were part of this ongoing bargaining. Outcault's comic strip character was the basis for the label *yellow papers*, applied to Hearst's and Pulitzer's newspapers; this tag evolved into the term *yellow journalism.*

During the prime of yellow journalism, its characteristic techniques were practiced across the country—in Cincinnati, St. Louis, San Francisco, Denver and Boston, as well as in New York; but widespread use of such techniques had disappeared by 1910.

The banner headline and the Sunday magazine, which are now professionally accepted practices, are two surviving characteristics of yellow journalism. The term *yellow journalism*, as used today, refers to sensational reporting or photographs.

Young adult. A term used by librarians, book publishers and booksellers to refer to the books published for young people between the ages of twelve and seventeen. Some publishers and librarians have lowered the minimum age level to ten, recognizing the interest of some of today's younger people in more adult themes. As Clarion Books' editor and publisher James Cross Giblin pointed out in a *Writer's Digest* article:

Fifteen years ago, the taboo barriers in this field, which had stood for generations, broke down right and left. Authors rushed into the breach with realistic novels that treated such hitherto "forbidden" subjects as premarital sex, child abuse, homosexuality, drug use, alcoholism, madness and incest. . . . Judy Blume, Paul Zindel, S.E. Hinton and many other authors successfully rode this wave of "new realism," establishing their reputations. . . .

Meanwhile, opponents of realism in young adult fiction, reflecting the new conservatism in the country, are mounting campaigns to have books they find offensive removed from the shelves of school and public libraries.

A new trend emerged in the early 1990s in young adult books: the horror novel. Written by authors such as Christopher Pike and R.L. Stine, these books are wildly popular. Pat McDonald, editorial director of Archway Paperbacks and Minstrel Books at Pocket, says the books offer "a wonderfully scary time—and at the end you're [readers] safe." (*See: Censorship, literary; Novels for young people; Romance novel.*)

Zeitgeist. The general intellectual, moral and cultural climate of an era. Jay McInerny's novel *Bright Lights, Big City* is said to have captured the zeitgeist of 1980s' America.

ZIP Code information. The ZIP Code for a particular city or town can be determined by using one of two sources. The U.S. Postal Service publishes an annual directory of ZIP Codes, called the *National ZIP Code & Post Office Directory*, which is available for public use at post office branches. This book is also sold at post offices, though it may not be available at small branches.

In addition, local telephone directories list the number of the government's 24-hour ZIP Code information service. The telephone number is given in the white pages under "United States Government" in the listing for the "U.S. Postal Service."

BIBLIOGRAPHY

Of the thousands of sources we consulted in preparing this book, the following are some books we came back to again and again. Within individual entries in *Writer's Encyclopedia—Third Edition*, you'll also find specialized titles cited and both they and the following books contain bibliographies that provide further resources on the art, craft and business of writing.

The ABC of Copyright. Paris: United Nations Educational, Scientific and Cultural Organization, 1981.

The Art and Craft of Poetry. Michael Bugeja. Cincinnati: Writer's Digest Books, 1994.

Benet's Reader's Encyclopedia. Carol Cohen, ed. New York: Harper & Row, Publishers, 1987.

Benet's Reader's Encyclopedia of American Literature. George Perkins, Barbara Perkins and Phillip Leininger, eds. New York: HaperCollins Publishers, 1991.

The Book Market: How to Write, Publish and Market Your Book. Aron Mathieu. New York: Andover Press, Inc., 1981.

The Book of Jargon: An Essential Guide to the Inside Languages of Today. Don Ethan Miller. New York: Macmillan, Inc., 1982.

Book Publishing Encyclopedia: Whom to Call, What to Do. Ronald T. Smith. Sarasota, FL; Bookworld Press, 1994.

Books In Print, 10 vols. New York: R.R. Bowker Co., annual.

Business Organizations, Agencies and Publications Directory, 7th ed. Donald P. Boyden and Robert Wilson, eds. Detroit: Gale Research, 1993.

Children's Writer's and Illustrator's Market. Christine Martin and Alice Buening, eds. Cincinnati: Writer's Digest Books, annual.

Comedy Writing Secrets. Mel Helitzer. Cincinnati: Writer's Digest Books, 1993.

The Complete Guide to Magazine Article Writing. John M. Wilson. Cincinnati: Writer's Digest Books, 1993.

The Craft of Writing Science Fiction That Sells. Ben Bova. Cincinnati: Writer's Digest Books, 1994.

Dare to be a Great Writer. Leonard Bishop. Cincinnati: Writer's Digest Books, 1992.

Dictionary of Media and Communications. Richard Weiner. New York: Simon and Schuster, 1990.

Directory of Corporate Affiliations. New Providence, NJ: National Register Publishing Co., Inc., 1994.

Discovering the Writer Within. Bruce Ballenger and Barry Lane. Cincinnati: Writer's Digest Books, 1989.

Editing Your Newsletter. Mark Beach. Cincinnati: Writer's Digest Books, 1995.

Encyclopedia of Associations. Deborah M. Burek, ed. Detroit: Gale Research, 1995.

Essentials of English, 4th ed. Vincent F. Hopper. Hauppauge, NY: Barron's Educational Series, Inc., 1990.

Eye of the Heart. Barbara Howes, ed. New York: Avon Books, 1976.

The Fiction Dictionary. Laurie Henry. Cincinnati: Story Press, 1995.

Fiction Writer's Workshop. Josip Novakovich. Cincinnati: Story Press, 1995.

Freeing Your Creativity. Marshall J. Cook. Cincinnati: Writer's Digest Books, 1995.

The Golden Bough, abr. ed. Sir James G. Frazer. New York: Macmillan, 1985.

Guide to Literary Agents. Kirsten Holm, ed. Cincinnati: Writer's Digest Books, 1994.

Guide to Religious and Inspirational Magazines. Elizabeth Gould and Livia Fiordelisi. Milton, MA: Writer's Resources, 1993.

Harbrace College Handbook, 11th ed. John C. Hodges. New York: Harcourt Brace Jovanovich, Inc., 1990.

How to Lie With Statistics. Darrell Huff. New York: W.W. Norton & Co., Inc., 1993.

How to Make Money Writing About Fitness and Health. Celia G. Scully and Thomas J. Scully, M.D. Cincinnati: Writer's Digest Books, 1986.

How to Market Your Own Book With Your Pocket in Mind. Norfolk, VA: RMK Publishing, 1992.

How to Pitch and Sell Your TV Script. David Silver. Cincinnati: Writer's Digest Books, 1991.

How to Put Your Book Together and Get a Job in Advertising, rev. ed. Maxine Paetro. Bruce Bendinger, ed. Chicago: Copy Workshop, 1991.

How to Write and Sell Children's Picture Books. Jean E. Karl. Cincinnati: Writer's Digest Books, 1994.

How to Write and Sell True Crime. Gary Provost. Cincinnati: Writer's Digest Books, 1989.

How to Write Science Fiction and Fantasy. Orson Scott Card. Cincinnati: Writer's Digest Books, 1990.

Intellectual Adventure of Ancient Man. Henri Frankfort. Chicago: University of Chicago Press, 1977.

International Copyright Law. Paul E. Geller. New York: Bender, 1988.

International Literary Market Place. New York: R.R. Bowker Co., 1995.

Investigative Reporting. Peter Benjaminson and David Anderson. Ames, IA: Iowa State University Press, 1990.

Knowing Where to Look: The Ultimate Guide to Research. Lois Horowitz. Cincinnati: Writer's Digest Books, 1988.

Latin American Writers. Stanley H. Barkan et al. Merrick, NY: Cross-cultural, 1991.

Literary Market Place. New York: R.R. Bowker Co., 1995.

Magazines in the Twentieth Century, 2nd ed. Theodore Peterson. Champaign, IL: University of Illinois Press, 1964.

Make Your Words Work. Gary Provost. Cincinnati: Writer's Digest Books, 1994.

Martin's Magic Formula for Getting the Right Job, rev. Phyllis Martin. New York: St. Martin's Press, 1987.

Mass Media Law and Regulation, 6th rev. ed. William E. Francois. Prospect Heights, IL: Waveland, 1993.

Mystery Writer's Marketplace and Sourcebook. Donna Collingwood, ed. Cincinnati: Writer's Digest Books, 1993.

The National Directory of Addresses and Telephone Numbers. Kay Gill, ed. dir. Detroit: Omnigraphics, Inc., 1995.

National Zip Code and Post Office Directory. Retail Operations Division, Delivery Services Department, U.S. Postal Service. Washington, DC: United States Postal Service, annual.

The New Everyman Dictionary of Music. David Cummings, ed. New York: Grove Weldenfeld, 1988.

Novel & Short Story Writer's Market. Barb Kuroff, ed. Cincinnati: Writer's Digest Books, annual.

Opportunities in Journalism Careers. Lincolnwood, IL: NTC Publishing Group, 1990.

Photographer's Market. Michael Willins, ed. Cincinnati: Writer's Digest Books, annual.

Playwriting for Theater, Film and Television. Laura Shamas. Cincinnati: Writer's Digest Books, 1991.

The Poet's Handbook. Judson Jerome. Cincinnati: Writer's Digest Books, 1986.

Poet's Market. Chris Martin, ed. Cincinnati: Writer's Digest Books, annual.

Practical Tips for Writing Popular Fiction. Barnaby Conrad and the staff of the Santa Barbara Writer's Conference. Cincinnati: Writer's Digest Books, 1990.

Professional's Guide to Publicity, 3rd rev. ed. Richard Weiner. New York: Public Relations Publishing, 1982.

Publish It Yourself. Charles Chickadel. El Sobrante, CA: Meridian Learning Systems, 1984.

The Publish-It-Yourself Handbook: Literary Tradition and How-To. Bill Henderson, ed. Yonkers, NY: The Pushcart Press, and New York: Harper & Row, Publishers, Inc., 1987.

The Relaxation Response. Herbert Benson, M.D. New York: Random House Value, 1992.

The Religious Writers Marketplace. William H. Gentz and Sandra H. Brooks. Nashville: Abingdon, 1994.

Resume Writing: A Comprehensive, How-To-Do-It Guide, 4th ed. Burdette E. Bostwick. New York: John Wiley & Sons, Inc., 1990.

The Sacred and the Profane: The Nature of Religion. Mircea Eliade. Magnolia, MA: Peter Smith, 1983.

Science Fiction, Fantasy and Horror, 1991: A Comprehensive Bibliography of Books and Short Fiction Published in the English Language. Charles N. Brown and William G. Contento. Oakland, CA: Locus Press, 1991.

Science Fiction Writer's Workshop. Barry B. Longyear. Philadelphia: Owlswick Press, 1980.

Self-Publishing Made Simple. Lori A. Patterson. Cupertino, CA: Step-by-Step, 1994.

The Self-Publishing Manual: How To Write, Print and Sell Your Own Book, 7th rev. ed. Dan Poynter. Santa Barbara: Para Publishing, 1992.

Shift Your Writing Career Into High Gear. Gene Perret. Cincinnati: Writer's Digest Books, 1993.

Silences. Tillie Olsen. New York: Dell Publishing Co., Inc., 1989.

Slang Dictionary. Dan Kikuchi. Skokie, IL: Daian International, 1993.

Songwriter's Market. Cindy Laufenberg, ed. Cincinnati: Writer's Digest Books, annual.

Standard Directory of Advertisers: Classified Edition. New Providence, NJ: National Register Publishing Co., Inc., 1994.

Standard Directory of Advertisers: Geographical Edition. New Providence, NJ: National Register Publishing Co., Inc., 1994.

Standard Directory of Advertising Agencies. New Providence, NJ: National Register Publishing Co., Inc., 1994.

The Stress of Life, 2nd ed. Hans Selye, M.D. New York: McGraw-Hill Book Co., 1978.

Stress: What It Is, What It Can Do to Your Health, How to Handle It. Walter McQuade and Ann Aikman. New York: NAL-Dutton, 1993.

Subject Guide to Books in Print, 5 vols. New York: R.R. Bowker Co., 1994-95.

Successful Scriptwriting. Jurgen Wolff and Kerry Cox. Cincinnati: Writer's Digest Books, 1991.

Synopsis of the Law of Libel and the Right of Privacy, rev. ed. Bruce W. Sanford. New York: Newspaper Enterprises, 1986.

30 Steps to Becoming a Writer. Scott Edelstein. Cincinnati: Writer's Digest Books, 1993.

This Business of Writing. Gregg Levoy. Cincinnati: Writer's Digest Books, 1992.

Ulrich's International Periodicals Directory, 5 vols. New York: R.R. Bowker Co., 1994.

Understanding Science Fiction. Thomas D. Clarenson. Columbia: University of South Carolina Press, 1990.

What Color Is Your Parachute?, rev. ed. Richard N. Bolles. Berkeley: Ten Speed Press, 1984.

Who's Hiring Who. Richard Lathrop. Berkeley: Ten Speed Press, 1989.

Word Processing for Beginners. Elza Dinwiddle-Boyd. Berkeley: Berkeley Publishing, 1991.

The Writer's Complete Guide to Conducting Interviews. Michael Schumacher. Cincinnati: Writer's Digest Books, 1993.

The Writer's Digest Handbook of Magazine Article Writing. Jean M. Fredette, ed. Cincinnati: Writer's Digest Books, 1993.

A Writer's Guide to Book Publishing, 3rd rev. ed. Richard Balkan. New York: NAL-Dutton, 1994.

The Writer's Guide to Conquering the Magazine Market. Connie Emerson. Cincinnati: Writer's Digest Books, 1991.

Writer's Legal Companion. Brad Bunnin and Peter Beren. Redding, MA: Addison-Wesley, 1988.

The Writer's Manual, rev. ed. Roy E. Porter et al. Palm Springs: ETC Publications, 1979.

Writer's Market. Mark Garvey, ed. Cincinnati: Writer's Digest Books, annual.

Writing Articles From the Heart: How to Write Your Life Experiences. Marjorie Holmes. Cincinnati: Writer's Digest Books, 1993.

Writing for Children. Catherine Woolley. New York: NAL-Dutton, 1991.

Writing for Children and Teenagers, 3rd rev. ed. Lee Wyndham and Arnold Madison, eds. Cincinnati: Writer's Digest Books, 1985.

Writing for Money. Loriann Hoff Oberlin. Cincinnati: Writer's Digest Books, 1995.

Writing the Blockbuster Novel. Albert Zuckerman. Cincinnati: Writer's Digest Books, 1994.

Writing the Broadway Musical. Aaron Frankel. New York: Drama Book Publishers, 1981.

Writing the Short Story: A Hands-On Writing Program. Jack M. Bickham. Cincinnati: Writer's Digest Books, 1994.

More Great Books
for Writers!

1996 Writer's Market—Celebrating 75 years of helping writers realize their dreams, this newest edition contains information on 4,000 writing opportunities. You'll find all the facts vital to the success of your writing career, including an up-to-date listing of buyers of books, articles and stories, listings of contests and awards, plus articles and interviews with top professionals. *#10432/$27.99/1008 pages*

Aliens and Alien Societies—Gain a better understanding of extraterrestrial life to develop viable creatures and cultures using this fascinating reference. You'll have science on your side as you uncover the secrets of biochemistry, engineering and space travel. Plus, you'll learn to portray aliens as individuals, true to their species. *#10469/$17.99/240 pages*

The Writer's Digest Sourcebook for Building Believable Characters—Create unforgettable characters as you "attend" a roundtable where six novelists reveal their approaches to characterization. You'll probe your characters' backgrounds, beliefs and desires with a fill-in-the-blanks questionnaire. And a thesaurus of characteristics will help you develop the many other features no character should be without. *#10463/$17.99/288 pages*

The Writer's Legal Guide, Revised Edition—Now the answer to all your legal questions is right at your fingertips! The updated version of this treasured desktop companion contains essential information on business issues, copyright protection and registration, contract negotiation, income taxation, electronic rights and much, much more. *#10478/$19.95/256 pages/paperback*

How to Write Attention-Grabbing Query & Cover Letters—Use the secrets Wood reveals to write queries perfectly tailored, too good to turn down! In this guidebook, you will discover why boldness beats blandness in queries every time, ten basics you *must* have in your article queries, ten query blunders that can destroy publication chances and much more. *#10462/$17.99/208 pages*

Writing to Sell—You'll discover high-quality writing and marketing counsel in this classic writing guide from well-known agent Scott Meredith. His timeless advice will guide you along the professional writing path as you get help with creating characters, plotting a novel, placing your work, formatting a manuscript, deciphering a publishing contract—even combating a slump! *#10476/$17.99/240 pages*

Discovering the Writer Within: 40 Days to More Imaginative Writing—Uncover the creative individual inside who will, with encouragement, turn secret thoughts and special moments into enduring words. You'll learn how to find something exciting in unremarkable places, write punchy first sentences for imaginary stories, give a voice to inanimate objects and much more! *#10472/$14.99/192 pages/paperback*

World-Building—Write fiction that transports readers from this world to another . . . of your making. You'll mix elements and build planets with chemically credible and geologically accurate characteristics as you uncover a myriad of topics including facts on gravity, atmospheric science, star types and much more! *#10470/$17.99/224 pages/14 b&w illus.*

1996 Novel & Short Story Writer's Market—Get the information you need to get your short stories and novels published. You'll discover 1,900 listed fiction publishers in this new edition, plus original articles on fiction writing technique; detailed subject categories to help you target appropriate publishers; and interviews with writers, publishers and editors! *#10441/$22.99/624 pages/paperback*

Writing the Blockbuster Novel—Let a top-flight agent show you how to weave the essential elements of a blockbuster into your own novels with memorable characters, exotic settings, clashing conflicts and more! *#10393/$18.99/224 pages*

The Writer's Digest Guide to Manuscript Formats—Don't take chances with your hard work! Learn how to prepare and submit books, poems, scripts, stories and more with the professional look editors expect from a good writer. *#10025/$19.99/200 pages*

Getting the Words Right: How to Rewrite, Edit & Revise—Reduction, rearrangement, rewording and rechecking—the four Rs of powerful writing. This book provides concrete instruction with dozens of exercises and pages of samples to help you improve your writing through effective revision. *#10172/$14.99/218 pages/paperback*

Malicious Intent: A Writer's Guide to How Criminals Think—Find all the details you need to create chillingly believable villains. You'll get a compelling look into the criminal mind: who they are, why they commit crimes, how they choose their victims—even how police catch them. *#10413/$16.99/240 pages/paperback*

The Writer's Ultimate Research Guide—Save research time and frustration with the help of this guide. Three hundred fifty-two information-packed pages will point you straight to the information you need to create better, more accurate fiction and nonfiction. With hundreds of listings of books and databases, each entry reveals how current the information is, what the content and organization is like and much more! *#10447/$19.99/352 pages*

How to Write Like an Expert About Anything—Find out how to use new technology and traditional research methods to get the information you need, envision new markets and write proposals that sell, find and interview experts on any topic and much more! *#10449/$17.99/224 pages*

Beginning Writer's Answer Book—This book answers 900 of the most often asked questions about every stage of the writing process. You'll find business advice, tax tips, plus new information about on-line networks, databases and more. *#10394/$17.99/336 pages*

Writing for Money—Discover where to look for writing opportunities—and how to make them pay off. You'll learn how to write for magazines, newspapers, radio and TV, newsletters, greeting cards and a dozen other hungry markets! *#10425/$17.99/256 pages*

How to Write Fast (While Writing Well)—Discover what makes a story and what it takes to research and write one. Then, learn step by step how to cut wasted time and effort by planning interviews for maximum results, beating writer's block with effective plotting, getting the most information from traditional library research and on-line computer databases and much more! Plus, a complete chapter loaded with tricks and tips for faster writing. *#10473/$15.99/208 pages/ paperback*

How to Write Irresistible Query Letters—Don't shortchange your idea with a lukewarm query! Cool shows how to select a strong slant, hook an editor with a tantalizing lead, sell yourself as the expert for the job and more. *#10146/$11.99/136 pages/paperback*

Make Your Words Work—Loaded with samples and laced with exercises, this guide will help you clean up your prose, refine your style, strengthen your descriptive powers, bring music to your words and much more! *#10399/$14.99/304 pages/paperback*

The Best Writing on Writing, Volume 2—This year's best collection of memorable essays, book excerpts and lectures on fiction, nonfiction, poetry, screenwriting and the writing life. *#48013/$16.99/224 pages/paperback*

The Complete Guide to Writing Fiction—This concise guide will help you develop the skills you need to write and sell long and short fiction. You'll get a complete rundown on outlining, narrative writing details, description, pacing and action. *#10158/$18.95/312 pages*

30 Steps to Becoming a Writer and Getting Published—This informational and inspirational guide helps you get started as a writer, develops your skills and style and gets your work ready for submission. *#10367/$16.99/176 pages*

The Fiction Dictionary—The essential guide to the inside language of fiction. You'll discover genres you've never explored, writing devices you'll want to attempt, fresh characters to populate your stories. *The Fiction Dictionary* dusts off the traditional concept of "dictionary" by giving full, vivid descriptions, and by using lively examples from classic and contemporary fiction . . . turning an authoritative reference into a can't-put-it-down browser. *#48008/$18.99/336 pages*

Writing the Short Story: A Hands-On Program—With Bickham's unique "workshop on paper" you'll plan, organize, write, revise and polish a short story. Clear instruction, helpful charts and practical exercises will lead you every step of the way! *#10421/$16.99/224 pages*

Creating Characters: How to Build Story People—Grab the empathy of your reader with characters so real they'll jump off the page. You'll discover how to make characters come alive with vibrant emotion, quirky personality traits, inspiring heroism, tragic weaknesses and other uniquely human qualities. *#10417/$14.99/192 pages/paperback*

Description—Discover how to use detailed description to awaken the reader's senses; advance the story using only relevant description; create original word depictions of people, animals, places, weather and much more! *#10451/$15.99/176 pages*

The Writer's Digest Guide to Good Writing—In one book, you'll find the best in writing instruction gleaned from the past 75 years of *Writer's Digest* magazine! Successful authors like Vonnegut, Steinbeck, Oates, Michener and over a dozen others share their secrets on writing technique, idea generation, inspiration and getting published. *#10391/$18.99/352 pages*

The Wordwatcher's Guide to Good Writing and Grammar—Avoid embarrassing grammar mistakes with this handy volume. Freeman gives hundreds of examples to clarify word usage, meaning, spelling and pronunciation. *#10197/$16.99/320 pages/paperback*

The Craft of Writing Science Fiction That Sells by Ben Bova—You'll discover how to fascinate audiences (and attract editors) with imaginative, well-told science fiction. Bova shows you how to market your ideas, submit your manuscripts and more! *#10395/$16.99/224 pages*

The Writer's Digest Guide to Manuscript Formats—Don't take chances with your hard work! Learn how to prepare and submit books, poems, scripts, stories and more with the professional look editors expect from a good writer. *#10025/$19.99/200 pages*

Fiction Writer's Workshop—Explore each aspect of the art of fiction including point of view, description, revision, voice and more. At the end of each chapter you'll find more than a dozen writing exercises to help you put what you've learned into action. *#48003/$17.99/256 pages*

Write Tight: How to Keep Your Prose Sharp, Focused and Concise—Discover how to say exactly what you want with grace and power, using not only the right word, but also the right number of words. Specific instructions and helpful exercises explain and demonstrate the process for you. *#10360/$16.99/192 pages*